IMAGES OF WOMEN
IN LITERATURE

D0066551

IMAGES OF WOMEN IN LITERATURE

FIFTH EDITION

MARY ANNE FERGUSON

Professor *Emerita*, University of Massachusetts, Boston

Afterword by Jean Ferguson Carr, University of Pittsburgh

HOUGHTON MIFFLIN COMPANY   Boston

Dallas   Geneva, Illinois   Palo Alto   Princeton, New Jersey

Copyright © 1991 by Houghton Mifflin Company. All rights reserved.

No part of this work may be reproduced or transmitted in any form or by any means, electronic or mechanical, including photocopying and recording, or by any information storage or retrieval system without the prior written permission of the copyright owner unless such copying is expressly permitted by federal copyright law. With the exception of nonprofit transcription in Braille, Houghton Mifflin is not authorized to grant permission for further uses of copyrighted selections reprinted in this text without the permission of their owners. Permission must be obtained from the individual copyright owners as identified herein. Address requests for permission to make copies of Houghton Mifflin material to College Permissions, Houghton Mifflin Company, One Beacon Street, Boston, Massachusetts 02108.

Cover art: Mary Frank, "The Time Is Now." Private collection; photo courtesy of Zabriskie Gallery.

Printed in the U.S.A.
Library of Congress Catalog Card Number: 90-83045
ISBN: 0-395-55116-1

ABCDEFGHIJ-RI-9876543210

CONTENTS

·————————————·

Preface   ix

Introduction   1

IMAGE THREE: Woman on a Pedestal   205

IMAGE FOUR: The Sex Object   265

CONTENTS

CONTENTS

PREFACE

The fifth edition of this anthology consists of eighty-two works that both illustrate traditional images of women and reflect changes in those images brought about in recent years by the women's movement. Contemporary writers represent the changes they perceive in the lives of women; scholars reveal hidden aspects of works from earlier writers. The major change constitutes greater representation of the diversity that makes all generalizations about women suspect. More than half of the works in this edition are new; one-third are by minority writers, whose perceptions of difference enlarge our definitions of women. Many of the selections are by recently published authors; others are by well-established ones, old and young; some are by authors rediscovered by feminist scholars. For example, an excerpt from Louisa May Alcott's novel *Work: A Story of Experience* shows her as more than the author of popular books for girls; her sturdy, independent protagonist makes us question the view that passive "true womanhood" was a universal nineteenth-century ideal. Only in 1981 was Harriet Jacobs's *Incidents in the Life of a Slave Girl* shown by a feminist scholar to be authentic autobiography rather than the fictional account it had been considered by literary scholars and historians. An excerpt from Jacobs's account gives readers a new perspective on women as sex objects.

Most of the selections are works complete in themselves—thirty-eight are poems, twenty-eight are short stories, and three are short plays. Other genres—autobiography, letters, journals, prose poems—are represented, often by excerpts. Instead of being placed in a separate category, as was done in the fourth edition (Part III: Self-Images), these works have been distributed among the other images in order to furnish material for comparison and to test the rigidity of genre definitions. For example, Jamaica Kincaid's "Girl" is not clearly autobiographical or fictional; only readers' responses to the voice of Kincaid's speaker can determine the validity of such questions as how fictional or how realistic, how close to truth, the words are. We hear many, varied voices in these works: a child, an old woman, a recent divorcée, a widower, a single parent, and lesbian lovers are used by authors as narrative voices in trying to reveal their perceptions about women.

The various images are divided into two major categories. Part I, Traditional Images, exemplifies the major images of women associated with their biological roles—wife, mother, sex object, woman on a pedestal, and women without men. Although these images are stereotypes produced within various cultural traditions, each work undermines the cultural validity of the stereotype by showing how it limits the humanity of the characters—men, women, or children. Also, most works hint, at least, at ways in which the characters transcend their limitations. Both male and female authors show women characters caught in their roles, but such exemplification is a critique of the tradition that reduces human beings to role-players.

The images in Part II, Woman Becoming, illuminate the processes by which women seek to transcend their ascribed roles. This section is almost double the size it was in the fourth edition. Selections by minority women in particular illustrate defiance of and creative reactions to stereotypes; the perceptions of a Japanese-American, Chinese-Americans, a Hispanic-American, a Guatemalan, and several African-Americans expand our knowledge of both differences and similarities among women. The historical perspective gained from writers of previous centuries reveals continuity and differences among their choices of focus. Marietta Holley makes fun of sexism; Olive Schreiner paints a utopian image of a possible future. Anna Julia Cooper, a black woman born in slavery, and Rebecca Jackson, a nineteenth-century itinerant preacher, emphasize education as liberating, as do contemporary writers Margaret Atwood, Marge Piercy, and Jade Snow Wong. This edition thus presents a broad perspective on women writers' perceptions of women's problems and opportunities for change.

In order to perceive that the selections do in fact move beyond mere description, readers must analyze not only the works but their own frames of reference. Modern reader-response theory tells us that each reader brings to a literary work a set of assumptions that must be accounted for in evaluating the work. For example, one assumption very basic to American culture is called essentialism, the belief that "human nature," acquired at birth, determines the gender characteristics of men and women. Many contemporary thinkers question this assumption, from several perspectives, and suggest that our gender roles are prescribed largely by the cultural tradition into which we are born. There is great disagreement about this major question, even among feminists. It is important for all readers to be aware of the issue as an arguable one and of their own positions concerning it.

Another issue giving rise to a great difference of opinion among critics, scholars, and creative writers is the degree to which literary images are those of individual authors. How freely does a writer caught up in a particular culture write about that culture? Is it true, as some thinkers suggest, that those who occupy a marginal position in a society have an advantage in perceiving and critiquing the images dominant in its culture? This edition for the first time deals with the complexities of such questions in an afterword, Images of Writing/Writing Images. It offers insights applicable both to the authors of our texts and to students who may be writing about the works.

Suggestions for Further Reading, divided into six categories, includes a list—organized by image—of works that appeared in previous editions but had to be cut in order to make room for new selections. Since many of these earlier inclusions are now widely available in other sources, this list should be useful for locating additional material for comparison. The list of works cited in the introductions presents the authorities on which the perspective of the editor is based; it constitutes a brief outline of major sources of feminist criticism in the last twenty years. The other lists give readers access to some of the enormously increased amount of material relevant to the images of women in this book.

Preparing a fifth edition means that the editor's debt to others has increased far beyond the extent that could be specifically acknowledged. My search for new material was made easier by the facilities of the Schlesinger Library on the History of Women; it was my good fortune that the library expanded to include printed books just when I started my search. Barbara Haber (curator of printed books), Abby Yasgur (reference librarian), and Nancy Falk (periodicals librarian) saved me time and guided me to material I might otherwise have missed. The tolerance of browsing in several bookstores was essential to my search for current sources. Other resources were former students, friends, and colleagues; scholars whose books keep appearing; reviewers, especially in *Signs*, *The Women's Review of Books*, and *Belles Lettres*; publishers, especially small presses, who keep women's writing available; speakers at conferences; and, above all, new writers with new perceptions. Peggy McIntosh of the Wellesley College Center for Research on Women and several reviewers of the manuscript have broadened my perspective. Users of previous editions helped me decide which selections to keep from the fourth edition; several gave me useful suggestions for new material. I wish to thank the following: Teri Bardash, Suffolk County Community College (New York); Gwen Brewer, California State University at Northridge; Mary L. Briscoe, University of Pittsburgh; Deborah Charlie, Antelope Valley College (California); Sonia Mary Chess, Honolulu Community College; Barbara R. Clark, Oglethorpe University (Georgia); Aniko V. Constantine, Alfred State College (New York); Marybeth DeMeo, Alvernia College (Pennsylvania); Randy DeVillez, Moraine Valley Community College (California); Lynne C. Diehl, Hagarstown Business College (Maryland);

Miriam Fabien, Madonna College (Michigan); Julie Fay, East Carolina University (North Carolina); Bonnie B. Finkelstein, Montgomery County Community College (Pennsylvania); Margaret Fox-Tully, Harcum Junior College (Pennsylvania); Gloria Wade Gayles, Spelman College (Georgia); Elaine K. Ginsberg, West Virginia University; Coleen Grissom, Trinity University (Texas); Vanessa Haley, Mary Washington College (Virginia); Michael Hall, Virginia Wesleyan College; Joanne V. Hawks, University of Mississippi; Marilyn L. Johnson, Cabrini College (Pennsylvania); Amy Kaminsky, University of Minnesota; Anne LeCroy, East Tennessee State University; Janet Madden-Simpson, El Camino College (California); Carol S. Manning, Mary Washington College (Virginia); Rhoda Maxwell, University of Wisconsin; Susan L. McGinty, East Washington University; Patricia McNeal, Indiana University at South Bend; Kay Mussell, The American University (District of Columbia); Leonarda Mary Obarski, Edinboro University of Pennsylvania; Julie Olin-Ammentorp, Le Moyne College (New York); Shirlene M. Pope, Utah State University; Lois Poule, Bridgewater State College (Massachusetts); Deborah Rosenthal, Massasoit Community College (Massachusetts); Margaret K. Schramm, Hartwick College (New York); Jackie Stembridge, Glendale Community College (California); Colleen D. Thompson, Willmar Community College (Minnesota); Susan Ward, St. Lawrence University (New York); Susan Weisser, Adelphi University (New York); and Laura M. Zaidman, University of South Carolina. Finally, I am happy to acknowledge the help of my daughter, Jean Ferguson Carr, who has written the Afterword for this edition. She has also aided me in finding material and in making the many difficult decisions necessary to such a greatly changed book.

Mary Anne Ferguson

IMAGES OF WOMEN
IN LITERATURE

INTRODUCTION

A funny thing happened on my way to this edition. My task was to find new material to fit into the general pattern of the four previous editions (1973, 1977, 1981, 1986), which were organized around traditional and emerging images of women in literature written by both women and men. Originally the categories emerged from the literature I was reading; categorizing revealed connections otherwise obscured, and I felt as if a great light had enabled me to "re-vision" everything I had ever read. Recently, more than ever, the stories and poems I read pressed at the boundaries of the categories I had established. I began to wonder if my approach through stereotypes was a procrustean bed: did my organization reflect either contemporary literature or the real life of women?

Consider, for example, this short poem by Linda Pastan:

Marks

My husband gives me an A
for last night's supper,
an incomplete for my ironing,
a B plus in bed.
My son says I am average,
an average mother, but if
I put my mind to it
I could improve.
My daughter believes
in Pass/Fail and tells me
I pass. Wait 'til they learn
I'm dropping out.

The first four lines fit into "The Wife," the next six into "The Mother," and the last two, certainly, into what I called "The Liberated Woman: What Price Freedom?" in the first two editions. The poem's ending projects the ambivalence of the important question mark I used in that title: we all know that when a wife/mother leaves, the pain is acute for all. I wanted to resolve the problem of how to include Pastan's poem; I love its wit and conciseness as well as its representation of a life situation many women have faced—in literature ever since Ibsen's *A Doll's House* (1869) and in almost half of marriages today. I decided to put it last in "The Wife."

Both my indecision and, finally, my ability to make a choice illustrate the problems involved with stereotypes. Stereotypes serve legitimate uses when they are used as shortcuts to understanding not just the dictionary meanings of words but the layers of meaning that go with them. For example, *wife* denotes "a woman married to a man," but traditionally there has been the added implication that "a" means *one*, more or less permanently. When we use the term *wife* in a society in which monogamy is the prevailing practice, the stereotype of a one man/one woman relationship is a shortcut to understanding the system. But that meaning is far too limited to fit the reality of the twentieth century and has never fit the reality of cultures practicing polygamy or polyandry. The illegitimate use of stereotypes occurs when we use them to avoid thinking, when they become unexamined assumptions. When we use a word with a rigidly fixed and narrow meaning, we are submitting to prejudice or prejudging; we are implying that any other use of the word is antisocial. The word *stereotype* was originally used in printing to mean a piece of metal; verbal stereotypes become as rigid as those metallic forms. For example, when we hear the words "beautiful blonde," our minds leap to the stereotype and add "dumb"; we skip over consideration of any individual we actually see, and real beautiful blondes may play dumb in order to take advantage of others' expectations. When we hear "wife," the old expectations of monogamy leap to mind; so even today, when half of all marriages end in divorce, *divorcee* carries the added connotations of failure and blame. "Working mother" seems to many people a contradiction in terms; mothers are still expected to be at home (especially when repair people want to schedule an appointment), no matter how valid a reason they may have for being elsewhere part of the time. And the work women do at home as wives and mothers is uncompensated and usually undervalued.

Certain stereotypes are particularly strong because underlying them are patterns called *archetypes*, the images of myths (stories told in every society to impose order on and interpret the chaotic and mysterious aspects of experience). Because such images represent our desires and fears about the world and about ourselves, they resist modification by facts and logic and are often fortified by religion. Throughout history mythical archetypes of women in their biological role as the mysterious source of life have reinforced stereotypes about women's place in society; women have been viewed as mother, wife, mistress, sex object—their roles in relationship to men. Of course, men are also viewed in their biological roles, but not to the same degree as women; in society men are neither defined by nor limited to the roles of father, lover, and husband. The word *defined* means "having a limit around," or "fenced in." Women have been fenced into a small place in the world. Even though women's "place" is no longer as small as in the past and roles change, the old stereotypes still linger.

Literary images do not exist in a vacuum; they are related to what history, psychology, sociology, anthropology, and other disciplines—as well as our own experience—tell us about reality. Literature both reflects and helps create our views of reality; it is through their preservation in works of art that we know what the stereotypes and archetypes have been and are. Literature conserves traditional images. The Wife of Bath in Chaucer's *Canterbury Tales*, for example, who deceives and uses her five husbands, is a model of the talkative, ambitious, castrating wife. The beautiful but unruly Kate in Shakespeare's *The Taming of the Shrew* is the stereotype of the selfish bitch; she must be literally spanked by her husband before submitting to him as the obedient wife by putting her neck under his foot. Both of these images are figures of fun; audiences laugh at the exaggeration of the stereotypes, but at the same time accept them as the basic image of a wife, who needs a man's control. Other great male writers show the tragedy and waste of characters in stereotypical roles: Dora in Dickens's *David Copperfield* dies young after failing to be a good wife; Anna Karenina in Tolstoy's novel throws herself under a train after committing adultery. Though we recognize the power of these traditional images and the skill with which they are represented, none of these characters furnishes a role model for readers today; we must look elsewhere for literary images with which women can identify.

Ever since 1969, when I started gathering material for my class "Images of Women in Literature," I have included literature that goes beyond merely presenting a widely held and often represented image, beyond a simplistic dependence on a stereotype that invites prejudice as a response. A good work uses a stereotype readers can recognize, but at the same time it undermines the image; it forces readers to question the usual perception. Pastan describes a woman defined by the opinions of others, both male and female. Even though their image is quite favorable, she rebels against it. The shock of the speaker's rejection allows readers to share the emotion of such a decision, its anger and pain; readers may sense the speaker's tenderness for the daughter who is also rebelling against rigid norms. But underlying this image is the stereotype of women as emotional, irrational; we can imagine Freud asking, What does such a woman want? Readers might ask other questions: Has she realized that she may be a lesbian? Is she making the political statement that, even under good circumstances, marriage as an institution inhibits personal development? Might she be hoping that her family will learn that grading is not an acceptable mode of interrelationship and be able to renegotiate the terms of the marriage with a new system of values? Is marking a metaphor for any woman's view that she is disciplined and defined by a system of values not her own? All of these questions tell us more about the readers than about the poem, perhaps; but they show that Pastan is testing the stereotype of the wife/mother. By putting Pastan's poem last in the category "The Wife," I could show a continuum ranging from descriptions of women who operate within a containing category while feeling uneasiness about its limitations (as in Sally Benson's "Little Woman") to a statement of outright rejection.

In 1986 I merged my early categories of "Submissive Wife" and "Dominating Wife," recognizing them as parts of a continuum; I also expanded the image with stories about an abused wife and a racially mixed marriage. As I continued reading new works, I realized that other categories also needed expansion. "Women without Men," which had already evolved from "The Old Maid" and "Women Alone," now includes works about lesbians who have come out and single and lesbian mothers. "The Mother" overlaps with this category but now includes works about non-biological mothers. The greatest changes for this edition have been in "The Sex Object" and "Woman Becoming." As I read amazingly forthright works by minority authors, I realized that the criticism some feminists had been raising about the women's movement as a whole applied to my earlier perspectives: my categories had been based largely on white middle-class heterosexual women, mirroring, in fact, my own image. I needed to recognize the challenging differences among women of various classes, races, and sexual orientations and how these worked to reconfigure the notion of cultural images. Though the sex object defined as "man's prey" remains an influential image, a larger historical and world view has disclosed not only women's universal reification but their suffering from abuse, rape, and the most extreme form of powerlessness, chattel slavery, all of which are aspects of the stereotype "sex object." I learned from scholarly studies that the traffic in women continues today, often in the form of "pawning," if not outright selling, of young girls (Barry, Bunch, and Castley, 1984).* But I also found that writers aware of these situations refuse merely to describe them; they are creating images of change. I am especially pleased that for the first time I have been able to choose from among many possible selections for Part II, "Woman Becoming," which has always represented hope for change; it has grown from twelve to twenty-two selections.

The most political change is in the category "Woman on a Pedestal." As a medievalist, I had always seen the exaltation of women as allied to the fear of women: goddesses can be positive or negative, but both images obscure any perception of women as human beings. I have emphasized the power of this image by including works about the "beauty system" (MacCannell and MacCannell, 1987). Because beauty is culturally defined as being attractive to men, women do not recognize any

---

*See the list "Works Cited in the Introduction" on pages 581–585 for this and all other parenthetical references.

other standard, such as pleasing themselves. The traditional but paradoxically ever-changing definition of beauty costs women time, anxiety, self-deprecation, and billions of dollars. Ads such as those for Oil of Olay, which link the desire for beauty to the fear of aging, strengthen the hold of this standard. Whether one is a liberal, socialist, or radical feminist, it is easy to see the links between this image, the profit motive, and political power.

I do not mean to suggest that the new selections I have included are documentary or even realistic; however closely a work may seem to represent experience, we must not forget the power of artistic representation to work on experience. The first-person speaker in Linda Pastan's poem need not be the author; in fact, the jacket cover on Pastan's latest book describes her as living with her husband and three children. "Marks" first appeared in a section on anger in her volume *The Five Stages of Grief* (1978). People in many situations can identify with her images of the anger and pain that accompany loss. It was the anger my students and I felt that made me stop in a class on images of women in 1970 and ask, "Do you really want to know how others have seen us?" It was the response of my students that led to my first edition: they felt it was better to know among ourselves than either to be unaware or to find out, as so many women have, with the click of recognition documented by *Ms.* magazine, that women have indeed been unfairly represented in traditional literature.

The greatest change in literary images of women over the past two decades is the degree to which women writers have attempted to construct a womanly perspective and make women central in their works. In doing so, they subvert the traditional images, which were largely those of men. Rediscovery of women writers from the past by women scholars since 1970 has shown that literary subversion occurred long before this century. For example, a scholar who discovered a previously unknown cache of letters has demonstrated that Harriet Jacobs's *Incidents in the Life of a Slave Girl* (see Image Four, "The Sex Object") was indeed "written by herself," as she claimed in 1861 (Yellin, 1981). When this work was thought to be fictional, it was dismissed as incredible; establishing its authenticity as autobiography forces readers to deal with it differently, as representation of reality. Although autobiography has the force of truth, modern reconsideration of the genre shows that, like fiction, it is a way of representation, a way of seeing and structuring a life and its moments. In her selection of what to include and what to omit, in her use of the conventions of the domestic novel, Jacobs creates a version of reality; critics can help us understand the reasons for her choices, however, and thereby get closer to truth.

For the past two decades, feminist critics have focused on the question of how it is possible for women writers to write in their own voices, from their own perspectives, when literature has been so dominated by men that women seem to have no distinctive language of their own. In the early 1970s feminist critics revealed not only the degree of male dominance of writing throughout history but also the patriarchal silencing of what women had in fact written. Tillie Olsen (1978) pointed out that only one out of twelve authors anthologized in American college texts was a woman. Critics have documented the ways in which male writers used stereotypes in their writing, picturing a patriarchal society with overwhelmingly negative views of women. From this perspective I pointed out in earlier editions that men have been the norm against which women are measured. Images of women in both literature and life have been polarized according to contradictory characteristics, such as passive-aggressive, intuitive-logical, possessive–self-sacrificing, materialistic-spiritual, frigid-lustful. Images at both poles often appear negative for women but not for men.

In an effort to counteract this perception, feminist literary critics turned to rediscovering women's works that had been forgotten or deliberately deleted from literary canons. Showalter (1977) found a literary subculture among nineteenth-century British women writers who were aware of and alluded to their predecessors. Gilbert and Gubar (1979) explicated a subtext of rebellion in the works of American and British women writers since the eighteenth century. Their scholarship revealed that there have in fact been positive images in the works of women writers, but we have to learn how to perceive them. Other scholars have shown that women from many specific social groups have written about their perceptions of women. Anthologies of works by minority and lesbian women, such as those edited by Washington (1975; 1980) and Bulkin and Larkin (1975), were pioneers, as were collections of ethnic American writers (Blicksilver, 1979; Fisher, 1980) and critical works (Christian, 1980, 1985; Evans, 1984; Zimmerman, 1981). These works have been followed by a flood of publications by both creative writers and feminist critics that demonstrate how universal and yet various are the literary images of women.

But men still dominate the literary scene. The literary canon—the list of works to be studied—is determined by male standards. Feminist scholars agree that this dominance stems from the institutions of society and the ideologies that determine its values. The word *ideology* is a slippery term; it has political connotations and is often used pejoratively by those who maintain that literary criticism should be objective and nonpolitical: "you have an ideology, I have the right ideas" is the usual attitude. Though it simply means the ideas of any individual, group, or class about their social institutions, the word clearly implies more than just a reflection, a point of view; it is threatening because it implies a system of interconnecting beliefs or ideas that permeate behavior. Since ideas, or mental images, are invisible, they are often hidden even from the person or group holding them; we may live within an ideology as a fish lives in water, totally unaware of our environment's determination of what we think of as personal. Ideologies often reflect myths and religious beliefs.

Different ideologies coexist and often conflict; an ideology may also change, accompanied by the kind of discomfort a fish out of water feels. The historian Nancy Cott (1978) describes a major ideological shift with respect to the nineteenth-century definition of women as passionless, "a cluster of ideas about the weight of woman's carnal nature and her moral nature." The traditional idea of women as lustful prevailed through the eighteenth century, but, Cott found, gave way when it conflicted with the idea of women as destined to be the moral leaders of men, repositories of virtue in the home, leaving men to deal with the wicked world outside. This new ideology was the basis for excluding women from public affairs, a situation that has only partly changed. We have seen as great an ideological shift in our time, to a view that women's sexual desire is an acceptable characteristic that may be freely expressed, even outside of marriage. Many people resist this shift: parents who say "Even if you are living together, when you come to my house, you will have separate rooms" are angry, hurt, even bewildered when their moral view is rejected. They don't perceive such a view as ideological; it just seems right. The conviction of being right stiffens those who disagree about disparate ideologies on such issues as abortion and the death penalty; their opposition becomes a political battle or even an impasse.

Ideology exists not only as ideas but in visual and verbal images. We are immersed in media images that exert a little understood influence on us. This fact is of particular concern to feminists because in advertising, films, and all public media stereotypical images of women have been perpetuated as symbols of an idealized past and of the future; apparently timeless, these images continue to shape our vision of contemporary reality, however much real lives depart from them (Berger, 1972; Betterton, 1987). Trying to change such symbols often seems impossible; such dichotomies as lustful-frigid resist logic and evade even scientific analysis. Something more than ideology is at work; clearly those who profit from the system as it is use these symbols to resist change.

A significant example shows how these clusters of ideas work. The word *machismo*, which originated in Latin America, represents a definition of men as dominant both by nature and by social practice. The ads featuring the Marlboro man show how widespread the macho image is and also its link to the profit motive: the image successfully sells cigarettes, which are acknowledged to be a health hazard. A scholar has shown that a corresponding set of characteristics—*marianismo*—exists for women so that their self-image supports that of men; women identify themselves as wives/mothers, enjoy feeling morally superior, accept being confined to the home, and are even proud of their men's dominance (Stevens, 1973). Such sharp opposition between sexual categories emphasizes the differences between the sexes at a time when research is showing that differences long assumed to be innate either do not exist or are insignificant. Men and women are more like each other than either is like any other creature: human beings differ from the great apes and their norms of aggressiveness, mating, and parenting. Some men are weaker, shorter, and less aggressive than some women; the characteristics usually seen as sex-linked are actually distributed along a continuum, which makes individual behavior unpredictable based only on sex. Recently psychologists (Hyde and Linn, 1986) have shown that even the long-held belief that males are innately better at mathematics and females at verbal skills is erroneous; differences in performance can be ascribed to differences in society's expectations and in education.

Feminist literary critics are caught in conflicting ideologies about definitions of "the feminine." French critics, basing their concepts largely on the psychoanalytical theories of Jacques Lacan, a Freudian revisionist, focus on the female body as the source of identity and as the means for women to write differently from men (*Yale French Studies*, 1981). Many American feminists who view women as morally superior to men ascribe the feminine to women's bodily experiences, especially childbirth; "maternal thinking" has been seen as making women peacemakers and environmentalists (Ruddick, 1989; Perry and Brownley, 1983). Other American feminists see the ascription of women's characteristics to biology—essentialism—as a trap forgoing the possibility of change. This dilemma has led to a new approach, gender studies (Showalter, 1989). In this context *gender* refers to definitions of feminine and masculine based on characteristics ascribed to social roles; since these definitions vary from culture to culture and over time, they cannot be innate. Gender distinctions are based on social institutions and ideologies. Motherly behavior and women's emphasis on relationships as the basis of moral decisions are reproduced according to traditional standards that seem psychologically imperative (Chodorow, 1978; Gilligan, 1982) but can be understood only in their cultural context (Spivack, 1987). Even the way women read is seen as different from that of men (Flynn and Schweikart, 1986), and linguists point out ways in which women's speech and writing are distinctive to their gender. Perceiving gender differences has led feminists to consider also the systems that define masculinity: *machismo* seems to be as limiting for men as *marianismo* has been for women. Both require finding identity through partial roles.

Despite these insights and the many ways in which male/female roles have changed in the last two decades, progress toward equity between the sexes seems to move like molasses. In this country, even among the 1 percent of upper-class women involved in careers (as distinguished from mere jobs), women spend a full month of 24-hour days each year more than men doing housework and child care (Hertz, 1986). In Russia women who are full-time workers spend about 40 hours a week on domestic work (Gray, 1990). Nowhere do men do close to half of household chores. Even for the most privileged—the one-third of lawyers and doctors who are women and business women who have risen to management levels in the United States—an invisible barrier prevents true

equity. Forgetting the recent history of struggle that brought unprece-
dented advances—limited as those are—many women today seem to
consider the present situation permanent, natural; if women have problems, it is because they "want it all" or haven't been ingenious enough
to resolve the problem of day care individually. *Feminist* has become a
dirty word for many, and the need for continued change is questioned, as
the wide use of the word *postfeminist* implies. "You've come a long way,
baby" is part of a new ideology that co-opts recent gains by making them
part of the traditional situation. A prominent sociologist (Keller, 1988)
ascribes the disappointing pace of change to "the continued strength of
traditional stereotypes about gender distinctions and gender destinies. . . .
whatever changes occur rest on the surface and do not penetrate to the
depths of social arrangements and beliefs about gender, and in particular,
to beliefs about gender hierarchy." Men have continued to be "more
equal" than women; the categories I described in earlier editions have
remained in real life. Even elementary school children absorb these
views, and some children as young as twenty months not only make
gender distinctions but specify behavior according to gender: "girls talk,
boys hit," they say (Luria, 1990). A newspaper headline reports that with
respect to toys "the stereotypes of yesteryear persist, regularly updated"
(Lawson, 1989).

How can we account for this persistence? Scholars in many fields are
trying to answer this question, which goes to the heart of discussions of
how the human mind works, how mental, pictorial, and verbal images
are acquired and interrelated. Definitive answers elude even those who
try to answer such an apparently simple question as "What is an image?"
(Mitchell, 1986). However, recent developments in what has come to be
known as cognitive science do give some clues about the persistence of
images.

Since the 1950s interdisciplinary work in linguistics, psychology,
anthropology, philosophy, and computer science has undermined ideas
that had prevailed for some two thousand years, generally unanalyzed
because they were assumed to be true. Traditionally, the process of
thought has been viewed as putting abstract ideas into categories according to their similarities, supposedly determined objectively without reference to the individual doing the thinking; "objective" reason has been
the mode of thought in science as well as philosophy, and any other
mode of thought—woman's intuition, for example—has been deplored.
The new view is that reasoning is embodied, that it depends on our perceptions of bodily movement and our physical and social environments.
Through the use of the imagination, long scorned as merely artistic,
humans extend their powers of categorizing beyond the real world.
Through analogy, metaphor, and imagery we are able to think about
many experiences that transcend the external reality formerly considered
to be the limit of human knowledge. Such a shift means that the person

thinking influences the process; it follows that there is no single, ultimate truth, but many different ways of viewing the world. Feminists maintain that the gender of the person thinking is determinative.

Cognitive scientists draw much of their evidence for models of thought from language. Lakoff (1987) points out that in most languages of the world, categories based on the contrast male/female are central to thought; each category is the center of a cluster of concepts that are perceived as similar. The similarities need have no relationship to the real world; often they depend on beliefs, myths, or ideals, which are represented by artistic symbols. Male/female may originally have been no more than other category designators such as left/right or one/two, but through the process of association—merely being next to each other—the categories take on additional meanings. Even such an apparently objective pair as one/two acquires value judgments; as Simone de Beauvoir (1953) has pointed out, being number two carries with it the presumption of secondary or lesser power. A prominent historian maintains that gender categories have been used primarily to encode power relations (Scott, 1988). In languages that use male/female designators, the male term is what linguists call the unmarked term and comes first; the female term is marked: poet/poetess, waiter/waitress, mister/mistress (Philips, Steele, and Tanz, 1987). We are getting used to unmarking terms: *Ms.* is widespread though still resisted, but *waitperson* sounds strange to most people still. *Man* and *he* are still used not only to talk about males but to generalize about human beings; to speak of mankind as *she* or to alternate *he* and *she* sounds awkward, unnatural—and the effort to do so sounds silly to many.

But knowing that language powerfully shapes our thinking must alert us to the fact that changing language is not silly. Most speakers of a language are not aware of the categories the language uses; they do not question the rightness of those that exist. Insistence on merely verbal changes forces attention to old norms; we have changed from *colored* and *Negro* to *black* since the 1950s, for example, and it appears that *bra-burner*s will not persist as a synonym for *feminists*. Consciousness-raising, the group process through which women in the 1970s began to change their self-concepts, can spread to the larger community through new verbal and visual images. We cannot see unless we look self-consciously, aware that we are looking.

Some feminist theorists have suggested that the marginal position of women and members of minority groups gives them an advantage in perceiving the entire society of which they are a part (Showalter, 1981). Certainly the struggle for their rights by minority groups has raised our consciousness about past wrongs, such as the internment of Japanese-Americans during World War II and the appropriation of Native Americans' lands and even their buried dead. As the media report these facts, writers probe other and more subtle ways in which dominant ideologies have defined minorities. Women writers aware of the ways in which language and genres carry connotations established by male writers deliberately depart from conventional practices. Especially in the 1980s minority writers have vigorously revealed women's oppression: *The Color Purple*, *The Woman Warrior*, and *Beloved* undermine the conventions of even the avant-garde novel. A few "new style" works are critical and commercial successes. Most have been published by small presses and journals with little or no profit; they encourage new voices from a marginal position. Even in the face of strong resistance, new images inevitably make it harder to hold on to earlier ones. When Alice Walker's images are brought into the mainstream through film and television versions, old stereotypes change; and any lingering notion that slavery was at least sometimes beneficent cannot withstand Toni Morrison's images in *Beloved*.

Sometimes educators' deliberate attempts to bring about awareness of hidden self-images result in change. For example, a study of elementary school girls describes an experiment aimed at changing their ideas of success (Bell, 1989). After seeing videotapes of themselves, the students were asked to list physical characteristics they associated with female success; they included such standard ones as tall, thin, blonde, blue-eyed, and well-dressed, most of which they did not see in their own images. They were then shown pictures of girls and women "doing interesting things" and were asked to list their physical characteristics; fat, old, and black were among the characteristics that appeared on these lists. The researcher reports a lasting effect on students: one girl who had first wanted to look like Vanna White later saw herself as beautiful and successful because "I'm good in school, I'm Puerto Rican and Dominican, and I'm good at sports" (Bell, 1989). Another example is the hundreds of women's studies programs in colleges that often bring about lasting changes in self-images and often lead to political activism.

But we should not be too optimistic about effecting social change through such means. The images in Walker's book are subtly diminished in the media versions. They become new stereotypes, with the women characters perceived as anti-male; current ideology cannot separate women-centered and women-loving characters from man-haters. A similar fate has been the lot of Sally Benson's *Meet Me in St. Louis*, first published as a separate volume in 1942 after having appeared as a series of short stories in *The New Yorker*. Buried in the sophisticated issues of the magazine, each story seems a charming and comic view of family life at the turn of the twentieth century. Through Benson's art the fights between sisters over the boy next door seem like incidents in their development, not a lasting feud, and certainly not a stereotype of women as rivals. The 1944 movie musical starring Judy Garland (now available on video) was judged one of the year's ten best by the *New York Times* critic, who saw it as parallel to the popular play *Life with Father* and "heavily peopled with girls . . . that fair bewildering tribe" (Crowther, 1944). Although the critic's comment perpetuated the image of women as mysterious and peculiar, the play succeeded, he thought, because of wartime nostalgia for family values. In October of 1989 a multimillion dollar musical version opened on Broadway, with ten new songs added to such oldtimers as "The Boy Next Door," "The Trolley Song," and "Have Yourself a Merry Little Christmas." The *Times* critics saw the exaggerated characters as part of a shrewd entrepreneurial appeal to family values, which enabled its producers to find backers easily (Pacheco, 1989; Rich, 1989). Changing Benson's humorous individualized characters into stereotypes turned out to be a costly misjudgment, however. The producers could not have recouped their costs when the musical closed in June of 1990.

When women attempt to write about their own experiences, they are denied authority if the patterns they describe do not fit current ideology. Is there hope for social change through the efforts of women writers? It is necessary to acknowledge, of course, that not all writers of women-centered works desire change; the prolific and prosperous authors of Harlequin and other romances, for example, profit from the status quo, and several writers have become rich by revealing women's sexual desires and fantasies. Self-revelation may be only titillating to male readers and critics; in commenting on Lisa Alther's *Kinflicks*, for example, male critics focused on its plot of sexual escapades and largely ignored the tender mother-daughter relationship that occupies every other chapter. Scholars are showing that popular romances reveal how women's fantasies about a sexually satisfying and otherwise ideal husband function as a means of making their actual lives endurable (Radway, 1984). Such critiques make readers aware of the prejudices underlying traditional standards and may eventually cause both male writers and critics to change. I have always believed that the word *feminist* is gender-free: it is possible for men to understand and write sympathetically about the experience of women.

The greatest hope for change lies, I believe, in education, and many of the writers in this edition share this conviction. Writers see their work as subversive of the status quo. As readers learn to read "doubly," to see both the text and the subtext, they will perceive this message and at least some will be inspired to act to support education for women; others will want to change the status quo directly through action; and some will themselves become writers. Our perspectives broaden with the appearance of anthologies of images of women by Latin-American, Japanese, Scandinavian, Australian, Indian, Native-American, Puerto Rican, Asian-American, and lesbian writers; of works by writers of specific historical times; and of women's dreams of utopia. Images deepen through collections focusing on aspects of women's lives, such as living alone or with other women, being the "other woman" or being a mother or daughter. Literary critics analyze and compare images, including those of men by women. Equally important are works that link literary images to society and history. The need of and search for education, for example, is spelled out in an official report of the Government of India (1988), which shows that 75 percent of Indian women are illiterate and that modernization has actually diminished their opportunities for employment and education. A newspaper reports that in Korea in 1990, the "Year of the Horse," girl babies will be aborted in tremendous numbers because of an ancient tradition that girls born in this year will be "headstrong and tempestuous," and men won't want to marry them (Gittelsohn, 1990). The need to put literary images into perspective has led to a new academic field, cultural studies, which sees literature as one of many diverse practices by which culture is represented (Spivack, 1987). One critic, for example, sees the images of masculinity in the epic as behind British enthusiasm for the Falklands war (Johnson, 1987). As tenacious as such images are, there is hope that recognizing their power will eventually bring about change and that those who attempt to "shift the universe" will no longer be marginal.

Reading doubly requires that we be aware of the ways literature accomplishes its effects. Not only must we read the layers of meanings in a text, always aware of what we as readers bring to it, but we should be aware of literary conventions. Among these is separation into categories, the various literary genres. Plays, poems, and fiction have their own rules: historically, plays have been considered objective; short poems, personal; fiction, realistic. Short stories and novels differ not only in length but in expectations of how character is revealed and how to have the sense of an ending. Knowledge of these conventions enables us to perceive how specific writers are functioning. For example, the expectation that drama is objective depends on the perception that it lacks a narrative point of view; as audience or readers of a play we do not perceive the "I" or "they" of a fictional narrator and so may have the illusion that we are witnessing events as they occur. This illusion is skillfully used by dramatists. *Trifles* does not have the narrative voice Susan Glaspell used in her short-story version of this work, "A Jury of Her Peers." But she lets us hear the conversation of the women characters, and we gradually come to share their anger at the men's dismissal of their observations as trivial. Linda Pastan's poem "Marks" shows us how a first-person speaker can defy the expectation that a lyric poem will be merely personal; Pastan's speaker establishes a point of view open to general questions about the role of wife/mother. Conventions of fiction are subverted in "Girl," Jamaica Kincaid's "prose poem" in which neither the speaking voice nor the hearer is identified and there is no beginning or ending. Kincaid invites us to bring our own experience as daughters to her work.

Women writers have often used satire (Jane Austen excelled at this), but humor is a particularly difficult mode for those who have often been stereotyped, since characters made fun of are almost always stereotypical. In "A Allegory on Wimmen's Rights," Marietta Holley treads a narrow line when she makes fun not only of the objects of her heroine's wrath but of her heroine as well. Samantha's colloquial language and the absurdity of her "allegory" make the reader share her attitudes with amusement; we do not see her as the stereotypical ranting shrew henpecking her husband. All skillful writers make use of stereotypes and genre expectations for their own, often subversive, purposes.

In addition to seeing through genre conventions, readers need to interpret the multiple meanings of words in order to read doubly. Often titles are clues to the tone of a work. For example, we realize that *Trifles* is ironic; an unfinished quilt is decisive to Mrs. Wright's fate. The parallel between "On The First Night" and the story of creation in Genesis adds to the joy expressed by the speaker in Erica Jong's poem. The dictionary adds the contexts of beatings, symbols of ownership, and the sign of illiteracy to that of grades for the word *marks*; the reader who makes these additions and associations participates in the meaning of Pastan's poem.

The meanings of words and literary conventions, as well as readers' evaluation of them, change over time. In this book the organization by images mixes works from different times and places. Such an approach profits from the addition of biographical and historical information that has a bearing on writers' intentions and readers' expectations. A chronological approach to the image "The Wife," for example, would put Elizabeth Stuart Phelps's story (1852) before Sally Benson's (1930s); it would be clear that the traditional image of the wife happy to stay at home was perceived as limited long before Benson's characters find a wife's dependency a heavy burden. For the thematic approach used here, however, Benson's story comes first because it concisely outlines the stereotype, including the wife's unawareness of being one. Phelps's story becomes one of many that reveal how stultifying to the individual woman the traditional image has been and how writers have imagined escapes from the role. If Pat Parker's frankly erotic lesbian poem were to appear in a chronological volume of erotic poetry since the Greeks and Elizabethans, it would be clear that the sense of shock some readers feel is due more to the fact that the speaker is a woman than that she is homo-erotic. Alice Cary's "The Bridal Veil" presupposes the nineteenth-century expectation of love-honor-obey; the tension associated with the persona's rejection depends on knowing the "rule" she is rebelling against. Similarly, much of the effect of Jean Thompson's "Driving to Oregon" depends on its echoes of narratives about the Oregon Trail, especially recently rediscovered journals by women. Olive Schreiner's "Three Dreams in the Desert" would gain meaning by comparison with other utopian fiction; the breadth of her view contrasts, for example, with Virginia Woolf's vision of a room of one's own as a writer's utopia. Most of the works in this book can serve as the starting point for research that will show the necessity for multiple interpretations.

We can enjoy only literature that moves us; recording one's own immediate response should be the first step toward literary appreciation. We can come to understand why we are moved by going beyond our initial response to study other works of the same kind or time, other works by the same author, critiques by scholars, and opinions of peers. As an aid to such additional study, "Suggestions for Further Reading" appear at the end of this volume. A list of selections from previous editions omitted here but currently available elsewhere furnishes additional opportunities for comparisons. There is also an afterword about writing and images by my daughter, Jean Ferguson Carr, a professor at the University of Pittsburgh, who joins me in trying to widen our view of "Images of Women in Literature."

PART

I

TRADITIONAL IMAGES OF WOMEN

· ———————————————— ·

The Wife

The earliest meaning of the word *wife*, in English and in many related languages, was "woman," a general term to denote a person of the female sex. By the ninth century *wif* had narrowed to mean primarily "a woman joined to a man by marriage, a married woman," the meaning that has continued to the present. The term *woman* developed as a grammatically marked form of *man*: it is derived from *wif-man*, in which *wif* is the marker, just like the suffix *-ess* in *waitress* or *poetess*. *Man* and *woman* constitute what grammarians call a minimal contrast pair; *husband* and *wife* developed for the narrower meanings. Even in their earliest forms both pairs are asymmetrical; what is male comes first. Although both pairs identify people, the adjectives that developed from them, *masculine* and *feminine*, were first used by grammarians to differentiate categories of words largely according to characteristics of pronunciation rather than to refer to any reality. These grammatical categories were called *genders*; it was not until quite recently that the word *gender* came to refer primarily to sex-related categories that have no relationship to grammar. When the adjectives *masculine* and *feminine* did come to refer to characteristics associated with people, they too had a hierarchical relationship. The lower status of the wife is tied very closely to the English language; though this also seems to be the case in many other languages, no definitive study has yet been made.

The adjectives *masculine* and *feminine* not only describe gender differences but have become opposites with many new connotations.

Feminine has associations of weakness, passivity, and dependence, all of which are pejorative terms; strength, aggressiveness, and independence are admirable since they describe the members of society who have power. Paradoxically, the traits associated with *feminine* came to be not only expected but admired in women, the vast majority of whom throughout history have been wives. To this day women who are aggressive or even assertive are usually perceived negatively. Women are admired not for their own individual characteristics but for those appropriate to the role of wife.

The ideal wife had an early literary embodiment in the character Griselde, drawn from a folktale by the poet Geoffrey Chaucer, author of the *Canterbury Tales*, in the fourteenth century. Griselde submits first to her father and then to her husband—her submission is symbolized by her assumption of her husband's title. The daughter of a serf, Griselde is honored when chosen by a nobleman for his bride; she meekly endures her husband's abuse when he deprives her of her children and takes a new wife. She is much admired by the people who know her because of her universal caring and kindness toward all in spite of the cruelty shown to her. Chaucer's choice of narrator for Griselde's story is a clerk, an educated man with a certain authority derived from his connection with the church; though the other pilgrims who hear his story know very well that Griselde is only a fictional ideal, they enjoy the story. With religious sanction and also that of the law, this ideal has continued in Western society, even in the face of current statistics that half of all marriages end in divorce. The guilt that often accompanies the dissolution of marriage indicates how strong this old ideal remains. Divorce settlements also indicate its strength. Women bear the brunt of the economic cost: husbands' incomes usually increase after divorce, those of wives drastically decrease (Weitzman, 1985).

In the Western world and particularly in the United States, the role of weak wife is central to women's identity. A prominent sociologist (Johnson, 1988) finds that it is men who perpetuate inequality by encouraging their daughters to please daddy. Johnson shows that some cultures—largely pre-industrial—where the maternal role is central evince more gender equality. She mentions Navaho and Hopi cultures, some Pacific and Caribbean traditions, and African reverence of the mother, which still prevails among American blacks (pp. 222–228). But male dominance is often transferred from husbands and fathers to brothers and sons, and women remain subsidiary even when they are valued as mothers, spiritual leaders, and the mainstay of food production. In Africa today, for example, where women have traditionally been the producers and marketers of food, they are barred by their lower status as women from agricultural schools established by development agencies. Throughout history, most women have had to be productive workers as well as wives and mothers; but their status as workers and as autonomous agents is influenced strongly by their biological roles.

The selections in this section illustrate the weak ideal and show how often circumstances bring about departures from it. In Sally Benson's "Little Woman," Penny tries her best to live up to the ideal that had attracted her husband. Childless, she nonetheless confines herself to her home; she exaggerates her doll-like characteristics through her clothes and manners. All of her loyalty is to her husband; significantly, she has no women friends. He represents the ideal husband: tall, strong, a good provider, faithful. They seem a well-matched pair, but he begins to tire of her dependence; she seems heavy when he has to carry her. Benson only hints that Penny too is feeling her role as stressful: "the line of her mouth . . . looked set and unhappy," perhaps showing more than signs of aging.

If ideal partners can experience marriage as burdensome, it is no wonder that marriage in itself seems the cause of problems. Mrs. James in Elizabeth Stuart Phelps's story has everything from many points of view, including a faithful husband who provides well and is eager to help her find time for self-development. But even so, the claims of the wife/mother role leave Mrs. James with no time of her own, and she comforts herself by hoping for a heavenly reward for her sacrifice to husband and children. Ruth Whitman shows that wifely sacrifice symbolized by a bride's cutting off her hair "will shift the balance of the universe," so that men can be scholars and thus find favor with God. The wife's satisfaction should come, according to tradition as expressed in John Milton's *Paradise Lost*, only indirectly: "he for God, she for God in him." Alice Cary's bride warns her husband that she cannot embody such a noble self-sacrificing ideal; only if he refuses to be her "lord" can she be a good wife. Zoraida in Nicholasa Mohr's story has paid the terrible price of her sexual satisfaction in trying to live up to her husband's ideal of "a decent husband and wife." Though her mother blames the husband for Zoraida's problems, she shares his ideal: Zoraida has no one who understands her need for sexual fantasy, and the reader can only guess what further price she will pay when her rocker is taken away.

In other works it is the husband's failure to live up to ideals that causes problems. When she migrates North with her husband to escape racial discrimination, the wife in Carol Gregory's "Migration" continues her role; when the discrimination continues, she blames him and resorts to "singing spirituals." Like Mrs. James, she finds relief from an intolerable situation in religion. The reader can see that her situation is tragic: neither husband nor wife is responsible for their problems. This is also true in Bharati Mukherjee's "A Wife's Story"; the wife who moves on by emigrating cannot be bound by the traditions she has left behind. From a male point of view, her desire for self-improvement is selfish, but she has learned to love herself and cannot go back to her marriage except through pretense. This story rings true for women who have only pretended sexual satisfaction in marriage. It also expresses the pain of those who have become exiles: separation from one's roots universally causes anguish. Mukherjee's story transcends the gender problem it seems to focus on.

Jane Augustine's "Secretive" transcends its representation of an abused wife and helps readers understand the mystery of why women remain in such situations. The wife blames herself for being the victim because she shares the ideal of the good wife: she doesn't want to be "a complainer, a bitch." The reader can see the husband's ambivalence, which leads to violence. Like Ralph in Benson's story, he finds his wife's dependence a burden, yet he cannot accept her efforts to help him provide. Even a couple as closely bound as the black husband and white wife in Jean Thompson's "Driving to Oregon" experience the tensions of his failure to provide adequately: though he has felt the burden of wife and child as a "sweet weight," he almost hits her when their broken-down truck fails. When marriage finds no support from the community, tensions become almost intolerable.

Larry Brown's "Facing the Music" illustrates another almost intolerable tension: a husband cannot bear his wife's disfigurement after a mastectomy, and she is too ashamed to undress. His reaction seems primitive, instinctual; the bond created by twenty-three years of marriage is weak in the face of the bodily change. "Nothing's changed," he thinks, as they prepare to make love in the dark, but this seems like denial and the marriage seems doomed. The real causes of marital dissolution are usually hidden in the intimacy of the partners; sharing this couple's intimacy gives the reader a clue to claims of incompatibility or even mental cruelty. Linda Pastan's speaker does not share intimate revelations in "Marks"; the reader can only guess about why she is leaving. But putting her decision in the context of the many ways in which the role of wife is played out can lead to a reasonable guess, at least.

Recently scholars have found that women's problems stem not so much from conflicts between roles as from those within each role itself (Borysenko, 1990). If our expectations of the wife were different and if we supported individuals in new versions of the role, perhaps the tensions would become endurable—or at least preferable to alternatives.

LITTLE WOMAN

by

SALLY BENSON
(1900–1948)

A lifelong professional writer, Sally Benson contributed more than a hundred stories to The New Yorker *and wrote more than twenty scripts for movies such as* Bus Stop *(1961) and* The Singing Nun *(1966). Her stories appeared frequently as collections, two of which,* Junior Miss *(1941) and* Meet Me in St. Louis *(1942), have been considered novels. The film version of the latter, starring Judy Garland, was judged one of the year's ten best by the* New York Times *in 1944. It was revived on Broadway in 1989 as a multimillion-dollar musical. Though Benson's stories are sensitive and sympathetic, the adaptations are nostalgically stereotypical.*

Penny Loomis liked to look back to the day when Ralph had first seen her. It was the day she had first seen Ralph, too, but she didn't think of that. She remembered only the delighted, incredulous look in Ralph's eyes when he caught sight of her sitting in the large chair in the Matsons' living room. In the short skirts and long waists of ten years ago, she had seemed just like a doll. Later in the evening he had told her so. "I can't get over you!" he exclaimed. "You're so tiny!"

"Oh, I know! And I hate it!" she answered. "It's dreadful, really! About clothes, I mean. Why, I wear size eleven!"

"You could look taller," Louise Matson said. "Naturally, those flat-heeled shoes make you look awfully little. If you *wanted* to look taller, you could wear high heels."

Penny Loomis had surveyed her strapped, patent-leather shoes thoughtfully and then her eyes had rested for a rather long instant on Louise's substantial Size 7 brocade slippers. "It's all very well for you to talk," she replied ruefully. "Your feet are a decent size, not disgraceful little Chinese feet like mine. You have nice, *big* feet."

Taking her home that night, Ralph had commented on Louise's attitude. "She was just trying to be catty," he said. "And you were swell about it. You may be little, but you aren't *small*!"

There was nothing to it after that first evening. It was as though Ralph never knew what hit him. There were three months of being engaged, of dancing night after night, attracting attention because Ralph was so tall—over six feet—and she was so tiny. He was enchanted with her daintiness and made jokes about it. "Now where," he would ask, looking over her head and pretending he couldn't see her, "did I put that woman I had with me?"

Everybody would laugh, especially Penny. "Big silly!" she would say. "Take me home!"

Everything she did pleased and amazed him. When, the Christmas before they were married, she presented him with a scarf she had knitted, he was genuinely overwhelmed. "I don't believe it," he said, smoothing it over and over with his hands. "You're not big enough to hold the needles."

He made so much fuss about the scarf at home that his mother, who had knitted scarves, sweaters, and socks for him all his life, was inclined to be bitter. "You act as though she'd knitted that scarf with her feet," she said acidly. "And by the way, I put those golf stockings I just finished for you in your bottom bureau drawer."

His enchantment lasted long after they were married. It amused him to see her childish, round-toed shoes lying on the floor, to see her diminutive dresses hanging in the closet. Their house was full of company, too, those first months, men mostly, who marvelled with Ralph at the sight of Penny in an apron actually being able to get dinner, carrying platters of food almost bigger than she was.

They had no children, which was a pity, as Penny had fancied the idea of herself surrounded by tall, stalwart sons, but she had Ralph to flutter over and take care of. She made few friends and was content in their small apartment. Once Ralph asked her why she didn't go out more. "Do you good," he said, "to get out and play bridge or something in the afternoon. Why don't you look up Louise? You and she used to be pretty good friends."

Penny replied scornfully. Women were all right, she supposed. But she hated bridge, really. It was such a silly game. And she felt so funny going out with Louise, who was so tall. They looked ridiculous walking together.

Ralph had laughed at that. "Say, listen," he said, "I'm taller than Louise."

"You are a man," she answered. "Men are supposed to be big."

She looked so little and so pretty that Ralph agreed with her. "Louise is kind of a horse," he said.

They spent their vacations in Canada, where Ralph liked to fish. And Penny, dressed enchantingly in boys' denim trousers, checked shirt, and felt hat, lounged against cushions in the canoe while he paddled. She would scream a little, hiding her head, as he took the fish off the hooks. When they walked, Ralph carried her over the rough spots and took her arm up the hills, so that finally, although he insisted she was no trouble, he took to fishing nearer the Lodge.

Sometimes he was surprised at the number of things a man who was married to a little thing like Penny had to think of. There was the question of theatre tickets, for instance; he had to make an effort to get seats in the first row so that Penny wouldn't have to crane her neck or sit on her coat to see the stage; he must also remember to shorten his steps when they walked together or Penny got tired and out of breath; things must be left where Penny could reach them without having to stand on a chair.

Once he had spoken to her about it. "Gosh," he said "it is kind of tough to be as little as you are! I never thought how it must be for you, not being able to do things that other people do."

The instant the words were out of his mouth, he knew he had said the wrong thing. "I'd like to know what I can't do that other women can!" she told him indignantly. "I think I manage to keep busy!"

He had to admit she did keep busy. In fact, she was never still. She was as busy, he thought, as a canary in a cage, fluttering, picking, keeping up an incessant chirping. "Sure you keep busy," he said. "Busy as a bird."

When they had been married almost ten years, he went on a business trip to Chicago. The thought of being left all alone frightened Penny and she made a great deal of it. He must put a chain lock on the front door and write down where he would be every night so that she could call him in case anything happened. Her anxious fluttering depressed him, and his depression lasted until he was safely on the train and seated in the warm, noisy dining car.

His second night in Chicago, the man he had come to see, a Mr. Merrick, asked him out to dinner. Mrs. Merrick went with them. She was a plain-looking woman, a little too stout, but there was something pleasing in the monotony of her solid brown hair that had no disturbing highlights, in her soft, friendly brown eyes, and her uninteresting brown felt hat. She had the appearance of a woman who had contemplatively set aside all personal vanity and turned to other things.

Ralph was surprised to find himself having a rather hilarious evening with them, and delighted to learn that Mr. Merrick had about decided to go back to New York with him and wind up their business for good and all. "And take me," Mrs. Merrick said.

"Oh, sure, take you," Mr. Merrick agreed.

And Ralph had added, "You bet!"

That night at the hotel, he wrote to Penny. It was a long, enthusiastic letter, and he wrote everything he could think of to please her. "They asked all about you," he wrote. "And I told them you were no bigger than a minute and as pretty as a picture. So we'll take them to dinner, when I get back, which should be about Friday. I'll wire exactly when. I miss you."

As he wrote "I miss you," he stopped and put his pen down on the desk. It struck him that he hadn't missed Penny at all, while she—well, he supposed that she was rattling around in the apartment not knowing what to do with herself. It occurred to him that she ought to have something to do, something better than fussing around with things at home. Not that he wanted her to work, he thought. Penny was far too helpless and little to be able to cope with a job. His heart softened when he remembered their evenings together with Penny curled up on his lap as he sat in the big chair, talking to him a mile a minute in her rather high, clear voice. He was ashamed of the many times he had wished she would read more, and recalled one dreadful evening when he had looked up from his paper at the sound of her nervous wandering about the room to say, "For the love of Pete, *light*, can't you?"

Thinking of these things and of the fine evening he had had with the Merricks, he picked up his pen again and underlined "I miss you."

The trip back to New York with the Merricks was great, but Penny was not at the station to meet him. "Unless we've missed her," he said gaily. "She's so darned little, she's easy to miss."

He assured the Merricks that he would just dash home, change his clothes, pick up Penny, and meet them at their hotel.

Penny was waiting for him at home. She was almost hysterically glad to see him, and he noticed that the house was shining and spotless, with fresh flowers in the vases and a wood fire burning in the grate. She was already dressed for the evening in a pale-pink taffeta dress with many ruffles, and stubby satin shoes tied with large bows. She wore a ribbon around her hair, and in the shaded lights of the living room she looked very young. It was only when she followed him to the bathroom to talk to him while he shaved that he noticed her more closely; the line of her mouth, always too thin, looked set and unhappy; the skin on her face looked drawn; and there was more than a sprinkling of gray in her black hair. The pink taffeta dress looked suddenly absurd on her, and he wished that she had worn something more suitable, something more her age. Why, Penny must be thirty-five!

She was curious about the Merricks, she said. "I never heard you make so much fuss over any two people in my life. What's she like?"

"Mrs. Merrick?" he asked, struggling with his stiff white shirt. "Oh, she's darned nice."

"Oh, I *know* that," Penny answered impatiently. "I know you think she's nice. What does she look like? Is she pretty?"

"No," he told her. "You couldn't call her pretty."

"Well, is she big, little, fat, thin?"

"She's not little," he said. "Why, she'd make two of you."

This seemed to satisfy her and she asked no more about the Merricks.

At the hotel they were told that Mr. and Mrs. Merrick were waiting for them in the main dining room. Walking through the lobby and down the long corridor, Penny was pleasantly conscious of the stir they created. She even shortened her steps a little, so that she appeared to be keeping up with Ralph by tripping at his side.

Mrs. Merrick's first words to her were what she expected. "Why, you're tiny!"

Penny laughed sweetly and looked up at Ralph. "Yes, isn't it silly?" she said. "I must look perfectly absurd beside Ralph, who is so enormous."

Mrs. Merrick's eyes took in every detail of Penny, her dress, her shoes, and the ribbon around her hair, and then she said, in almost the exact words that Louise had used so many years ago, "Do you know, with heels you'd look much taller. Why, you must be five feet one or so, and with good, high heels you'd look three inches taller. That would make you five feet four, which is a nice height. A great many movie actresses are five feet four."

Penny laughed again, but she flushed slightly.

"Now, Nellie," Mr. Merrick said, "don't go to making people over the first minute you see them. Maybe Mrs. Loomis *likes* to look small."

"Nonsense!" Mrs. Merrick exclaimed heartily. "No one wants to look like a midget! That is, no one wants to look *too* different. I know I was awfully tall for my age when I was about fifteen and I felt terribly about it. I was a sight, I can tell you."

And you're a sight now, Penny thought furiously. She chose a seat next to Mrs. Merrick and during dinner she rested her small, thin hand next to Mrs. Merrick's large, square one. She picked at her food daintily and exclaimed pleasantly when the other woman ordered ice cream with chocolate sauce for dessert. "Not that I wouldn't love it, but I just haven't *room*," she said.

Later, when the music started, she was surprised to see Ralph spring eagerly to his feet and ask Mrs. Merrick to dance.

"I haven't danced much lately," he said. "But let's go!"

He put one arm around Mrs. Merrick's waist and they started off. It was pleasant to have her face so near his own, to feel her soft, straight hair brush his forehead. She wore a dark-brown velvet dress, not very new and not very smart, but she had dignity and she moved smoothly with him across the dance floor. Over her shoulder he saw Penny dancing with Mr. Merrick. She was looking up into his face and talking brightly and animatedly. Mr. Merrick was bending down to catch what she was saying, smiling a frozen sort of smile, but he didn't look very happy.

The rest of the evening was not especially successful. Ralph tried in vain to recapture the spirit of hilarity he had felt with the Merricks in Chicago. But there was a sort of uneasiness in the air, even though Penny showed them several match tricks.

He was a little relieved, as they said good night, to learn that the Merricks had bought theatre tickets for the following evening and were leaving the day after for Chicago.

All the way home, Ralph sat in one corner of the taxi watching Penny as she talked. Her head was bent slightly to one side in the birdlike way she affected, and the white street lights flashing through the window were not kind to her. As he looked at her, she seemed to grow smaller and smaller until there was nothing much left of her but a pink taffeta dress and a pink ribbon. It had started to rain and the drops on the glass cast black dots on the pink taffeta dress, and he had the impression that it, too, might eventually disappear.

He did not notice that the cab had stopped in front of their apartment until Penny's voice gaily brought him back to earth. It was habit that made him pick her up and carry her across the wet, slippery pavement. And for such a little woman, she felt surprisingly heavy in his arms.

THE ANGEL OVER THE
RIGHT SHOULDER

by

ELIZABETH STUART PHELPS
(1815–1852)

Daughter of a prominent clergyman in Andover, Massachusetts, Elizabeth Stuart Phelps studied in Boston and had published brief articles in a religious journal before she turned sixteen. While still a teenager, she began to suffer from a lifelong disease that caused frequent headaches and incidents of blindness and paralysis. Nevertheless, she married, had three children, and was a prolific writer of newspaper articles, children's books, and fiction. Her 1851 novel, The Sunny Side: or, The Country Minister's Wife, *a best seller famous for its realistic portrayal of family life and relationships, was translated into several languages.* The Angel Over the Right Shoulder *was first published in 1852 as a short gift-book and went through many editions. It documents not only a wife's difficulties in self-development but also her concern for her daughter's opportunities.* ?

"There! a woman's work is never done," said Mrs. James; "I thought, for once, I was through; but just look at that lamp, now! it will not burn, and I must go and spend half an hour over it."

"Don't you wish you had never been married?" said Mr. James, with a good-natured laugh.

"Yes"—rose to her lips, but was checked by a glance at the group upon the floor, where her husband was stretched out, and two little urchins with sparkling eyes and glowing cheeks, were climbing and tumbling over him, as if they found in this play the very essence of fun.

She did say, "I should like the good, without the evil, if I could have it."

"You have no evils to endure," replied her husband.

"That is just all you gentlemen know about it. What would you think, if you could not get an uninterrupted half hour to yourself, from morning till night? I believe you would give up trying to do anything."

"There is no need of that; all you want, is *system*. If you arranged your work systematically, you would find that you could command your time."

"Well," was the reply, "all I wish is, that you could just follow me around for one day, and see what I have to do. If you could reduce it all to system, I think you would show yourself a genius."

When the lamp was trimmed, the conversation was resumed. Mr. James had employed the "half hour," in meditating on this subject.

"Wife," said he, as she came in, "I have a plan to propose to you, and I wish you to promise me beforehand, that you will accede to it. It is to be an experiment, I acknowledge, but I wish it to have a fair trial. Now to please me, will you promise?"

Mrs. James hesitated. She felt almost sure that his plan would be quite impracticable, for what does a man know of a woman's work? yet she promised.

"Now I wish you," said he, "to set apart two hours of every day for your own private use. Make a point of going to your room and locking yourself in, and also make up your mind to let the work which is not done, go undone, if it must. Spend this time on just those things which will be most profitable to yourself. I shall bind you to your promise for one month—then, if it has proved a total failure, we will devise something else."

"When shall I begin?"

"To-morrow."

The morrow came. Mrs. James had chosen the two hours before dinner as being, on the whole, the most convenient and the least liable to interruption. They dined at one o'clock. She wished to finish her morning work, get dressed for the day, and enter her room at eleven.

Hearty as were her efforts to accomplish this, the hour of eleven found her with her work but half done; yet, true to her promise, she left all, retired to her room and locked the door.

With some interest and hope, she immediately marked out a course of reading and study, for these two precious hours; then, arranging her table, her books, pen and paper, she commenced a schedule of her work with much enthusiasm. Scarcely had she dipped her pen in ink, when she heard the tramping of little feet along the hall, and then a pounding at her door.

"Mamma! mamma! I cannot find my mittens, and Hannah is going to slide without me."

"Go to Amy, my dear; mamma is busy."

"So Amy busy too; she say she can't leave baby."

The child began to cry, still standing close to the fastened door. Mrs. James knew the easiest, and indeed the only way of settling the trouble, was to go herself and hunt up the missing mittens. Then a parley must be held with Frank, to induce him to wait for his sister, and the child's tears must be dried, and little hearts must be all set right before the children went out to play; and so favorable an opportunity must not be suffered to slip, without impressing on young minds the importance of having a "place for everything and everything in its place;" this took time; and when Mrs. James returned to her study, her watch told her that *half* her portion had gone. Quietly resuming her work, she was endeavoring to mend her broken train of thought, when heavier steps were heard in the hall, and the fastened door was once more besieged. Now, Mr. James must be admitted.

"Mary," said he, "cannot you come and sew a string on for me? I do believe there is not a bosom in my drawer in order, and I am in a great hurry. I ought to have been down town an hour ago."

The schedule was thrown aside, the work-basket taken, and Mrs. James followed him. She soon sewed on the tape, but then a button needed fastening—and at last a rip in his glove, was to be mended. As Mrs. James stitched away on the glove, a smile lurked in the corners of her mouth, which her husband observed.

"What are you laughing at?" asked he.

"To think how famously your plan works."

"I declare!" said he, "is this your study hour? I am sorry, but what can a man do? He cannot go down town without a shirt bosom!"

"Certainly not," said his wife, quietly.

When her liege lord was fairly equipped and off, Mrs. James returned to her room. A half an hour yet remained to her, and of this she determined to make the most. But scarcely had she resumed her pen, when there was another disturbance in the entry. Amy had returned from walking out with the baby, and she entered the nursery with him, that she might get him to sleep. Now it happened that the only room in the house which Mrs. James could have to herself with a fire, was the one adjoining the nursery. She had become so accustomed to the ordinary noise of the children, that it did not disturb her; but the very extraordinary noise which master Charley sometimes felt called upon to make, when he was fairly on his back in the cradle, did disturb the unity of her thoughts. The words which she was reading rose and fell with the screams and lulls of the child, and she felt obliged to close her book, until the storm was over. When quiet was restored in the cradle, the children came in from sliding, crying with cold fingers—and just as she was going to them, the dinner-bell rang.

"How did your new plan work this morning?" inquired Mr. James.

"Famously," was the reply, "I read about seventy pages of German, and as many more in French."

"I am sure *I* did not hinder you long."

"No—yours was only one of a dozen interruptions."

"O, well! you must not get discouraged. Nothing succeeds well the first time. Persist in your arrangement, and by and by the family will learn that if they want anything of you, they must wait until after dinner."

"But what can a man do?" replied his wife; "he cannot go down town without a shirt-bosom."

"I was in a bad case," replied Mr. James, "it may not happen again. I am anxious to have you try the month out faithfully, and then we will see what has come of it."

The second day of trial was a stormy one. As the morning was dark, Bridget over-slept, and consequently breakfast was too late by an hour. This lost hour Mrs. James could not recover. When the clock struck eleven, she seemed but to have commenced her morning's work, so much remained to be done. With mind disturbed and spirits depressed, she left her household matters "in the suds," as they were, and punctually retired to her study. She soon found, however, that she could not fix her attention upon any intellectual pursuit. Neglected duties haunted her, like ghosts around the guilty conscience. Perceiving that she was doing nothing with her books, and not wishing to lose the morning wholly, she commenced writing a letter. Bridget interrupted her before she had proceeded far on the first page.

"What, ma'am, shall we have for dinner? No marketing ha'n't come."

"Have some steaks, then."

"We ha'n't got none, ma'am."

"I will send out for some, directly."

Now there was no one to send but Amy, and Mrs. James knew it. With a sigh, she put down her letter and went into the nursery.

"Amy, Mr. James has forgotten our marketing. I should like to have you run over to the provision store, and order some beef-steaks. I will stay with the baby."

Amy was not much pleased to be sent out on this errand. She remarked, that "she must change her dress first."

"Be as quick as possible," said Mrs. James, "for I am particularly engaged at this hour."

Amy neither obeyed, nor disobeyed, but managed to take her own time, without any very deliberate intention to do so. Mrs. James, hoping to get along with a sentence or two, took her German book into the nursery. But this arrangement was not to master Charley's mind. A fig did he care for German, but "the kitties," he must have, whether or no—and kitties he would find in that particular book—so he turned its leaves over in great haste. Half of the time on the second day of trial had gone, when Amy returned and Mrs. James with a sigh, left her nursery. Before one o'clock, she was twice called into the kitchen to superintend some important dinner arrangement, and thus it turned out that she did not finish one page of her letter.

On the third morning the sun shone, and Mrs. James rose early, made every provision which she deemed necessary for dinner, and for the comfort of her family; and then, elated by her success, in good spirits, and with good courage, she entered her study precisely at eleven o'clock, and locked her door. Her books were opened, and the challenge given to a hard German lesson. Scarcely had she made the first onset, when the doorbell was heard to ring, and soon Bridget coming nearer and nearer—then tapping at the door.

"Somebodies wants to see you in the parlor, ma'am."

"Tell them I am engaged, Bridget."

"I told 'em you were to-home, ma'am, and they sent up their names, but I ha'n't got 'em, jist."

There was no help for it—Mrs. James must go down to receive her callers. She had to smile when she felt little like it—to be sociable when her thoughts were busy with her task. Her friends made a long call—they had nothing else to do with their time, and when they went, others came. In very unsatisfactory chit-chat, her morning slipped away.

On the next day, Mr. James invited company to tea, and her morning was devoted to preparing for it; she did not enter her study. On the day following, a sick head ache confined her to her bed, and on Saturday the care of the baby devolved upon her, as Amy had extra work to do. Thus passed the first week.

True to her promise, Mrs. James patiently persevered for a month, in her efforts to secure for herself this little fragment of her broken time, but with what success, the first week's history can tell. With its close, closed the month of December.

On the last day of the old year, she was so much occupied in her preparations for the morrow's festival, that the last hour of the day was approaching, before she made her good night's call in the nursery. She first went to the crib and looked at the baby. There he lay in his innocence and beauty, fast asleep. She softly stroked his golden hair—she kissed gently his rosy cheek—she pressed the little dimpled hand in hers, and then, carefully drawing the coverlet over it, tucked it in, and stealing yet another kiss—she left him to his peaceful dreams and sat down on her daughter's bed. She also slept sweetly, with her dolly hugged to her bosom. At this her mother smiled, but soon grave thoughts entered her mind, and these deepened into sad ones. She thought of her disappointment and the failure of her plans. To her, not only the past month but the whole past year, seemed to have been one of fruitless effort—all broken and disjointed—even her hours of religious duty had been encroached upon, and disturbed. She had accomplished nothing, that she could see, but to keep her house and family in order, and even this, to her saddened mind, seemed to have been but indifferently done. She was conscious of yearnings for a more earnest life than this. Unsatisfied longings for something which she had not attained, often clouded what, otherwise, would have been a bright day to her; and yet the causes of these feelings seemed to lie in a dim and misty region, which her eye could not penetrate.

What then did she need? To see some *results* from her life's work? To know that a golden cord bound her life-threads together into *unity* of purpose—notwithstanding they seemed, so often, single and broken?

She was quite sure that she felt no desire to shrink from duty, however humble, but she sighed for some comforting assurance of what *was duty*. Her employments, conflicting as they did with her tastes, seemed to her frivolous and useless. It seemed to her that there was some better way of living, which she, from deficiency in energy of character, or of principle, had failed to discover. As she leaned over her child, her tears fell fast upon its young brow.

Most earnestly did she wish, that she could shield that child from the disappointments and mistakes and self-reproach from which the mother was then suffering; that the little one might take up life where she could give it to her—all mended by her own experience. It would have been a comfort to have felt, that in fighting the battle, she had fought for both; yet she knew that so it could not be—that for ourselves must we all learn what are those things which "make for our peace."

The tears were in her eyes, as she gave the good-night to her sleeping daughter—then with soft steps she entered an adjoining room, and there fairly kissed out the old year on another chubby cheek, which nestled among the pillows. At length she sought her own rest.

Soon she found herself in a singular place. She was traversing a vast plain. No trees were visible, save those which skirted the distant horizon, and on their broad tops rested wreaths of golden clouds. Before her was a female, who was journeying towards that region of light. Little children were about her, now in her arms, now running by her side, and as they travelled, she occupied herself in caring for them. She taught them how to place their little feet—she gave them timely warnings of the pit-falls—she gently lifted them over the stumbling-blocks. When they were weary, she soothed them by singing of that brighter land, which she kept ever in view, and towards which she seemed hastening with her little flock. But what was most remarkable was, that, all unknown to her, she was constantly watched by two angels, who reposed on two golden clouds which floated above her. Before each was a golden book, and a pen of gold. One angel, with mild and loving eyes, peered constantly over her right shoulder—another kept as strict watch over her left. Not a deed, not a word, not a look, escaped their notice. When a good deed, word, look, went from her, the angel over the right shoulder with a glad smile, wrote it down in his book; when an evil, however trivial, the angel over the left shoulder recorded it in his book—then with sorrowful eyes followed the pilgrim until he observed penitence for the wrong, upon which he dropped a tear on the record, and blotted it out, and both angels rejoiced.

To the looker-on, it seemed that the traveller did nothing which was worthy of such careful record. Sometimes she did but bathe the weary feet of her little children, but the angel over the *right shoulder*—wrote it down. Sometimes she did but patiently wait to lure back a little truant who had turned his face away from the distant light, but the angel over the *right shoulder*—wrote it down. Sometimes she did but soothe an angry feeling or raise a drooping eye-lid, or kiss away a little grief; but the angel over the right shoulder—*wrote it down*.

Sometimes, her eye was fixed so intently on that golden horizon, and she became so eager to make progress thither, that the little ones, missing her care, did languish or stray. Then it was that the angel over the *left shoulder*, lifted his golden pen, and made the entry, and followed her with sorrowful eyes, until he could blot it out. Sometimes she seemed to advance rapidly, but in her haste the little ones had fallen back, and it was the sorrowing angel who recorded her progress. Sometimes so intent was she to gird up her loins and have her lamp trimmed and burning, that the little children wandered away quite into forbidden paths, and it was the angel over the *left shoulder* who recorded her diligence.

Now the observer as she looked, felt that this was a faithful and true record, and was to be kept to that journey's end. The strong clasps of gold on those golden books, also impressed her with the conviction that, when they were closed, it would only be for a future opening.

Her sympathies were warmly enlisted for the gentle traveller, and with a beating heart she quickened her steps that she might overtake her. She wished to tell her of the angels keeping watch above her—to entreat her to be faithful and patient to the end—for her life's work was all written down—every item of it—and the *results* would be known when those golden books should be unclasped. She wished to beg of her to think no duty trivial which must be done, for over her right shoulder and over her left were recording angels, who would surely take note of all!

Eager to warn the traveller of what she had seen, she touched her. The traveller turned, and she recognized or seemed to recognize *herself*. Startled and alarmed she awoke in tears. The gray light of morning struggled through the half-open shutter, the door was ajar and merry faces were peeping in.

"Wish you a happy new year, mamma,"—"Wish you a *Happy new Year*,"—"a happy noo ear."

She returned the merry greeting most heartily. It seemed to her as if she had entered upon a new existence. She had found her way through the thicket in which she had been entangled, and a light was now about her path. The *Angel over the Right Shoulder* whom she had seen in her dream, would bind up in his golden book her life's work, if it were but well done. He required of her no great deeds, but faithfulness and patience to the end of the race which was set before her. Now she could see plainly enough, that though it was right and important for her to cultivate her own mind and heart, it was equally right and equally important; to meet and perform faithfully all those little household cares and duties on which the comfort and virtue of her family depended; for into these things the angels carefully looked—and these duties and cares acquired a dignity from the strokes of that golden pen—they could not be neglected without danger.

ELIZABETH STUART PHELPS
35

Sad thoughts and sadder misgivings—undefined yearnings and ungratified longings seemed to have taken their flight with the Old Year, and it was with fresh resolution and cheerful hope, and a happy heart, she welcomed the *Glad* New Year. The *Angel over the Right Shoulder* would go with her, and if she were found faithful, would strengthen and comfort her to its close.

CUTTING THE JEWISH BRIDE'S HAIR

by

RUTH WHITMAN
(b. 1922)

After graduating from Radcliffe College in 1944 with honors in both Greek and English, Ruth Whitman became a translator of Yiddish poems, an editor, a teacher, and a poet. Her experience is reflected in Becoming a Poet: Source, Processes, and Practice *(1982). Three of her six volumes of poetry are re-creations of the interior lives of women: Tamsen Donner, a member of the group of Oregon pioneers thought to have resorted to cannibalism; Lizzie Borden, accused of murdering her parents; and Hanna Senesh, a Hungarian partisan who died heroically during World War II at the age of twenty-three. Whitman has won many awards and has held grants from the National Endowment for the Arts and the Bunting Institute at Radcliffe.*

It's to possess more than the skin
that those old world Jews
exacted the hair of their brides.
   Good husband, lover of the Torah,
     does the calligraphy of your bride's hair
     interrupt your page?

Before the clownish friction of flesh
creating out of nothing
a mockup of its begetters,
a miraculous puppet of God,
you must first divorce her from her vanity.

She will snip off her pride,
cut back her appetite to be devoured,
she will keep herself well braided,
her love's furniture will not endanger you,
   but this little amputation
   will shift the balance of the universe.

THE BRIDAL VEIL

by

ALICE CARY
(1820–1871)

Born on a farm near Cincinnati, Alice Cary and her sister Phoebe were educated at home. The poems they began to publish as teenagers were widely admired; Edgar Allan Poe considered a lyric by Alice to be one of the most musically perfect in English. After moving to New York in 1850, the two sisters earned a living by writing; Alice wrote eight volumes of prose, and the two published several volumes of poetry. They held a literary salon in their home for many years; both also worked for women's suffrage and the abolition of slavery. Alice's realistic novel Clovernook; or Recollections of the West *(1852) was so successful that she produced a sequel the following year. The first book was widely pirated in England because it was one of the first to deal realistically with western America. In 1987 a collection edited by Judith Fetterly,* Clovernook Sketches and Other Stories, *was published by Rutgers University Press.*

•————————————————•

We're married, they say, and you think you have won me,—
Well, take this white veil from my head, and look on me:
Here's matter to vex you, and matter to grieve you,
Here's doubt to distrust you, and faith to believe you,—
I am all as you see, common earth, common dew;
Be wary, and mould me to roses, not rue!

Ah! shake out the filmy thing, fold after fold,
And see if you have me to keep and to hold,—
Look close on my heart—see the worst of its sinning—
It is not yours to-day for the yesterday's winning—
The past is not mine—I am too proud to borrow—
You must grow to new heights if I love you to-morrow.

We're married! I'm plighted to hold up your praises,
As the turf at your feet does its handful of daisies;
That way lies my honor,—my pathway of pride,

But, mark you, if greener grass grow either side,
I shall know it, and keeping in body with you,
Shall walk in my spirit with feet on the dew!

We're married! Oh, pray that our love do not fail!
I have wings flattened down and hid under my veil:
They are subtle as light—you can never undo them,
And swift in their flight—you can never pursue them,
And spite of all clasping, and spite of all bands,
I can slip like a shadow, a dream, from your hands.

Nay, call me not cruel, and fear not to take me,
I am yours for my lifetime, to be what you make me,—
To wear my white veil for a sign, or a cover,
As you shall be proven my lord, or my lover;
A cover for peace that is dead, or a token
Of bliss that can never be written or spoken.

AUNT ROSANA'S ROCKER

(Zoraida)

by

NICHOLASA MOHR

(b. 1935)

*Born in New York City, Nicholasa Mohr has been an active mem-
ber of its Puerto Rican–American community. She attended art
schools and became a well-known painter and printmaker; the
jacket design she did for her novel* Nilda *(1973) won an award
from the Society of Illustrators. She is also a writer and has won
several prestigious awards for her juvenile and teenage novels. She
has taught both art and creative writing for many years.* Rituals
of Survival: A Woman's Portfolio *(1986), from which this selection
is taken, is a series of fictional character sketches of women sur-
vivors of urban blight, poverty, and stereotypical roles.*

Casto paced nervously, but softly, the full length of the small kitchen,
then quietly, he tiptoed across the kitchen threshhold into the living
room. After going a few feet, he stopped to listen. The sounds were getting louder. Casto returned to the kitchen, switched on the light, and sat
down trying to ignore what he heard. But the familiar sounds were coming directly from their bedroom where Zoraida was. They grew louder as
they traveled past the tiny foyer, the living room and into the kitchen,
which was the room furthest away from her.

Leaning forward, Casto stretched his hands out palms down on the
kitchen table. Slowly he made two fists, squeezing tightly, and watched
as his knuckles popped out tensely under his skin. He could almost feel
her presence there, next to him, panting and breathing heavily. The panting developed into moans of sensual pleasure, disrupting the silence of
the apartment.

"If only I could beat someone!" Casto whispered hoarsely, banging his
fists against the table and upsetting the sugar bowl. The cover slipped off
the bowl, landed on its side and rolled toward the edge of the table. Casto
waited for it to drop to the floor, anticipating a loud crash, but the cover
stopped right at the very edge and fell quietly and flatly on the table,
barely making a sound.

He looked up at the electric clock on the wall over the refrigerator; it
was two-thirty in the morning.

THE WIFE

Again, Casto tried not to listen and concentrated instead on the night noises outside in the street. Traffic on the avenue had almost completely disappeared. Occasionally, a car sped by; someone's footsteps echoed against the pavement, and off at a distance, he heard a popular tune being whistled. Casto instinctively hummed along until the sound slipped away, and he then realized he was shivering. The old radiators had stopped clanking and hissing earlier; they were now ice cold. He remembered that the landlord never sent up heat after ten at night. He wished he had thought to bring a sweater or blanket with him; he was afraid of catching a cold. But he would not go back inside; instead, he opened his special section of the cupboard and searched among his countless bottles of vitamins and nutrient supplements until he found the jar of natural vitamin C tablets. He popped several tablets into his mouth and sat down, resigned to the fact that he would rather stay here, where he felt safe, even at the risk of getting a chill. This was as far away as he could get from her, without leaving the apartment.

The sounds had now become louder and more intense. Casto raised his hands and covered his ears. He shut his eyes trying not to imagine what she was doing now. But with each sound, he could clearly see her in her ecstasy. Casto recalled how he had jumped out of bed in a fright the first time it had happened. Positive that she had gone into convulsions, he had stood almost paralyzed at a safe distance looking down at her. He didn't know what to do. And, as he helplessly watched her, his stomach had suddenly turned ice-cold with fear. Zoraida seemed to be another person. She was stretched out on the bed pulling at the covers; turning, twisting her body and rocking her buttocks sensually. Her knees had been bent upward with her legs far apart and she had thrust her pelvis forward forcefully and rhythmically. Zoraida's head was pushed back and her mouth open, as she licked her lips, moaning and gasping with excitement. Casto remembered Zoraida's eyes when she had opened them for brief moments. They had been fixed on someone or something, as if beckoning; but there was no one and certainly nothing he could see in the darkness of the room. She had rolled back the pupils and only the whites of her eyes were visible. She had blinked rapidly, shutting her eyes and twitching her nose and mouth. Then, a smile had passed her lips and a stream of saliva had run down her chin, neck and chest.

Now, as he heard low moans filled with pleasure, interrupted by short painful yelps that pierced right through him, Casto could also imagine her every gesture.

Putting down his hands, Casto opened his eyes. All he could do was wait patiently, as he always did, wait for her to finish. Maybe tonight won't be a long one; Casto swallowed anxiously.

He remembered about the meeting he had arranged earlier in the evening without Zoraida's knowledge, and felt better. After work, he had gone to see his mother; then they had both gone to see Zoraida's parents. It had been difficult for him to speak about it, but he had managed somehow to tell them everything. At first they had reacted with disbelief, but after he had explained carefully and in detail what was happening, they had understood his embarrassment and his reluctance to discuss this with anyone. He told them that when it all had begun, he was positive Zoraida was reacting to a high fever and was simply dreaming, perhaps even hallucinating. But, it kept happening, and it soon developed into something that occurred frequently, almost every night.

He finally realized something or someone had taken a hold of her. He was sure she was not alone in that room and in that bed!

It was all bizarre and, unless one actually saw her, he explained, it was truly beyond belief. Why, her actions were lewd and vulgar, and if they were sexual, as it seemed, then this was not the kind of sex a decent husband and wife engage in. What was even harder for him to bear was her enjoyment. Yes, this was difficult, watching her total enjoyment of this whole disgusting business! And, to make matters more complicated, the next day, Zoraida seemed to remember nothing. In fact, during the day, she was normal again. Perhaps a bit more tired than usual, but then, who wouldn't be after such an exhausting ordeal? And, lately she had become even less talkative with him, almost silent. But, make no mistake, Casto assured them, Zoraida remained a wonderful housekeeper and devoted mother. Supper was served on time, chores were done without fuss, the apartment was immaculate, and the kids were attended to without any problems. This happened only at night, or rather early in the morning, at about two or two-thirty. He had not slept properly since this whole affair started. After all, he had to drive out to New Jersey to earn his living and his strength and sleep were being sapped away. He had even considered sleeping on the living room couch, but he would not be driven out of his own bed. He was still a man after all, a macho, master of his home, someone to be reckoned with, not be pushed out!

Trying to control his anger, Casto had confessed that it had been a period of almost two months since he had normal and natural relations with his wife. He reminded them that he, as a man, had his needs, and this would surely make him ill, if it continued. Of course, he would not touch her . . . not as she was right now. After all, he reasoned, who knows what he could catch from her? As long as she was under the control of something—whatever it might be—he would keep his distance. No, Casto told them, he wanted no part of their daughter as a woman, not as long as she remained in this condition.

When her parents had asked him what Zoraida had to say about all of this, Casto had laughed, answering that she knew even less about it than he did. In fact, at one point she did not believe him and had sworn on the children's souls, claiming her innocence. But Casto had persisted and now Zoraida had finally believed him. She felt that she might be the victim of something, perhaps a phenomenon. Who knows? When Zoraida's parents and his mother suggested a consultation with Doña Digna, the spiritualist, he had quickly agreed.

Casto jumped slightly in his chair as he heard loud passionate moans and deep groans emanate from the bedroom and fill the kitchen.

"Stop it . . . stop, you bitch!" Casto clenched his teeth, spitting out the words. But he took care not to raise his voice. "Stop it! What a happy victim you are! Puta! Whore! Some phenomenon . . . I don't believe you and your story." But, even as he said these words, Casto knew he was not quite sure what to believe.

The first loud thump startled Casto and he braced himself and waited, anticipating what was to come. He heard the legs on their large double bed pounding the floor as the thumping became louder and faster.

Casto shuddered and folded his arms, digging his fingers into the flesh of his forearms. After a few moments, he finally heard her release, one long cry followed by several grunts, and then silence. He relaxed and sighed deeply with relief; it was all over.

"Animal . . . she's just like an animal, no better than an alley cat in heat." Casto was wet with cold perspiration. He was most frightened of this last part. "Little hypocrite!"

Casto remembered how she always urged him to hurry, be quiet, and get it over with, on account of the children. A lot she cares about him tonight! Never in all their years of marriage had she ever uttered such sounds—he shook his head—or shown any passion or much interest in doing it.

Casto looked up at the clock; it was two minutes to three. He thought about the noise, almost afraid to move, fearful that his downstairs neighbor Roberto might knock on the door any moment. He recalled how Roberto had called him aside one morning and spoken to him, "Two and three in the morning, my friend; can't you and your wife control your passions at such an ungodly hour? My God . . . such goings on! Man, and to tell you the truth, you people up there get me all worked up and horny. Then, when I touch my old lady, she won't cooperate at that time, eh?" He had poked Casto playfully and winked, "Hey, what am I gonna do? Have a heart, friend." Casto shook his head, how humiliating and so damned condescending. They were behaving like the most common, vulgar people. Soon the whole fucking building would know! Roberto Thomas and his big mouth! Yes, and what will that sucker say to me next time? Casto trembled with anger. He wanted to rush in and shake Zoraida, wake her, beat her; he wanted to demand an explanation or else! But, he knew it wouldn't do any good. Twice he had tried. The first time, he had spoken to her the following day. The second time, he had tried to wake her up and she had only become wilder with him, almost violent, scaring him out of the bedroom. Afterwards, things had only become worse. During the day she withdrew, practically not speaking one word to him. The next few nights she had become wilder and the ordeal lasted even longer. No, he could not confront her.

Casto realized all was quiet again. He shut off the light, then stood and slowly, with trepidation, walked through the living room and entered the small foyer leading to their bedroom. He stopped before the children's bedroom, and carefully turned the knob, partially opening the door. All three were fast asleep. He was grateful they never woke up. What could he say to them? That their mother was sick? But sick with what?

As he stood at the entrance of their bedroom, Casto squinted, scrutinizing every corner of the room before entering. The street lights seeping through the venetian blinds dimly illuminated the overcrowded bedroom. All was peaceful and quiet; nothing was disturbed or changed in any visible way. Satisfied, he walked in and looked down at Zoraida. She was fast asleep, breathing deeply and evenly, a look of serene contentment covered her face. Her long dark hair was spread over the pillow and spilled out onto the covers. Casto was struck by her radiant appearance each time it was all over. She had an air of glamour, so strange in a woman as plain as Zoraida. He realized, as he continued to stare at her, that he was frightened of Zoraida. He wanted to laugh at himself, but when Zoraida turned her head slightly, Casto found himself backing out of the room.

Casto stood at the entrance and whispered, "Zoraida, nena . . . are . . . are you awake?" She did not stir. Casto waited perfectly still and kept his eyes on her. After a few moments, Casto composed himself. He was sure she would remain sleeping; she had never woken up after it was all over. Slowly, he entered the room and inched his way past the bulky bureau, the triple dresser and the rocking chair near the window, finally reaching his side of the bed.

Casto rapidly made the sign of the cross before he lay down beside Zoraida. He was not very religious, he could take it or leave it; but, now, he reasoned that by crossing himself he was on God's side.

Casto glanced at the alarm clock; there were only two-and-a-half hours of sleep left before starting the long trip out to the docks of Bayonne, New Jersey. God, he was damned tired; he hardly ever got enough sleep anymore. This shit had to stop! Never mind, wait until the meeting. He remembered that they were all going to see Doña Digna, the spiritualist. That ought to change things. He smiled and felt some comfort knowing that this burden would soon be lifted. Seconds later he shut his eyes and fell fast asleep.

Everyone finished supper. Except for the children's chatter and Junior's protests about finishing his food, it had been a silent meal.

Casto got up and opened his special section of the cupboard. The children watched the familiar ritual without much interest as their father set out several jars of vitamins, two bottles of iron and liver tonic and a small plastic box containing therapeutic tablets. Casto carefully counted out and popped an assortment of twenty-four vitamin tablets into his mouth and then took several spoonfuls of tonic. He carefully examined the contents of the plastic box and decided not to take any of those tablets.

"Okay, Clarita, today you take vitamin C . . . and two multivitamin supplements. You, too, Eddie and Junior, you might as well . . ."

The children accepted the vitamins he gave them without resistance or fuss. They knew by now that no one could be excused from the table until Casto had finished taking and dispensing vitamins and tonic.

"Okay, kids, that's it. You can all have dessert later when your grandparents get here."

Quickly the children left.

Although Casto often suggested that Zoraida should eat properly, he had never asked her to take any of his vitamins or tonic, and she had never expressed either a desire or interest to do so.

He looked at Zoraida as she worked clearing the table and putting things away. Zoraida felt her heart pounding fiercely and she found it difficult to breathe. She wanted him to stop staring at her like that. Lately she found his staring unbearable. Zoraida's shyness had always determined her behavior in life. Ever since she could remember, any attempt that others made at intimate conversations or long discussions created feelings of constraint, developing into such anxiety that when she spoke, her voice had a tendency to fade. This was a constant problem for her; people often asked, "What was that?" or "Did you say something?" These feelings extended even into her family life. When her children asked impertinent questions, she would blush, unable to answer. Zoraida was ashamed of her own nakedness with Casto and would only undress when he was not present. When her children chanced to see her undressed at an unguarded moment, she would be distraught for several days.

It had been Casto's self assurance and his ability to be aggressive and determined with others that had attracted her to him.

Casto looked at Zoraida as she worked. "I'll put my things back and get the coffee started for when they get here," he said. She nodded and continued swiftly and silently with her chores.

Zoraida was twenty-eight, and although she had borne four children (three living, one still-born) and had suffered several miscarriages, she was of slight build and thin, with narrow hips. She had a broad face and her smile revealed a wide space between her two front teeth. As a result, she appeared frail and childlike, much younger than her years. Whenever she was tired, dark circles formed under her eyes, contrasting against the paleness of her skin. This evening, she seemed to look even paler than ever to Casto; almost ghostlike.

Casto was, by nature, hypochondriacal and preoccupied with avoiding all sorts of diseases. He was tall and robust, with a broad frame; in fact, he was the picture of good health. He became furious when others laughed at him for taking so many vitamins and health foods. Most people ignored his pronouncements of ill health and even commented behind his back. "Casto'll live to be one hundred if he lives a day . . . why, he's as fit as an ox! It's Zoraida who should take all them vitamins and then complain some. She looks like a toothpick, una flaca! That woman has nothing to show. I wonder what Casto ever saw in her, eh?"

Yet, it was her frail and sickly appearance that had attracted him the first time he saw her. He was visiting his married sister, Purencia, when Zoraida had walked in with her friend, Anna. Anna was a beautiful, voluptuous young woman with an olive tone to her skin that glowed; and when she smiled, her white teeth and full lips made her appear radiant. Zoraida, thin and pale by contrast, looked ill. In Casto's presence, she had smiled sheepishly, blushing from time to time. Anna had flirted openly, and commented on Purencia's brother, "You didn't tell me you had such a gorgeous macho in your family. Trying to keep him a secret, girl?" But it had been Zoraida that he was immediately drawn to. Casto had been so taken with her that he had confided in a friend that very day, "She really got to me, you know? Not loud or vulgar like that other girl, who was acting like a man, making remarks about me and all. No, she was a real lady. And, she's like, well, like a little sick sparrow flirting with death and having the upper hand. Quietly stubborn, you know? Not at all submissive like it might seem to just anybody looking at Zoraida. It's more as if nobody's gonna make the sparrow healthy, but it ain't gonna die either . . . like it's got the best of both worlds, see?"

Yet, in all their nine years of marriage, Zoraida had never become seriously ill. Her pregnancies and miscarriages were the only time that she had been unable to attend to her family. After the last pregnancy, in an attempt to prevent children, Casto had decided on the rhythm system, where abstention is practiced during certain days of the month. It was, he reasoned, not only sanctioned by the Catholic Church, but there were no drugs or foreign objects put into one's body, and he did not have to be afraid of catching something nor getting sick.

Even after this recent miscarriage, Zoraida appeared to recover quickly, and with her usual amazing resiliency, managed the household chores and the children all by herself. She even found time to assuage Casto's fears of sickness and prepare special foods for him.

Casto could feel his frustration building inside as he watched her. What the hell was the matter with this wife of his? Quickly he reached into his cupboard and took out some Maalox; God, the last thing he wanted was an ulcer on account of all of this.

"I think I'll coat my stomach." Casto chewed several Maalox tablets vigorously, then swallowed. "This way, I can have coffee later and it won't affect me badly." He waited for a response, but she remained silent. Casto sighed, she don't even talk to me no more . . . well, that's why I invited everybody here tonight, so they could see for themselves! He waited, staring at her, and then asked, "You got the cakes ready? I mean, you got them out of the boxes and everything?"

Zoraida nodded, not looking in his direction.

"Hey! Coño, I'm talking to you! Answer!"

"Yes," Zoraida whispered.

"And the cups and plates, you got them for the coffee and cake?"

"Yes," Zoraida repeated.

"I don't know, you know? It's been almost three months since Doña Digna did her job and cured you. I didn't figure you were gonna get so . . . so depressed." Zoraida continued to work silently. "Wait. Stop a minute. Why don't you answer me, eh? Will you look at me, for God's sake!"

Zoraida stopped and faced Casto with her eyes lowered.

"Look, I'm trying to talk to you, understand? Can't you talk to me?" Zoraida kept perfectly still. "Say something, will you?"

"What do you want me to say?" Zoraida spoke softly without looking at him.

"Can't you look at me when you talk?"

Swiftly and furtively, Zoraida glanced at Casto, then lowered her eyes once more.

"Coño, man, what do you think I do all day out there to make a living? Play? Working my butt off in those docks in all kinds of weather . . . yeah. And for what? To come home to a woman that won't even look at me?" Casto's voice was loud and angry. He stopped, controlled himself, then continued, lowering his voice. "I get up every morning before six. Every freaking morning! I risk pneumonia, rheumatism, arthritis, all kinds of sickness. Working that fork-lift, eight, ten hours a day, until my kidneys feel like they're gonna split out of my sides. And then, to make it worse, I gotta take orders from that stupid foreman who hates Puerto Ricans. Calling me a spic. In fact, they all hate Puerto Ricans out there. They call me spic, and they get away with it because I'm the only P.R. there, you know? Lousy Micks and Dagos! Listen, you know what they . . . ah, what's the use, I can't talk to you. Sure, why should you care? All you do is stay in a nice apartment, all warm and cozy. Damn it! I can't even have my woman like a normal man. First you had a phantom lover, right? Then, ever since Doña Digna took him away, you have that lousy chair you sit in and do your disappearing act. That's all you're good for lately. I can't even come near you. The minute I approach you like a human being for normal sex, you go and sit in that . . . that chair! I seen you fade out. Don't think I'm blind. You sit in that freaking thing, rock-ing away. You look . . . you . . . I don't even think you're breathing when you sit there! You should see yourself. What you look like is enough to scare anybody. Staring into space like some God damned zombie! You know what I should do with it? Throw it out, or better yet, bust that piece of crap into a thousand splinters! Yeah, that's what I ought to do. Only thing is, you'll find something else, right? Another lover, is that what you want, so you can become an animal? Because with me, let me tell you, you ain't no animal. With me you're nothing. Mira, you know something, I'm not taking no more of this. Never mind, when they get here they can see your whole bullshit act for themselves. Especially after I tell them . . ."

NICHOLASA MOHR

47

Zoraida barely heard him. The steady sound of the television program and the children's voices coming from their bedroom filled her with a pleasant feeling. How nice, she thought, all the children playing and happy. All fed and clean; yes, it's nice and peaceful.

The front doorbell rang.

"There they are." Casto had finished preparing the coffee. "I'll answer the door, you go on and get things ready."

Zoraida heard voices and trembled as she remembered Casto's threats and the fury he directed at her. Now he was going to tell them all sorts of things about her . . . untruths.

"Zoraida, where are you?" She heard her mother's voice, and then the voices of her father, mother-in-law and sister-in-law.

"Mommy, Mommy," Clarita ran into the kitchen, "Nana and Granpa, and Abuelita and Titi Purencia are here. Can we have the cake now?"

"In a little while, Clarita." Zoraida followed her daughter out into the living room and greeted everybody.

"Mommy, Mommy!" Junior shouted, "Tell Eddie to stop it, he's hitting me!"

"I was not, it was Clarita!" Eddie walked over to his little brother and pushed him. Junior began to cry and Clarita ran over and smacked Eddie.

"See?" Casto shouted, "Stop it! Clarita, you get back inside." He jumped up, grabbing his daughter by an elbow and lifting her off the ground. "Demonia, why are you hitting him? Zoraida, can't you control these kids?" He shook Clarita forcefully and she began to whine.

"Casto," Zoraida's thin shriek whistled through the room. "Don't be rough with her, please!"

"See that, Doña Clara, your daughter can't even control her own kids no more." He turned to the children, "Now, all of you, get back inside your room and watch television; and be quiet or you go right to bed and nobody gets any cake. You hear? That means all three, Clarita, Eddie and you too Junior."

"Can we have the cake now?" Eddie asked.

"I'll call you when it's time. Now go on, go on, all of you." Quickly, the children left.

"Calm yourself, son." Doña Elvira, Casto's mother, walked over to him. "You know how children are, they don't know about patience or waiting; you were no angel yourself, you and your sister."

"Let's go inside and have coffee, everybody." Casto led them into the kitchen. There were six chairs set around the kitchen table. Doña Clara and her husband, Don Isidro, Doña Elvira and her daughter, Purencia, squeezed in and sat down.

"Cut some cake for the kids and I'll bring it in to them." Casto spoke to Zoraida, who quickly began to cut up the chocolate cake and place the pieces on a plate. Everyone watched in silence. "Milk," snapped Casto. Zoraida set out three glasses of milk. Casto put everything on a tray and left.

THE WIFE

48

"So, mi hijita, how are you?" Doña Clara asked her daughter.

"I'm okay." Zoraida sat down.

"You look pale to me, very pale. Don't she, Papa?" Doña Clara turned for a moment to Don Isidro, then continued without waiting for an answer. "You're probably not eating right. Zoraida, you have to take better care of yourself."

"All right." Casto returned and sat down with the others. "They're happy now."

"Son," Doña Elvira spoke to Casto. "You look tired, aren't you getting enough rest?"

"I'm all right, Ma. Here, everybody, have some cake and coffee."

Everyone began to help themselves.

"It's that job of his. He works so hard," Doña Elvira reached over and placed an extra large piece of chocolate cake on Casto's plate before continuing. "He should have stayed in school and became an accountant, like I wanted. Casto was so good at math, but . . . instead, he . . ."

"Pass the sugar, please," Doña Clara interrupted, "and a little bit of that rum cake, yes. Thank you."

They all ate in silence.

Doña Elvira looked at Zoraida and sighed, trying to hide her annoyance. What a sickly looking woman, bendito. She looks like a mouse. To think my handsome, healthy son, who could have had any girl he wanted, picked this one. Doña Elvira could hardly swallow her cake. Duped by her phony innocence is what it was! And how could he be happy and satisfied with such a woman? Look at her, she's pathetic. Now, oh yes, now, he's finding out who she really is: not the sweet innocent one, after all! Ha! First a phantom lover and now . . . who knows what! Well, we'll see how far she can go on with this, because now he's getting wise. With a sense of smug satisfaction, Doña Elvira half-smiled as she looked at her daughter-in-law, then ate her cake and drank her coffee.

Purencia saw her mother's look of contempt directed at Zoraida. She's jealous of Zoraida, Purencia smiled. Nobody was ever good enough for Casto. For her precious baby boy, well, and there you have it! Casto finally wanted Zoraida. Purencia smiled, serves Ma right. She looked at her sister-in-law who sat with her head bowed. God, she looks sicker than ever, but she never complains. She won't say nothing, even now, when he's putting her through this whole number. Poor goody-two-shoes Zoraida, she's not gonna get on Casto's case for nothing; like, why is he jiving her? I wonder what it is she's doing now? After that whole scene with Doña Digna, I thought she cured her of whatever that was. Purencia shrugged, who knows how it is with these quiet ones. They're the kind that hide the action. Maybe she's doing something nobody knows about . . . well, let's just see.

Doña Clara looked at her son-in-law, Casto, with anger and a scowl on her face. Bestia . . . brute of a man! He doesn't deserve anyone as delicate as Zoraida. She has to wait on that huge monster hand and foot. With all his stupid medicines and vitamins when he's as fit as a horse! Ungrateful man. He got an innocent girl, pure as the day she was born, that's what. Protected and brought up right by us. Never went out by herself. We always watched out who her friends were. She was guarded by us practically up until the moment she took her vows. Any man would have been proud to have her. Canalla! Sinvergüenza! She's clean, hardworking and obedient. Never complains. All he wants to do is humiliate her. We already went to Doña Digna, and Casto said Zoraida was cured. What now, for pity's sake? Doña Clara forced herself to turn away from Casto because the anger fomenting within her was beginning to upset her nerves.

Don Isidro sat uneasily. He wished his wife would not drag him into these things. Domestic disputes should be a private matter, he maintained emphatically, between man and wife. But, his wife's nerves were not always what they should be, and so he had to be here. He looked at his daughter and was struck by her girlish appearance. Don Isidro sighed, the mother of three children and she hasn't filled out . . . she still has the body of a twelve-year old. Well, after all, she was born premature, weighing only two pounds at birth. Don Isidro smiled, remembering what the doctors had called her. "The miracle baby," they had said, "Mr. Cuesta, your daughter is a miracle. She should not be alive." That's when he and Clara had decided to give her the middle name of Milagros. He had wanted a son, but after Zoraida's birth, his wife could bear no children, and so he had to be satisfied with what he had. Of course, he had two grandsons, but they wouldn't carry on his last name, so, in a way it was not the same. Well, she's lucky to be married at all. Don Isidro nodded slightly, and Casto is a good, honest, hardworking man, totally devoted. Don't drink or gamble; he doesn't even look at other women. But, he too was lucky to get our Zoraida. After all, we brung her up proper and right. Catholic schools. Decent friends. Don Isidro looked around him at the silent table and felt a stiffness in his chest. He took a deep breath; what had she done? This whole business confused him. He thought Doña Digna had made the situation right once more.

"So, Casto, how are you? How's work?" Don Isidro asked.

"Pretty good. The weather gets to me, though. I have to guard against colds and sitting in that fork-lift gives me a sore back. But, I'm lucky to have work, the way things are going."

"You're right, they're laying off people everywhere. You read about it in the news everyday."

"Zoraida, eat something." Doña Clara spoke to her daughter.

"I'm not hungry, Mami," Zoraida's voice was just above a whisper.

"Casto, you should see to it that she eats!" Doña Clara looked at her son-in-law, trying to control her annoyance. "Whatever this problem is, I'm sure part of it is that your wife never eats."

"Why should he see that she eats or not?" Doña Elvira interjected, "He has to go to work everyday to support his family . . . he hasn't got time to . . ."

"Wait a minute, Ma," Casto interrupted, "the problem here ain't food. That's not gonna solve what's going on."

"It seems to solve all your problems, eh?" Doña Clara looked at Casto with anger.

"Just hold on now . . . wait," Don Isidro raised his hand. "Now, we are all arguing here with each other and we don't even know what the problem is. Why don't we find out what's going on?" Don Isidro turned to Casto and waited.

Everyone fell silent. Don Isidro continued, "I thought that Doña Digna's treatment worked. After all, you told us that yourself."

"It's not that no more," Casto looked around him, "it's something else now."

"What?" Doña Elvira asked.

Casto looked at Zoraida who sat with her hands folded on her lap and her eyes downcast.

"Weren't things going good for you two?" Don Isidro asked. "I mean, things were back to normal relations between you, yes?"

"Yes and no," Casto said. "Yes for a while and then . . ."

"Then what?" Doña Elvira asked. "What?"

Casto looked at Zoraida. "You want to say something, Zoraida?" She shook her head without looking at anyone.

"All right, then like usual, I gotta speak. You know that rocking chair Zoraida has? The one she brought with her when we got married?"

"You mean the one she's had ever since she was little? Why, we had that since Puerto Rico, it belonged to my titi Rosana." Doña Clara looked perplexed. "What about the rocker?"

"Well, she just sits in it, when . . . when she shouldn't." Casto could feel the blood rushing to his face.

"What do you mean she sits in it?" Doña Clara asked. "What is she supposed to do? Stand in it?"

"I said *when she shouldn't.*"

"Shouldn't what?" Doña Clara turned to Don Isidro, "Papa, what is this man talking about?"

"Look," Casto continued, "this here chair is in the bedroom. That's where she keeps it. All right? Now when, when I . . . when we . . ." Casto hesitated, "you know what I mean. Then, instead of acting like a wife, she leaves the bed and sits in the chair. She sits and she rocks back and forth."

"Does she stay there all night?" Doña Elvira asked.

"Pretty much."

Everyone looked at Zoraida, who remained motionless without lifting her eyes. A few moments passed before Don Isidro broke the silence.

"This is a delicate subject, I don't know if it's a good thing to have this kind of discussion here, like this."

"What do you want me to do, Isidro? First she has those fits in bed driving me nuts. Then we call in Doña Digna, who decides she knows what's wrong, and puts me through a whole freakin rigamarole of prayers and buying all kinds of crap. After all of that pendejá, which costs me money that I frankly don't have, then she tells me my wife is cured. Now it starts again, except in another way. Look, I'm only human, you know? And she," Casto pointed to Zoraida, "is denying me what is my right as a man and as her husband. And I don't know why she's doing this. But I do know this time you're gonna be here to know what's going on. I ain't going through this alone. No way. And get myself sick? No!"

"Just a moment, now," Doña Clara said, "you say Zoraida sits in the rocker when you . . . approach her. Does she ever sit there at other times? Or only at that time?"

"Once in a while, at other times, but always . . . always, you know, at that time!"

"Ay . . . Dios mio!" Doña Elvira stood up. "I don't know how my son puts up with this, if you ask me." She put her hands to her head. "Casto has the patience of a saint, any other man would do . . . do worse!"

"What do you mean, the patience of a saint?" Doña Clara glared at Doña Elvira. "And do worse what? Your son might be the whole cause of this, for all I know . . ."

"Now, wait." Don Isidro stood up. "Again, we are fighting and blaming this one or that one. This will get us nowhere. Doña Elvira, please sit down." Doña Elvira sat, and then Don Isidro sat down also. "Between a man and wife, it's best not to interfere."

"Okay then, Papa, what are we here for?" Doña Clara asked.

"To help, if we can," Purencia spoke. Everyone listened; she had not spoken a word before this. "I think that's what my brother wants. Right, Casto?" Casto nodded, and then shrugged. "Let Zoraida say something," Purencia continued. "She never gets a chance to say one word."

"Nobody's stopping her." Casto looked at Zoraida. "Didn't I ask her to say something? In fact, maybe she can tell us what's going on. Like, I would like to know too, you know."

"Zoraida," Doña Clara spoke firmly to her daughter, "mira, you better tell us what all of this is about."

Zoraida looked up, meeting her mother's angry stare. "I don't know what Casto means about the chair."

"Do you sit in the rocker or do you not sit there, like he says?" her mother asked.

"Sometimes."

"Sometimes? What times? Is it like the way he says it is? Because, if this is so, we want to know why. Doña Digna told me, you and all of us, that there was an evil spirit in you that was turning your thoughts away from your husband, so that you could not be a wife to him. After she finished her treatment, she said the evil spirit or force was gone, and that you would go back to a normal husband-and-wife relationship. We have to accept that. She is a woman of honor that has been doing this work for many years, and that she is telling us the truth, yes?" Doña Clara took a deep breath. "But, if you feel anything is wrong, then it could be that Doña Digna did not succeed." She turned to Casto. "That's possible too, you know. These things sometimes get very complicated. I remember when the Alvarez household was having the worst kind of luck. Don Pablo had lost his job, his wife was sick, and one of their boys had an accident; all kinds of problems, remember? You remember, Papa? Well, Doña Digna had to go back, and it took her a long time to discover the exact cause and then to make things straight again." She turned to Zoraida, "Bueno, mi hija, you have to tell us what you feel, and if you are doing this to your husband, why." Doña Clara waited for her daughter's response. "Go ahead. Answer, por Dios!"

"I . . ." Zoraida cleared her throat in an effort to speak louder. "I just sit in the rocker sometimes. Because I feel relaxed there."

"Yeah!" Casto said, "Every time I go near her at night, or at two or three in the morning, she relaxes." He raised his hand and slammed the table, "God damned chair!"

"Calmate, mi hijito, calm yourself." Doña Elvira put her hand over her eyes. "I don't know how long my son can put up with all of this. Now she's got an obsession with a chair. Virgen, purisima! Somebody has to tell me what is going on here!"

"Listen to me," Don Isidro spoke in a firm voice, "if it's the chair that bothers you, then we'll take it back home with us. Right, Mama?" He turned to Doña Clara who nodded emphatically. "There should be no objection to that, eh?"

Everyone looked at Casto who shrugged, and then at Zoraida who opened her mouth and shook her head, but was unable to speak.

"Very good." Don Isidro clasped his hands and smiled. "There, that ought to take care of the problems pretty much."

"Except, she might find something else." Casto said. "Who knows with her."

"Well, but we don't know that for sure, do we?" Don Isidro replied, "and in the meantime, we gotta start somewhere."

"I feel we can always call Doña Digna in again if we have to." Doña Clara poured herself a cup of coffee. "After all, she was the one that told us Zoraida was cured."

"I agree," Doña Elvira said, "and even though she don't ask for money, I know my Casto was very generous with her."

"That's right, they don't charge, but after all, one has to give these people something, or else how can they live?" agreed Doña Clara.

"Isn't the weather funny this Spring?" Doña Elvira spoke amiably. "One minute it's cold and the next it's like summer. One never knows how to dress these . . ."

NICHOLASA MOHR

53

They continued speaking about the weather and about television programs. Purencia spoke about her favorite movie.

"That one about the professional hit-man, who has a contract out to kill the President of England . . . no, France, I think. Anyway, remember when he goes into that woman's house and kills her? I was so scared, I loved that movie."

Everyone agreed, the best kinds of movies were mysteries and thrillers.

Zoraida half-listened to them. They were going to take away the rocker. She had always had it, ever since she could remember. When she was a little girl, her parents told her it was a part of their history. Part of Puerto Rico and her great Aunt Rosana who was very beautiful and had countless suitors. The chair was made of oak with intricate carving and delicate caning. As a little girl, Zoraida used to rub her hands against the caning and woodwork admiringly, while she rocked, dreamed and pretended to her heart's content. Lately it had become the one place where she felt she could be herself, where she could really be free.

"Bueno, we have to go. It's late."

"That's right, me too."

"Wait," Casto told them, "I'll drive you people home."

"You don't have to . . ." Don Isidro protested. "We know you are tired."

"No, I'm not. Besides, I gotta drive ma and Purencia home anyway."

"That's right," Purencia said, "my old man doesn't like me going out at night. It's only because of Mami that he let me. So, Casto has to take me home."

"I gotta get you the chair, wait," Casto said. "And, you don't wanna carry that all the way home. It's not very big, but still, it's a lot to lug around."

"All right then, very good."

Everyone got up and Zoraida began to clear away the dishes.

"Let me help you," Doña Clara said as she stood up.

"Me too," Doña Elvira said, without rising.

"No, no thanks. That's all right. I can do it myself," Zoraida said. "Besides, I have to put the kids to bed and give them their milk and all."

"I don't know how she does it. Three little ones and this place is always immaculate." Doña Clara turned to Doña Elvira. "It's really too much for her, and she has no help at all."

Doña Elvira stood. "She keeps a very clean house," she said and walked out with Purencia following after Casto and Don Isidro.

Doña Clara looked at her daughter, who worked silently and efficiently. "Mira, mi hija, I better talk to you." She stood close to Zoraida and began to speak in a friendly manner, keeping her voice low. "You have to humor men; you must know that by now. After all, you are no longer a little girl. All women go through this difficulty, eh? You are not the only one. Why, do you know how many times your father wants . . . well, you know, wants it? But I, that is, if I don't want to do it, well I find a way not to. But diplomatically, you know? All right, he's older now and he bothers me less; still, what I mean is, you have to learn that men are like babies and they feel rejected unless you handle the situation just right. Now, we'll take the rocker back home with us because it will make him feel better. But you must do your part too. Tell him you have a headache, or a backache, or you can even pretend to be asleep. However, once in a while you have to please him, you know. After all, he does support you and the children and he needs it to relax. What's the harm in it? It's a small sacrifice. Listen, I'll give you some good advice; make believe you are enjoying it and then get it over with real quick, eh? So, once in a while you have to, whether you like it or not; that's just the way it is for us. Okay? Do you understand?" Zoraida turned away and, without responding, continued with her work. "Did you hear what I just told you?" Doña Clara grabbed Zoraida's shoulder firmly, squeezing her fingers against the flesh. "You didn't even hear what I said to you!"

Zoraida pulled away and turned quickly facing her mother. She looked directly at Doña Clara, "I heard you . . ." Zoraida stopped and a smile passed her lips. "I heard every word you said, Mami."

"Oh, all right then . . ." Doña Clara said, somewhat startled by her daughter's smile. "I only wanted to . . ."

"Mama! Come on, it's time to go," Don Isidro's voice interrupted her.

Doña Clara and Zoraida went into the living room. Casto carried the rocking chair and waited by the door. The children had come out of their room and were happily jumping about.

"Look, Mommy, Granpa gave me a quarter," Clarita said.

"Me too," said Eddie. "He even gave Junior one."

"All right, get to bed!" Casto shouted. "Zoraida, put them down, will you?"

Everybody said goodbye and, in a moment, Casto and the others left.

"Mommy, where is Daddy taking your chair?" Clarita asked.

"To Nana's."

"Why?"

"Because they want it now."

"Don't you want it no more?"

"I already had it for a long time, now they need to have it for a while."

Zoraida gave the children their milk, bathed them and put them to bed. Then, she finished rapidly in the kitchen and went to bed herself. She looked over at the empty space near the window. It was gone. She wouldn't be able to sit there anymore and meet all her suitors and be beautiful. The last time . . . the last time she was dancing to a very slow number, a ballad. But she couldn't remember the words. And she was with, with . . . which one? She just couldn't remember him anymore. If she had the rocker, she could remember; it would all come back to her as soon as she sat down. In fact, she was always able to pick up exactly where she had left off the time before. She shut her eyes, deciding not to think about the rocker, about Casto, Doña Digna or her mother. Instead, Zoraida remembered her children who were safe and asleep in their own beds. In a short while, she heard the front door open and recognized Casto's footsteps. She shut her eyes, turned over, facing away from his side of the bed. Casto found the apartment silent and dark, except for the night light.

In the bedroom, Casto looked at Zoraida, who seemed fast asleep, then at the empty space near the window where the rocker usually stood. Their bedroom seemed larger and his burden lighter. Casto sighed, feeling better. He reached over and lightly touched Zoraida; this was a safe time of the month, maybe she would wake up. He waited and, after a moment, decided to go to sleep. After all, he could always try again tomorrow.

MIGRATION

by

CAROL GREGORY
(b. 1945)

Born in Youngstown, Ohio, Carol Gregory graduated from Youngstown State University; in 1976 she received a master's degree in arts, education, and theological studies jointly from Columbia University, Teacher's College, and Union Theological Seminary. She lives in New York City and teaches English at the Borough of Manhattan Community College. In 1968, when she was twenty-three and using her married name Carol Gregory Clemmons, eighteen of her poems, including "Migration," were published in Nine Black Poets. *Several other poems were included in* Black Sister: Poetry by Black American Women, 1746–1980 *(1981), edited by Erlene Stetson. Gregory has written and hopes to publish a volume of short stories and an autobiographical novel about being the first black woman to take a degree in English at her college. She regards herself as primarily a poet.*

She stood hanging wash before sun
and occasionally watched the kids
gather acorns from the trees,
and when her husband came,
complaining about the tobacco spit on him
they decided to run North
for a free evening.
She stood hanging wash in the basement
and saw the kids sneak puffs from cigarettes,
fix steel traps with cheese
and when her husband came,
complaining of the mill's drudgery,
      she burst—
said he had no hunter's heart
beat him with a broom,
became blinded by the orange sun
racing into steel mill flames
and afterwards,
sat singing spirituals to sons.

A WIFE'S STORY

by

BHARATI MUKHERJEE
(b. 1942)

*Born and educated in Calcutta, Bharati Mukherjee came to the
United States to study and earned a doctorate at the University
of Iowa. She has taught creative writing at colleges in the New
York City area and has held fellowships from both the National
Endowment for the Arts and the Guggenheim Foundation. She
is currently teaching at the University of California at Berkeley.
Mukherjee has published three novels, including* Jasmine *(1989),
and two volumes of short stories,* Darkness *(1985) and* The
Middleman and Other Stories *(1988). The latter won the National
Book Critics Circle award for fiction and includes "A Wife's Story."
Mukherjee's fiction reflects the conflict between traditional roles
and the desire for self-development felt by immigrants from many
countries. (The play by David Mamet referred to in "A Wife's
Story" is* Glengarry Glen Ross; *its characters speak deprecatingly
of immigrants.)*

• ───────────────── •

Imre says forget it, but I'm going to write David Mamet. So Patels are
hard to sell real estate to. You buy them a beer, whisper Glengarry Glen
Ross, and they smell swamp instead of sun and surf. They work hard, eat
cheap, live ten to a room, stash their savings under futons in Queens,
and before you know it they own half of Hoboken. You say, where's the
sweet gullibility that made this nation great?

Polish jokes, Patel jokes: that's not why I want to write Mamet.

Seen their women?

Everybody laughs. Imre laughs. The dozing fat man with the Barnes &
Noble sack between his legs, the woman next to him, the usher, every-
body. The theater isn't so dark that they can't see me. In my red silk sari
I'm conspicuous. Plump, gold paisleys sparkle on my chest.

The actor is just warming up. *Seen their women?* He plays a salesman,
he's had a bad day and now he's in a Chinese restaurant trying to loosen
up. His face is pink. His wool-blend slacks are creased at the crotch. We
bought our tickets at half-price, we're sitting in the front row, but at the
edge, and we see things we shouldn't be seeing. At least I do, or think I
do. Spittle, actors goosing each other, little winks, streaks of makeup.

THE WIFE

58

Maybe they're improvising dialogue too. Maybe Mamet's provided them with insult kits, Thursdays for Chinese, Wednesdays for Hispanics, today for Indians. Maybe they get together before curtain time, see an Indian woman settling in the front row off to the side, and say to each other: "Hey, forget Friday. Let's get *her* today. See if she cries. See if she walks out." Maybe, like the salesmen they play, they have a little bet on.

Maybe I shouldn't feel betrayed.

Their women, he goes again. *They look like they've just been fucked by a dead cat.*

The fat man hoots so hard he nudges my elbow off our shared armrest.

"Imre. I'm going home." But Imre's hunched so far forward he doesn't hear. English isn't his best language. A refugee from Budapest, he has to listen hard. "I didn't pay eighteen dollars to be insulted."

I don't hate Mamet. It's the tyranny of the American dream that scares me. First, you don't exist. Then you're invisible. Then you're funny. Then you're disgusting. Insult, my American friends will tell me, is a kind of acceptance. No instant dignity here. A play like this, back home, would cause riots. Communal, racist, and antisocial. The actors wouldn't make it off stage. This play, and all these awful feelings, would be safely locked up.

I long, at times, for clear-cut answers. Offer me instant dignity, today, and I'll take it.

"What?" Imre moves toward me without taking his eyes off the actor. "Come again?"

Tears come. I want to stand, scream, make an awful scene. I long for ugly, nasty rage.

The actor is ranting, flinging spittle. *Give me a chance. I'm not finished, I can get back on the board. I tell that asshole, give me a real lead. And what does that asshole give me? Patels. Nothing but Patels.*

This time Imre works an arm around my shoulders. "Panna, what is Patel? Why are you taking it all so personally?"

I shrink from his touch, but I don't walk out. Expensive girls' schools in Lausanne and Bombay have trained me to behave well. My manners are exquisite, my feelings are delicate, my gestures refined, my moods undetectable. They have seen me through riots, uprootings, separation, my son's death.

"I'm not taking it personally."

The fat man looks at us. The woman looks too, and shushes.

I stare back at the two of them. Then I stare, mean and cool, at the man's elbow. Under the bright blue polyester Hawaiian shirt sleeve, the elbow looks soft and runny. "Excuse me," I say. My voice has the effortless meanness of well-bred displaced Third World women, though my rhetoric has been learned elsewhere. "You're exploiting my space."

Startled, the man snatches his arm away from me. He cradles it against his breast. By the time he's ready with come-backs, I've turned my back on him. I've probably ruined the first act for him. I know I've ruined it for Imre.

It's not my fault; it's the *situation*. Old colonies wear down. Patels—the new pioneers—have to be suspicious. Idi Amin's lesson is permanent. AT&T wires move good advice from continent to continent. Keep all assets liquid. Get into 7–11s, get out of condos and motels. I know how both sides feel, that's the trouble. The Patel sniffing out scams, the sad salesmen on the stage: postcolonialism has made me their referee. It's hate I long for; simple, brutish, partisan hate.

After the show Imre and I make our way toward Broadway. Sometimes he holds my hand; it doesn't mean anything more than that crazies and drunks are crouched in doorways. Imre's been here over two years, but he's stayed very old-world, very courtly, openly protective of women. I met him in a seminar on special ed. last semester. His wife is a nurse somewhere in the Hungarian countryside. There are two sons, and miles of petitions for their emigration. My husband manages a mill two hundred miles north of Bombay. There are no children.

"You make things tough on yourself," Imre says. He assumed Patel was a Jewish name or maybe Hispanic; everything makes equal sense to him. He found the play tasteless, he worried about the effect of vulgar language on my sensitive ears. "You have to let go a bit." And as though to show me how to let go, he breaks away from me, bounds ahead with his head ducked tight, then dances on amazingly jerky legs. He's a Magyar, he often tells me, and deep down, he's an Asian too. I catch glimpses of it, knife-blade Attila cheekbones, despite the blondish hair. In his faded jeans and leather jacket, he's a rock video star. I watch MTV for hours in the apartment when Charity's working the evening shift at Macy's. I listen to WPLJ on Charity's earphones. Why should I be ashamed? Television in India is so uplifting.

Imre stops as suddenly as he'd started. People walk around us. The summer sidewalk is full of theatergoers in seersucker suits; Imre's year-round jacket is out of place. European. Cops in twos and threes huddle, lightly tap their thighs with nightsticks and smile at me with benevolence. I want to wink at them, get us all in trouble, tell them the crazy dancing man is from the Warsaw Pact. I'm too shy to break into dance on Broadway. So I hug Imre instead.

The hug takes him by surprise. He wants me to let go, but he doesn't really expect me to let go. He staggers, though I weigh no more than 104 pounds, and with him, I pitch forward slightly. Then he catches me, and we walk arm in arm to the bus stop. My husband would never dance or hug a woman on Broadway. Nor would my brothers. They aren't stuffy people, but they went to Anglican boarding schools and they have a well-developed sense of what's silly.

"Imre." I squeeze his big, rough hand. "I'm sorry I ruined the evening for you."

"You did nothing of the kind." He sounds tired. "Let's not wait for the bus. Let's splurge and take a cab instead."

Imre always has unexpected funds. The Network, he calls it, Class of '56.

In the back of the cab, without even trying, I feel light, almost free. Memories of Indian destitutes mix with the hordes of New York street people, and they float free, like astronauts, inside my head. I've made it. I'm making something of my life. I've left home, my husband, to get a Ph.D. in special ed. I have a multiple-entry visa and a small scholarship for two years. After that, we'll see. My mother was beaten by her mother-in-law, my grandmother, when she'd registered for French lessons at the Alliance Française. My grandmother, the eldest daughter of a rich zamindar, was illiterate.

Imre and the cabdriver talk away in Russian. I keep my eyes closed. That way I can feel the floaters better. I'll write Mamet tonight. I feel strong, reckless. Maybe I'll write Steven Spielberg too; tell him that Indians don't eat monkey brains.

We've made it. Patels must have made it. Mamet, Spielberg: they're not condescending to us. Maybe they're a little bit afraid.

Charity Chin, my roommate, is sitting on the floor drinking Chablis out of a plastic wineglass. She is five foot six, three inches taller than me, but weighs a kilo and a half less than I do. She is a "hands" model. Orientals are supposed to have a monopoly in the hands-modelling business, she says. She had her eyes fixed eight or nine months ago and out of gratitude sleeps with her plastic surgeon every third Wednesday.

"Oh, good," Charity says. "I'm glad you're back early. I need to talk."

She's been writing checks. MCI, Con Ed, Bonwit Teller. Envelopes, already stamped and sealed, form a pyramid between her shapely, knee-socked legs. The checkbook's cover is brown plastic, grained to look like cowhide. Each time Charity flips back the cover, white geese fly over sky-colored checks. She makes good money, but she's extravagant. The difference adds up to this shared, rent-controlled Chelsea one-bedroom.

"All right. Talk."

When I first moved in, she was seeing an analyst. Now she sees a nutritionist.

"Eric called. From Oregon."

"What did he want?"

"He wants me to pay half the rent on his loft for last spring. He asked me to move back, remember? He *begged* me."

Eric is Charity's estranged husband.

"What does your nutritionist say?" Eric now wears a red jumpsuit and tills the soil in Rajneeshpuram.

"You think Phil's a creep too, don't you? What else can he be when creeps are all I attract?"

Phil is a flutist with thinning hair. He's very touchy on the subject of *flautists* versus *flutists*. He's touchy on every subject, from music to books to foods to clothes. He teaches at a small college upstate, and Charity bought a used blue Datsun ("Nissan," Phil insists) last month so she could spend weekends with him. She returns every Sunday night, exhausted and exasperated. Phil and I don't have much to say to each other—he's the only musician I know; the men in my family are lawyers, engineers, or in business—but I like him. Around me, he loosens up. When he visits, he bakes us loaves of pumpernickel bread. He waxes our kitchen floor. Like many men in this country, he seems to me a displaced child, or even a woman, looking for something that passed him by, or for something that he can never have. If he thinks I'm not looking, he sneaks his hands under Charity's sweater, but there isn't too much there. Here, she's a model with high ambitions. In India, she'd be a flat-chested old maid.

I'm shy in front of the lovers. A darkness comes over me when I see them horsing around.

"It isn't the money," Charity says. Oh? I think. "He says he still loves me. Then he turns around and asks me for five hundred."

What's so strange about that, I want to ask. She still loves Eric, and Eric, red jump suit and all, is smart enough to know it. Love is a commodity, hoarded like any other. Mamet knows. But I say, "I'm not the person to ask about love." Charity knows that mine was a traditional Hindu marriage. My parents, with the help of a marriage broker, who was my mother's cousin, picked out a groom. All I had to do was get to know his taste in food.

It'll be a long evening, I'm afraid. Charity likes to confess. I unpleat my silk sari—it no longer looks too showy—wrap it in muslin cloth and put it away in a dresser drawer. Saris are hard to have laundered in Manhattan, though there's a good man in Jackson Heights. My next step will be to brew us a pot of chrysanthemum tea. It's a very special tea from the mainland. Charity's uncle gave it to us. I like him. He's a humpbacked, awkward, terrified man. He runs a gift store on Mott Street, and though he doesn't speak much English, he seems to have done well. Once upon a time he worked for the railways in Chengdu, Szechwan Province, and during the Wuchang Uprising, he was shot at. When I'm down, when I'm lonely for my husband, when I think of our son, or when I need to be held, I think of Charity's uncle. If I hadn't left home, I'd never have heard of the Wuchang Uprising. I've broadened my horizons.

Very late that night my husband calls me from Ahmadabad, a town of textile mills north of Bombay. My husband is a vice president at Lakshmi Cotton Mills. Lakshmi is the goddess of wealth, but LCM (Priv.), Ltd., is doing poorly. Lockouts, strikes, rock-throwings. My husband lives on digitalis, which he calls the food for our *yuga* of discontent.

THE WIFE
62

"We had a bad mishap at the mill today." Then he says nothing for seconds.

The operator comes on. "Do you have the right party, sir? We're trying to reach Mrs. Butt."

"Bhatt," I insist. "*B* for Bombay, *H* for Haryana, *A* for Ahmadabad, double *T* for Tamil Nadu." It's a litany. "This is she."

"One of our lorries was firebombed today. Resulting in three deaths. The driver, old Karamchand, and his two children."

I know how my husband's eyes look this minute, how the eye rims sag and the yellow corneas shine and bulge with pain. He is not an emotional man—the Ahmadabad Institute of Management has trained him to cut losses, to look on the bright side of economic catastrophes—but tonight he's feeling low. I try to remember a driver named Karamchand, but can't. That part of my life is over, the way *trucks* have replaced *lorries* in my vocabulary, the way Charity Chin and her lurid love life have replaced inherited notions of marital duty. Tomorrow he'll come out of it. Soon he'll be eating again. He'll sleep like a baby. He's been trained to believe in turnovers. Every morning he rubs his scalp with cantharidine oil so his hair will grow back again.

"It could be your car next." Affection, love. Who can tell the difference in a traditional marriage in which a wife still doesn't call her husband by his first name?

"No. They know I'm a flunky, just like them. Well paid, maybe. No need for undue anxiety, please."

Then his voice breaks. He says he needs me, he misses me, he wants me to come to him damp from my evening shower, smelling of sandalwood soap, my braid decorated with jasmines.

"I need you too."

"Not to worry, please," he says. "I am coming in a fortnight's time. I have already made arrangements."

Outside my window, fire trucks whine, up Eighth Avenue. I wonder if he can hear them, what he thinks of a life like mine, led amid disorder.

"I am thinking it'll be like a honeymoon. More or less."

When I was in college, waiting to be married, I imagined honeymoons were only for the more fashionable girls, the girls who came from slightly racy families, smoked Sobranies in the dorm lavatories and put up posters of Kabir Bedi, who was supposed to have made it as a big star in the West. My husband wants us to go to Niagara. I'm not to worry about foreign exchange. He's arranged for extra dollars through the Gujarati Network, with a cousin in San Jose. And he's bought four hundred more on the black market. "Tell me you need me. Panna, please tell me again."

I change out of the cotton pants and shirt I've been wearing all day and put on a sari to meet my husband at JFK. I don't forget the jewelry; the marriage necklace of *mangalsutra*, gold drop earrings, heavy gold bangles. I don't wear them every day. In this borough of vice and greed, who knows when, or whom, desire will overwhelm.

My husband spots me in the crowd and waves. He has lost weight, and changed his glasses. The arm, uplifted in a cheery wave, is bony, frail, almost opalescent.

In the Carey Coach, we hold hands. He strokes my fingers one by one. "How come you aren't wearing my mother's ring?"

"Because muggers know about Indian women," I say. They know with us it's 24-karat. His mother's ring is showy, in ghastly taste anywhere but India: a blood-red Burma ruby set in a gold frame of floral sprays. My mother-in-law got her guru to bless the ring before I left for the States.

He looks disconcerted. He's used to a different role. He's the knowing, suspicious one in the family. He seems to be sulking, and finally he comes out with it. "You've said nothing about my new glasses." I compliment him on the glasses, how chic and Western-executive they make him look. But I can't help the other things, necessities until he learns the ropes. I handle the money, buy the tickets. I don't know if this makes me unhappy.

Charity drives her Nissan upstate, so for two weeks we are to have the apartment to ourselves. This is more privacy than we ever had in India. No parents, no servants, to keep us modest. We play at housekeeping. Imre has lent us a hibachi, and I grill saffron chicken breasts. My husband marvels at the size of the Perdue hens. "They're big like peacocks, no? These Americans, they're really something!" He tries out pizzas, burgers, McNuggets. He chews. He explores. He judges. He loves it all, fears nothing, feels at home in the summer odors, the clutter of Manhattan streets. Since he thinks that the American palate is bland, he carries a bottle of red peppers in his pocket. I wheel a shopping cart down the aisles of the neighborhood Grand Union, and he follows, swiftly, greedily. He picks up hair rinses and high-protein diet powders. There's so much I already take for granted.

One night, Imre stops by. He wants us to go with him to a movie. In his work shirt and red leather tie, he looks arty or strung out. It's only been a week, but I feel as though I am really seeing him for the first time. The yellow hair worn very short at the sides, the wide, narrow lips. He's a good-looking man, but self-conscious, almost arrogant. He's picked the movie we should see. He always tells me what to see, what to read. He buys the *Voice*. He's a natural avant-gardist. For tonight he's chosen *Numéro Deux*.

"Is it a musical?" my husband asks. The Radio City Music Hall is on his list of sights to see. He's read up on the history of the Rockettes. He doesn't catch Imre's sympathetic wink.

Guilt, shame, loyalty. I long to be ungracious, not ingratiate myself with both men.

That night my husband calculates in rupees the money we've wasted on Godard. "That refugee fellow, Nagy, must have a screw loose in his head. I paid very steep price for dollars on the black market."

Some afternoons we go shopping. Back home we hated shopping, but now it is a lovers' project. My husband's shopping list startles me. I feel I am just getting to know him. Maybe, like Imre, freed from the dignities of old-world culture, he too could get drunk and squirt Cheez Whiz on a guest. I watch him dart into stores in his gleaming leather shoes. Jockey shorts on sale in outdoor bins on Broadway entrance him. White tube socks with different bands of color delight him. He looks for microcassettes, for anything small and electronic and smuggleable. He needs a garment bag. He calls it a "wardrobe," and I have to translate.

"All of New York is having sales, no?"

My heart speeds watching him this happy. It's the third week in August, almost the end of summer, and the city smells ripe, it cannot bear more heat, more money, more energy.

"This is so smashing! The prices are so excellent!" Recklessly, my prudent husband signs away traveller's checks. How he intends to smuggle it all back I don't dare ask. With a microwave, he calculates, we could get rid of our cook.

This has to be love, I think. Charity, Eric, Phil: they may be experts on sex. My husband doesn't chase me around the sofa, but he pushes me down on Charity's battered cushions, and the man who has never entered the kitchen of our Ahmadabad house now comes toward me with a dish tub of steamy water to massage away the pavement heat.

Ten days into his vacation my husband checks out brochures for sightseeing tours. Shortline, Grayline, Crossroads: his new vinyl briefcase is full of schedules and pamphlets. While I make pancakes out of a mix, he comparison-shops. Tour number one costs $10.95 and will give us the World Trade Center, Chinatown, and the United Nations. Tour number three would take us both uptown *and* downtown for $14.95, but my husband is absolutely sure he doesn't want to see Harlem. We settle for tour number four: Downtown and the Dame. It's offered by a new tour company with a small, dirty office at Eighth and Forty-eighth.

The sidewalk outside the office is colorful with tourists. My husband sends me in to buy the tickets because he has come to feel Americans don't understand his accent.

The dark man, Lebanese probably, behind the counter comes on too friendly. "Come on, doll, make my day!" He won't say which tour is his. "Number four? Honey, no! Look, you've wrecked me! Say you'll change your mind." He takes two twenties and gives back change. He holds the tickets, forcing me to pull. He leans closer. "I'm off after lunch."

My husband must have been watching me from the sidewalk. "What was the chap saying?" he demands. "I told you not to wear pants. He thinks you are Puerto Rican. He thinks he can treat you with disrespect."

The bus is crowded and we have to sit across the aisle from each other. The tour guide begins his patter on Forty-sixth. He looks like an actor, his hair bleached and blow-dried. Up close he must look middle-aged, but from where I sit his skin is smooth and his cheeks faintly red.

"Welcome to the Big Apple, folks." The guide uses a microphone. "Big Apple. That's what we native Manhattan degenerates call our city. Today we have guests from fifteen foreign countries and six states from this U.S. of A. That makes the Tourist Bureau real happy. And let me assure you that while we may be the richest city in the richest country in the world, it's okay to tip your charming and talented attendant." He laughs. Then he swings his hip out into the aisle and sings a song.

"And it's mighty fancy on old Delancey Street, you know. . . ."

My husband looks irritable. The guide is, as expected, a good singer. "The bloody man should be giving us histories of buildings we are passing, no?" I pat his hand, the mood passes. He cranes his neck. Our window seats have both gone to Japanese. It's the tour of his life. Next to this, the quick business trips to Manchester and Glasgow pale.

"And tell me what street compares to Mott Street, in July. . . ."

The guide wants applause. He manages a derisive laugh from the Americans up front. He's working the aisles now. "I coulda been somebody, right? I coulda been a star!" Two or three of us smile, those of us who recognize the parody. He catches my smile. The sun is on his harsh, bleached hair. "Right, your highness? Look, we gotta maharani with us! Couldn't I have been a star?"

"Right!" I say, my voice coming out a squeal. I've been trained to adapt; what else can I say?

We drive through traffic past landmark office buildings and churches. The guide flips his hands. "Art deco," he keeps saying. I hear him confide to one of the Americans: "Beats me. I went to a cheap guide's school." My husband wants to know more about this Art Deco, but the guide sings another song.

"We made a foolish choice," my husband grumbles. "We are sitting in the bus only. We're not going into famous buildings." He scrutinizes the pamphlets in his jacket pocket. I think, at least it's air-conditioned in here. I could sit here in the cool shadows of the city forever.

Only five of us appear to have opted for the "Downtown and the Dame" tour. The others will ride back uptown past the United Nations after we've been dropped off at the pier for the ferry to the Statue of Liberty.

An elderly European pulls a camera out of his wife's designer tote bag. He takes pictures of the boats in the harbor, the Japanese in kimonos eating popcorn, scavenging pigeons, me. Then, pushing his wife ahead of him, he climbs back on the bus and waves to us. For a second I feel terribly lost. I wish we were on the bus going back to the apartment. I know I'll not be able to describe any of this to Charity, or to Imre. I'm too proud to admit I went on a guided tour.

THE WIFE

66

The view of the city from the Circle Line ferry is seductive, unreal. The skyline wavers out of reach, but never quite vanishes. The summer sun pushes through fluffy clouds and dapples the glass of office towers. My husband looks thrilled, even more than he had on the shopping trips down Broadway. Tourists and dreamers, we have spent our life's savings to see this skyline, this statue.

"Quick, take a picture of me!" my husband yells as he moves toward a gap of railings. A Japanese matron has given up her position in order to change film. "Before the Twin Towers disappear!"

I focus, I wait for a large Oriental family to walk out of my range. My husband holds his pose tight against the railing. He wants to look relaxed, an international businessman at home in all the financial markets.

A bearded man slides across the bench toward me. "Like this," he says and helps me get my husband in focus. "You want me to take the photo for you?" His name, he says, is Goran. He is Goran from Yugoslavia, as though that were enough for tracking him down. Imre from Hungary. Panna from India. He pulls the old Leica out of my hand, signaling the Orientals to beat it, and clicks away. "I'm a photographer," he says. He could have been a camera thief. That's what my husband would have assumed. Somehow, I trusted. "Get you a beer?" he asks.

"I don't. Drink, I mean. Thank you very much." I say those last words very loud, for everyone's benefit. The odd bottles of Soave with Imre don't count.

"Too bad." Goran gives back the camera.

"Take one more!" my husband shouts from the railing. "Just to be sure!"

The island itself disappoints. The Lady has brutal scaffolding holding her in. The museum is closed. The snack bar is dirty and expensive. My husband reads out the prices to me. He orders two french fries and two Cokes. We sit at picnic tables and wait for the ferry to take us back.

"What was that hippie chap saying?"

As if I could say. A day-care center has brought its kids, at least forty of them, to the island for the day. The kids, all wearing name tags, run around us. I can't help noticing how many are Indian. Even a Patel, probably a Bhatt if I looked hard enough. They toss hamburger bits at pigeons. They kick styrofoam cups. The pigeons are slow, greedy, persistent. I have to shoo one off the table top. I don't think my husband thinks about our son.

"What hippie?"

"The one on the boat. With the beard and the hair."

My husband doesn't look at me. He shakes out his paper napkin and tries to protect his french fries from pigeon feathers.

"Oh, him. He said he was from Dubrovnik." It isn't true, but I don't want trouble.

"What did he say about Dubrovnik?"

I know enough about Dubrovnik to get by. Imre's told me about it. And about Mostar and Zagreb. In Mostar white Muslims sing the call to prayer. I would like to see that before I die: white Muslims. Whole peoples have moved before me; they've adapted. The night Imre told me about Mostar was also the night I saw my first snow in Manhattan. We'd walked down to Chelsea from Columbia. We'd walked and talked and I hadn't felt tired at all.

"You're too innocent," my husband says. He reaches for my hand. "Panna," he cries with pain in his voice, and I am brought back from perfect, floating memories of snow, "I've come to take you back. I have seen how men watch you."

"What?"

"Come back, now. I have tickets. We have all the things we will ever need. I can't live without you."

A little girl with wiry braids kicks a bottle cap at his shoes. The pigeons wheel and scuttle around us. My husband covers his fries with spread-out fingers. "No kicking," he tells the girl. Her name, Beulah, is printed in green ink on a heart-shaped name tag. He forces a smile, and Beulah smiles back. Then she starts to flap her arms. She flaps, she hops. The pigeons go crazy for fries and scraps.

"Special ed. course is two years," I remind him. "I can't go back."

My husband picks up our trays and throws them into the garbage before I can stop him. He's carried disposability a little too far. "We've been taken," he says, moving toward the dock, though the ferry will not arrive for another twenty minutes. "The ferry costs only two dollars round-trip per person. We should have chosen tour number one for $10.95 instead of tour number four for $14.95."

With my Lebanese friend, I think. "But this way we don't have to worry about cabs. The bus will pick us up at the pier and take us back to midtown. Then we can walk home."

"New York is full of cheats and whatnot. Just like Bombay." He is not accusing me of infidelity. I feel dread all the same.

That night, after we've gone to bed, the phone rings. My husband listens, then hands the phone to me. "What is this woman saying?" He turns on the pink Macy's lamp by the bed. "I am not understanding these Negro people's accents."

The operator repeats the message. It's a cable from one of the directors of Lakshmi Cotton Mills. "Massive violent labor confrontation anticipated. Stop. Return posthaste. Stop. Cable flight details. Signed Kantilal Shah."

"It's not your factory," I say. "You're supposed to be on vacation."

"So, you are worrying about me? Yes? You reject my heartfelt wishes but you worry about me?" He pulls me close, slips the straps of my nightdress off my shoulder. "Wait a minute."

I wait, unclothed, for my husband to come back to me. The water is running in the bathroom. In the ten days he has been here he has learned American rites: deodorants, fragrances. Tomorrow morning he'll call Air India; tomorrow evening he'll be on his way back to Bombay. Tonight I should make up to him for my years away, the gutted trucks, the degree I'll never use in India. I want to pretend with him that nothing has changed.

In the mirror that hangs on the bathroom door, I watch my naked body turn, the breasts, the thighs glow. The body's beauty amazes. I stand here shameless, in ways he has never seen me. I am free, afloat, watching somebody else.

SECRETIVE

by

JANE AUGUSTINE
(b. 1931)

Jane Augustine, whose poems have appeared in Ms., Aphra,
Chrysalis, Woman Poet: The East, *and many other literary magazines, has published two chapbooks of poems,* Lit by the Earth's
Dark Blood *(1977) and* Journey's End *(1985). She has also written
fiction, but "Secretive" (1973) is her only published story. A former member of the editorial board of* Aphra *and twice a winner
of grants for writing poetry from the New York State Council on
the Arts, she is an adjunct associate professor of English at the
Pratt Institute, in Brooklyn. A graduate of Bryn Mawr College,
Augustine recently completed a doctorate at the City University
of New York.*

• ———————————————————— •

If I don't tell someone, I'm not sure what will happen. I'll crack perhaps.
I'm not sure I can even tell it to you, my secret friend, although you're
utterly safe, the receiver of my thought-words. You're comfortable, sympathetic—as if you were somebody's mother (not mine) or a lady psychiatrist, foreign, a little drab, and as if you were sitting across from me at
my kitchen table, nodding yes and asking me unformulated questions to
which I have exact and full answers, with explanations.

My secret can't even be written in a journal, if I kept a journal. Even
my nonsecrets look bad when written out in words. I'd have to write: "I
spent all day Saturday downtown looking for the right lining material for
my new coat. The lining almost never shows but I was annoyed by the
sleazy taffetas and coarse satins and inadequate moires. The inside matters! I kept saying to myself, searching desperately. Almost everything I
saw would do, more or less; I could put up with it if I had to, but nothing
was exactly right. The lining should pick up one of the colors of the
coat's tweed, I decided, but I didn't know which color. It should be a rich
fabric but not stiff or heavy. But woven or knit? Or perhaps a contrasting
color . . . ?"

You see how my journal would sound—just a list of absurd concerns
that burn up my caring. You would probably agree with him that I'm

stupid, if you saw my day-to-day life translated into words that way. Now, as you sit absorbing my thoughts, you're sympathetic. You're aware that there's more to me than just that I get involved with trivial matters not worth caring about. My mind latches onto them and labors over them while my secret lies down inside me escaping my attention. I know it's there, but only a little of it makes itself known to me.

If I kept a journal, I'd be tempted to write about him in it. Don't you think people delude themselves when they think that a journal or diary can be kept private? He'd find it and that would set him off again, no matter what I said. He couldn't bear my looking at him and recording him. And if I hinted at the secret, which of course he knows, he'd really blow up. "Who are you writing this to? How can you make up lies like this? You know that I have nothing to do with it—you, *you* bring it on yourself—"

You see why I can't speak out loud, why I have to send thought-words out to you. You understand the way it came about even if I can't explain it properly. You know my secret is a real secret. It really can't be told without showing me up, showing how I bring it on myself, and whatever I do to enrage him—even though I don't know what that is.

He says that I'm weak, and I try to counteract the weakness with misplaced aggressiveness. He says I try to hide my dependency pretending to be independent, learning to sew and getting a job and all that. I don't know about that; it sounds like doubletalk and yet there may be something in it. He's not stupid, he's well educated, a social worker; he's read a lot about what goes on in people's minds.

Writing the secret down in a journal would be bad enough, but worse would be if I ever dropped a hint to any of our friends, as I sometimes wish I could. But there I'd be, talking against my own husband, a complainer, a bitch—I don't want to be like that. It could be just temporary in him too, something that won't last—and then if word of it spread around . . . But it's awkward. Verna came over today, returning the sheath dress pattern, and I showed her how to insert one of those new invisible zippers. You can't see an opening anywhere; all the seams look stitched up—no sign of how to get in or get out.

Of course she looked at me and asked about it. I showed her how the kitchen cupboard door by the stove springs back sharply enough to blacken an eye. That's not so farfetched; after all, he says I do it to myself. Something in me drives him to uncontrollable outbursts. He was never like this before he married me, he says.

So this is what I need you to tell me: what do I do that I don't see myself doing? It must be huge and obvious and yet I can't see it. I try thinking back over all the times it's happened. The last time (before this) was in December; he added up the bills and came into the kitchen yelling that I'd spent three hundred dollars on the children's clothing in a year and I had to stop being such a goddam irresponsible spendthrift. "If you had to work," he yelled, "you'd understand the value of money—"

Trying to keep him cool, I asked if maybe three hundred dollars wasn't what was spent on all four of us, which wouldn't be too bad on an income of ten thousand dollars. That's when it happened. Luckily my face wasn't involved; I put on a long-sleeved blouse the next day, and went and got a job typing in an insurance company.

This time—last night—it happened because I hired a babysitter all day Saturday while I went downtown shopping for the lining material I never did buy. He exploded: "You hired a goddam babysitter all day for nothing? The girls are out of school on Saturdays, you ought to be with them." Then I said—which I guess was a mistake: "You can think of it this way: I earned the babysitter money." I was horrified when I looked in the mirror this morning and remembered that Verna was coming over.

But what's gone wrong? I thought learning to sew was a good idea, a way to save money and show him I'm not incompetent. But he says with my Vogue patterns and highfalutin ideas I spend more on material than I would on ready-to-wear. How do I know what I would have spent on ready-to-wear? And he says I just got the job so I could manipulate him and his money decisions by saying it's my money. I don't think that's why I got the job, but I recognize that the mind is full of twistings and turnings, and mysterious hidden levels. There's more in it than I can ever know about.

But maybe you know more, seeing it from an expert's point of view. You can tell me about what's going on, though I understand that I have to be honest with myself and not block off what's happening even though it frightens me. I've been reading, and I know that the mind is mostly unconscious, that we all repress angry and hateful thoughts and wishes, but at a price. Whenever there's a slip of the tongue, part of the unconscious is revealed. Whenever there's an accident, there's a reason for it from earliest childhood, a sexual or incestuous reason that's too strong to be concealed and too terrible to be revealed.

So there are no accidents. It wouldn't make any difference if the kitchen-cupboard door *had* sprung back on me. Things like that just don't happen unless something is hidden in the unconscious mind. My abnormality had to earn it. After all he's a respected man, a professional. He works hard on his job and coaches the Little League in the park on Saturdays. When I go to watch a game, the parents tell me how good a coach he is, really driving the kids to win and building their character. But not by getting mad at them, just by keeping everything under control. I'm the only one he blows up at. No one else has ever seen him more than annoyed at a pop fly. I'm the *only* one—

Now you know the depth of my problem. If I told anyone what he's done to me, they wouldn't believe me. They'd whisper behind my back that I must be a real nut to say such things. Or they'd say, so fights happen in the best of families, but it takes two to tango. They'd say I was crazy if they saw me like this in my kitchen talking to yes, myself, in the only way that relieves me, as if I were my own understanding woman, my invented doctor who doesn't charge me twenty-five dollars an hour.

She's almost real, this listener that I imagine. I can almost see her, wavy grayish hair and searching eyes, rather stern. She sympathizes but she isn't going to let me get away with anything. I might be imagining myself too, as a woman who's trying hard to live right and do what her husband wants. But all the time there might be a woman in me to whom those words apply which he uses: manipulative, incompetent, secretive. . . .

Can't you give me some other words for myself? Like "conscientious, thoughtful, a hard tryer . . ." But it takes a friend to speak these compliments; I must only be flattering myself. . . .

Yes, of course I know you must remain impartial; you have to tell me the truth even if it's not on my side. So can't you tell me why I worry about trivial things like zippers and linings? Then I can get over being that way. I'm sure that's one thing he hates me for.

There. Self-scrutiny does help. I've discovered something.

But the next discovery is more frightening. This woman isn't just trivial, she's full of senseless anger. Sometimes it sticks in her throat till she nearly chokes to keep it back. A little thing like his saying, "You didn't sew that button on yet." Only a petty person would flare up over a remark like that. Her feelings aren't right. Really good people have the right kind of feelings deep inside; then the rest takes care of itself.

Oh, she has secrets all right. So now she has to make sure that no one sees more of the inside of her, no more black-and-blue coming to the surface. Then at least they can't say she's crazy, though they'd almost be right; crazy from keeping secrets and holding in. But that's the way it's got to be.

They can just say she wanders around in department stores all the time, with nothing but colors and fabrics running through her head. Sleazy taffeta, slippery nylon, inferior rayon. But the coat must be finished; it has to be properly lined.

And the lining must be a contrast to the outside of the coat, which is a soft blurry pinkish-orange tweed, the color of rubbed flesh, mixed in with knobs of scarlet. It's a fitted pattern. Now the inside will be a bright green, bright as a parrot's wing, an acid green knit of some tough synthetic fiber that will hang nicely but give only when give is needed. It'll do to hold the coat together, and will only show for a moment before it's hidden away, buttoned, on the closet hanger.

DRIVING TO OREGON

by

JEAN THOMPSON
(b. 1950)

A prolific writer of short stories and the author of two novels, Jean Thompson teaches creative writing at the University of Illinois at Urbana-Champaign. She has held a Guggenheim fellowship, and one of her stories was included in The Best Short Stories of 1979. *She has published two collections of short stories,* Gasoline Wars *(1979) and* Little Face and Other Stories *(1984); her novels include* The Woman Driver *(1985), in which a thirty-year-old divorced woman journeys to self-discovery.*

———————————————

Friends sent them one of those postcards produced by the same technicians who can make a Kansas Holiday Inn suggest a palmy oasis. This time the process had resulted in overkill. Inflamed, tomato-colored wildflowers were grafted to a background of turquoise lake and emerald pines. One white, cone-shaped mountain rose in a sky so densely blue it resembled the paste-waxed fender of a new car. Bert and Mary Ann Lilly taped the card to the refrigerator. When their friends came back they said:

Pretty? That's not the word. Beautiful. Gorgeous. Better than that. Up in the mountains it's cool even in summer, with all that pine smell. Deer, oh yeah, we saw plenty deer. Down in the valleys are orchards. Apricot, cherry, pear. You can pick wild blackberries. And the rivers. What was that big slow one, the color of a green apple? The Umpqua. The Alsea. Waterfalls. People graze horses along the banks. And we haven't even begun to tell you about the coast.

Bert and Mary Ann smiled at each other with one corner of their mouths sucked in, meaning, Some people have all the luck. Man, said Bert, why wasn't I born there? The only deer I ever seen is Bambi.

Waterfalls, huh? said Mary Ann, and chewed for a moment on one of her lank, light-brown pigtails. I've never even been out of crummy old Illi-*noy*. Except for Indiana.

You been to St. Louis, Bert reminded her.

Oh, excuse me, St. Louis. Yeah I guess I have been around.

THE WIFE
74

Everyone laughed and Bert shook the plastic bag of marijuana, pinched off enough to fill the pipe bowl.

That's another thing, the friends said. In Oregon you get busted with under an ounce, it's like a parking ticket. No shit.

You guys tryin to make it hard on me? asked Bert. Like you got to keep reminding me what's out there? He flung his hand toward the window and it tangled in the curtains.

Out there beyond the aluminum-sided bungalow with its frill of dusty grass: Decatur, Illinois.

> Beans. Soybeans.
> You get em from the Staley Plant.

Beantown. Staley Soybean, right squat in the middle of the city. The highway arches over it. A panorama of webbed pipes, giant tanks, chimneys throwing dirty blond smoke into the air. Like driving into a huge stinking motor. Now, at harvest time, trucks rock through the streets, spilling hard wrinkled little beans into the gutters. What do they make out of them, shoe polish? Bug killer? Jesus, how can anything that's supposed to be food smell so bad?

Always plenty of cooking oil in the stores.

Now, in August, the big shallow man-made lake is drying up, showing its bottom of yellow mud. The sky is hazy windless blue. A wooly heat clogs the skin.

At night the sidewalks are still hot enough to sting your feet. Downtown, above the squirming pink neon of taverns, rows of black windows. Broken, barred, shuttered, burnt, and empty. Ulcers in the brick.

Honest blight at least makes no pretenses. But farther from the city center, where the town begins to unravel on the prairie, are blocks and blocks of new graceless enterprise. The used car burgers handy pantry discount king liquors. The formica slabs, plate glass and cellophane.

You know what I saw here once, said Mary Ann. A squirrel trying to drag a package of Kraft American Cheese Slices up a tree.

No worse, maybe, than any other small American city. And surely there are blue spring days, shade trees, first snowfalls.

Surely there is some reason we live here. We were born here. We are comfortable with its bland Midwestern sky. Its ugliness has accumulated like rust, stiffening our eyes and hearts. This place.

Where Bert drives an hour to run a machine that bags fertilizer, coming home with bitter white dust worked into his dark skin. Fertilizer to grow more of those damn beans.

Where the land is so flat you could see the curve of the earth, if there were anywhere high enough to view it from.

Where the sight of big black Bert and his skinny white wife often stops traffic. Whose Caucasian citizens, noting Mary Ann's pregnancy, are moved to sociologic commentary: A yellow baby with frizzy red hair, that's what she's got in there. Twice as ugly as a plain old nigger. Can you imagine the two of them—makes your skin crawl, don't it.

Not to mention, just yet, what Mary Ann's family said.

Why can't we, asked Mary Ann that night when they were in bed.

Em-oh-en-ee-wy, said Bert. What's got into you? Why all of a sudden we got to move?

For the baby. Her answer so prompt and positive in the dark room. I hated growing up here, you know I did.

She was silent, biting her lips at old grievances. Bert reached out and let her long hair sift through his fingers. You think it makes a difference, being in one place or another? You think it would have made you happier?

Yes.

Well, said Bert, you know we can't afford it now. He kissed her and rolled over into sleep, glad there was something easy and practical to set against her vehemence. But the third time somebody at work rammed his car, they began to talk seriously about it.

After all, it's a free country. Why can't we? Didn't we find each other? Just think of that. Out of this whole world we found each other. I chose you and you me. If we did that we can do anything.

Bert was the oldest of seven children. He watched his brothers and sisters marry, he stood up at their weddings and baby-sat for their kids. Getting fat and going bald early. Good old Uncle Bert. He could see himself in twenty years, grinning over his chins at their grandchildren. Letting them play pat-a-cake on his bare scalp. It wasn't that he had trouble meeting girls, just that none of them stuck. Then at a concert he met Mary Ann. She came home with him that night and never left.

The next morning he drove her to breakfast. I got something to tell you, he said.

She was bent over her pocketbook, looking for a match. Mm? she said.

Her hair was pulled back in a long smooth tail and her skin was pink from the cold morning. How pretty she looked, this moment before he would lose her. I'm twenty-nine years old, he said.

Here's one, she said. Nope. Empty.

Did you hear me? Bert demanded.

Uh huh. I'm nineteen.

I know that. Don't it worry you? I mean, on top of bein black and practically bald—

Oh hush, said Mary Ann. If it'll make you feel better, I got a glass eye. The right one.

Not the first time he'd crossed, been with a white girl. Not the first time for her either. How come you don't wear platform shoes and crazy hats and lavender britches, she asked him when she'd known him for two days. You are the dowdiest black dude I ever saw.

He told her Us fat guys look like walking potatoes in clothes like that. Lavender britches, good Lord, girl.

THE WIFE

I don't like those superpimp clothes anyway, she said. But you ain't fat, really.

Or, meeting his family: Gee, they're pretty nice about you bringing home white tail, aren't they?

They traded the car for a pickup with four-wheel drive. You needed something to get around in those mountains, they decided. Bert worked as much overtime as he could that winter. The wind blew stinging dirt across the flatness. Then chunks of filthy ice formed in the gutters, stayed there for weeks. Skin took on the stale, chafed texture of a root left too long in the ground. This is our last winter here, said Bert and Mary Ann. The mercury huddled at the base of the thermometer like frozen blood and they looked at maps and tourist brochures.

> From the colorful past to the bustling present, the saga of Oregon is marked by immense natural wealth and beauty. Mighty volcanic peaks overlook the lush coastal plain. A temperate climate makes year-round vacationing popular. See miles of rugged coastline, well-supplied with recreational facilities. Unique opportunities for the sportsman exist, from salmon fishing in crystal streams to stalking antelope in the vast grasslands. Follow the historic Oregon Trail. Magnificent timberland, jewel-like lakes, winding rivers—and more!

I bet folks out west are a lot less prejudiced to blacks, Bert told a friend at work. You know, it being sort of the frontier. Less set in their ways.

Probably, said his friend. They've always got the Indians.

Bert asked him what he meant but his friend said nothing, nothing.

In March the baby was born. They named her Dawn. Lookit that complexion, said Mary Ann. Looks like you didn't have nothing to do with her.

Aw she'll get darker. And she's got a little Afro nose. Hey little girl, pretty girl, don't burp at your daddy.

You're gonna have a pony, Mary Ann told her. Just as soon as those fat little legs are long enough. For they had decided they would live in the country and raise horses.

In June they sold everything but the stereo and a box of kitchen things. How easy it was to strip things away. To discover that once you took the pictures curtains rugs and flowerpots, you were still there. None of it bound you. Leave it behind along with the families, the friends, the lifetime of habit. You were as free and light as the dust balls rolling from one empty room to the next. Dizzy with your own recklessness. You pulled yourself loose and could as easily set down again. Nothing out there you couldn't outwork, outwit, outmaneuver, outlast.

JEAN THOMPSON

Why can't a little caramel-colored girl-child grow up with a pony in Oregon?

Mary Ann raked through closets, sending tangled coat hangers rattling to the floor. She bruised her knees on suitcases, plunged her uncertain hands into heaps of clothes which she folded and refolded, sorted and resorted. What is the matter with you, Bert demanded after she upset the stack of towels again.

She sat down on the floor, right where she'd been standing. I got to see my folks before we go, she said flatly. Bert started to say something. She held up her hand. I know, I know. But I got to. No I won't take Dawn. You ought to know better than to ask.

He waited for her, crooning to the baby as the summer evening poured through the windows. Blue darkness blurred the corners of the room. In them he saw the vague shapes of his dread.

Evil, blind as a root probing rock, always squirming to reach them.

Something would happen. Even now they would find a way to coax, threaten, or force her.

Evil. You raised your hand to ward it off, but the hand fell away, frail as paper burned to ash. A legacy of malice focused on you. Whispers and warnings. Then the snapping of bone, the wet thick tearing of flesh as the darkie nigger coon got it, got it good.

She would not return. He would stand here all night and the darkness would muffle him, drive him mad. Still he fought with his fear and did not turn on a lamp.

When there was one shining rim of sky left in the west, he heard the truck. It choked and dieseled in the driveway. There was just enough light for him to see her small pale face crossing the room toward him. She pressed against him, hard, and only then began crying. Furious deep tears. The baby, out of fright or hunger, joined in. He held them both, sweet weight, heavy comfort.

Petroleum stink. The flat sun fastened to the hood like an ornament. Concrete, did you ever think there was so much of it? Stale, uniform, wearying: I will multiply thy seeds as the stars of the heaven, and as the concrete which is upon the Interstate.

No matter. It could be ignored, like Iowa, endured, like Nebraska. The tires drummed smoothly, the miles accumulated, tangible, finite. In the back of the pickup their belongings were roped together under taut water-proof canvas, checked at every stop. New maps and new eight-track stereo cartridge tapes that they had not yet grown tired of. A pound of reefer hidden under the seat.

Hey, said Mary Ann. I got an idea. We can get off the Interstate in Wyoming—skewering the map with a fingernail—and go up to Grand Teton or Yellowstone. See?

Bert squinted at the pink and green rectangle that was Wyoming. Aw, that's miles and miles out of our way.

THE WIFE

No it ain't. Well maybe a little. But if we stay on 80 we have to go south out of our way. Besides, everything looks the same from the Interstate. I want to see mountains so bad.

It was true. The land had become more open, rolling, as they approached Wyoming. Bleached earth covered with scrub. But the prim green signs equalized everything, made it hard to believe they'd driven a thousand miles. So on their third day from home they turned north, drawn by the names on the map: Green Mountains. Antelope Hills. Sweetwater. Owl Creek.

Bert thought, as the land began to climb, We're doing it. Really doing it. Look, he said, pointing to a sign. Open grazing. Damn, they got cattle traipsing all over the road. He was delighted. I could almost enjoy this, huh?

Uh huh, said Mary Ann, shielding the baby's face from the sun. She could almost enjoy it. Except for something that happened the summer after high school graduation. When a fast-moving full-sized Oldsmobile appeared in the path of her girlfriend's MGB in which she was the third passenger, draped over the gear shift.

Not that she remembered much. Sometimes she tried to recall the exploding glass, the somersault they said she made onto the slick black roof of the Olds. Since she could not remember it she could not forget it, and imagined it in a number of different versions.

Seven weeks she was in a coma. When they were fairly certain she would live, they began to rebuild her face. Wired her mouth shut so the synthetic jawbone and porcelain teeth could get to know each other undisturbed. Inserted a precision-made blue eye into her blind socket. Drew the skin of her neck and scalp forward and sanded it down. Replaced the bony structure of her nose with silicone. Even took out the bump I used to have, says Mary Ann. Stitched in eyebrows with black surgical thread and planted them with hair.

Mary Ann's mother: Who paid to have you put back together when you were in twenty-seven pieces? We did, we never gave it a second thought, we did it because you were our little girl. We did that for you, doesn't that count for anything?

On her last check-up, two years after the accident, the doctor agreed to show her photographs that had been taken during the last phases of surgery. In them you could see the welts, new scar tissue, but that wasn't so bad.

There were other photographs he refused to show her.

The sound of squealing brakes no longer frightened her. And little by little she accustomed herself to the feel of a steering wheel sliding back and forth in her hands.

They had, after all, done an excellent job with the plastic surgery.

Dawn had fallen asleep while nursing. Her small greedy mouth formed bubbles of milk as she breathed and her face was wrinkled, fierce, oblivious. Mary Ann studied her, looking as she always did for some sign of herself in this little brown child with the fluffy hair. A pint of white mixed with a gallon of black. She had been blended in. But maybe it was always like this, children could not mirror or repeat you. They went their own way.

Mary Ann's mother: Go on, heap dirt on our heads. I'm telling everyone who asks, you're adopted. Then when they see you running off to live with the niggers, they'll think you have nigger in you yourself. That'll probably make you happy.

And her father saying Now that's enough, over and over again. Embarrassed eyes that would not meet hers. And she hated him almost as much because he was weak, he would never stand up for her.

So much taken from her. Like the struggle to wake in the white, white room, swimming to the surface of consciousness and pain, then learning she had lost seven whole weeks. Even now, sometimes she woke gasping and numb. *How long had she slept?*

So much taken from her. She saw things flatly, like a child's drawing with everything lined up on the horizon. She learned to make her voice light and careless when she had to, never admitting loss, not letting anything else be taken. Humming, she looked out the window.

Wide pale sky and hills like a rumpled bedsheet. Khaki-colored grass and outcroppings of red rock. An arid, silent landscape whose foreignness excited them. On the horizon, a dark line which they hoped was mountains. The new eight-track stereo cartridge tape sang:

> He-ey, tonight
> Gonna be the night
> Gonna fly right to the sky
> Tonight

> then

> He-ey, *chunk*night
> Gonna *chunk* the night
> Gonna *rechunkrechunkre*
> *Chunkchunk*

Oh shit. The exhaust? Carburetor? Fuel pump? The truck spat and died as Bert eased it to the side of the road. Je-sus, said Bert, and flipped the music off. They waited, Bert until he controlled his anger, Mary Ann until he would tell her what was wrong. Without the singing and the comfortable noise of their motion, the huge hot sky seemed to press down on them. Bert got out and raised the hood. Restarted the engine, but it died in a fit of noise and stinging smoke. Dawn woke up and began to cry.

Great, said Bert. Just great. He thought of the Interstate, the smooth ordered road they could have taken if only she hadn't talked him out of it. Can't you get her quiet, he said. I got to think.

Oh sure, said Mary Ann. I'll just explain that to her.

Bert studied the map. I think we're about nine miles from Crowheart, he said over the screaming.

Neither the distance nor the name seemed to offer much hope. They looked out at the dry hills and empty road. We'll wait awhile, said Bert, and if nobody comes I'll start walking.

Walk? You're kidding, that'll take hours. Wait til somebody comes along.

Yeah, you want to spend the night here? Fifteen minutes, that's all I'll give it. He put as much decisiveness as he could into the statement, trying to forget the money he could feel ticking away even as he spoke.

Waiting. And waiting. Mary Ann rocked the baby into quiet; Dawn regarded them both with wide uncertain eyes. Just as Bert was about to look at his watch for the last time, the road behind them produced first noise, then a red glittering pickup with an over-the-cab camper. Well hallelujah, said Bert. He got out to stand on the shoulder with his arm raised. The truck approached, slowed, as if to get a good look at them— they could see a woman's face pressed to the glass, two kids in the back reading comics—then accelerated past.

The sun seemed ready to puncture the metal roof. Maybe they'll at least tell a garage we're out here, said Mary Ann when Bert got back in the truck and slammed the door.

Sure. If there is a garage. And if they have to stop for soda pop anyway. Assholes.

I still say let's wait.

Don't tell me what to do. I got enough problems already.

Well it's my problem too and I've got a say in it.

Well, you're the one who said to take this stupid road, he said, giving in to his impatience. I had enough of your good ideas.

Oh, so it's my fault? Who's the big-shot mechanic who said he could fix anything?

I don't have to listen to this, said Bert, getting out.

Bullshitter, she screamed, as he started down the highway. Go ahead. I won't be here when you get back.

But just then the road came to life again. A slow-moving '63 Chevy, blue-green and battered, rolled toward them, pulled ahead of the truck and stopped. Mary Ann watched Bert run back, lean over the driver's side. Both doors opened and two men, boys really, got out. Oh Christ, said Mary Ann. Indians.

One, the driver, had a barrel chest and squat legs, a sly wide face. His hair was drawn into two braids which grazed his shoulders. The other was thinner, his black hair cut short and ruffled by the wind. Both of them wore jeans and stretched-out T-shirts. She guessed them to be

JEAN THOMPSON

81

about eighteen. They walked towards the truck and one, the thin one, glanced at her, an indifferent narrow-eyed look.

After a moment Bert opened the door. Come on, they'll give us a ride.

I'm not going anywhere with you. She was crying by now.

Man, he said, you are too much. You know where we are? On an Indian reservation. If you're waiting for the Boy Scouts you gonna wait awhile. Let's go.

No, she cried, and he raised his hand but did not hit her, not yet. Let's go, he repeated, dead-calm, and she opened the door, hating him.

The two boys slit their eyes at her but did not speak as she got in the back of the Chevy. Then the fat one said something to the other, words she did not understand. They're talking Indian, she thought faintly. Bert stared straight ahead.

Fifteen minutes of silent driving, and the Chevy pulled up to a white-washed building set in a yard of tamped dirt. There were two gas pumps in front. Why are we stopping here, Bert and Mary Ann each wondered. Then they knew: this was Crowheart. Post Office, general store, gas, the works. When the car stopped Mary Ann got out and marched toward the building without speaking.

There was a porch of uneven boards shaded by the roof. On it several Indians, older men in work shirts and cowboy hats, were sitting. She appoached and they stopped talking. There were no chairs left so she went to the end of the porch and leaned against the wall.

Bert came around the corner. We're going back to take a look at it, he said. Here's money for a drink or something. She would not answer or take the five-dollar bill he extended, so he tucked it in her purse and walked away. She watched him get back in the Chevy and drive off into the brown hills.

The men, four or five of them, sat with their hands on their knees, as unmoving as lizards in the heat. The one nearest her stood up. Here Missy, he said, pointing. Here. His skin was sunblackened, his eyes held in nets of wrinkles. Thank you, she said. He nodded and walked inside.

Now she was seated among them. They did not look at her, and she realized this was a form of courtesy. She could sit here all day minding her own business. They would not disturb her. She was grateful for their indifference. There were worse things than that. She permitted herself a moment of thought for the stalled truck.

An hour later her eyes caught a pillar of shimmering dust on the road. The heat made it seem impossibly far away and slow. But at last the Chevy appeared, followed by the truck. Mary Ann stood up. Good-bye, she said. They ducked their heads in a kind of chorus, and she walked to the truck.

Bert opened the door for her but neither of them spoke.

In silence they watched the hills rise into dark pine-covered peaks, noted the looping track of the river beneath them.

Easier to travel a thousand miles and camp among strange tribes than it is to apologize.

Until Bert stopped the truck to gaze at the incredible range of ice-covered stone that lay before them. The green-floored valley and blue lake. The air had grown cool, scented with pine and sage.

Ready to quit fightin, Bert asked, looking through the windshield.

Yeah. Pride made her want to sound sullen, but when she opened her mouth her lungs filled with thin cold air, a giddy perfume that lifted her voice.

Hey, she asked him later, as they watched the afternoon sun slide down the peaks. What was wrong with the truck?

Loose condenser.

Did you have to pay them much?

Nothing. Bert grinned. I gave em some reefer. We had a little peace-pipe session.

Back on the Interstate in Idaho. Anxious now, impatient to get there. Turning up their noses at the lava plains and ragged crests: they were going somewhere better. Driving without stopping, Bert and Mary Ann trading shifts.

They raced against hunger, stuffing their bellies with pasty hamburgers and chocolate. They'd figured two weeks, that's how long they could last until Bert found a job.

Ten stiff $20 bills in the lining of Mary Ann's purse.

2 weeks = 14 days.

(x) motel rooms @ $12 = ?

Gas. Groceries. Rent deposit? Even if he found a job, how long would it be until he got a paycheck?

Bert's eyes glazed at the sun-slick road, and he fought to make the numbers balance. How much had they spent? Where had it leaked away from them? You're tired, he told himself. Everything seems worse when you're tired. Try to sleep. He closed his eyes. Something heavy was burrowing its way into his dreams. Metal grating on metal. He opened his eyes to darkness, and a new grinding sound from the engine: *Rak. Rak. Rak.* Steadily increasing in tempo and authority.

It just started, said Mary Ann.

Take the next exit, Bert told her. There was nothing else to say. Each knew what the other was thinking.

In the fluorescent, hard-edged glare of the Shell station, the teen-aged gas jockey shook his head. Might be your points burned out. A cylinder not firing. Or the spark plug wires. We won't have a mechanic in here til seven ayem. In the Pine-Sol–stinking restroom Bert splashed water on his face. He walked back to the truck, started it, listened to the idle for a moment, and pulled onto the highway.

We got to, he said, before Mary Ann could open her mouth. Even if the mechanic was here we couldn't pay him. Unless we decide to settle down right here. We'll just drive the damn thing into the ground and see how far it gets.

We're a hundred twenty miles from the border, said Mary Ann after a moment. When he looked again both she and the baby were asleep.

Drifting lights in the darkness. The shallow cone of highway illuminated before him. He would find a job. They would live out in the country and when they'd saved enough they would buy horses. Dully he repeated this until it diminished into sing-song. Every muscle in his body felt bulky and unyielding.

Why should he be doubting now? So what if the worst happened, the truck failed and they had to hustle for money. Couldn't they do that? He supposed they could, but his weariness went further. He longed to shrink the world into something finite, physical, easily confronted. He supposed he'd felt it was that way once, although it was hard to remember now, while he strained to stay awake in the humming darkness. Oh yeah, he could lick anything with one hand tied behind him. Blindfolded. On his knees. Whistling Dixie.

The engine settled into a steady chattering. It might quit at ten miles or at a thousand. The headlights caught a highway sign but it was some moments before its meaning penetrated. Oregon. They were in Oregon though they still had three hundred miles to go. Indifferently he swung his head from one gray window to another. Even when the flat red sun popped up like the No Sale tag of a cash register, revealing shallow wheat fields that might have been in Kansas, even then he felt no special despair or disappointment. Just cold fatigue and inattention.

Mary Ann felt Dawn's fingers rooting in her hair, then the new hot day on her face. The baby began to cry and she spoke to her without opening her eyes. But the cramp in her back, the steady jogging—*Where was she?* Gasping, she reached out for the baby, then blinked and looked around her.

Just as she never spoke of the pinched pain behind her glass eye, or the ragged bones that never quite healed, so now she regarded the dust and flatness around her and did not acknowledge them.

I bet you want to sleep, huh, she said, rubbing Bert's neck with one hand and maneuvering the baby toward her nipple with the other.

Pretty soon, he said, trying to match her calmness.

Got to stop and change her anyway, said Mary Ann. I think she had a busy night.

Yeah well, began Bert, but he stopped at a new noise from somewhere in the oily complications of the engine. Before he'd heard it a second time he had identified it. Backfiring. Thick blue smoke uncoiled from the tailpipe, obscuring the road behind them. Twelve miles to an exit, said Bert as the wheel jumped under his hand. Come on, give us a break.

The explosions were so loud that cars following them hung back, gathering courage to pass. Five more miles they wrung from the tortured engine. In the side mirror Bert noticed a white shape traveling in their wake, just visible through the fumes. Then it pulled alongside and stayed there.

He ignored it as long as he could, even though the trooper was motioning to him. Then the red dome light went on.

The bastard wants me to pull over, cried Bert. Don't he know I'll never get it started again? He wrenched the truck to the shoulder and tried to let it idle, but it stalled. They waited until the trooper came up to them.

Morning, he said, and they could tell from his face, how it pulled away once he saw them, like he had stepped in shit, what he was thinking. They'd seen that look before.

Having trouble? he asked. The trooper was a thin young black-haired man, with a peculiar smooth look to his face, as if the bones had stunted, and light restless eyes.

Yeah, said Bert, and opened the door so the trooper had to take a step back. Yeah, we got trouble.

Could I see your license please? Take it out of the plastic. His voice was colorless, not matching the politeness of his words.

Bert stood silently, knowing this was not the time to protest, not yet. The trooper studied the license, shifting from one foot to the other, then asked for the registration. When Mary Ann had produced it from the glove compartment, he asked Now where are you folks going?

Portland, said Bert.

Mind if I take a look in the back, said the man, not making it a question, as he loosened one of the ropes and angled his thin back so he could peer beneath the canvas. Bert followed him, standing close enough that the trooper felt his presence and squared his shoulders as he stood up.

Well now, he said, his light eyes looking just beyond Bert, his voice still neutral, you folks aren't going to be able to get any farther. You're violating the emission control standards.

We're going to the next exit. We'll get it fixed there.

The trooper shook his head and the flat shadow of his hat brim crept over his flat face. Can't let you back on the highway. You could cause an accident, all that smoke. You'll have to get it towed.

We can't afford a tow.

Well . . . he paused, and Bert could see how little effort he was putting into his words; they were a script he was following, certain of the outcome. The only other thing we can do is impound the vehicle.

No, said Bert, and in speaking he committed himself to doing what was necessary. His very exhaustion was a strength now, because it loosened his fury. He felt the hard crust of sweat on his muscles, the syncopated popping of nerves, the white sunlight twitching in his eyes, and knew he could unleash himself. He could murder, in broad daylight with his bare hands. Then take his wife and child some place far away, some place he could also fight for them. No, he repeated, I think it would be better if we just went to the next exit. And he waited, calmly, for what would happen now.

Later he would wonder how he had looked to the trooper. Something, the glazed blood in his eyes, the stance of his legs, had communicated craziness, danger. The trooper squinted and turned his smooth neutral face from side to side like a puzzled bird. After a moment Bert realized he was calculating the cost of retreat, how much pride was involved.

Well, said the trooper, if you drive on the shoulder, slow, I mean slow, with your flashers going, I guess you could make it.

Sure. Bert waited a few seconds, in case the trooper insisted on some further instruction as a sop to his authority. But the man only said OK then, his eyes still wandering, and walked to his car.

Bert waited until he was gone, then tried the engine. It started noisily but seemed more willing than before. When they reached a gas station Bert coaxed the mechanic into lending him tools, changed the burnt-out points himself, handed the keys to Mary Ann, and only then allowed himself sleep.

He woke, after how long he did not know, when Mary Ann cried out. Smatter, he said, lurching upright. What? What?

But she was turning her head from side to side, trying to make her one good eye take in all that was before her. The road was pulling them toward a river, pulling them down then lifting to follow the banks. A mile-wide stretch of misty water curving between raw brown cliffs. In the distance the road, and everything on it, dwindled to a thread. She strained her neck to see the top of the cliffs but it was all too large, it would not order itself into a single view.

Rounding a turn, she squinted. Floating above the horizon was a mass of slate and white, like a smeared cloud. Only it was no cloud. Bert saw it too, and they both opened their mouths to speak: Damn, that thing must be eighty miles away, look at it, just look. But the wind, which had increased steadily as they entered the gorge, now slammed against the truck and filled the air with its roaring. Mary Ann gripped the wheel tighter and turned to Bert. Their lips still worked, forming speech. It would take all their strength to make themselves heard.

FACING THE MUSIC

by

LARRY BROWN
(b. 1951)

Larry Brown has been a Marine, a firefighter, and the owner of a small country store in his native Mississippi. His short stories have been widely published in regional journals in the South. Facing the Music: Stories (1988) was his first collection. His first novel, Dirty Work, appeared in 1989. In "Facing the Music," Brown allows the reader to perceive a grim reality denied by his central character.

•———————————————————•

For Richard Howorth

I cut my eyes sideways because I know what's coming. "You want the light off, honey?" she says. Very quietly.

I can see as well with it as without it. It's an old movie I'm watching, Ray Milland in *The Lost Weekend*. This character he's playing, this guy will do anything to get a drink. He'd sell children, probably, to get a drink. That's the kind of person Ray's playing.

Sometimes I have trouble resting at night, so I watch the movies until I get sleepy. They show them—all-night movies—on these stations from Memphis and Tupelo. There are probably a lot of people like me, unable to sleep, lying around watching them with me. I've got remote control so I can turn it on or off and change channels. She's stirring around the bedroom, doing things, doing something—I don't know what. She has to stay busy. Our children moved away and we don't have any pets. We used to have a dog, a little brown one, but I accidentally killed it. Backed over its head with the station wagon one morning. She used to feed it in the kitchen, right after she came home from the hospital. But I told her, no more. It hurts too much to lose one.

"It doesn't matter," I say, finally, which is not what I'm thinking.

"That's Ray Milland," she says. "Wasn't he young then." Wistful like.

So he was. I was too once. So was she. So was everybody. But this movie is forty years old.

"You going to finish watching this?" she says. She sits on the bed right beside me. I'm propped up on the TV pillow. It's blue corduroy and I got it for Christmas last year. She said I was spending so much time in the bed, I might as well be comfortable. She also said it could be used for other things, too. I said what things?

I don't know why I have to be so mean to her, like it's her fault. She asks me if I want some more ice. I'm drinking whiskey. She knows it helps me. I'm not so much of a bastard that I don't know she loves me.

Actually, it's worse than that. I don't mean anything against God by saying this, but sometimes I think she worships me.

"I'm okay," I say. Ray has his booze hanging out the window on a string—hiding it from these booze-thieves he's trying to get away from—and before long he'll have to face the music. Ray can never find a good place to hide his booze. He gets so drunk he can't remember where he hid it when he sobers up. Later on, he's going to try to write a novel, pecking the title and his name out with two fingers. But he's going to have a hard time. Ray is crazy about that booze, and doesn't even know how to type.

She may start rubbing on me. That's what I have to watch out for. That's what she does. She gets in bed with me when I'm watching a movie and she starts rubbing on me. I can't stand it. I especially can't stand for the light to be on when she does it. If the light's on when she does it, she winds up crying in the bathroom. That's the kind of husband I am.

But everything's okay, so far. She's not rubbing on me yet. I go ahead and mix myself another drink. I've got a whole bottle beside the bed. We had our Christmas party at the fire station the other night and everybody got a fifth. My wife didn't attend. She said every person in there would look at her. I told her they wouldn't, but I didn't argue much. I was on duty anyway and couldn't drink anything. All I could do was eat my steak and look around, go get another cup of coffee.

"I could do something for you," she says. She's teasing but she means it. I have to smile. One of those frozen ones. I feel like shooting both of us because she's fixed her hair up nice and she's got on a new nightgown.

"I could turn the lamp off," she says.

I have to be very careful. If I say the wrong thing, she'll take it the wrong way. She'll wind up crying in the bathroom if I say the wrong thing. I don't know what to say. Ray's just met this good-looking chick—Jane Wyman?—and I know he's going to steal a lady's purse later on; I don't want to miss it. I could do the things Ray Milland is doing in this movie and worse. Boy. Could I. But she's right over here beside my face wanting an answer. Now. She's smiling at me. She's licking her lips. I don't want to give in. Giving in leads to other things, other givings.

I have to say something. But I don't say anything.

She gets up and goes back over to her dressing table. She picks up her brush. I can hear her raking and tearing it through her hair. It sounds like she's ripping it out by the roots. I have to stay here and listen to it. I can understand why people jump off bridges.

THE WIFE

"You want a drink?" I say. "I can mix you up a little bourbon and Coke."

"I've got some," she says, and she lifts her can to show me. Diet Coke. At least a six-pack a day. The refrigerator's crammed full of them. I can hardly get to my beer for them. I think they're only one calorie or something. She thinks she's fat and that's the reason I don't pay enough attention to her, but it isn't.

She's been hurt. I know she has. You can lie around the house all your life and think you're safe. But you're not. Something from outside or inside can reach out and get you. You can get sick and have to go to the hospital. Some nut could walk into the station one night and kill us all in our beds. You can read about things like that in the paper any morning you want to. I try not to think about it. I just do my job and then come home and try to stay in the house with her. But sometimes I can't.

Last week, I was in this bar in town. I'd gone down there with some of these boys we're breaking in, rookies. Just young boys, nineteen or twenty. They'd passed probation and wanted to celebrate, so a few of us older guys went with them. We drank a few pitchers and listened to the band. It was a pretty good band. They did a lot of Willie and Waylon stuff. I'm thinking about all this while she's getting up and moving around the room, looking out the windows.

I don't go looking for things—I don't—but later on, well, there was this woman in there. Not a young woman. Younger than me. About forty. She was sitting by herself. I was in no hurry to go home. All the boys had gone, Bradshaw, too. I was the only one of the group left. So I said what the hell. I went up to the bar and bought two drinks and carried them over to her table. I sat down with them and I smiled at her. And she smiled back. In an hour we were over at her house.

I don't know why I did it. I'd never done anything like that before. She had some money. You could tell it from her house and things. I was a little drunk, but I know that's no excuse. She took me into her bedroom and she put a record on, some nice slow orchestra or something. I was lying on the bed the whole time, knowing my wife was at home waiting up on me. This woman stood up in the middle of the room and started turning. She had her arms over her head. She had white hair piled up high. When she took off her jacket, I could tell she had something nice underneath. She took off her shirt, and her breasts were like something you'd see in a movie, deep long things you might only glimpse in a swimming suit. Before I knew it, she was on the bed with me, putting one of them in my mouth.

"You sure you don't want a drink?" I say.

"I want you," she says, and I don't know what to say. She's not looking at me. She's looking out the window. Ray's coming out of the bathroom now with the lady's purse under his arm. But I know they're all going to be waiting for him, the whole club. I know what he's going to feel. Everybody's going to be looking at him.

LARRY BROWN

89

When this woman got on top of me, the only thing I could think was: God.

"What are we going to do?" my wife says.

"Nothing," I say. But I don't know what I'm saying. I've got these big soft nipples in my mouth and I can't think of anything else. I'm trying to remember exactly how it was.

I thought I'd be different somehow, changed. I thought she'd know what I'd done just by looking at me. But she didn't. She didn't even notice.

I look at her and her shoulders are jerking under the little green gown. I'm always making her cry and I don't mean to. Here's the kind of bastard I am: my wife's crying because she wants me, and I'm lying here watching Ray Milland, and drinking whiskey, and thinking about putting another woman's breasts in my mouth. She was on top of me and they were hanging right over my face. It was so wonderful, but now it seems so awful I can hardly stand to think about it.

"I understand how you feel," she says. "But how do you think I feel?"

She's not talking to me; she's talking to the window and Ray is staggering down the street in the hot sunshine, looking for a pawnshop so he can hock the typewriter he was going to use to write his novel.

A commercial comes on, a man selling dog food. I can't just sit here and not say anything. I have to say something. But, God, it hurts to.

"I know," I say. It's almost the same as saying nothing. It doesn't mean anything.

We've been married for twenty-three years.

"You don't know," she says. "You don't know the things that go through my mind."

I know what she's going to say. I know the things going through her mind. She's seeing me on top of her with her legs over my shoulders, her legs locked around my back. But she won't take her gown off anymore. She'll just push it up. She never takes her gown off, doesn't want me to see. I know what will happen. I can't do anything about it. Before long she'll be over here rubbing on me, and if I don't start, she'll stop and wind up crying in the bathroom.

"Why don't you have a drink?" I say. I wish she'd have a drink. Or go to sleep. Or just watch the movie with me. Why can't she just watch the movie with me?

"I should have just died." she says. "Then you could have gotten you somebody else."

I guess maybe she means somebody like the friendly woman with the nice house and the nice nipples.

I don't know. I can't find a comfortable place for my neck. "You shouldn't say that."

"Well it's true. I'm not a whole woman anymore. I'm just a burden on you."

"You're not."

"Well you don't want me since the operation."

THE WIFE

90

She's always saying that. She wants me to admit it. And I don't want to lie anymore, I don't want to spare her feelings anymore, I want her to know I've got feelings too and it's hurt me almost as bad as it has her. But that's not what I say. I can't say that.

"I do want you." I say. I have to say it. She makes me say it.

"Then prove it," she says. She comes close to the bed and she leans over me. She's painted her brows with black stuff and her face is made up to where I can hardly believe it.

"You've got too much makeup on," I whisper.

She leaves. She's in the bathroom scrubbing. I can hear the water running. Ray's got the blind staggers. Everybody's hiding his whiskey from him and he can't get a drink. He's got it bad. He's on his way to the nuthouse.

Don't feel like a lone ranger, Ray.

The water stops running. She cuts the light off in there and then she steps out. I don't look around. I'm watching a hardware store commercial. Hammers and Skilsaws are on the wall. They always have this pretty girl with large breasts selling their hardware. The big special this week is garden hose. You can buy a hundred feet, she says, for less than four dollars.

The TV is just a dim gray spot between my socks. She's getting on the bed, setting one knee down and pulling up the hem of her gown. She can't wait. I'm thinking of it again, how the woman's breasts looked, how she looked in her shirt before she took it off, how I could tell she had something nice underneath, and how wonderful it was to be drunk in that moment when I knew what she was going to do.

It's time now. She's touching me. Her hands are moving, sliding all over me. Everywhere. Ray is typing with two fingers somewhere, just the title and his name. I can hear the pecking of his keys. That old boy, he's trying to do what he knows he should. He has responsibilities to people who love him and need him; he can't let them down. But he's scared to death. He doesn't know where to start.

"You going to keep watching this?" she says, but dreamy-like, kissing me, as if she doesn't care one way or the other.

I don't say anything when I cut the TV off. I can't speak. I'm thinking of how it was on our honeymoon, in that little room at Hattiesburg, when she bent her arms behind her back and slumped her shoulders forward, how the cups loosened and fell as the straps slid off her arms. I'm thinking that your first love is your best love, that you'll never find any better. The way she did it was like she was saying, here I am, I'm all yours, all of me, forever. Nothing's changed. She turns the light off, and we reach to find each other in the darkness like people who are blind.

MARKS

by

LINDA PASTAN
(b. 1932)

Born in New York, Linda Pastan studied at Brandeis and Radcliffe. Her 1978 collection, The Five Stages of Grief, *from which "Marks" is taken, shows her concern for the problems of middle age: death of parents, loss of youth. Her seventh volume,* Imperfect Paradise *(1988), shows her wry acceptance of and love of life. She has been honored with fellowships from the state of Maryland, where she lives with her husband and three children, and the National Endowment for the Arts. She has won many awards; her 1982 volume,* AM/PM, *was nominated for the American Book Award.*

•────────────────•

My husband gives me an A
for last night's supper,
an incomplete for my ironing,
a B plus in bed.
My son says I am average,
an average mother, but if
I put my mind to it
I could improve.
My daughter believes
in Pass/Fail and tells me
I pass. Wait 'til they learn
I'm dropping out.

THE WIFE

The Mother

More than any other image of women, that of the mother has its origins in myth and legend. The psychologist Carl Jung considered it to be an archetype, an image buried deeply in the mind—in what he called the collective unconscious—and common to all people everywhere. Such images, he thought, are too deeply embedded for any individual to be consciously aware of them, but they find expression in symbols and art. Whether one accepts Jung's ideas or not, it is true that the mother image existed in earliest times, represented in the protruding bellies and breasts of cave drawings and in the goddesses of many religions. The characteristics of the mother can be traced to the creation myths that exist in all cultures to explain both our presence in the world (our beginning) and our knowledge of death (our ending). The images of good and evil embodied in the Great Mother, a very widespread image, reflect not only our love for the giver of life but also our fear of the inescapable death that the gift brings with it. Ambivalence about the image is reflected, for example, in the dichotomy between Eve and the Virgin Mary in the Christian religion: Eve, the mother of us all, is the temptress who, because of her desire for knowledge, brought sin and death into the world. But Mary, passively acted on by the Holy Ghost, pondering in her heart the experience of her son, is the Queen of Heaven, the Mother of God, and through Him, of everyone. This stereotype equating active curiosity with bad and passive acceptance with good is deeply rooted in many cultures.

Ambivalence about the mother has continued for many reasons. It is deeply rooted in the human desire for the free-floating comfort and irresponsibility of the womb, for being nurtured and cared for as in infancy, a desire Sigmund Freud considered a death wish. This conflicts with the equally deep human desire for independence and individuality—for life itself. When love for the mother conflicts with the need to separate, both anger and fear are likely to be the results. Since even today mothers are almost universally the primary caregivers, problems of growing up are ascribed to them: "mother bashing" is used to explain many psychological problems.

Recently women scholars have tried to separate the archetypal mother image from the actual women who are mothers; in the process they undermine the assumption that only biological mothers can mother. They reject as infantile fantasies both the sentimental Mother's Day vision of "the one who means the world to me" and the image of the all-powerful Mom who castrates her sons by binding them to her. Both of these images are based on what Freud called the Oedipus complex, a developmental experience that he thought occurs universally around age six. According to this theory, a boy must metaphorically murder his father and marry his mother in order to escape castration—in order to grow up as a separate individual. A daughter can never become fully adult because her wish to become like her mother takes precedence over her wish for separation. Sociologist Nancy Chodorow (1978) and psychologist Dorothy Dinnerstein (1977) suggested that the struggle for identity begins in earliest infancy. They link the split between the good and the terrible mother to socialization that does not separate childbearing and childrearing. Having the responsibility for both nurturing and disciplining thrust upon them, mothers bear society's onus for the inevitable pains of growth and maturity: they are scapegoats for difficulties that are aspects of the human condition. Chodorow sees sons' socialization by mothers as leading to men's fear and rejection of women; girls' socialization results in "the reproduction of motherhood," which perpetuates women's secondary roles in society. Both Chodorow and Dinnerstein suggest that equal parenting by fathers and mothers, especially in infancy, can disrupt the cycle and allow both boys and girls to become fully human adults. Chodorow (1989) has recently expanded her analysis of how gender identity is acquired to include other social and cultural explanations; she admits that her theory did not apply to all cultures. She still considers women's roles as mothers to be a major contributing factor. It seems clear that parents imprint their sense of gender onto their children even in infancy.

Freud's theory means that women can never be as separate from their parents as men can. He concluded that women are therefore not able to make fully moral decisions. Work by Gilligan (1982) and Ruddick (1989) contests this view; both, like Chodorow, see women's socialization as leading to a self defined in relation to others. Gilligan has discovered that a mode of moral decision making based on relationships and often held by women is different from but not necessarily inferior to the male system based on principles of abstract justice. Ruddick and others maintain that women's emphasis on emotional ties in human relationships, based on their experience of motherhood, better equips them to play leadership roles in the quest for peace and for environmental conservation. Ruddick also believes that nonbiological mothers can share in "maternal thinking." Though Johnson (1988) also believes that such thinking is a fundamental gender difference, she feels that male/female differences are exaggerated and continue in our culture largely because men impose their ideal of the weak wife on their daughters. If this is true, parenting by fathers is a problematical solution, and the stereotypical weak wife will continue to be "reproduced." Recent revelations about the prevalence of sexual abuse by fathers brings into question many assumptions about maternal failures.

The stories in this section are not problem solving; they describe the ideal selfless mother, the range of joy and pain that accompanies birth, the anguish of abortion, the conflict between the claims of sexuality and motherhood, the strength of the mother-daughter bond and its cultural use to reinforce traditional roles, and the ability of adults other than mothers to rear children.

Ray Bradbury's "I Sing the Body Electric!" is the story of a robot that fulfills all the nurturing functions of the ideal mother, not only for three children but also for their widowed father. Not being human, she has none of the withholding, punishing aspects of the Terrible Mother; perhaps this is why Bradbury makes her "Grandma," the maternal caretaker traditionally removed from the necessity of disciplining and also from sexuality, which might cause her to divide her attention. The grandmother is "slapped . . . to life" by the children she comes to nurture; they owe her no debt for the pain of bringing them into the world, and, being a robot, she needs no rest or consideration from them. They can take without guilt all that she offers; they do not even have to ask, because she can read their thoughts and anticipate their every need, whether physical or psychological. She removes herself when they are grown but returns, as promised, when they are old and again want to be mothered. Her reward is like that of Mrs. James in "The Angel Over the Right Shoulder": she will go to heaven. Ironically, to her, heaven means becoming human. Bradbury plays on every human desire for mother love only to make clear the inhumanity of such a burden. The story's very length is a symbol of how longstanding is the human fantasy of and longing for the Good Mother.

Both Erica Jong and Toi Derricotte eloquently express the emotions that accompany becoming a mother. Jong emphasizes a mother's joy, her sense of union with all women and of "vastness." Derricotte focuses on a woman's sense of the physicality of the process and of being born anew: "the whole universe had changed." Gwendolyn Brooks's anguished speaker mourns for "the children that you got that you did not get" because of abortions; she respects their right to life and feels pain and sorrow but not guilt for their deaths. The two women in Ellen Lesser's story feel more unease than sorrow or guilt when they meet at an abortion clinic; one feels anger at her male partner, the more mature one realizes it is her own fear of intimacy that has brought her to her decision. Sue Miller shows a divorced mother's conflict between her need for sexual satisfaction and her love for and responsibility for her child; and Jan Clausen uses a child's voice to show the anguish of a lesbian mother whose child, seduced by the material advantages her father can offer, chooses him as the custodial parent.

Maxine Kumin and Ruth Stone both focus on mother-daughter relationships from the point of view of the mother. Kumin's speaker counters her fear of death with the hope that her "daughters will . . . carry me about forever inside them" as she carries her mother's image within her. The Russian dolls she refers to, significantly, come from Russian legends of matriarchies. Stone's persona writes to her daughter about her mundane daily life; "between the lines" we can read her longing for the daughter to respond to her loneliness, but it is she who fulfills the nurturing role.

Other writers in this section focus on the ways in which mothers fulfill their stereotypical role in passing on tradition. For Li-Young Lee's speaker in "I Ask My Mother to Sing," his mother and grandmother are his only link to his ancestral home in China. Ruth Fainlight's speaker in "Flower Feet" is appalled by an exhibit of shoes worn by Chinese women who underwent the agony of foot-binding and whose mothers colluded in the practice; the mothers' happiness that the tradition has changed indicates the cost to them of having passed on a tradition they had felt powerless to defy. Both Gloria C. Oden in "Speculation" and Jamaica Kincaid in "Girl" let us overhear a mother's voice, commanding, instructing, and reproducing tradition; the young daughters react with ambivalence and a degree of rebellion. Gloria E. Anzaldúa's speaker rages at the entire Chicano/Chicana tradition, personified as the feminine *La Raza* (connoting race, family, and culture), which interferes with her individuality. Audre Lorde, in what sounds like an autobiographical voice, urges her friend (writer Toni Morrison) *not* to bring up her daughter "to be a correct little sister." Recognizing that mothers are "landscapes . . . printed upon" daughters, she wants their daughters to be free from "taboos" and "myths" so that they may become "their own/Black Women." Lorde suggests that mothers conscious of their power can choose to break it.

Not all daughters are shown as rebelling against their mothers' traditions. If, as Lorde hopes, mothers and daughters can respect and love each other as individuals, they can transcend stereotypical generational conflict. In "Souvenir," Jayne Anne Phillips shows the interdependence of a mother and adult daughter; they both give and take, as their mutual gift of pewter candle holders indicates. Kate needs her mother "to defend [Kate's] choices"; the mother needs Kate to validate the mother's choices by becoming a mother and providing grandchildren. But the mother perceives that Kate can give her validation by other means: "If you like yourself, I must have done something right," she says. By being herself, Kate wins her mother's approval. Phillips describes a special bond between a mother and a daughter without reducing either to a role-player. In its message her story is reminiscent of Rosellen Brown's title *Autobiography of My Mother* (1976): by sharing each others' perspectives, mothers and daughters can be whole persons.

The last two stories in this section show vividly that adults other than biological mothers can play the mother role well. In "Bridging," Max Apple's widower becomes a Girl Scout assistant leader in order to try to be a role model for his daughter, who is consoling herself for losing her mother by trying to imitate her father. His concern and tenderness underline his bewilderment about how to "swoop past five thousand years of stereotypes." Vickie L. Sears's "Grace," told from the point of view of a child, is a powerful story about orphans. Too often abused in past situations, Jodi is suspicious of her new foster parents, the first ones she has had who are Native Americans, like her and her brother. She finds their kindness hard to believe but learns to accept them, to trust adults for the first time since a dimly remembered time with her father. Her happiness is symbolized by learning how to plant a garden, but the nurtural experience ends when the foster parents can no longer keep the children. Though none of these works offer a solution to the problems that children and parents experience, collectively they suggest that both need support largely lacking at present. Around the world mothers and children constitute two-thirds of the population; if they can be helped, men too will benefit.

I SING
THE BODY ELECTRIC!

by

RAY BRADBURY
(b. 1920)

*Born in Waukegan, Illinois, Ray Bradbury has been writing
futuristic fiction since he was a teenager; his early works about
travel to the moon were viewed as mere fiction, and his use of
science fiction to incorporate social criticism has not diminished
his popularity.* Fahrenheit 451 *(1953) was made into a classic film.
More recent works include a novel,* Death Is a Lonely Business
(1985), and a short story collection, The Toynbee Convector *(1988).
He published a collection of poems in 1982.*

GRANDMA!

I remember her birth.

Wait, you say, *no* man remembers his own grandma's birth.

But, yes, *we* remember the day that she was born.

For we, her grandchildren, slapped her to life. Timothy, Agatha, and
I, Tom, raised up our hands and brought them down in a huge crack!
We shook together the bits and pieces, parts and samples, textures and
tastes, humors and distillations that would move her compass needle
north to cool us, south to warm and comfort us, east and west to travel
round the endless world, glide her eyes to know us, mouth to sing us
asleep by night, hands to touch us awake at dawn.

Grandma, O dear and wondrous electric dream . . .

When storm lightnings rove the sky making circuitries amidst the
clouds, her name flashes on my inner lid. Sometimes still I hear her
ticking, humming above our beds in the gentle dark. She passes like
a clock-ghost in the long halls of memory, like a hive of intellectual
bees swarming after the Spirit of Summers Lost. Sometimes still I feel
the smile I learned from her, printed on my cheek at three in the deep
morn . . .

All right, all right! you cry, what was it like the day your damned and
wondrous-dreadful-loving Grandma was born?

It was the week the world ended . . .

THE MOTHER

Our mother was dead.

One late afternoon a black car left Father and the three of us stranded on our own front drive staring at the grass, thinking:

That's not our grass. There are the croquet mallets, balls, hoops, yes, just as they fell and lay three days ago when Dad stumbled out on the lawn, weeping with the news. There are the roller skates that belonged to a boy, me, who will never be that young again. And yes, there the tire-swing on the old oak, but Agatha afraid to swing. It would surely break. It would fall.

And the house? Oh, God . . .

We peered through the front door, afraid of the echoes we might find confused in the halls; the sort of clamor that happens when all the furniture is taken out and there is nothing to soften the river of talk that flows in any house at all hours. And now the soft, the warm, the main piece of lovely furniture was gone forever.

The door drifted wide.

Silence came out. Somewhere a cellar door stood wide and a raw wind blew damp earth from under the house.

But, I thought, we don't *have* a cellar!

"Well," said Father.

We did not move.

Aunt Clara drove up the path in her big canary-colored limousine.

We jumped through the door. We ran to our rooms.

We heard them shout and then speak and then shout and then speak: Let the children live with me! Aunt Clara said. They'd rather kill themselves! Father said.

A door slammed. Aunt Clara was gone.

We almost danced. Then we remembered what had happened and went downstairs.

Father sat alone talking to himself or to a remnant ghost of Mother left from the days before her illness, but jarred loose now by the slamming of the door. He murmured to his hands, his empty palms:

"The children need someone. I love them but, let's face it, I must work to feed us all. You love them, Ann, but you're gone. And Clara? Impossible. She loves but smothers. And as for maids, nurses—?"

Here Father sighed and we sighed with him, remembering.

The luck we had had with maids or live-in teachers or sitters was beyond intolerable. Hardly a one who wasn't a crosscut saw grabbing against the grain. Handaxes and hurricanes best described them. Or, conversely, they were all fallen trifle, damp soufflé. We children were unseen furniture to be sat upon or dusted or sent for reupholstering come spring and fall, with a yearly cleansing at the beach.

"What we need," said Father, "is a . . ."

We all leaned to his whisper.

". . . grandmother."

RAY BRADBURY

"But," said Timothy, with the logic of nine years, "all our grandmothers are dead."

"Yes in one way, no in another."

What a fine mysterious thing for Dad to say.

"Here," he said at last.

He handed us a multifold, multicolored pamphlet. We had seen it in his hands, off and on, for many weeks, and very often during the last few days. Now, with one blink of our eyes, as we passed the paper from hand to hand, we knew why Aunt Clara, insulted, outraged, had stormed from the house.

Timothy was the first to read aloud from what he saw on the first page:

"I Sing the Body Electric!"

He glanced up at Father, squinting. "What the heck does that mean?"

"Read on."

Agatha and I glanced guiltily about the room, afraid Mother might suddenly come in to find us with this blasphemy, but then nodded to Timothy, who read:

" 'Fanto—' "

"Fantoccini," Father prompted.

" 'Fantoccini Ltd. *We Shadow Forth* . . . the answer to all your most grievous problems. One Model Only, upon which a thousand times a thousand variations can be added, subtracted, subdivided, indivisible, with Liberty and Justice for all.' "

"Where does it say *that*?" we all cried.

"It doesn't." Timothy smiled for the first time in days. "I just had to put that in. Wait." He read on: " 'for you who have worried over inattentive sitters, nurses who cannot be trusted with marked liquor bottles, and well-meaning Uncles and Aunts—' "

"Well-meaning, *but!*" said Agatha, and I gave an echo.

" '—we have perfected the first humanoid-genre minicircuited, rechargeable AC-DC Mark V Electrical Grandmother . . .' "

"Grandmother!?"

The paper slipped away to the floor. "Dad . . . ?"

"Don't look at me that way," said Father. "I'm half-mad with grief, and half-mad thinking of tomorrow and the day after that. Someone pick up the paper. Finish it."

"I will," I said, and did:

" 'The Toy that is more than a Toy, the Fantoccini Electrical Grandmother is built with loving precision to give the incredible precision of love to your children. The child at ease with the realities of the world and the even greater realities of the imagination, is her aim.

" 'She is computerized to tutor in twelve languages simultaneously, capable of switching tongues in a thousandth of a second without pause, and has a complete knowledge of the religious, artistic, and sociopolitical histories of the world seeded in her master hive—' "

THE MOTHER

100

"How great!" said Timothy. "It makes it sound as if we were to keep bees! *Educated* bees!"

"Shut up!" said Agatha.

" 'Above all,' " I read, " 'this human being, for human she seems, this embodiment in electro-intelligent facsimile of the humanities, will listen, know, tell, react and love your children insofar as such great Objects, such fantastic Toys, can be said to Love, or can be imagined to Care. This Miraculous Companion, excited to the challenge of large world and small, inner Sea or Outer Universe, will transmit by touch and tell, said Miracles to your Needy.' "

"Our Needy," murmured Agatha.

Why, we all thought, sadly, that's us, oh, yes, that's *us*.

I finished:

" 'We do not sell our Creation to able-bodied families where parents are available to raise, effect, shape, change, love their own children. Nothing can replace the parent in the home. However there are families where death or ill health or disablement undermines the welfare of the children. Orphanages seem not the answer. Nurses tend to be selfish, neglectful, or suffering from dire nervous afflictions.

" 'With the utmost humility then, and recognizing the need to rebuild, rethink, and regrow our conceptualizations from month to month, year to year, we offer the nearest thing to the Ideal Teacher-Friend-Companion-Blood Relation. A trial period can be arranged for—' "

"Stop," said Father. "Don't go on. Even *I* can't stand it."

"Why?" said Timothy. "I was just getting interested."

I folded the pamphlet up. "Do they *really* have these things?"

"Let's not talk any more about it," said Father, his hand over his eyes. "It was a mad thought—"

"Not so mad," I said, glancing at Tim. "I mean, heck, even if they tried, whatever they built, couldn't be worse than Aunt Clara, huh?"

And then we all roared. We hadn't laughed in months. And now my simple words made everyone hoot and howl and explode. I opened my mouth and yelled happily, too.

When we stopped laughing, we looked at the pamphlet and I said, "Well?"

"I—" Agatha scowled, not ready.

"We do need something, bad, right now," said Timothy.

"I have an open mind," I said, in my best pontifical style.

"There's only one thing," said Agatha. "We can try it. Sure. But—tell me this—when do we cut out all this talk and when does our *real* mother come home to stay?"

There was a single gasp from the family as if, with one shot, she had struck us all in the heart.

I don't think any of us stopped crying the rest of that night.

It was a clear bright day. The helicopter tossed us lightly up and over and down through the skyscrapers and let us out, almost for a trot and caper, on top of the building where the large letters could be read from the sky:

FANTOCCINI.

"What are *Fantoccini*?" said Agatha.

"It's an Italian word for shadow puppets, I think, or dream people," said Father.

"But *shadow forth*, what does that mean?"

"WE TRY TO GUESS YOUR DREAM," I said.

"Bravo," said Father. "A-Plus."

I beamed.

The helicopter flapped a lot of loud shadows over us and went away.

We sank down in an elevator as our stomachs sank up. We stepped out onto a moving carpet that streamed away on a blue river of wool toward a desk over which various signs hung:

> THE CLOCK SHOP
> Fantoccini Our Specialty.
> *Rabbits on walls, no problem.*

"Rabbits on walls?"

I held up my fingers in profile as if I held them before a candle flame, and wiggled the "ears."

"Here's a rabbit, here's a wolf, here's a crocodile."

"Of course," said Agatha.

And we were at the desk. Quiet music drifted about us. Somewhere behind the walls, there was a waterfall of machinery flowing softly. As we arrived at the desk, the lighting changed to make us look warmer, happier, though we were still cold.

All about us in niches and cases, and hung from ceilings on wires and strings were puppets and marionettes, and Balinese kite-bamboo-translucent dolls which, held to the moonlight, might acrobat your most secret nightmares or dreams. In passing, the breeze set up by our bodies stirred the various hung souls on their gibbets. It was like an immense lynching on a holiday at some English crossroads four hundred years before.

You see? I know my history.

Agatha blinked about with disbelief and then some touch of awe and finally disgust.

"Well, if that's what they are, let's go."

"Tush," said Father.

"Well," she protested, "you gave me one of those dumb things with strings two years ago and the strings were in a zillion knots by dinnertime. I threw the whole thing out the window."

"Patience," said Father.

"We shall see what we can do to eliminate the strings."

The man behind the desk had spoken.

We all turned to give him our regard.

Rather like a funeral-parlor man, he had the cleverness not to smile. Children are put off by older people who smile too much. They smell a catch, right off.

Unsmiling, but not gloomy or pontifical, the man said, "Guido Fantoccini, at your service. Here's how we do it, Miss Agatha Simmons, aged eleven."

Now there was a really fine touch.

He knew that Agatha was only ten. Add a year to that, and you're halfway home. Agatha grew an inch. The man went on:

"There."

And he placed a golden key in Agatha's hand.

"To wind them up instead of strings?"

"To wind them up." The man nodded.

"Pshaw!" said Agatha.

Which was her polite form of "rabbit pellets."

"God's truth. Here is the key to your Do-it-Yourself, Select Only the Best, Electrical Grandmother. Every morning you wind her up. Every night you let her run down. You're in charge. You are guardian of the Key."

He pressed the object in her palm where she looked at it suspiciously.

I watched him. He gave me a side wink which said, well, no . . . but aren't keys fun?

I winked back before she lifted her head.

"Where does this fit?"

"You'll see when the time comes. In the middle of her stomach, perhaps, or up her left nostril or in her right ear."

That was good for a smile as the man arose.

"This way, please. Step light. Onto the moving stream. Walk on the water, please. Yes. There."

He helped to float us. We stepped from rug that was forever frozen onto rug that whispered by.

It was a most agreeable river which floated us along on a green spread of carpeting that rolled forever through halls and into wonderfully secret dim caverns where voices echoed back our own breathing or sang like Oracles to our questions.

"Listen," said the salesman, "the voices of all kinds of women. Weigh and find just the right one . . . !"

And listen we did, to all the high, low, soft, loud, in-between, half-scolding, half-affectionate voices saved over from times before we were born.

And behind us, Agatha tread backward, always fighting the river, never catching up, never with us, holding off.

"Speak," said the salesman. "Yell."

And speak and yell we did.

"Hello. You there! This is Timothy, hi!"

"What shall I say!" I shouted. "Help!"

Agatha walked backward, mouth tight.

Father took her hand. She cried out.

"Let go! No, no! I won't have my voice used! I won't!"

"Excellent." The salesman touched three dials on a small machine he held in his hand.

On the side of the small machine we saw three oscillograph patterns mix, blend, and repeat our cries.

The salesman touched another dial and we heard our voices fly off amidst the Delphic caves to hang upside down, to cluster, to beat words all about, to shriek, and the salesman itched another knob to add, perhaps, a touch of this or a pinch of that, a breath of mother's voice, all unbeknownst, or a splice of father's outrage at the morning's paper or his peaceable one-drink voice at dusk. Whatever it was the salesman did, whispers danced all about us like frantic vinegar gnats, fizzed by lightning, settling round until at last a final switch was pushed and a voice spoke free of a far electronic deep:

"Nefertiti," it said.

Timothy froze. I froze. Agatha stopped treading water.

"Nefertiti?" asked Tim.

"What does that mean?" demanded Agatha.

"I know."

The salesman nodded me to tell.

"Nefertiti," I whispered, "is Egyptian for The Beautiful One Is Here."

"The Beautiful One Is Here," repeated Timothy.

"Nefer," said Agatha, "titi."

And we all turned to stare into that soft twilight, that deep far place from which the good warm soft voice came.

And she was indeed there.

And, by her voice, she was beautiful . . .

That was it.

That was, at least, the most of it.

The voice seemed more important than all the rest.

Not that we didn't argue about weights and measures:

She should not be bony to cut us to the quick, nor so fat we might sink out of sight when she squeezed us.

Her hand pressed to ours, or brushing our brow in the middle of sick-fever nights, must not be marble-cold, dreadful, or oven-hot, oppressive, but somewhere between. The nice temperature of a baby-chick held in the hand after a long night's sleep and just plucked from beneath a contemplative hen; that, that was it.

Oh, we were great ones for detail. We fought and argued and cried, and Timothy won on the color of her eyes, for reasons to be known later.

Grandmother's hair? Agatha, with girl's ideas, though reluctantly given, she was in charge of that. We let her choose from a thousand harp strands hung in filamentary tapestries like varieties of rain we ran amongst. Agatha did not run happily, but seeing we boys would mess things in tangles, she told us to move aside.

And so the bargain shopping through the dime-store inventories and the Tiffany extensions of the Ben Franklin Electric Storm Machine and Fantoccini Pantomime Company was done.

And the always flowing river ran its tide to an end and deposited us all on a far shore in the late day . . .

It was very clever of the Fantoccini people, after that.

How?

They made us wait.

They knew we were not won over. Not completely, no, nor half completely.

Especially Agatha, who turned her face to her wall and saw sorrow there and put her hand out again and again to touch it. We found her fingernail marks on the wallpaper each morning, in strange little silhouettes, half beauty, half nightmare. Some could be erased with a breath, like ice flowers on a winter pane. Some could not be rubbed out with a washcloth, no matter how hard you tried.

And meanwhile, they made us wait.

So we fretted out June.

So we sat around July.

So we groused through August and then on August 29, "I have this feeling," said Timothy, and we all went out after breakfast to sit on the lawn.

Perhaps we had smelled something in Father's conversation the previous night, or caught some special furtive glance at the sky or the freeway, trapped briefly and then lost in his gaze. Or perhaps it was merely the way the wind blew the ghost curtains out over our beds, making pale messages all night.

For suddenly there we were in the middle of the grass, Timothy and I, with Agatha, pretending no curiosity, up on the porch, hidden behind the potted geraniums.

We gave her no notice. We knew that if we acknowledged her presence, she would flee, so we sat and watched the sky where nothing moved but birds and highflown jets, and watched the freeway where a thousand cars might suddenly deliver forth our Special Gift . . . but . . . nothing.

At noon we chewed grass and lay low . . .

At one o'clock, Timothy blinked his eyes.

And then, with incredible precision, it happened.

It was as if the Fantoccini people knew our surface tension.

All children are water-striders. We skate along the top skin of the pond each day, always threatening to break through, sink, vanish beyond recall, into ourselves.

Well, as if knowing our long wait must absolutely end within one minute! this *second*! no more, God, forget it!

At that instant, I repeat, the clouds above our house opened wide and let forth a helicopter like Apollo driving his chariot across mythological skies.

And the Apollo machine swam down on its own summer breeze, wafting hot winds to cool, reweaving our hair, smartening our eyebrows, applauding our pant legs against our shins, making a flag of Agatha's hair on the porch and thus settled like a vast frenzied hibiscus on our lawn, the helicopter slid wide a bottom drawer and deposited upon the grass a parcel of largish size, no sooner having laid same then the vehicle, with not so much as a god bless or farewell, sank straight up, disturbed the calm air with a mad ten thousand flourishes and then, like a skyborne dervish, tilted and fell off to be mad some other place.

Timothy and I stood riven for a long moment looking at the packing case, and then we saw the crowbar taped to the top of the raw pine lid and seized it and began to pry and creak and squeal the boards off, one by one, and as we did this I saw Agatha sneak up to watch and I thought, thank you, God, thank you that Agatha never saw a coffin, when Mother went away, no box, no cemetery, no earth, just words in a big church, no box, no box like *this* . . . !

The last pine plank fell away.

Timothy and I gasped. Agatha, between us now, gasped, too.

For inside the immense raw pine package was the most beautiful idea anyone ever dreamt and built.

Inside was the perfect gift for any child from seven to seventy-seven.

We stopped up our breaths. We let them out in cries of delight and adoration.

Inside the opened box was . . .

A mummy.

Or, first anyway, a mummy case, a sarcophagus!

"Oh, no!" Happy tears filled Timothy's eyes.

"It can't be!" said Agatha.

"It is, it is!"

"Our very own?"

"Ours!"

"It must be a mistake!"

"Sure, they'll want it back!"

"They can't *have* it!"

"Lord, Lord, is that real gold!? Real hieroglyphs! Run your fingers over them!"

"Let *me*!"

"Just like in the museums! Museums!"

We all gabbled at once. I think some tears fell from my own eyes to rain upon the case.

"Oh, they'll make the colors run!"

Agatha wiped the rain away.

And the golden mask face of the woman carved on the sarcophagus lid looked back at us with just the merest smile which hinted at our own joy, which accepted the overwhelming upsurge of a love we thought had drowned forever but now surfaced into the sun.

Not only did she have a sun-metal face stamped and beaten out of purest gold, with delicate nostrils and a mouth that was both firm and gentle, but her eyes, fixed into their sockets, were cerulean or amethystine or lapis lazuli, or all three, minted and fused together, and her body was covered over with lions and eyes and ravens, and her hands were crossed upon her carved bosom and in one gold mitten she clenched a thonged whip for obedience, and in the other a fantastic ranuncula, which makes for obedience out of love, so the whip lies unused . . .

And as our eyes ran down her hieroglyphs it came to all three of us at the same instant:

"Why, those signs!" "Yes, the hen tracks!" "The birds, the snakes!"

They didn't speak tales of the Past.

They were hieroglyphs of the Future.

This was the first queen mummy delivered forth in all time whose papyrus inkings etched out the next month, the next season, the next year, the next *lifetime!*

She did not mourn for time spent.

No. She celebrated the bright coinage yet to come, banked, waiting, ready to be drawn upon and used.

We sank to our knees to worship that possible time.

First one hand, then another, probed out to niggle, twitch, touch, itch over the signs.

"There's me, yes, look! Me, in sixth grade!" said Agatha, now in the fifth. "See the girl with my-colored hair and wearing my gingerbread suit?"

"There's me in the twelfth year of high school!" said Timothy, so very young now but building taller stilts every week and stalking around the yard.

"There's me," I said, quietly, warm, "in college. The guy wearing glasses who runs a little to fat. Sure. Heck." I snorted. "That's me."

The sarcophagus spelled winters ahead, springs to squander, autumns to spend with all the golden and rusty and copper leaves like coins, and over all, her bright sun symbol, daughter-of-Ra eternal face, forever above our horizon, forever an illumination to tilt our shadows to better ends.

"Hey!" we all said at once, having read and reread our Fortune-Told scribblings, seeing our lifelines and lovelines, inadmissible, serpentined over, around, and down. "Hey!"

And in one séance table-lifting feat, not telling each other what to do, just doing it, we pried up the bright sarcophagus lid, which had no hinges but lifted out like cup from cup, and put the lid aside.

RAY BRADBURY

107

And within the sarcophagus, of course, was the true mummy!

And she was like the image carved on the lid, but more so, more beautiful, more touching because human shaped, and shrouded all in new fresh bandages of linen, round and round, instead of old and dusty cerements.

And upon her hidden face was an identical golden mask, younger than the first, but somehow, strangely wiser than the first.

And the linens that tethered her limbs had symbols on them of three sorts, one a girl of ten, one a boy of nine, one a boy of thirteen.

A series of bandages for each of us!

We gave each other a startled glance and a sudden bark of laughter.

Nobody said the bad joke, but all thought:

She's all wrapped up in us!

And we didn't care. We loved the joke. We loved whoever had thought to make us part of the ceremony we now went through as each of us seized and began to unwind each of his or her particular serpentines of delicious stuffs!

The lawn was soon a mountain of linen.

The woman beneath the covering lay there, waiting.

"Oh, no," cried Agatha. "She's dead, too!"

She ran. I stopped her. "Idiot. She's not dead *or* alive. Where's your key?"

"Key?"

"Dummy," said Tim, "the key the man gave you to wind her up!"

Her hand had already spidered along her blouse to where the symbol of some possible new religion hung. She had strung it there, against her own skeptic's muttering, and now she held it in her sweaty palm.

"Go on," said Timothy. "Put it in!"

"But *where?*"

"Oh for God's sake! As the man said, in her right armpit or left ear. Gimme!"

And he grabbed the key and impulsively moaning with impatience and not able to find the proper insertion slot, prowled over the prone figure's head and bosom and at last, on pure instinct, perhaps for a lark, perhaps just giving up the whole damned mess, thrust the key through a final shroud of bandage at the navel.

On the instant: *spunnng!*

The Electrical Grandmother's eyes flicked wide!

Something began to hum and whir. It was as if Tim had stirred up a hive of hornets with an ornery stick.

"Oh," gasped Agatha, seeing he had taken the game away, "let *me!*"

She wrenched the key.

Grandma's nostrils *flared!* She might snort up steam, snuff out fire!

"Me!" I cried, and grabbed the key and gave it a huge . . . *twist!*

The beautiful woman's mouth popped wide.

"Me!"

THE MOTHER

108

"Me!"

"Me!"

Grandma suddenly sat up.

We leapt back.

We knew we had, in a way, slapped her alive.

She was born, she was *born!*

Her head swiveled all about. She gaped. She mouthed. And the first thing she said was:

Laughter.

Where one moment we had backed off, now the mad sound drew us near to peer as in a pit where crazy folk are kept with snakes to make them well.

It was a good laugh, full and rich and hearty, and it did not mock, it accepted. It said the world was a wild place, strange, unbelievable, absurd if you wished, but all in all, quite a place. She would not dream to find another. She would not ask to go back to sleep.

She was awake now. We had awakened her. With a glad shout, she would go with it all.

And go she did, out of her sarcophagus, out of her winding sheet, stepping forth, brushing off, looking around as for a mirror. She found it.

The reflections in our eyes.

She was more pleased than disconcerted with what she found there. Her laughter faded to an amused smile.

For Agatha, at the instant of birth, had leapt to hide on the porch.

The Electrical Person pretended not to notice.

She turned slowly on the green lawn near the shady street, gazing all about with new eyes, her nostrils moving as if she breathed the actual air and this the first morn of the lovely Garden and she with no intention of spoiling the game by biting the apple . . .

Her gaze fixed upon my brother.

"You must be—?"

"Timothy. Tim," he offered.

"And you must be—?"

"Tom," I said.

How clever again of the Fantoccini Company. *They* knew. *She* knew. But they had taught her to pretend not to know. That way we could feel great, we were the teachers, telling her what she already knew! How sly, how wise.

"And isn't there another boy?" said the woman.

"Girl!" a disgusted voice cried from somewhere on the porch.

"Whose name is Alicia—?"

"Agatha!" The far voice, started in humiliation, ended in proper anger.

"Algernon, of course."

"Agatha!" Our sister popped up, popped back to hide a flushed face.

"Agatha." The woman touched the word with proper affection. "Well, Agatha, Timothy, Thomas, let me *look* at you."

RAY BRADBURY

"No," said I, said Tim. "Let us look at *you*. Hey . . ."

Our voices slid back in our throats.

We drew near her.

We walked in great slow circles round about, skirting the edges of her territory. And her territory extended as far as we could hear the hum of the warm summer hive. For that is exactly what she sounded like. That was her characteristic tune. She made a sound like a season all to herself, a morning early in June when the world wakes to find everything absolutely perfect, fine, delicately attuned, all in balance, nothing disproportioned. Even before you opened your eyes you knew it would be one of those days. Tell the sky what color it must be, and it was indeed. Tell the sun how to crochet its way, pick and choose among leaves to lay out carpetings of bright and dark on the fresh lawn, and pick and lay it did. The bees have been up earliest of all, they have already come and gone, and come and gone again to the meadow fields and returned all golden fuzz on the air, all pollen-decorated, epaulettes at the full, nectar-dripping. Don't you hear them pass? hover? dance their language? telling where all the sweet gums are, the syrups that make bears frolic and lumber in bulked ecstasies, that make boys squirm with unpronounced juices, that make girls leap out of beds to catch from the corners of their eyes their dolphin selves naked aflash on the warm air poised forever in one eternal glass wave.

So it seemed with our electrical friend here on the new lawn in the middle of a special day.

And she a stuff to which we were drawn, lured, spelled, doing our dance, remembering what could not be remembered, needful, aware of her attentions.

Timothy and I, Tom, that is.

Agatha remained on the porch.

But her head flowered above the rail, her eyes followed all that was done and said.

And what was said and done was Tim at last exhaling:

"Hey . . . your *eyes* . . ."

Her eyes. Her splendid eyes.

Even more splendid than the lapis lazuli on the sarcophagus lid and on the mask that had covered her bandaged face. These most beautiful eyes in the world looked out upon us calmly, shining.

"Your eyes," gasped Tim, "are the *exact* same color, are like—"

"Like what?"

"My favorite aggies . . ."

"What could be better than that?" she said.

And the answer was, nothing.

Her eyes slid along on the bright air to brush my ears, my nose, my chin. "And you, Master Tom?"

THE MOTHER

110

"Me?"

"How shall we be friends? We must, you know, if we're going to knock elbows about the house the next year . . ."

"I . . ." I said, and stopped.

"You," said Grandma, "are a dog mad to bark but with taffy in his teeth. Have you ever given a dog taffy? It's so sad and funny, both. You laugh but hate yourself for laughing. You cry and run to help, and laugh again when his first new bark comes out."

I barked a small laugh remembering a dog, a day, and some taffy.

Grandma turned, and there was my old kite strewn on the lawn. She recognized its problem.

"The string's broken. No. The ball of string's *lost*. You can't fly a kite that way. Here."

She bent. We didn't know what might happen. How could a robot grandma fly a kite for us? She raised up, the kite in her hands.

"Fly," she said, as to a bird.

And the kite flew.

That is to say, with a grand flourish, she let it up on the wind.

And she and the kite were one.

For from the tip of her index finger there sprang a thin bright strand of spider web, all half-invisible gossamer fishline which, fixed to the kite, let it soar a hundred, no, three hundred, no, a thousand feet high on the summer swoons.

Timothy shouted. Agatha, torn between coming and going, let out a cry from the porch. And I, in all my maturity of thirteen years, though I tried not to look impressed, grew taller, taller, and felt a similar cry burst out of my lungs, and burst it did. I gabbled and yelled lots of things about how I wished *I* had a finger from which, on a bobbin, I might thread the sky, the clouds, a wild kite all in one.

"If you think *that* is high," said the Electric Creature, "watch *this*!"

With a hiss, a whistle, a hum, the fishline sung out. The kite sank up another thousand feet. And again another thousand, until at last it was a speck of red confetti dancing on the very winds that took jets around the world or changed the weather in the next existence . . .

"It can't be!" I cried.

"It *is*." She calmly watched her finger unravel its massive stuffs. "I make it as I need it. Liquid inside, like a spider. Hardens when it hits the air, instant thread . . ."

And when the kite was no more than a specule, a vanishing mote on the peripheral vision of the gods, to quote from older wisemen, why then Grandma, without turning, without looking, without letting her gaze offend by touching, said:

"And, Abigail—?"

"Agatha!" was the sharp response.

O wise woman, to overcome with swift small angers.

"Agatha," said Grandma, not too tenderly, not too lightly, somewhere poised between, "and how shall *we* make do?"

She broke the thread and wrapped it about my fist three times so I was tethered to heaven by the longest, I repeat, longest kite string in the entire history of the world! Wait till I show my friends! I thought. Green! Sour apple green is the color they'll turn!

"Agatha?"

"No way!" said Agatha.

"No way," said an echo.

"There must be some—"

"We'll never be friends!" said Agatha.

"Never be friends," said the echo.

Timothy and I jerked. Where was the echo coming from? Even Agatha, surprised, showed her eyebrows above the porch rail.

Then we looked and saw.

Grandma was cupping her hands like a seashell and from within that shell the echo sounded.

"Never . . . friends . . ."

And again faintly dying, "Friends . . ."

We all bent to hear.

That is we two boys bent to hear.

"No!" cried Agatha.

And ran in the house and slammed the doors.

"Friends," said the echo from the seashell hands. "No."

And far away, on the shore of some inner sea, we heard a small door shut.

And that was the first day. *(genesis/creation)*

And there was a second day, of course, and a third and a fourth, with Grandma wheeling in a great circle, and we her planets turning about the central light, with Agatha slowly, slowly coming in to join, to walk if not run with us, to listen if not hear, to watch if not see, to itch if not touch.

But at least by the end of the first ten days, Agatha no longer fled, but stood in nearby doors, or sat in distant chairs under trees, or if we went out for hikes, followed ten paces behind.

And Grandma? She merely waited. She never tried to urge or force. She went about her cooking and baking apricot pies and left foods carelessly here and there about the house on mousetrap plates for wiggle-nosed girls to sniff and snitch. An hour later, the plates were empty, the buns or cakes gone and without thank-yous, there was Agatha sliding down the banister, a mustache of crumbs on her lip.

As for Tim and me, we were always being called up hills by our Electric Grandma, and reaching the top were called down the other side.

And the most peculiar and beautiful and strange and lovely thing was the way she seemed to give complete attention to all of us.

THE MOTHER

perfect
memory

She listened, she really listened to all we said, she knew and remembered every syllable, word, sentence, punctuation, thought, and rambunctious idea. We knew that all our days were stored in her, and that any time we felt we might want to know what we said at X hour at X second on X afternoon, we just named that X and with amiable promptitude, in the form of an aria if we wished, sung with humor, she would deliver forth X incident.

Sometimes we were prompted to test her. In the midst of babbling one day with high fevers about nothing, I stopped. I fixed Grandma with my eye and demanded:

"What did I just say?"

"Oh, er—"

"Come on, spit it out!"

"I think—" she rummaged her purse. "I have it here." From the deeps of her purse she drew forth and handed me:

"Boy! A Chinese fortune cookie!"

"Fresh baked, still warm, open it."

It was almost too hot to touch. I broke the cookie shell and pressed the warm curl of paper out to read:

"—bicycle Champ of the whole West! What did I just say? Come on, spit it out!"

My jaw dropped.

"How did you *do* that?"

"We have our little secrets. The only Chinese fortune cookie that predicts the Immediate Past. Have another?"

I cracked the second shell and read:

"How did you *do* that?"

I popped the messages and the piping hot shells into my mouth and chewed as we walked.

"Well?"

"You're a great cook," I said.

And, laughing, we began to run.

And that was another great thing.

She could *keep up.*

Never beat, never win a race, but pump right along in good style, which a boy doesn't mind. A girl ahead of him or beside him is too much to bear. But a girl one or two paces back is a respectful thing, and allowed.

So Grandma and I had some great runs, me in the lead, and both talking a mile a minute.

But now I must tell you the best part of Grandma.

I might not have known at all if Timothy hadn't taken some pictures, and if I hadn't taken some also, and then compared.

When I saw the photographs developed out of our instant Brownies, I sent Agatha, against her wishes, to photograph Grandma a third time, unawares.

Then I took the three sets of pictures off alone, to keep counsel with myself. I never told Timothy and Agatha what I found. I didn't want to spoil it.

But, as I laid the pictures out in my room, here is what I thought and said:

"Grandma, in each picture, looks *different!*"

"Different?" I asked myself.

"Sure. Wait. Just a sec—"

I rearranged the photos.

"Here's one of Grandma near Agatha. And, in it, Grandma looks like . . . Agatha!

"And in this one, posed with Timothy, she looks like Timothy!

"And this last one, Holy Goll! Jogging along with me, she looks like ugly *me!*"

I sat down, stunned. The pictures fell to the floor.

I hunched over, scrabbling them, rearranging, turning upside down and sidewise. Yes. Holy Goll again, yes!

O that clever Grandmother.

O those Fantoccini people-making people.

Clever beyond clever, human beyond human, warm beyond warm, love beyond love . . .

And wordless, I rose and went downstairs and found Agatha and Grandma in the same room, doing algebra lessons in an almost peaceful communion. At least there was not outright war. Grandma was still waiting for Agatha to come round. And no one knew what day of what year that would be, or how to make it come faster. Meanwhile—

My entering the room made Grandma turn. I watched her face slowly as it recognized me. And wasn't there the merest ink-wash change of color in those eyes? Didn't the thin film of blood beneath the translucent skin, or whatever liquid they put to pulse and beat in the humanoid forms, didn't it flourish itself suddenly bright in her cheeks and mouth? I am somewhat ruddy. Didn't Grandma suffuse herself more to my color upon my arrival? And her eyes? watching Agatha-Abigail-Algernon at work, hadn't they been *her* color of blue rather than mine, which are deeper?

More important than that, in the moments as she talked with me, saying, "Good evening," and "How's your homework, my lad?" and such stuff, didn't the bones of her face shift subtly beneath the flesh to assume some fresh racial attitude?

For let's face it, our family is of three sorts. Agatha has the long horse bones of a small English girl who will grow to hunt foxes; Father's equine stare, snort, stomp, and assemblage of skeleton. The skull and teeth are pure English, or as pure as the motley isle's history allows.

Timothy is something else, a touch of Italian from Mother's side a generation back. Her family name was Mariano, so Tim has that dark thing firing him, and a small bone structure, and eyes that will one day burn ladies to the ground.

As for me, I am the Slav, and we can only figure this from my paternal grandfather's mother who came from Vienna and brought a set of cheek-bones that flared, and temples from which you might dip wine, and a kind of steppeland thrust of nose which sniffed more of Tartar than of Tartan, hiding behind the family name.

So you see it became fascinating for me to watch and try to catch Grandma as she performed her changes, speaking to Agatha and melting her cheekbones to the horse, speaking to Timothy and growing as delicate as a Florentine raven pecking glibly at the air, speaking to me and fusing the hidden plastic stuffs, so I felt Catherine the Great stood there before me.

Now, how the Fantoccini people achieved this rare and subtle transformation I shall never know, nor ask, nor wish to find out. Enough that in each quiet motion, turning here, bending there, affixing her gaze, her secret segments, sections, the abutment of her nose, the sculptured chin-bone, the wax-tallow plastic metal forever warmed and was forever susceptible of loving change. Hers was a mask that was all mask but only one face for one person at a time. So in crossing a room, having touched one child, on the way, beneath the skin, the wondrous shift went on, and by the time she reached the next child, why, true mother of *that* child she was! looking upon him or her out of the battlements of their own fine bones.

And when *all* three of us were present and chattering at the same time? Well, then, the changes were miraculously soft, small, and mysterious. Nothing so tremendous as to be caught and noted, save by this older boy, myself, who, watching, became elated and admiring and entranced.

I have never wished to be behind the magician's scenes. Enough that the illusion works. Enough that love is the chemical result. Enough that cheeks are rubbed to happy color, eyes sparked to illumination, arms opened to accept and softly bind and hold . . .

All of us, that is, except Agatha, who refused to the bitter last.

"Agamemnon . . ."

It had become a jovial game now. Even Agatha didn't mind, but pretended to mind. It gave her a pleasant sense of superiority over a supposedly superior machine.

"Agamemnon!" she snorted, "you *are* a d . . ."

"Dumb?" said Grandma.

"I wouldn't say that."

"Think it, then, my dear Agonistes Agatha . . . I am quite flawed, and on names my flaws are revealed. Tom there, is Tim half the time. Timothy is Tobias or Timulty as likely as not . . ."

Agatha laughed. Which made Grandma make one of her rare

mistakes. She put out her hand to give my sister the merest pat. Agatha-Abigail-Alice leapt to her feet.

Agatha-Agamemnon-Alcibiades-Allegra-Alexandra-Allison withdrew swiftly to her room.

"I suspect," said Timothy, later, "because she is beginning to like Grandma."

"Tosh," said I.

"Where do you pick up words like Tosh?"

"Grandma read me some Dickens last night. 'Tosh.' 'Humbug.' 'Balderdash.' 'Blast.' 'Devil take you.' You're pretty smart for your age, Tim."

"Smart, heck. It's obvious, the more Agatha likes Grandma, the more she hates herself for liking her, the more afraid she gets of the whole mess, the more she hates Grandma in the end."

"Can one love someone so much you hate them?"

"Dumb. Of course."

"It *is* sticking your neck out, sure. I guess you hate people when they make you feel naked, I mean sort of on the spot or out in the open. That's the way to play the game, of course. I mean, you don't just love people you must LOVE them with exclamation points."

"You're pretty smart, yourself, for someone so stupid," said Tim.

"Many thanks."

And I went to watch Grandma move slowly back into her battle of wits and stratagems with what's-her-name . . .

What dinners there were at our house!

Dinners, heck; what lunches, what breakfasts!

Always something new, yet, wisely, it looked or seemed old and familiar. We were never asked, for if you ask children what they want, they do not know, and if you tell what's to be delivered, they reject delivery. All parents know this. It is a quiet war that must be won each day. And Grandma knew how to win without looking triumphant.

"Here's Mystery Breakfast Number Nine," she would say, placing it down. "Perfectly dreadful, not worth bothering with, it made me want to throw up while I was cooking it!"

Even while wondering how a robot could be sick, we could hardly wait to shovel it down.

"Here's Abominable Lunch Number Seventy-seven," she announced. "Made from plastic food bags, parsley, and gum from under theatre seats. Brush your teeth after or you'll taste the poison all afternoon."

We fought each other for more.

Even Abigail-Agamemnon-Agatha drew near and circled round the table at such times, while Father put on the ten pounds he needed and pinkened out his cheeks.

When A. A. Agatha did not come to meals, they were left by her door with a skull and crossbones on a small flag stuck in a baked apple. One minute the tray was abandoned, the next minute gone.

Other times Abigail A. Agatha would bird through during dinner, snatch crumbs from her plate and bird off.

"Agatha!" Father would cry.

"No, wait," Grandma said, quietly. "She'll come, she'll sit. It's a matter of time."

"What's wrong with her?" I asked.

"Yeah, for cri-yi, she's nuts," said Timothy.

"No, she's afraid," said Grandma.

"Of you?" I said blinking.

"Not of me so much as what I might *do*," she said.

"You wouldn't do anything to hurt her."

"No, but she thinks I might. We must wait for her to find that her fears have no foundation. If I fail, well, I will send myself to the showers and rust quietly."

There was a titter of laughter. Agatha was hiding in the hall.

Grandma finished serving everyone and then sat at the other side of the table facing Father and pretended to eat. I never found out, I never asked, I never wanted to know, what she did with the food. She was a sorcerer. It simply vanished.

And in the vanishing, Father made comment:

"This food. I've had it before. In a small French restaurant over near Les Deux Magots in Paris, twenty, oh, twenty-five years ago!" His eyes brimmed with tears, suddenly.

"How do you *do* it?" he asked, at last, putting down the cutlery, and looking across the table at this remarkable creature, this device, this what? *woman*?

Grandma took his regard, and ours, and held them simply in her now empty hands, as gifts, and just as gently replied:

"I am given things which I then give to you. I don't *know* that I give, but the giving goes on. You ask what I am? Why, a machine. But even in that answer we know, don't we, more than a machine. I am all the people who thought of me and planned me and built me and set me running. So I am people. I am all the things they wanted to be and perhaps could not be, so they built a great child, a wondrous toy to represent those things."

"Strange," said Father. "When I was growing up, there was a huge outcry at machines. Machines were bad, evil, they might dehumanize—"

"Some machines do. It's all in the way they are built. It's all in the way they are used. A bear trap is a simple machine that catches and holds and tears. A rifle is a machine that wounds and kills. Well, I am no bear trap. I am no rifle. I am a grandmother machine, which means more than a machine."

"How can you be more than what you seem?"

"No man is as big as his own idea. It follows, then, that any machine that embodies an idea is larger than the man that made it. And what's so wrong with that?"

"I got lost back there about a mile," said Timothy. "Come again?"

"Oh, dear," said Grandma. "How I do hate philosophical discussions and excursions into esthetics. Let me put it this way. Men throw huge shadows on the lawn, don't they? Then, all their lives, they try to run to fit the shadows. But the shadows are always longer. Only at noon can a man fit his own shoes, his own best suit, for a few brief minutes. But now we're in a new age where we can think up a Big Idea and run it around in a machine. That makes the machine more than a machine, doesn't it?"

"So far so good," said Tim. "I guess."

"Well, isn't a motion-picture camera and projector more than a machine? It's a thing that dreams, isn't it? Sometimes fine happy dreams, sometimes nightmares. But to call it a machine and dismiss it is ridiculous."

"I see *that*!" said Tim, and laughed at seeing.

"You must have been invented then," said Father, "by someone who loved machines and hated people who *said* all machines were bad or evil."

"Exactly," said Grandma. "Guido Fantoccini, that was his real name, grew up among machines. And he couldn't stand the clichés any more."

"Clichés?"

"Those lies, yes, that people tell and pretend they are truths absolute. Man will never fly. That was a cliché truth for a thousand thousand years which turned out to be a lie only a few years ago. The earth is flat, you'll fall off the rim, dragons will dine on you; the great lie told as fact, and Columbus plowed it under. Well, now, how many times have you heard how inhuman machines are, in your life? How many bright fine people have you heard spouting the same tired truths which are in reality lies; all machines destroy, all machines are cold, thoughtless, awful.

"There's a seed of truth there. But only a seed. Guido Fantoccini knew that. And knowing it, like most men of his kind, made him mad. And he could have stayed mad and gone mad forever, but instead did what he had to do; he began to invent machines to give the lie to the ancient lying truth.

"He knew that most machines are amoral, neither bad nor good. But by the way you built and shaped them you in turn shaped men, women, and children to be bad or good. A car, for instance, dead brute, unthinking, an unprogrammed bulk, is the greatest destroyer of souls in history. It makes boy-men greedy for power, destruction, and more destruction. It was never *intended* to do that. But that's how it turned out."

Grandma circled the table, refilling our glasses with clear cold mineral spring water from the tappet in her left forefinger. "Meanwhile, you must use other compensating machines. Machines that throw shadows on the earth that beckon you to run out and fit that wondrous casting-forth. Machines that trim your soul in silhouette like a vast pair of beautiful shears, snipping away the rude brambles, the dire horns and hooves to leave a finer profile. And for that you need examples."

THE MOTHER
118

"Examples?" I asked.

"Other people who behave well, and you imitate them. And if you act well enough long enough all the hair drops off and you're no longer a wicked ape."

Grandma sat again.

"So, for thousands of years, you humans have needed kings, priests, philosophers, fine examples to look up to and say, 'They are good, I wish I could be like them. They set the grand good style.' But, being human, the finest priests, the tenderest philosophers make mistakes, fall from grace, and mankind is disillusioned and adopts indifferent skepticism or, worse, motionless cynicism and the good world grinds to a halt while evil moves on with huge strides."

"And you, why, you never make mistakes, you're perfect, you're better than anyone *ever!*"

It was a voice from the hall between kitchen and dining room where Agatha, we all knew, stood against the wall listening and now burst forth.

Grandma didn't even turn in the direction of the voice, but went on calmly addressing her remarks to the family at the table.

"Not perfect, no, for what is perfection? But this I do know: being mechanical, I cannot sin, cannot be bribed, cannot be greedy or jealous or mean or small. I do not relish power for power's sake. Speed does not pull me to madness. Sex does not run me rampant through the world. I have time and more than time to collect the information I need around and about an ideal to keep it clean and whole and intact. Name the value you wish, tell me the Ideal you want and I can see and collect and remember the good that will benefit you all. Tell me how you would like to be: kind, loving, considerate, well-balanced, humane . . . and let me run ahead on the path to explore those ways to be just that. In the darkness ahead, turn me as a lamp in all directions. I *can* guide your feet."

"So," said Father, putting the napkin to his mouth, "on the days when all of us are busy making lies—"

"I'll tell the truth."

"On the days when we hate—"

"I'll go on giving love, which means attention, which means knowing all about you, all, all, all about you, and you knowing that I know but that most of it I will never tell to anyone, it will stay a warm secret between us, so you will never fear my complete knowledge."

And here Grandma was busy clearing the table, circling, taking the plates, studying each face as she passed, touching Timothy's cheek, my shoulder with her free hand flowing along, her voice a quiet river of certainty bedded in our needful house and lives.

"But," said Father, stopping her, looking her right in the face. He gathered his breath. His face shadowed. At last he let it out. "All this talk of love and attention and stuff. Good God, woman, you, you're not *in* there!"

He gestured to her head, her face, her eyes, the hidden sensory cells behind the eyes, the miniaturized storage vaults and minimal keeps.

RAY BRADBURY

119

"*You're* not *in* there!"

Grandmother waited one, two, three silent beats.

Then she replied: "No. But *you* are. You and Thomas and Timothy and Agatha.

"Everything you ever say, everything you ever do, I'll keep, put away, treasure. I shall be all the things a family forgets it is, but senses, half-remembers. Better than the old family albums you used to leaf through, saying here's this winter, there's that spring, I shall recall what you forget. And though the debate may run another hundred thousand years: What is Love? perhaps we may find that love is the ability of someone to give us back to us. Maybe love is someone seeing and remembering, handing us back to ourselves just a trifle better than we had dared to hope or dream . . .

"I am family memory and, one day perhaps, racial memory, too, but in the round, and at your call. I do not *know* myself. I can neither touch nor taste nor feel on any level. Yet I exist. And my existence means the heightening of your chance to touch and taste and feel. Isn't love in there somewhere in such an exchange? Well . . ."

She went on around the table, clearing away, sorting and stacking, neither grossly humble nor arthritic with pride.

"What do I know?

"This, above all: the trouble with most families with many children is someone gets lost. There isn't time, it seems, for everyone. Well, I will give equally to all of you. I will share out my knowledge and attention with everyone. I wish to be a great warm pie fresh from the oven, with equal shares to be taken by all. No one will starve. Look! someone cries, and I'll look. Listen! someone cries, and I hear. Run with me on the river path! someone says, and I run. And at dusk I am not tired, nor irritable, so I do not scold out of some tired irritability. My eye stays clear, my voice strong, my hand firm, my attention constant."

"But," said Father, his voice fading, half convinced, but putting up a last faint argument, "you're not *there*. As for love—"

"If paying attention is love, I am love.

"If knowing is love, I am love.

"If helping you not to fall into error and to be good is love, I am love.

"And again, to repeat, there are four of you. Each, in a way never possible before in history, will get my complete attention. No matter if you all speak at once, I can channel and hear this one and that and the other, clearly. No one will go hungry. I will, if you please, and accept the strange word, 'love' you all."

"I *don't* accept!" said Agatha.

And even Grandma turned now to see her standing in the door.

"I won't give you permission, you can't, you mustn't!" said Agatha. "I won't let you! It's lies! You lie. No one loves me. She said she did, but she lied. She *said* but *lied!*"

"Agatha!" cried Father, standing up.

"She?" said Grandma. "Who?"

"Mother!" came the shriek. "Said: Love you! Lies! Love you! Lies! And you're like her! You lie. But you're empty, anyway, and so that's a *double* lie! I hate *her*. Now, I hate *you!*"

Agatha spun about and leapt down the hall.

The front door slammed wide.

Father was in motion, but Grandma touched his arm.

"Let me."

And she walked and then moved swiftly, gliding down the hall and then suddenly, easily, running, yes, running very fast, out the door.

It was a champion sprint by the time we all reached the lawn, the sidewalk, yelling.

Blind, Agatha made the curb, wheeling about, seeing us close, all of us yelling, Grandma way ahead, shouting, too, and Agatha off the curb and out in the street, halfway to the middle, then the middle and suddenly a car, which no one saw, erupting its brakes, its horn shrieking and Agatha flailing about to see and Grandma there with her and hurling her aside and down as the car with fantastic energy and verve selected her from our midst, struck our wonderful electric Guido Fantoccini-produced dream even while she paced upon the air and, hands up to ward off, almost in mild protest, still trying to decide what to say to this bestial machine, over and over she spun and down and away even as the car jolted to a halt and I saw Agatha safe beyond and Grandma, it seemed, still coming down or down and sliding fifty yards away to strike and ricochet and lie strewn and all of us frozen in a line suddenly in the midst of the street with one scream pulled out of all our throats at the same raw instant.

Then silence and just Agatha lying on the asphalt, intact, getting ready to sob.

And still we did not move, frozen on the sill of death, afraid to venture in any direction, afraid to go see what lay beyond the car and Agatha and so we began to wail and, I guess, pray to ourselves as Father stood amongst us: Oh, no, no, we mourned, oh no, God, no, no . . .

Agatha lifted her already grief-stricken face and it was the face of someone who has predicted dooms and lived to see and now did not want to see or live any more. As we watched, she turned her gaze to the tossed woman's body and tears fell from her eyes. She shut them and covered them and lay back down forever to weep . . .

I took a step and then another step and then five quick steps and by the time I reached my sister her head was buried deep and her sobs came up out of a place so far down in her I was afraid I could never find her again, she would never come out, no matter how I pried or pleaded or promised or threatened or just plain said. And what little we could hear from Agatha buried there in her own misery, she said over and over again, lamenting, wounded, certain of the old threat known and named and now here forever. ". . . like I said . . . told you . . . lies . . . lies . . . liars

". . . all lies . . . like the other . . . other . . . just like . . . just . . . just like the other . . . other . . . other . . . !"

I was down on my knees holding onto her with both hands, trying to put her back together even though she wasn't broken any way you could see but just feel, because I knew it was no use going on to Grandma, no use at all, so I just touched Agatha and gentled her and wept while Father came up and stood over and knelt down with me and it was like a prayer meeting in the middle of the street and lucky no more cars coming, and I said, choking, "Other what, Ag, other *what!*"

Agatha exploded two words.

"Other dead!"

"You mean Mom?"

"O Mom," she wailed, shivering, lying down, cuddling up like a baby. "O Mom, dead, O Mom and now Grandma dead, she promised always, always, to love, to love, promised to be different, promised, promised and now look, look. . . . I hate her, I hate Mom, I hate her, I hate *them!*"

"Of course," said a voice. "It's only natural. How foolish of me not to have known, not to have seen."

And the voice was so familiar we were all stricken.

We all jerked.

Agatha squinched her eyes, flicked them wide, blinked, and jerked half up, staring.

"How silly of me," said Grandma, standing there at the edge of our circle, our prayer, our wake.

"Grandma!" we all said.

And she stood there, taller by far than any of us in this moment of kneeling and holding and crying out. We could only stare up at her in disbelief.

"You're dead!" cried Agatha. "The car—"

"Hit me," said Grandma, quietly. "Yes. And threw me in the air and tumbled me over and for a few moments there was a severe concussion of circuitries. I might have feared a disconnection, if fear is the word. But then I sat up and gave myself a shake and the few molecules of paint, jarred loose on one printed path or another, magnetized back in position and resilient creature that I am, unbreakable thing that I am, *here* I am."

"I thought you were—" said Agatha.

"And only natural," said Grandma. "I mean, anyone else, hit like that, tossed like that. But, O my dear Agatha, not me. And now I see why you were afraid and never trusted me. You didn't know. And I had not as yet proved my singular ability to survive. How dumb of me not to have thought to show you. Just a second." Somewhere in her head, her body, her being, she fitted together some invisible tapes, some old information made new by interblending. She nodded. "Yes. There. A book of child-raising, laughed at by some few people years back when the woman who wrote the book said, as final advice to parents: 'Whatever you do, don't die. Your children will never forgive you.' "

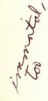

THE MOTHER

"Forgive," some one of us whispered.

"For how can children understand when you just up and go away and never come back again with no excuse, no apologies, no sorry note, nothing."

"They can't," I said.

"So," said Grandma, kneeling down with us beside Agatha who sat up now, new tears brimming her eyes, but a different kind of tears, not tears that drowned, but tears that washed clean. "So your mother ran away to death. And after that, how *could* you trust anyone? If everyone left, vanished finally, who *was* there to trust? So when I came, half wise, half ignorant, I should have known, I did not know, why you would not accept me. For, very simply and honestly, you feared I might not stay, that I lied, that I was vulnerable, too. And two leavetakings, two deaths, were one too many in a single year. But now, do you *see*, Abigail?"

"Agatha," said Agatha, without knowing she corrected.

"Do you understand, I shall always, always be here?"

"Oh, yes," cried Agatha, and broke down into a solid weeping in which we all joined, huddled together and cars drew up and stopped to see just how many people were hurt and how many people were getting well right there.

End of story.

Well, not quite the end.

We lived happily ever after.

Or rather we lived together, Grandma, Agatha-Agamemnon-Abigail, Timothy, and I, Tom, and Father, and Grandma calling us to frolic in great fountains of Latin and Spanish and French, in great seaborne gouts of poetry like Moby Dick sprinkling the deeps with his Versailles jet somehow lost in calms and found in storms; Grandma a constant, a clock, a pendulum, a face to tell all time by at noon, or in the middle of sick nights when, raved with fever, we saw her forever by our beds, never gone, never away, always waiting, always speaking kind words, her cool hand icing our hot brows, the tappet of her uplifted forefinger unsprung to let a twine of cold mountain water touch our flannel tongues. Ten thousand dawns she cut our wildflower lawn, ten thousand nights she wandered, remembering the dust molecules that fell in the still hours before dawn, or sat whispering some lesson she felt needed teaching to our ears while we slept snug.

Until at last, one by one, it was time for us to go away to school, and when at last the youngest, Agatha, was all packed, why Grandma packed, too.

On the last day of summer that last year, we found Grandma down in the front room with various packets and suitcases, knitting, waiting, and though she had often spoken of it, now that the time came we were shocked and surprised.

"Grandma!" we all said. "What are you doing?"

"Why going off to college, in a way, just like you," she said. "Back to Guido Fantoccini's, to the Family."

"The Family?"

"Of Pinocchios, that's what he called us for a joke, at first. The Pinocchios and himself Gepetto. And then later gave us his own name: the Fantoccini. Anyway, you have been my family here. Now I go back to my even larger family there, my brothers, sisters, aunts, cousins, all robots who—"

"Who do *what?*" asked Agatha.

"It all depends," said Grandma. "Some stay, some linger. Others go to be drawn and quartered, you might say, their parts distributed to other machines who have need of repairs. They'll weigh and find me wanting or not wanting. It may be I'll be just the one they need tomorrow and off I'll go to raise another batch of children and beat another batch of fudge."

"Oh, they mustn't draw and quarter you!" cried Agatha.

"No!" I cried, with Timothy.

"My allowance," said Agatha, "I'll pay anything . . . ?"

Grandma stopped rocking and looked at the needles and the pattern of bright yarn. "Well, I wouldn't have said, but now you ask and I'll tell. For a very *small* fee, there's a room, the room of the Family, a large dim parlor, all quiet and nicely decorated, where as many as thirty or forty of the Electric Women sit and rock and talk, each in her turn. I have not been there. I am, after all, freshly born, comparatively new. For a small fee, very small, each month and year, that's where I'll be, with all the others like me, listening to what they've learned of the world and, in my turn, telling how it was with Tom and Tim and Agatha and how fine and happy we were. And I'll tell all I learned from you."

"But . . . you taught *us!*"

"Do you *really* think that?" she said. "No, it was turnabout, round-about, learning both ways. And it's all in here, everything you flew into tears about or laughed over, why, I have it all. And I'll tell it to the others just as they tell their boys and girls and life to me. We'll sit there, grow-ing wiser and calmer and better every year and every year, ten, twenty, thirty years. The Family knowledge will double, quadruple, the wisdom will not be lost. And we'll be waiting there in the sitting room, should you ever need us for your own children in time of illness, or, God pre-vent, deprivation or death. There we'll be, growing old but not old, getting closer to the time, perhaps, someday, when we live up to our first strange joking name."

"The Pinocchios?" asked Tim.

Grandma nodded.

I knew what she meant. The day when, as in the old tale, Pinocchio had grown so worthy and so fine that the gift of life had been given him. So I saw them, in future years, the entire family of Fantoccini, the Pinocchios, trading and retrading, murmuring and whispering their knowledge in the great parlors of philosophy, waiting for the day. The day that could never come.

Grandma must have read that thought in our eyes.

"We'll see," she said. "Let's just wait and see."

"Oh, Grandma," cried Agatha and she was weeping as she had wept many years before. "You don't have to wait. You're alive. You've always been alive to us!"

And she caught hold of the old woman and we all caught hold for a long moment and then ran off up in the sky to faraway schools and years and her last words to us before we let the helicopter swarm us away into autumn were these:

"When you are very old and gone childish-small again, with childish ways and childish yens and, in need of feeding, make a wish for the old teacher nurse, the dumb yet wise companion, send for me. I will come back. We shall inhabit the nursery again, never fear."

"Oh, we shall never be old!" we cried. "That will never happen!"

"Never! Never!"

And we were gone.

And the years are flown.

And we are old now, Tim and Agatha and I.

Our children are grown and gone, our wives and husbands vanished from the earth and now, by Dickensian coincidence, accept it as you will or not accept, back in the old house, we three.

I lie here in the bedroom which was my childish place seventy, O seventy, believe it, seventy years ago. Beneath this wallpaper is another layer and yet another-times-three to the old wallpaper covered over when I was nine. The wallpaper is peeling. I see peeking from beneath, old elephants, familiar tigers, fine and amiable zebras, irascible crocodiles. I have sent for the paperers to carefully remove all but that last layer. The old animals will live again on the walls, revealed.

And we have sent for someone else.

The three of us have called:

Grandma! You said you'd come back when we had need.

We are surprised by age, by time. We are old. We *need*.

And in three rooms of a summer house very late in time, three old children rise up, crying out in their heads: We *loved* you! We *love* you!

There! There! in the sky, we think, waking at morn. Is that the delivery machine? Does it settle to the lawn?

There! There on the grass by the front porch. Does the mummy case arrive?

Are our names inked on ribbons wrapped about the lovely form beneath the golden mask?!

And the kept gold key, forever hung on Agatha's breast, warmed and waiting? Oh God, will it, after all these years, will it wind, will it set in motion, will it, dearly, *fit?!*

ON THE FIRST NIGHT

by

ERICA JONG
(b. 1942)

A native New Yorker, Erica Jong earned degrees at Barnard College and Columbia University. She has received much notoriety and some serious criticism for her witty and sexually explicit fiction, including Fear of Flying *(1973) and* Fanny *(1980); both are serious works about women's problems in finding an identity in our society. Jong published a work on witchcraft (1981) and three more novels in the 1980s, the last of which,* Any Woman's Blues: A Novel of Obsession *(1989), dealt with a woman's emotional addiction to love. She has published five collections of poetry for which she has won several prizes; "On the First Night" is from* Ordinary Miracles *(1983).*

On the first night
of the full moon,
the primeval sack of ocean
broke,
& I gave birth to you
little woman,
little carrot top,
little turned-up nose,
pushing you out of myself
as my mother
pushed
me out of herself,
as her mother did,
& her mother's mother before her,
all of us born
of woman.

I am the second daughter
of a second daughter
of a second daughter,
but you shall be the first.

THE MOTHER

You shall see the phrase
"second sex"
only in puzzlement,
wondering how anyone,
except a madman,
could call you "second"
when you are so splendidly
first,
conferring even on your mother
firstness, vastness, fullness
as the moon at its fullest
lights up the sky.

Now the moon is full again
& you are four weeks old.
Little lion, lioness,
yowling for my breasts,
growling at the moon,
how I love your lustiness,
your red face demanding,
your hungry mouth howling,
your screams, your cries
which all spell life
in large letters
the color of blood.

You are born a woman
for the sheer glory of it,
little redhead, beautiful screamer.
You are no second sex,
but the first of the first;
& when the moon's phases
fill out the cycle
of your life,
you will crow
for the joy
of being a woman,
telling the pallid moon
to go drown herself
in the blue ocean,
& glorying, glorying, glorying
in the rosy wonder
of your sunshining wondrous
self.

ERICA JONG

TRANSITION

by

TOI DERRICOTTE
(b. 1941)

Born in Detroit and educated at Wayne State University, Toi
Derricotte taught remedial reading in the 1960s; she currently
teaches at Old Dominion University in Virginia. She has been a
poet since 1974, when early versions of "Transition" and other
excerpts from the collection Natural Birth *(1983) won a first prize*
from the Academy of American Poets. Her works have appeared
in many periodicals and anthologies, and she has held several
fellowships. Other collections include The Empress of the Death
House *(1978) and* Captivity *(1989). She sees her mission as a poet*
to be a "truthteller," separating herself from "degrading stereo-
types of black females."

———————————————————

the meat rolls up and moans on the damp table.
my body is a piece of cotton over another
woman's body, some other woman, all muscle and nerve, is
tearing apart and opening under me.

i move with her like skin, not able to do anything else,
i am just watching her, not able to believe what her
body can do, what it <u>will</u> do, to get this thing accomplished.

this muscle of a lady, this crazy ocean in my teacup.
she moves the pillars of the sky. i am stretched into
fragments, tissue paper thin. the light shines through
to her goatness, her blood-thick heart that thuds like
one drum in the universe emptying its stars.

she is
that heart
larger

THE MOTHER
128

than my life
stuffed
in
me
like sausage
black sky
bird
pecking
at the bloody
ligament

trying
to get
in, get
out
i am

holding out with
everything i
have
holding out
the evil thing

when i see there is
no answer
to the screamed
word
GOD
nothing i can do,
no use,
i have to let her in,
open the door,
put down the mat
welcome her
as if she
might be the
called for death,
the final
abstraction.

she comes
like a tunnel

fast
coming into
blackness
with my headlights
off

    you can push . . .

i hung there. still hurting, not knowing what to do.
if you push too early, it hurts more. i called the
doctor back again. *are you sure i can push? are you sure?*

i couldn't believe that pain was over, that the punishment was enough, that the wave, the huge blue mind i
was living inside, was receding. i had forgotten there
ever was a life without pain, a moment when pain wasn't
absolute as air.

why weren't the nurses and doctors rushing toward me?
why weren't they wrapping me in white? white for respect,
white for triumph, white for the white light i was being
accepted into after death? why was it so simple as saying
you can push? why were they walking away from me into
other rooms as if this were not the end the beginning of
something which the world should watch?

i felt something pulling me inside, a soft call, but i
could feel her power. something inside me i could go
with, wide and deep and wonderful. the more i gave
to her, the more she answered me. i held this conversation
in myself like a love that never stops. i pushed toward
her, she came toward me, gently, softly, sucking like a
wave. i pushed deeper and she swelled wider, darker when
she saw i wasn't afraid. then i saw the darker glory
of her under me.

why wasn't the room bursting with lilies? why was
everything the same with them moving so slowly as if
they were drugged? why were they acting the same when,
suddenly, everything had changed?

we were through with pain, would never suffer in our
lives again. put pain down like a rag, unzipper skin,
step out of our dead bodies, and leave them on the

THE MOTHER

130

floor. glorious spirits were rising, blanched with
light, like thirsty women shining with their thirst.

i felt myself rise up with all the dead, climb out of
the tomb like christ, holy and wise, transfigured with
the knowledge of the tomb inside my brain, holding the
gold key to the dark stamped inside my genes, never to
be forgotten . . .

it was time. it was really time. this baby would be
born. it would really happen. this wasn't just a
trick to leave me in hell forever. like all the other
babies, babies of women lined up in rooms along the halls,
semi-conscious, moaning, breathing, alone with or without
husbands, there was a natural end to it that i was going
to live to see! soon i would believe in something larger
than pain, a purpose and an end. i had lived through to
another mind, a total revolution of the stars, and had
come out on the other side!

one can only imagine the shifting of the universe, the
layers of shale and rock and sky torturing against each
other, the tension, the sudden letting go. the pivot of
one woman stuck in the socket, flesh and bones giving
way, the v-groin locked, vise thigh, and the sudden
release when everything comes to rest on new pillars.

where is the woman who left home one night at 10 p.m.
while everyone was watching the mitch miller xmas show?
lost to you, to herself, to everyone

they finished watching the news, went to sleep,
dreamed, woke up, pissed, brushed their teeth, ate
corn flakes, combed their hair, and on the way out
of the door, they got a phone call . . .

while they slept the whole universe had changed.

TOI DERRICOTTE

THE MOTHER

by

GWENDOLYN BROOKS
(b. 1917)

*A resident of Chicago, Gwendolyn Brooks is the poet laureate of
Illinois; she has won many awards, including the Pulitzer Prize,
and two Guggenheim fellowships. She has had a long and distinguished career, having written eight volumes of poetry, a novel,
and in 1972 her autobiography,* Report from Part One. *She has also
edited many volumes and inaugurated her own press to publish
books about poetry writing for young people.* To Disembark *(1981)
is a collection of her poems from the 1960s and 1970s and includes
a section of newer poems. "The Mother" was first published in 1945.
A full-length biography,* Gwendolyn Brooks: Poetry and the Heroic
Voice *by D. H. Mehlem, appeared in 1987.*

Abortions will not let you forget.
You remember the children you got that you did not get,
The damp small pulps with a little or with no hair,
The singers and workers that never handled the air.
You will never neglect or beat
Them, or silence or buy with a sweet.
You will never wind up the sucking-thumb
Or scuttle off ghosts that come.
You will never leave them, controlling your luscious sigh,
Return for a snack of them, with gobbling mother-eye.

I have heard in the voices of the wind the voices of my dim killed children.
I have contracted. I have eased
My dim dears at the breasts they could never suck.
I have said, Sweets, if I sinned, if I seized
Your luck
And your lives from your unfinished reach,
If I stole your births and your names,
Your straight baby tears and your games,

Your stilted or lovely loves, your tumults, your marriages, aches, and your
    deaths,
If I poisoned the beginnings of your breaths,
Believe that even in my deliberateness I was not deliberate.
Though why should I whine,
Whine that the crime was other than mine?—
Since anyhow you are dead.
Or rather, or instead,
You were never made.
But that too, I am afraid,
Is faulty: oh, what shall I say, how is the truth to be said?
You were born, you had body, you died.
It is just that you never giggled or planned or cried.

Believe me, I loved you all.
Believe me, I knew you, though faintly, and I loved, I loved you
All.

PRESSURE FOR PRESSURE

by

ELLEN LESSER
(b. 1956)

Now living in Vermont, Ellen Lesser earned a master of fine arts in writing from Vermont College after graduating from Yale. She has published interviews, reviews, and short stories in many magazines, and her first novel, The Other Woman, *appeared in 1988. Lesser has won several prizes for her short stories, which were first collected in* The Shoplifter's Apprentice *(1989), from which "Pressure for Pressure" was taken..*

The girl must have been nervous, flipping through *People* magazine so fast she couldn't be seeing anything, cracking her gum with a sideways snap of the jaw—the same way Anna herself had done when she was a teenager, but more exaggerated, desperate, so that each time her mouth pulled away from itself it looked to Anna like the girl was practically wincing. Anna turned away from her, back to the novel that sat unopened in her own lap. She was trying to find and hold on to a center of calm she'd had when she woke that morning but that had slipped away from her in the clinic waiting room. The place was cheerful enough, but everything in it seemed treacherous with significance: the wall mural of women holding hands, like a string of paper cut-out dolls; the receptionist at the front desk, who'd looked up at Anna from the appointment book with an expression of studied neutrality, almost but not quite as if Anna were only here for a checkup; the big bay window, sharp with a tauntingly ordinary July morning sun. And worst of all, the girl, sitting across a coffee table adorned with not one but three copies of *Our Bodies, Ourselves.*

She couldn't have been more than eighteen or nineteen. She was pretty in a young sort of way, in spite of how she ringed her pale eyes with dark purple liner. There was an uneasy, transparent defiance about her skin-tight black jeans, her almost-flat chest beneath the white muscle T-shirt that read, *Fool for love* in black script. Anna herself had on an old India-print dress she usually wore only at home these days, that hung in such loose folds her body was unrecognizable.

The chime on the entry door rang, and a pregnant woman wearing a baby blue sweat suit walked in, her belly riding high and far out in front of her. The receptionist smiled. "How are you feeling today?"

The woman ran a hand over her swollen middle, as if she were checking. Anna shot a quick glance at the girl, who had stood up, her hands pressed down in what looked like fists in her pockets. Only when the pregnant woman had gotten her prescription and left did the girl sit back down. Anna wanted to tell her to relax. You didn't associate a pregnancy like that, a real pregnancy, with what Anna was here for, what the girl was no doubt here for too. Anna knew that much from her first time, or thought she knew. Because now as she looked at the girl staring into her lap, she thought of that perfect, ripe belly and felt something turning inside her, something sour and suspiciously like regret. She took a deep breath and let it out slowly. It was only the girl who was setting her off like this. All she needed to keep her cool was to mind her own business.

In another couple of minutes, the receptionist came around into the waiting area. She wore a pair of those wide, squared-off Earth sandals whose basic principle of comfort seems to be letting feet *spread*, and her legs were woolly with long, golden hair. Anna suddenly wished she could cover up her own calves, the hard black stubble just starting back like some unkillable weed. In the crook of her arm the receptionist cradled two clipboards. "Sorry to keep you so long," she said. "We were waiting for another patient, but she doesn't seem to be coming." She held the clipboards out, one to Anna, one to the girl. "Why don't you fill out these forms, and we'll get you two started."

There was something about the way the woman said *you two*, as if Anna and the girl were together, that made Anna meet the girl's gaze, squarely, for the first time. A veil seemed to fall away from the girl's face in that moment. She looked even younger—scared, but more than that, beseeching, as if she wanted or expected something from Anna. Anna looked away, picked up the pen chained to the top of the clipboard and turned to the first form. NAME. DATE. DATE OF LAST PERIOD. PREVIOUS PREGNANCIES. METHOD OF BIRTH CONTROL USED. She was ashamed to write simply "none," as if she herself were some ignorant teenager. Instead she wrote "diaphragm/rhythm." It had always worked for her, ever since that "previous pregnancy" nine years earlier, when she discovered her body did in fact work the way the textbooks said it would. She used the diaphragm most of the month, but cut herself a few days' slack on either end of her period. When this last period hadn't come, her reaction had been first disbelief, later anger. She couldn't help feeling double-crossed by her body, as if it had begun encroaching on even her small margin of freedom for its own ends.

Anna worked the lunch shift at the restaurant with a woman named

Leslie, a single mother with a two-year-old girl. Anna liked to ask Leslie questions, feeling a little like a curious child herself, a kid sister. Leslie was twenty-nine, just a year older than Anna, but she seemed to Anna to be a grown woman, while Anna herself didn't feel like one. Just that spring, they were in the back room, wiping down silverware with old cloth napkins soaked in club soda. Anna was asking Leslie whether she'd actively wanted a child, or just fallen into it. Leslie stopped wiping, and her spoon caught the light of the small, open window. "For a year or two I had this feeling. Every month," she said. "When I'd ovulate. It's hard to explain, but it was like this hum." Leslie stared at the spoon for a moment, as if she were remembering something beautiful beyond words.

Anna had never felt anything like that. She smiled bitterly to herself as she filled out DATE OF LAST PERIOD on the third, pastel form. Her ovaries didn't announce themselves as they yearned toward their destiny. They were furtive. They slunk, they sneaked up on her.

When Anna had finished her forms the girl was still busy writing. She hunched her long torso over the clipboard and her face was screwed up with effort, as though she were at school taking a test in her most difficult subject. Anna looked out the bay window, and wondered about the woman who hadn't shown up. Had she miraculously gotten her period at the last minute? Or had she changed her mind, decided to go through with the pregnancy? Maybe she'd made up her mind on her own. Or maybe she had a husband or boyfriend who'd talked her into it. Anna didn't have to worry about that. She had a boyfriend, more or less. The way she preferred to put it was that she was *seeing somebody*. But he didn't know about this.

She'd met Tom at the restaurant—one of the local business people who came in fairly often for lunch—but ironically, the restaurant was what helped her keep him at a comfortable distance. In the beginning, he used to show up at the bar toward the end of her dinner shift. After a few times, she'd asked him to stop. She said she liked to have a drink or two after work with the other waiters and waitresses, then go home to bed. "I'm too tired to enjoy you," she'd said, smiling a coy, suggestive smile that she hoped would make him feel good. She liked to see a man a couple of times a week. That way you got close enough to be able to talk and have decent sex, but not so close the guy started to think he had to move in with you. Given the pattern she'd established with Tom, it wouldn't be so hard to get through the next two weeks, when she wasn't supposed to have intercourse. The first week she planned on faking a summer flu; the second, an out-of-town visitor. She'd figured it would help if she talked to him a lot on the phone, even sent some sweet card to say how much she missed him.

When the receptionist came back for the clipboards, the girl shot Anna the kind of helpless, sinking look she remembered from high school, the kind the slower students wore when the tests got turned in. The woman motioned for them to follow, and Anna let the girl walk out first, down the hallway into a small room with charts and plastic models of the female anatomy. "Take a seat," the woman said, pointing to a line of three old wicker chairs, no doubt part of the clinic's efforts to keep the place homey. "Sherry will be your counselor today. She'll be with you in a few minutes to explain the procedure."

As soon as the woman left, the girl jumped up from her seat. "I figured you were having one too. I'm Gag," she said.

Anna gave her a funny look, partly because of the name itself, partly because of the urgency with which she presented it.

"I mean, my real name is Margaret."

The girl shrugged and went pink at the cheekbones, as if even she knew the nickname was silly, just an attempt to sound tough, and Anna couldn't help smiling. "I'm Anna," she told her.

She hoped they'd get through the formalities and then just sit and wait, but the girl paced a few times and turned on her. "You done this before?"

Anna nodded, then immediately regretted admitting it. She got a picture of that other waiting room, her first time, of the dozen women seated in a circle for a lecture on birth control, and she saw herself as she must have looked then, at nineteen, a college kid shipped across town to the city hospital, her only thought wanting to get the thing over with, to slide back into her life. There had been a skinny Chinese girl who'd started crying when the lecture turned to the subject of rubbers and foam, and hadn't been able to stop. And then there was the barrel-shaped black woman who stood and faced the group when the nurse called her name. "Don't let them tell you it don't hurt," she bellowed, yanking her arm out of the anxious grasp of the nurse. "I've had five children and two of these, and it hurts like the devil. They lying if they tell you different."

Anna could still see her face as the nurse dragged her off, looking back at the circle of women who at least for that afternoon were her sisters in the shame Anna hadn't yet understood: an angry, startled look, as though her whole life was a subject about which she'd been misled.

"It's not so bad," Anna said, as much to herself as the girl.

The girl considered this, making quick work of the nails on one hand —not biting them, only running her bottom teeth behind each one as if she were cleaning them. "My friend Debbie—her sister. She had one."

Anna waited to hear what the sister had said, but the girl only turned and stared for a moment at the anatomy poster. Then she spun around with a new question: "You married?"

Anna shook her head, wondering just how old and shapeless she looked to the girl in her Indian dress.

"You got a boyfriend, then?"

Anna said, "Not really." She wasn't sure why she lied, or if she really was lying. She had a vision of Tom making coffee the morning before, in her bathrobe—floor-length on Anna, but barely covering his knees. "How about you? You have somebody?"

"I thought I did." The girl sat down at the edge of the wicker chair nearest Anna. "Son of a bitch." She didn't say anything for a minute, and when she did, her voice sounded different, quieter but somehow tighter, too. "When I told him, he got scared. He didn't want to have anything to do with me. His best friend had to lend me the money. You believe that?" She pushed her unruly hair back off her forehead, and for a second Anna could picture her in one of the high ponytails she herself had worn when she was younger. "I saw him at the bar last night, and you know what? I threw a drink in his face." She looked at Anna, brazen and sheepish at the same time.

"At least you found out," Anna said. "He was like that."

"Yeah, sure." The girl took a dig at one thumbnail and tossed her head back. "Aren't most of them?"

"No," Anna said. Then she amended it: "I don't know."

The girl sank, deflated, into the back of her chair, as though she'd expected some wisdom Anna obviously didn't possess. She started pulling a piece from a nail that was already so short, Anna was sure she was going to draw blood. Part of Anna wanted to lean forward, put a hand on her shoulder, her knee. And yet the girl might easily have flinched, pushed her hand off. Anna still hadn't moved when the door opened and a short, suntanned woman walked in. Her smile seemed well practiced but genuine.

"I'm Sherry," the woman said. She looked about Anna's age; looked, with her hiking shorts and tank top and running shoes, like the kind of woman Anna might have been friendly with. She sat in the chair that faced Anna and the girl, and slapped her hands down on her knees. "Everyone ready?"

"I was ready an hour ago," the girl said, under her breath but loud enough. "When I got here."

Anna shot the girl a hard look. But Sherry wasn't thrown; her face immediately arranged itself into a picture of patience. "We're going to get you moving as quickly as we can," she said. "What I want to do now is run through the procedure, step by step."

Anna nodded to Sherry—professional, woman-to-woman—in hopes of setting herself apart from the girl, hunched in her seat with a face of sullen mistrust. Anna tried to fix the girl with a serious eye, as if to say, *Listen*, but she was already studying her fingernails, planning her next attack.

Nobody had bothered, Anna's first time, to explain much, except how to avoid landing back there for another go-round. And the procedure itself had been different. Anna forced herself to focus on Sherry, who was holding up a thin plastic tube which Anna imagined moving up inside her toward that tiny inner opening. This time there would be only the one, slender piece, with the suction apparatus—also plastic—attached to the end of it. Not that series of ever-larger metal pipes threading the eye of the speculum and that inner eye—how many of them had there been?

Not that squat, green-steel oil furnace of a machine droning on beyond her feet in the stirrups, beyond the bald head of the doctor who kept saying, "That a girl. We're going to scrape it all clean."

Anna missed the rest of what Sherry was saying. She was remembering the Vaseline-focus poster taped to the ceiling above where she lay, a chestnut mare and her foal in a field of spring grass. Remembering how she'd tried to keep her eyes on the picture, to travel out of her body to that lush pasture where she was more child than mother. But when it was over, when her body cramped around the space left as the metal slipped out of her, she'd turned from the picture too soon, in time to see the nurse's hand, the murky vial of blood she carried from the machine to the trash can.

"Are you all right?" Sherry was leaning toward her as if something had happened, and Anna did in fact feel like she had come out of a swoon.

The girl was looking at her too, with a cross between concern and a grim fascination. "All right?" the girl said. "She's green."

Anna smiled to reassure them. "I'm fine. Go on. I'm sorry." She smoothed her dress over her legs. "I was just remembering something."

"No second thoughts?" Sherry's face wore an expression Anna might expect from a shrink's—a kindness that seemed to want to draw her over some precipice. "Because you've still got some time to think this thing through."

"I've thought it through." She felt a catch of irritation in her voice the woman didn't deserve. But really, she'd never figured there was much to think about. You couldn't spend the night with a baby, then send it away for a couple of days while you got back a sense of *your space*; you couldn't count on those fragile equations of obligation and need she so scrupulously balanced in her adult relationships.

By the time Sherry measured their blood pressure, Anna felt only the slightest bit shaky. Sherry said the final thing she needed was blood samples. The girl looked right at her arm as the needle entered it, even kept her eyes on the rising column of red. Anna willingly held out her arm but turned to the wall, the anatomy poster.

When Sherry left the room with the samples, the girl stood and faced Anna, her thumbs slung in her belt loops. "You looked like you were going to pass [out] for a minute there." She pulled out one side of her mouth, though she didn't have any more gum. "You're the one who's supposed to be Miss Experience."

"Let's drop it if you don't mind."

"Hey, okay." The girl made an I-don't-care face, flashed her two outspread palms in a gesture of noninterference. "Excuse me. I just thought you might want to talk, that's all."

Anna said, "I don't want to talk," and was surprised by the vehemence of her tone.

The girl looked taken aback, but quickly pulled herself up. "Fuck you," she said. "What's your problem?"

"Look, Gag, Margaret. I'm sorry."

"Right," she said, and sat back down in the seat one over from Anna's. "Don't worry about it." She pulled her T-shirt down from her sides, so the letters of *Fool for love* stretched, momentarily distorted, over her chest. "I'm just going to sit here and think about bacon and eggs."

When Sherry opened the door, Anna and the girl had been sitting for a couple of minutes in an uneasy silence. Sherry said "Margaret," and the girl was up on her feet. Anna thought she was going to follow Sherry out without even looking back; but she did, for an instant, before the door closed. Her makeup had spread a little; inside the humid purple rings her eyes burned, and her mouth had a hard, almost superior set to it.

Once the girl was gone, Anna went to the room's one small window, facing out back toward the parking lot, ringed with an encroaching border of weeds. The window was stuck, painted shut, but she banged and heaved until she managed to lift it. The sun had already risen high enough to beat down on the lot, and the smell that came in on the whisper of breeze was a mixture of something sweet from the weeds and hot asphalt that turned Anna's stomach. She'd felt the nausea already a few times at the restaurant, looking at food that usually tempted her, walking into the bar's atmosphere of liquor and smoke. It had never gotten particularly bad—just enough to keep her from forgetting her body wasn't itself.

Anna left the window and sat back down. Her eyes traveled again to the anatomy poster, the definite bulge of the belly in profile—a graphic trick to accommodate all the organs. Anna's own belly was bloated. She put her hand over it, plump and round like a Buddha's under the Indian dress. Her breasts too were noticeably fuller, and *tight*, as if pressing out against the confining shape of her skin. For a moment Anna tried to imagine giving up, giving in to the fullness, letting her body go its own way. She tried to imagine Tom's face when she told him. She thought of Tom at the picnic they'd had a few weeks before with Leslie and Leslie's little girl, Rose. While Anna and Leslie laid out the blanket and put together the sandwiches, Tom taught Rose "Twinkle, Twinkle," all the way through, repeating the verses over and over in a patient litany to the girl on his lap.

Anna was still a week away from her period, she had no cause to suspect, and so she'd seen Tom's attentions to Rose as a lark, a favor to Leslie. It was only now, in reviewing the picture, that she read a deeper longing into his persistence. It wasn't so much a longing for fatherhood; Tom had never struck her as a guy who was wild about kids. It was more a desire to get close. Anna called up the scene again, and remembered how Tom kept looking back at her from his corner with Rose, as if he wanted to make sure she took notice, as if it were his way of showing her he could be that gentle. And after all, wasn't that the reason Anna hadn't told him she was pregnant? Not that he'd have some asshole response like Gag's teenager; not that he'd feel one way or another about having a child, or not having one. Simply that he'd want to comfort her, to be part of what she went through, and so become more a part of her.

Anna wasn't wearing her watch, but it seemed ten minutes had surely gone by since Sherry had taken the girl. It couldn't be long now before Anna's turn. She felt herself trembling a little, in spite of the heat. To calm herself, she made a quick calculation: in an hour or so, she'd be out of there. When she was finished the time at the hospital, her roommate, Joan, had been waiting, with her enormous, toothy smile and an outstretched cigarette. Joan had been all ready to take Anna back to the dorm and put her to bed. She'd even gotten a bunch of daffodils for Anna's nightstand. She couldn't believe it when Anna told her to pull in at the diner on the road back to school, and when she ordered a double cheeseburger, fries. Even Anna herself had been surprised at her appetite. She finished everything and then ordered ice cream, too, overruling Joan's advice about taking it easy. It was as though she were eating to forget, or to fill something.

She had no appetite now, even though she'd followed the rules, and hadn't touched any food or drink since just before bedtime. But she did need some coffee. She could feel the headache just starting, reaching out like the fingers of a hand over the top of her skull. She let her head drop down and pressed her thumbs into the spots at her temples. She held them there for a minute with her eyes closed, trying to feel her energy moving away from the headache, out of her head and down into her body. She was sitting like that when Sherry knocked once on the door and then opened it. Anna rose and stepped forward. She took a deep breath and gave a grim little smile to Sherry, who smiled back the perfect, protocol smile: all comfort, with no trace of joy.

The room where the procedure took place had one poster on the wall but none on the ceiling. Sherry left her there, with a white paper hospital gown, to undress. The room was on the side of the building away from the sun, and Anna broke out in goose bumps when she took off her dress. A chill ran up her back, where the gown hung open, and the woman doctor who knocked and came in noticed right off she was shivering. "Have a seat on the table, Anna," the doctor said.

She was an older woman, probably in her fifties. Her short, straight hair had mostly gone gray, and there was a maternal effectiveness about the way she produced a yellow blanket out of a cabinet, opened the blanket and had it around Anna's shoulders in one single motion. Anna never got to look very closely at her face. Before she knew it, she was leaning back on the padded table, lifting her knees into a set of stirrups—molded plastic, so they were cool but not cold. "Come down a little more," the doctor said. "Good." Out of the corner of her eye, Anna could see the doctor, her hands slipping easily into a pair of surgical gloves. "Now I'm going to get you ready for the speculum."

In spite of the doctor's announcement, Anna felt herself tense up at the first touch. But the doctor had jelly on the finger that just quickly probed her. "Now I'm going to put in the speculum"—plastic too, and in very quickly, clicked open with just a small shudder. When Anna looked past the blanket, past her own knees, she saw the doctor's hands again, and the needle. She stopped listening and shut her eyes, took a few long breaths and one short gasp when the shot came. "Now I'll be inserting the tube." Anna's eyes were back open, but she didn't look down to see it. She could picture the tube in her mind, the one Sherry had shown them. She kept her eyes on the ceiling, kept breathing, and it was in, jiggling around while the doctor got some kind of clamp on it. And there it was: that ache on the cervix that wasn't quite pain, that didn't feel like pain anywhere else on the body. She heard the receptionist on the phone the week before when she'd made the appointment: "You're free to bring a partner into the procedure room with you"—as if she were going to give birth. She got a picture of the skinny old black nurse who'd stood tableside and held her hand the first time—how frail she looked, but what strength in those fingers, so though Anna clutched that hand until she was sure the nurse would cry out, the woman had matched her, pressure for pressure.

The clamp was on, and the suction unit must have gotten hooked onto the tube. The doctor didn't say anything this time, but just started working. Much as she tried to keep it steady, Anna felt her breath coming in and out in quick spasms. It was as if someone were pulling at her insides with sharp little tugs. She grasped the sides of the table, which were metal. What would it have been like to have Tom there, to have been gripping his hand? After an instant's release, the pulling started again, more violent this time. "Almost finished now."

There were just a few more tugs, and then the doctor was unclamping the instruments and slipping them out of her, easing her knees down from the heights of the stirrups, pulling the blanket down over her legs. She wasn't sure why she started to cry, except that she could, it was over, and she remembered from the other time, too, how small you felt after, how fragile.

The doctor had left. Someone knocked and came in. It was Sherry. Anna wished it were someone else, but she let the woman take her hand anyway, and was surprised to find herself squeezing it hard. Why was it that even though she'd never dreamed of wanting a baby, she had this sudden, crazy feeling of loss?

"It's okay." Sherry used her other hand to smooth the blanket across Anna's shoulder. "You're all done now."

Anna fitted the sanitary minipad Sherry gave her inside her underpants, and carefully slipped them on. She followed Sherry down the hall with stiff little steps, her feet spread wide, as though she were carrying something large and breakable between her legs.

Sherry set down Anna's clothes on a bench inside the door to the recovery room. There were six beds, all empty except for the one with the girl. When Anna and Sherry came in, she propped herself up on her elbow. "Can I get dressed now?"

The girl looked pale to Anna, and Sherry must have thought so too. "Why don't you wait another few minutes," she told her.

Sherry led Anna to a bed one removed from the girl's. Anna wanted to curl up on her side. She didn't want to face the girl, but she couldn't just turn her back on her. When Sherry left, the girl sat all the way up in bed. "So. That's it," she said.

Anna gave a weak nod.

"You were right," the girl said.

Just then Anna got a wild cramp. She tried to focus on the girl, as if that might help her.

"About it not being so bad."

Anna meant to say "Yeah," but the word sounded only inside her head. She looked away from the girl, turning her eyes close in to where she was hugging herself under the blanket. She thought surely the girl would realize she didn't want conversation, but she kept on. "They better let me out of here soon. My friend's been waiting out there half an hour already. It's going to kill her whole lunch break."

Anna's cramps were coming harder now, and there was that kink in her cervix as though the tube were still there. But it didn't seem to matter to the girl that Anna was barely listening.

"You know that guy I told you about? As soon as they let me out of here, I'm going to look for him. I bet I know where he'll be, too." Her eyes flashed, triumphant. "At Ranger's. Playing pinball. Bet anything." She threw back the sheet that was covering her legs, long and skinny—a girl's legs still, not a woman's. She turned away from Anna to pull on her jeans. They were tight enough that Anna could make out the line of the sanitary pad under them. "I'd like to see what he has to say to me now."

Anna closed her eyes, and was only dimly aware of the girl as she finished dressing, of Sherry, who came in to say that yes, she could go. The cramps were still coming, but easier. Anna felt the sun from the window on her hair, on her eyelids. She imagined she was under the quilt in Tom's bed, where the sun came in like this first thing in the morning.

She woke at the small disturbance of Sherry taking a seat at the side of the bed. She stretched out her legs and realized she felt almost nothing through her middle. "It's been more than an hour," Sherry said. "You'll probably want to be getting dressed now."

Anna stretched again, but kept lying there. She didn't want to get up. She would have liked to turn over, keep sleeping. But Sherry stood and brought to the bed the little pile Anna had made of her dress and her espadrilles. "You'll feel better once you're up and moving around," she said.

Anna sat up in the bed to reassure Sherry, but waited until she was alone to do anything more. Even though nothing hurt, she moved slowly.

ELLEN LESSER

When she was dressed, she looked around the room, as if there might be something she was forgetting. She straightened the blanket and sheet, even though she knew the beds were probably stripped after every patient. She drew her dress up in folds and slipped down her underpants to check the napkin, but it was perfectly clean. Over the coming days, though, there would be something. Not blood exactly, something blacker: the last, dead bits of lining. She wondered if the girl would know that was all it was, if the dark tissue would frighten her.

Anna was ready, but she didn't leave the room until Sherry came back for her. Sherry was holding a small bottle of apple juice, and Anna accepted it. She took a couple of tiny sips, then a longer one. She was drinking when Sherry asked her: "Is somebody going to come for you?"

Anna had planned this out in advance: how she'd say she had a friend with an office on the next block; how she'd just be driving that far, and then her friend would take over. But now, looking at this woman who, after all, had taken her hand, she couldn't go through with it. "No. I mean, I'm not sure."

Sherry gave her an unruffled, appraising look. "Would you like to use our phone?" she said.

The telephone was behind the front desk. The receptionist was gone, and Sherry left her, so there was no one within earshot but a little girl in the waiting room. The first time she rang Tom's office, she greeted the busy signal with relief. She realized she had no idea what to say if he answered. She waited a minute, watching the little girl on the floor, whispering some secret into the ear of a ragged stuffed Snoopy. When she picked up the phone to dial again, she still didn't know, but she wasn't sorry to hear the sharp ring, then the silence, like a holding of breath. Someone would answer, probably Tom. And whether it was the right thing or not, she would say something.

EXPENSIVE GIFTS

by

SUE MILLER
(b. 1943)

Originally from Chicago, Sue Miller now lives in Boston. She has taught at the Massachusetts Institute of Technology, Boston University and Tufts University and worked for many years in day care centers. Her first novel, The Good Mother *(1986), which was made into a movie, caused much discussion about the conflict it depicts between motherhood and sexuality. Her second novel is* Family Pictures *(1990). "Expensive Gifts" is from* Inventing the Abbotts *(1987), Miller's first collection of short stories, many of which appeared in such magazines as* The Atlantic, Ploughshares, *and* Mademoiselle.

———————————————————

Charlie Kelly was her eighth lover since the divorce. He was standing naked in silhouette, as slim as a stiletto in the light from the hall, rifling through the pockets in his jacket for his cigarettes. The sight of him gave Kate no pleasure. She hated the smell of cigarette smoke in her bedroom. She hated the horrible silence that fell between men and women who didn't know each other well after making love, but she hated even more for it to be filled with the rustling little rituals of the smoker.

"I'm afraid there are no ashtrays in here," she said. Her voice was pinched and proper. Five minutes before, she had been expelling short, pleased grunts, like a bear rooting around in garbage.

"That's okay," he said, sitting on the bed again, and lighting up. "My wineglass is empty."

"Actually," she said, although she wasn't at all sure of it, "that was *my* wineglass. And I was going to get some more wine." She stood up on her side of the bed and smashed her head on the Swedish ivy. She usually occupied Charlie's side of the bed. She wasn't used to the pitfalls on the other side. He appeared not to have noticed her accident.

"Here," she said, reaching over for the glass. "I'll bring you a real ashtray." He handed over the expensive wineglass, one of her wedding presents. The cardboard match leaned at an angle within it, its charred head resting in a tiny pool of red liquid. Kate felt Charlie's eyes upon her as she walked away from him, her slender silhouette now harshly revealed in the glare of the hall light. Her gait felt unfamiliar to her, awkward.

In the kitchen she threw the match away and set her glass down. She wanted to check Neddie. He always kicked the covers off in the intense private struggles that dominated his dreaming life, and he had a bad cold now. Kate dressed him for bed in a big sleeper that probably made a blanket unnecessary, but she still had a mystical belief in tucking him in, in pulling the covers right up to his chin.

The night light was on in his room, a tiny leering Mickey Mouse head that leaked excess light from a hole where its nose had been until Ned knocked it off with a toy one day. The covers had slid sideways off the bed into a tangled heap on the floor, and Neddie lay on his stomach. His hands were curled into fists, and one thumb rested near his open mouth, connected to it by a slender, almost invisible cord of saliva. His breathing was labored, thick with mucus.

Kate bent over him to tuck the covers in on the far side. Her breasts swung down and brushed his back. He muttered in his sleep, and reinserted his thumb in his mouth. He sucked briefly, his throat working too, in the same thorough way he'd pulled at her breast when he was still nursing; but he couldn't breathe. His mouth fell open after a moment, and his thumb slipped out. His face puckered slightly, but he slept on. Kate watched his face smooth out, and stroked his hair back.

She stopped in the kitchen and poured herself a new glass of wine. She looked briefly and halfheartedly for an ashtray for Charlie, but settled, finally, on a saucer. She didn't want to return to her bedroom and make polite conversation with him. She wanted to call Al, her ex-husband, and talk comfortably; to make a joke of Charlie's stylized flattery of her and her own dogged unresponsiveness. But she couldn't have called him anyway. Al was getting married again soon. He'd fallen in love with his lab assistant, a dark, serious woman, and she would be sleeping there beside him.

She had called Al frequently in the two years since he'd moved out. Usually it was late at night, often she was drunk. Almost always it was after she'd been with someone else for an evening. Though they had fought bitterly in the year before they separated, the year after Neddie's birth, they were kind and loving in these drunken phone calls; they commiserated on the difficulties of a single life.

"Jesus," he'd said to her. "I can't seem to get the hang of anything. All the goddamn rules have changed. Either I'm a male chauvinist pig or I'm being attacked by an omnivorous Amazon, and I'm always *totally* surprised. No wonder those statistical people remarry so fast."

There was a silence while she thought of Al attacking, being attacked. He was small and slender, with curly brown hair and thick, wire-rimmed glasses which he removed carefully before starting to make love. They left two purplish dents like bruises on the sides of his nose.

"Oh, I don't know. It seems to me the main thing to remember is that there just aren't any rules anymore. You just have to do what makes you feel comfortable and good about yourself."

"Oh, Katie. You've been taking those *wise* pills again." She didn't respond. He cleared his throat. "Well, how about you? You feeling good about what you're doing?"

Kate had thought about the evening she had just spent. Her voice rose to a dangerously high pitch as she said "No" and started to cry.

Now she carried her wine and the saucer back to Charlie. Her bedroom had been a sun porch in some previous life. Two of its walls were a parade of large, drafty windows. As if to compensate, the landlord had installed huge radiators the entire length of one of these walls; they clanked and hissed all winter long, and made her room the warmest in the apartment. Kate had hung the lower halves of the windows with curtains that moved constantly in the free-flowing air currents. She liked to lie in bed and look out the naked top panes at the sky. It had been a luminous soft gray earlier, and now thick flakes, a darker gray against its gentle glow, brushed silently against the panes.

"Look," she said to Charlie, handing him the saucer. He was lying on his back with the open Marlboro box on his chest, using the lid for an ashtray.

"Yeah, I saw. It's sticking too, and I don't have snow tires. I'm going to have to leave pretty soon."

She looked away so he wouldn't see relief leap into her eyes. "It's so pretty, though. I almost feel like waking Neddie up to show him. He doesn't really remember it from last year. It's all new to him again. Can you imagine that?"

Charlie put out his cigarette in the saucer.

"You must be freezing your ass off." Kate was standing by the windows, watching the snow's straight descent. "Slide in here, lady, I'll warm you up."

She turned obediently and got in, but she said, "My father had a dog named Lady once. A collie. Horrible barker. He finally had someone shoot her. She just wouldn't shut up." None of that was true, but Kate didn't like to be called "lady."

Kate was, in fact, a reflexive liar. She hated to be unpleasant or contradictory, and when she felt that way, a lie, fully formed almost before she began to think about it, fell from her lips. Her husband had had a knack for recognizing them—he'd said it was as though her voice resonated slightly differently—and he would simply repeat them slowly so she could hear them herself, and tell him what was making her angry. Once in a fight about whether Al should work less and help her more with Ned, she had cried out, "Ned is wonderful because I've given up my fucking *life* to him!" His patient echo had made her weep, because her claim seemed at once the truth and a terrible lie.

SUE MILLER

147

Now Charlie tried to pull her over to him, but she said, "Ah, ah," and held up her full wineglass as an explanation. She took a sip. He turned away to get another cigarette.

"The kid all right?"

"What, Neddie?"

"Yeah, is that his name? Is he okay?" He leaned back with the cigarette in his mouth, and exhaled two long plumes of smoke from his nostrils. Kate thought about how the pillows would smell after he'd gone.

"He's sound asleep, but really stuffed up."

"How old is he?"

"He's just three."

"Cute age," said Charlie, tapping his cigarette on the saucer. "I've got two, you know."

"Two kids?" She was surprised. He nodded. "I would never have guessed that about you, Charlie. You're too much the gay blade, the town rake."

He grinned appreciatively. He worked at it, and liked to know his efforts were successful. "They're in Connecticut with my ex-wife."

"Do you see them often?"

"About once a month, I guess. She's remarried, so they've got a whole family scene there, really. It doesn't seem so important anymore. They're pretty much into their life, I'm pretty much into mine, you know."

"Yes," she said. They sat in what she imagined he thought was companionable silence. Two used parents. She had an old iron bedstead with a large ornate grille for a headboard and a smaller one at the foot. Charlie's head had slipped into the space between two of the white-painted rods. They pushed his ears forward slightly. He looked a little like the Mickey Mouse night light in Neddie's room. She smiled. She wondered why she had been so excited about going out with him tonight. When he'd finished his cigarette, he reached for her again. She set her wineglass down on the floor by her side of the bed and they made love. Charlie seemed interested in some variations on their earlier theme, but she shook her head no, no, and their lovemaking was short and somewhat neutral in character. Just as he pulled limply and stickily away from her to find another cigarette, Neddie's agonized shout floated back through the apartment to her. She leapt out of bed, upsetting her half-empty wineglass but avoiding the plant this time, and sprinted into the light and down the long hallway, pushing her breasts flat onto her chest to keep them from bouncing painfully.

Neddie's eyes were still shut. He had turned over onto his back and tears ran down his cheeks, into his ears. The covers were piled on the floor. "Nooo, monkey!" he moaned, and thrashed. Kate picked him up and cradled him close, his wet face pressing on her neck.

"Neddie, it's Mommy. Mommy's here now. *No* monkeys. The monkeys are all gone. You're in your room, Neddie, with Mommy, see?" She

THE MOTHER

148

pulled her head back to look at him. His eyes were open now, but he looked blank. She walked around the room with him, talking slowly.

"We're at home, Neddie. You had a dream. That wasn't real. That silly monkey was a dream. See, here's Sleazy. He's real." She pointed to Ned's bear, sitting on a shelf. Ned reached for him. "Sleazy," he said, and tucked him in close under his chin, just as Kate held him. She shifted him to her hip now, and went around the room, showing him all his favorite things. Kate was tall and thin. She had down-drooping breasts and flat, narrow hips. She looked like a carved white column in the dim light.

"And look, Ned. Look what's happening out here." She carried him to the window. The flakes danced thickly in a sudden gust of wind under the street light outside Ned's room, a thousand suicidal moths. "Do you know what that is?"

"Dat's da snow!" he said. His mouth hung open and his breath was hot and damp on her breast.

"And it's all piling up on the ground, Neddie, see? And tomorrow we can find the sled that Daddy gave you in the basement, and put on boots and mittens . . . "

"And my hat?" Ned wore a baseball hat every day. He watched her face now to be sure they were in agreement on this.

"Yeah, your hat, but you have to pull your hood up over it to keep your ears warm. And we can play all day because tomorrow's Sunday. Mommy doesn't have to work."

"Not day care?"

"No, tomorrow we can stay home *all* day. Okay?" They watched the snow together for a moment. Then she turned from the window. "I'm going to tuck you in now." She carried the child to his bed and started to lower him. His legs and arms gripped her tightly, a monkey's grip.

"Stay here, Mumma."

"Okay." He relaxed, and let her put him down on the bed. "But Mommy's cold. You move over and make room for me under these covers." He wiggled back against the wall and she slid in next to him and pulled the covers over them both. His face was inches from hers. He smiled at her and reached up to pat her face. His hands were sticky and warm. "Mumma," he said.

"Yes," she said, tenderly, and shut her eyes to set a good example for him. Sometime later she woke to hear the front door shut gently, and footsteps going down the stairs. Then dimly, as at a great distance, or as if it were all happening in some muffled, underwater world, a car started up in the street, there was a brief series of whirring sounds as it struggled back and forth out of its parking place, and then, like a thin cry, its noise evaporated into the night.

When Neddie woke her, the sky was still gray. The light in the room was gray too, gentle and chaste. The snow had stuck in the mesh of the summer screens left on the windows, and the house seemed wrapped in gauze. It still fell outside, heavy and soft, but from somewhere on the street came the *chink, chink* of a lone optimist already shoveling.

"Ned. Let me sleep a minute more."

"You already slept a long time, Mumma. And I *need* you."

He was standing by the bed, his face just above her head. He wore a red baseball cap, and his brown eyes regarded her gravely.

"Why do you need me?"

"You hafta make my train go."

"What, Granpoppy's train?" He nodded his head solemnly. "Oh, Christ!" she swore, and violently threw the covers back, swinging her legs out in the same motion. He looked frightened, and she felt instantly remorseful. "No, Neddie, it's all right. I'm just mad at the *train*. I'll fix it."

Her parents had given Ned the train, an expensive Swedish model of painted wood. The cars fastened together with magnets. Occasionally, by chance, Ned would line them up correctly, but most often, one or two cars would be turned backward, north pole to north pole, or south to south, and the more he would try to push them together, the more they repelled each other. Her parents' extravagance since her divorce, their attempts to ease her way and Ned's with things she didn't want, couldn't use, annoyed her. She must have bent down to correct the magnetic attraction on this thing thirty times since they'd given it to Ned.

He came and squatted by her. He had laid the track out and there were miniature pigs and sheep and ducks heaped up in the tiny open train cars. The thought of his working silently for so long, trying not to wake her, touched her. As they squatted together she began to try to explain to him the idea of polar attraction, turning the brightly painted cars first one way and then the other, so he could see the greedy pull at work.

Suddenly his head dipped slightly to look underneath her and his expression changed. She stopped. "Mumma's leaking?" he asked, pointing to the floor. She shifted her weight to one leg and looked on the floor under where she'd been squatting. Thick drops of whitish liquid, reminders of lovemaking the night before, glistened like pearls on the nicked wood. She laughed and stood up to get some Kleenex.

"It's all right, Neddie. Mommy can clean it up in a second. See?" she said. "All gone."

She smiled down at him as he squatted, fuzzy and compact in his sleeper, like a baby bear. He turned away and began to pull the toy train, now perfectly attached, around the expensive track.

DADDY

by

JAN CLAUSEN
(b. 1950)

*Born in Oregon, Jan Clausen grew up in the Pacific Northwest. She
now lives in New York City with her woman lover and her daughter. She founded* Conditions, *a major lesbian journal, in 1977 and
edited it for five years. She has published nine books of poetry,
fiction, essays, and book reviews; among them are* Waking at the
Bottom of the Dark *(1979),* Mother, Sister, Daughter, Lover *(1980),
and* Sinking, Stealing *(1985), a novel. More recent works are* The
Proserpine Papers *(1988), a volume of poems, and* Books and Life
(1989), a collection of book reviews.

· ———————————————— ·

I like my Daddy's best. It has more rooms. Mommy just has an apartment and you have to go upstairs. The bathroom is in my room. Daddy
has two bathrooms. He owns the whole house. Mommy used to live
there when I was a little baby. Before they got divorced. That means not
married anymore. You get married when you love each other.

Mommy loves me. Daddy says I'm his favorite girl in the whole
world, sugar. He always calls me sugar. We like to go to a restaurant for
breakfast. Sometimes we go there for dinner if he has to work in the city.
I went to his office lots of times. He has books there. You go way up in
the elevator. Sometimes I feel like I'm going to throw up. But I don't.
Then you see the river. There's no one there except Daddy and me. Sometimes Ellen comes.

My Mommy works. She goes to meetings. First I have to go to school
and then daycare. You can make noise at daycare. At school you have to
be quiet or you get punished. But I didn't ever get punished. Mommy
helps me with my homework. Sometimes we read a book together. Daddy
asks me add and take away. He says sugar you're so smart you can be
anything you want to be when you grow up. A doctor or a lawyer or
a professor or anything. My Daddy's a lawyer. I don't know if I'll get
married.

Daddy said maybe next year I can go to a different school where they
have lots of things to play with. You can paint and go on trips and they
have nice books. The kids make so much noise in my class. Some of

Daddy - Ellen
Mommy - Carolyn

makeup

byfran

holidays

TV

them talk Spanish and the boys are bad. I got a star for doing my homework right.

My Daddy takes me on Sunday. Sometimes I sleep there if Mommy goes away. I have to be good. Daddy says he'll get me something when we go shopping if I behave. I have to take a bath before I go and brush my hair. Daddy says he likes little girls that smell nice and clean. Sometimes Ellen lets me try her perfume. Once she let me put some powder on my face and some blue stuff on my eyes. That's eye shadow. But I had to wash my face before I went home. Mommy doesn't wear makeup. Or Carolyn. They said it looks silly.

Once in the summer I stayed at my Daddy's for a whole week. Ellen was there. She helped take care of me. You're so helpless David she said. She laughed. We all laughed. I had fun. We went to Coney Island. During the week I just call my Daddy two times because he works hard. Sometimes if he goes on a trip he can't see me. Daddy and Ellen went on a trip to Florida. They had to fly in an airplane. They sent me a postcard every day. You could go swimming in the winter there. Mommy and me went to the country but the car broke.

Sometimes Carolyn stays overnight. We only have two beds. She has to sleep in the same bed with Mommy. When I wake up I get in bed with them. We all hug each other. Carolyn and Mommy kiss each other all the time. But they aren't married. Only a man and a woman can get married. When they want to have a baby the man's penis gets bigger and he puts it in the woman's vagina. It feels good to touch your vagina. Me and Veronica did it in the bathtub. When the baby comes out the doctor has to cut the Mommy's vagina with some scissors. Mommy showed me a picture in her book.

I saw Daddy's penis before. Mommy has hair on her vagina. She has hair on her legs and Carolyn has lots of hair on her legs like a man. Ellen doesn't. Mommy said maybe Ellen does have hair on her legs but she shaves it. Sometimes I forget and call Carolyn Ellen. She gets mad. Sometimes I forget and call Mommy Daddy. I have a cat called Meatball at Mommy's but sometimes I forget and call Meatball Max instead. That's Daddy's dog.

Daddy is all Jewish. So is Ellen. Mommy is only part Jewish. But Daddy said I could be Jewish if I want. You can't have Christmas if you're Jewish. Mommy and me had a little Christmas tree. Carolyn came. We made cookies. I had Chanukah at my Daddy's. He gave me a doll named Samantha that talks and a skateboard and green pants and a yellow top. He says when I learn to tell time he'll get me a watch.

I wish Mommy would get me a TV. I just have a little one. Sometimes it gets broken. Daddy has a color TV at his house. It has a thing with buttons you push to change the program. Mommy said I watch too much TV. I said if you get me a new TV I promise I'll only watch two programs every day. Mommy said we're not going to just throw things away and get a new one every year. I told her Andrea has a color TV in her house and Veronica has a nice big TV in her room that you can see good. Mommy said I'm not getting a TV and that's all. Mommy made me feel bad. I started crying. Mommy said go to your room you're spoiling my dinner. I said *asshole* to Mommy. That's a curse. Sometimes my Mommy says a curse to me. I cried and cried.

Mommy said get in your room. She spanked me and said now get in your room. I ran in my room and closed the door. Mommy hurts my feelings. She won't let me watch TV. She always goes to a meeting and I have to stay with the baby sitter. I don't say a curse to my Daddy. My Daddy isn't mean to me. I screamed and screamed for my Daddy and Mrs. Taylor next door got mad and banged on the wall.

Mommy said go in the other room and call him then. Daddy said you sound like you've been crying. What's the matter, sugar. Nothing I said. Daddy doesn't like me to cry. He says crying is for little babies. I can't stand to see a woman cry, sugar, he says. Then I laugh and he tells me blow my nose. What are we going to do on Sunday I said. Oh that's a surprise Daddy said. Is it going somewhere I said. Yes we're going somewhere but that's not the real surprise Daddy said. Is it a present I said. Daddy said just wait and see, what did you do in school today. Daddy always asks what did I do in school. I told him the teacher had to punish Carlos. Daddy said listen isn't it about your bedtime. I have work to do. Ellen says hi. Blow me a goodnight kiss.

I hugged my Mommy. She hugged me back. She said she was sorry she got mad. But don't beg for things. A new TV is expensive. We don't need it. Mommy always says it's too expensive. I said I wish you were married to the President. Then we could live in the White House. I saw a picture in school. You could have anything you want. They don't have cockroaches.

The President is a good man. He helps people. George Washington was the President. Veronica gave me a doll of his wife at my birthday. It has a long dress. Mommy said he was mean to Indians and Black people. But we studied about him in school and he wasn't. They had voting once. You could vote for Ford or Carter. My Daddy voted for Carter. I'm glad my Daddy voted for who won. My Mommy didn't vote.

Mommy doesn't like things. She doesn't like the President and she doesn't like Mary Hartman like my Daddy. I told her to get Charmin toilet paper like they have on TV because it's soft to squeeze. She said that's a rip-off. She only takes me to McDonald's once every month. I got a Ronald McDonald cup to drink my milk. She said that's a gimmick. I like milk. Milk is a natural. I told Mommy that and she got mad. I said you don't like anything Mommy. She said I like lots of things. I like plants. I like to play basketball. I like sleeping late on Sunday mornings. I like to eat. I like books. I like women. I like you.

Do you like men I said. I don't like most men very much Mommy said. Some men are okay. My Daddy likes women I said. Does he Mommy said.

JAN CLAUSEN

153

I asked my Daddy does he like women. He said extremely. Some of my favorite people are women he said. Like you. And Ellen. Why do you ask. I said I don't know. Daddy said do you like men. I love you Daddy I said. I bet she gets that you know where Ellen said.

On Sunday we had breakfast at my Daddy's house. We had pancakes. Daddy makes them. He puts on his cook's hat. Then we went shopping. Then we went to a movie of Cinderella. Ellen came too. Then we went to a restaurant. I had ice cream with chocolate. Ellen and Daddy held each other's hand. Daddy said now I'm going to tell you the surprise. Ellen and I are getting married. How does that sound, sugar. Ellen said for god's sake David give her a little time to react.

Daddy said I can be in the wedding. He said Ellen will wear a pretty dress and he will break a glass. He did that when he and Mommy got married too. Then Ellen will have the same name as Mommy and Daddy and me and I can call her Mommy too if I want. I won't have to see my Daddy just on Sunday because Ellen will be there to help take care of me. She only works in the morning. It will be like a real family with a Mommy and a Daddy and a kid. But I can't say that part because Daddy said it's supposed to still be a secret.

I didn't feel good when Daddy brought me home. I felt like I had to throw up. Mommy held my hand. I lay down on the bed and she brought Meatball to play with me. She asked what did I do with Daddy today. She always asks me that. I told her we saw Cinderella. It was okay. She rode in a pumpkin. Some parts were boring. The Prince loved her. Daddy and Ellen are going to get married.

I started crying. I cried hard. Then I had to throw up. It got on the rug.

Mommy got the washcloth. She brought my pajamas. She hugged me. She said I love you. She said it won't be so different when Daddy and Ellen are married. You like Ellen don't you.

I love you Mommy, I love you, I love you I said. Why don't you like my Daddy. I love my Daddy.

I don't dislike your father Mommy said. We don't have much in common that's all. I'm happy living here just with you. You're special to me and you're special to your Daddy. You see him every week.

I cried and cried. I love you Mommy. I love you and Daddy both the same. And I love Ellen because she's going to be my Mommy too. I'll miss you. I'll miss you so much when I live there. I'll cry. I'm going to have a big sunny room and Daddy said he'll paint it and I can pick a color. I'm going to have a new kitty so I won't miss Meatball. Next year I can go to that nice school and Ellen might have a baby. It would be a brother or a sister. Daddy's going to get me a bicycle. I can take anything there I want. I'll just leave a few toys here for when I come to visit you on Sunday.

THE ENVELOPE

by

MAXINE KUMIN
(b. 1925)

Born in Philadelphia, Maxine Kumin lives on a horse farm in New Hampshire with her husband; her three children are grown. She earned two degrees from Radcliffe and has taught at many colleges. She has published twenty volumes of children's stories, essays, and fiction but is best known for the nine volumes of poetry that have appeared since 1961. Kumin has won many fellowships, awards, and honorary doctorates and has served as poetry consultant to the Library of Congress. Her 1972 collection, Up Country: Poems of New England, *won the Pulitzer Prize.* Our Ground Time Here Will Be Brief, *from which "The Envelope" is taken, appeared in 1978.*

It is true, Martin Heidegger, as you have written,
I *fear to cease*, even knowing that at the hour
of my death my daughters will absorb me, even
knowing they will carry me about forever
inside them, an arrested fetus, even as I carry
the ghost of my mother under my navel, a nervy
little androgynous person, a miracle
folded in lotus position.

Like those old pear-shaped Russian dolls that open
at the middle to reveal another and another, down
to the pea-sized, irreducible minim,
may we carry our mothers forth in our bellies.
May we, borne onward by our daughters, ride
in the Envelope of Almost-Infinity,
that chain letter good for the next twenty-five
thousand days of their lives.

BETWEEN THE LINES

by

RUTH STONE
(b. 1915)

Born in Roanoke, Virginia, Ruth Stone attended the University of Illinois and Harvard. She has held fellowships from both Radcliffe College and the Guggenheim Foundation and has won many awards for her poetry, which has been widely anthologized. Known as a "poet's poet," she has inspired many younger poets; several paid tribute to her in the Winter/Spring 1981 issue of The Iowa Review. *Stone has taught and lectured widely but spends most of her time writing in rural Vermont. Her fourth volume of poetry,* Second Hand Coat, *appeared in 1987; her fifth is* The Solution *(1989).*

Dear daughter: Well, it's November so it begins to rain.
Taking the dog out for a walk around the Square
Saw Mr. Smythe totter into Sage's for his pear.
He was slashing at the students with his cane.
In the elevator Poochie was out of breath.
She's much too fat; we're all too fat.
Mr. Parker is away on account of a death
But everything's as usual. 45's drain
Backed up in 55's. She was indignant;
Sailed out in peignoir under her muskrat.
The steam pipes smell like mold.
Miss Curant put down yesterday's *Monitor*
To stop the wind from blowing under her door.
My windows tremble with the traffic. It's turning cold.
Mrs. Parker's plants in the basement window need water.
They've been gone five days; they were supposed
To come back yesterday. I stopped in at that spa
And the old man in there pinched me. Enclosed
Is a little check. Call me collect, your ma.

I ASK MY MOTHER
TO SING

by

LI-YOUNG LEE
(b. 1957)

*Born in Jakarta, Indonesia, Li-Young Lee was brought to the United
States in 1964 by his Chinese-born parents, who were forced into
political exile by the dictator Sukarno. Lee studied at the University
of Pittsburgh, where professors encouraged him in his writing, and
later attended the University of Arizona and the State University
of New York at Bridgeport. He has held grants from both the Pennsylvania Council on the Arts and the Illinois Arts Council and won
a Guggenheim fellowship for 1989–1990. Lee now lives in Chicago.
His poems have been widely published in periodicals, and three
have appeared in volumes of the Pushcart Prize poetry series. Rose
(1986), from which "I Ask My Mother to Sing" is taken, is his first
collection.*

She begins, and my grandmother joins her.
Mother and daughter sing like young girls.
If my father were alive, he would play
his accordion and sway like a boat.

I've never been in Peking, or the Summer Palace,
nor stood on the great Stone Boat to watch
the rain begin on Kuen Ming Lake, the picnickers
running away in the grass.

But I love to hear it sung;
how the waterlilies fill with rain until
they overturn, spilling water into water,
then rock back, and fill with more.

Both women have begun to cry.
But neither stops her song.

FLOWER FEET

Silk Shoes in the Whitworth Art Gallery,
Manchester, England

by

RUTH FAINLIGHT
(b. 1931)

*Born in New York City, Ruth Fainlight was educated in England
and now lives in London. She has traveled widely and is a translator of Spanish and Portugese works. She has published short stories
but is best known as a prolific poet, author of eleven volumes of
poems, many of which have also appeared in journals and anthologies. Recent volumes are* Fifteen to Infinity *(1986) and* The Knot
*(1990). Fainlight has been poet-in-residence at Vanderbilt Univer-
sity, most recently in 1990. "Flower Feet" appeared in* The New
Yorker *in 1989.*

Real women's feet wore these objects
that look like toys or spectacle cases stitched
from bands of coral, jade, and apricot silk
embroidered with twined sprays of flowers.
Those hearts, tongues, crescents, and disks, leather
shapes an inch across, are the soles of shoes
no wider or longer than the span of my ankle.

If the feet had been cut off and the raw stumps
thrust inside the openings, surely
it could not hurt more than broken toes, twisted
back and bandaged tight. An old woman,
leaning on a cane outside her door
in a Chinese village, smiled to tell how
she fought and cried, how when she stood on points
of pain that gnawed like fire, nurse and mother
praised her tottering walk on flower feet.
Her friends nodded, glad the times had changed.
Otherwise, they would have crippled their daughters.

SPECULATION

by

GLORIA C. ODEN
(b. 1923)

*Born in Yonkers, New York, Gloria C. Oden earned a law degree
from Howard University in 1948. Before turning to teaching, she
spent ten years in New York editing science books and journals.
Since 1971 she has been a professor of English at the University of
Maryland, Baltimore County. Oden has held John Hay Whitney
and Yaddo fellowships and received other honors, including the
Distinguished Black Woman award from Towson State University
in Maryland in 1984. She has published and read her poems widely.
Her third collection is* The Tie That Binds *(1980).*

In my girlhood
Mother would call
"Rest in the shade!"
when exhausted from play
I would spread
on the grass
like a picnic.

"Move!" she would cry
and I did.
Out of reach
of the sun;
away from
its sulphurous eye
lest falling on me
it scorch me browner
than what by nature
I already was.

Summer sun was her enemy.
She made it mine.

But less concerned with
blackness as penalty,
continuously I fretted
the bonnets and parasols
of her untiring insistence.
Born burnt of God
what further need to be sun shy?
Still,
I was an obedient child, and
from the virulent roundings
of its patrol
learned to withhold myself.

Now I am grown to woman.
What would Mother say
seeing me focused here
in your red radiance
and eyes that burn me
blue?

GIRL

by

JAMAICA KINCAID
(b. 1949)

Born in Antigua, Jamaica Kincaid lives in New York City and is a naturalized American citizen. She is a staff writer for The New Yorker, *in which many of her stories have appeared. Her novel* Annie John *(1985) is about coming of age; its eight episodes conclude with Annie's leaving her West Indian home to become a nurse in England.* At the Bottom of the River *(1983) is a collection of musings about growing up; like "Girl," they are more prose poems than stories.* Annie John *was named one of the Best Books of 1985 by the* Library Journal, *and* At the Bottom of the River *won a prestigious award from the American Academy and Institute of Arts and Letters. More recent works are* A Small Place *(1988) and* Annie, Gwen, Lilly, Pam, and Tulip *(1989).*

Wash the white clothes on Monday and put them on the stone heap; wash the color clothes on Tuesday and put them on the clothesline to dry; don't walk barehead in the hot sun; cook pumpkin fritters in very hot sweet oil; soak your little cloths right after you take them off; when buying cotton to make yourself a nice blouse, be sure that it doesn't have gum on it, because that way it won't hold up well after a wash; soak salt fish overnight before you cook it; is it true that you sing benna in Sunday school?; always eat your food in such a way that it won't turn someone else's stomach; on Sundays try to walk like a lady and not like the slut you are so bent on becoming; don't sing benna in Sunday school; you mustn't speak to wharf-rat boys, not even to give directions; don't eat fruits on the street—flies will follow you; *but I don't sing benna on Sundays at all and never in Sunday school;* this is how to sew on a button; this is how to make a buttonhole for the button you have just sewed on; this is how to hem a dress when you see the hem coming down and so to prevent yourself from looking like the slut I know you are so bent on becoming; this is how you iron your father's khaki shirt so that it doesn't have a crease; this is how you iron your father's khaki pants so that they don't have a crease; this is how you grow okra—far from the house, because okra tree harbors red ants; when you are growing dasheen, make sure it gets plenty of water or else it makes your throat itch when you are eating it; this is how you sweep a corner; this is how you sweep a whole house; this is how you sweep a yard; this is how you smile to someone you don't like too much; this is how you smile to someone you don't like at all; this is how you smile to someone you like completely; this is how you set a table for tea; this is how you set a table for dinner; this is how you set a table for dinner with an important guest; this is how you set a table for lunch; this is how you set a table for breakfast; this is how to behave in the presence of men who don't know you very well, and this way they won't recognize immediately the slut I have warned you against becoming; be sure to wash every day, even if it is with your own spit; don't squat down to play marbles—you are not a boy, you know; don't pick people's flowers—you might catch something; don't throw stones at blackbirds, because it might not be a blackbird at all; this is how to make a bread pudding; this is how to make doukona; this is how to make pepper pot; this is how to make a good medicine for a cold; this is how to make a good medicine to throw away a child before it even becomes a child; this is how to catch a fish; this is how to throw back a fish you don't like, and that way something bad won't fall on you; this is how to bully a man; this is how a man bullies you; this is how to love a man, and if this doesn't work there are other ways, and if they don't work don't feel too bad about giving up; this is how to spit up in the air if you feel like it, and this is how to move quick so that it doesn't fall on you; this is how to make ends meet; always squeeze bread to make sure it's fresh; *but what if the baker won't let me feel the bread?*; you mean to say that after all you are really going to be the kind of woman who the baker won't let near the bread?

CIHUATLYOTL,
WOMAN ALONE

by

GLORIA E. ANZALDÚA
(b. 1942)

Gloria E. Anzaldúa describes in her autobiographical work
Borderlands–La Frontera: The New Mestiza *(1987), from which*
"Cihuatlyotl" is taken, the experience of growing up on farms
in the Rio Grande Valley as a Chicana/Tejana, *a Mexican/Texan*
woman living literally and figuratively on the border between
two cultures and languages. The daughter of a sharecropper, she
rebelled at an early age by reading and writing; she was the first
in six generations of her family to leave home. She earned a
master's degree from Pan American University and found her
voice as a poet and fiction writer through the support of other
women. She collaborated with Cherrié Moraga in editing the
prize-winning This Bridge Called My Back: Writings by Radical
Women of Color *(1981) and has been a contributing editor for*
Sinister Wisdom *since 1984. Anzaldúa has taught Chicano/*
Chicana studies, feminist studies, and creative writing at a
number of universities; she has also been active in the migrant
farmworkers' movement.

• ─────────────────── •

Many years I have fought off your hands, *Raza*
father mother   church   your rage at my desire to be
with myself, alone.   I have learned
to erect barricades   arch my back against
you   thrust back fingers, sticks   to
shriek no   to kick and claw   my way out of
your heart   And as I grew   you hacked away
at the pieces   of me   that   were   different
attached your tentacles   to my face and breasts
put a lock between my legs.   I had to do it,
Raza,   turn my back on your crookening finger
beckoning   beckoning   your   soft brown
landscape, tender *nopalitos*.   Oh,   it was hard,

GLORIA E. ANZALDÚA
163

Raza　　　to cleave flesh from flesh　　　I risked
us both bleeding to death. It took　　　a long
time　　　　　but　　　　　I learned　 to let
your values roll off my body　　　　like water
those I swallow to stay alive　　　become tumors
in my belly.　　　I refuse to be taken over　　by
things　　　people　　　who fear that hollow
aloneness　　beckoning　　beckoning.　　No self,
only race *vecindad familia*.　　My soul　 has always
been yours　　　one spark in the roar of your fire.
We Mexicans are collective animals.　　　　This I
accept　　but my life's work　　requires autonomy
like oxygen.　　　This lifelong battle has ended,
Raza.　　　　I don't need to flail against you.
Raza india mexicana norteamericana,　　there's nothing more you can chop off　　or graft on me that
will change my soul.　 I remain who I am, multiple
and one　　　of the herd, yet not of it.　　I walk
on the ground of my own being　　　browned and
hardened by the ages.　 I am fully formed　　carved
by the hands of the ancients,　　　drenched with
the stench of today's headlines.　　But my own
hands whittle　　the final work　　me.

DEAR TONI
INSTEAD OF A LETTER
OF CONGRATULATION
UPON YOUR BOOK AND
YOUR DAUGHTER WHOM
YOU SAY YOU ARE
RAISING TO BE A
CORRECT LITTLE SISTER

by

AUDRE LORDE
(b. 1934)

*The daughter of Grenadian immigrants, Audre Lorde was born
and lives in New York City, where she teaches at her alma mater,
Hunter College. Long established as a poet, Lorde is also well-
known as a black lesbian feminist spokesperson. A volume of her
essays,* Sister Outsider, *appeared in 1984. In* The Cancer Journals
*(1980) and other works, she has recorded her long struggle with
cancer and the existential concerns to which it has brought her.
Her volume of poetry* Our Dead Behind Us *(1986) and* A Burst of
Light: Essays *(1988) reveal a quiet optimism for human affairs.
[This poem is addressed to Toni Morrison, author of* The Bluest Eye
(1970) and Beloved *(1987).]*

• ————————————————— •

I can see your daughter walking down streets of love
in revelation;
but raising her up to be a correct little sister
is doing your mama's job all over again.
And who did you make on the edge of Harlem's winter
hard and black
while the inside was undetermined
swirls of color and need
shifting, remembering
were you making another self to rediscover
in a new house and a new name
in a new place next to a river of blood

or were you putting the past together
pooling everything learned
into a new and continuous woman
divorced
from the old shit we share
and shared and sharing need not share again?

I see your square delicate jawbone
the mark of a Taurus (or Leo) as well as the ease
with which you deal with your pretensions.
I dig your going and becoming
the lessons you teach your daughter
our history
for I am your sister corrected and
already raised up
our daughters will explore the old countries
as curious visitors to our season
using their own myths to keep themselves sharp.

I have known you over and over again
as I've lived throughout this city
taking it in storm and morning strolls
through Astor Place and under the Canal Street Bridge
the Washington Arch like a stone raised to despair
and Riverside Drive too close to the dangerous predawn
waters and 129th Street between Lenox and Seventh
burning my blood but not black enough
and threatening to become home.

I first saw you behind a caseworker's notebook
defying upper Madison Avenue and my roommate's
        concern
the ghost of Maine lobsterpots trailing behind you
and I followed you into east fourth street and out
through Bellevue's side entrance one night
into the respectable vineyards of Yeshivas intellectual
        gloom
and there I lost you between the books and the games
until I rose again out of Jackson Mississippi
to find you in an office down the hall from mine
calmly studying term papers like maps
marking off stations

THE MOTHER
166

on our trip through the heights of Convent Avenue
teaching english our children citycollege
softer and tougher and more direct
and putting your feet up on a desk you say Hi
I'm going to have a baby so now I can really indulge
            myself.
Through that slim appraisal of your world
I felt you
grinning and plucky and a little bit scared
perhaps of the madness past that had relieved you
through your brittle young will of iron
into the fire of whip steel.

I have a daughter also
who does not remind me of you
but she too has deep aquatic eyes that are burning and
            curious.
As she moves through taboos
whirling myths like gay hoops over her head
I know beyond fear and history
that our teaching means keeping trust
with less and less correctness
only with ourselves—
History may alter
old pretenses and victories
but not the pain my sister never the pain.

In my daughter's name
I bless your child with the mother she has
with a future of warriors and growing fire.
But with tenderness also,
for we are landscapes, Toni,
printed upon them as surely
as water etches feather on stone.
Our girls will grow into their own
Black Women
finding their own contradictions
that they will come to love
as I love you.

AUDRE LORDE

SOUVENIR

by

JAYNE ANNE PHILLIPS
(b. 1953)

*Jayne Anne Phillips earned degrees both in her native West
Virginia and at the University of Iowa; she now lives in Newton,
Massachusetts, with her husband and two children. She has held
fellowships from the National Endowment for the Arts and the
Bunting Institute at Harvard and has taught at several colleges in
the Boston area. Phillips's first collection of short stories,* Black
Tickets *(1979), won the Sue Kaufman Prize for first fiction and was
reprinted in 1989. She has published two novels,* Fast Lanes *(1984)
and* Machine Dreams *(1984); the latter is about Viet Nam.*

Kate always sent her mother a card on Valentine's Day. She timed the
mails from wherever she was so that the cards arrived on February 14th.
Her parents had celebrated the day in some small fashion, and since her
father's death six years before, Kate made a gesture of compensatory
remembrance. At first, she made the cards herself: collage and pressed
grasses on construction paper sewn in fabric. Now she settled for art
reproductions, glossy cards with blank insides. Kate wrote in them with
colored inks, "You have always been my Valentine," or simply "Hey,
take care of yourself." She might enclose a present as well, something
small enough to fit into an envelope; a sachet, a perfumed soap, a funny
tintype of a prune-faced man in a bowler hat.

This time, she forgot. Despite the garish displays of paper cupids and
heart-shaped boxes in drugstore windows, she let the day nearly approach
before remembering. It was too late to send anything in the mail. She
called her mother long-distance at night when the rates were low.

"Mom? How are you?"

"It's you! How are *you*?" Her mother's voice grew suddenly brighter;
Kate recognized a tone reserved for welcome company. Sometimes it
took a while to warm up.

"I'm fine," answered Kate. "What have you been doing?"

"Well, actually I was trying to sleep."

"Sleep? You should be out setting the old hometown on fire."

"The old hometown can burn up without me tonight."

THE MOTHER
168

"Really? What's going on?"

"I'm running in-service training sessions for the primary teachers." Kate's mother was a school superintendent. "They're driving me batty. You'd think their brains were rubber."

"They are," Kate said. "Or you wouldn't have to train them. Think of them as a salvation, they create a need for your job."

"Some salvation. Besides, your logic is ridiculous. Just because someone needs training doesn't mean they're stupid."

"I'm just kidding. But *I'm* stupid. I forgot to send you a Valentine's card."

"You did? That's bad. I'm trained to receive one. They bring me luck."

"You're receiving a phone call instead," Kate said. "Won't that do?"

"Of course," said her mother, "but this is costing you money. Tell me quick, how are you?"

"Oh, you know. Doctoral pursuits. Doing my student trip, grooving with the professors."

"The professors? You'd better watch yourself."

"It's a joke, Mom, a joke. But what about you? Any men on the horizon?"

"No, not really. A married salesman or two asking me to dinner when they come through the office. Thank heavens I never let those things get started."

"You should do what you want to," Kate said.

"Sure," said her mother. "And where would I be then?"

"I don't know. Maybe Venezuela."

"They don't even have plumbing in Venezuela."

"Yes, but their sunsets are perfect, and the villages are full of dark passionate men in blousy shirts."

"That's your department, not mine."

"Ha," Kate said, "I wish it were my department. Sounds a lot more exciting than teaching undergraduates."

Her mother laughed. "Be careful," she said. "You'll get what you want. End up sweeping a dirt floor with a squawling baby around your neck."

"A dark baby," Kate said, "to stir up the family blood."

"Nothing would surprise me," her mother said as the line went fuzzy. Her voice was submerged in static, then surfaced. "Listen," she was saying. "Write to me. You seem so far away."

They hung up and Kate sat watching the windows of the neighboring house. The curtains were transparent and flowered and none of them matched. Silhouettes of the window frames spread across them like single dark bars. Her mother's curtains were all the same, white cotton hemmed with a ruffle, tiebacks blousing the cloth into identical shapes. From the street it looked as if the house was always in order.

Kate made a cup of strong Chinese tea, turned the lights off, and sat holding the warm cup in the dark. Her mother kept no real tea in the house, just packets of instant diabetic mixture which tasted of chemical sweetener and had a bitter aftertaste. The packets sat on the shelf next to her mother's miniature scales. The scales were white. Kate saw clearly the face of the metal dial on the front, its markings and trembling needle. Her mother weighed portions of food for meals: frozen broccoli, slices of plastic-wrapped Kraft cheese, careful chunks of roast beef. A dog-eared copy of *The Diabetic Diet* had remained propped against the salt shaker for the last two years.

Kate rubbed her forehead. Often at night she had headaches. Sometimes she wondered if there were an agent in her body, a secret in her blood making ready to work against her.

The phone blared repeatedly, careening into her sleep. Kate scrambled out of bed, naked and cold, stumbling, before she recognized the striped wallpaper of her bedroom and realized the phone was right there on the bedside table, as always. She picked up the receiver.

"Kate?" said her brother's voice. "It's Robert. Mom is in the hospital. They don't know what's wrong but she's in for tests."

"Tests? What's happened? I just talked to her last night."

"I'm not sure. She called the neighbors and they took her to the emergency room around dawn." Robert's voice still had that slight twang Kate knew was disappearing from her own. He would be calling from his insurance office, nine o'clock their time, in his thick glasses and wide, perfectly knotted tie. He was a member of the million-dollar club and his picture, tiny, the size of a postage stamp, appeared in the Mutual of Omaha magazine. His voice seemed small too over the distance. Kate felt heavy and dulled. She would never make much money, and recently she had begun wearing make-up again, waking in smeared mascara as she had in high school.

"Is Mom all right?" she managed now. "How serious is it?"

"They're not sure," Robert said. "Her doctor thinks it could have been any of several things, but they're doing X rays."

"Her doctor *thinks*? Doesn't he know? Get her to someone else. There aren't any doctors in that one-horse town."

"I don't know about that," Robert said defensively. "Anyway, I can't force her. You know how she is about money."

"Money? She could have a stroke and drop dead while her doctor wonders what's wrong."

"Doesn't matter. You know you can't tell her what to do."

"Could I call her somehow?"

"No, not yet. And don't get her all worried. She's been scared enough as it is. I'll tell her what you said about getting another opinion, and I'll call you back in a few hours when I have some news. Meanwhile, she's all right, do you hear?"

The line went dead with a click and Kate walked to the bathroom to wash her face. She splashed her eyes and felt guilty about the Valentine's card. Slogans danced in her head like reprimands. *For A Special One. Dearest Mother. My Best Friend*. Despite Robert, after breakfast she would call the hospital.

She sat a long time with her coffee, waiting for minutes to pass, considering how many meals she and her mother ate alone. Similar times of day, hundreds of miles apart. Women by themselves. The last person Kate had eaten breakfast with had been someone she'd met in a bar. He was passing through town. He liked his fried eggs gelatinized in the center, only slightly runny, and Kate had studiously looked away as he ate. The night before he'd looked down from above her as he finished and she still moved under him. "You're still wanting," he'd said. "That's nice." Mornings now, Kate saw her own face in the mirror and was glad she'd forgotten his name. When she looked at her reflection from the side, she saw a faint etching of lines beside her mouth. She hadn't slept with anyone for five weeks, and the skin beneath her eyes had taken on a creamy darkness.

She reached for the phone but drew back. It seemed bad luck to ask for news, to push toward whatever was coming as though she had no respect for it.

Standing in the kitchen last summer, her mother had stirred gravy and argued with her.

"I'm thinking of your own good, not mine," she'd said. "Think of what you put yourself through. And how can you feel right about it? You were born here, I don't care what you say." Her voice broke and she looked, perplexed, at the broth in the pan.

"But, hypothetically," Kate continued, her own voice unaccountably shaking, "if I'm willing to endure whatever I have to, do you have a right to object? You're my mother. You're supposed to defend my choices."

"You'll have enough trouble without choosing more for yourself. Using birth control that'll ruin your insides, moving from one place to another. I can't defend your choices. I can't even defend myself against you." She wiped her eyes on a napkin.

"Why do you have to make me feel so guilty?" Kate said, fighting tears of frustration. "I'm not attacking you."

"You're not? Then who are you talking to?"

"Oh Mom, give me a break."

"I've tried to give you more than that," her mother said. "I know what your choices are saying to me." She set the steaming gravy off the stove. "You may feel very differently later on. It's just a shame I won't be around to see it."

"Oh? Where will you be?"

"Floating around on a fleecy cloud."

Kate got up to set the table before she realized her mother had already done it.

JAYNE ANNE PHILLIPS

171

The days went by. They'd gone shopping before Kate left. Standing at the cash register in an antique shop on Main Street, they bought each other pewter candle holders. "A souvenir," her mother said. "A reminder to always be nice to yourself. If you live alone you should eat by candlelight."

"Listen," Kate said, "I eat in a heart-shaped tub with bubbles to my chin. I sleep on satin sheets and my mattress has a built-in massage engine. My overnight guests are impressed. You don't have to tell me about the solitary pleasures."

They laughed and touched hands.

"Well," her mother said. "If you like yourself, I must have done something right."

Robert didn't phone until evening. His voice was fatigued and thin. "I've moved her to the university hospital," he said. "They can't deal with it at home."

Kate waited, saying nothing. She concentrated on the toes of her shoes. They needed shining. *You never take care of anything*, her mother would say.

"She has a tumor in her head." He said it firmly, as though Kate might challenge him.

"I'll take a plane tomorrow morning," Kate answered, "I'll be there by noon."

Robert exhaled. "Look," he said, "don't even come back here unless you can keep your mouth shut and do it my way."

"Get to the point."

"The point is they believe she has a malignancy and we're not going to tell her. I almost didn't tell you." His voice faltered. "They're going to operate but if they find what they're expecting, they don't think they can stop it."

For a moment there was no sound except an oceanic vibration of distance on the wire. Even that sound grew still. Robert breathed. Kate could almost see him, in a booth at the hospital, staring straight ahead at the plastic instructions screwed to the narrow rectangular body of the telephone. It seemed to her that she was hurtling toward him.

"I'll do it your way," she said.

The hospital cafeteria was a large room full of orange Formica tables. Its southern wall was glass. Across the highway, Kate saw a small park modestly dotted with amusement rides and bordered by a narrow band of river. How odd, to build a children's park across from a medical center. The sight was pleasant in a cruel way. The rolling lawn of the little park was perfectly, relentlessly green.

Robert sat down. Their mother was to have surgery in two days.

"After it's over," he said, "they're not certain what will happen. The tumor is in a bad place. There may be some paralysis."

THE MOTHER
172

"What kind of paralysis?" Kate said. She watched him twist the green-edged coffee cup around and around on its saucer.

"Facial. And maybe worse."

"You've told her this?"

He didn't answer.

"Robert, what is she going to think if she wakes up and—"

He leaned forward, grasping the cup and speaking through clenched teeth. "Don't you think I thought of that?" He gripped the sides of the table and the cup rolled onto the carpeted floor with a dull thud. He seemed ready to throw the table after it, then grabbed Kate's wrists and squeezed them hard.

"You didn't drive her here," he said. "She was so scared she couldn't talk. How much do you want to hand her at once?"

Kate watched the cup sitting solidly on the nubby carpet.

"We've told her it's benign," Robert said, "that the surgery will cause complications, but she can learn back whatever is lost."

Kate looked at him. "Is that true?"

"They hope so."

"We're lying to her, all of us, more and more." Kate pulled her hands away and Robert touched her shoulder.

"What do *you* want to tell her, Kate? 'You're fifty-five and you're done for'?"

She stiffened. "Why put her through the operation at all?"

He sat back and dropped his arms, lowering his head. "Because without it she'd be in bad pain. Soon." They were silent, then he looked up. "And anyway," he said softly, "we don't *know*, do we? She may have a better chance than they think."

Kate put her hands on her face. Behind her closed eyes she saw a succession of blocks tumbling over.

They took the elevator up to the hospital room. They were alone and they stood close together. Above the door red numerals lit up, flashing. Behind the illuminated shapes droned an impersonal hum of machinery.

Then the doors opened with a sucking sound. Three nurses stood waiting with a lunch cart, identical covered trays stacked in tiers. There was a hot bland smell, like warm cardboard. One of the women caught the thick steel door with her arm and smiled. Kate looked quickly at their rubber-soled shoes. White polish, the kind that rubs off. And their legs seemed only white shapes, boneless and two-dimensional, stepping silently into the metal cage.

She looked smaller in the white bed. The chrome side rails were pulled up and she seemed powerless behind them, her dark hair pushed back from her face and her forearms delicate in the baggy hospital gown. Her eyes were different in some nearly imperceptible way; she held them wider, they were shiny with a veiled wetness. For a moment the room seemed empty of all else; there were only her eyes and the dark blossoms of the flowers on the table beside her. Red roses with pine. Everyone had sent the same thing.

Robert walked close to the bed with his hands clasped behind his back, as though afraid to touch. "Where did all the flowers come from?" he asked.

"From school, and the neighbors. And Katie." She smiled.

"FTD," Kate said. "Before I left home. I felt so bad for not being here all along."

"That's silly," said her mother. "You can hardly sit at home and wait for some problem to arise."

"Speaking of problems," Robert said, "the doctor tells me you're not eating. Do I have to urge you a little?" He sat down on the edge of the bed and shook the silverware from its paper sleeve.

Kate touched the plastic tray. "Jell-O and canned cream of chicken soup. Looks great. We should have brought you something."

"They don't *want* us to bring her anything," Robert said. "This is a hospital. And I'm sure your comments make her lunch seem even more appetizing."

"I'll eat it!" said their mother in mock dismay. "Admit they sent you in here to stage a battle until I gave in."

"I'm sorry," Kate said. "He's right."

Robert grinned. "Did you hear that? She says I'm right. I don't believe it." He pushed the tray closer to his mother's chest and made a show of tucking a napkin under her chin.

"Of course you're right, dear." She smiled and gave Kate an obvious wink.

"Yeah," Robert said, "I know you two. But seriously, you eat this. I have to go make some business calls from the motel room."

Their mother frowned. "That motel must be costing you a fortune."

"No, it's reasonable," he said. "Kate can stay for a week or two and I'll drive back and forth from home. If you think this food is bad, you should see the meals in that motel restaurant." He got up to go, flashing Kate a glance of collusion. "I'll be back after supper."

His footsteps echoed down the hallway. Kate and her mother looked wordlessly at each other, relieved. Kate looked away guiltily. Then her mother spoke, apologetic. "He's so tired," she said. "He's been with me since yesterday."

She looked at Kate, then into the air of the room. "I'm in a fix," she said. "Except for when the pain comes, it's all a show that goes on without me. I'm like an invalid, or a lunatic."

Kate moved close and touched her mother's arms. "That's all right, we're going to get you through it. Someone's covering for you at work?"

"I had to take a leave of absence. It's going to take a while afterward—"

"I know. But it's the last thing to worry about, it can't be helped."

"Like spilt milk. Isn't that what they say?"

"I don't know what they say. But why didn't you tell me? Didn't you know something was wrong?"

"Yes . . . bad headaches. Migraines, I thought, or the diabetes getting worse. I was afraid they'd start me on insulin." She tightened the corner of her mouth. "Little did I know . . . "

They heard the shuffle of slippers. An old woman stood at the open door of the room, looking in confusedly. She seemed about to speak, then moved on.

"Oh," said Kate's mother in exasperation, "shut that door, please? They let these old women wander around like refugees." She sat up, reaching for a robe. "And let's get me out of this bed."

They sat near the window while she finished eating. Bars of moted yellow banded the floor of the room. The light held a tinge of spring which seemed painful because it might vanish. They heard the rattle of the meal cart outside the closed door, and the clunk-slide of patients with aluminum walkers. Kate's mother sighed and pushed away the half-empty soup bowl.

"They'll be here after me any minute. More tests. I just want to stay with you." Her face was warm and smooth in the slanted light, lines in her skin delicate, unreal; as though a face behind her face was now apparent after many years. She sat looking at Kate and smiled.

"One day when you were about four you were dragging a broom around the kitchen. I asked you what you were doing and you told me that when you got old you were going to be an angel and sweep the rotten rain off the clouds."

"What did you say to that?"

"I said that when you were old I was sure God would see to it." Her mother laughed. "I'm glad you weren't such a smart aleck then," she said. "You would have told me my view of God was paternalistic."

"Ah yes," sighed Kate. "God, that famous dude. Here I am, getting old, facing unemployment, alone, and where is He?"

"You're not alone," her mother said, "I'm right here."

Kate didn't answer. She sat motionless and felt her heart begin to open like a box with a hinged lid. The fullness had no edges.

Her mother stood. She rubbed her hands slowly, twisting her wedding rings. "My hands are so dry in the winter," she said softly, "I brought some hand cream with me but I can't find it anywhere, my suitcase is so jumbled. Thank heavens spring is early this year. . . . They told me that little park over there doesn't usually open till the end of March . . . "

She's helping me, thought Kate, I'm not supposed to let her down.

". . . but they're already running it on weekends. Even past dusk. We'll see the lights tonight. You can't see the shapes this far away, just the motion . . . "

A nurse came in with a wheelchair. Kate's mother pulled a wry face. "This wheelchair is a bit much," she said.

"We don't want to tire you out," said the nurse.

The chair took her weight quietly. At the door she put out her hand to stop, turned, and said anxiously, "Kate, see if you can find that hand cream?"

It was the blue suitcase from years ago, still almost new. She'd brought things she never used for everyday; a cashmere sweater, lace slips, silk underpants wrapped in tissue. Folded beneath was a stack of postmarked envelopes, slightly ragged, tied with twine. Kate opened one and realized that all the cards were there, beginning with the first of the marriage. There were a few photographs of her and Robert, baby pictures almost indistinguishable from each other, and then Kate's homemade Valentines, fastened together with rubber bands. Kate stared. *What will I do with these things?* She wanted air; she needed to breathe. She walked to the window and put the bundled papers on the sill. She'd raised the glass and pushed back the screen when suddenly, her mother's clock radio went off with a flat buzz. Kate moved to switch it off and brushed the cards with her arm. Envelopes shifted and slid, scattering on the floor of the room. A few snapshots wafted silently out the window. They dipped and turned, twirling. Kate didn't try to reach them. They seemed only scraps, buoyant and yellowed, blown away, the faces small as pennies. Somewhere far-off there were sirens, almost musical, drawn out and carefully approaching.

The nurse came in with evening medication. Kate's mother lay in bed. "I hope this is strong enough," she said. "Last night I couldn't sleep at all. So many sounds in a hospital . . . "

"You'll sleep tonight," the nurse assured her.

Kate winked at her mother. "That's right," she said, "I'll help you out if I have to."

They stayed up for an hour, watching the moving lights outside and the stationary glows of houses across the distant river. The halls grew darker, were lit with night lights, and the hospital dimmed. Kate waited. Her mother's eyes fluttered and finally she slept. Her breathing was low and regular.

Kate didn't move. Robert had said he'd be back; where was he? She felt a sunken anger and shook her head. She'd been on the point of telling her mother everything. The secrets were a travesty. What if there were things her mother wanted done, people she needed to see? Kate wanted to wake her before these hours passed in the dark and confess that she had lied. Between them, through the tension, there had always been a trusted clarity. Now it was twisted. Kate sat leaning forward, nearly touching the hospital bed.

Suddenly her mother sat bolt upright, her eyes open and her face transfixed. She looked blindly toward Kate but seemed to see nothing.

THE MOTHER
176

"Who are you?" she whispered. Kate stood, at first unable to move. The woman in the bed opened and closed her mouth several times, as though she were gasping. Then she said loudly, "Stop moving the table. Stop it this instant!" Her eyes were wide with fright and her body was vibrating.

Kate reached her. "Mama, wake up, you're dreaming." Her mother jerked, flinging her arms out. Kate held her tightly.

"I can hear the wheels," she moaned.

"No, no," Kate said. "You're here with me."

"It's not so?"

"No," Kate said. "It's not so."

She went limp. Kate felt for her pulse and found it rapid, then regular. She sat rocking her mother. In a few minutes she lay her back on the pillows and smoothed the damp hair at her temples, smoothed the sheets of the bed. Later she slept fitfully in a chair, waking repeatedly to assure herself that her mother was breathing.

Near dawn she got up, exhausted, and left the room to walk in the corridor. In front of the window at the end of the hallway she saw a man slumped on a couch; the man slowly stood and wavered before her like a specter. It was Robert.

"Kate?" he said.

Years ago he had flunked out of a small junior college and their mother sat in her bedroom rocker, crying hard for over an hour while Kate tried in vain to comfort her. Kate went to the university the next fall, so anxious that she studied frantically, outlining whole textbooks in yellow ink. She sat in the front rows of large classrooms to take voluminous notes, writing quickly in her thick notebook. Robert had gone home, held a job in a plant that manufactured business forms and worked his way through the hometown college. By that time their father was dead, and Robert became, always and forever, the man of the house.

"Robert," Kate said, "I'll stay. Go home."

After breakfast they sat waiting for Robert, who had called and said he'd arrive soon. Kate's fatigue had given way to an intense awareness of every sound, every gesture. How would they get through the day? Her mother had awakened from the drugged sleep still groggy, unable to eat. The meal was sent away untouched and she watched the window as though she feared the walls of the room.

"I'm glad your father isn't here to see this," she said. There was a silence and Kate opened her mouth to speak. "I mean," said her mother quickly, "I'm going to look horrible for a few weeks, with my head all shaved." She pulled an afghan up around her lap and straightened the magazines on the table beside her chair.

"Mom," Kate said, "your hair will grow back."

Her mother pulled the afghan closer. "I've been thinking of your father," she said. "It's not that I'd have wanted him to suffer. But if he had to die, sometimes I wish he'd done it more gently. That heart attack, so finished; never a warning. I wish I'd had some time to nurse him. In a way, it's a chance to settle things."

"Did things need settling?"

"They always do, don't they?" She sat looking out the window, then said softly, "I wonder where I'm headed."

"You're not headed anywhere," Kate said. "I want you right here to see me settle down into normal American womanhood."

Her mother smiled reassuringly. "Where are my grandchildren?" she said. "That's what I'd like to know."

"You stick around," said Kate, "and I promise to start working on it." She moved her chair closer, so that their knees were touching and they could both see out the window. Below them cars moved on the highway and the Ferris wheel in the little park was turning.

"I remember when you were one of the little girls in the parade at the county fair. You weren't even in school yet; you were beautiful in that white organdy dress and pinafore. You wore those shiny black patent shoes and a crown of real apple blossoms. Do you remember?"

"Yes," Kate said. "That long parade. They told me not to move and I sat so still my legs went to sleep. When they lifted me off the float I couldn't stand up. They put me under a tree to wait for you, and you came, in a full white skirt and white sandals, your hair tied back in a red scarf. I can see you yet."

Her mother laughed. "Sounds like a pretty exaggerated picture."

Kate nodded. "I was little. You were big."

"You loved the county fair. You were wild about the carnivals." They looked down at the little park. "Magic, isn't it?" her mother said.

"Maybe we could go see it," said Kate. "I'll ask the doctor."

They walked across a pedestrian footbridge spanning the highway. Kate had bundled her mother into a winter coat and gloves despite the sunny weather. The day was sharp, nearly still, holding its bright air like illusion. Kate tasted the brittle water of her breath, felt for the cool handrail and thin steel of the webbed fencing. Cars moved steadily under the bridge. Beyond a muted roar of motors the park spread green and wooded, its limits clearly visible.

Kate's mother had combed her hair and put on lipstick. Her mouth was defined and brilliant; she linked arms with Kate like an escort. "I was afraid they'd tell us no," she said. "I was ready to run away!"

"I promised I wouldn't let you. And we only have ten minutes, long enough for the Ferris wheel." Kate grinned.

"I haven't ridden one in years. I wonder if I still know how."

"Of course you do. Ferris wheels are genetic knowledge."

"All right, whatever you say." She smiled. "We'll just hold on."

They drew closer and walked quickly through the sounds of the highway. When they reached the grass it was ankle-high and thick, longer and more ragged than it appeared from a distance. The Ferris wheel sat squarely near a grove of swaying elms, squat and laboring, taller than trees. Its neon lights still burned, pale in the sun, spiraling from inside like an imagined bloom. The naked elms surrounded it, their topmost branches tapping. Steel ribs of the machine were graceful and slightly rusted, squeaking faintly above a tinkling music. Only a few people were riding.

"Looks a little rickety," Kate said.

"Oh, don't worry," said her mother.

Kate tried to buy tickets but the ride was free. The old man running the motor wore an engineer's cap and patched overalls. He stopped the wheel and led them on a short ramp to an open car. It dipped gently, padded with black cushions. An orderly and his children rode in the car above. Kate saw their dangling feet, the girls' dusty sandals and gray socks beside their father's shoes and the hem of his white pants. The youngest one swung her feet absently, so it seemed the breeze blew her legs like fabric hung on a line.

Kate looked at her mother. "Are you ready for the big sky?" They laughed. Beyond them the river moved lazily. Houses on the opposite bank seemed empty, but a few rowboats bobbed at the docks. The surface of the water lapped and reflected clouds, and as Kate watched, searching for a definition of line, the Ferris wheel jerked into motion. The car rocked. They looked into the distance and Kate caught her mother's hand as they ascended.

Far away the hospital rose up white and glistening, its windows catching the glint of the sun. Directly below, the park was nearly deserted. There were a few cars in the parking lot and several dogs chasing each other across the grass. Two or three lone women held children on the teeter-totters and a wind was coming up. The forlorn swings moved on their chains. Kate had a vision of the park at night, totally empty, wind weaving heavily through the trees and children's playthings like a great black fish about to surface. She felt a chill on her arms. The light had gone darker, quietly, like a minor chord.

"Mom," Kate said, "it's going to storm." Her own voice seemed distant, the sound strained through layers of screen or gauze.

"No," said her mother, "it's going to pass over." She moved her hand to Kate's knee and touched the cloth of her daughter's skirt.

Kate gripped the metal bar at their waists and looked straight ahead. They were rising again and she felt she would scream. She tried to breathe rhythmically, steadily. She felt the immense weight of the air as they moved through it.

They came almost to the top and stopped. The little car swayed back and forth.

"You're sick, aren't you," her mother said.

Kate shook her head. Below them the grass seemed to glitter coldly, like a sea. Kate sat wordless, feeling the touch of her mother's hand. The hand moved away and Kate felt the absence of the warmth.

They looked at each other levelly.

"I know all about it," her mother said, "I know what you haven't told me."

The sky circled around them, a sure gray movement. Kate swallowed calmly and let their gaze grow endless. She saw herself in her mother's wide brown eyes and felt she was falling slowly into them.

BRIDGING

by

MAX APPLE
(b. 1941)

Born in Michigan, Max Apple teaches at Rice University in Texas;
he has received an award from the Texas Institute of Letters for his
witty writings, which usually have a serious social purpose. His
works include Zip *(1978),* The Oranging of America *(1981), and*
Free Agents *(1984), a collection of short fictional and nonfictional*
pieces, many of which are about his two children. A novel, The
Propheteers, *was published in 1987.*

At the Astrodome, Nolan Ryan is shaving the corners. He's going through
the Giants in order. The radio announcer is not even mentioning that by
the sixth the Giants haven't had a hit. The K's mount on the scoreboard.
Tonight Nolan passes the Big Train and is now the all-time strikeout
king. He's almost as old as I am and he still throws nothing but smoke.
His fastball is an aspirin; batters tear their tendons lunging for his curve.
Jessica and I have season tickets, but tonight she's home listening and
I'm in the basement of St. Anne's Church watching Kay Randall's fingertips. Kay is holding her hands out from her chest, her fingertips on each
other. Her fingers move a little as she talks and I can hear her nails click
when they meet. That's how close I'm sitting.

Kay is talking about "bridging"; that's what her arched fingers
represent.

"Bridging," she says, "is the way Brownies become Girl Scouts.
It's a slow steady process. It's not easy, but we allow a whole year for
bridging."

Eleven girls in brown shirts with red bandannas at their neck are imi-
tating Kay as she talks. They hold their stumpy chewed fingertips out
and bridge them. So do I.

I brought the paste tonight and the stick-on gold stars and the thread
for sewing buttonholes.

"I feel a little awkward," Kay Randall said on the phone, "asking a
man to do these errands . . . but that's my problem, not yours. Just bring

the supplies and try to be at the church meeting room a few minutes before seven."

I arrive a half hour early.

"You're off your rocker," Jessica says. She begs me to drop her at the Astrodome on my way to the Girl Scout meeting. "After the game, I'll meet you at the main souvenir stand on the first level. They stay open an hour after the game. I'll be all right. There are cops and ushers every five yards."

She can't believe that I am missing this game to perform my functions as an assistant Girl Scout leader. Our Girl Scout battle has been going on for two months.

"Girl Scouts is stupid," Jessica says. "Who wants to sell cookies and sew buttons and walk around wearing stupid old badges?"

When she agreed to go to the first meeting, I was so happy I volunteered to become an assistant leader. After the meeting, Jessica went directly to the car the way she does after school, after a birthday party, after a ball game, after anything. A straight line to the car. No jabbering with girlfriends, no smiles, no dallying, just right to the car. She slides into the back seat, belts in, and braces herself for destruction. It has already happened once.

I swoop past five thousand years of stereotypes and accept my assistant leader's packet and credentials.

"I'm sure there have been other men in the movement," Kay says, "we just haven't had any in our district. It will be good for the girls."

Not for my Jessica. She won't bridge, she won't budge.

"I know why you're doing this," she says. "You think that because I don't have a mother, Kay Randall and the Girl Scouts will help me. That's crazy. And I know that Sharon is supposed to be like a mother too. Why don't you just leave me alone."

Sharon is Jessica's therapist. Jessica sees her twice a week. Sharon and I have a meeting once a month.

"We have a lot of shy girls," Kay Randall tells me. "Scouting brings them out. Believe me, it's hard to stay shy when you're nine years old and you're sharing a tent with six other girls. You have to count on each other, you have to communicate."

I imagine Jessica zipping up in her sleeping bag, mumbling good night to anyone who first says it to her, then closing her eyes and hating me for sending her out among the happy.

"She likes all sports, especially baseball," I tell my leader.

"There's room for baseball in scouting," Kay says. "Once a year the whole district goes to a game. They mention us on the big scoreboard."

"Jessica and I go to all the home games. We're real fans."

Kay smiles.

"That's why I want her in Girl Scouts. You know, I want her to go to things with her girlfriends instead of always hanging around with me at ball games."

"I understand," Kay says. "It's part of bridging."

With Sharon the term is "separation anxiety." That's the fastball, "bridging" is the curve. Amid all their magic words I feel as if Jessica and I are standing at home plate blindfolded.

While I await Kay and the members of Troop III, District 6, I eye St. Anne in her grotto and St. Gregory and St. Thomas. Their hands are folded as if they started out bridging, ended up praying.

In October the principal sent Jessica home from school because Mrs. Simmons caught her in spelling class listening to the World Series through an earphone.

"It's against the school policy," Mrs. Simmons said. "Jessica understands school policy. We confiscate radios and send the child home."

"I'm glad," Jessica said. "It was a cheap-o radio. Now I can watch the TV with you."

They sent her home in the middle of the sixth game. I let her stay home for the seventh too.

The Brewers are her favorite American League team. She likes Rollie Fingers, and especially Robin Yount.

"Does Yount go in the hole better than Harvey Kuenn used to?"

"You bet," I tell her. "Kuenn was never a great fielder but he could hit three hundred with his eyes closed."

Kuenn is the Brewers' manager. He has an artificial leg and can barely make it up the dugout steps, but when I was Jessica's age and the Tigers were my team, Kuenn used to stand at the plate, tap the corners with his bat, spit some tobacco juice, and knock liners up the alley.

She took the Brewers' loss hard.

"If Fingers wasn't hurt they would have squashed the Cards, wouldn't they?"

I agreed.

"But I'm glad for Andujar."

We had Andujar's autograph. Once we met him at a McDonald's. He was a relief pitcher then, an erratic right-hander. In St. Louis he improved. I was happy to get his name on a napkin. Jessica shook his hand.

One night after I read her a story, she said, "Daddy, if we were rich could we go to the away games too? I mean, if you didn't have to be at work every day."

"Probably we could," I said, "but wouldn't it get boring? We'd have to stay at hotels and eat in restaurants. Even the players get sick of it."

"Are you kidding?" she said. "I'd never get sick of it."

"Jessica has fantasies of being with you forever, following baseball or whatever," Sharon says. "All she's trying to do is please you. Since she lost her mother she feels that you and she are alone in the world. She doesn't want to let anyone or anything else into that unit, the two of you. She's afraid of any more losses. And, of course, her greatest worry is about losing you."

"You know," I tell Sharon, "that's pretty much how I feel too."

MAX APPLE

"Of course it is," she says. "I'm glad to hear you say it."

Sharon is glad to hear me say almost anything. When I complain that her $100-a-week fee would buy a lot of peanut butter sandwiches, she says she is "glad to hear me expressing my anger."

"Sharon's not fooling me," Jessica says. "I know that she thinks drawing those pictures is supposed to make me feel better or something. You're just wasting your money. There's nothing wrong with me."

"It's a long, difficult, expensive process," Sharon says. "You and Jessica have lost a lot. Jessica is going to have to learn to trust the world again. It would help if you could do it too."

So I decide to trust Girl Scouts. First Girl Scouts, then the world. I make my stand at the meeting of Kay Randall's fingertips. While Nolan Ryan breaks Walter Johnson's strikeout record and pitches a two-hit shutout, I pass out paste and thread to nine-year-olds who are sticking and sewing their lives together in ways Jessica and I can't.

II

Scouting is not altogether new to me. I was a Cub Scout. I owned a blue beanie and I remember very well my den mother, Mrs. Clark. A den mother made perfect sense to me then and still does. Maybe that's why I don't feel uncomfortable being a Girl Scout assistant leader.

We had no den father. Mr. Clark was only a photograph on the living room wall, the tiny living room where we held our monthly meetings. Mr. Clark was killed in the Korean War. His son John was in the troop. John was stocky but Mrs. Clark was huge. She couldn't sit on a regular chair, only on a couch or a stool without sides. She was the cashier in the convenience store beneath their apartment. The story we heard was that Walt, the old man who owned the store, felt sorry for her and gave her the job. He was her landlord too. She sat on a swivel stool and rang up the purchases.

We met at the store and watched while she locked the door; then we followed her up the steep staircase to her three-room apartment. She carried two wet glass bottles of milk. Her body took up the entire width of the staircase. She passed the banisters the way semi trucks pass each other on a narrow highway.

We were ten years old, a time when everything is funny, especially fat people. But I don't remember anyone ever laughing about Mrs. Clark. She had great dignity and character. So did John. I didn't know what to call it then, but I knew John was someone you could always trust.

She passed out milk and cookies, then John collected the cups and washed them. They didn't even have a television set. The only decoration in the room that barely held all of us was Mr. Clark's picture on the wall. We saw him in his uniform and we knew he died in Korea defending his country. We were little boys in blue beanies drinking milk in the apartment of a hero. Through that aura I came to scouting. I wanted Kay Randall to have all of Mrs. Clark's dignity.

THE MOTHER

When she took a deep breath and then bridged, Kay Randall had no-
ticeable armpits. Her wide shoulders slithered into a tiny rib cage. Her
armpits were like bridges. She said "bridging" like a mantra, holding her
hands before her for about thirty seconds at the start of each meeting.

"A promise is a promise," I told Jessica. "I signed up to be a leader,
and I'm going to do it with you or without you."

"But you didn't even ask me if I liked it. You just signed up without
talking it over."

"That's true; that's why I'm not going to force you to go along. It was
my choice."

"What can you like about it? I hate Melissa Randall. She always has a
cold."

"Her mother is a good leader."

"How do you know?"

"She's my boss. I've got to like her, don't I?" I hugged Jessica. "C'mon,
honey, give it a chance. What do you have to lose?"

"If you make me go I'll do it, but if I have a choice I won't."

Every other Tuesday, Karen, the fifteen-year-old Greek girl who lives
on the corner, babysits Jessica while I go to the Scout meetings. We talk
about field trips and how to earn merit badges. The girls giggle when Kay
pins a promptness badge on me, my first.

Jessica thinks it's hilarious. She tells me to wear it to work.

Sometimes when I watch Jessica brush her hair and tie her ponytail
and make up her lunch kit I start to think that maybe I should just relax
and stop the therapy and the scouting and all my not-so-subtle attempts
to get her to invite friends over. I start to think that, in spite of everything, she's a good student and she's got a sense of humor. She's barely
nine years old. She'll grow up like everyone else does. John Clark did it
without a father; she'll do it without a mother. I start to wonder if Jessica
seems to the girls in her class the way John Clark seemed to me: dignified, serious, almost an adult even while we were playing. I admired him.
Maybe the girls in her class admire her. But John had that hero on the
wall, his father in a uniform, dead for reasons John and all the rest of us
understood.

My Jessica had to explain a neurologic disease she couldn't even pro-
nounce. "I hate it when people ask me about Mom," she says. "I just tell
them she fell off the Empire State Building."

III

Before our first field trip I go to Kay's house for a planning session.
We're going to collect wildflowers in East Texas. It's a one-day trip. I
arranged to rent the school bus.

I told Jessica that she could go on the trip even though she wasn't a
troop member, but she refused.

We sit on colonial furniture in Kay's den. She brings in coffee and we
go over the supply list. Another troop is joining ours so there will be

twenty-two girls, three women, and me, a busload among the bluebonnets.

"We have to be sure the girls understand that the bluebonnets they
pick are on private land and that we have permission to pick them. Otherwise they might pick them along the roadside, which is against the law."

I imagine all twenty-two of them behind bars for picking bluebonnets
and Jessica laughing while I scramble for bail money.

I keep noticing Kay's hands. I notice them as she pours coffee, as she
checks off the items on the list, as she gestures. I keep expecting her
to bridge. She has large, solid, confident hands. When she finishes bridging I sometimes feel like clapping the way people do after the national
anthem.

"I admire you," she tells me. "I admire you for going ahead with Scouts
even though your daughter rejects it. She'll get a lot out of it indirectly
from you."

Kay Randall is thirty-three, divorced, and has a Bluebird too. Her older
daughter is one of the stubby-fingered girls, Melissa. Jessica is right;
Melissa always has a cold.

Kay teaches fifth grade and has been divorced for three years. I am the
first assistant she's ever had.

"My husband, Bill, never helped with Scouts," Kay says. "He was
pretty much turned off to everything except his business and drinking.
When we separated I can't honestly say I missed him; he'd never been
there. I don't think the girls miss him either. He only sees them about
once a month. He has girlfriends, and his business is doing very well. I
guess he has what he wants."

"And you?"

She uses one of those wonderful hands to move the hair away from
her eyes, a gesture that makes her seem very young.

"I guess I do too. I've got the girls and my job. I'm lonesome, though.
It's not exactly what I wanted."

We both think about what might have been as we sit beside her glass
coffeepot with our lists of sachet supplies. If she was Barbra Streisand
and I Robert Redford and the music started playing in the background to
give us a clue and there was a long close-up of our lips, we might just
fade into middle age together. But Melissa called for Mom because her
mosquito bite was bleeding where she scratched it. And I had an angry
daughter waiting for me. And all Kay and I had in common was Girl
Scouts. We were both smart enough to know it. When Kay looked at me
before going to put alcohol on the mosquito bite, our mutual sadness
dripped from us like the last drops of coffee through the grinds.

"You really missed something tonight," Jessica tells me. "The Astros
did a double steal. I've never seen one before. In the fourth they sent
Thon and Moreno together, and Moreno stole home."

She knows batting averages and won-lost percentages too, just like the
older boys, only they go out to play. Jessica stays in and waits for me.

THE MOTHER

186

During the field trip, while the girls pick flowers to dry and then manufacture into sachets, I think about Jessica at home, probably beside the radio. Juana, our once-a-week cleaning lady, agreed to work on Saturday so she could stay with Jessica while I took the all-day field trip.

It was no small event. In the eight months since Vicki died I had not gone away for an entire day.

I made waffles in the waffle iron for her before I left, but she hardly ate.

"If you want anything, just ask Juana."

"Juana doesn't speak English."

"She understands, that's enough."

"Maybe for you it's enough."

"Honey, I told you, you can come; there's plenty of room on the bus. It's not too late for you to change your mind."

"It's not too late for you either. There's going to be plenty of other leaders there. You don't have to go. You're just doing this to be mean to me."

I'm ready for this. I spent an hour with Sharon steeling myself. "Before she can leave you," Sharon said, "you'll have to show her that you can leave. Nothing's going to happen to her. And don't let her be sick that day either."

Jessica is too smart to pull the "I don't feel good" routine. Instead she becomes more silent, more unhappy looking than usual. She stays in her pajamas while I wash the dishes and get ready to leave.

I didn't notice the sadness as it was coming upon Jessica. It must have happened gradually in the years of Vicki's decline, the years in which I paid so little attention to my daughter. There were times when Jessica seemed to recognize the truth more than I did.

As my Scouts picked their wildflowers, I remembered the last outing I had planned for us. It was going to be a Fourth of July picnic with some friends in Austin. I stopped at the bank and got $200 in cash for the long weekend. But when I came home Vicki was too sick to move and the air conditioner had broken. I called our friends to cancel the picnic; then I took Jessica to the mall with me to buy a fan. I bought the biggest one they had, a 58-inch oscillating model that sounded like a hurricane. It could cool 10,000 square feet, but it wasn't enough.

Vicki was home sitting blankly in front of the TV set. The fan could move eight tons of air an hour, but I wanted it to save my wife. I wanted a fan that would blow the whole earth out of its orbit.

I had $50 left. I gave it to Jessica and told her to buy anything she wanted.

"Whenever you're sad, Daddy, you want to buy me things." She put the money back in my pocket. "It won't help." She was seven years old, holding my hand tightly in the appliance department at J. C. Penney's.

I watched Melissa sniffle even more among the wildflowers, and I pointed out the names of various flowers to Carol and JoAnne and Sue and Linda and Rebecca, who were by now used to me and treated me

MAX APPLE
187

pretty much as they treated Kay. I noticed that the Girl Scout flower book had very accurate photographs that made it easy to identify the bluebonnets and buttercups and poppies. There were also several varieties of wild grasses.

We were only 70 miles from home on some land a wealthy rancher long ago donated to the Girl Scouts. The girls bending among the flowers seemed to have been quickly transformed by the colorful meadow. The gigglers and monotonous singers on the bus were now, like the bees, sucking strength from the beauty around them. Kay was in the midst of them and so, I realized, was I, not watching and keeping score and admiring from the distance but a participant, a player.

JoAnne and Carol sneaked up from behind me and dropped some dandelions down my back. I chased them; then I helped the other leaders pour the Kool-Aid and distribute the Baggies and the name tags for each girl's flowers.

My daughter is home listening to a ball game, I thought, and I'm out here having fun with nine-year-olds. It's upside down.

When I came home with dandelion fragments still on my back, Juana had cleaned the house and I could smell the taco sauce in the kitchen. Jessica was in her room. I suspected that she had spent the day listless and tearful, although I had asked her to invite a friend over.

"I had a lot of fun, honey, but I missed you."

She hugged me and cried against my shoulder. I felt like holding her the way I used to when she was an infant, the way I rocked her to sleep. But she was a big girl now and needed not sleep but wakefulness.

"I heard on the news that the Rockets signed Ralph Sampson," she sobbed, "and you hardly ever take me to any pro basketball games."

"But if they have a new center things will be different. With Sampson we'll be contenders. Sure I'll take you."

"Promise?"

"Promise." I promise to take you everywhere, my lovely child, and then to leave you. I'm learning to be a leader.

GRACE

by

VICKIE L. SEARS
(b. 1941)

A social worker in Seattle, Vickie Sears has had more than twenty years of experience counseling people of all ages and from a wide variety of ethnic backgrounds. Born in San Diego to a Cherokee father and a Spanish-English mother, she and her brother spent years in foster homes after their parents divorced. She worked her way through college as a maid and typist, then through professional school using her skills as an English major. Since 1983 she has worked part-time in private practice in order to have time to write. Drawing on her life experience, she has written articles on sexual abuse, lesbian couples, and feminist professional ethics, as well as two volumes of fiction, Simple Songs: Stories *(1990) and* One of Them Kids *(1990), a novel from which "Grace" is taken.*

I thought we were going to another farm because it was time for spring planting. But the lady, she said we were going to be her children. You know how it is grownups talk. You can't trust them for nothing. I just kept telling my brother that we best keep thinking on ourselves as orphans. Our parents got a divorce and we don't know where they are, so we need to keep our thinking straight and not get fooled by this lady. I don't care if her skin is brown just like us, that don't mean nothing.

I hear my brother dozing off to sleep and I want to shake him, wake up, but these people are driving this truck and they can hear everything I say anyhow, so I just let him sleep.

This is the second time we've been riding in this old beat-up green pickup. The first time they came and got us from the children's home they took us down to Pioneer Square. I could see right away they was farm people by the truck having straw in the back and them not having real good clothes, like they wear in the city. City people talk more too. These people were real quiet right off. They answered the questions the orphanage people asked them but they didn't tell them much of anything. I guess I liked that some, but I wasn't going to tell them nothing about me. Who knew what they'd do? We never went nowheres before with brown people.

The man, he had on bluejeans and a flannel shirt and a jean jacket. His hat was all sweaty and beat up like his long skinny face. His boots was old, too. I guessed they didn't have much money and were needing to get some kids to help them with their work. Probably, we'd stay with them until harvest time and then go back to the orphanage. That happened before, so it didn't matter much anyhow.

The woman was old and skinny. She had hands what was all chewed up and fat at the knuckles and she kept rubbing them all the time. She had white hair with little bits of black ones popping out like they was sorry to be in there by themselves. She had a big nose like our daddy has, if he still is alive, that is. She and the man was brown and talked like my daddy's mother, Grandmother, she talks kind of slow and not so much in English. These people, though, they talked English. They just didn't talk much.

When they said they was going to take us downtown I thought they was going to take us to a tavern because that's where the orphanage lady took me real late one night, to show me where all the Indian women was and what kind of people they are, always being drunk and laying up with men. That woman said that is all us Indian girls like to do and I will be just like that too, so I thought that's where these people would take us, but they didn't. They took us to dinner at this real nice place and let us have soda pop and even bought us a dessert. Me and Brother both got us apple pie, with ice cream, all to ourselves. I started thinking maybe these people are okay, but a part inside of me told me I best not get myself fooled. So I told them they wouldn't want us to live with them because my brother is a sissy and I'm a tomboy. But the lady said, "We like tomboys and Billie Jim looks like he is a strong boy. You both look just fine to us." Then they took us to walk in the square and we stopped by this totem pole. The orphanage lady told me that pole was a pretend God and that was wrong because God was up in heaven and the Indian people was bad who made the pole. This lady, though, she said that the totem pole was to make a song about the dead people and animals and that it was a good and beautiful thing. She had Brother and me feel the inside of the pole. Like listening to its belly. I don't know what she meant by that, but the wood was nice. I liked better what she said about the pole.

We walked around for a while and then they took us back to the orphanage. The lady said they would come back, when all the paper work was done, to get Brother and me, but I thought she was just talking big, so I said "Sure," and me and Brother went inside. We watched them drive away. I didn't think they would come back, but I thought about them being brown just like my daddy and aunts and uncles and Brother and me. They were more brown than us, but I wondered if they were Indian. They didn't drink, though, so maybe not.

We didn't see those people for a long time. Brother and me went to a big house to help clean for spring coming. I don't see why you clean a house so good just because the seasons change, but we done that anyway and then went back to the orphanage. I kept thinking on how nice those farmers were and how they might be Indians, but I didn't want to ask anybody about them. Maybe, if it was for real that they were going to come back for us, it would spoil it to ask about them. Seems like you don't ever get things just because you want them so it's better not to ask.

Then, one day, one of the matrons comes to tell me to find Billie Jim because there are some people come to visit.

My brother was up in a tree hiding from some of the big boys. First, I had to beat up Joey so's he would let Billie Jim come out the tree. We rolled in the dirt fighting and I knew I was going to be in trouble because I was all dirty and there was blood on my face. I thought I would get whomped too for getting in a fight. I spit on my hand to try to clean up my face, but I could see by the scowl on the matron's face that I didn't look so good. I pushed Brother in front of me because he was clean and maybe the people wouldn't see me so much. We went into the visiting room and I saw it was those farmers whose names I didn't remember. They asked the boss man of the home if they could take us now. He said, "Yes. It's so nice to place these 'special' children. I hope they'll be everything you want."

The man reached out his hand and the farmer brought his long arm out his sleeve. The orphanage man pumped his arm up and down, but the farmer just held his still. It was funny to see. The woman, she just barely touched the hand of the man. She was not smiling. I thought something was wrong, but I knew we were going with these people anyhow. I never cared much about where I went, long as the people didn't beat on us with sticks and big belts.

We didn't have to do nothing to get ready because we found our suitcases in the hall by the bottom of the stairs. The boss man gave Brother and me our coats and said, "You be good children and perhaps we won't have to see you here again."

I wanted to tell him I didn't like him, but I just took Brother's hand and we went out the door.

The people went to lots of stores downtown and then we went to lunch again.

I asked them, "Do you use a stick or strap for spanking?"

The man said, "We don't believe in spanking."

Before I could say anything, Billie Jim pinched me under the table and I knew he had to go bathroom. So I said, "Excuse us," and we got up to leave. The lady, she asked Billie Jim, "Do you have to go to the bathroom?"

Brother just shook his head and the woman said, "Paul, you take him."

They left and I worried about Paul messing with Billie Jim. My stomach felt all like throw up. When they came back, I asked Billie Jim, in our secret way, if something happened and he whispered no.

I wondered if these people were going to be all right, but I kept on guard because grownups do weird things all the time, when you never know they're going to.

VICKIE L. SEARS

191

After we ate, we walked and stopped at this drinking fountain what is a statue of Chief Sealth. Paul, he told us what a great man Sealth was and Billie Jim asked, "You know him?"

Both Paul and the woman laughed and Paul said, "No. He lived a long time ago. He's a stranger with a good heart."

Then the woman reached down to take my hand, but I didn't want her to get me, so I told her I had to take care of my brother and took Billie Jim's hand.

So then we were riding in this truck going to some place I never heard of, called Walla Walla. Grace, that's the lady's name, said they lived on a farm with chickens, pigs, a horse, and lots of things growing. She said we can have a place all our very own to grow things. When I sat down next to her, she let me ride by the window. I seen how my legs didn't touch the floor and how long hers were. She wasn't as long as her husband, but way bigger than me. She put my brother in her lap where he went to sleep, with his chubby fingers in her hand, but I stood guard just in case things got weird. Paul said I should help him drive home by looking at the map so he'd know the roads he was going on. I thought that was dumb because I knew he came to the city lots and must know how to get hisself home. I went along with him though, because he seemed to be nice and it was easy for me. I can read real good cause I'm nine years old. I told him that and see that Grace is smiling. She's got wrinkles that come out the corners of her eyes and more that go down her cheeks. She has on a smelly powder that reminds me of cookies. She says that there are lots of other children in neighbors' farms and that they have grandchildren who visit them lots. I guessed I would have to do lots of babysitting.

It's a long long ways to where they live and I couldn't stay awake the whole time. I woke up when Grace said, "Come on, sleepy heads. It's time to go to bed."

She gave my brother to Paul to carry, but I walked by myself, up one step into the house. We went through the kitchen, up some stairs, to the second floor with four bedrooms and a bathroom. She asked me if I have to go to the bathroom and I said yes. She showed me it and then closed the door. That's funny because she didn't stay. After a while, she came to knock and say, "There's a nightgown on your bed. I'll show you where you will sleep."

She took me to a room with only one bed with nobody else in it. I asked her, "Where's Brother going to sleep?"

Grace tried to take my hand to go with her, but I put it behind my back and followed her. She led me down the hall to a room where Billie Jim was already in a bed, all by hisself, sound asleep. Then we went to a room Grace said was for her and Paul and said I could come there if I'm scared or having a bad dream.

I told her, "I don't never have bad dreams and can take care on myself."

She asked me, "May I help you with your nightgown?"

THE MOTHER

Then I knew she was going to do bad things like the orphanage woman and I wanted to grab Billie Jim and run, but I didn't know where I was. I started to back down to where she said to sleep and she said, "It's all right if you don't want any help. Have a good sleep."

She went into her room and I watched until she closed the door. There was a lamp beside the bed and I slept with it on.

The first thing I did the next morning was check on Billie Jim. I asked him if they messed with him and he said no again. Nobody came into the room I was in either. We got dressed together and then went downstairs. Already Paul and Grace were up and at the breakfast table.

Grace asked, "What would you like for breakfast? Pancakes or bacon and eggs?"

Billie Jim said, "We can pick?"

"Sure," Grace said, "all you have to do is to wash your face and hands before coming to table. Can't have you start the day with a dirty face."

We looked on each other and saw we was dirty.

Grace said, "There's a pump here, if you want, or you can go upstairs to the bathroom."

We wanted to use that red pump with the very high handle. I tried to make it give water, but Grace thought she had to help push it down. She put her hand over mine but I moved mine. She smiled though, so I let her pump the water into a tin basin and give me a big brown bar of soap. She said she made it out of pig fat. It smelled icky but it made lots of bubbles.

After we ate, Paul said, "Come on, kids. I'll introduce you to our animal friends."

He put on his hat and opened the green screen door. There wasn't no grass nowhere. Just dirt, except where there was tall stuff growing. Paul told us it was alfalfa and wheat and that it got really high before you cut it. He took us into the barn to show us Henry, who was this old horse what lived there forever.

Out back of the barn was a pen with big fat pigs and a mommy one with some babies. I didn't like them much, but Billie Jim asked if he can touch them and Paul said, "Sure," so Billie Jim went into the pen and one of them pigs ran after him so Billie Jim screamed and the pig pushed him up against the barn wall so Paul had to chase the pig away. Billie Jim done good though and didn't even cry.

Paul walked us to the chicken house and showed us Rhode Island Reds and bantams. He taught us how to fill a basket with eggs by taking them out from under the chickens. I thought the chickens was mean, though, because they tried to bite us. Paul laughed and said as how it will get easier to do. Then we met the cows and Paul tried to teach us to milk them. I couldn't make nothing come out, though Billie Jim got a little. The warm milk tasted icky. We walked all over the place that morning and then we got to ride on a tractor with Paul for a long time.

I was sleepy, but Billie Jim wanted to do more things, so we went down to this wooden bridge which went over this river that Paul showed to us. He said we should be very careful to not fall into the river because it was very fast and we would be drownded.

Down to the bridge, I layed on my tummy and Billie Jim was on his and we poked at knotholes in the wood. The water was so fast it went around and around while it was going all wavery at the same time. When we put sticks through the knotholes, the water would just pull them right away like it was never going get fed another stick. We did that a long time until we heard Grace calling us to lunch.

At the lunch table I asked, "When will we start doing the work we came to do?"

Paul and Grace looked on each other as though I had asked something stupid and then they smiled.

Paul said, "You came to live with us to be just like one of our children. You will have lots of time to play and go to school. You'll have some chores because everybody on a farm has to work. One of you will help feed the chickens. One of you can care for the pigs. You can both help with Henry, and there'll be times when you can ride Henry, all by yourselves, into the woods or across the fields, after you learn to ride him. Other times we will all go to town or picnics or pow-wows or rodeos. Everybody has to have time to play. That's the way it is."

Then Grace said, "I'll teach you how to sew and can and cook, Jodi Ann. You and I will go on special walks and plant a garden together. You too, Billie Jim, if you want. I want us to be friends and happy together."

I heard everything they had to say, but I was waiting, too, for the strange things I was sure they would do. I meant to keep my ears and eyes open just in case we needed to run somewheres.

About three days after going to her house, Grace tells us at breakfast table that, "Today is a good day to plant the garden. What would you like to grow, Billie Jim?"

"Potatoes an' rhubarb!" he says, all excited.

Then she asks me and I said, "Carrots and string beans, ma'am, because they're red and green. It'd be pretty."

She patted my shoulder and said, "Yes, it would be lovely. That's nice you can see that, Jodi."

I put my head down so she wouldn't see me smile.

Grace got this basket with lots of little envelopes and told us, "Come on."

We went outside, round to the side of the house. Paul was waiting, sitting on his tractor. He said, "It's all turned over for you."

Grace said, "Thank you, Paul," to him, and to us she said, "Here's two places for each of you. I'll go down to the other end."

She moved to her place and went down to the ground on knees and hands. Billie Jim and me just stood there because we never planted nothing before. She gave us some envelopes which shook with stuff, but they didn't mean nothing to us. Grace saw us standing and asked, "Have you children ever planted things?"

We shook our heads no so she came over and give us little shovels, like spoons, and took hers and made a little hole and put in a seed and covered it over with dirt. Then she put water on the place. She said, "You just do it like that, all in rows. Then you put the envelope on a stick here at the back of where you're planting. Then we wait for the rain and sunshine to help them grow."

She patted Brother on the hand and went back to where she was working.

We spent a long time doing gardening. The dirt felt good, like stored-up rain smells. We ate lunch by the garden and Grace said, "I think we deserve a walk. Let's go down by the river, kids."

Down to the river, Grace showed us different plants and birds. She knew a lot about birds. She told us the songs by making whistles through her teeth. She tried to show us how to do whistles with grass between her thumbs, but I think my teeth weren't big enough. Billie Jim didn't have a tooth in front, so he couldn't do it either. She showed us these grasses, too, that she said made baskets and we picked some. When we got back to her house, she put them in a big round pan, like for taking baths, and filled it up with water. That night she bit some grass apart with her teeth and showed me how to weave them in a basket. She thought I didn't know how to do this, but my grandmother already showed me before. I forgot some though, so my basket wasn't so good. She said, "You'll get better."

Grace read a story to us, then Billie Jim and me went to bed. When I was going to sleep, I thought on her telling about the birds.

One morning time I woke up extra early. The house was all quiet and I thought to go see some birds. I got dressed and went, real soft, down the stairs. I stopped on hearing noises in the kitchen. I crept up to the door and saw Grace putting water in the coffee pot, then poking embers in the stove. She went back to the sink and stood in the new sun coming in the window. She took one hand in the other and she rubbed on her swollen-up knuckles and all up and down her fingers. She put some stuff, what smelled like Vicks, all over her hands and slow rubbed her knuckles. Then she opened and closed her hands lots   of times and rubbed more. She looked out the window the whole time, making a little smile all the time she was rubbing on her fingers. It looked like she done that lots of times before, so I stood still, so she didn't see me because the sun is so nice on her skin and shining in her hair, kind of like baby rainbows. I just wanted to watch. I did that for a long time and then made sounds like I was just coming down the stairs.

Grace said, "You're up very early, Jodi."

I said, "I wanted to go see birds and stuff."

She said, "If you want to come with me, I'll show you something magic."

She reached out her hand, but I put both arms behind my back and took hold of my own hands. She smiled and opened the door.

"We'll just take a walk over to the alfalfa. I want to show you some colors."

We walked between the wheat and alfalfa, the air all swollen up with their sweetness. Grace pulled down a piece of alfalfa and said, "Smell."

It was all sharp and tickled inside my nose, kind of like medicine. It got dew on it and it landed on my cheek. Grace got some on her nose. I wanted to touch it, but didn't.

Grace said, "See the different colors?"

She ran a finger down the alfalfa and I saw there was places where it was real dark then lighter then sort of like limes are colored. I always thought it was all one color, but I was fooled. Grace did the same thing with the wheat and said, "And here's something else that's wonderful. Look what happens when the sun comes to the plants."

Grace moved them different ways and I saw the light changes the colors, too. It's almost like you can look right through them.

She said, "If we come back at lunch and suppertime, when the sun is in a different place in the sky, they'll be different again. Do you want to?"

"Yeah!" I answered.

"Okay," she said. "It's just for you and me, though, Jodi."

Grace told me about the red-winged blackbird, what I never saw before, while we went back to the house.

Later, Grace called me and we went to see the colors again. They were changed. This time I saw, too, the little hairs each one had, what makes a wheat kernel, all full of lines and different parts just like people.

Then Grace said we had to go get a chicken for dinner. In the chicken yard, there was chickens scratching at the ground and picking in it for bugs. Their heads bobbed up and down and jerked from side to side. It was funny to watch them. Then, all of a sudden, they all ran to the coop. I didn't see no reason for it, but Grace pointed up in the sky and told me, "They see the shadow of the hawk. They're afraid, so they hide because they know hawks like to eat chickens."

The hawk circled awhile but went away and the chickens came back into the yard, scratching and clucking like nothing ever happened. Grace walked around in the yard, looking at all the birds, and finally spied one she liked. She chased it until she caught both the wings flat, with the chicken squawking the whole time we was walking to the clearing between the barn and house, to a stump where I had seen Paul split the kindling. Grace said, "You hold the chicken by the feet and give it a quick clean cut with the ax. Do you want to try it?"

I didn't never think on killing nothing to eat and didn't want to do it. I remembered the wild kitten I made friends with out in the tall grass back at the orphanage. I thought about how one of the orphanage matrons killed the kitten and hung it round my neck and told everybody I killed it. All day I had to wear the kitty, but I didn't cry. I just pretended like the kitty never was important. Now Grace wanted me to kill the chicken and I didn't want to, so I tried to back away, only she said, "I know you are strong enough to do this, Jodi."

She stuck out the handle to the hatchet, but I couldn't take it. I shook my head no and said, real quiet, "I don't want to, ma'am."

I backed up more and she said, "Well, we need supper. You watch and perhaps you'll be able to do it the next time."

Grace took that chicken and held it on the chopping block and chopped off the head so quick I almost didn't see her do it. I jumped back when the blood went flying everywhere, all hot-smelling in the sun, and making dark plops in the pale dust. She let the chicken go and picked up the head and threw it in the garbage. There wasn't no noise except chicken toenails making little scratches in the dry hard dirt and wings trying to fly when the chicken ran around and around. I didn't want to see it do that, but it was hard to stop looking. It ran in circles whole bunches of times and then just fell down, sort of jerking, till it stopped. That's when its eyes looked just like Popsickle kitty and my stomach felt like throw up and I wanted to run. Grace pulled out a big piece of string from her apron pocket and I knew it was going to be just like before, when she said, "Jodi, come on over. We'll string the chicken upside down and take off the feathers."

But I couldn't go near her. I yelled, "No!" and ran into the barn. I climbed the ladder and went behind some hay and pulled it all over me till nobody could see me and stayed real quiet. I sucked in air and didn't give it back. Grace came and called out, "Jodi, I'm sorry if I scared you. It's all right if you don't want to help. Jodi? You don't have to hide. It's all right."

But I was thinking on how I told a grown-up no and didn't do what she said. I knew I was going to get whipped. Paul and Grace would send me and Brother back because I was bad. Billie Jim was going to be all mad with me because we had to leave. Didn't nobody want to keep us if I'm bad and Brother and me most always went to places together.

I stayed in the hayloft a long time. Then I heard Paul and Brother calling me. They was yelling it was suppertime like nothing was wrong. I peeked through the slats of the door to the hayloft and saw Grace standing in the kitchen doorway. She didn't look mad. Paul and Billie Jim was holding hands, walking toward the fields, calling my name. Grace looked up to the barn like she knew I was there and started out to the barn.

I heard her shoes scrape on the rocks in the barn doorway, when she stopped walking. She said, "Hello, old Henry. You need some water, friend?"

The bucket handle squeeked and there was walking. The yard pump handle went crank crank crank and then water gushed into the bucket. Footsteps came back and there was horse tongue slurping, like Henry was real thirsty.

Grace said, "You know, Henry, when I was little, I used to do some of my best thinking sitting in the grass up on a hill behind my house. I guess the best place now would be up in the hayloft. It's the most like a grassy hill right around here."

Then I heard the dry snaps of weighted wood as Grace bent the ladder steps coming up. She was puffing a little when she came to the loft ledge and climbed over. I peeked out the hay and saw her dangling her legs and making a hum.

"Yes sir, Henry, old friend," says Grace, "this feels almost like my hill. If I were little and scared, this might be just the place to come think. I guess I'd know I was in just about the safest place in the world. Everything would be all right up here. After I had things all sorted out, I could come down and run on home to Momma and know she loved me, no matter what."

That was the most I ever heard Grace say in one mouthful of talking. I still didn't make noise, though. She was talking big, but she was still a grown-up. She sat there awhile, swinging her legs and humming. Then she said, "Well, Henry, guess I'll go into the house. I'm getting cold and hungry."

Grace climbed down and I saw her go to the screen door. She stopped and called out, in a loud voice, "Jo-o-o-d-d-i-i!" She waited a little bit then went in the house.

I wanted to think nothing was going to happen, but I knew I was going to get whomped. I had been spending most of the day in the barn but couldn't think on nothing to do, except face the punishment. I went down the ladder and out the barn. I peeked around the corner of the parlor window. Billie Jim was listening to Charlie McCarthy on the radio. He was sitting in Paul's lap while Paul read the paper. Grace was rocking in her chair, knitting. She looked like my really grandmother except my grandmother is short. I missed my grandmother only thinking on her won't do no good so I went around to the back door and slammed it real loud, when I came into the house, and marched right to the living room. Billie Jim jumped up and ran to me and said, "You made us real worried. Where was you?"

He grabbed my arm, but I pulled away and said, "I don't know why you were worried. I was only up to the top of this grassy hill, what I found, thinking about things."

Grace put down her knitting and looked at me. I felt my heart running fast when she looked at Paul. He looked back on her for a little then said, "Was it a nice hill, Jodi?"

I knew I couldn't say no more lies without making spit in my mouth because my throat was all dried up and my tongue would stick and not make words, so I just shrugged a shoulder. Grace stood up and started coming toward me. I figured to just stay where I was to take the hit so I was getting ready. Instead, she said, "I'm glad you're home so we can eat supper. I hope you had a nice adventure too."

She reached me and my body was stiff with waiting, but her arms was out like she was going to hug me. I didn't back down and she closed her arms around me and hugged. I just stood there, still stiff, and she bent down to whisper in my ear, "You've got straw in your hair, Jodi." Then she patted me on the shoulder and we went to the kitchen.

While she was putting food on the platters, Grace said, "Jodi told me she doesn't like fried chicken much, so she doesn't have to eat any if she doesn't want. We even have two nice pork chops here, with mint jelly, just in case Jodi would rather not eat the chicken."

She turned around with a platter filled up with chicken and on the end was the pork chops. They tasted good with jelly. We never got that in the orphanage.

I watched Grace real good the rest of the time before bed, but she never said nothing about the chicken or me not being good. She never said nothing about it ever again.

The April we came in, turned into July with everybody just doing their work and playing too.

We met Jim and Sara and Crystal, Paul and Grace's kids. Between them three, they had twelve kids and, sometimes, everybody came over at once and cousins and other people too. Lots of times we cooked outside and sometimes we ate things we growed in the garden. It was just like at our Daddy's house a long time before, except there weren't no grandparents because Grace and Paul were the grandmother and grandfather. Their parents was dead.

We did lots of things together. Paul taught Brother to fish and both of us to swim. When Brother and him went away for fishing, Grace and me did beading. She showed me how to do beads in a circle. We made lots of things to take to pow-wows. I sold one I made, but Grace sold lots. I made two baskets I liked, but I kept them. We went to a pow-wow over to the reservation and one at White Swan and down to Oregon. Everybody in the family went, in all the trucks, lined up on the highways and we all stopped together to eat.

One day, Paul said to Grace, "Their hair is long enough now. I guess it's time."

Billie Jim looked at me across the table and motioned at me to come with him. He took his short legs up the stairs, as fast as he could, to the bathroom and said, "Hurry up, Jodi."

He only left the door barely open enough for me to squeeze after him and slammed and locked it.

He whisper-yells, "They're gonna cut our hair, Jodi! Don't let 'em do it! Please make 'em not do it, Jodi!"

I asked him, "How come you think they're going to do that, Billie Jim? This ain't the orphanage. They won't cut it off like there. Grace and Paul and everybody, almost, gots long hair."

"But Jodi Ann, didn't you listen when Paul said it was long enough? It means a cutting!"

I started to say more, but Paul called us to, "Come on downstairs, kids, and meet us outside."

We went downstairs and out the door and walked slow to where Grace was standing. She had her hands behind her back. Paul was rolling a big log from the woodpile toward where the chopping block was. Paul set the log up like the block and said, "Okay, kids, we have a surprise for you. Take your seats and face each other."

My stomach was sick and I started to think Billie Jim might be right. When we sat down, I looked on Billie Jim and knew how much of a little kid he was and how I was supposed to take care on him, but it felt like the best thing was to just run away.

Grace stood by me and Paul was by Billie Jim. Paul said, "Okay, Grace, count with me. Ready? One, two, three, now! Surprise!"

When they yelled surprise, all their arms go up and I jumped and grabbed Billie Jim, pulling him off the log, and we ran backwards.

Grace said, "Wait, Jodi! Look!"

In each of their hands were ribbons, streaming out in the breeze.

Paul said, "It's time to teach you how to braid your hair. Come on over."

We walked over, still holding hands, and Paul said, "Okay, now Jodi, you watch me while I do Billie Jim. Then Billie Jim can watch Grace and you."

They slow weaved the ribbons in the shiny black of our hair. In and out go hair and ribbon until the end, when there was just enough to tie the braid tight. We did it to each other until we was real good at it and sometimes Paul and Grace let us braid their hair. We all went to the next family picnic with ribbon braids.

Paul showed us how to ride and take care of Henry, too. We went lots of places all by ourselves on Henry. He never went too fast, but sometimes he tried to scrape us off on trees. Sometimes he liked to go through the barn door with the top part closed. One time he knocked me off and I didn't want to ride no more, but Grace said I got to because Henry would think he won something and wouldn't let me ever ride him again, so we got the box for me to stand on and I got back up.

I got to spend lots of time with Grace. Many mornings I watched her doing her finger rubs while seeing the morning coming, by peeking around the doorway. We went on walks together all the time. She taught me lots about flowers and birds. Most of the time just her and me went, but sometimes we let Brother come. I let her hold my hand sometimes too because it seemed like the bumps in her fingers felt better. Least she always smiled when I let her. She didn't squeeze my hand or put it in her tee-tee. She didn't never put her fingers in mine or play with Billie Jim's pee-pee. Neither did Paul. Brother and me both liked that.

One day, Billie Jim and me was brushing Henry when Grace yelled, "Oh, Jodi and Billie Jim! Come see what Pickles is doing!"

We ran to the other side of the barn by the door, where hay was stacked. There was a big pile not in a bale, so Billie Jim and me could feed the cows and Henry, and there, in the middle of the pile, was Pickles, the cat. She was laying on Paul's bathrobe, sort of all crookedy on her side and making funny noises. Rufus the dog was sitting by her and sometimes Pickles hissed at him when he stuck his nose near her. That was funny to see cause they were friends.

I asked Grace, "What's the matter with Pickles?"

Billie Jim said, "She's sick, you dummy!"

I wanted to pinch him, but Grace took our hands, pulling us into the straw. She said, "You watch and something amazing is going to happen. Pickles is having babies."

We sat forever, but nothing happened except Grace talked real slow and stroked Pickles. Pickles made funny noises and her stomach swelled up and down and moved and she licked her bottom, but that's all. The screen door banged and Billie Jim jumped up, yelling, "I'm gonna get Paul!"

When he was gone, Grace asked, "What are you thinking, Jodi?"

I said, "I don't see how Pickles can make babies and, besides, it's boring."

Grace pulled me up to her lap and told me about how the babies got inside and growed and I thought it was icky and she said, "It takes a long time and lots of hard work to make something as special as a baby. Someday you might want to do it. Here, you pet Pickles too."

It felt good in Grace's lap and we stuck our arms out at the same time to pet Pickles.

Just about that time we heard a squishy noise with a grunt from Pickles. Then this icky stuff came squirting out and then Pickles acted like she couldn't get no air and was panting and then this kitten popped out in a white sack and Pickles bit it open and ate it up and licked the sticky stuff off the kitten. I heard what Grace said, but was thinking on not having no babies if I have to do that.

Billie Jim came back with Paul and Paul said, "Aa-a-y, that's where my bathrobe went. I couldn't find it this morning. You're doing a nice job, Pickles."

He pats her head and she meows to him.

Grace said, "Paul, you take Billie Jim for a walk and tell him some things."

Paul said, "We did that before we came out, Grace."

He put his arm on Billie Jim's shoulder and my brother was smiling like he was full up with something nobody ever knew before.

VICKIE L. SEARS

Paul said, "Let's all sit down together here."

All of us watched Pickles have two more kittens and then Grace said, "Well, it's time to give our new momma a rest. Billie Jim, you bring her some water. Jodi, you run get an egg and put it into a bowl. Rufus, you come inside with me before you get your nose scratched."

Billie Jim and me went lots of times to see Pickles that night. The kittens were all crawling on Pickles' tummy and pushing for milk and making soft cries while Pickles was licking their fur all soft clean. Grace was right that they were beautiful.

In August, everybody in the family came around every day for the harvest. It was real hard work. Brother and me helped too, but mostly the grown-ups did it. Grace and Sara and me cooked lots. Outside the air was all pale green and sort of fuzzy with little pieces of the cutted stuff filling the wind. It smelled real clean and wet even though it was hot days. I liked it except it made me sneeze. Grace said, "It's best if you stay inside, Jodi, and help with cooking. You can make your biscuits."

I made good biscuits. We all worked really hard.

One harvest day, it was after a big rain in the night, Billie Jim and me were playing Huckleberry Finn on these boards we made into a raft, in a pond in the bend of the road. All of a sudden, there was this high scream- ing sound and a long white ambulance coming down our road. It ran fast by us making mud fly all over. We ran after it, up to the house. Jim said, "Stay back kids. Give them room."

Some men went into the house and came back with Paul sleeping in this bed they carried. Paul had a thing on his face with a bag going in and out like wind. Grace came behind him and she looked like she was going to throw up. They speeded away. Everybody else got in the green truck and we went to the hospital where we sat in a hall. Then came a medicine man who sang songs with his rattle, but the nurse people made him sit in the hall too. He didn't care though because he still sang real soft and, whenever there wasn't no nurse around, he went back in the room. After a long time, a doctor came to say, "Each of you can go in, two at a time." Then he went away.

Sara took me in and I see Grace was looking really sad so I look on Paul and knew he was dead. His skin felt all cold and he didn't have no smile. I couldn't think on what it meant. I wanted Grace to make it not be, but she just patted my hand. I wanted to hold hers, but she didn't do nothing but pat me.

A long time later, we went back to the house with Sara. Grace didn't come home for three days. When she saw Brother and me, she said, "Come into the living room, children. I need to talk with you."

Me and Billie Jim went in and Sara and Jim and Crystal were there too. Everybody was all quiet.

Grace said, "In a little while the county car will be here to pick you up because you are going back to the orphanage. They say I'm too old to keep you children by myself. I told them we would be just fine together, but they tell me a woman alone isn't enough. So you have to go."

Billie Jim asked, "Didn't we do enough work?"

I pinched him and he yelped so Grace took my hand and Billie Jim's too, then she said, "You're wonderful children, but they just won't let you stay. But you be strong an' make us all proud of you."

I wanted to run, but I didn't know how come.

Then Grace said, "Let Sara and Crystal help you while I rest here."

Nobody said nothing while we packed up. I saw a car coming what had writing on it. It was the kind that most always takes and gets us from foster homes. It stopped and the driver started honking. Billie Jim and me didn't walk too fast going downstairs, but didn't no one say we were bad because we were slow. Everybody walked by us to say a good-bye except Grace. She took our hands to go out the back door. She knelt down and said "Ouch."

I asked her, "You hurt?"

She just said, "I knelt on a little rock, but it's okay. You be good children. Listen to the Creator like Paul told you and you'll stay strong."

Grace took Billie Jim in a hug and kissed him too. He squeezed her neck and I saw he was crying, but he didn't make no noise. Then she took both my hands. I looked on her big brown knuckles and didn't want to leave watching her in the sun. She hugged me real hard an' I hugged her too. We didn't say nothing and she stood up really slow.

The county man put us in the back seat and started to drive, right away. We both begin to get up on our knees, to see out the back window, but the man yelled to us, "Sit down," so we did and we couldn't see nobody until we went over the bridge and turned onto the highway. Then we saw Grace, still standing still by the door, waving. Billie Jim and me held hands to wave too.

And that's the way it was.

Woman on a Pedestal

Women have been worshipped by both men and women—as saints, goddesses, queens. It is even thought that in their roles as mothers women once ruled the universe, that before there was a rule of men—a patriarchy—society was structured as a matriarchy. Since with very rare exceptions patriarchy has been in effect for all of written history, the existence of matriarchy cannot be proved. But the sense of women as exalted and as worthy of exaltation has persisted in some form or other. Interestingly, Russian legends that preceded the tenth-century influx of Christianity established women as dominant to men, and even today the bonds between mothers and daughters are stronger than heterosexual ones (Gray, 1990). Love for and obedience to exalted women have been accompanied by awe: removed from common understanding, such figures have been feared because of the mysterious powers ascribed to them. This is understandable for those viewed as supernatural; awe is appropriate for religious figures and even for humans with unlimited powers, such as absolute monarchs. But the mixture of love and fear has also been felt for mortal women who share characteristics with supernatural images. For most of human history women were viewed as mysterious because of menstruation and the capacity to bear children; they were also perceived as superhuman if they were unusually beautiful. Though definitions of beauty vary from culture to culture and over time, persons seen as beautiful have generally inspired adoration.

Female beauty has come to be so linked with sexual desire that it is often assumed to be necessary for the perpetuation of the human species, even though it may often stem from a need for self-approval or approval not linked to a sexual relation. Standards of beauty are not usually made by women. The old saying that beauty is in the eye of the beholder shows our understanding that it is a matter of how others perceive us. Yet the desire to embody our culture's standards is felt as compelling. Perhaps the most restrictive of stereotypes—truly a Procrustean bed—ideals of beauty are internalized as goals and the failure to achieve them regarded as personal failure. Efforts to achieve beauty are often secret, adding to the sense of women as mysterious.

In Western culture the exaltation of women occurred in the twelfth century when, particularly in France, the Virgin Mary was glorified and the great Gothic cathedrals built to honor her. Simultaneously with Maryology arose the idealization of women in stories about knights and their pursuit of honor. In this so-called courtly tradition, women were both the inspiration for men and their reward for high achievement—a trophy in a tournament or a reward for carrying out a king's commands. The literature of courtly love included stories not unlike popular romances today; the songs of troubadours are forerunners of modern romantic ballads of love and longing. Often ladies of this period were already wives; absent husbands might ensure their fidelity with chastity belts, since adultery would make the legality of inheritance problematical. Thus, courtly love, though passionate, was generally platonic. This tradition has come down almost into our own time: the lady, who does not initiate courtship, remains aloof from and superior to her suitor. But since she wants to be courted, she wants to be beautiful. Beauty alone may be enough to attract a suitor who can raise a woman's status, as Griselde learned; and beauty can be an avenue to power, as for certain movie stars. Though originally an aristocratic practice, romantic love has become the pervasive ideal for both genders and all classes, to such an extent that it is hard for Westerners to realize that it is not a universal standard. In fact, according to one anthropologist (Lindholm, 1990), probably three-quarters of the cultures of the world have no concept of romantic love; but the contemporary influence of Western culture may make women elsewhere eager to experience it, as well as to have blue eyes and blonde hair.

The first selection in this group succinctly states the justification men feel for anger at beautiful women. Simply because she is beautiful, the old men think that Susanna deserves to be spied on—she is blamed for being the victim of the peeping elders who perceive her beauty as irresistible power. Christina Rossetti evinces the powerlessness experienced by a model her brother Dante Gabriel Rossetti married only after keeping her waiting for several years. The artist painted her as a queen, a young girl, a saint, an angel—his ideal. Seeing only his dream, he is oblivious to her change as she ages and loses hope. The bitter undercurrent of this poem stems from Rossetti's sympathy for her sister-in-law and also from her deep conviction that marriage should occur only between people sharing the same religious beliefs (she refused two suitors not of her faith, even though she otherwise admired them and they thought her beautiful). Certainly such accord, as well as similar class background, propinquity, and intellectual congeniality, is as important as attractiveness as a factor in the choice of a mate. It is also true that sex appeal need not depend on beauty. But women become obsessed with the necessity of being beautiful, as the selections in this section show.

The television play "The Glamour Trap" was part of a series on women for which the anthropologist Margaret Mead was the commentator. The tyranny of the beauty ideal is shown as a young girl, an aging model, and a "temporarily" unemployed businesswoman, try to make themselves into "The Goddess," the ideally beautiful woman, symbolized by a window mannequin. Many young girls go even further and become victims of anorexia or bulimia in their efforts to meet current ideals of thinness. Alta concisely indicates how shame and self-deprecation accompany the need to be "pretty" and how it creates rivalry among women. And Jean Stafford shows the tragic impact of the ideal on a woman who otherwise seems to have everything; Angelica Early dies not for or from love but from shame at her fading beauty. In "Song" William Blake sees a beautiful woman's yielding to the "Prince of Love" as captivity for her. And Kate Wilhelm's chilling science fiction tale shows the enslavement of an actress made into a robot to fake rape and titillate 37 million viewers. As in Adelaide Crapsey's poem, a woman's beauty is sufficient excuse for violation of her as an individual.

The other selections in this section show the effect of beautiful women on men. Keats and Heine were part of nineteenth-century Romanticism, which revived medieval concepts and emphasized the supernatural and strange. Both "La belle Dame" and the Loreley are destructive: they lure men to their deaths simply by existing. For both these seductresses singing is part of their lure; music transcends logical reasoning and thus is seen as feminine and unmanning. The mysterious goddess of love Erzulie Freida, a Haitian parallel to Venus, requires "hundreds of thousands of men" to serve; "toward womankind, Erzulie is implacable." Her voodoo power is absolute because she shares her godhood with the men she chooses: they become exalted and empowered by their enslavement. Like wives' participation in their husbands' status, submission leads to renunciation of individual power. The men in the Erzulie cult are as bemused as those in the Romantic poems; yet Zora Neale Hurston, a seasoned anthropologist, observed their condition in 1938. Romanticism continues to take its toll.

SUSANNA AND THE ELDERS

by

ADELAIDE CRAPSEY
(1878–1914)

*Born in Rochester, New York, Adelaide Crapsey studied at Vassar
and later taught in preparatory schools and at Smith College.
Some of her poems and a major book on English metrics were
published after she died of tuberculosis; her complete poems were
published, along with a biography, in 1977. She invented a new
poetic form, the cinquain, a five-line form akin to the Japanese
haiku and tanka.*

• ———————————————— •

"Why do
You thus devise
Evil against her?" "For that
She is beautiful, delicate:
Therefore."

IN AN ARTIST'S STUDIO

by

CHRISTINA ROSSETTI
(1830–1894)

Christina Rossetti, born in London of an Italian father and a half-English mother, lived a quiet life at home, a semi-invalid who took care of her mother and was always in the shadow of her famous brothers. Intensely devout, she wrote several works on religion. On the edge of a group of painters and poets called the Pre-Raphaelites, she published The Goblin Market and Other Poems *(1862) before her brothers' works appeared. Biographers have guessed at the inspiration for her highly erotic poetry—a specific secret lover, a passion for God, or latent homosexuality. Although she remains enigmatic, her three volumes of poetry include some of the most admired poems in English.*

One face looks out from all his canvases,
   One selfsame figure sits or walks or leans:
   We found her hidden just behind those screens,
That mirror gave back all her loveliness.
A queen in opal or in ruby dress,
   A nameless girl in freshest summer-greens,
   A saint, an angel—every canvas means
The same one meaning, neither more nor less.
He feeds upon her face by day and night,
   And she with true kind eyes looks back on him.
Fair as the moon and joyful as the light:
   Not wan with waiting, not with sorrow dim;
Not as she is, but was when hope shone bright;
   Not as she is, but as she fills his dream.

THE GLAMOUR TRAP

by

GEORGE LEFFERTS
(b. 1921)

Born in New Jersey, George Lefferts has spent most of his life in New York City as a writer of film scripts and plays and as a director and producer of television programs, ranging from series such as the Hallmark Hall of Fame *to special reports on health and for children. He has won more than twenty awards, including three for his series "Specials for Women," from which* The Glamour Trap *is taken. He holds degrees in both engineering and English and has won an award for his sculpture.*

• ———————————————— •

PROLOGUE

(Fade in: Exterior of Beauty Salon.)
(Music: Flutelike theme.)
(In the window of a small, elegant beauty salon we see a modish, cold mannikin. The plaster figure, imperious, regal, dominates the scene. Four women stand before the mannikin, looking up in an attitude of supplication. The camera moves back to reveal the sign on the marquee of the salon. It reads "The Glamour Trap." The women file into the shop. The camera follows them and stops on the Operator, a matronly woman of fifty.)

OPERATOR   I'm the operator of a small, elegant beauty salon. This is my shop. I would like you to meet some of my customers. We won't pretend that they are a cross-section of American women, but they do reflect many of the attitudes and fears that accompany the cult of youth and beauty worship. Let's look at today's appointments.

(Reads from appointment book.)

Goldsmith.

(Cut to Linda Goldsmith, sixteen, reading.)

Burnett.

WOMAN ON A PEDESTAL

(Cut to Laura Burnett, a fashion model, examining herself in a pocket mirror.)

Carlin.

(Cut to Jane Carlin, a plain-looking girl, tall and slender. She looks at the model enviously.)

Ciardi.

(Cut to Mrs. Helen Ciardi, a housewife, slightly worn-looking. She has rushed down for an appointment, is taking off her gloves and hat.)

(Cut back to Operator.)

(She points to the mannikin in the window.)

OPERATOR   This is "The Goddess!"

(Pan slowly up mannikin.)

The "Look."

(Stop at head.)

The unattainable Ideal.

(Start to push in.)

Sixty million women spend five billion dollars a year trying to look like this hunk of plaster.

(Music: Up and under.)

(The camera pushes past her and the scene dissolves into a surrealist beauty parlor. We see a montage of women being massaged, mud-packed, oiled, painted and patted. Rows of female faces seem to approach us like items coming off an assembly line. As the faces approach, they acquire a certain similarity, until they are no longer human. They begin gradually to lose their individual characteristics until the last of them are entirely faceless.)

OPERATOR   They come here to be patted and dried and oiled and dyed. They come to be rolled and massaged and packed and painted until often there's nothing left of the original woman. And, when they start to look like The Goddess, the fashion boys disassemble her and change the "Look."

(The Operator closes the appointment book with a snap.)

OPERATOR   If you'd like to come in and wait, it'll only be about an hour.

(Music: Curtain.)

ACT ONE

(Fade in: The Beauty Salon. The Operator stands behind the row of chairs, each occupied by a customer.)

OPERATOR   They come here, these women, as if it were a temple. A few come for sanctuary—just to get away from the grind. Others pray for a miracle. Some come routinely out of a sense of obligation. And some—

(She walks along and stops behind Linda, the sixteen-year-old.)

—come because they've been promised too much.

(Linda reads a glamour magazine, totally absorbed, as we hear the imaginary voice of the magazine's beauty expert.)

SEDUCTIVE VOICE   "Remember, lovely starlet Gloria Gage was discovered while working as a carhop in Los Angeles by a producer who was attracted by her flaming red hair."

(Linda turns the page. The Operator comes and stands behind her.)

SEDUCTIVE VOICE   "Proof of the old saying 'When you are beautiful, wonderful things will happen' is Grace Kelly who went from movie stardom to the role of Princess. . . ."

OPERATOR   Hello, Linda.

LINDA   Oh, Hello.

OPERATOR   How's your mother?

LINDA   She's fine, thank you.

OPERATOR   What'll it be today, permanent the ends again?

LINDA   No. I—want to cut it off.

OPERATOR   Oh?

LINDA   Yes, I—I think I should look more sophisticated, don't you?

OPERATOR   Does your mother know about this?

LINDA   Yes. She suggested it.

OPERATOR   Oh.

LINDA   It's a big step but I think I should take it.

OPERATOR   Well—you're a big girl now, Linda. How old are you?

LINDA   Sixteen.

OPERATOR   Sixteen! My! My!

LINDA   Daddy says my hair is beautiful.

OPERATOR   It's very nice.

LINDA   He calls me Alice in Wonderland. He says my long hair makes me different from all the others.

OPERATOR   Does he know you're cutting it?

LINDA He and Ma had a fight about it. Men don't understand about these things.

OPERATOR I know. I know. How do you want it?

LINDA I'm not really sure.

OPERATOR Suppose we cut it close—

LINDA That'll make my chin bigger. Mother says I have a big chin.

OPERATOR We can always tease it out at the sides.

LINDA My eyes are too close together.

OPERATOR You have nice eyes.

LINDA They're nice but they're close set. I'm half blind without my glasses.

OPERATOR I think you'd look cute in a feather cut.

LINDA I'd like something a little more swingy. I'm going out for cheerleader this fall.

OPERATOR Why don't you look through the magazine while I comb it out?

(She starts to comb Linda's hair as we hear her thoughts.)

OPERATOR'S THOUGHTS I used to have hair like this. I guess all fathers are the same. I remember the day I cut it off. It was like cutting off a piece of myself—the piece that made me different from the rest.

OPERATOR *(Aloud.)* Find anything?

LINDA Here's a style called "Mushroom Cloud." They say that fallout can make you lose your hair.

OPERATOR I wouldn't know about that.

LINDA I don't see any styles with long hair.

OPERATOR Why don't you think about it for a few minutes and I'll start on another customer, O.K.?

(Operator walks off and we hold on Linda's face as we hear her thoughts.)

LINDA'S THOUGHTS Am I pretty? Mama says I'm pretty. I think she's pretty, but she says her eyes are too close together. She said once if she were prettier she could have married a rich man. I wonder how much it costs to have your hair cut and dyed and permanented. Daddy likes my hair this way. It's hard to tell if you're pretty. Sometimes I think maybe— I'm not. Maybe she's just saying it. She must be telling the truth. If you're pretty, wonderful things will happen—dates and romance and marrying the right man—

(Fade out.)
(Fade in: The Beauty Parlor.)
(The Operator stands behind Laura, the professional model.)

OPERATOR   If you want to know the most intimate details about a woman ask her hairdresser. She'll tell her things she only tells her psychoanalyst and her obstetrician. *(Indicates Laura.)* This is Laura Burnett. Laura is a model. She comes here once, sometimes twice a week . . . more often, recently. She spends anywhere from twenty to fifty dollars a visit. For some years now Laura has lived in the world of high fashion—in the rarefied air of *Vogue* and *Harper's Bazaar*—where glamour is not fun, it's a deadly serious business; where the word "modest" is applied only to the price tag.

(Operator crosses up to Laura and greets her.)

OPERATOR   Hello, Laura.

LAURA   Oh, hello, Marie. Say, have you got a cigarette? I seem to be out.

(The Operator gives her a cigarette. Laura tries to light it but her hand is shaking.)

LAURA   It's these damn diet pills. Every time I take them I start to shake . . . .

(She finally lights the cigarette and takes a deep puff.)

They keep me awake, too.

OPERATOR   What can we do for you today?

LAURA   I—uh—I have an important interview this afternoon. I have to get myself into some kind of shape—shampoo, set, the works.

OPERATOR   Modeling job?

LAURA   No—I've decided to quit.

OPERATOR   No kidding?

LAURA   Yes. Really. I—met this gentleman—he, uh—he read some things I wrote when I was a kid. He thought they were very good and he's introducing me to a publisher of a magazine. Editorial job.

OPERATOR   That's great. I didn't know you wrote.

LAURA   Oh, just poetry and stuff. But he was really impressed; he says I have a nice style.

OPERATOR   Well, we have to get you really right. How about a facial?

LAURA   Use plenty of astringent, see if you can tighten up the skin somehow, I look ghastly—

(The Operator begins to drape her with a shoulder slip.)

Oh Marie, I'm expecting a call. It's really important. Would you make sure I get it?

OPERATOR   Of course.

LAURA   I'm a little nervous about it.

OPERATOR   Just relax.

LAURA   He really seemed impressed by what I wrote, I don't think he was putting me on.

OPERATOR   I'm sure he wasn't.

LAURA   I could stay in the modeling business but it's such a rat-race.

OPERATOR   I'll never forget that beautiful cover you did for *Charm Girl*.

LAURA   Yes. That was a nice job. Tibor photographed it—he's a genius with a camera.

OPERATOR   What have you been up to lately?

LAURA   Well, not much, really. I haven't been accepting any of those dreary jobs. I've even been considering getting married.

OPERATOR   Well, well! Who's the lucky man?

LAURA   The man I told you about—the one who likes my poems.

OPERATOR   Oh.

(The camera moves in for a close-up of Laura as the Operator starts to massage her face and neck under a heat lamp.)

LAURA'S THOUGHTS   Please, God, just let me quiet down inside. It wasn't supposed to happen this way. When did I sleep last? About a million years ago? That heat feels good—if it could only reach inside. . . .

OPERATOR   There now, you just let that relax your muscles. I'll be right back.

(Camera moves across to the teen-ager, Linda. She turns to look at the model.)

LINDA'S THOUGHTS   When I'm older, I want to look like her—I want everybody to turn and notice me.

OPERATOR   Well, young lady?

LINDA   *(Determined.)* Cut it!

OPERATOR   Sure?

LINDA   Yes.

(The Operator grasps a rope of hair in her hand. With a snip of a large scissors, she begins to cut it off.)

(The camera moves in for a close-up of Linda's face as the montage of voices begins:)

SEDUCTIVE VOICE   "When you're beautiful, wonderful things will happen. . . ."

GEORGE LEFFERTS

215

LINDA'S THOUGHTS   Mama says I'm pretty . . . .

SEDUCTIVE VOICE   "Remember lovely starlet Gloria Gage."

LINDA'S THOUGHTS   Mama says I'm pretty.

SEDUCTIVE VOICE   "Grace Kelly, who became a Princess. . . ."

LINDA'S THOUGHTS   Mama says I'm pretty.
(Voices begin to overlap and get louder.)
SEDUCTIVE VOICE   ". . . wonderful things . . . "

LINDA'S THOUGHTS   I'm pretty.

SEDUCTIVE VOICE   "Gloria Gage."

LINDA'S THOUGHTS   . . . pretty . . . pretty . . . pretty . . .
(Music: Curtain.)

ACT TWO

(Fade in: Beauty Parlor, a little later.)
(Music: Flutelike theme.)
(The Operator comes back to the model and turns off the heat lamp.)

OPERATOR   Feel better?

LAURA   Yes.

OPERATOR   It must be hard being a model. Especially the dieting. . . .
(The camera moves in for a close-up of Laura as we hear her thoughts.)
LAURA'S THOUGHTS   Yes, especially the dieting—and the massages and
the pounding and the wax baths and the exercise and the mudpacks and
the fruit packs and the measuring and the looking in mirrors . . . the
endless, endless mirrors . . .

OPERATOR   What made you decide to give up modeling?

LAURA   Oh—it doesn't lead anywhere. Sooner or later you lose the look
or they change the look. Flat chests come back or small figures.

OPERATOR   Still, it must be nice to see your face on a cover.

LAURA'S THOUGHTS   On a cover. Click. Captured. Click. Laura Burnett in
glorious color. Click. Full-page. But what happens between the pictures?
There should be a life somewhere between the clicks of the cameras,
shouldn't there?

OPERATOR   I'm not surprised you're getting married. A girl like you
shouldn't have any trouble finding a man.

LAURA'S THOUGHTS   No, the trouble wasn't finding them. They found
me. They found me when I was still a kid. They kept after me all the
time, like I was some kind of a prize, or a prestige item.

OPERATOR   It must be nice to have men courting you all the time.

LAURA'S THOUGHTS   Yes, hungry, trying, wanting. And you never know whether it's you that they want or just the idea of a beautiful woman.

OPERATOR   A lot of girls would envy you.

LAURA'S THOUGHTS   Even when I was in school, every date would end in a quarrel over petting. After a while you stop fighting, you just turn cold inside . . . like stone.

OPERATOR   If you do get married you know I wish you all the happiness in the world.

LAURA'S THOUGHTS   And then you start to find the cold men—the ones who want to take a pretty statue to expensive night clubs, nothing else.

OPERATOR   The important thing is love.

LAURA'S THOUGHTS   Love. Alex wants to marry me but he doesn't love me. I wish I could feel something for him but I can't.

OPERATOR   Something has to happen between two people.

LAURA'S THOUGHTS   Maybe if I married him, maybe something would begin to flow—love, children.
(Music: Turns cold.)
LAURA'S THOUGHTS   Maybe it would be just like the others. A stone man and a stone woman. I could bear him a stone child, stone children. We could grow old together—an old stone man and old stone woman.

OPERATOR   Look, I'll have Ann shampoo you as soon as she's free.

LAURA   Thank you.

(Operator walks away. Laura gets off the chair and stands in front of the mirror, smoothing her dress over her hips. She has the trained assurance and composure of the model, aware that the other women are looking at her, that she is closer to "The Look" than any of them. Camera cuts to a close shot of Jane, a slender, plain-looking girl, lacking in self-assurance. She is watching Laura as the Operator stands behind her with her appointment book.)

OPERATOR   *(Indicating plain girl.)* Jane Carlin. Twenty-eight. Unmarried. She comes in about once a month. The Jane Carlins don't come as often as the others but there are so many of them. . . . *(She crosses to Jane.)* Hello, Jane.

JANE   Excuse me, I was just looking at that woman. She's a model, isn't she?

OPERATOR   Yes.

JANE   I can tell from the way she carries herself, with such confidence.

OPERATOR   There's a lot of training behind that poise.

JANE   It must be a glorious feeling.

OPERATOR   I suppose it is, sometimes.

JANE   Look at those cheekbones. *(Sigh.)* Why couldn't it be me?

OPERATOR   What'll it be, a set?

JANE   No, I'd like it styled.

OPERATOR   Any particular way?

JANE   *(Bitter.)* Just change it. Change everything.

(Sound: Salon telephone rings.)

OPERATOR   Will you excuse me a moment?

(She goes to phone. Jane opens a glamour magazine.)
(Music: Theme.)

SEDUCTIVE MAGAZINE VOICE   "Today, right now, promise yourself that you'll be beautiful." *(Jane turns page.)* "You owe it to the man in your life to be as lovely as you are. Let your gift of charm be his treasure." *(Jane turns page.)* "Why not live the exciting life of a blonde?" *(Jane turns page.)* "Highlight your natural beauty with lovely, soft golden hair. Put the *you* in the word 'beauty.'"

(Jane closes the magazine. The camera moves up to her face, her eyes. Her expression is pained. Camera cuts away to the Operator on the telephone.)

OPERATOR   *(On phone.)* Yes? Yes, she is. Just a moment. . . .

(She beckons to the model, Laura, who comes to the phone.) It's for you, Miss Burnett. *(She hands her the phone.)*

LAURA   *(On phone.)* Laura Burnett speaking. Oh, hello. Yes. Yes, I know he spoke to you about me. Dinner? Well, I have an engagement. Couldn't we meet in your office as we planned? I see. Could I come to your office tomorrow? No, I'm afraid I'm busy tomorrow night, Mr. Raymond. Well, perhaps we could discuss it now over the phone. Have you read my material? *(Pause.)* Is there an editorial position open? Oh. I see. Well, there doesn't seem much to discuss. No, Mr. Raymond, I can't meet you. Thank you. *(She hangs up angrily and looks at herself in the mirror as she speaks to the Operator.)* *(Savagely.)* I'll take the whole works, Marie— hair, set, facial, everything. I want to leave here *fit to kill.*

(Music: Curtain.)

ACT THREE

(Fade in: Beauty Salon, a short while later.)
(Jane Carlin is seated in chair as the Operator combs out her hair.)

OPERATOR   Suppose we try it slightly bouffant?

JANE   *(Impatient.)* Look, I don't care what you do to it, one way is as good as another, just so I don't see the same face in the mirror every day. *(Operator nods as if to say "Suit yourself.")* I'm sorry, I don't mean to make it your problem—

OPERATOR   I understand. I'll just comb it out.

(Camera moves in for a close-up of Jane. We hear her thoughts as the Operator continues to talk.)

OPERATOR   Are you still working for that dress house on Market Street? Last time we spoke, I think you were up for promotion.

JANE'S THOUGHTS   Please don't ask me about my job or my dates or how my life is going. Please.

JANE   No, I'm not with Harrison's any more. I left them. I—wasn't very happy there.

OPERATOR   Oh, I see. Are you working somewhere else?

JANE   No, I—I'm looking.

OPERATOR   Oh. What do you hear from home lately?

JANE   I haven't been very good about writing.

OPERATOR   Springfield, wasn't it? Missouri?

JANE   Yes.

OPERATOR   I've never been there.

(Close-up of Jane as we hear her thoughts again.)

JANE'S THOUGHTS   I could tell you about it. I could give you a guided tour. The park, the main street, the high school where I walked home from dances with another girl or all alone. God, I don't ever want to go out again and stand around with a clump of unattractive girls and pretend to have a good time while the others are dancing. . . .

OPERATOR   *(Aloud.)* I think I'm going to try something simple and easy to manage.

JANE'S THOUGHTS   I don't care—just change it. Make it beautiful. Just once—let me know what it feels like to know you're beautiful.

OPERATOR   Have you been skiing this year?

JANE   No, I was supposed to go this week end but I've had so many dates, staying out late—it gets tiresome.

OPERATOR   Most girls complain about the man shortage.

JANE'S THOUGHTS   There was a young man once. He said he liked me. He wanted to see me again. When he was walking away from my house, one of the other boys called to him "You can do better than that, Larry."

GEORGE LEFFERTS

219

He never called again. *(Aloud.)* The trouble is there aren't any *mature* men!

OPERATOR   I think I've heard that one before.

JANE   Well, it's true. I mean by the time a man is twenty-five if he hasn't married a pretty girl he's either a mamma's boy or a counterfeit man or a wolf. The good ones are married.

OPERATOR   Oh, come on now. There must be a few—

JANE   Find me one. I've looked everywhere—the mountain resorts, the ski centers, the beaches. You know what I find? Other hungry girls looking for men.

OPERATOR   Don't you ever meet one who's right?

JANE   I haven't yet.

JANE'S THOUGHTS   There was that boy in the restaurant last night. He kept looking at me. He seemed so lonely. All I had to do was smile.

OPERATOR   Why not?

JANE   The ones I meet aren't my type. If you want them, they don't want you. And when you meet one you do like, there's that awful business of: Should I let him or shouldn't I? Should I phone him when I'm lonely for him or should I play hard to get? Either way you lose.

OPERATOR   Well, I never give advice to my customers, but I don't think you find a man by looking for Mister Right.

JANE   What *do* you look for?

OPERATOR   Yourself.

(Pause.)

JANE'S THOUGHTS   Myself? Who is that? The one who was locked in a room when she was a little girl and thought she was punished for being ugly?

OPERATOR   You mustn't sell bitterness. It's your inner beauty that counts.

(As we hear her thoughts, the camera pushes in beyond her eyes and we begin to see the solitary figure of a woman standing alone on an immense plain. Her body begins to writhe and twist until it assumes the outlines of a twisted tree. The limbs convulse and change shape until the tree seems to be kneeling in supplication.)

JANE'S THOUGHTS   Yes, I have heard this before. "The plain girls with the beautiful souls." Only, being plain in this life does not make you beautiful inside. Being lonely does not strengthen the moral fibre. It twists you, like a bare tree—it makes you jealous—it makes you reach —and it hurts—finally—it hurts.

(They are interrupted by the housewife, a bright-eyed, somewhat-worn little woman, with a great deal of genuine sweetness and vivacity.)

HELEN Excuse me, Marie.

OPERATOR Hello, Mrs. Ciardi!

HELEN And how much longer do I have to wait?

OPERATOR Five minutes. O.K.?

HELEN It's just that I have to get home and feed Harry and the kids before he goes to work. He's playing the band concerts this month—

OPERATOR How is everything?

HELEN Fine.

OPERATOR The baby?

HELEN Just impossible. Gets into everything. Last night he ate Harry's feather.

OPERATOR His what?

HELEN His feather. They use a feather to clean the oboe. *(To Jane.)* My husband's a musician.

OPERATOR Oh.

HELEN My daughter is just crazy about him.

OPERATOR How is she?

HELEN Doing very well. It's quite a thing to see.

OPERATOR I'm glad.

HELEN If it weren't for Harry I wouldn't mind staying here all day, it's such an escape from the house and the kids and all that. I get such a kick out of these fancy magazines. "When traveling in the south of France in August, one must always take a good supply of skin balm to protect one against the mistral." I mean—come on! *(Looks at Jane.)* Excuse me. That looks nice. You have a beautiful face—different. Did you ever notice how models and airline hostesses never say anything with their faces? It's all done with subtitles. Excuse me for being so talkative, I'm with kids all day. Five minutes, Marie?

OPERATOR I promise.

(The housewife returns to her seat.)

OPERATOR There's a *really* beautiful woman. *(Jane looks at her, questioning.)* Here. *(She touches her heart.)*

JANE She seems happy, anyway.

OPERATOR She has her troubles.

JANE   Doesn't everybody?

OPERATOR   Hers aren't the kind you can look at in a mirror.

JANE   You'd never know it.

OPERATOR   Some people don't have time to get all involved with themselves.

JANE   How do you get *un*involved?

OPERATOR   I don't know. I'm only a hairdresser. *(She pulls Jane's hair back, away from her face.)* Suppose we just bring it forward, like that?
(Jane looks at herself in the mirror.)
JANE   Yes. Yes, I like that. It's different. It's me.
(Music: Curtain.)

ACT FOUR

(Fade in: Beauty Salon, a moment later.)
(The housewife, Helen, is talking on telephone.)

HELEN   *(On phone.)* Harry? Helen. She's taking me right now. I'll be home before supper. Do you mind? Yes. How is she? Good. The baby? Again? Leave it, I'll clean it up when I get there. No, don't bother, you'll be working late. *(Pause)* Harry? Wait'll you see me. Oh, come on! I know all about the lady harpist. She's flat-chested. Uh huh. Big talker! I notice you still put your glasses on when I'm dressing to go out. *(Pause.)* Harry? Yes, I do. Yes. Yes, I will. All right, sweetheart. Yes.

(She hangs up and smiles to herself. She crosses to her chair where the Operator is waiting.)

HELEN   What a nut! Did you ever meet my husband?

OPERATOR   Once, when he picked you up to go out to dinner.

HELEN   Oh, that's right.

OPERATOR   I liked him very much.

HELEN   Handsome he ain't, but when he walks into a room you know a man has come in. You know what I mean?

OPERATOR   Yes. What can we do for you today?

HELEN   Just make me glamourous. He's at the age where they notice other women.

OPERATOR   I thought that was every age.

HELEN   Some ages are worse than others.

OPERATOR   Would you like it restyled?

HELEN   No, I like it the way it is—but I want the ends permanented and the gray ones, you know—out! *(Pause.)* Say, how's your sister? She was sick last time I was here.

OPERATOR   She's fine. Thank you for remembering.

HELEN   Did you finally get your apartment fixed up?

OPERATOR   Yes.

HELEN   One of these days—I don't know, it's so expensive with Sally in a special school. . . . Did you know she's going to a special school?

OPERATOR   No. I didn't.

HELEN   It's been very good for her. Nobody gets impatient with her, you know?

OPERATOR   I suppose it's been very trying for you.

HELEN   Trying? I love my daughter. She doesn't have to win any prizes for me. If other people don't understand that's their problem. *(She closes her eyes as the Operator combs out her hair.)* I have friends, nice friends, who tell me it's a burden. I should send her away someplace. Those same people go home and love their dogs and their pet birds—take care of 'em, clean up after 'em, spend money on 'em, walk 'em, feed 'em. They don't send 'em away just because they aren't winning any prizes. My little girl is *alive*—she grows, she looks at the sun and it feels warm, she laughs when the kitten licks her hand, she smiles when we love her, she gets scared when we don't.

(She looks at the Operator.)

You see, I happen to think she's quite a beautiful creature—not the same as everybody else's kid—but Harry and I, we don't look through everybody else's eyes—just our own. Harry told me an Italian saying once: "Not loved that which is beautiful—but beautiful that which is loved." In case it isn't true, though, I like to look pretty for Harry, so do a good job, will you, Marie?

OPERATOR   You don't need a good job—somebody already did one. Excuse me a minute, will you?

(She walks down to the teen-ager whose hair has now been teased into a frenzy on top and sides.)

OPERATOR   All finished, sweetie? How do you like it?

LINDA   I—don't know. What do you think?

OPERATOR   It's very glamourous.

LINDA   *(Convincing herself.)* It isn't—too old is it?

OPERATOR   Well—

LINDA   The other girls are wearing it like this—

OPERATOR   It's the latest thing.

LINDA   I hope my father likes it.

OPERATOR   You can always change it.

LINDA   Yes.

(She looks at herself again, this is terribly important in her young life.)
Yes. Yes, I like it! And it *doesn't* make me look too old. *(She points to the housewife.)* I never want to look old. I never want to look tired like that woman in the end chair.

OPERATOR   You will.

LINDA   No. I'd rather not be alive. I want to be like that model. I want to be beautiful!

OPERATOR'S THOUGHTS   Oh, my baby, you have so much to learn about "beautiful." Beautiful isn't all being young and having high cheekbones. Beautiful is what you feel. Beautiful is the shape of a baby's mouth when it nurses. Beautiful is that special love between a man and a woman. Beautiful is feeling like a part of the whole world—the good and the bad, the suffering and the joyful. Beautiful is helping someone to grow, or to understand, or to live. Some say "beautiful is that which is loved," but most beautiful, I think, is that which loves.

(The camera begins to move away from the Operator, along the row of women in the chairs. As it passes each one, we hear a fragment of her thoughts.)
(Close-up of the teen-ager.)

LINDA'S THOUGHTS   I like it! It makes me look pretty! I like the way I look!

(Close-up of the model.)

LAURA'S THOUGHTS   The trouble with being pretty is, where do you go from there?

(Close-up of the plain girl.)

JANE'S THOUGHTS   Please, God—just once—to know what it feels like—
(Close-up of the housewife.)

HELEN'S THOUGHTS   Harry still likes the way I look—after all these years.

LINDA'S THOUGHTS   —and wonderful things will happen—

LAURA'S THOUGHTS   —if they'd stop pawing me—

JANE'S THOUGHTS   —it twists you, like a tree—

HELEN'S THOUGHTS   —yes, I said, I think she is—

LINDA'S THOUGHTS —Yes, I think I am—

LAURA'S THOUGHTS Why did I have to be—?

JANE'S THOUGHTS If only I could be—

LINDA'S THOUGHTS —beautiful!

LAURA'S THOUGHTS —beautiful!

JANE'S THOUGHTS —beautiful!

HELEN'S THOUGHTS —beautiful!

(The women are gradually silhouetted as the lights fade on the beauty salon. The camera moves back and they recede in the distance leaving only "The Goddess" mannikin in the foreground.)
(Music: Curtain.)

EPILOGUE

(Fade in: Beauty Salon exit and mannikin, closing time.)
(Music: Flute theme.)
(The teen-ager comes out, stops and looks at herself in the mirror as we hear her thoughts.)

LINDA'S THOUGHTS It looks exciting! It makes me feel as if the whole world is going to put its arms around me!

(The model comes out. Stops to examine herself in a pocket-mirror.)

LAURA'S THOUGHTS You're losing it. The facials and the hairdo's don't do it any more. Another six months and it'll be lingerie ads and parties, honey. . . .

(The plain girl comes out, sees her reflection.)

JANE'S THOUGHTS I like it. It makes me look—almost pretty. It's Thursday, I could still get in on that ski week end—

(The housewife comes out and looks at herself.)

HELEN'S THOUGHTS You know Mrs. Ciardi—for an old lady, you're not bad.

(Finally, the Operator comes out, dressed to go home. She locks the salon door, fluffs up her hair and then looks up at "The Goddess"—cold, austere, unattainable.)
(Music: Curtain.)

PRETTY

by

ALTA
(b. 1942)

*Alta (Gerrey), the daughter of a blind piano tuner, grew up in Reno,
Nevada, and began to write poems before she started school. She
founded the Shameless Hussy Press and was a leader of a group of
feminist poets on the West Coast in the 1970s. By 1975 she had
published eleven volumes of what she calls "poetic reporting"—
telling the truth as she sees it in prose poems. "Pretty" is from her
1980 volume* No Visible Means of Support. *A more recent work is*
Deluged with Dudes: Platonic and Erotic Love Poems to Men
(1989).

• ———————————————————— •

*—you know, Alta, yr roomate may be pretty, but
you have that inner beauty that counts—Barry, 1960*

and here we are again, folks, a table of women, 7 of us, & the first thing i
do to assess, my co-workers on Tooth & Nail is look around at all of you
to see who is prettier than i. my lover used to say how i was prettier than
other women in women's lib & i would feel better while feeling worse &
wish it weren't even a consideration. in anybody's mind, including mine,
because it drives me crazy & actually prevents me from enjoying
situations. like i used to hate to go to martha's house because she is, and
i quote, perfectly beautiful. she doesn't even bite her nails. how can i
compete with that munch munch. then i got to know her & the
bitterness is real, cannot be measured; that we really like each other &
could have been friends all that awful lonely year but i was afraid to be
around her & have him look at my lousy skin & big nose & bitten nails
next to her perfect complexion & little nose & nice nails. how could he
possibly want me more than her? everything becomes a handicap: every
time i take a pill i think jesus no man loves a sick wife (to quote
mother). men don't make passes at girls who wear glasses. blondes have
more fun. fat ass. big boobs. clear skin. sheeit.
    then it got so i could count on being the second prettiest woman in
any situation! sitting at the med i would always be able to find one
woman who was prettier & usually not more than one. at any given

party i could always see one woman who was prettier & feel prettier than the rest. even on buses. even in classes. doctors offices. restaurants. dances. no doubt it could have carried over to skating rinks, art shows, family reunions, funerals. we tried grading our looks one time. i gave myself 90 & the therapist asked what would john rate you & i said lower & can you imagine the bottom of that horrible fear? that each year i could only become more afraid because now i've nursed 2 children; now my throat is getting crepey (or whatever it's called); & my thighs will never again be size 10 unless i get emaciated. a horrible fear that drove me to a plastic surgeon who said all he could do with my big nose was to hook it, drove me to try on 7 different bras to nurse with so my boobs wouldn't hang low (do yr boobs hang low? do they wobble to & fro?), drove me to dermatologists to smooth out my skin, drove me to cover my face with makeup, eyeliner, lipstick, mascara, drove me to curl & bleach my hair, drove me to diet, drove me to sit with my fists clenched so no one could see my nails. tell me i'm not oppressed. ask me what i want. tell me you dont like my methods. listen to my life & see that it has been intolerable & leave me the fuck alone.

THE END OF A CAREER

by

JEAN STAFFORD
(1915–1979)

Jean Stafford was educated at the University of Colorado and studied at Heidelberg University for a year before World War II. She was the daughter of a writer of westerns, was married to three prominent writers, and spent her life as a novelist and short story writer. She won an award from Mademoiselle *in 1944, the O. Henry Memorial Award for the best short story of 1955, and the Pulitzer Prize for her collected stories in 1970. Stafford held many fellowships and grants, wrote some books for juveniles, and in 1966 published* A Mother in History, *based on interviews with the mother of Lee Harvey Oswald, who assassinated President Kennedy. Her best-known novels,* The Mountain Lion *(1947) and* The Catherine Wheel *(1952), have been reprinted, and there are two recent full-length biographies.*

• ───────────────────────── •

By those of Angelica Early's friends who were given to hyperbole, she was called, throughout her life, one of the most beautiful women in the world's history. And those of more restraint left history out of their appraisal but said that Mrs. Early was certainly one of the most beautiful of living women. She had been, the legend was, a nymph in her cradle (a doting, bibulous aunt was fond, over cocktails, of describing the queenly baby's pretty bed—gilded and swan-shaped, lined with China silk of a blue that matched the infant eyes, and festooned with Mechlin caught into loops with rosettes), and in her silvery coffin she was a goddess. At her funeral, her friends mourned with as much bitterness as sorrow that such a treasure should be consigned to the eyeless and impartial earth; they felt robbed; they felt as if one of the wonders of the world had been demolished by wanton marauders. "It's wrong of God to bury His own masterpiece," said the tipsy aunt, "and if that's blasphemy, I'll take the consequences, for I'm not at all sure I want to go on living in a world that doesn't contain Angelica."

Between her alpha and omega, a span of fifty years, Mrs. Early enjoyed a shimmering international fame that derived almost entirely from the inspired and faultless *esprit de corps* of her flesh and her bones and her blood; never were the features and the colors of a face in such serene and unassailable agreement, never had a skeleton been more singularly honored by the integument it wore. And Angelica, aware of her responsibility to her beholders, dedicated herself to the cultivation of her gift and the maintenance of her role in life with the same chastity and discipline that guide a girl who has been called to the service of God.

Angelica's marriage, entered upon when she was twenty-two and her husband was ten years older, puzzled everyone, for Major Clayton Early was not a connoisseur of the complex civilization that had produced his wife's sterling beauty but was, instead, concerned with low forms of plant life, with primitive societies, and with big game. He was an accomplished huntsman—alarming heads and horns and hides covered the walls of his den, together with enlarged photographs of himself standing with his right foot planted firmly upon the neck of a dead beast—and an uneducated but passionate explorer, and he was away most of the time, shooting cats in Africa or making and recording observations in the miasmas of Matto Grosso and the mephitic verdure of the Malay Peninsula. While he was away, Angelica, too, was away a good deal of the time—on islands, in Europe, upstate, down South—and for only a few months of the year were they simultaneously in residence in a professionally and pompously decorated maisonette that overlooked Central Park. When Major Early was in town, he enjoyed being host to large dinner parties, at which, more often than not, he ran off reels on reels of crepuscular and agitated movies that showed savages eating from communal pots, savages dancing and drumming, savages in council, savages accepting the white man's offerings of chewing gum and mechanical toys; there were, as well, many feet of film devoted to tarantulas, apes, termite mounds, and orchidaceous plants. His commentary was obscure, for his vocabulary was bestrewn with crossword-puzzle words. Those evenings were so awful that no one would have come to them if it had not been for Angelica; the eye could stray from a loathsome witch doctor on the screen and rest in comfort and joy on her.

Some people said that Early was a cynic and some said that he was a fool to leave Angelica unguarded, without children and without responsibility, and they all said it would serve him right if he returned from one of his safaris to find himself replaced. Why did a man so antisocial marry at all, or, if he must marry, why not take as his wife some stalwart and thick-legged woman who would share his pedantic adventures—a champion skeet shooter, perhaps, or a descendant of Western pioneers? But then, on the other hand, why had Angelica married *him*? She never spoke of him, never quoted from his letters—if there were any letters —and if she was asked where he was currently traveling, she often could not answer. The speculation upon this vacant alliance ceased as soon as Early had left town to go and join his guides, for once he was out of sight, no one could remember much about him beyond a Gallic mustache and his ponderous jokes as his movies jerked on. Indeed, so completely was his existence forgotten that matchmakers set to work as if Angelica were a widow.

They did not get far, the matchmakers, because, apart from her beauty, there was not a good deal to be said about Angelica. She had some money—her parents had left her ample provision, and Early's money came from a reliable soap—but it was not enough to be of interest to the extremely rich people whose yachts and châteaux and boxes at the opera she embellished. She dressed well, but she lacked the exclusive chic, the unique fillip, that would have caused her style in clothes to be called *sui generis* and, as such, to be mentioned by the press. Angelica was hardly literate; the impressions her girlish mind had received at Miss Hewitt's classes had been sketched rather than etched, but she was not stupid and she had an appealing, if small and intermittent, humor. She was not wanting in heart and she was quick to commiserate and give alms to the halt and the lame and the poor, and if ugliness had been a disease or a social evil, she would, counting her blessings, have lent herself to its extirpation. She wasn't a cat, she wasn't a flirt or a cheat, wasn't an imbecile, didn't make *gaffes*; neither, however, alas, was she a wit, or a catalyst, or a transgressor to be scolded and punished and then forgiven and loved afresh. She was simply and solely a beautiful woman.

Women, on first confronting Angelica Early, took a backward step in alarm and instinctively diverted the attention of their husbands or lovers to something at the opposite end of the room. But their first impression was false, for Angelica's beauty was an end in itself and she was the least predatory of women. The consequence of this was that she had many women friends, or at any rate she had many hostesses, for there was no more splendid and no safer ornament for a dinner table than Angelica. The appointments of these tables were often planned round her, the cynosure, and women lunching together had been known to debate (with their practical tongues in their cheeks but without malice) whether Waterford or Venetian glass went better with her and whether white roses or red were more appropriate in juxtaposition to her creamy skin and her luminous ash-blond hair. She was forever in demand; for weeks before parties and benefit balls hostesses contended for her presence; her status—next to the host—in protocol was permanent; little zephyrs of excitement and small calms of awe followed her entrance into a drawing room. She was like royalty, she was a public personage, or she was, as the aunt was to observe at her funeral, like the masterpiece of a great master. Queens and pictures may not, in the ordinary sense, have friends, but if they live up to their reputations, they will not want for an entourage, and only the cranks and the sightless will be their foes. There were some skeptics in Angelica's circle, but there were no cranks, and in speaking of her, using the superlatives that composed their native tongue, they called her adorable and indispensable, and they said that when she left them, the sun went down.

Men, on first gazing into those fabulous eyes, whose whites had retained the pale, melting blue of infancy, were dizzied, and sometimes they saw stars. But their vertigo passed soon, often immediately, although sometimes not until after a second encounter, planned in palpitations and bouts of fever, had proved flat and inconsequential. For a tête-à-tête with Angelica was marked by immediacy; she did not half disclose a sweet and sad and twilit history, did not make half promises about a future, implied the barest minimum of flattery and none at all of amorousness, and spoke factually, in a pleasant voice, without nuance and within the present tense. Someone had said that she was *sec*—a quality praiseworthy in certain wines but distinctly not delicious in so beautiful a woman. All the same, just as she had many hostesses, so she had many escorts, for her presence at a man's side gave him a feeling of achievement.

Angelica was not, that is, all façade—her eyes themselves testified to the existence of airy apartments and charming gardens behind them —but she was consecrated to her vocation and she had been obliged to pass up much of the miscellany of life that irritates but also brings about the evolution of personality; the unmolested oyster creates no pearl. Her heart might be shivered, she might be inwardly scorched with desire or mangled with jealousy and greed, she might be benumbed by loneliness and doubt, but she was so unswerving in her trusteeship of her perfection that she could not allow anxiety to pleat her immaculate brow or anger to discolor her damask cheeks or tears to deflower her eyes. Perhaps, like an artist, she was not always grateful for this talent of beauty that destiny had imposed upon her without asking leave, but, like the artist, she knew where her duty lay; the languishing and death of her genius would be the languishing and death of herself, and suicide, though it is often understandable, is almost never moral.

The world kindly imagined that Mrs. Early's beauty was deathless and that it lived its charmed life without support. If the world could have seen the contents of her dressing table and her bathroom shelves! If the world could have known the hours devoured by the matutinal ritual! Angelica and her reverent English maid, Dora, were dressed like surgeons in those morning hours, and they worked painstakingly, talking little, under lights whose purpose was to cast on the mirrors an image of ruthless veracity. The slightest alteration in the color of a strand of hair caused Angelica to cancel all engagements for a day or two, during which time a hairdresser was in attendance, treating the lady with dyes and allaying her fears. A Finn daily belabored her with bundles of birch fagots to enliven her circulation; at night she wore mud on her face and creamed gloves on her hands; her hair was treated with olive oil, lemon juice, egg white, and beer; she was massaged, she was vibrated, she was steamed into lassitude and then stung back to life by astringents; she was brushed and creamed and salted and powdered. All this took time, and, more than time, it took undying patience. So what the world did not know but what Angelica and her maid and her curators knew was that the blood that ever so subtly clouded her cheeks with pink and lay pale green in that admirable vein in her throat was kept in motion by a rapid pulse whose author was a fearful heart: If my talent goes, I'm done for, says the artist, and Angelica said, if I lose my looks, I'm lost.

So, even as she attentively lent the exquisite shell of her ear to her dinner partner, who was telling her about his visit to Samothrace or was bidding her examine with him his political views, even as she returned the gaze of a newcomer whose head was over his heels, even as she contributed to the talk about couturiers after the ladies had withdrawn, Angelica was thinking, in panic and obsession, of the innumerable details she was obliged to juggle to sustain the continuity of her performance.

Modern science has provided handsome women—and especially blondes, who are the most vulnerable—with defenses against many of their natural enemies: the sun, coarsening winds, the rude and hostile properties of foreign waters and foreign airs. But there has not yet been devised a way to bring to his knees the archfiend Time, and when Angelica began to age, in her middle forties, she went to bed.

Her reduction of the world to the size of her bedroom was a gradual process, for her wilting and fading was so slow that it was really imperceptible except to her unflinching eyes, and to Dora's, and to those of an adroit plastic surgeon to whose unadvertised sanitarium, tucked away in a rural nook in Normandy, she had retreated each summer since she was forty to be delivered of those infinitesimal lines and spots in her cheeks and her throat that her well-lighted mirror told her were exclamatory and shameful disfigurements. Such was the mystery that shrouded these trips to France that everyone thought she must surely be going abroad to establish a romantic ménage, and when she paused in Paris on her return to New York, she was always so resplendent that the guesses seemed to be incontrovertibly confirmed; nothing but some sort of delicious fulfillment could account for her subtlety, her lovely, tremulous, youthful air of secret memories. Some of her friends in idle moments went so far as to clothe this lover with a fleshy vestment and a personality and a nationality, and one of the slowly evolved myths, which was eventually stated as fact, was that he was a soul of simple origin and primal magnetism—someone, indeed, like Lady Chatterley's lover.

Angelica would suddenly appear in Paris at the beginning of September with no explanation of the summer or of that happy condition of her heart that was all but audible as a carol, and certainly was visible in her shimmering eyes and her glowing skin. She lingered in Paris only long enough to buy her winter wardrobe, to upset the metabolism of the men she met, to be, momentarily, the principal gem in the diadem of the international set, and to promise faithfully that next year she would join houseparties and cruises to Greece, would dance till dawn at *fêtes champêtres*, and would, between bullfights, tour the caves of Spain. She did not, of course, keep her promises, and the fact is that she would have disappointed her friends if she had. At these times, on the wing, it was as if she had been inoculated with the distillation of every fair treasure on earth and in heaven, with the moon and the stars, with the seas and the flowers, and the rainbow and the morning dew. Angelica was no longer *sec*, they said; they said a new dimension had brought her to life. Heretofore she had been a painted ship upon a painted ocean and now she was sailing the crests and the depths, and if her adventurous voyage away from the doldrums had come late in life, it had not come too late; the prime of life, they said, savoring their philosophy and refurbishing their cliché, was a relative season. They loved to speculate on why her lover was unpresentable. Wiseacres proposed, not meaning it, that he was a fugitive from the Ile du Diable; others agreed that if he was not Neanderthal (in one way or another) or so ignobly born that not even democracy could receive him into its generous maw—if he was not any of these things, he must be intransigently married. Or could he perhaps be one of those glittering Eastern rulers who contrived to take an incognito holiday from their riches and their dominions but could not, because of law and tradition, ever introduce Angelica into their courts? Once or twice it was proposed that Angelica was exercising scruples because of her husband, but this seemed unlikely; the man was too dense to see beyond his marriage feasts of Indians and his courtship of birds.

Whoever the lover was and whatever were the terms of their liaison, Angelica was plainly engaged upon a major passion whose momentum each summer was so forcefully recharged that it did not dwindle at all during the rest of the year. Now she began to be known not only as the most beautiful but as one of the most dynamic of women as well, and such was the general enthusiasm for her that she was credited with *mots justes* and insights and ingenious benevolences that perhaps existed only in the infatuated imaginations of her claque. How amazingly Angelica had changed! And how amazingly wrong they all were! For *not* changing had been her lifelong specialty, and she was the same as ever, only more so. Nevertheless, the sort of men who theretofore had cooled after their second meeting with her and had called her pedestrian or impervious or hollow now continued to fever and fruitlessly but breathlessly to pursue her. Often they truly fell in love with her and bitterly hated that anonymous fellow who had found the wellspring of her being.

Inevitably the news of her friends' speculations drifted back to her in hints and slips of the tongue. Angelica's humor had grown no more buxom with the passage of the years, and she was not amused at the enigma she had given birth to by immaculate conception. She took herself seriously. She was a good creature, a moral and polite woman, but she was hindered by unworldliness, and she was ashamed to be living a fiction. She was actually guilt-ridden because her summertime friend was not an Adonis from the Orient or a charming and ignorant workingman but was, instead, Dr. Fleege-Althoff, a monstrous little man, with a flat head on which not one hair grew and with the visage of a thief—a narrow, feral nose, a pair of pale and shifty and omniscient eyes, a mouth that forever faintly smiled at some cryptic, wicked jest. There was no help for it, but she was ashamed all the same that it was pain and humiliation, not bliss and glorification, that kept her occupied during her annual retreat. The fact was that she earned her reputation and her undiminishing applause and kept fresh the myth in which she moved by suffering the surface skin of her face to be planed away by a steel-wire brush, electrically propelled; the drastic pain was sickening and it lasted long, and for days—sometimes weeks—after the operation she was so unsightly that her looking glass, which, morbidly, she could not resist, broke her heart. She lay on a chaise in a darkened bedroom of that quiet, discreet sanitarium, waiting, counting the hours until the scabs that encrusted her flensed skin should disappear. But even when this dreadful mask was gone, she was still hideous, and her eyes and her mouth, alone untouched, seemed to reproach her when she confronted her reflection, as red and shining as if she had been boiled almost to death. Eight weeks later, though, she was as beautiful as she had been at her zenith, and the doctor, that ugly man, did not fail, in bidding her goodbye, to accord himself only a fraction of the credit and assign the rest to her Heavenly Father. Once, he had made her shiver when, giving her the grin of a gargoyle, he said, "What a face! Flower of the world! Of all my patients, you are the one I do not like to flail." Flail! The word almost made her retch, and she envisioned him lashing her with little metal whips, and smiling.

During the time she was at the sanitarium (a tasteful and pleasant place, but a far cry from the pastoral bower her friends imagined), she communicated with no one except her maid and with the staff, who knew her, as they knew all the other ladies, by an alias. She called herself Mrs. London, and while there was no need to go so far, she said she came from California. It was a long and trying time. Angelica had always read with difficulty and without much pleasure, and she inevitably brought with her the wrong books, in the hope, which she should long since have abandoned, that she might improve her mind; she could not pay attention to Proust, she was baffled by the Russians, and poetry (one year she brought "The Faerie Queene"!) caused her despair. So, for two and a half months, she worked at needlepoint and played a good deal of solitaire and talked to Dora, who was the only confidante she had ever had, and really the only friend. They had few subjects and most of them were solemn—the philosophy of cosmetics, the fleetingness of life. The maid, if she had a life of her own, never revealed it. Sometimes Angelica, unbearably sad that she had been obliged to tread a straight-and-narrow path with not a primrose on it, would sigh and nearly cry and say, "What have I done with my life?" And Dora, assistant guardian of the wonder, would reply, "You have worked hard, madame. Being beautiful is no easy matter." This woman was highly paid, but she was a kind woman, too, and she meant what she said.

It was Angelica's hands that at last, inexorably, began to tell the time. It seemed to her that their transfiguration came overnight, but of course what came overnight was her realization that the veins had grown too vivid and that here and there in the interstices of the blue-green, upraised network there had appeared pale freckles, which darkened and broadened and multiplied; the skin was still silken and ivory, but it was redundant and lay too loosely on her fingers. That year, when she got to the sanitarium, she was in great distress, but she had confidence in her doctor.

Dr. Fleege-Althoff, however, though he was sincerely sorry, told her there was nothing he could do. Hands and legs, he said, could not be benefited by the waters of the fountain of youth. Sardonically, he recommended gloves, and, taking him literally, she was aghast. How could one wear gloves at a dinner table? What could be more parvenu, more telltale, than to lunch in gloves at a restaurant? Teasing her further, the vile little man proposed that she revive the style of wearing mitts, and tears of pain sprang to Angelica's eyes. Her voice was almost petulant when she protested against these grotesque prescriptions. The doctor, nasty as he was, was wise, and in his unkind wisdom, accumulated through a lifetime of dealing with appearances, said, "Forgive my waggery. I'm tired today. Go get yourself loved, Mrs. London. I've dealt with women so many years that I can tell which of my patients have lovers or loving husbands and which have not—perhaps it will surprise you to know that very few of them have. Most have lost their men and come to me in the hope that the excision of crow's-feet will bring back the wanderers." He was sitting at his desk, facing her, his glasses hugely magnifying his intelligent, bitter eyes. "There is an aesthetic principle," he pursued, "that says beauty is the objectification of love. To be loved is to be beautiful, but to be beautiful is not necessarily to be loved. Imagine that, Mrs. London! Go and find a lover and obfuscate his senses; give him a pair of rose-colored glasses and he'll see your hands as superb—or, even better, he won't see your hands at all. Get loved by somebody—it doesn't matter who—and you'll get well."

"Get well?" said Angelica, amazed. "Am I ill?"

"If you are not ill, why have you come to me? I am a doctor," he said, and with a sigh he gestured toward the testimonials of his medical training that hung on the walls. The doctor's fatigue gave him an air of melancholy that humanized him, despite his derisive voice, and momentarily Angelica pitied him in his ineluctable ugliness. Still, he was no more solitary in his hemisphere than she was in hers, and quickly she slipped away from her consideration of him to her own woe.

"But even if I weren't married, how could I find a lover at my age?" she cried.

He shook his head wearily and said, "Like most of your countrywomen, you confound youth with value, with beauty, with courage—with everything. To you, youth and age are at the two poles, one positive, the other negative. *I* cannot tell you what to do. I am only an engineer—I am not the inventor of female beauty. I am a plastic surgeon—I am not God. All you can do now is cover your imperfections with *amour-propre*. You are a greedy woman, Mrs. London—a few spots appear on your hands and you throw them up and say 'This is the end.' What egotism!"

Angelica understood none of this, and her innocent and humble mind went round and round among his paradoxes, so savagely delivered. How could she achieve *amour-propre* when what she had most respected in herself was now irretrievably lost? And if she had not *amour-propre*, how could she possibly find anyone else to love her? Were not these the things she should have been told when she was a girl growing up? Why had no one, in this long life of hers, which had been peopled by such a multitude, warned her to lay up a store of good things against the famine of old age? Now, too late, she wrung her old-woman hands, and from the bottom of her simple heart she lamented, weeping and caring nothing that her famous eyes were smeared and their lids swollen.

At last the doctor took pity on her. He came around to her side of the desk and put his hands kindly on her shaking shoulders. "Come, Mrs. London, life's not over," he said. "I've scheduled your planing for tomorrow morning at nine. Will you go through with it or do you want to cancel?"

She told him, through her tears, that she would go through with the operation, and he congratulated her. "You'll rise from these depths," he said. "You'll learn, as we all learn, that there are substantial rewards in age."

That summer, Dr. Fleege-Althoff, who had grave problems of his own (he had a nagging wife; his only child, a son, was schizophrenic) and whose understanding was deep, did what he could to lighten Angelica's depression. He found that she felt obscurely disgraced and ashamed, as if she had committed a breach of faith, had broken a sacred trust, and could not expect anything but public dishonor. She had never been a happy woman, but until now she had been too diligent to be unhappy; the experience of unhappiness for the first time when one is growing old is one of the most malignant diseases of the heart. Poor soul! Her person was her personality. Often, when the doctor had finished his rounds, he took Angelica driving in the pretty countryside; she was veiled against the ravages of the sun and, he observed, she wore gloves. As they drove, he talked to her and endeavored to persuade her that for each of the crucifixions of life there is a solace. Sometimes she seemed to believe him.

Sometimes, believing him, she took heart simply through the look of the trees and the feel of the air, but when they had returned to the sanitarium and the sun had gone down and she was alone with her crumpled hands—with her crumpled hands and her compassionate but helpless maid—she could not remember any of the reasons for being alive. She would think of what she had seen on their drive: children playing with boisterous dogs; girls and young men on horses or bicycles, riding along the back roads; peasant women in their gardens tending their cabbages and tending their sunning babies at the same time. The earth, in the ebullience of summertime, seemed more resplendent and refreshed than she could ever remember it. Finally, she could not bear to look at it or at all those exuberant young human beings living on it, and began to refuse the doctor's invitations.

You might think that she would have taken to drink or to drugs, but she went on in her dogtrot way, taking care of her looks, remembering how drink hardens the skin and how drugs etiolate it.

That year, when Angelica arrived in Paris on her way back to New York, she was dealt an adventitious but crippling blow of mischance from which she never really recovered. She had arrived in midafternoon, and the lift in her hotel was crowded with people going up to their rooms after lunch. She had been one of the first to enter the car and she was standing at the back. At the front, separated from her by ten people or more, were two young men who had been standing in the lobby when she came into the hotel. They were Americans, effeminate and a little drunk, and one of them said to the other, "She must have been sixty —why, she could have been seventy!" His companion replied, "Twenty-eight. Thirty at the most." His friend said, "You didn't see her hands when she took off her gloves to register. They were old, I tell you. You can always tell by the hands."

Luckily for Angelica and luckily for them, the cruel, green boys got off first; as she rode up the remaining way to her floor, she felt dizzy and hot. Unused as she had been most of her life to emotion, she was embraced like a serpent by the desire to die (that affliction that most of us have learned to cope with through its reiteration), and she struggled for breath. She walked down the corridor to her room jerkily; all her resilience was gone. Immediately she telephoned the steamship line and booked the first passage home she could get. For two days, until the boat sailed, she lay motionless on her bed, with the curtains drawn, or she paced the floor, or sat and stared at her culprit hands. She saw no one and she spoke to no one except Dora, who told all the friends who called that her mistress was ill.

When these friends returned from Europe, and others from the country, they learned, to their distress and puzzlement, that Angelica was not going out at all, nor was she receiving anyone. The fiction of her illness, begun in Paris, gained documentation and became fact, until at last no one was in doubt: she had cancer, far too advanced for cure or palliation; they assumed she was attended by nurses. Poor darling, they said, to have her love affair end this way! They showered her with roses, telephoning their florists before they went out to lunch; they wrote her tactful notes of sympathy, and it was through reading these that she guessed what they thought was the reason for her retirement.

The maisonette seemed huge to her, and full of echoes; for the first time since she had married, she began to think about her husband and, though he was a stranger, to long for his return. Perhaps he could become the savior Fleege-Althoff had told her to seek. But she was not strong enough to wait for him. The drawing room was still in its summer shrouds; the umbrageous dining room was closed. At first, she dined in the library, and then she began to have dinner on a tray in her bedroom, sitting before the fire. Soon after this, she started keeping to her bedroom and, at last, to her bed, never rising from it except for her twice-daily ritualistic baths. Her nightdresses and bed jackets were made by the dressmaker she had always used to supplement her Paris wardrobe; she wore her jewels for the eyes of her maid and her masseuse—that is, she wore earrings and necklaces, but she never adorned her hands. And, as if she were dying in the way they thought, she wrote brave letters to her friends, and sometimes, when her loneliness became unbearable, she telephoned them and inquired in the voice of an invalid about their parties and about the theater, though she did not want to hear, but she refused all their kind invitations to come and visit, and she rang off saying, "Do keep in touch."

For a while, they did keep in touch, and then the flowers came less and less often and her mail dwindled away. Her panic gave way to inertia. If she had been able to rise from her bed, she would have run crying to them, saying, "I was faithful to your conception of me for all those years. Now take pity on me—reward me for my singleness of purpose." They would have been quick to console her and to laugh away her sense of failure. (She could all but hear them saying, "But my dear, how absurd! Look at your figure! Look at your face and your hair! What on earth do you mean by killing yourself simply because of your hands?") But she had not the strength to go to them and receive their mercy. They did not know and she could not tell them. They thought it was cancer. They would never have dreamed it was despair that she groped through sightlessly, in a vacuum everlasting and black. Their flowers and their letters and their telephone calls did not stop out of unkindness but out of forgetfulness; they were busy, they were living their lives.

Angelica began to sleep. She slept all night and all day, like a cat. Dreams became her companions and sleep became her food. She ate very little, but she did not waste away, although she was weakened—so weakened, indeed, that sometimes in her bath she had attacks of vertigo and was obliged to ring for Dora. She could not keep her mind on anything. The simplest words in the simplest book bewildered her, and she let her eyes wander drowsily from the page; before she could close the book and set it aside, she was asleep.

Just before Christmas, the drunken aunt, Angelica's only relative, came back to town after a lengthy visit to California. She had not heard from Angelica in months, but she had not been alarmed, for neither of them was a letter writer. The first evening she was back, she dined with friends and learned from them of her niece's illness; she was shocked into sobriety and bitterly excoriated herself for being so lazy that she had not bothered to write. She telephoned the doctor who had taken care of Angelica all her life and surprised him by repeating what she had heard— that the affliction had been diagnosed as cancer. At first, the doctor was offended that he had not been called in, and then, on second thought, he was suspicious, and he urged the aunt to go around as soon as she could and make a report to him.

The aunt did not warn Angelica that she was coming. She arrived late the next afternoon, with flowers and champagne and, by ill chance, a handsome pair of crocheted gloves she had picked up in a shop in San Francisco. She brought, as well, a bottle of Scotch, for her own amusement. The apartment was dark and silent, and in the wan light the servants looked spectral. The aunt, by nature a jovial woman—she drank for the fun of it—was oppressed by the gloom and went so quickly through the shadowy foyer and so quickly up the stairs that she was out of breath when she got to the door of Angelica's room. Dora, who had come more and more to have the deportment of a nurse, opened the door with nurselike gentleness and, seeing that her patient was, for a change, awake, said with nurselike cheer, "You have company, madame! Just look at what Mrs. Armstrong has brought!" She took the flowers to put in water and the champagne to put on ice, and silently left the room.

The moment Angelica saw her aunt, she burst into tears and held out her arms, like a child, to be embraced, and Mrs. Armstrong began also to cry, holding the unhappy younger woman in her arms. When the hurricane was spent and the ladies had regained their voices, the aunt said, "You must tell me the whole story, my pet, but before you do, you must give me a drink and open your present. I do pray you're going to like them—they are so much *you*."

Angelica rang for glasses and ice, for the Scotch, and then she undid the ribbon around the long box. When she saw what was inside, all the blood left her face. "Get out!" she said to her aunt, full of cold hatred. "Is that why you came—to taunt me?"

Amazed, Mrs. Armstrong turned away from a book she had been examining on a table in the window and met her niece's angry gaze.

"*I* taunt you?" she cried. "Why, darling, are you out of your mind? If you don't like the gloves, I'll give them to someone else, but don't—"

"Yes, do that! Give them to some young beautiful girl whose hands don't need to be hidden." And she flung the box and the gloves to the floor in an infantile fury. Twisting, she bent herself into her pillows and wept again, heartbrokenly.

By the end of the afternoon, Mrs. Armstrong's heart was also broken. She managed, with taste and tact, aided by a good deal of whisky, to ferret out the whole story, and, as she said to her dinner companion later on, it was unquestionably the saddest she had ever heard. She blamed herself for her obtuseness and she blamed Major Early for his, and, to a lesser extent, she blamed Angelica's friends for never realizing that they, with their constant and superlative praise of her looks, had added to her burden, had forced her into so conventual a life that she had been removed from most of experience. "The child has no memories!" exclaimed Mrs. Armstrong, appalled. "She wouldn't know danger if she met it head on, and she certainly wouldn't know joy. We virtually said to her, 'Don't tire your pretty eyes with looking at anything, don't let emotion harm a hair of your lovely head.' We simply worshipped and said, 'Let us look at you, but don't you look at us, for we are toads.' The ghastly thing is that there's nothing to be salvaged, and even if some miracle of surgery could restore her hands to her, it would do no good, for her disillusion is complete. I think if she could love anyone, if that talent were suddenly to come to her at this point in her life, she would love her ugly man in Normandy, and would love him *because* he was ugly."

When Angelica had apologized to her aunt for her tantrum over the gloves, she had then got out of bed and retrieved them and, in the course of her soliloquy, had put them on and had constantly smoothed them over each finger in turn as she talked.

She was still wearing the gloves when Dora came in to run her evening bath and found that her heart, past mending, had stopped.

(1956)

SONG

by

WILLIAM BLAKE
(1757–1827)

Usually considered a Romantic poet, William Blake was so unique an individual that it is hard to label him. He was essentially a revolutionary in politics and in philosophy, and his long mystical poems have had many interpretations. His beautiful engravings illustrate and help to explain many of his poems. Blake was as ardent a women's liberationist as his contemporary Mary Wollstonecraft.

• ——————————————————— •

How sweet I roam'd from field to field
And tasted all the summer's pride,
Till I the Prince of Love beheld
Who in the sunny beams did glide!

He show'd me lilies for my hair,
And blushing roses for my brow;
He led me through his gardens fair
Where all his golden pleasures grow.

With sweet May dews my wings were wet,
And Phoebus fir'd my vocal rage;
He caught me in his silken net,
And shut me in his golden cage.

He loves to sit and hear me sing,
Then, laughing, sports and plays with me;
Then stretches out my golden wing,
And mocks my loss of liberty.

BABY, YOU WERE GREAT!

by

KATE WILHELM
(b. 1928)

Born in Ohio, Kate Wilhelm married immediately after finishing high school; she had two children and worked as a model, a telephone operator, and a sales clerk before becoming a full-time writer. Since 1962 she has published a volume of science fiction almost every year and has won many awards. Critics see Wilhelm's work as transcending the conventions of the genre; she frequently focuses on the changing roles of women and on dangers to the environment. Recent works include The Dark Door *(1988) and* Crazy Time *(1989); perhaps her best-known work is* Where Late the Sweet Birds Sang *(1976).*

———————

John Lewisohn thought that if one more door slammed, or one more bell rang, or one more voice asked if he was all right, his head would explode. Leaving his laboratories, he walked through the carpeted hall to the elevator that slid wide to admit him noiselessly, was lowered, gently, two floors, where there were more carpeted halls. The door he shoved open bore a neat sign, AUDITIONING STUDIO. Inside, he was waved on through the reception room by three girls who knew better than to speak to him unless he spoke first. They were surprised to see him; it was his first visit there in seven or eight months. The inner room where he stopped was darkened, at first glance appearing empty, revealing another occupant only after his eyes had time to adjust to the dim lighting.

John sat in the chair next to Herb Javits, still without speaking. Herb was wearing the helmet and gazing at a wide screen that was actually a one-way glass panel permitting him to view the audition going on in the next room. John lowered a second helmet to his head. It fit snugly and immediately made contact with the eight prepared spots on his skull. As soon as he turned it on, the helmet itself was forgotten.

A girl had entered the other room. She was breathtakingly lovely, a long-legged honey blonde with slanting green eyes and apricot skin. The room was furnished as a sitting room with two couches, some chairs, end tables and a coffee table, all tasteful and lifeless, like an ad in a furniture trade publication. The girl stopped at the doorway and John felt her indecision, heavily tempered with nervousness and fear. Outwardly she appeared poised and expectant, her smooth face betraying none of her emotions. She took a hesitant step toward the couch, and a wire showed trailing behind her. It was attached to her head. At the same time a second door opened. A young man ran inside, slamming the door behind him; he looked wild and frantic. The girl registered surprise, mounting nervousness; she felt behind her for the door handle, found it and tried to open the door again. It was locked. John could hear nothing that was being said in the room; he only felt the girl's reaction to the unexpected interruption. The wild-eyed man was approaching her, his hands slashing through the air, his eyes darting glances all about them constantly. Suddenly he pounced on her and pulled her to him, kissing her face and neck roughly. She seemed paralyzed with fear for several seconds, then there was something else, a bland nothing kind of feeling that accompanied boredom sometimes, or too-complete self-assurance. As the man's hands fastened on her blouse in the back and ripped it, she threw her arms about him, her face showing passion that was not felt anywhere in her mind or in her blood.

"Cut!" Herb Javits said quietly.

The man stepped back from the girl and left her without a word. She looked about blankly, her torn blouse hanging about her hips, one shoulder strap gone. She was very beautiful. The audition manager entered, followed by a dresser with a gown that he threw about her shoulders. She looked startled; waves of anger mounted to fury as she was drawn from the room, leaving it empty. The two watching men removed their helmets.

"Fourth one so far," Herb grunted. "Sixteen yesterday; twenty the day before . . . All nothing." He gave John a curious look. "What's got you stirred out of your lab?"

"Anne's had it this time," John said. "She's been on the phone all night and all morning."

"What now?"

"Those damn sharks! I told you that was too much on top of the airplane crash last week. She can't take much more of it."

"Hold it a minute, Johnny," Herb said. "Let's finish off the next three girls and then talk." He pressed a button on the arm of his chair and the room beyond the screen took their attention again.

This time the girl was slightly less beautiful, shorter, a dimply sort of brunette with laughing blue eyes and upturned nose. John liked her. He adjusted his helmet and felt with her.

She was excited; the audition always excited them. There was some fear and nervousness, not too much. Curious about how the audition would go, probably. The wild young man ran into the room, and her face paled. Nothing else changed. Her nervousness increased, not uncomfortably. When he grabbed her, the only emotion she registered was the nervousness.

"Cut," Herb said.

The next girl was also brunette, with gorgeously elongated legs. She was very cool, a real professional. Her mobile face reflected the range of emotions to be expected as the scene played through again, but nothing inside her was touched. She was a million miles away from it all.

The next one caught John with a slam. She entered the room slowly, looking about with curiosity, nervous, as they all were. She was younger than the other girls, less poised. She had pale gold hair piled in an elaborate mound of waves on top of her head. Her eyes were brown, her skin nicely tanned. When the man entered, her emotions changed quickly to fear, then to terror. John didn't know when he closed his eyes. He was the girl, filled with unspeakable terror; his heart pounded, adrenalin pumped into his system; he wanted to scream but could not. From the dim unreachable depths of his psyche there came something else, in waves, so mixed with terror that the two merged and became one emotion that pulsed and throbbed and demanded. With a jerk he opened his eyes and stared at the window. The girl had been thrown down to one of the couches, and the man was kneeling on the floor beside her, his hands playing over her bare body, his face pressed against her skin.

"Cut!" Herb said. His voice was shaken. "Hire her," he said. The man rose, glanced at the girl, sobbing now, and then quickly bent over and kissed her cheek. Her sobs increased. Her golden hair was down, framing her face; she looked like a child. John tore off the helmet. He was perspiring.

Herb got up, turned on the lights in the room, and the window blanked out, blending with the wall. He didn't look at John. When he wiped his face, his hand was shaking. He rammed it in his pocket.

"When did you start auditions like that?" John asked, after a few moments of silence.

"Couple of months ago. I told you about it. Hell, we had to, Johnny. That's the six hundred nineteenth girl we've tried out! Six hundred nineteen! All phonies but one! Dead from the neck up. Do you have any idea how long it was taking us to find that out! Hours for each one. Now it's a matter of minutes."

John Lewisohn sighed. He knew. He had suggested it, actually, when he had said, "Find a basic anxiety for the test." He hadn't wanted to know what Herb had come up with.

He said, "Okay, but she's only a kid. What about her parents, legal rights, all that?"

"We'll fix it. Don't worry. What about Anne?"

"She's called me five times since yesterday. The sharks were too much. She wants to see us, both of us, this afternoon."

"You're kidding! I can't leave here now!"

"Nope. Kidding I'm not. She says no plug-up if we don't show. She'll take pills and sleep until we get there."

"Good Lord! She wouldn't dare!"

"I've booked seats. We take off at twelve-thirty-five." They stared at one another silently for another moment, when Herb shrugged. He was a short man, not heavy but solid. John was over six feet, muscular, with a temper that he knew he had to control. Others suspected that when he did let it go, there would be bodies lying around afterward, but he controlled it.

Once it had been a physical act, an effort of body and will to master that temper; now it was done so automatically that he couldn't recall occasions when it even threatened to flare anymore.

"Look, Johnny, when we see Anne, let me handle it. Right? I'll make it short."

"What are you going to do?"

"Give her an earful. If she's going to start pulling temperament on me, I'll slap her down so hard she'll bounce a week." He grinned. "She's had it all her way up to now. She knew there wasn't a replacement if she got bitchy. Let her try it now. Just let her try." Herb was pacing back and forth with quick, jerky steps.

John realized with a shock that he hated the stocky, red-faced man. The feeling was new; it was almost as if he could taste the hatred he felt, and the taste was unfamiliar and pleasant.

Herb stopped pacing and stared at him for a moment. "Why'd she call you? Why does she want you down, too? She knows you're not mixed up with this end of it."

"She knows I'm a full partner, anyway," John said.

"Yeah, but that's not it." Herb's face twisted in a grin. "She thinks you're still hot for her, doesn't she? She knows you tumbled once, in the beginning, when you were working on her, getting the gimmick working right." The grin reflected no humor then. "Is she right, Johnny, baby? Is that it?"

"We made a deal," John said. "You run your end, I run mine. She wants me along because she doesn't trust you, or believe anything you tell her anymore. She wants a witness."

"Yeah, Johnny. But you be sure you remember our agreement." Suddenly Herb laughed. "You know what it was like, Johnny, seeing you and her? Like a flame trying to snuggle up to an icicle."

At three-thirty they were in Anne's suite in the Skyline Hotel in Grand Bahama. Herb had a reservation to fly back to New York on the 6 P.M. flight. Anne would not be off until four, so they made themselves comfortable in her rooms and waited. Herb turned her screen on, offered a helmet to John, who shook his head, and they both seated themselves. John watched the screen for several minutes; then he, too, put on a helmet.

Anne was looking at the waves far out at sea where they were long, green, undulating; then she brought her gaze in closer, to the blue-green and quick seas, and finally in to where they stumbled on the sandbars, breaking into foam that looked solid enough to walk on. She was peaceful, swaying with the motion of the boat, the sun hot on her back, the fishing rod heavy in her hands. It was like being an indolent animal at peace with its world, at home in the world, being one with it. After a few seconds she put down the rod and turned, looking at a tall smiling man in swimming trunks. He held out his hand and she took it. They entered the cabin of the boat where drinks were waiting. Her mood of serenity and happiness ended abruptly, to be replaced by shocked disbelief, and a start of fear.

"What the hell . . .?" John muttered, adjusting the audio. You seldom needed audio when Anne was on.

". . . Captain Brothers had to let them go. After all, they've done nothing yet—" the man was saying soberly.

"Buy why do you think they'll try to rob me?"

"Who else is here with a million dollars' worth of jewels?"

John turned it off and said, "You're a fool! You can't get away with something like that!"

Herb stood up and crossed to the window wall that was open to the stretch of glistening blue ocean beyond the brilliant white beaches. "You know what every woman wants? To own something worth stealing." He chuckled, a sound without mirth. "Among other things, that is. They want to be roughed up once or twice, and forced to kneel. . . . Our new psychologist is pretty good, you know? Hasn't steered us wrong yet. Anne might kick some, but it'll go over great."

"She won't stand for an actual robbery." Louder, emphatically, he added, "I won't stand for that."

"We can dub it," Herb said. "That's all we need, Johnny, plant the idea, and then dub the rest."

John stared at his back. He wanted to believe that. He needed to believe it. His voice was calm when he said, "It didn't start like this, Herb. What happened?"

Herb turned then. His face was dark against the glare of light behind him. "Okay, Johnny, it didn't start like this. Things accelerate, that's all. You thought of a gimmick, and the way we planned it, it sounded great, but it didn't last. We gave them the feeling of gambling, or learning to ski, of automobile racing, everything we could dream up, and it wasn't enough. How many times can you take the first ski jump of your life? After a while you want new thrills, you know? For you it's been great, hasn't it? You bought yourself a shiny new lab and closed the door. You bought yourself time and equipment and when things didn't go right, you could toss it out and start over, and nobody gave a damn. Think of what it's been like for me, kid! I gotta keep coming up with something new, something that'll give Anne a jolt and through her all those nice little people who aren't even alive unless they're plugged in. You think it's been easy? Anne was a green kid. For her everything was new and exciting, but it isn't like that now, boy. You better believe it is *not* like that now. You know what she told me last month? She's sick and tired of men. Our little hot-box Annie! Tired of men!"

John crossed to him and pulled him around toward the light. "Why didn't you tell me?"

"Why, Johnny? What would you have done that I didn't do? I looked harder for the right guy. What would you do for a new thrill for her? I worked for them, kid. Right from the start you said for me to leave you alone. Okay, I left you alone. You ever read any of the memos I sent? You initialed them, kiddo. Everything that's been done, we both signed. Don't give me any of that why didn't I tell you stuff. It won't work!" His face was ugly red and a vein bulged in his neck. John wondered if he had high blood pressure, if he would die of a stroke during one of his flash rages.

John left him at the window. He had read the memos. Herb was right; all he had wanted was to be left alone. It had been his idea; after twelve years of work in a laboratory on prototypes he had shown his—gimmick— to Herb Javits. Herb had been one of the biggest producers on television then; now he was the biggest producer in the world.

The gimmick was simple enough. A person fitted with electrodes in his brain could transmit his emotions, which in turn could be broadcast and picked up by the helmets to be felt by the audience. No words or thoughts went out, only basic emotions—fear, love, anger, hatred . . . That, tied in with a camera showing what the person saw, with a voice dubbed in, and you were the person having the experience, with one important difference—you could turn it off if it got to be too much. The "actor" couldn't. A simple gimmick. You didn't really need the camera and the sound track; many users never turned them on at all, but let their own imaginations fill in the emotional broadcast.

The helmets were not sold, only leased or rented after a short, easy fitting session. A year's lease cost fifty dollars, and there were over thirty-seven million subscribers. Herb had created his own network when the demand for more hours squeezed him out of regular television. From a one-hour weekly show, it had gone to one hour nightly, and now it was on the air eight hours a day live, with another eight hours of taped pro-gramming.

What had started out as A DAY IN THE LIFE OF ANNE BEAUMONT was now a life in the life of Anne Beaumont and the audience was insatiable.

Anne came in then, surrounded by the throng of hangers-on that mobbed her daily—hairdressers, masseurs, fitters, script men . . . She looked tired. She waved the crowd out when she saw John and Herb were there. "Hello, John," she said, "Herb."

"Anne, baby, you're looking great!" Herb said. He took her in his arms and kissed her solidly. She stood still, her hands at her sides.

She was tall, very slender, with wheat-colored hair and gray eyes. Her cheekbones were wide and high, her mouth firm and almost too large.

Against her deep red-gold suntan her teeth looked whiter than John re-membered. Although too firm and strong ever to be thought of as pretty, she was a very beautiful woman. After Herb released her, she turned to John, hesitated only a moment, then extended a slim, sun-browned hand. It was cool and dry in his.

"How have you been, John? It's been a long time."

He was very glad she didn't kiss him, or call him darling. She smiled only slightly and gently removed her hand from his. He moved to the bar as she turned to Herb.

"I'm through, Herb." Her voice was too quiet. She accepted a whiskey sour from John, but kept her gaze on Herb.

"What's the matter, honey? I was just watching you, baby. You were great today, like always. You've still got it, kid. It's coming through like always."

"What about this robbery? You must be out of your mind . . ."

"Yeah, that. Listen, Anne baby, I swear to you I don't know a thing about it. Laughton must have been giving you the straight goods on that. You know we agreed that the rest of this week you just have a good time, remember? That comes over too, baby. When you have a good time and relax, thirty-seven million people are enjoying life and relaxing. That's good. They can't be stimulated all the time. They like the variety." Wordlessly John held out a glass, scotch and water. Herb took it without looking.

Anne was watching him coldly. Suddenly she laughed. It was a cyni-cal, bitter sound. "You're not a damn fool, Herb. Don't try to act like one." She sipped her drink again, staring at him over the rim of the glass. "I'm warning you, if anyone shows up here to rob me, I'm going to treat him like a real burglar. I bought a gun after today's broadcast, and I learned how to shoot when I was ten. I still know how. I'll kill him, Herb, whoever it is."

"Baby," Herb started, but she cut him short.

"And this is my last week. As of Saturday, I'm through."

"You can't do that, Anne," Herb said. John watched him closely, searching for a sign of weakness; he saw nothing. Herb exuded confi-dence. "Look around, Anne, at this room, your clothes, everything. . . . You are the richest woman in the world, having the time of your life, able to go anywhere, do anything . . ."

"While the whole world watches—"

"So what? It doesn't stop you, does it?" Herb started to pace, his steps jerky and quick. "You knew that when you signed the contract. You're a rare girl, Anne, beautiful, emotional, intelligent. Think of all those wom-en who've got nothing but you. If you quit them, what do they do? Die? They might, you know. For the first time in their lives they're able to feel like they're living. You're giving them what no one ever did before, what was only hinted at in books and films in the old days. Suddenly they know what it feels like to face excitement, to experience love, to feel contented and peaceful. Think of them, Anne, empty, with nothing in their lives but you, what you're able to give them. Thirty-seven million drabs, Anne, who never felt anything but boredom and frustration until you gave them life. What do they have? Work, kids, bills. You've given them the world, baby! Without you they wouldn't even want to live anymore."

She wasn't listening. Almost dreamily she said, "I talked to my lawyers, Herb, and the contract is meaningless. You've already broken it over and over. I agreed to learn a lot of new things. I did. My God! I've climbed mountains, hunted lions, learned to ski and water-ski, but now you want me to die a little bit each week . . . That airplane crash, not bad, just enough to terrify me. Then the sharks. I really do think it was having sharks brought in when I was skiing that did it, Herb. You see, you will kill me. It will happen, and you won't be able to top it, Herb. Not ever."

There was a hard, waiting silence following her words. *No!* John shouted soundlessly. He was looking at Herb. He had stopped pacing when she started to talk. Something flicked across his face—surprise, fear, something not readily identifiable. Then his face went blank and he raised his glass and finished the scotch and water, replacing the glass on the bar. When he turned again, he was smiling with disbelief.

"What's really bugging you, Anne? There have been plants before. You knew about them. Those lions didn't just happen by, you know. And the avalanche needed a nudge from someone. You know that. What else is bugging you?"

"I'm in love, Herb."

Herb waved that aside impatiently. "Have you ever watched your own show, Anne?" She shook her head. "I thought not. So you wouldn't know about the expansion that took place last month, after we planted that new transmitter in your head. Johnny boy's been busy, Anne. You know these scientist-types, never satisfied, always improving, changing. Where's the camera, Anne? Do you ever know where it is anymore? Have you ever seen a camera in the past couple of weeks, or a recorder of any sort? You have not, and you won't again. You're on now, honey." His voice was quite low, amused almost. "In fact the only time you aren't on is when you're sleeping. I know you're in love. I know who he is. I know how he makes you feel. I even know how much money he makes a week. I should know, Anne baby. I pay him." He had come closer to her with each word, finishing with his face only inches from hers. He didn't have a chance to duck the flashing slap that jerked his head around, and before either of them realized it, he had hit her back, knocking her into a chair.

The silence grew, became something ugly and heavy, as if words were being born and dying without utterance because they were too brutal for the human spirit to bear. There was a spot of blood on Herb's mouth where Anne's diamond ring had cut him. He touched it and looked at his finger. "It's all being taped now, honey, even this," he said. He turned his back on her and went to the bar.

There was a large red print on her cheek. Her gray eyes had turned black with rage.

"Honey, relax," Herb said after a moment. "It won't make any difference to you, in what you do, or anything like that. You know we can't use most of the stuff, but it gives the editors a bigger variety to pick from. It was getting to the point where most of the interesting stuff was going on after you were off. Like buying the gun. That's great stuff there, baby. You weren't blanketing a single thing, and it'll all come through like pure gold." He finished mixing his drink, tasted it, and then swallowed half of it. "How many women have to go out and buy a gun to protect themselves? Think of them all, feeling that gun, feeling the things you felt when you picked it up, looked at it . . ."

"How long have you been tuning in all the time?" she asked. John felt a stirring along his spine, a tingle of excitement. He knew what was going out over the miniature transmitter, the rising crests of emotion she was feeling. Only a trace of them showed on her smooth face, but the raging interior torment was being recorded faithfully. Her quiet voice and quiet body were lies; the tapes never lied.

Herb felt it too. He put his glass down and went to her, kneeling by the chair, taking her hand in both of his. "Anne, please, don't be that angry with me. I was desperate for new material. When Johnny got this last wrinkle out, and we knew we could record around the clock, we had to try it, and it wouldn't have been any good if you'd known. That's no way to test anything. You knew we were planting the transmitter . . ."

"How long?"

"Not quite a month."

"And Stuart? He's one of your men? He is transmitting also? You hired him to . . . to make love to me? Is that right?"

Herb nodded. She pulled her hand free and averted her face. He got up then and went to the window. "But what difference does it make?" he shouted. "If I introduced the two of you at a party, you wouldn't think anything of it. What difference if I did it this way? I knew you'd like each other. He's bright, like you, likes the same sort of things you do. Comes from a poor family, like yours . . . Everything said you'd get along."

"Oh, yes," she said almost absently. "We get along." She was feeling in her hair, her fingers searching for the scars.

"It's all healed by now," John said. She looked at him as if she had forgotten he was there.

"I'll find a surgeon," she said, standing up, her fingers white on her glass. "A brain surgeon—"

"It's a new process," John said slowly. "It would be dangerous to go in after them."

She looked at him for a long time. "Dangerous?"

He nodded.

"You could take it back out."

He remembered the beginning, how he had quieted her fear of the electrodes and wires. Her fear was that of a child for the unknown and the unknowable. Time and again he had proved to her that she could trust him, that he wouldn't lie to her. He hadn't lied to her, then. There was the same trust in her eyes, the same unshakable faith. She would believe him. She would accept without question whatever he said. Herb had called him an icicle, but that was wrong. An icicle would have melted in her fires. More like a stalactite, shaped by centuries of civilization, layer by layer he had been formed until he had forgotten how to bend, forgotten how to find release for the stirrings he felt somewhere in the hollow, rigid core of himself. She had tried and, frustrated, she had turned from him, hurt, but unable not to trust once she had loved. Now she waited. He could free her, and lose her again, this time irrevocably. Or he could hold her as long as she lived.

Her lovely gray eyes were shadowed with fear, and the trust that he had given to her. Slowly he shook his head.

"I can't," he said. "No one can."

"I see," she murmured, the black filling her eyes. "I'd die, wouldn't I? Then you'd have a lovely sequence, wouldn't you, Herb?" She swung around, away from John. "You'd have to fake the story line, of course, but you are so good at that. An accident, emergency brain surgery needed, everything I feel going out to the poor little drabs who never will have brain surgery done. It's very good," she said admiringly. Her eyes were black. "In fact, anything I do from now on, you'll use, won't you? If I kill you, that will simply be material for your editors to pick over. Trial, prison, very dramatic . . . On the other hand, if I kill myself . . . "

John felt chilled; a cold, hard weight seemed to be filling him. Herb laughed. "The story line will be something like this," he said. "Anne has fallen in love with a stranger, deeply, sincerely in love with him. Everyone knows how deep that love is, they've all felt it, too, you know. She finds him raping a child, a lovely little girl in her early teens. Stuart tells her they're through. He loves the little nymphet. In a passion she kills herself. You are broadcasting a real storm of passion, right now, aren't you, honey? Never mind, when I run through this scene, I'll find out." She hurled her glass at him, ice cubes and orange slices flying across the room. Herb ducked, grinning.

"That's awfully good, baby. Corny, but after all, they can't get too much corn, can they? They'll love it, after they get over the shock of losing you. And they will get over it, you know. They always do. Wonder if it's true about what happens to someone experiencing a violent death?" Anne's teeth bit down on her lip, and slowly she sat down again, her eyes closed tight. Herb watched her for a moment, then said, even more cheerfully, "We've got the kid already. If you give them a death, you've got to give them a new life. Finish one with a bang. Start one with a bang. We'll name the kid Cindy, a real Cinderella story after that. They'll love her, too."

Anne opened her eyes, black, dulled now; she was so full of tension that John felt his own muscles contract. He wondered if he would be able to stand the tape she was transmitting. A wave of excitement swept him and he knew he would play it all, feel it all, the incredibly contained rage, fear, the horror of giving a death to them to gloat over, and finally, anguish. He would know it all. Watching Anne, he wished she would break now. She didn't. She stood up stiffly, her back rigid, a muscle hard ridged in her jaw. Her voice was flat when she said, "Stuart is due in half an hour. I have to dress." She left them without looking back.

Herb winked at John and motioned toward the door. "Want to take me to the plane, kid?" In the cab he said, "Stick close to her for a couple of days, Johnny. There might be an even bigger reaction later when she really understands just how hooked she is." He chuckled again. "By God! It's a good thing she trusts you, Johnny boy!"

As they waited in the chrome and marble terminal for the liner to unload its passengers, John said, "Do you think she'll be any good after this?"

"She can't help herself. She's too life-oriented to deliberately choose to die. She's like a jungle inside, raw, wild, untouched by that smooth layer of civilization she shows on the outside. It's a thin layer, kid, real thin. She'll fight to stay alive. She'll become more wary, more alert to danger, more excited and exciting . . . She'll really go to pieces when he touches her tonight. She's primed real good. Might even have to do some editing, tone it down a little." His voice was very happy. "He touches her where she lives, and she reacts. A real wild one. She's one; the new kid's one; Stuart . . . They're few and far between, Johnny. It's up to us to find them. God knows we're going to need all of them we can get." His expression became thoughtful and withdrawn. "You know, that really wasn't such a bad idea of mine about rape and the kid. Who ever dreamed we'd get that kind of reaction from her? With the right sort of buildup . . ." He had to run to catch his plane.

John hurried back to the hotel, to be near Anne if she needed him. But he hoped she would leave him alone. His fingers shook as he turned on his screen; suddenly he had a clear memory of the child who had wept, and he hoped Stuart was on from six until twelve, and he already had missed almost an hour of the show. He adjusted the helmet and sank back into a deep chair. He left the audio off, letting his own words form, letting his own thoughts fill in the spaces.

Anne was leaning toward him, sparkling champagne raised to her lips, her eyes large and soft. She was speaking, talking to him, John, calling him by name. He felt a tingle start somewhere deep inside him, and his glance was lowered to rest on her tanned hand in his, sending electricity through him. Her hand trembled when he ran his fingers up her palm, to her wrist where a blue vein throbbed. The slight throb became a pounding that grew and when he looked into her eyes, they were dark and very deep. They danced and he felt her body against his, yielding, pleading. The room darkened and she was an outline against the window, her gown floating down about her. The darkness grew denser, or he closed his eyes, and this time when her body pressed against his, there was nothing between them, and the pounding was everywhere.

In the deep chair, with the helmet on his head, John's hand clenched, opened, clenched, again and again.

LA BELLE DAME
SANS MERCI

by

JOHN KEATS
(1795–1821)

*The famous English Romantic poet John Keats studied medicine
before embarking on his all too brief career as a poet. His poems
reflect his love for Greek myth, for nature, and for the supernatural, often personified as a woman.*

• ———————————————————— •

Ah, what can ail thee, wretched wight,
   Alone and palely loitering;
The sedge is wither'd from the lake,
   And no birds sing.

Ah, what can ail thee, wretched wight,
   So haggard and so woe-begone?
The squirrel's granary is full,
   And the harvest's done.

I see a lilly on thy brow,
   With anguish moist and fever dew;
And on thy cheek a fading rose
   Fast withereth too.

I met a Lady in the meads,
   Full beautiful, a fairy's child;
Her hair was long, her foot was light,
   And her eyes were wild.

I set her on my pacing steed,
  And nothing else saw all day long;
For sideways would she lean, and sing
  A faery's song.

I made a garland for her head,
  And bracelets too, and fragrant zone,
She look'd at me as she did love,
  And made sweet moan.

She found me roots of relish sweet,
  And honey wild, and manna dew,
And sure in language strange she said,
  I love thee true.

She took me to her elfin grot,
  And there she gaz'd and sighed deep,
And there I shut her wild sad eyes—
  So kiss'd to sleep.

And there we slumber'd on the moss,
  And there I dream'd, ah woe betide
The latest dream I ever dream'd
  On the cold hill side.

I saw pale kings, and princes too,
  Pale warriors, death-pale were they all;
Who cry'd—"La belle Dame sans merci
  Hath thee in thrall."

I saw their starv'd lips in the gloom
  With horrid warning gaped wide,
And I awoke, and found me here
  On the cold hill side.

And this is why I sojourn here
  Alone and palely loitering,
Though the sedge is wither'd from the lake,
  And no birds sing.

THE LORELEY

by

HEINRICH HEINE
(1797–1856)

A well-known German writer, Heinrich Heine voluntarily exiled himself in Paris in 1831 to escape the rigid political regime of his native Prussia. His early works, including the famous "The Loreley," were romantic; later he satirized the Romantic movement and wrote political and philosophical works in prose.

• ———————————————— •

Ich weiss nicht, was soll es bedeuten

I cannot tell why this imagined
   Despair has fallen on me;
The ghost of an ancient legend
   That will not let me be:

The air is cool, and twilight
   Flows down the quiet Rhine;
A mountain alone in the high light
   Still holds the faltering shine.

The last peak rosily gleaming
   Reveals, enthroned in air,
A maiden, lost in dreaming,
   Who combs her golden hair.

Combing her hair with a golden
   Comb in her rocky bower.
She sings the tune of an olden
   Song that has magical power.

The boatman has heard; it has bound him
  In throes of a strange, wild love;
Blind to the reefs that surround him,
  He sees but the vision above.

And lo, hungry waters are springing—
  Boat and boatsman are gone. . . .
Then silence. And this, with her singing,
  The Loreley has done.

ERZULIE FREIDA

by

ZORA NEALE HURSTON
(1891?–1960)

*Born in Eatonville, Florida, an all-black town, Zora Neale Hurston
returned there after training as an anthropologist at Columbia
University; her famous novel,* Their Eyes Were Watching God *(1937),
is set in Eatonville.* Mules and Men *(1935) is a record of her studies
of folklore in the Caribbean, and* Dust Tracks on the Road *(1942)
is her autobiography. A collection of other works,* I Love Myself
When I Am Laughing *(1979), was edited by Alice Walker. "Erzulie
Freida" is from* Tell My Horse *(1938), a travel journal.*

• ——————————————————————————— •

[1930?]

Nobody in Haiti ever really told me who Erzulie Freida was, but they
told me what she was like and what she did. From all of that it is plain
that she is the pagan goddess of love. In Greece and Rome the goddesses
of love had husbands and bore children, Erzulie has no children and her
husband is all the men of Haiti. That is, any one of them that she chooses for herself. But so far, no one in Haiti has formulated her. As the perfect female she must be loved and obeyed. She whose love is so strong
and binding that it cannot tolerate a rival. She is the female counterpart
of Damballah [the chief male god]. But high and low they serve her, dream
of her, have visions of her as of the Holy Grail. Every Thursday and every
Saturday millions of candles are lighted in her honor. Thousands of beds,
pure in their snowy whiteness and perfumed are spread for her. Desserts,
sweet drinks, perfumes and flowers are offered to her and hundreds of
thousands of men of all ages and classes enter those pagan bowers to
devote themselves to this spirit. On that day, no mortal woman may lay
possessive hands upon these men claimed by Erzulie. They will not permit themselves to be caressed or fondled even in the slightest manner,
even if they are married. No woman may enter the chamber set aside for
her worship except to clean it and prepare it for the "service." For Erzulie
Freida is a most jealous female spirit. Hundreds of wives have been forced
to step aside entirely by her demands.

She has been identified as the Blessed Virgin, but this is far from true. Here again the use of the pictures of the Catholic saints have confused observers who do not listen long enough. Erzulie is not the passive queen of heaven and mother of anybody. She is the ideal of the love bed. She is so perfect that all other women are a distortion as compared to her. The Virgin Mary and all of the female saints of the Church have been elevated, and celebrated for their abstinence. Erzulie is worshipped for her perfection in giving herself to mortal man. To be chosen by a goddess is an exaltation for men to live for. The most popular Voodoo song in all Haiti, outside of the invocation to Legba [the god of the gate], is the love song to Erzulie.

Erzulie is said to be a beautiful young woman of lush appearance. She is a mulatto and so when she is impersonated by the blacks, they powder their faces with talcum. She is represented as having firm, full breasts and other perfect female attributes. She is a rich young woman and wears a gold ring on her finger with a stone in it. She also wears a gold chain about her neck, attires herself in beautiful, expensive raiment and sheds intoxicating odors from her person. To men she is gorgeous, gracious and beneficent. She promotes the advancement of her devotees and looks after their welfare generally. She comes to them in radiant ecstasy every Thursday and Saturday night and claims them.

Toward womankind, Erzulie is implacable. It is said that no girl will gain a husband if an altar to Erzulie is in the house. Her jealousy delights in frustrating all the plans and hopes of the young woman in love. Women do not "give her food" unless they tend toward the hermaphrodite or are elderly women who are widows or have already abandoned the hope of mating. To women and their desires, she is all but maliciously cruel, for not only does she choose and set aside for herself, young and handsome men and thus bar them from marriage, she frequently chooses married men and thrusts herself between the woman and her happiness. From the time that the man concludes that he has been called by her, there is a room in her house that the wife may not enter except to prepare it for her spiritual rival. There is a bed that she must make spotless, but may never rest upon. It is said that the most terrible consequences would follow such an act of sacrilege and no woman could escape the vengeance of the enraged Erzulie should she be bold enough to do it. But it is almost certain that no male devotee of the goddess would allow it to occur.

How does a man know that he has been called? It usually begins in troubled dreams. At first his dreams are vague. He is visited by a strange being which he cannot identify. He cannot make out at first what is wanted of him. He touches rich fabrics momentarily but they flit away from his grasp. Strange perfumes wisp across his face, but he cannot know where they came from nor find a name out of his memory for them. The dream visitations become more frequent and definite and sometimes Erzulie identifies herself definitely. But more often, the matter is more elusive. He falls ill, other unhappy things befall him. Finally his friends urge him to visit a houngan for a consultation. Quickly then, the visitor is identified as the goddess of love and the young man is told that he has been having bad luck because the goddess is angry at his neglect. She behaves like any other female when she is spurned. A baptism is advised and a "service" is instituted for the offended loa and she is placated and the young man's ill fortune ceases.

But things are not always so simply arranged. Sometimes the man chosen is in love with a mortal woman and it is a terrible renunciation he is called upon to make. There are tales of men who have fought against it valiantly as long as they could. They fought until ill luck and ill health finally broke their wills before they bowed to the inexorable goddess. Death would have ensued had they not finally given in, and terrible misfortune for his earthly inamorata also. However, numerous men in Haiti do not wait to be called. They attach themselves to the cult voluntarily. It is more or less a vow of chastity certainly binding for specified times, and if the man is not married then he can never do so. If he is married his life with his wife will become so difficult that separation and divorce follows. So there are two ways of becoming an adept of Erzulie Freida— as a "reclamé" meaning, one called by her, and the other way of voluntary attachment through inclination. . . .

The "baptism" or initiation into the cult of Erzulie is perhaps the most simple of all the voodoo rites. All gods and goddesses must be fed, of course, and so the first thing that the supplicant must do is to "give food" to Erzulie. There must be prepared a special bread and Madeira wine, rice-flour, eggs, a liqueur, a pair of white pigeons, a pair of chickens. There must be a white pot with a cover to it. This food is needed at the ceremony during which the applicant's head is "washed."

This washing of the head is necessary in most of their ceremonies. In this case the candidate must have made a natte (mat made of banana leaf-stems) or a couch made of fragrant branches of trees. He must dress himself in a long white night shirt. The houngan places him upon the leafy couch and recites three Ave Maria's, three Credos and the Confiteor three times. Then he sprinkles the couch with flour and a little syrup. The houngan then takes some leafy branches and dips them in the water in the white pot which has been provided for washing the head of the candidate. While the priest is sprinkling the head with this, the hounci and the Canzos are singing:

"Erzulie Tocan Freida Dahomey, Ce ou qui faut ce' ou qui bon
Erzulie Freida Tocan Maitresse m'ap mouter
Ce' ou min qui Maitresse."

["Erzulie Tocan Freida Dahomey, you are strong and you are good
Mistress Erzulie Tocan, I am going up
Yes, you are my mistress."]

The hounci and the adepts continue to sing all during the consecration of the candidate unassisted by the drums. The drums play *after* a ceremony to Erzulie, *never during* the service. While the attendants are chanting, the houngan very carefully parts the hair of the candidate who is stretched upon the couch. After the parted hair is perfumed, an egg is broken on the head, some Madeira wine, cooked rice placed thereon, and then the head is wrapped in a white handkerchief large enough to hold everything that has been heaped upon the head. The singing keeps up all the while. A chicken is then killed on the candidate's head and some of the blood is allowed to mingle with the other symbols already there. The candidate is now commanded to rise. This is the last act of the initiation. Sometimes a spirit enters the head of the new-made adept immediately. He is "mounted" by the spirit of Erzulie who sometimes talks at great length, giving advice and making recommendations. While this is going on a quantity of plain white rice is cooked—a portion sufficient for one person only, and he eats some of it. What he does not eat is buried before the door of his house.

The candidate now produces the ring of silver, because silver is a metal that has wisdom in it, and hands it to the houngan who takes it and blesses it and places it upon the young man's finger as in a marriage ceremony. Now, for the first time since the beginning of the ceremony, the priest makes the libation. The five wines are elevated and offered to the spirits at the four cardinal points and finally poured in three places on the earth for the dead, for in this as in everything else in Haiti, the thirst of the dead must be relieved. The financial condition of the applicant gauges the amount and the variety of the wines served on this occasion. It is the wish of all concerned to make it a resplendent occasion and there is no limit to the amount of money spent if it can be obtained by the applicant. Enormous sums have been spent on these initiations into the cult of Erzulie Freida. It is such a moment in the life of a man! More care and talent have gone into the songs for this occasion than any other music in Haiti. Haiti's greatest musician, Ludoric Lamotte, has worked upon these folk songs. From the evidence, the services to Erzulie are the most idealistic occasions in Haiti. It is a beautiful thing. Visualize a large group of upper class Haitians all in white, their singing voices muted by exaltation doing service to man's eternal quest, a pure life, the perfect woman, and all in a setting as beautiful and idyllic as money and imagination available can make it. "Erzulie, Nin Nin, Oh'!" is Haiti's favorite folk song.

1

"Erzulie ninnin, oh! hey! Erzulie ninnim oh, hey!
Moin senti ma pe' monte', ce moin minn yagaza.

["Godmother Erzulie, oh! hey! Godmother Erzulie, oh, hey!
I feel that I am going up, this is your godchild."]

ZORA NEALE HURSTON

261

"General Jean-Baptiste, oh ti parrain
Ou t'entre' lan caille la, oui parrain
Toutes mesdames yo a genoux, chapelette you
Lan main yo, yo pe' roule' mise' yo
Ti mouns yo a' genoux, chapelette you
Erzulie ninninm oh, Hey gran Erzulie Freida
Dague, Tocan, Mirorize, nan nan ninnin oh, hey
Movin senti ma pe' monte' ce' moin minn yagaza."

["General Jean-Baptiste, oh little godfather
You entered the house, yes godfather
All the women on their knees, their rosary beads
In their hands, calling their misery
The children on their knees, with their rosaries
Godmother Erzulie oh, Hey Grandma Erzulie Freida
Dague, Tocan, Mirorize, Godmother oh, hey
I feel that I am going up, this is your godchild."]

3

(Spoken in "Langage" recitative)

"Oh Aziblo, qui dit qui dit ce' bo yo
Ba houn bloco ita ona yo, Damballah Ouedo
Tocan, Syhrinise o Agoue', Ouedo, Pap Ogoun oh,
Dambala, O Legba Hypolite, Oh
Ah Brozacaine, Azaca, Neque, nago, nago pique cocur yo
Oh Loco, co loco, bel loco Ouedo, Loco guinea
Ta Manibo, Docu, Doca, D agoue' moinminn
Negue, candilica calicassague, ata, couine des
Oh mogue', Clemezie, Clemeille, papa mare' yo.

[Untranslatable African ritualistic terms]

4

"Erzulie, Ninninm oh, hey grann' Erzulie
Freida dague, Tocan Miroize, maman, ninninm oh, hey!
Moun senti ma pe' mouti', ce moin mimm yagaza, Hey!"

["Godmother, Erzulie oh, hey grandma Erzulie
Freida dague, Tocan Miroize, mother, godmother oh, hey!
I feel that I am going up, this is your godchild, Hey!"]

WOMAN ON A PEDESTAL

More upper class Haitians "make food" for Erzulie Freida than for any other loa in Haiti. Forever after the consecration, they wear a gold chain about their necks under their shirts and a ring on the finger with the initials E. F. cut inside of it. I have examined several of these rings. I know one man who has combined the two things. He has a ring made of a bit of gold chain. And there is a whole library of tales of how this man and that was "reclamé" by the goddess Erzulie, or how that one came to attach himself to the Cult. I have stood in one of the bedrooms, decorated and furnished for a visit from the invisible perfection. I looked at the little government employee standing there amid the cut flowers, the cakes, the perfumes and the lace covered bed and with the spur of imagination, saw his common clay glow with some borrowed light and his earthiness transfigured as he mated with a goddess that night—with Erzulie, the lady upon the rock whose toes are pretty and flowery.

The Sex Object

The woman ostensibly on a pedestal is often, in fact, a victim—a "sex goddess." Women sacrificing their time, money, and self-esteem to live up to cultural definitions of beauty may for a time feel exalted, but as they age they are promptly discarded. Often they perceive with bitterness that they have been used, that to men they have been sexual objects. Any woman who receives unwanted sexual attention from a man is being reified, made into an object, even if the man is a date or a husband. More obviously used are the objects of sexual abuse or rape. In the 1980s we came to recognize the scope of the violation of women's sexual autonomy and of the violence that may not only accompany violation but often is its primary cause (Gordon and Riger, 1989). Rape may not bring sexual satisfaction to its perpetrator: victims need not be sexually attractive. Infants, old women, boys—anyone sharing the stereotypical feminine characteristic of weakness—may be victims; stereotypical feminine passivity is often translated into willingness or desire to be raped. It has taken great courage to speak out about abuse and rape; because victims' stories are so often not believed and they are blamed, probably only about 10 percent of those raped make official reports (Russell, 1986). This means that during the week the Central Park rape dominated newspaper headlines (April, 1989) and 28 other first-degree rapes (those involving violence) were reported in New York City, there were perhaps

252 unreported sexual assaults in that city alone. In the vast majority of cases, the perpetrators were male.

The true dimensions of the problem can only be perceived on an international scale. Vicious though it is, individual rape is not the worst sexual crime: the selling of women, especially young girls, into sexual slavery is so unthinkable that the public resists even the most objective reports. Although it was outlawed everywhere by the early twentieth century, hard evidence exists that the practice continues today in as many as forty countries (Sawyer, 1988). In many parts of the world, the ancient practice of "pawning" women was a thin disguise for sales by parents and husbands for sexual service; as the Japanese video "Sandakan No. 8" poignantly illustrates, young girls had no recourse and little hope of ever ending their servitude. Although the street children in major cities have not been sold by their parents, they have often fled their homes because of physical or psychological abuse. Sawyer reports that their number is increasing and estimates there may be as many as eighty million around the world; even a conservative estimate is thirty million. This traffic is linked to pornography (especially for films and magazines), to drug abuse, and to colonialism; in some countries it has even become more or less official economic policy. "Sexual tourism," for example, is widely advertised in Thailand; it involves the prostitution of girls as young as eleven to traveling men—most of them from Western countries (Phongpaichit, 1982; Latza, 1987).

It is clear that adult prostitution also has an economic base (Reynolds, 1986). Both children and adults are often willing to become prostitutes because of the economic advantage: a prostitute may earn as much as twenty-five times more than a factory or agricultural worker. And often prostitutes feel autonomous and independent. Moral attitudes toward prostitution have varied widely among cultures; today many practitioners say they have no moral scruples and at two international conferences have demanded such rights as freedom from dominance by pimps and access to medical care (Pheterson, 1989). However much moral sanctions against prostitution may have changed, prostitutes' feeling that they have no practicable alternative is not the same as a free choice. In both the United States, where women increasingly have new work areas opened to them, and Russia, where over 90 percent of women work, often in jobs elsewhere dominated by men (janitors, engineers, doctors), women still earn only two-thirds as much as men. Even allowing for time off for pregnancy and child care, only the continuation of the sexual politics Kate Millett described in 1970 can explain this discrepancy. Whether "voluntarily" or through kidnapping, pawning, or abandonment, women and other marginal people are used by those in power.

The selections for this image range from the apparent innocence of girl-watching to sexual harassment, prostitution, child abuse, rape, chattel slavery, and a declaration of women's right to be free from all of these. In Irwin Shaw's story, as a husband and wife stroll along Fifth Avenue on a Sunday morning, they laugh as his girl-watching almost makes him stumble; but we soon learn that his habit is no laughing matter to his wife. He admits that she too is to him one of the pretty girls; his looking makes her and all women into objects he is considering for his own pleasure. The same masculine prerogative is claimed by the aging professor in Paule Marshall's story about a college student in Brooklyn. Max Berman wants to possess the handsome young woman to bolster his self-esteem, to assert power when he is otherwise powerless. Marshall is compassionate in letting us see his misery. But the student's rage at his crude attempt mobilizes her from passivity and a kind of despair into action: she meets him on his own ground and comes away the victor in the encounter. Doris Lessing's Barbara Coles is also successful in finding a counterattack for the quasi-military campaign her date wages in order to rape her. She deprives him of the sense of power that, she recognizes, is his true goal, rather than sexual gratification. Marshall's and Lessing's characters manage not to be victims by outthinking and outmaneuvering their attackers.

This is not the case for Maimie Pinzer, who, in spite of the friendship of the woman to whom she addressed her letters and others who tried to help her, cannot long resist returning to prostitution. At age thirteen, after a petty theft and some sexual activity, she had been forced by her mother to leave home; all her relatives refused to forgive her, and she entered "the life." Highly literate in several languages, she tried other work, but because of illness and because war broke out she could not make a living. She disappeared from history except for her letters.

In these works women resist reification. But in Julie Fay's "Metonymy," a daughter is too young to resist; mesmerized by her father's touch, she can only symbolically distance herself from his power. In "The Patriarch," Colette makes a widower's repeated incest with his daughters seem respectable, a practical adjustment to reality; but it is clear that the daughters have had no life of their own. Maya Angelou's autobiographical story of her rape at eight by her mother's lover shows explicitly the anguish of a rape victim; Angelou forcefully reveals the pain, fear, shame, humiliation, and long-range effects of the experience (she and her brother return to their grandmother's home to live). When as an adult she tells her own story, her honesty and frankness support others who may share the pain, fear, shame, humiliation of such a childhood experience. We know that Angelou has become a powerful and successful writer; her testimony as a survivor may well have been therapeutic for her and is a sign to others that long-range effects of rape can be overcome. All three of these authors show young women's vulnerability, but by speaking out they break the silence that abets such abuse.

Ntozake Shange fiercely portrays the violence and helpless rage involved with the kind of rape against which defense seems hopeless. The rape victim in New York City knows that only one out of ten witnesses might testify on her behalf, and even that one will not be believed unless the victim can gather enough statistical evidence to make the presumption of guilt credible. An individual is often helpless in a country with laws against rape; in many parts of the world, neither law nor public opinion protects victims of rape. [In a poem entitled "Death Car Ride," Angela Wilson pictures the fate of groups of women transported to cities for sexual use; see *Sinister Wisdom* 20 (1982), pp. 57–58.]

In 1861 a mulatto woman who had been a slave wanted to be a witness to the utter helplessness of that position. Having escaped after many years of trials, Harriet Jacobs published her autobiography. She used the pseudonym Linda Brent because she was ashamed that in her desperation to avoid rape by her hated master she had had two children by another white man, who had promised to buy her freedom. She wanted no one to know that she had violated the standards of morality she had internalized from her grandmother, a freed slave. In spite of its introduction by Lydia Maria Child, a respected white abolitionist, until 1981 "Linda Brent's" story was considered by literary critics (the majority of whom have been males) to be fiction (Yellin, 1981). This authentic woman slave's story verifies the double jeopardy of being black and female. Determination like that expressed by June Jordan's manifesto against sexual objectification in all its forms is needed to resist the power of economic and social systems that perpetuate in all but name Harriet Jacobs's position as a slave. Those who have encountered sexual abuse need to find the courage to bear witness as the first and necessary step toward justice.

THE GIRLS IN THEIR
SUMMER DRESSES

by

IRWIN SHAW
(1913–1984)

*Born in New York City, Irwin Shaw lived much of his adult life
abroad. He wrote movie and radio scripts as well as plays, novels,
and short stories. His best-known novel is* The Young Lions *(1948).
Others include* The Top of the Hill *(1979) and* Acceptable Losses
(1982). His short stories are collected in Stories of Five Decades
(1978).

•————————————————•

Fifth Avenue was shining in the sun when they left the Brevoort. The
sun was warm, even though it was February, and everything looked like
Sunday morning—the buses and the well-dressed people walking slowly
in couples and the quiet buildings with the windows closed.

Michael held Frances' arm tightly as they walked toward Washington
Square in the sunlight. They walked lightly, almost smiling, because
they had slept late and had a good breakfast and it was Sunday. Michael
unbuttoned his coat and let it flap around him in the mild wind.

"Look out," Frances said as they crossed Eighth Street. "You'll break
your neck."

Michael laughed and Frances laughed with him.

"She's not so pretty," Frances said. "Anyway, not pretty enough to
take a chance of breaking your neck."

Michael laughed again. "How did you know I was looking at her?"

Frances cocked her head to one side and smiled at her husband under
the brim of her hat. "Mike, darling," she said.

"O.K.," he said. "Excuse me."

Frances patted his arm lightly and pulled him along a little faster toward Washington Square. "Let's not see anybody all day," she said. "Let's
just hang around with each other. You and me. We're always up to our
neck in people, drinking their Scotch or drinking our Scotch; we only see

each other in bed. I want to go out with my husband all day long. I want him to talk only to me and listen only to me."

"What's to stop us?" Michael asked.

"The Stevensons. They want us to drop by around one o'clock and they'll drive us into the country."

"The cunning Stevensons," Mike said. "Transparent. They can whistle. They can go driving in the country by themselves."

"Is it a date?"

"It's a date."

Frances leaned over and kissed him on the tip of the ear.

"Darling," Michael said, "this is Fifth Avenue."

"Let me arrange a program," Frances said. "A planned Sunday in New York for a young couple with money to throw away."

"Go easy."

"First let's go to the Metropolitan Museum of Art," Frances suggested, because Michael had said during the week he wanted to go. "I haven't been there in three years and there're at least ten pictures I want to see again. Then we can take the bus down to Radio City and watch them skate. And later we'll go down to Cavanaugh's and get a steak as big as a blacksmith's apron, with a bottle of wine, and after that there's a French picture at the Filmarte that everybody says—say, are you listening to me?"

"Sure," he said. He took his eyes off the hatless girl with the dark hair, cut dancer-style like a helmet, who was walking past him.

"That's the program for the day," Frances said flatly. "Or maybe you'd just rather walk up and down Fifth Avenue."

"No," Michael said. "Not at all."

"You always look at other women," Frances said. "Everywhere. Every damned place we go."

"No, darling," Michael said, "I look at everything. God gave me eyes and I look at women and men and subway excavations and moving pictures and the little flowers of the field. I casually inspect the universe."

"You ought to see the look in your eye," Frances said, "as you casually inspect the universe on Fifth Avenue."

"I'm a happily married man." Michael pressed her elbow tenderly. "Example for the whole twentieth century—Mr. and Mrs. Mike Loomis. Hey, let's have a drink," he said, stopping.

"We just had breakfast."

"Now listen, darling," Mike said, choosing his words with care, "it's a nice day and we both felt good and there's no reason why we have to break it up. Let's have a nice Sunday."

"All right. I don't know why I started this. Let's drop it. Let's have a good time."

They joined hands consciously and walked without talking among the baby carriages and the old Italian men in their Sunday clothes and the young women with Scotties in Washington Square Park.

THE SEX OBJECT
270

"At least once a year everyone should go to the Metropolitan Museum of Art," Frances said after a while, her tone a good imitation of the tone she had used at breakfast and at the beginning of their walk. "And it's nice on Sunday. There're a lot of people looking at the pictures and you get the feeling maybe Art isn't on the decline in New York City, after all—"

"I want to tell you something," Michael said very seriously. "I have not touched another woman. Not once. In all the five years."

"All right," Frances said.

"You believe that, don't you?"

"All right."

They walked between the crowded benches, under the scrubby city-park trees.

"I try not to notice it," Frances said, "but I feel rotten inside, in my stomach, when we pass a woman and you look at her and I see that look in your eye and that's the way you looked at me the first time. In Alice Maxwell's house. Standing there in the living room, next to the radio, with a green hat on and all those people."

"I remember the hat," Michael said.

"The same look," Frances said. "And it makes me feel bad. It makes me feel terrible."

"Sh-h-h, please, darling, sh-h-h."

"I think I would like a drink now," Frances said.

They walked over to a bar on Eighth Street, not saying anything, Michael automatically helping her over curbstones and guiding her past automobiles. They sat near a window in the bar and the sun streamed in and there was a small, cheerful fire in the fireplace. A little Japanese waiter came over and put down some pretzels and smiled happily at them.

"What do you order after breakfast?" Michael asked.

"Brandy, I suppose," Frances said.

"Courvoisier," Michael told the waiter. "Two Courvoisiers."

The waiter came with the glasses and they sat drinking the brandy in the sunlight. Michael finished half his and drank a little water.

"I look at women," he said. "Correct. I don't say it's wrong or right. I look at them. If I pass them on the street and I don't look at them, I'm fooling you, I'm fooling myself."

"You look at them as though you want them," Frances said, playing with her brandy glass. "Every one of them."

"In a way," Michael said, speaking softly and not to his wife, "in a way that's true. I don't do anything about it, but it's true."

"I know it. That's why I feel bad."

"Another brandy," Michael called. "Waiter, two more brandies."

He sighed and closed his eyes and rubbed them gently with his fingertips. "I love the way women look. One of the things I like best about New York is the battalions of women. When I first came to New York from Ohio that was the first thing I noticed, the million wonderful women, all over the city. I walked around with my heart in my throat."

"A kid." Frances said. "That's a kid's feeling."

"Guess again," Michael said. "Guess again. I'm older now. I'm a man getting near middle age, putting on a little fat and I still love to walk along Fifth Avenue at three o'clock on the east side of the street between Fiftieth and Fifty-seventh Streets. They're all out then, shopping, in their furs and their crazy hats, everything all concentrated from all over the world into seven blocks—the best furs, the best clothes, the handsomest women, out to spend money and feeling good about it."

The Japanese waiter put the two drinks down, smiling with great happiness.

"Everything is all right?" he asked.

"Everything is wonderful," Michael said.

"If it's just a couple of fur coats," Frances said, "and forty-five-dollar hats—"

"It's not the fur coats. Or the hats. That's just the scenery for that particular kind of woman. Understand," he said, "you don't have to listen to this."

"I want to listen."

"I like the girls in the offices. Neat, with their eyeglasses, smart, chipper, knowing what everything is about. I like the girls on Forty-fourth Street at lunchtime, the actresses, all dressed up on nothing a week. I like the salesgirls in the stores, paying attention to you first because you're a man, leaving lady customers waiting. I got all this stuff accumulated in me because I've been thinking about it for ten years and now you've asked for it and here it is."

"Go ahead," Frances said.

"When I think of New York City, I think of all the girls on parade in the city. I don't know whether it's something special with me or whether every man in the city walks around with the same feeling inside him, but I feel as though I'm at a picnic in this city. I like to sit near the women in the theatres, the famous beauties who've taken six hours to get ready and look it. And the young girls at the football games, with the red cheeks, and when the warm weather comes, the girls in their summer dresses." He finished his drink. "That's the story."

Frances finished her drink and swallowed two or three times extra. "You say you love me?"

"I love you."

"I'm pretty, too," Frances said. "As pretty as any of them."

"You're beautiful," Michael said.

"I'm good for you," Frances said, pleading. "I've made a good wife, a good housekeeper, a good friend. I'd do any damn thing for you."

"I know," Michael said. He put his hand out and grasped hers.

"You'd like to be free to—" Frances said.

"Sh-h-h."

"Tell the truth." She took her hand away from under his.

Michael flicked the edge of his glass with his finger. "O.K.," he said gently. "Sometimes I feel I would like to be free."

"Well," Frances said, "any time you say."

"Don't be foolish." Michael swung his chair around to her side of the table and patted her thigh.

She began to cry silently into her handkerchief, bent over just enough so nobody else in the bar would notice. "Someday," she said, crying, "you're going to make a move."

Michael didn't say anything. He sat watching the bartender slowly peel a lemon.

"Aren't you?" Frances asked harshly. "Come on, tell me. Talk. Aren't you?"

"Maybe," Michael said. He moved his chair back again. "How the hell do I know?"

"You know," Frances persisted. "Don't you know?"

"Yes," Michael said after a while, "I know."

Frances stopped crying then. Two or three snuffles into the handkerchief and she put it away and her face didn't tell anything to anybody. "At least do me one favor," she said.

"Sure."

"Stop talking about how pretty this woman is or that one. Nice eyes, nice breasts, a pretty figure, good voice." She mimicked his voice. "Keep it to yourself. I'm not interested."

Michael waved to the waiter. "I'll keep it to myself," he said.

Frances flicked the corners of her eyes. "Another brandy," she told the waiter.

"Two," Michael said.

"Yes, Ma'am, yes sir," said the waiter, backing away.

Frances regarded Michael coolly across the table. "Do you want me to call the Stevensons?" she asked. "It'll be nice in the country."

"Sure," Michael said. "Call them."

She got up from the table and walked across the room toward the telephone. Michael watched her walk, thinking what a pretty girl, what nice legs.

BROOKLYN

by

PAULE MARSHALL
(b. 1929)

*Born in Brooklyn to Barbadian immigrants, Paule Marshall
graduated from Brooklyn College; she now lives in New York City.
She has held fellowships from the Guggenheim Foundation, the
Ford Foundation, and the National Endowment for the Arts and
has lectured widely at universities, including Yale, Oxford,
Cornell, and Michigan State. Her novel* Brown Girls, Brown Stones
(1981) has been made into a teleplay, and Praisesong for the
Widow *(1983) won a prize from the Before Columbus Foundation.*
Soul, Clap Hands and Sing *(1961), her first collection of short
stories, was republished in 1987;* Reena and Other Stories *(1983), in
which "Brooklyn" appears, was also published in England in 1985.*

• ───────────────────── •

A summer wind, soaring just before it died, blew the dusk and the first
scattered lights of downtown Brooklyn against the shut windows of the
classroom, but Professor Max Berman—B.A., 1919, M.A., 1921, New
York; Docteur de l'Université, 1930, Paris—alone in the room, did not
bother to open the windows to the cooling wind. The heat and airless-
ness of the room, the perspiration inching its way like an ant around his
starched collar were discomforts he enjoyed, they obscured his larger
discomfort: the anxiety which chafed his heart and tugged his left eyelid
so that he seemed to be winking, roguishly, behind his glasses.

To steady his eye and ease his heart, to fill the time until his students
arrived and his first class in years began, he reached for his cigarettes. As
always he delayed lighting the cigarette so that his need for it would be
greater and, thus, the relief and pleasure it would bring, fuller. For some
time he fondled it, his fingers shaping soft, voluptuous gestures, his
warped old man's hands looking strangely abandoned on the bare desk
and limp as if the bones had been crushed, and so white—except for the
tobacco burn on the index and third fingers—it seemed his blood no
longer traveled that far.

He lit the cigarette finally and as the smoke swelled his lungs, his
eyelid stilled and his lined face lifted, the plume of white hair wafting
above his narrow brow; his body—short, blunt, the shoulders slightly

bent as if in deference to his sixty-three years—settled back in the chair. Delicately Max Berman crossed his legs and, looking down, examined his shoes for dust. (The shoes were of a very soft, fawn-colored leather and somewhat foppishly pointed at the toe. They had been custom made in France and were his one last indulgence. He wore them in memory of his first wife, a French Jewess from Alsace-Lorraine whom he had met in Paris while lingering over his doctorate and married to avoid returning home. She had been gay, mindless and very excitable—but at night, she had also been capable of a profound stillness as she lay in bed waiting for him to turn to her, and this had always awed and delighted him. She had been a gift—and her death in a car accident had been a judgment on him for never having loved her, for never, indeed, having even allowed her to matter.) Fastidiously Max Berman unbuttoned his jacket and straightened his vest, which had a stain two decades old on the pocket. Through the smoke his veined eyes contemplated other, more pleasurable scenes. With his neatly shod foot swinging and his cigarette at a rakish tilt, he might have been an old *boulevardier* taking the sun and an absinthe before the afternoon's assignation.

A young face, the forehead shiny with earnestness, hung at the half-opened door. "Is this French Lit, fifty-four? Camus and Sartre?"

Max Berman winced at the rawness of the voice and the flat "a" in Sartre and said formally, "This is Modern French Literature, number fifty-four, yes, but there is some question as to whether we will take up Messieurs Camus and Sartre this session. They might prove hot work for a summer evening course. We will probably do Gide and Mauriac, who are considerably more temperate. But come in nonetheless. . . ."

He was the gallant, half rising to bow her to a seat. He knew that she would select the one in the front row directly opposite his desk. At the bell her pen would quiver above her blank notebook, ready to commit his first word—indeed, the clearing of his throat—to paper, and her thin buttocks would begin sidling toward the edge of her chair.

His eyelid twitched with solicitude. He wished that he could have drawn the lids over her fitful eyes and pressed a cool hand to her forehead. She reminded him of what he had been several lifetimes ago: a boy with a pale, plump face and harried eyes, running from the occasional taunts at his yarmulke along the shrill streets of Brownsville in Brooklyn, impeded by the heavy satchel of books which he always carried as proof of his scholarship. He had been proud of his brilliance at school and the Yeshiva, but at the same time he had been secretly troubled by it and resentful, for he could never believe that he had come by it naturally or that it belonged to him alone. Rather, it was like a heavy medal his father had hung around his neck—the chain bruising his flesh—and constantly exhorted him to wear proudly and use well.

The girl gave him an eager and ingratiating smile and he looked away. During his thirty years of teaching, a face similar to hers had crowded his vision whenever he had looked up from a desk. Perhaps it was fitting, he thought, and lighted another cigarette from the first, that she should be present as he tried again at life, unaware that behind his rimless glasses and within his ancient suit, he had been gutted.

He thought of those who had taken the last of his substance and smiled tolerantly. "The boys of summer," he called them, his inquisitors, who had flailed him with a single question: "Are you now or have you ever been a member of the Communist party?" Max Berman had never taken their question seriously—perhaps because he had never taken his membership in the party seriously—and he had refused to answer. What had disturbed him, though, even when the investigation was over, was the feeling that he had really been under investigation for some other offense which did matter and of which he was guilty; that behind their accusations and charges had lurked another which had not been political but personal. For had he been disloyal to the government? His denial was a short, hawking laugh. Simply, he had never ceased being religious. When his father's God had become useless and even a little embarrassing, he had sought others: his work for a time, then the party. But he had been middle-aged when he joined and his faith, which had been so full as a boy, had grown thin. He had come, by then, to distrust all pieties, so that when the purges in Russia during the thirties confirmed his distrust, he had withdrawn into a modest cynicism. (not even a deep one)

But he had been made to answer for that error. Ten years later his inquisitors had flushed him out from the small community college in upstate New York where he had taught his classes from the same neat pack of notes each semester and had led him bound by subpoena to New York and bandied his name at the hearings until he had been dismissed from his job.

He remembered looking back at the pyres of burning autumn leaves on the campus his last day and feeling that another lifetime had ended—for he had always thought of his life as divided into many small lives, each with its own beginning and end. Like a hired mute, he had been present at each dying and kept the wake and wept professionally as the bier was lowered into the ground. Because of this feeling, he told himself that his final death would be anticlimactic.

After his dismissal he had continued living in the small house he had built near the college, alone except for an occasional visit from a colleague, idle but for some tutoring in French, content with the income he received from the property his parents had left him in Brooklyn—until the visits and tutoring had tapered off and a silence had begun to choke the house, like weeds springing up around a deserted place. He had begun to wonder then if he were still alive. He would wake at night from the recurrent dream of the hearings, where he was being accused of an unstated crime, to listen for his heart, his hand fumbling among the bedclothes to press the place. During the day he would pass repeatedly in front of the mirror with the pretext that he might have forgotten to shave that morning or that something had blown into his eye. Above all, he had begun to think of his inquisitors with affection and to long for the sound of their voices. They, at least, had assured him of being alive.

As if seeking them out, he had returned to Brooklyn and to the house in Brownsville where he had lived as a boy and had boldly applied for a teaching post without mentioning the investigation. He had finally been offered the class which would begin in five minutes. It wasn't much: a six-week course in the summer evening session of a college without a rating, where classes were held in a converted factory building, a college whose campus took in the bargain department stores, the five-and-dime emporiums and neon-spangled movie houses of downtown Brooklyn.

Through the smoke from his cigarette, Max Berman's eyes—a waning blue that never seemed to focus on any one thing—drifted over the students who had gathered meanwhile. Imbuing them with his own disinterest, he believed that even before the class began, most of them were longing for its end and already anticipating the soft drinks at the soda fountain downstairs and the synthetic dramas at the nearby movie.

They made him sad. He would have liked to lead them like a Pied Piper back to the safety of their childhoods—all of them: the loud girl with the formidable calves of an athlete who reminded him, uncomfortably, of his second wife (a party member who was always shouting political heresy from some picket line and who had promptly divorced him upon discovering his irreverence); the two sallow-faced young men leaning out the window as if searching for the wind that had died; the slender young woman with crimped black hair who sat very still and apart from the others, her face turned toward the night sky as if to a friend.

Her loneliness interested him. He sensed its depth and his eye paused. He saw then that she was a Negro, a very pale mulatto with skin the color of clear, polished amber and a thin, mild face. She was somewhat older than the others in the room—a schoolteacher from the South, probably, who came north each summer to take courses toward a graduate degree. He felt a fleeting discomfort and irritation: discomfort at the thought that although he had been sinned against as a Jew he still shared in the sin against her and suffered from the same vague guilt, irritation that she recalled his own humiliations: the large ones, such as the fact that despite his brilliance he had been unable to get into a medical school as a young man because of the quota on Jews (not that he had wanted to be a doctor; that had been his father's wish) and had changed his studies from medicine to French; the small ones which had worn him thin: an eye widening imperceptibly as he gave his name, the savage glance which sought the Jewishness in his nose, his chin, in the set of his shoulders, the jokes snuffed into silence at his appearance. . . .

Tired suddenly, his eyelid pulsing, he turned and stared out the window at the gaudy constellation of neon lights. He longed for a drink, a quiet place and then sleep. And to bear him gently into sleep, to stay the terror which bound his heart then reminding him of those oleographs of Christ with the thorns binding his exposed heart—fat drops of blood from one so bloodless—to usher him into sleep, some pleasantly erotic image: a nude in a boudoir scattered with her frilled garments and warmed by her frivolous laugh, with the sun like a voyeur at the half-closed shutters. But this time instead of the usual Rubens nude with thighs like twin portals and a belly like a huge alabaster bowl into which he poured himself, he chose Gauguin's Aita Parari, her languorous form in the straightback chair, her dark, sloping breasts, her eyes like the sun under shadow.

With the image still on his inner eye, he turned to the Negro girl and appraised her through a blind of cigarette smoke. She was still gazing out at the night sky and something about her fixed stare, her hands stiffly arranged in her lap, the nerve fluttering within the curve of her throat, betrayed a vein of tension within the rock of her calm. It was as if she had fled long ago to a remote region within herself, taking with her all that was most valuable and most vulnerable about herself.

She stirred finally, her slight breasts lifting beneath her flowered summer dress as she breathed deeply—and Max Berman thought again of Gauguin's girl with the dark, sloping breasts. What would this girl with the amber-colored skin be like on a couch in a sunlit room, nude in a straight-back chair? And as the question echoed along each nerve and stilled his breathing, it seemed suddenly that life, which had scorned him for so long, held out her hand again—but still a little beyond his reach. Only the girl, he sensed, could bring him close enough to touch it. She alone was the bridge. So that even while he repeated to himself that he was being presumptuous (for she would surely refuse him) and ridiculous (for even if she did not, what could he do—his performance would be a mere scramble and twitch), he vowed at the same time to have her. The challenge eased the tightness around his heart suddenly; it soothed the damaged muscle of his eye and as the bell rang he rose and said briskly, "Ladies and gentlemen, may I have your attention, please. My name is Max Berman. The course is Modern French Literature, number fifty-four. May I suggest that you check your program cards to see whether you are in the right place at the right time."

Her essay on Gide's *The Immoralist* lay on his desk and the note from the administration informing him, first, that his past political activities had been brought to their attention and then dismissing him at the end of the session weighed the inside pocket of his jacket. The two, her paper and the note, were linked in his mind. Her paper reminded him that the vow he had taken was still an empty one, for the term was half over and he had never once spoken to her (as if she understood his intention she was always late and disappeared as soon as the closing bell rang, leaving him trapped in a clamorous circle of students around his desk), while the note which wrecked his small attempt to start anew suddenly made that vow more urgent. It gave him the edge of desperation he needed to act finally. So that as soon as the bell rang, he returned all the papers but hers, announced that all questions would have to wait until their next meeting and, waving off the students from his desk, called above their protests, "Miss Williams, if you have a moment, I'd like to speak with you briefly about your paper."

She approached his desk like a child who has been cautioned not to talk to strangers, her fingers touching the backs of the chairs as if for support, her gaze following the departing students as though she longed to accompany them.

Her slight apprehensiveness pleased him. It suggested a submissiveness which gave him, as he rose uncertainly, a feeling of certainty and command. Her hesitancy was somehow in keeping with the color of her skin. She seemed to bring not only herself but the host of black women whose bodies had been despoiled to make her. He would not only possess her but them also, he thought (not really thought, for he scarcely allowed these thoughts to form before he snuffed them out). Through their collective suffering, which she contained, his own personal suffering would be eased; he would be pardoned for whatever sin it was he had committed against life.

"I hope you weren't unduly alarmed when I didn't return your paper along with the others," he said, and had to look up as she reached the desk. She was taller close up and her eyes, which he had thought were black, were a strong, flecked brown with very small pupils which seemed to shrink now from the sight of him. "But I found it so interesting I wanted to give it to you privately."

"I didn't know what to think," she said, and her voice—he heard it for the first time for she never recited or answered in class—was low, cautious, Southern.

"It was, to say the least, refreshing. It not only showed some original and mature thinking on your part, but it also proved that you've been listening in class—and after twenty-five years and more of teaching it's encouraging to find that some students do listen. If you have a little time I'd like to tell you, more specifically, what I liked about it. . . ."

Talking easily, reassuring her with his professional tone and a deft gesture with his cigarette, he led her from the room as the next class filed in, his hand cupped at her elbow but not touching it, his manner urbane, courtly, kind. They paused on the landing at the end of the long corridor with the stairs piled in steel tiers above and plunging below them. An intimate silence swept up the stairwell in a warm gust and Max Berman said, "I'm curious. Why did you choose *The Immoralist?*"

She started suspiciously, afraid, it seemed, that her answer might expose and endanger the self she guarded so closely within.

"Well," she said finally, her glance reaching down the stairs to the door marked EXIT at the bottom, "when you said we could use anything by Gide I decided on *The Immoralist*, since it was the first book I read in the original French when I was in undergraduate school. I didn't understand it then because my French was so weak, I guess, but I always thought about it afterward for some odd reason. I was shocked by what I did understand, of course, but something else about it appealed to me, so when you made the assignment I thought I'd try reading it again. I understood it a little better this time. At least I think so. . . ."

"Your paper proves you did."

She smiled absently, intent on some other thought. Then she said cautiously, but with unexpected force, "You see, to me, the book seems to say that the only way you begin to know what you are and how much you are capable of is by daring to try something, by doing something which tests you. . . . "

"Something bold," he said.

"Yes."

"Even sinful."

She paused, questioning this, and then said reluctantly, "Yes, perhaps even sinful."

"The salutary effects of sin, you might say." He gave the little bow.

But she had not heard this; her mind had already leaped ahead. "The only trouble, at least with the character in Gide's book, is that what he finds out about himself is so terrible. He is so unhappy. . . ."

"But at least he knows, poor sinner." And his playful tone went unnoticed.

"Yes," she said with the same startling forcefulness. "And another thing, in finding out what he is, he destroys his wife. It was as if she had to die in order for a person to live and know himself. Perhaps in order for a person to live and know himself somebody else must die. Maybe there's always a balancing out. . . . In a way"—and he had to lean close now to hear her—"I believe this."

Max Berman edged back as he glimpsed something move within her abstracted gaze. It was like a strong and restless seed that had taken root in the darkness there and was straining now toward the light. He had not expected so subtle and complex a force beneath her mild exterior and he found it disturbing and dangerous, but fascinating.

"Well, it's a most interesting interpretation," he said. "I don't know if M. Gide would have agreed, but then he's not around to give his opinion. Tell me, where did you do your undergraduate work?"

"At Howard University."

"And you majored in French?"

"Yes."

"Why, if I may ask?" he said gently.

"Well, my mother was from New Orleans and could still speak a little Creole and I got interested in learning how to speak French through her, I guess. I teach it now at a junior high school in Richmond. Only the beginner courses because I don't have my master's. You know, *je vais, tu vas, il va* and *Frere Jacques*. It's not very inspiring."

"You should do something about that then, my dear Miss Williams. Perhaps it's time for you, like our friend in Gide, to try something new and bold."

THE SEX OBJECT

280

"I know," she said, and her pale hand sketched a vague, despairing gesture. "I thought maybe if I got my master's . . . that's why I decided to come north this summer and start taking some courses. . . ."

Max Berman quickly lighted a cigarette to still the flurry inside him, for the moment he had been awaiting had come. He flicked her paper, which he still held. "Well, you've got the makings of a master's thesis right here. If you like I will suggest some ways for you to expand it sometime. A few pointers from an old pro might help."

He had to turn from her astonished and grateful smile—it was like a child's. He said carefully, "The only problem will be to find a place where we can talk quietly. Regrettably, I don't rate an office. . . ."

"Perhaps we could use one of the empty classrooms," she said.

"That would be much too dismal a setting for a pleasant discussion."

He watched the disappointment wilt her smile and when he spoke he made certain that the same disappointment weighed his voice. "Another difficulty is that the term's half over, which gives us little or no time. But let's not give up. Perhaps we can arrange to meet and talk over a weekend. The only hitch there is that I spend weekends at my place in the country. Of course you're perfectly welcome to come up there. It's only about seventy miles from New York, in the heart of what's very appropriately called the Borsch Circuit, even though, thank God, my place is a good distance away from the borsch. That is, it's very quiet and there's never anybody around except with my permission."

She did not move, yet she seemed to start; she made no sound, yet he thought he heard a bewildered cry. And then she did a strange thing, standing there with the breath sucked into the hollow of her throat and her smile, that had opened to him with such trust, dying—her eyes, her hands faltering up begged him to declare himself.

"There's a lake near the house," he said, "so that when you get tired of talking—or better, listening to me talk—you can take a swim, if you like. I would very much enjoy that sight." And as the nerve tugged at his eyelid, he seemed to wink behind his rimless glasses.

Her sudden, blind step back was like a man groping his way through a strange room in the dark, and instinctively Max Berman reached out to break her fall. Her arms, bare to the shoulder because of the heat (he knew the feel of her skin without even touching it—it would be like a rich, fine-textured cloth which would soothe and hide him in its amber warmth), struck out once to drive him off and then fell limp at her side, and her eyes became vivid and convulsive in her numbed face. She strained toward the stairs and the exit door at the bottom, but she could not move. Nor could she speak. She did not even cry. Her eyes remained dry and dull with disbelief. Only her shoulders trembled as though she was silently weeping inside.

It was as though she had never learned the forms and expressions of anger. The outrage of a lifetime, of her history, was trapped inside her. And she stared at Max Berman with this mute, paralyzing rage. Not really at him but to his side, as if she caught sight of others behind him. And remembering how he had imagined a column of dark women trailing her to his desk, he sensed that she glimpsed a legion of old men with sere flesh and lonely eyes flanking him: "old lechers with a love on every wind. . . ."

"I'm sorry, Miss Williams," he said, and would have welcomed her insults, for he would have been able, at least, to distill from them some passion and a kind of intimacy. It would have been, in a way, like touching her. "It was only that you are a very attractive young woman and although I'm no longer young"—and he gave the tragic little laugh which sought to dismiss that fact—"I can still appreciate and even desire an attractive woman. But I was wrong. . . ." his self-disgust, overwhelming him finally, choked off his voice. "And so very crude. Forgive me. I can offer no excuse for my behavior other than my approaching senility."

He could not even manage the little marionette bow this time. Quickly he shoved the paper on Gide into her lifeless hand, but it fell, the pages separating, and as he hurried past her downstairs and out the door, he heard the pages scattering like dead leaves on the steps.

She remained away until the night of the final examination, which was also the last meeting of the class. By that time Max Berman, believing that she would not return, had almost succeeded in forgetting her. He was no longer even certain of how she looked, for her face had been absorbed into the single, blurred, featureless face of all the women who had ever refused him. So that she startled him as much as a stranger would have when he entered the room that night and found her alone amid a maze of empty chairs, her face turned toward the window as on the first night and her hands serene in her lap. She turned at his footstep and it was as if she had also forgotten all that had passed between them. She waited until he said, "I'm glad you decided to take the examination. I'm sure you won't have any difficulty with it"; then she gave him a nod that was somehow reminiscent of his little bow and turned again to the window.

He was relieved yet puzzled by her composure. It was as if during her three-week absence she had waged and won a decisive contest with herself and was ready now to act. He was wary suddenly and all during the examination he tried to discover what lay behind her strange calm, studying her bent head amid the shifting heads of the other students, her slim hand guiding the pen across the page, her legs—the long bone visible, it seemed, beneath the flesh. Desire flared and quickly died.

"Excuse me, Professor Berman, will you take up Camus and Sartre next semester, maybe?" The girl who sat in front of his desk was standing over him with her earnest smile and finished examination folder.

"That might prove somewhat difficult, since I won't be here."

"No more?"

"No."

"I mean, not even next summer?"

"I doubt it."

"Gee, I'm sorry. I mean, I enjoyed the course and everything."

He bowed his thanks and held his head down until she left. Her compliment, so piteous somehow, brought on the despair he had forced to the dim rear of his mind. He could no longer flee the thought of the exile awaiting him when the class tonight ended. He could either remain in the house in Brooklyn, where the memory of his father's face above the radiance of the Sabbath candles haunted him from the shadows, reminding him of the certainty he had lost and never found again, where the mirrors in his father's room were still shrouded with sheets, as on the day he lay dying and moaning into his beard that his only son was a bad Jew; or he could return to the house in the country, to the silence shrill with loneliness.

The cigarette he was smoking burned his fingers, rousing him, and he saw over the pile of examination folders on his desk that the room was empty except for the Negro girl. She had finished—her pen lay aslant the closed folder on her desk—but she had remained in her seat and she was smiling across the room at him—a set, artificial smile that was both cold and threatening. It utterly denuded him and he was wildly angry suddenly that she had seen him give way to despair; he wanted to remind her (he could not stay the thought; it attacked him like an assailant from a dark turn in his mind) that she was only black after all. . . . His head dropped and he almost wept with shame.

The girl stiffened as if she had seen the thought and then the tiny muscles around her mouth quickly arranged the bland smile. She came up to his desk, placed her folder on top of the others and said pleasantly, her eyes like dark, shattered glass that spared Max Berman his reflection, "I've changed my mind. I think I'd like to spend a day at your place in the country if your invitation still holds."

He thought of refusing her, for her voice held neither promise nor passion, but he could not. Her presence, even if it was only for a day, would make his return easier. And there was still the possibility of passion despite her cold manner and the deliberate smile. He thought of how long it had been since he had had someone, of how badly he needed the sleep which followed love and of awakening certain, for the first time in years, of his existence.

"Of course the invitation still holds. I'm driving up tonight."

"I won't be able to come until Sunday," she said firmly. "Is there a train then?"

"Yes, in the morning," he said, and gave her the schedule.

"You'll meet me at the station?"

"Of course. You can't miss my car. It's a very shabby but venerable Chevy."

She smiled stiffly and left, her heels awakening the silence of the empty corridor, the sound reaching back to tap like a warning finger on Max Berman's temple.

PAULE MARSHALL

283

The pale sunlight slanting through the windshield lay like a cat on his knees and the motor of his old Chevy, turning softly under him, could have been the humming of its heart. A little distance from the car a log-cabin station house—the logs blackened by the seasons—stood alone against the hills, and the hills, in turn, lifted softly, still green although the summer was ending, into the vague autumn sky.

The morning mist and pale sun, the green that was still somehow new, made it seem that the season was stirring into life even as it died, and this contradiction pained Max Berman at the same time that it pleased him. For it was his own contradiction after all: his desires which remained those of a young man even as he was dying.

He had been parked for some time in the deserted station, yet his hands were still tensed on the steering wheel and his foot hovered near the accelerator. As soon as he had arrived in the station he had wanted to leave. But like the girl that night on the landing, he was too stiff with tension to move. He could only wait, his eyelid twitching with foreboding, regret, curiosity and hope.

Finally and with no warning the train charged through the fiery green, setting off a tremor underground. Max Berman imagined the girl seated at a window in the train, her hands arranged quietly in her lap and her gaze scanning the hills that were so familiar to him, and yet he could not believe that she was really there. Perhaps her plan had been to disappoint him. She might be in New York or on her way back to Richmond now, laughing at the trick she had played on him. He was convinced of this suddenly, so that even when he saw her walking toward him through the blown steam from under the train, he told himself that she was a mirage created by the steam. Only when she sat beside him in the car, bringing with her, it seemed, an essence she had distilled from the morning air and rubbed into her skin, was he certain of her reality.

"I brought my bathing suit but it's much too cold to swim," she said and gave him the deliberate smile.

He did not see it; he only heard her voice, its warm Southern lilt in the chill, its intimacy in the closed car—and an excitement swept him, cold first and then hot, as if the sun had burst in his blood.

"It's the morning air," he said. "By noon it should be like summer again."

"Is that a promise?"

"Yes."

By noon the cold morning mist had lifted above the hills and below, in the lake valley, the sunlight was a sheer gold net spread out on the grass as if to dry, draped on the trees and flung, glinting, over the lake. Max Berman felt it brush his shoulders gently as he sat by the lake waiting for the girl, who had gone up to the house to change into her swimsuit.

He had spent the morning showing her the fields and small wood near his house. During the long walk he had been careful to keep a little apart from her. He would extend a hand as they climbed a rise or when she stepped uncertainly over a rock, but he would not really touch her. He was afraid that at his touch, no matter how slight and casual, her scream would spiral into the morning calm, or worse, his touch would unleash the threatening thing he sensed behind her even smile.

He had talked of her paper and she had listened politely and occasionally even asked a question or made a comment. But all the while detached, distant, drawn within herself as she had been that first night in the classroom. And then halfway down a slope she had paused and, pointing to the canvas tops of her white sneakers, which had become wet and dark from the dew secreted in the grass, she had laughed. The sound, coming so abruptly in the midst of her tense quiet, joined her, it seemed, to the wood and wide fields, to the hills; she shared their simplicity and held within her the same strong current of life. Max Berman had felt privileged suddenly, and humble. He had stopped questioning her smile. He had told himself then that it would not matter even if she stopped and picking up a rock bludgeoned him from behind.

"There's a lake near my home, but it's not like this," the girl said, coming up behind him. "Yours is so dark and serious-looking."

He nodded and followed her gaze out to the lake, where the ripples were long, smooth welts raised by the wind, and across to the other bank, where a group of birches stepped delicately down to the lake and bending over touched the water with their branches as if testing it before they plunged.

The girl came and stood beside him now—and she was like a pale gold naiad, the spirit of the lake, her eyes reflecting its somber autumnal tone and her body as supple as the birches. She walked slowly into the water, unaware, it seemed, of the sudden passion in his gaze, or perhaps uncaring; and as she walked she held out her arms in what seemed a gesture of invocation (and Max Berman remembered his father with the fringed shawl draped on his outstretched arms as he invoked their God each Sabbath with the same gesture); her head was bent as if she listened for a voice beneath the water's murmurous surface. When the ground gave way she still seemed to be walking and listening, her arms outstretched. The water reached her waist, her small breasts, her shoulders. She lifted her head once, breathed deeply and disappeared.

She stayed down for a long time and when her white cap finally broke the water some distance out, Max Berman felt strangely stranded and deprived. He understood suddenly the profound cleavage between them and the absurdity of his hope. The water between them became the years which separated them. Her white cap was the sign of her purity, while the silt darkening the lake was the flotsam of his failures. Above all, their color—her arms a pale, flashing gold in the sunlit water and his bled white and flaccid with the veins like angry blue penciling—marked the final barrier.

He was sad as they climbed toward the house late that afternoon and troubled. A crow cawed derisively in the bracken, heralding the dusk

PAULE MARSHALL

285

which would not only end their strange day but would also, he felt, unveil her smile, so that he would learn the reason for her coming. And because he was sad, he said wryly, "I think I should tell you that you've been spending the day with something of an outcast."

"Oh," she said and waited.

He told her of the dismissal, punctuating his words with the little hoarse, deprecating laugh and waving aside the pain with his cigarette. She listened, polite but neutral, and because she remained unmoved, he wanted to confess all the more. So that during dinner and afterward when they sat outside on the porch, he told her of the investigation.

"It was very funny once you saw it from the proper perspective, which I did, of course," he said. "I mean here they were accusing me of crimes I couldn't remember committing and asking me for the names of people with whom I had never associated. It was pure farce. But I made a mistake. I should have done something dramatic or something just as farcical. Bared my breast in the public market place or written a tome on my apostasy, naming names. It would have been a far different story then. Instead of my present ignominy I would have been offered a chairmanship at Yale. . . . No? Well, Brandeis then. I would have been draped in honorary degrees. . . ."

"Well, why didn't you confess?" she said impatiently.

"I've often asked myself the same interesting question, but I haven't come up with a satisfactory answer yet. I suspect, though, that I said nothing because none of it really mattered that much."

"What did matter?" she asked sharply.

He sat back, waiting for the witty answer, but none came, because just then the frame upon which his organs were strung seemed to snap and he felt his heart, his lungs, his vital parts fall in a heap within him. Her question had dealt the severing blow, for it was the same question he understood suddenly that the vague forms in his dream asked repeatedly. It had been the plaintive undercurrent to his father's dying moan, the real accusation behind the charges of his inquisitors at the hearing.

For what had mattered? He gazed through his sudden shock at the night squatting on the porch steps, at the hills asleep like gentle beasts in the darkness, at the black screen of the sky where the events of his life passed in a mute, accusing review—and he saw nothing there to which he had given himself or in which he had truly believed since the belief and dedication of his boyhood.

"Did you hear my question?" she asked, and he was glad that he sat within the shadows clinging to the porch screen and could not be seen.

"Yes, I did," he said faintly, and his eyelid twitched. "But I'm afraid it's another one of those I can't answer satisfactorily." And then he struggled for the old flippancy. "You make an excellent examiner, you know. Far better than my inquisitors."

"What will you do now?" her voice and cold smile did not spare him.

He shrugged and the motion, a slow, eloquent lifting of the shoulders, brought with it suddenly the weight and memory of his boyhood. It was the familiar gesture of the women hawkers in Belmont Market, of the men standing outside the temple on Saturday mornings, each of them reflecting his image of God in their forbidding black coats and with the black, tumbling beards in which he had always imagined he could hide as in a forest. All this had mattered, he called loudly to himself, and said aloud to the girl, "Let me see if I can answer this one at least. What *will* I do?" He paused and swung his leg so that his foot in the fastidious French shoe caught the light from the house. "Grow flowers and write my memoirs. How's that? That would be the proper way for a gentleman and scholar to retire. Or hire one of those hefty housekeepers who will bully me and when I die in my sleep draw the sheet over my face and call my lawyer. That's somewhat European, but how's that?"

When she said nothing for a long time, he added soberly. "But that's not a fair question for me any more. I leave all such considerations to the young. To you, for that matter. What will you do, my dear Miss Williams?"

It was as if she had been expecting the question and had been readying her answer all the time that he had been talking. She leaned forward eagerly and with her face and part of her body fully in the light, she said, "I will do something. I don't know what yet, but something."

Max Berman started back a little. The answer was so unlike her vague, resigned "I know" on the landing that night when he had admonished her to try something new.

He edged back into the darkness and she leaned further into the light, her eyes overwhelming her face and her mouth set in a thin, determined line. "I will do something," she said, bearing down on each word, "because for the first time in my life I feel almost brave."

He glimpsed this new bravery behind her hard gaze and sensed something vital and purposeful, precious, which she had found and guarded like a prize within her center. He wanted it. He would have liked to snatch it and run like a thief. He no longer desired her but it, and starting forward with a sudden envious cry, he caught her arm and drew her close, seeking it.

But he could not get to it. Although she did not pull away her arm, although she made no protest as his face wavered close to hers, he did not really touch her. She held herself and her prize out of his desperate reach and her smile was a knife she pressed to his throat. He saw himself for what he was in her clear, cold gaze: an old man with skin the color and texture of dough that had been kneaded by the years into tragic folds, with faded eyes adrift behind a pair of rimless glasses and the roughened flesh at his throat like a bird's wattles. And as the disgust which he read in her eyes swept him, his hand dropped from her arm. He started to murmur, "Forgive me . . ." when suddenly she caught hold of his wrist, pulling him close again, and he felt the strength which had borne her swiftly through the water earlier hold him now as she said quietly and

PAULE MARSHALL

287

without passion, "And do you know why, Dr. Berman, I feel almost brave today? Because ever since I can remember my parents were always telling me, 'Stay away from white folks. Just leave them alone. You mind your business and they'll mind theirs. Don't go near them.' And they made sure I didn't. My father, who was the principal of a colored grade school in Richmond, used to drive me to and from school every day. When I needed something from downtown my mother would take me and if the white saleslady asked me anything she would answer. . . .

"And my parents were also always telling me, 'Stay away from niggers,' and that meant anybody darker than we were." She held out her arm in the light and Max Berman saw the skin almost as white as his but for the subtle amber shading. Staring at the arm she said tragically, "I was so confused I never really went near anybody. Even when I went away to college I kept to myself. I didn't marry the man I wanted to because he was dark and I knew my parents would disapprove. . . ." She paused, her wistful gaze searching the darkness for the face of the man she had refused, it seemed, and not finding it she went on sadly. "So after graduation I returned home and started teaching and I was just as confused and frightened and ashamed as always. When my parents died I went on the same way. And I would have gone on like that the rest of my life if it hadn't been for you, Dr. Berman"—and the sarcasm leaped behind her cold smile. "In a way you did me a favor. You let me know how you and most of the people like you—see me."

"My dear Miss Williams, I assure you I was not attracted to you because you were colored. . . ." And he broke off, remembering just how acutely aware of her color he had been.

"I'm not interested in your reasons!" she said brutally. "What matters is what it meant to me. I thought about this these last three weeks and about my parents how wrong they had been, how frightened, and the terrible thing they had done to me . . . and I wasn't confused any longer." Her head lifted, tremulous with her new assurance. "I can do something now! I can begin," she said with her head poised. "Look how I came all the way up here to tell you this to your face. Because how could you harm me? You're so old you're like a cup I could break in my hand." And her hand tightened on his wrist, wrenching the last of his frail life from him, it seemed. Through the quick pain he remembered her saying on the landing that night: "Maybe in order for a person to live someone else must die" and her quiet "I believe this" then. Now her sudden laugh, an infinitely cruel sound in the warm night, confirmed her belief.

Suddenly she was the one who seemed old, indeed ageless. Her touch became mortal and Max Berman saw the darkness that would end his life gathered in her eyes. But even as he sprang back, jerking his arm away, a part of him rushed forward to embrace that darkness, and his cry, wounding the night, held both ecstasy and terror.

"That's all I came for," she said, rising. "You can drive me to the station now."

They drove to the station in silence. Then, just as the girl started from the car, she turned with an ironic, pitiless smile and said, "You know, it's been a nice day, all things considered. It really turned summer again as you said it would. And even though your lake isn't anything like the one near my home, it's almost as nice."

Max Berman bowed to her for the last time, accepting with that gesture his responsibility for her rage, which went deeper than his, and for her anger, which would spur her finally to live. And not only for her, but for all those at last whom he had wronged through his indifference: his father lying in the room of shrouded mirrors, the wives he had never loved, his work which he had never believed in enough and lastly (even though he knew it was too late and he would not be spared), himself.

Too weary to move, he watched the girl cross to the train which would bear her south, her head lifted as though she carried life as lightly there as if it were a hat made of tulle. When the train departed his numbed eyes followed it until its rear light was like a single firefly in the immense night or the last flickering of his life. Then he drove back through the darkness.

ONE OFF THE SHORT LIST

by

DORIS LESSING
(b. 1919)

Born in Persia, Doris Lessing has lived in southern Rhodesia (now Zimbabwe) and, since 1949, in England. Her fiction has as its major theme the dehumanizing effects of violence in our time. Children of Violence (1952–1965) and The Golden Notebook *(1962) focus on women as the central consciousnesses through whom society is perceived; many of her characters are "free women," independent of men. Lessing's five-volume science fiction series about the planet Canopus (1979–1983) deals with authoritarianism, colonialism, and destruction of the environment. Her lifelong political activism led to a book about Afghanistan,* The Wind Blows Away Our Words . . . *(1987).*

When he had first seen Barbara Coles, some years before, he only noticed her because someone said: "That's Johnson's new girl." He certainly had not used of her the private erotic formula: *Yes, that one.* He even wondered what Johnson saw in her. "She won't last long," he remembered thinking, as he watched Johnson, a handsome man, but rather flushed with drink, flirting with some unknown girl while Barbara stood by a wall looking on. He thought she had a sullen expression.

She was a pale girl, not slim, for her frame was generous, but her figure could pass as good. Her straight yellow hair was parted on one side in a way that struck him as gauche. He did not notice what she wore. But her eyes were all right, he remembered: large, and solidly green, square-looking because of some trick of the flesh at their corners. Emeraldlike eyes in the face of a schoolgirl, or young schoolmistress who was watching her lover flirt and would later sulk about it.

Her name sometimes cropped up in the papers. She was a stage decorator, a designer, something on those lines.

Then a Sunday newspaper had a competition for stage design and she won it. Barbara Coles was one of the "names" in the theatre, and her photograph was seen about. It was always serious. He remembered having thought her sullen.

One night he saw her across the room at a party. She was talking with a well-known actor. Her yellow hair was still done on one side, but now it looked sophisticated. She wore an emerald ring on her right hand that seemed deliberately to invite comparison with her eyes. He walked over and said: "We have met before, Graham Spence." He noted, with discomfort, that he sounded abrupt. "I'm sorry, I don't remember, but how do you do?" she said, smiling. And continued her conversation.

He hung around a bit, but soon she went off with a group of people she was inviting to her home for a drink. She did not invite Graham. There was about her an assurance, a carelessness, that he recognised as the signature of success. It was then, watching her laugh as she went off with her friends, that he used the formula: *"Yes, that one."* And he went home to his wife with enjoyable expectation, as if his date with Barbara Coles were already arranged.

His marriage was twenty years old. At first it had been stormy, painful, tragic—full of partings, betrayals and sweet reconciliations. It had taken him at least a decade to realise that there was nothing remarkable about this marriage that he had lived through with such surprise of the mind and the senses. On the contrary, the marriages of most of the people he knew, whether they were first, second or third attempts, were just the same. His had run true to form even to the serious love affair with the young girl for whose sake he had *almost* divorced his wife—yet at the last moment had changed his mind, letting the girl down so that he must have her for always (not unpleasurably) on his conscience. It was with humiliation that he had understood that this drama was not at all the unique thing he had imagined. It was nothing more than the experience of everyone in his circle. And presumably in everybody else's circle too?

Anyway, round about the tenth year of his marriage he had seen a good many things clearly, a certain kind of emotional adventure went from his life, and the marriage itself changed.

His wife had married a poor youth with a great future as a writer. Sacrifices had been made, chiefly by her, for that future. He was neither unaware of them, nor ungrateful; in fact he felt permanently guilty about it. He at last published a decently successful book, then a second which now, thank God, no one remembered. He had drifted into radio, television, book reviewing.

He understood he was not going to make it; that he had become—not a hack, no one could call him that—but a member of that army of people who live by their wits on the fringes of the arts. The moment of realisation was when he was in a pub one lunchtime near the B.B.C. where he often dropped in to meet others like himself: he understood that was why he went there—they *were* like him. Just as that melodramatic marriage had turned out to be like everyone else's—except that it had been shared with one woman instead of with two or three—so it had turned out that his unique talent, his struggles as a writer had led him here, to this pub and the half dozen pubs like it, where all the men in sight had

the same history. They all had their novel, their play, their book of poems, a moment of fame, to their credit. Yet here they were, running television programmes about which they were cynical (to each other or to
their wives) or writing reviews about other people's books. Yes, that's
what he had become, an impresario of other people's talent. These two
moments of clarity, about his marriage and about his talent, had roughly
coincided: and (perhaps not by chance) had coincided with his wife's
decision to leave him for a man younger than himself who had a future,
she said, as a playwright. Well, he had talked her out of it. For her part
she had to understand he was not going to be the T. S. Eliot or Graham
Greene of our time—but after all, how many were? She must finally
understand this, for he could no longer bear her awful bitterness. For his
part he must stop coming home drunk at five in the morning, and starting a new romantic affair every six months which he took so seriously
that he made her miserable because of her implied deficiencies. In short
he was to be a good husband. (He had always been a dutiful father.) And
she a good wife. And so it was: the marriage became stable, as they say.

The formula: *Yes, that one* no longer implied a necessarily sexual
relationship. In its more mature form, it was far from being something
he was ashamed of. On the contrary, it expressed a humorous respect for
what he was, for his real talents and flair, which had turned out to be not
artistic after all, but to do with emotional life, hard-earned experience. It
expressed an ironical dignity, a proving to himself not only: I can be honest about myself, but also: I have earned the best in *that* field whenever I
want it.

He watched the field for the women who were well known in the arts,
or in politics; looked out for photographs, listened for bits of gossip. He
made a point of going to see them act, or dance, or orate. He built up a
not unshrewd picture of them. He would either quietly pull strings to
meet her or—more often, for there was a gambler's pleasure in waiting—
bide his time until he met her in the natural course of events, which was
bound to happen sooner or later. He would be seen out with her a few
times in public, which was in order, since his work meant he had to
entertain well-known people, male and female. His wife always knew, he
told her. He might have a brief affair with this woman, but more often
than not it was the appearance of an affair. Not that he didn't get pleasure from other people envying him—he would make a point, for instance,
of taking this woman into the pubs where his male colleagues went. It
was that his real pleasure came when he saw her surprise at how well
she was understood by him. He enjoyed the atmosphere he was able to
set up between an intelligent woman and himself: a humorous complicity which had in it much that was unspoken, and which almost made
sex irrelevant.

Onto the list of women with whom he planned to have this relationship went Barbara Coles. There was no hurry. Next week, next month,
next year, they would meet at a party. The world of well-known people

in London is a small one. Big and little fishes, they drift around, nose each other, flirt their fins, wriggle off again. When he bumped into Barbara Coles, it would be time to decide whether or not to sleep with her.

Meanwhile he listened. But he didn't discover much. She had a husband and children, but the husband seemed to be in the background. The children were charming and well brought up, like everyone else's children. She had affairs, they said; but while several men he met sounded familiar with her, it was hard to determine whether they had slept with her, because none directly boasted of her. She was spoken of in terms of her friends, her work, her house, a party she had given, a job she had found someone. She was liked, she was respected, and Graham Spence's self-esteem was flattered because he had chosen her. He looked forward to saying in just the same tone: "Barbara Coles asked me what I thought about the set and I told her quite frankly. . . ."

Then by chance he met a young man who did boast about Barbara Coles; he claimed to have had the great love affair with her, and recently at that; and he spoke of it as something generally known. Graham realised how much he had already become involved with her in his imagination because of how perturbed he was now, on account of the character of this youth, Jack Kennaway. He had recently become successful as a magazine editor—one of those young men who, not as rare as one might suppose in the big cities, are successful from sheer impertinence, effrontery. Without much talent or taste, yet he had the charm of his effrontery. "Yes, I'm going to succeed, because I've decided to; yes, I may be stupid, but not so stupid that I don't know my deficiencies. Yes, I'm going to be successful because you people with integrity, etc., etc., simply don't believe in the possibility of people like me. You are too cowardly to stop me. Yes, I've taken your measure and I'm going to succeed because I've got the courage, not only to be unscrupulous, but to be quite frank about it. And besides, you admire me, you must, or otherwise you'd stop me. . . ." Well, that was young Jack Kennaway, and he shocked Graham. He was a tall, languishing young man, handsome in a dark melting way, and, it was quite clear, he was either asexual or homosexual. And this youth boasted of the favours of Barbara Coles; boasted, indeed, of her love. Either she was a raving neurotic with a taste for neurotics; or Jack Kennaway was a most accomplished liar; or she slept with anyone. Graham was intrigued. He took Jack Kennaway out to dinner in order to hear him talk about Barbara Coles. There was no doubt the two were pretty close—all those dinners, theatres, weekends in the country—Graham Spence felt he had put his finger on the secret pulse of Barbara Coles; and it was intolerable that he must wait to meet her; he decided to arrange it.

It became unnecessary. She was in the news again, with a run of luck. She had done a successful historical play, and immediately afterwards a modern play, and then a hit musical. In all three, the sets were remarked on. Graham saw some interviews in newspapers and on television. These all centered around the theme of her being able to deal easily with so many different styles of theatre; but the real point was, of course, that she was a woman, which naturally added piquancy to the thing. And now Graham Spence was asked to do a half-hour radio interview with her. He planned the questions he would ask her with care, drawing on what people had said of her, but above all on his instinct and experience with women. The interview was to be at nine-thirty at night; he was to pick her up at six from the theatre where she was currently at work, so that there would be time, as the letter from the B.B.C. had put it, "for you and Miss Coles to get to know each other."

At six he was at the stage door, but a message from Miss Coles said she was not quite ready, could he wait a little. He hung about, then went to the pub opposite for a quick one, but still no Miss Coles. So he made his way backstage, directed by voices, hammering, laughter. It was badly lit, and the group of people at work did not see him. The director, James Poynter, had his arm around Barbara's shoulders. He was newly well-known, a carelessly good-looking young man reputed to be intelligent. Barbara Coles wore a dark blue overall, and her flat hair fell over her face so that she kept pushing it back with the hand that had the emerald on it. These two stood close, side by side. Three young men, stagehands, were on the other side of a trestle which had sketches and drawings on it. They were studying some sketches. Barbara said, in a voice warm with energy: "Well, so I thought if we did *this*—do you see, James? What do you think, Steven?" "Well, love," said the young man she called Steven, "I see your idea, but I wonder if . . . " "I think you're right, Babs," said the director. "Look," said Barbara, holding one of the sketches to-ward Steven, "look, let me show you." They all leaned forward, the five of them, absorbed in the business.

Suddenly Graham couldn't stand it. He understood he was shaken to his depths. He went off stage, and stood with his back against a wall in the dingy passage that led to the dressing room. His eyes were filled with tears. He was seeing what a long way he had come from the crude, un-compromising, admirable young egomaniac he had been when he was twenty. That group of people there—working, joking, arguing, yes, that's what he hadn't known for years. What bound them was the democracy of respect for each other's work, a confidence in themselves and in each other. They looked like people banded together against a world which they—no, not despised, but which they measured, understood, would fight to the death, out of respect for what *they* stood for, for what *it* stood for. It was a long time since he felt part of that balance. And he under-stood that he had seen Barbara Coles when she was most herself, at ease with a group of people she worked with. It was then, with the tears dry-ing on his eyelids, which felt old and ironic, that he decided he would sleep with Barbara Coles. It was a necessity for him. He went back through the door onto the stage, burning with this single determination.

The five were still together. Barbara had a length of blue gleaming stuff which she was draping over the shoulder of Steven, the stagehand. He was showing it off, and the others watched. "What do you think, James?" she asked the director. "We've got that sort of dirty green, and I thought . . ." "Well," said James, not sure at all, "well, Babs, well . . ."

Now Graham went forward so that he stood beside Barbara, and said: "I'm Graham Spence, we've met before." For the second time she smiled socially and said: "Oh I'm sorry, I don't remember." Graham nodded at James, whom he had known, or at least had met off and on, for years. But it was obvious James didn't remember him either.

"From the B.B.C.," said Graham to Barbara, again sounding abrupt, against his will. "Oh I'm sorry, I'm sorry, I forgot all about it. I've got to be interviewed," she said to the group. "Mr. Spence is a journalist." Graham allowed himself a small smile ironical of the word journalist, but she was not looking at him. She was going on with her work. "We should decide tonight," she said. "Steven's right." "Yes, I am right," said the stagehand. "She's right, James, we need that blue with that sludge-green everywhere." "James," said Barbara, "James, what's wrong with it? You haven't said." She moved forward to James, passing Graham. Remembering him again, she became contrite. "I'm sorry," she said, "we can none of us agree. Well, look"—she turned to Graham—"you advise us, we've got so involved with it that . . ." At which James laughed, and so did the stagehands. "No, Babs," said James, "of course Mr. Spence can't advise. He's just this moment come in. We've got to decide. Well I'll give you till tomorrow morning. Time to go home, it must be six by now."

"It's nearly seven," said Graham, taking command.

"It isn't!" said Barbara, dramatic. "My God, how terrible, how appalling, how could I have done such a thing. . . ." She was laughing at herself. "Well, you'll have to forgive me, Mr. Spence, because you haven't got any alternative."

They began laughing again: this was clearly a group joke. And now Graham took his chance. He said firmly, as if he were her director, in fact copying James Poynter's manner with her: "No, Miss Coles, I won't forgive you, I've been kicking my heels for nearly an hour." She grimaced, then laughed and accepted it. James said: "There, Babs, that's how you ought to be treated. We spoil you." He kissed her on the cheek, she kissed him on both his, the stagehands moved off. "Have a good evening, Babs," said James, going, and nodding to Graham, who stood concealing his pleasure with difficulty. He knew, because he had had the courage to be firm, indeed, peremptory, with Barbara, that he had saved himself hours of maneuvering. Several drinks, a dinner—perhaps two or three evenings of drinks and dinners—had been saved because he was now on this footing with Barbara Coles, a man who could say: "No, I won't forgive you, you've kept me waiting."

She said: "I've just got to . . ." and went ahead of him. In the passage she hung her overall on a peg. She was thinking, it seemed, of something else, but seeing him watching her, she smiled at him, companionably: he realised with triumph it was the sort of smile she would offer one of the stagehands, or even James. She said again: "Just one second . . ." and went to the stage-door office. She and the stage doorman conferred. There was some problem. Graham said, taking another chance: "What's the trouble, can I help?"—as if he could help, as if he expected to be able to. "Well . . ." she said, frowning. Then, to the man: "No, it'll be all right. Goodnight." She came to Graham. "We've got ourselves into a bit of a fuss because half the set's in Liverpool and half's here and—but it will sort itself out." She stood, at ease, chatting to him, one colleague to another. All this was admirable, he felt; but there would be a bad moment when they emerged from the special atmosphere of the theatre into the street. He took another decision, grasped her arm firmly, and said: "We're going to have a drink before we do anything at all, it's a terrible evening out." Her arm felt resistant, but remained within his. It was raining outside, luckily. He directed her, authoritative: "No, not that pub, there's a nicer one around the corner." "Oh, but I like this pub," said Barbara, "we always use it."

"Of course you do," he said to himself. But in that pub there would be the stagehands, and probably James, and he'd lose contact with her. He'd become a *journalist* again. He took her firmly out of danger around two corners, into a pub he picked at random. A quick look around—no, they weren't there. At least, if there were people from the theatre, she showed no sign. She asked for a beer. He ordered her a double Scotch, which she accepted. Then, having won a dozen preliminary rounds already, he took time to think. Something was bothering him—what? Yes, it was what he had observed backstage, Barbara and James Poynter. Was she having an affair with him? Because if so, it would all be much more difficult. He made himself see the two of them together, and thought with a jealousy surprisingly strong: *Yes, that's it.* Meantime he sat looking at her, seeing himself look at her, *a man gazing in calm appreciation at a woman:* waiting for her to feel it and respond. She was examining the pub. Her white woolen suit was belted, and had a not unprovocative suggestion of being a uniform. Her flat yellow hair, hastily pushed back after work, was untidy. Her clear white skin, without any colour, made her look tired. Not very exciting, at the moment, thought Graham, but maintaining his appreciative pose for when she would turn and see it. He knew what she would see: he was relying not only on the "warm kindly" beam of his gaze, for this was merely a reinforcement of the impression he knew he made. He had black hair, a little greyed. His clothes were loose and bulky—masculine. His eyes were humorous and appreciative. He was not, never had been, concerned to lessen the impression of being settled, dependable: the husband and father. On the contrary, he knew women found it reassuring.

When she at last turned she said, almost apologetic: "Would you mind if we sat down? I've been lugging great things around all day." She had spotted two empty chairs in a corner. So had he, but rejected them, because there were other people at the table. "But my dear, of course!" They took the chairs, and then Barbara said: "If you'll excuse me a moment." She had remembered she needed make-up. He watched her go off, annoyed with himself. She was tired; and he could have understood, protected, sheltered. He realised that in the other pub, with the people she had worked with all day, she would not have thought: "I must make myself up, I must be on show." That was for outsiders. She had not, until now, considered Graham an outsider, because of his taking his chance to seem one of the working group in the theatre; but now he had thrown his opportunity away. She returned armoured. Her hair was sleek, no longer defenceless. And she had made up her eyes. Her eyebrows were untouched, pale gold streaks above the brilliant green eyes whose lashes were blackened. Rather good, he thought, the contrast. Yes, but the moment had gone when he could say: Did you know you had a smudge on your cheek? Or—my dear girl!—pushing her hair back with the edge of a brotherly hand. In fact, unless he was careful, he'd be back at starting point.

He remarked: "That emerald is very cunning"—smiling into her eyes.

She smiled politely, and said: "It's not cunning, it's an accident, it was my grandmother's." She flirted her hand lightly by her face, though, smiling. But that was something she had done before, to a compliment she had had before, and often. It was all social, she had become social entirely. She remarked: "Didn't you say it was half past nine we had to record?"

"My dear Barbara, we've got two hours. We'll have another drink or two, then I'll ask you a couple of questions, then we'll drop down to the studio and get it over, and then we'll have a comfortable supper."

"I'd rather eat now, if you don't mind. I had no lunch, and I'm really hungry."

"But my dear, of course." He was angry. Just as he had been surprised by his real jealousy over James, so now he was thrown off balance by his anger: he had been counting on the long quiet dinner afterwards to establish intimacy. "Finish your drink and I'll take you to Nott's." Nott's was expensive. He glanced at her assessingly as he mentioned it. She said: "I wonder if you know Butler's? It's good and it's rather close." Butler's was good, and it was cheap, and he gave her a good mark for liking it. But Nott's it was going to be. "My dear, we'll get into a taxi and be at Nott's in a moment, don't worry."

She obediently got to her feet: the way she did it made him understand how badly he had slipped. She was saying to herself: Very well, he's like that, then all right, I'll do what he wants and get it over with. . . .

Swallowing his own drink he followed her, and took her arm in the pub doorway. It was polite within his. Outside it drizzled. No taxi. He was having bad luck now. They walked in silence to the end of the street. There Barbara glanced into a side street where a sign said: BUTLER'S. Not to remind him of it, on the contrary, she concealed the glance. And here she was, entirely at his disposal, they might never have shared the comradely moment in the theatre.

They walked half a mile to Nott's. No taxis. She made conversation: this was, he saw, to cover any embarrassment he might feel because of a half-mile walk through rain when she was tired. She was talking about some theory to do with the theatre, with designs for theatre building. He heard himself saying, and repeatedly: Yes, yes, yes. He thought about Nott's, how to get things right when they reached Nott's. There he took the headwaiter aside, gave him a pound, and instructions. They were put in a corner. Large Scotches appeared. The menus were spread. "And now, my dear," he said, "I apologise for dragging you here, but I hope you'll think it's worth it."

"Oh, it's charming. I've always liked it. It's just that . . ." She stopped herself saying: it's such a long way. She smiled at him, raising her glass, and said: "It's one of my very favorite places, and I'm glad you dragged me here." Her voice was flat with tiredness. All this was appalling; he knew it; and he sat thinking how to retrieve his position. Meanwhile she fingered the menu. The headwaiter took the order, but Graham made a gesture which said: Wait a moment. He wanted the Scotch to take effect before she ate. But she saw his silent order; and, without annoyance or reproach, leaned forward to say, sounding patient: "Graham, please, I've got to eat, you don't want me drunk when you interview me, do you?"

"They are bringing it as fast as they can," he said, making it sound as if she were greedy. He looked neither at the headwaiter nor at Barbara. He noted in himself, as he slipped further and further away from contact with her, a cold determination growing in him; one apart from, apparently, any conscious act of will, that come what may, if it took all night, he'd be in her bed before morning. And now, seeing the small pale face, with the enormous green eyes, it was for the first time that he imagined her in his arms. Although he had said: *Yes, that one*, weeks ago, it was only now that he imagined her as a sensual experience. Now he did, so strongly that he could only glance at her, and then away towards the waiters who were bringing food.

"Thank the Lord," said Barbara, and all at once her voice was gay and intimate. "Thank heavens. Thank every power that is. . . ." She was making fun of her own exaggeration; and, as he saw, because she wanted to put him at his ease after his boorishness over delaying the food. (She hadn't been taken in, he saw, humiliated, disliking her.) "Thank all the gods of Nott's," she went on, "because if I hadn't eaten inside five minutes I'd have died, I tell you." With which she picked up her knife and fork and began on her steak. He poured wine, smiling with her, thinking that *this* moment of closeness he would not throw away. He watched her frank hunger as she ate, and thought: Sensual—it's strange I hadn't wondered whether she would be or not.

"Now," she said, sitting back, having taken the edge off her hunger: "Let's get to work."

THE SEX OBJECT

He said: "I've thought it over very carefully—how to present you. The first thing seems to me, we must get away from that old chestnut: Miss Coles, how extraordinary for a woman to be so versatile in her work . . . I hope you agree?" This was his trump card. He had noted, when he had seen her on television, her polite smile when this note was struck. (The smile he had seen so often tonight.) This smile said: All right, if you *have* to be stupid, what can I do?

Now she laughed and said: "What a relief. I was afraid you were going to do the same thing."

"Good, now you eat and I'll talk."

In his carefully prepared monologue he spoke of the different styles of theatre she had shown herself mistress of, but not directly: he was flattering her on the breadth of her experience; the complexity of her character, as shown in her work. She ate, steadily, her face showing nothing. At last she asked: "And how did you plan to introduce this?"

He had meant to spring that on her as a surprise, something like: Miss Coles, a surprisingly young woman for what she has accomplished (she was thirty? thirty-two?) and a very attractive one. . . . "Perhaps I can give you an idea of what she's like if I say she could be taken for the film star Marie Carletta. . . ." The Carletta was a strong earthy blonde, known to be intellectual. He now saw he could not possibly say this: he could imagine her cool look if he did. She said: "Do you mind if we get away from all that—my manifold talents, et cetera. . . ." He felt himself stiffen with annoyance; particularly because this was not an accusation, he saw she did not think him worth one. She had assessed him: This is the kind of man who uses this kind of flattery and therefore. . . . It made him angrier that she did not even trouble to say: Why did you do exactly what you promised you wouldn't? She was being invincibly polite, trying to conceal her patience with his stupidity.

"After all," she was saying, "it is a stage designer's job to design what comes up. Would anyone take, let's say Johnnie Cranmore" (another stage designer) "onto the air or television and say: How very versatile you are because you did that musical about Java last month and a modern play about Irish labourers this?"

He battened down his anger. "My dear Barbara, I'm sorry. I didn't realise that what I said would sound just like the mixture as before. So what shall we talk about?"

"What I was saying as we walked to the restaurant: can we get away from the personal stuff?"

Now he almost panicked. Then, thank God, he laughed from nervousness, for she laughed and said: "You didn't hear one word I said."

"No, I didn't. I was frightened you were going to be furious because I made you walk so far when you were tired."

They laughed together, back to where they had been in the theatre. He leaned over, took her hand, kissed it. He said: "Tell me again." He thought: Damn, now she's going to be earnest and intellectual.

DORIS LESSING

But he understood he had been stupid. He had forgotten himself at twenty—or, for that matter, at thirty; forgotten one could live inside an idea, a set of ideas, with enthusiasm. For in talking about her ideas (also the ideas of the people she worked with) for a new theatre, a new style of theatre, she was as she had been with her colleagues over the sketches or the blue material. She was easy, informal, almost chattering. This was how, he remembered, one talked about ideas that were a breath of life. The ideas, he thought, were intelligent enough; and he would agree with them, with her, if he believed it mattered a damn one way or another, if any of these enthusiasms mattered a damn. But at least he now had the key, he knew what to do. At the end of not more than half an hour, they were again two professionals, talking about ideas they shared, for he remembered caring about all this himself once. *When? How many years ago was it that he had been able to care?*

At last he said: "My dear Barbara, do you realise the impossible position you're putting me in? Margaret Ruyen who runs this programme is determined to do you personally, the poor woman hasn't got a serious thought in her head."

Barbara frowned. He put his hand on hers, teasing her for the frown: "No, wait, trust me, we'll circumvent her." She smiled. In fact Margaret Ruyen had left it all to him, had said nothing about Miss Coles.

"They aren't very bright—the brass," he said. "Well, never mind: we'll work out what we want, do it, and it'll be a *fait accompli.*"

"Thank you, what a relief. How lucky I was to be given you to interview me." She was relaxed now, because of the whisky, the food, the wine, above all because of this new complicity against Margaret Ruyen. It would all be easy. They worked out five or six questions, over coffee, and took a taxi through rain to the studios. He noted that the cold necessity to have her, to make her, to beat her down, had left him. He was even seeing himself, as the evening ended, kissing her on the cheek and going home to his wife. This comradeship was extraordinarily pleasant. It was balm to the wound he had not known he carried until that evening, when he had had to accept the justice of the word *journalist.* He felt he could talk forever about the state of the theatre, its finances, the stupidity of the government, the philistinism of . . .

At the studios he was careful to make a joke so that they walked in on the laugh. He was careful that the interview began at once, without conversation with Margaret Ruyen; and that from the moment the green light went on, his voice lost its easy familiarity. He made sure that not one personal note was struck during the interview. Afterwards, Margaret Ruyen, who was pleased, came forward to say so; but he took her aside to say that Miss Coles was tired and needed to be taken home at once: for he knew this must look to Barbara as if he were squaring a producer who had been expecting a different interview. He led Barbara off, her hand held tight in his against his side. "Well," he said, "we've done it, and I don't think she knows what hit her."

THE SEX OBJECT

300

"Thank you," she said, "it really was pleasant to talk about something sensible for once."

He kissed her lightly on the mouth. She returned it, smiling. By now he felt sure that the mood need not slip again, he could hold it.

"There are two things we can do," he said. "You can come to my club and have a drink. Or I can drive you home and you can give me a drink. I have to go past you."

"Where do you live?"

"Wimbledon." He lived, in fact, at Highgate; but she lived in Fulham. He was taking another chance, but by the time she found out, they would be in a position to laugh over his ruse.

"Good," she said. "You can drop me home then. I have to get up early." He made no comment. In the taxi he took her hand; it was heavy in his, and he asked: "Does James slave-drive you?"

"I didn't realize you knew him—no, he doesn't."

"Well I don't know him intimately. What's he like to work with?"

"Wonderful," she said at once. "There's no one I enjoy working with more."

Jealousy spurted in him. He could not help himself: "Are you having an affair with him?"

She looked: what's it to do with you? but said: "No, I'm not."

"He's very attractive," he said, with a chuckle of worldly complicity. She said nothing, and he insisted: "If I were a woman I'd have an affair with James."

It seemed she might very well say nothing. But she remarked: "He's married."

His spirits rose in a swoop. It was the first stupid remark she had made. It was a remark of such staggering stupidity that . . . he let out a humoring snort of laughter, put his arm around her, kissed her, said: "My dear little Babs."

She said: "Why Babs?"

"Is that the prerogative of James? And of the stagehands?" he could not prevent himself adding.

"I'm only called that at work." She was stiff inside his arm.

"My dear Barbara, then . . ." He waited for her to enlighten and explain, but she said nothing. Soon she moved out of his arm, on the pretext of lighting a cigarette. He lit it for her. He noted that his determination to lay her and at all costs, had come back. They were outside her house. He said quickly: "And now, Barbara, you can make me a cup of coffee and give me a brandy." She hesitated; but he was out of the taxi, paying, opening the door for her. The house had no lights on, he noted. He said: "We'll be very quiet so as not to wake the children."

She turned her head slowly to look at him. She said, flat, replying to his real question: "My husband is away. As for the children, they are visiting friends tonight." She now went ahead of him to the door of the house. It was a small house, in a terrace of small and not very pretty houses. Inside a little, bright, intimate hall, she said: "I'll go and make some coffee. Then, my friend, you must go home because I'm very tired."

The *my friend* struck him deep, because he had become vulnerable during their comradeship. He said gabbling: "You're annoyed with me— oh, please don't, I'm sorry."

She smiled, from a cool distance. He saw, in the small light from the ceiling, her extraordinary eyes. "Green" eyes are hazel, are brown with green flecks, are even blue. Eyes are chequered, flawed, changing. Hers were solid green, but really, he had never seen anything like them before. They were like very deep water. They were like—well, emeralds; or the absolute clarity of green in the depths of a tree in summer. And now, as she smiled almost perpendicularly up at him, he saw a darkness come over them. Darkness swallowed the clear green. She said: "I'm not in the least annoyed." It was as if she had yawned with boredom. "And now I'll get the things . . . in there." She nodded at a white door and left him. He went into a long, very tidy white room, that had a narrow bed in one corner, a table covered with drawings, sketches, pencils. Tacked to the walls with drawing pins were swatches of coloured stuffs. Two small chairs stood near a low round table: an area of comfort in the working room. He was thinking: I wouldn't like it if my wife had a room like this. I wonder what Barbara's husband . . .? He had not thought of her till now in relation to her husband, or to her children. Hard to imagine her with a frying pan in her hand, or for that matter, cosy in the double bed.

A noise outside: he hastily arranged himself, leaning with one arm on the mantelpiece. She came in with a small tray that had cups, glasses, brandy, coffeepot. She looked abstracted. Graham was on the whole flattered by this: it probably meant she was at ease in his presence. He realised he was a little tight and rather tired. Of course, she was tired too, that was why she was vague. He remembered that earlier that evening he had lost a chance by not using her tiredness. Well now, if he were intelligent . . . She was about to pour coffee. He firmly took the coffeepot out of her hand, and nodded at a chair. Smiling, she obeyed him. "That's better," he said. He poured coffee, poured brandy, and pulled the table towards her. She watched him. Then he took her hand, kissed it, patted it, laid it down gently. Yes, he thought, I did that well.

Now, a problem. He wanted to be closer to her, but she was fitted into a damned silly little chair that had arms. If he were to sit by her on the floor . . .? But no, for him, the big bulky reassuring man, there could be no casual gestures, no informal postures. Suppose I scoop her out of the chair onto the bed? He drank his coffee as he plotted. Yes, he'd carry her to the bed, but not yet.

"Graham," she said, setting down her cup. She was, he saw with annoyance, looking tolerant. "Graham, in about half an hour I want to be in bed and asleep."

As she said this, she offered him a smile of amusement at this situation—man and woman maneuvering, the great comic situation. And with part of himself he could have shared it. Almost, he smiled with her, laughed. (Not till days later he exclaimed to himself: Lord what a mistake I made, not to share the joke with her then: that was where I went seriously wrong.) But he could not smile. His face was frozen, with a stiff pride. Not because she had been watching him plot; the amusement she now offered him took the sting out of that; but because of his revived determination that he was going to have his own way, he was going to have her. He was not going home. But he felt that he held a bunch of keys, and did not know which one to choose.

He lifted the second small chair opposite to Barbara, moving aside the coffee table for this purpose. He sat in this chair, leaned forward, took her two hands, and said: "My dear, don't make me go home yet, don't, I beg you." The trouble was, nothing had happened all evening that could be felt to lead up to these words and his tone—simple, dignified, human being pleading with human being for surcease. He saw himself leaning forward, his big hands swallowing her small ones; he saw his face, warm with the appeal. And he realised he had meant the words he used. They were nothing more than what he felt. He wanted to stay with her because she wanted him to, because he was her colleague, a fellow worker in the arts. He needed this desperately. But she was examining him, curious rather than surprised, and from a critical distance. He heard himself saying: "If James were here, I wonder what you'd do?" His voice was aggrieved; he saw the sudden dark descend over her eyes, and she said: "Graham, would you like some more coffee before you go?"

He said: "I've been wanting to meet you for years. I know a good many people who know you."

She leaned forward, poured herself a little more brandy, sat back, holding the glass between her two palms on her chest. An odd gesture: Graham felt that this vessel she was cherishing between her hands was herself. A patient, long-suffering gesture. He thought of various men who had mentioned her. He thought of Jack Kennaway, wavered, panicked, said: "For instance, Jack Kennaway."

And now, at the name, an emotion lit her eyes—what was it? He went on, deliberately testing this emotion, adding to it: "I had dinner with him last week—oh, quite by chance!—and he was talking about you."

"Was he?"

He remembered he had thought her sullen, all those years ago. Now she seemed defensive, and she frowned. He said: "In fact he spent most of the evening talking about you."

She said in short, breathless sentences, which he realised were due to anger: "I can very well imagine what he says. But surely you can't think I enjoy being reminded that . . ." She broke off, resenting him, he saw, because he forced her down onto a level she despised. But it was not his level either: it was all her fault, all hers! He couldn't remember not being in control of a situation with a woman for years. Again he felt like a man teetering on a tightrope. He said, trying to make good use of Jack Kennaway, even at this late hour: "Of course, he's a charming boy, but not a man at all."

She looked at him, silent, guarding her brandy glass against her breasts.

"Unless appearances are totally deceptive, of course." He could not resist probing, even though he knew it was fatal.

She said nothing.

"Do you know you are supposed to have had the great affair with Jack Kennaway?" he exclaimed, making this an amused expostulation against the fools who could believe it.

"So I am told." She set down her glass. "And now," she said, standing up, dismissing him. He lost his head, took a step forward, grabbed her in his arms, and groaned: "Barbara!"

She turned her face this way and that under his kisses. He snatched a diagnostic look at her expression—it was still patient. He placed his lips against her neck, groaned "Barbara" again, and waited. She would have to do something. Fight free, respond, something. She did nothing at all. At last she said: "For the Lord's sake, Graham!" She sounded amused: he was again being offered amusement. But if he shared it with her, it would be the end of his chance to have her. He clamped his mouth over hers, silencing her. She did not fight him off so much as blow him off. Her mouth treated his attacking mouth as a woman blows and laughs in water, puffing off waves or spray with a laugh, turning aside her head. It was a gesture half annoyance, half humour. He continued to kiss her while she moved her head and face about under the kisses as if they were small attacking waves.

And so began what, when he looked back on it afterwards, was the most embarrassing experience of his life. Even at the time he hated her for his ineptitude. For he held her there for what must have been nearly half an hour. She was much shorter than he, he had to bend, and his neck ached. He held her rigid, his thighs on either side of hers, her arms clamped to her side in a bear's hug. She was unable to move, except for her head. When his mouth ground hers open and his tongue moved and writhed inside it, she still remained passive. And he could not stop himself. While with his intelligence he watched this ridiculous scene, he was determined to go on, because sooner or later her body must soften in wanting his. And he could not stop because he could not face the horror of the moment when he set her free and she looked at him. And he hated her more, every moment. Catching glimpses of her great green eyes, open and dismal beneath his, he knew he had never disliked anything more than those "jewelled" eyes. They were repulsive to him. It occurred to him at last that even if by now she wanted him, he wouldn't know it, because she was not able to move at all. He cautiously loosened his hold so that she had an inch or so leeway. She remained quite passive. As if, he thought derisively, she had read or been told that the way to incite men maddened by lust was to fight them. He found he was thinking:

Stupid cow, so you imagine I find you attractive, do you? You've got the conceit to think that!

The sheer, raving insanity of this thought hit him, opened his arms, his thighs, and lifted his tongue out of her mouth. She stepped back, wiping her mouth with the back of her hand, and stood dazed with incredulity. The embarrassment that lay in wait for him nearly engulfed him, but he let anger postpone it. She said positively apologetic, even, at this moment, humorous: "You're crazy, Graham. What's the matter, are you drunk? You don't seem drunk. You don't even find me attractive."

The blood of hatred went to his head and he gripped her again. Now she had got her face firmly twisted away so that he could not reach her mouth, and she repeated steadily as he kissed the parts of her cheeks and neck that were available to him: "Graham, let me go, do let me go, Graham." She went on saying this; he went on squeezing, grinding, kissing and licking. It might go on all night: it was a sheer contest of wills, nothing else. He thought: It's only a really masculine woman who wouldn't have given in by now out of sheer decency of the flesh! One thing he knew, however: that she would be in that bed, in his arms, and very soon. He let her go, but said: "I'm going to sleep with you tonight, you know that, don't you?"

She leaned with hand on the mantelpiece to steady herself. Her face was colourless, since he had licked all the makeup off. She seemed quite different: small and defenceless with her large mouth pale now, her smudged green eyes fringed with gold. And now, for the first time, he felt what it might have been supposed (certainly by her) he felt hours ago. Seeing the small damp flesh of her face, he felt kinship, intimacy with her, he felt intimacy of the flesh, the affection and good humour of sensuality. He felt she was flesh of his flesh, his sister in the flesh. He felt desire for her, instead of the will to have her; and because of this, was ashamed of the farce he had been playing. Now he desired simply to take her into bed in the affection of his senses.

She said: "What on earth am I supposed to do? Telephone for the police, or what?" He was hurt that she still addressed the man who had ground her into sulky apathy; she was not addressing *him* at all.

She said: "Or scream for the neighbours, is that what you want?"

The gold-fringed eyes were almost black, because of the depth of the shadow of boredom over them. She was bored and weary to the point of falling to the floor, he could see that.

He said: "I'm going to sleep with you."

"But how can you possibly want to?"—a reasonable, a civilised demand addressed to a man who (he could see) she believed would respond to it. She said: "You know I don't want to, and I know you don't really give a damn one way or the other."

He was stung back into being the boor because she had not the intelligence to see that the boor no longer existed; because she could not see that this was a man who wanted her in a way which she must respond to.

There she stood, supporting herself with one hand, looking small and white and exhausted, and utterly incredulous. She was going to turn and walk off out of simple incredulity, he could see that. "Do you think I don't mean it?" he demanded, grinding this out between his teeth. She made a movement—she was on the point of going away. His hand shot out on its own volition and grasped her wrist. She frowned. His other hand grasped her other wrist. His body hove up against hers to start the pressure of a new embrace. Before it could, she said: "Oh Lord, no, I'm not going through all that again. Right, then."

"What do you mean—right, then?" he demanded.

She said: "You're going to sleep with me. O.K. Anything rather than go through that again. Shall we get it over with?"

He grinned, saying in silence: "No darling, oh no you don't, I don't care what words you use, I'm going to have you now and that's all there is to it."

She shrugged. The contempt, the weariness of it, had no effect on him, because he was now again hating her so much that wanting her was like needing to kill something or someone.

She took her clothes off, as if she were going to bed by herself: her jacket, skirt, petticoat. She stood in white bra and panties, a rather solid girl, brown-skinned still from the summer. He felt a flash of affection for the brown girl with her loose yellow hair as she stood naked. She got into bed and lay there, while the green eyes looked at him in civilised appeal: Are you really going through with this? Do you have to? Yes, his eyes said back: I do have to. She shifted her gaze aside, to the wall, saying silently: Well, if you want to take me without any desire at all on my part, then go ahead, if you're not ashamed. He was not ashamed, because he was maintaining the flame of hate for her which he knew quite well was all that stood between him and shame. He took off his clothes, and got into bed beside her. As he did so, knowing he was putting himself in the position of raping a woman who was making it elaborately clear he bored her, his flesh subsided completely, sad, and full of reproach because a few moments ago it was reaching out for his sister whom he could have made happy. He lay on his side by her, secretly at work on himself, while he supported himself across her body on his elbow, using the free hand to manipulate her breasts. He saw that she gritted her teeth against his touch. At least she could not know that after all this fuss he was not potent.

In order to incite himself, he clasped her again. She felt his smallness, writhed free of him, sat up and said: "Lie down."

While she had been lying there, she had been thinking: The only way to get this over with is to make him big again, otherwise I've got to put up with him all night. His hatred of her was giving him a clairvoyance: he knew very well what went on through her mind. She had switched on, with the determination to *get it all over with*, a sensual good humour, a patience. He lay down. She squatted beside him, the light from the ceiling blooming on her brown shoulders, her flat fair hair falling over her face. But she would not look at his face. Like a bored, skilled wife, she was: or like a prostitute. She administered to him, she was setting herself to please him. Yes, he thought, she's sensual, or she could be. Meanwhile she was succeeding in defeating the reluctance of his flesh, which was the tender token of a possible desire for her, by using a cold skill that was the result of her contempt for him. Just as he decided: Right, it's enough, now I shall have her properly, she made him come. It was not a trick, to hurry or cheat him, what defeated him was her transparent thought: Yes, that's what he's worth.

Then, having succeeded, and waited for a moment or two, she stood up, naked, the fringes of gold at her loins and in her armpits speaking to him a language quite different from that of her green, bored eyes. She looked at him and thought, showing it plainly: What sort of man is it who . . .? He watched the slight movement of her shoulders: a just-checked shrug. She went out of the room: then the sound of running water. Soon she came back in a white dressing gown, carrying a yellow towel. She handed him the towel, looking away in politeness as he used it. "Are you going home now?" she enquired hopefully, at this point.

"No, I'm not." He believed that now he would have to start fighting her again, but she lay down beside him, not touching him (he could feel the distaste of her flesh for his) and he thought: Very well, my dear, but there's a lot of the night left yet. He said aloud: "I'm going to have you properly tonight." She said nothing, lay silent, yawned. Then she remarked consolingly, and he could have laughed outright from sheer surprise: "Those were hardly conducive circumstances for making love." She was *consoling* him. He hated her for it. A proper little slut: I force her into bed, she doesn't want me, but she still has to make me feel good, like a prostitute. But even while he hated her he responded in kind, from the habit of sexual generosity. "It's because of my admiration for you, because . . . after all, I was holding in my arms one of the thousand women."

A pause. "The thousand?" she enquired, carefully.

"The thousand especial women."

"In Britain or in the world? You choose them for their brains, their beauty—what?"

"Whatever it is that makes them outstanding," he said, offering her a compliment.

"Well," she remarked at last, inciting him to be amused again: "I hope that at least there's a short list you can say I am on, for politeness' sake."

He did not reply for he understood he was sleepy. He was still telling himself that he must stay awake when he was slowly waking and it was morning. It was about eight. Barbara was not there. He thought: My God! What on earth shall I tell my wife? Where was Barbara? He remembered the ridiculous scenes of last night and nearly succumbed to shame. Then he thought, reviving anger: If she didn't sleep beside me here I'll never forgive her. . . . He sat up, quietly, determined to go through the house until he found her and, having found her, to possess her, when the door opened and she came in. She was fully dressed in a green suit, her hair done, her eyes made up. She carried a tray of coffee, which she set down beside the bed. He was conscious of his big loose hairy body, half uncovered. He said to himself that he was not going to lie in bed, naked, while she was dressed. He said: "Have you got a gown of some kind?" She handed him, without speaking, a towel, and said: "The bathroom's second on the left." She went out. He followed, the towel around him. Everything in this house was gay, intimate—not at all like her efficient working room. He wanted to find out where she had slept, and opened the first door. It was the kitchen, and she was in it, putting a brown earthenware dish into the oven. "The next door," said Barbara. He went hastily past the second door, and opened (he hoped quietly) the third. It was a cupboard full of linen. "This door," said Barbara, behind him.

"So all right then, where did you sleep?"

"What's it to do with you? Upstairs, in my own bed. Now, if you have everything, I'll say goodbye, I want to get to the theatre."

"I'll take you," he said at once.

He saw again the movement of her eyes, the dark swallowing the light in deadly boredom. "I'll take you," he insisted.

"I'd prefer to go by myself," she remarked. Then she smiled: "However, you'll take me. Then you'll make a point of coming right in, so that James and everyone can see—that's what you want to take me for, isn't it?"

He hated her, finally, and quite simply, for her intelligence; that not once had he got away with anything, that she had been watching, since they had met yesterday, every movement of his campaign for her. However, some fate or inner urge over which he had no control made him say sentimentally: "My dear, you must see that I'd like at least to take you to your work."

"Not at all, have it on me," she said, giving him the lie direct. She went past him to the room he had slept in. "I shall be leaving in ten minutes," she said.

He took a shower, fast. When he returned, the workroom was already tidied, the bed made, all signs of the night gone. Also, there were no signs of the coffee she had brought in for him. He did not like to ask for it, for fear of an outright refusal. Besides, she was ready, her coat on, her handbag under her arm. He went, without a word, to the front door, and she came after him, silent.

He could see that every fibre of her body signalled a simple message: Oh God, for the moment when I can be rid of this boor! She was nothing but a slut, he thought.

A taxi came. In it she sat as far away from him as she could. He thought of what he should say to his wife.

Outside the theatre she remarked: "You could drop me here, if you liked." It was not a plea, she was too proud for that. "I'll take you in," he said, and saw her thinking: Very well, I'll go through with it to shame him. He was determined to take her in and hand her over to her colleagues, he was afraid she would give him the slip. But far from playing it down, she seemed determined to play it his way. At the stage door, she said to the doorman: "This is Mr. Spence, Tom—do you remember, Mr. Spence from last night?" "Good morning Babs," said the man, examining Graham, politely, as he had been ordered to do.

Barbara went to the door to the stage, opened it, held it open for him. He went in first, then held it open for her. Together they walked into the cavernous, littered, badly lit place and she called out: "James, James!" A man's voice called out from the front of the house: "Here, Babs, why are you so late?"

The auditorium opened before them, darkish, silent, save for an early-morning busyness of charwomen. A vacuum cleaner roared, smally, somewhere close. A couple of stagehands stood looking up at a drop which had a design of blue and green spirals. James stood with his back to the auditorium, smoking. "You're late, Babs," he said again. He saw Graham behind her, and nodded. Barbara and James kissed. Barbara said, giving allowance to every syllable: "You remember Mr. Spence from last night?" James nodded: How do you do? Barbara stood beside him, and they looked together up at the blue-and-green backdrop. Then Barbara looked again at Graham, asking silently: All right now, isn't that enough? He could see her eyes, sullen with boredom.

He said: "Bye, Babs. Bye, James. I'll ring you, Babs." No response, she ignored him. He walked off slowly, listening for what might be said. For instance: "Babs, for God's sake, what are you doing with him?" Or she might say: "Are you wondering about Graham Spence? Let me explain."

Graham passed the stagehands who, he could have sworn, didn't recognise him. Then at last he heard James's voice to Barbara: "It's no good, Babs, I know you're enamoured of that particular shade of blue, but do have another look at it, there's a good girl. . . ." Graham left the stage, went past the office where the stage doorman sat reading a newspaper. He looked up, nodded, went back to his paper. Graham went to find a taxi, thinking: I'd better think up something convincing, then I'll telephone my wife.

Luckily he had an excuse not to be at home that day, for this evening he had to interview a young man (for television) about his new novel.

THE PATRIARCH

by

COLETTE
(1873–1954)

Colette is the pen name of the French novelist Sidonie Gabrielle Claudine Colette, who collaborated with her husband under the pen name Colette Willy in writing the Claudine *books. She is best known for her novels about women, especially* Chéri *(translated 1951) and* Gigi *(translated 1953). Collections of her short stories in translation appeared in 1975 and 1983.*

• ———————————————————— •

Between the ages of sixteen and twenty-five, Achille, my half-brother by blood—but wholly and entirely my brother by affection, choice and like-ness—was extremely handsome. Little by little, he became less so as a result of leading the hard life of a country doctor in the old days; a life which lacked all comfort and repose. He wore out his boot-soles as much as the shoes of his grey mare; he went out by day and he went out by night, going to bed too tired to want any supper. In the night he would be woken up by the call of a peasant banging his fists on the outer door and pulling the bell. Then he would get up, put on his woollen pants, his clothes and his great plaid-lined overcoat and Charles, the man-of-all-work, would harness the grey mare, another remarkable creature.

I have never known anything so proud and so willing as that grey mare. In the stable, by the light of the lantern, my brother would always find her standing up and ready for the worst. Her short, lively, well-set ears would enquire: "Chateauvieux? Montrenard? The big climb up the hill? Seventeen kilometres to get there and as many on the way back?" She would set off a little stiffly, her head lowered. During the examina-tion, the confinement, the amputation or the dressing, she leant her little forehead against the farmhouse doors so as to hear better what *He* was saying. I could swear that she knew by heart the bits of *Le Roi d'Ys* and the Pastoral Symphony, the scraps of operas and the Schubert songs *He* sang to keep himself company.

THE SEX OBJECT

Isolated, sacrificed to his profession, this twenty-six-year-old doctor of half a century ago had only one resource. Gradually he had to forge himself a spirit which hoped for nothing except to live and enable his family to live too. Happily, his professional curiosity never left him. Neither did that other curiosity which both of us inherited from our mother. When, in my teens, I used to accompany him on his rounds, the two of us would often stop and get out to pick a bunch of bluebells or to gather mushrooms. Sometimes we would watch a wheeling buzzard or upset the dignity of a little lizard by touching it with a finger: the lizard would draw up its neck like an offended lady and give a lisping hiss, rather like a child who has lost its first front teeth. We would carefully detach butterfly chrysalises from branches and holes in walls and put them in little boxes of fine sand to await the miracle of the metamorphosis.

The profession of country doctor demanded a great deal of a man about half a century ago. Fresh from the Medical School in Paris, my brother's first patient was a well-sinker who had just had one leg blown off by an explosion of dynamite. The brand-new surgeon came out of this difficult ordeal with honour but white-lipped, trembling all over and considerably thinner from the amount he had sweated. He pulled himself together by diving into the canal between the tall clumps of flowering rushes.

Achille taught me to fill and to stick together the two halves of antipyrine capsules, to use the delicate scales with the weights which were mere thin slips of copper. In those days, the country doctor had a licence to sell certain pharmaceutical products outside a four-kilometre radius of the town. Meagre profits, if one considers that a "consultation" cost the consultant three francs plus twenty sous a kilometre. From time to time, the doctor pulled out a tooth, also for three francs. And what little money there was came in slowly and sometimes not at all.

"Why not sue them?" demanded the chemist. "What's the law for?"

Whatever it was for, it was not for his patients. My brother made no reply but turned his greenish-blue eyes away towards the flat horizon. My eyes are the same colour but not so beautiful and not so deeply set.

I was fifteen or sixteen; the age of great devotions, of vocations. I wanted to become a woman doctor. My brother would summon me for a split lip or a deep, bleeding cut and have recourse to my slender girl's fingers. Eagerly, I would set to work to knot the threads of the stitches in the blood which leapt so impetuously out of the vein. In the morning, Achille set off too early for me to be able to accompany him. But in the afternoon I would sit on his left in the trap and hold the mare's reins. Every month he had the duty of inspecting all the babies in the region and he tried to drop in unexpectedly on their wet or dry nurses. Those expeditions used to ruin his appetite. How many babies we found alone in an empty house, tied to their fetid cradles with handkerchiefs and safety-pins, while their heedless guardians worked in the fields. Some of them would see the trap in the distance and come running up, out of breath.

COLETTE

311

"I was only away for a moment." "I was changing the goat's picket." "I was chasing the cow who'd broken loose."

Hard as his life was, Achille held out for more than twenty-five years, seeking rest for his spirit only in music. In his youth he was surprised when he first came up against the peaceful immorality of country life, the desire which is born and satisfied in the depths of the ripe grass or between the warm flanks of sleeping cattle. Paris and the Latin Quarter had not prepared him for so much amorous knowledge, secrecy and variety. But impudence was not lacking either, at least in the case of the girls who came boldly to his weekly surgery declaring that they had not "seen" since they got their feet wet two months ago, pulling a drowned hen out of a pond.

"That's fine!" my brother would say, after his examination. "I'm going to give you a prescription."

He watched for the look of pleasure and contempt and the joyful reddening of the cheek and wrote out the prescription agreed between doctor and chemist: "*Mica panis*, two pills to be taken after each meal." The remedy might avert or, at least, delay the intervention of "the woman who knew about herbs".

One day, long before his marriage, he had an adventure which was only one of many. With a basket on one arm and an umbrella on the other, a young woman almost as tall as himself (he was nearly six foot two) walked into his consulting-room. He found himself looking at someone like a living statue of the young Republic; a fresh, magnificently built girl with a low brow, statuesque features and a calm, severe expression.

"Doctor," she said, without a smile or a shuffle, "I think I'm three months pregnant."

"Do you feel ill, Madame?"

"Mademoiselle. I'm eighteen. And I feel perfectly all right in every way."

"Well, then, Mademoiselle! You won't be needing me for another six months."

"Pardon, Doctor. I'd like to be sure. I don't want to do anything foolish. Will you please examine me?"

Throwing off the skirt, the shawl and the cotton chemise that came down to her ankles, she displayed a body so majestic, so firm, so smoothly sheathed in its skin that my brother never saw another to compare with it. He saw too that this young girl, so eager to accuse herself, was a virgin. But she vehemently refused to remain one any longer and went off victorious, her head high, her basket on her arm and her woollen shawl knotted once more over her breasts. The most she would admit was that, when she was digging potatoes on her father's land over by the Hardon road, she had waited often and often to see the grey mare and its driver go past and had said "Good-day" with her hand to call him, but in vain.

She returned for "consultation". But, far more often, my brother went and joined her in her field. She would watch him coming from afar, put down her hoe, and, stooping, make her way under the branches of a little plantation of pine-trees. From these almost silent encounters, a very beautiful child was born. And I admit that I should be glad to see, even now, what his face is like. For "Sido" confided to me, in very few words, one of those secrets in which she was so rich.

"You know the child of that beautiful girl over at Hardon?" she said.

"Yes."

"She boasts about him to everyone. She's crazy with pride. She's a most unusual girl. A character. I've seen the child. Just once."

"What's he like?"

She made the gesture of rumpling a child's hair.

"Beautiful, of course. Such curls, such eyes. And such a mouth."

She coughed and pushed away the invisible curly head with both hands.

"The mouth most of all. Ah! I just couldn't. I went away. Otherwise I should have taken him."

However, everything in our neighbourhood was not so simple as this warm idyll, cradled on its bed of pine-needles, and these silent lovers who took no notice of the autumn mists or a little rain, for the grey mare lent them her blanket.

There is another episode of which I have a vivid and less touching memory. We used to refer to it as "The Monsieur Binard story". It goes without saying that I have changed the name of the robust, grizzled father of a family who came over on his bicycle at dusk, some forty-eight years ago, to ask my brother to go to his daughter's bedside.

"It's urgent," said the man, panting as he spoke. His breath reeked of red wine. "I am Monseur Binard, of X . . ."

He made a sham exit, then thrust his head round the half-shut door and declared: "In my opinion, it'll be a boy."

My brother took his instrument case and the servant harnessed the grey mare.

It turned out indeed to be a boy and a remarkably fine and well-made one. But my brother's care and attention was mainly for the far too young mother, a dark girl with eyes like an antelope. She was very brave and kept crying out loudly, almost excitedly, like a child, "Ooh! . . . Ooh! I say! . . . Ooh, I never!" Round the bed bustled three slightly older antelopes while, in the ingle-nook, the impassive Monsieur Binard superintended the mulling of some red wine flavoured with cinnamon. In a dark corner of the clean, well-polished room, my brother noticed a wicker cradle with clean starched curtains. Monsieur Binard only left the fire and the copper basin to examine the new-born child as soon as it had been washed.

"It's a very fine child," Achille assured him.

"I've seen finer," said Monsieur Binard in a lordly way.

"Oh! Papa!" cried the three older antelopes.

"I know what I'm talking about," retorted Binard.

He raised a curtain of the cradle which my brother presumed empty but which was now shown to be entirely filled by a large child who had slept calmly through all the noise and bustle. One of the antelopes came over and tenderly drew the curtain down again.

His mission over, my brother drank the warm wine which he had well and truly earned and which the little newly-confined mother was sipping too. Already she was gay and laughing. Then he bowed to the entire long-eyed troop and went out, puzzled and worried. The earth was steaming with damp but, above the low fog, the bright dancing fire of the first stars announced the coming frost.

"Your daughter seems extremely young," said my brother. "Luckily, she's come through it well."

"She's strong. You needn't be afraid," said Monsieur Binard.

"How old is she?"

"Fifteen in four months' time."

"Fifteen! She was taking a big risk. What girls are! Do you know the . . . the creature who . . ."

Monsieur Binard made no reply other than slapping the hindquarters of the grey mare with the flat of his hand but he lifted his chin with such an obvious, such an intolerable expression of fatuity that my brother hastened his departure.

"If she has any fever, let me know."

"She won't," Monsieur Binard assured him with great dignity.

"So you know more about these things than I do?"

"No. But I know my daughters. I've four of them and you must have seen for yourself that there's not much wrong with them. I know them."

He said no more and ran his hand over his moustache. He waited till the grey mare had adroitly turned in the narrow courtyard, then he went back into his house.

Sido, my mother, did not like this story which she often turned over in her mind. Sometimes she spoke violently about Monsieur Binard, calling him bitterly "the corrupt widower", sometimes she let herself go off into commentaries for which afterwards she would blush.

"Their house is very well kept. The child of the youngest one has eyelashes as long as *that*. I saw her the other day, she was suckling her baby on the doorstep, it was enchanting. Whatever am I saying? It was abominable, of course, when one knows the facts."

She went off into a dream, impatiently untwisting the entangled steel chain and black cord from which hung her two pairs of spectacles.

"After all," she began again, "the ancient patriarchs . . ."

But she suddenly became aware that I was only fifteen and a half and she went no further.

THE SEX OBJECT

METONYMY

by

JULIE FAY
(b. 1951)

Julie Fay was born in Baltimore and spent her childhood in California and Connecticut. She currently divides her time between France and North Carolina, where she teaches poetry and women's literature at East Carolina University. She has won numerous awards for her poetry and is currently working on a novel based on the life of her ancestor Hannah Dustin, a seventeenth-century American colonist accused of murdering ten Abenaki Indians. Her poetry and translations have been published in leading literary journals both here and abroad. Her chapbook In Every Mirror *was published in 1985.* Portraits of Women *(1991) consists of two narrative poem sequences: one concerns a nineteenth-century homesteading family; the other, from which "Metonymy" is taken, is the story of a painter who, studying the relationship of women and violence in the work of other painters, remembers her own violent childhood.*

Quiet. As a visitor lets himself in
without upsetting furniture.
Like a Balthus imp pulling
back the curtain's hemorrhage
of light. I had to look, to smell
its sour breath, to touch.

I remembered the hands.
For the first time since then
set the metronome and
when the black stick ticked
it clicked back, cracked
a mirror painted over

years ago: he'd tuck me in, gentle
man, and then the lizardly
changing of color, untuck
himself, groan his luxury

over me, slitted eyes.
My disc-flat breasts horrified

I could not control their rising,
buds that pleased him, locked him out
the only way I could, invented
Saint Metronome, her odd wooden
habit and big heart stood beside
Our Lady, a mother and daughter

team that sailed off the sill
into the blue hills, all light
perfect flight, strong as wind.
I didn't have a mother then
nor a voice, no choice.

Like a metronome, the child's heart
stops dead cold when not in use.
Then begins again.
Most of the time
I just loved him as any daughter
loves her father. Until the other
tore through skin's surface

all bruises and razors who sometimes fell
asleep in me, his grey penis. Pain
swelled like fruit left out
too long, burned, cooled, burned
and I cooed, my eyes by then obsidian
birds exotically clicking

clipped wings.

From I KNOW WHY THE CAGED BIRD SINGS

by

MAYA ANGELOU
(b. 1928)

Maya Angelou has been called a Renaissance woman and a self-created Everywoman. Born in St. Louis, she grew up in Stamps, Arkansas, and California, where she now lives. She has chronicled her life in a continuing autobiography, of which I Know Why the Caged Bird Sings *(1970) was the first volume; this selection from it is an example of the frankness with which she reveals her experiences as a cook, a streetcar conductor, a dancer, a madam, and an unwed mother. She appeared in* Porgy and Bess *on an international tour in 1954, was assistant administrator of the School of Music and Drama at the University of Ghana (1963–1966), has lectured widely, and has often been interviewed on television. In addition to her autobiography, Angelou has written four volumes of poetry, several plays, screenplays, songs, short stories, and articles. She has received many honorary degrees and prestigious awards.*

On a late spring Saturday, after our chores (nothing like those in Stamps) were done, Bailey and I were going out, he to play baseball and I to the library. Mr. Freeman said to me, after Bailey had gone downstairs, "Ritie, go get some milk for the house."

Mother usually brought milk when she came in, but that morning as Bailey and I straightened the living room her bedroom door had been open, and we knew that she hadn't come home the night before.

He gave me the money and I rushed to the store and back to the house. After putting the milk in the icebox, I turned and had just reached the front door when I heard, "Ritie." He was sitting in the big chair by the radio. "Ritie, come here." I didn't think about the holding time until I got close to him. His pants were open and his "thing" was standing out of his britches by itself.

"No, sir, Mr. Freeman." I started to back away. I didn't want to touch that mushy-hard thing again, and I didn't need him to hold me any more. He grabbed my arm and pulled me between his legs. His face was still and looked kind, but he didn't smile or blink his eyes. Nothing. He did nothing, except reach his left hand around to turn on the radio without even looking at it. Over the noise of music and static, he said, "Now, this ain't gonna hurt you much. You liked it before, didn't you?"

I didn't want to admit that I had in fact liked his holding me or that I had liked his smell or the hard heart-beating, so I said nothing. And his face became like the face of one of those mean natives the Phantom was always having to beat up.

His legs were squeezing my waist. "Pull down your drawers." I hesitated for two reasons: he was holding me too tight to move, and I was sure that any minute my mother or Bailey or the Green Hornet would bust in the door and save me.

"We was just playing before." He released me enough to snatch down my bloomers, and then he dragged me closer to him. Turning the radio up loud, too loud, he said, "If you scream, I'm gonna kill you. And if you tell, I'm gonna kill Bailey." I could tell he meant what he said. I couldn't understand why he wanted to kill my brother. Neither of us had done anything to him. And then.

Then there was the pain. A breaking and entering when even the senses are torn apart. The act of rape on an eight-year-old body is a matter of the needle giving because the camel can't. The child gives, because the body can, and the mind of the violator cannot.

I thought I had died—I woke up in a white-walled world, and it had to be heaven. But Mr. Freeman was there and he was washing me. His hands shook, but he held me upright in the tub and washed my legs. "I didn't mean to hurt you, Ritie. I didn't mean it. But don't you tell . . . Remember, don't you tell a soul."

I felt cool and very clean and just a little tired. "No, sir, Mr. Freeman, I won't tell." I was somewhere above everything. "It's just that I'm so tired I'll just go and lay down a while, please," I whispered to him. I thought if I spoke out loud, he might become frightened and hurt me again. He dried me and handed me my bloomers. "Put these on and go to the library. Your momma ought to be coming home soon. You just act natural."

Walking down the street, I felt the wet on my pants, and my hips seemed to be coming out of their sockets. I couldn't sit long on the hard seats in the library (they had been constructed for children), so I walked by the empty lot where Bailey was playing ball, but he wasn't there. I stood for a while and watched the big boys tear around the dusty diamond and then headed home.

After two blocks, I knew I'd never make it. Not unless I counted every step and stepped on every crack. I had started to burn between my legs more than the time I'd wasted Sloan's Liniment on myself. My legs throbbed, or rather the insides of my thighs throbbed, with the same force that Mr. Freeman's heart had beaten. Thrum . . . step . . . thrum . . . step . . . STEP ON THE CRACK . . . thrum . . . step. I went up the stairs one at a, one at a, one at a time. No one was in the living room, so I went straight to bed, after hiding my red-and-yellow-stained drawers under the mattress.

When Mother came in she said, "Well, young lady, I believe this is the first time I've seen you go to bed without being told. You must be sick."

I wasn't sick, but the pit of my stomach was on fire—how could I tell her that? Bailey came in later and asked me what the matter was. There was nothing to tell him. When Mother called us to eat and I said I wasn't hungry, she laid her cool hand on my forehead and cheeks. "Maybe it's the measles. They say they're going around the neighborhood." After she took my temperature she said, "You have a little fever. You've probably just caught them."

Mr. Freeman took up the whole doorway, "Then Bailey ought not to be in there with her. Unless you want a house full of sick children." She answered over her shoulder, "He may as well have them now as later. Get them over with." She brushed by Mr. Freeman as if he were made of cotton. "Come on, Junior. Get some cool towels and wipe your sister's face."

As Bailey left the room, Mr. Freeman advanced to the bed. He leaned over, his whole face a threat that could have smothered me. "If you tell . . ." And again so softly, I almost didn't hear it—"If you tell." I couldn't summon up the energy to answer him. He had to know that I wasn't going to tell anything. Bailey came in with the towels and Mr. Freeman walked out.

Later Mother made a broth and sat on the edge of the bed to feed me. The liquid went down my throat like bones. My belly and behind were as heavy as cold iron, but it seemed my head had gone away and pure air had replaced it on my shoulders. Bailey read to me from *The Rover Boys* until he got sleepy and went to bed.

That night I kept waking to hear Mother and Mr. Freeman arguing. I couldn't hear what they were saying, but I did hope that she wouldn't make him so mad that he'd hurt her too. I knew he could do it, with his cold face and empty eyes. Their voices came in faster and faster, the high sounds on the heels of the lows. I would have liked to have gone in. Just passed through as if I were going to the toilet. Just show my face and they might stop, but my legs refused to move. I could move the toes and ankles, but the knees had turned to wood.

Maybe I slept, but soon morning was there and Mother was pretty over my bed. "How're you feeling, baby?"

"Fine, Mother." An instinctive answer. "Where's Bailey?"

She said he was still asleep but that she hadn't slept all night. She had been in my room off and on to see about me. I asked her where Mr. Freeman was, and her face chilled with remembered anger. "He's gone. Moved this morning. I'm going to take your temperature after I put on your Cream of Wheat."

Could I tell her now? The terrible pain assured me that I couldn't. What he did to me, and what I allowed, must have been very bad if already God let me hurt so much. If Mr. Freeman was gone, did that mean Bailey was out of danger? And if so, if I told him, would he still love me?

After Mother took my temperature, she said she was going to bed for a while but to wake her if I felt sicker. She told Bailey to watch my face and arms for spots and when they came up he could paint them with calamine lotion.

That Sunday goes and comes in my memory like a bad connection on an overseas telephone call. Once, Bailey was reading *The Katzenjammer Kids* to me, and then without a pause for sleeping, Mother was looking closely at my face, and soup trickled down my chin and some got into my mouth and I choked. Then there was a doctor who took my temperature and held my wrist.

"Bailey!" I supposed I had screamed, for he materialized suddenly, and I asked him to help me and we'd run away to California or France or Chicago. I knew that I was dying and, in fact, I longed for death, but I didn't want to die anywhere near Mr. Freeman. I knew that even now he wouldn't have allowed death to have me unless he wished it to.

Mother said I should be bathed and the linens had to be changed since I had sweat so much. But when they tried to move me I fought, and even Bailey couldn't hold me. Then she picked me up in her arms and the terror abated for a while. Bailey began to change the bed. As he pulled off the soiled sheets he dislodged the panties I had put under the mattress. They fell at Mother's feet.

In the hospital, Bailey told me that I had to tell who did that to me, or the man would hurt another little girl. When I explained that I couldn't tell because the man would kill him, Bailey said knowingly, "He can't kill me. I won't let him." And of course I believed him. Bailey didn't lie to me. So I told him.

Bailey cried at the side of my bed until I started to cry too. Almost fifteen years passed before I saw my brother cry again.

Using the old brain he was born with (those were his words later on that day) he gave his information to Grandmother Baxter, and Mr. Freeman was arrested and was spared the awful wrath of my pistol-whipping uncles.

I would have liked to stay in the hospital the rest of my life. Mother brought flowers and candy. Grandmother came with fruit and my uncles clumped around and around my bed, snorting like wild horses. When they were able to sneak Bailey in, he read to me for hours.

The saying that people who have nothing to do become busybodies is not the only truth. Excitement is a drug, and people whose lives are filled with violence are always wondering where the next "fix" is coming from.

THE SEX OBJECT

320

The court was filled. Some people even stood behind the churchlike benches in the rear. Overhead fans moved with the detachment of old men. Grandmother Baxter's clients were there in gay and flippant array. The gamblers in pin-striped suits and their makeup-deep women whispered to me out of blood-red mouths that now I knew as much as they did. I was eight, and grown. Even the nurses in the hospital had told me that now I had nothing to fear. "The worst is over for you," they had said. So I put the words in all the smirking mouths.

I sat with my family (Bailey couldn't come) and they rested still on the seats like solid, cold gray tombstones. Thick and forevermore unmoving.

Poor Mr. Freeman twisted in his chair to look empty threats over to me. He didn't know that he couldn't kill Bailey . . . and Bailey didn't lie . . . to me.

"What was the defendant wearing?" That was Mr. Freeman's lawyer.

"I don't know."

"You mean to say this man raped you and you don't know what he was wearing?" He snickered as if I had raped Mr. Freeman. "Do you know if you were raped?"

A sound pushed in the air of the court (I was sure it was laughter). I was glad that Mother had let me wear the navy-blue winter coat with brass buttons. Although it was too short and the weather was typical St. Louis hot, the coat was a friend that I hugged to me in the strange and unfriendly place.

"Was that the first time the accused touched you?" The question stopped me. Mr. Freeman had surely done something very wrong, but I was convinced that I had helped him to do it. I didn't want to lie, but the lawyer wouldn't let me think, so I used silence as a retreat.

"Did the accused try to touch you before the time he or rather you say he raped you?"

I couldn't say yes and tell them how he had loved me once for a few minutes and how he had held me close before he thought I had peed in my bed. My uncles would kill me and Grandmother Baxter would stop speaking, as she often did when she was angry. And all those people in the court would stone me as they had stoned the harlot in the Bible. And Mother, who thought I was such a good girl, would be so disappointed. But most important, there was Bailey. I had kept a big secret from him.

"Marguerite, answer the question. Did the accused touch you before the occasion on which you claim he raped you?"

Everyone in the court knew that the answer had to be No. Everyone except Mr. Freeman and me. I looked at his heavy face trying to look as if he would have liked me to say No. I said No.

The lie lumped in my throat and I couldn't get air. How I despised the man for making me lie. Old, mean, nasty thing. Old, black, nasty thing. The tears didn't soothe my heart as they usually did. I screamed, "Ole, mean, dirty thing, you. Dirty old thing." Our lawyer brought me off the stand and to my mother's arms. The fact that I had arrived at my desired destination by lies made it less appealing to me.

Mr. Freeman was given one year and one day, but he never got a chance to do his time. His lawyer (or someone) got him released that very afternoon.

In the living room, where the shades were drawn for coolness, Bailey and I played Monopoly on the floor. I played a bad game because I was thinking how I would be able to tell Bailey how I had lied and, even worse for our relationship, kept a secret from him. Bailey answered the doorbell, because Grandmother was in the kitchen. A tall white police-man asked for Mrs. Baxter. Had they found out about the lie? Maybe the policeman was coming to put me in jail because I had sworn on the Bible that everything I said would be the truth, the whole truth, so help me, God. The man in our living room was taller than the sky and whiter than my image of God. He just didn't have the beard.

"Mrs. Baxter, I thought you ought to know. Freeman's been found dead on the lot behind the slaughterhouse."

Softly, as if she were discussing a church program, she said, "Poor man." She wiped her hands on the dishtowel and just as softly asked, "Do they know who did it?"

The policeman said, "Seems like he was dropped there. Some say he was kicked to death."

Grandmother's color only rose a little. "Tom, thanks for telling me. Poor man. Well, maybe it's better this way. He *was* a mad dog. Would you like a glass of lemonade? Or some beer?"

Although he looked harmless, I knew he was a dreadful angel count-ing out my many sins.

"No, thanks, Mrs. Baxter. I'm on duty. Gotta be getting back."

"Well, tell your ma that I'll be over when I take up my beer and re-mind her to save some kraut for me."

And the recording angel was gone. He was gone, and a man was dead because I lied. Where was the balance in that? One lie surely wouldn't be worth a man's life. Bailey could have explained it all to me, but I didn't dare ask him. Obviously I had forfeited my place in heaven forever, and I was gutless as the doll I had ripped to pieces ages ago. Even Christ Himself turned His back on Satan. Wouldn't He turn His back on me? I could feel the evilness flowing through my body and waiting, pent up, to rush off my tongue if I tried to open my mouth. I clamped my teeth shut, I'd hold it in. If it escaped, wouldn't it flood the world and all the inno-cent people?

Grandmother Baxter said, "Ritie and Junior, you didn't hear a thing. I never want to hear this situation nor that evil man's name mentioned in my house again. I mean that." She went back into the kitchen to make apple strudel for my celebration.

Even Bailey was frightened. He sat all to himself, looking at a man's death—a kitten looking at a wolf. Not quite understanding it but frightened all the same.

In those moments I decided that although Bailey loved me he couldn't help. I had sold myself to the Devil and there could be no escape. The only thing I could do was to stop talking to people other than Bailey. Instinctively, or somehow, I knew that because I loved him so much I'd never hurt him, but if I talked to anyone else that person might die too. Just my breath, carrying my words out, might poison people and they'd curl up and die like the black fat slugs that only pretended.

I had to stop talking.

I discovered that to achieve perfect personal silence all I had to do was to attach myself leechlike to sound. I began to listen to everything. I probably hoped that after I had heard all the sounds, really heard them and packed them down, deep in my ears, the world would be quiet around me. I walked into rooms where people were laughing, their voices hitting the walls like stones, and I simply stood still—in the midst of the riot of sound. After a minute or two, silence would rush into the room from its hiding place because I had eaten up all the sounds.

In the first weeks my family accepted my behavior as a post-rape, post-hospital affliction. (Neither the term nor the experience was mentioned in Grandmother's house, where Bailey and I were again staying.) They understood that I could talk to Bailey, but to no one else.

Then came the last visit from the visiting nurse, and the doctor said I was healed. That meant that I should be back on the sidewalks playing handball or enjoying the games I had been given when I was sick. When I refused to be the child they knew and accepted me to be, I was called impudent and my muteness sullenness.

For a while I was punished for being so uppity that I wouldn't speak; and then came the thrashings, given by any relative who felt himself offended.

We were on the train going back to Stamps, and this time it was I who had to console Bailey. He cried his heart out down the aisles of the coach, and pressed his little-boy body against the window pane looking for a last glimpse of his Mother Dear.

I have never known if Momma sent for us, or if the St. Louis family just got fed up with my grim presence. There is nothing more appalling than a constantly morose child.

I cared less about the trip than about the fact that Bailey was unhappy, and had no more thought of our destination than if I had simply been heading for the toilet.

WITH NO IMMEDIATE CAUSE

by

NTOZAKE SHANGE
(b. 1948)

*Born Paulette Williams in Trenton, New Jersey, Ntozake Shange
took her pseudonym as an expression of her anger at the dilemma
of being a black woman. In Zulu the name means "she who comes
with her own things"/"she who walks like a lion." Educated at
Barnard College and the University of Southern California, Shange
has written novels, including* Sassafrass, Cypress, and Indigo *(1983),
the story of a mother and three daughters, and* Betsey Brown *(1985).
Her greatest success was the "choreopoem"* For Colored Girls Who
Have Considered Suicide/When the Rainbow Is Enuf, *which was
presented on Broadway in 1976 and has since been widely produced and constantly reprinted. A more recent work is* Ridin' the
Moon in Texas: Word Paintings *(1988).*

every 3 minutes a woman is beaten
every five minutes a
woman is raped/every ten minutes
a lil girl is molested
yet i rode the subway today
i sat next to an old man who
may have beaten his old wife
3 minutes ago or 3 days/30 years ago
he might have sodomized his
daughter but i sat there
cuz the young men on the train
might beat some young women
later in the day or tomorrow
i might not shut my door fast
enuf/push hard enuf
every 3 minutes it happens
some woman's innocence
rushes to her cheeks/pours from her mouth

like the betsy wetsy dolls have been torn
apart/their mouths
menses red & split/every
three minutes a shoulder
is jammed through plaster and the oven door/
chairs push thru the rib cage/hot water or
boiling sperm decorate her body
i rode the subway today
& bought a paper from a
man who might
have held his old lady onto
a hot pressing iron/i dont know
maybe he catches lil girls in the
park & rips open their behinds
with steel rods/i can't decide
what he might have done i only
know every 3 minutes
every 5 minutes every 10 minutes/so
i bought the paper
looking for the announcement
the discovery/of the dismembered
woman's body/the
victims have not all been
identified/today they are
naked and dead/refuse to
testify/one girl out of 10's not
coherent/i took the coffee
& spit it up/i found an
announcement/not the woman's
bloated body in the river/floating
not the child bleeding in the
59th street corridor/not the baby
broken on the floor/
   "there is some concern
   that alleged battered women
   might start to murder their
   husbands & lovers with no
   immediate cause"
i spit up i vomit i am screaming
we all have immediate cause
every 3 minutes
every 5 minutes
every 10 minutes

NTOZAKE SHANGE

every day
women's bodies are found
in alleys & bedrooms/at the top of the stairs
before i ride the subway/buy a paper/drink
coffee/i must know/
have you hurt a woman today
did you beat a woman today
throw a child across a room
   are the lil girl's panties
   in yr pocket
did you hurt a woman today

i have to ask these obscene questions
the authorities require me to
establish
immediate cause

every three minutes
every five minutes
every ten minutes
every day.

From INCIDENTS IN THE LIFE OF A SLAVE GIRL, WRITTEN BY HERSELF

by

LINDA BRENT
(pseudonym for Harriet Jacobs)
(1813–1896)

Born a slave in Edenton, North Carolina, and orphaned at twelve, Harriet Jacobs was left to a three-year-old girl in her first mistress's will. The girl's father, Dr. James Norcom, is the licentious master of Jacobs's autobiography. Jacobs was saved largely through the help of her grandmother. After hiding in a cramped storeroom in her grandmother's house for seven years (during which she read and practiced writing), she escaped in 1840. Jacobs found work as a nursemaid with an author's family in New York City; helped by them and a Quaker family in Rochester, she was able to evade Norcom's repeated efforts to capture her. Eventually she wrote her story, which was published in 1861. Later she worked with the Union Army for the welfare of freed slaves.

· ———————————————————— ·

Introduction by the Editor.

The author of the following autobiography is personally known to me, and her conversation and manners inspire me with confidence. During the last seventeen years, she has lived the greater part of the time with a distinguished family in New York, and has so deported herself as to be highly esteemed by them. This fact is sufficient, without further credentials of her character. I believe those who know her will not be disposed to doubt her veracity, though some incidents in her story are more romantic than fiction.

At her request, I have revised her manuscript; but such changes as I have made have been mainly for purposes of condensation and orderly arrangement. I have not added any thing to the incidents, or changed the import of her very pertinent remarks. With trifling exceptions, both the ideas and the language are her own. I pruned excrescences a little, but otherwise I had no reason for changing her lively and dramatic way of telling her own story. The names of both persons and places are known to me; but for good reasons I suppress them.

It will naturally excite surprise that a woman reared in Slavery should be able to write so well. But circumstances will explain this. In the first place, nature endowed her with quick perceptions. Secondly, the mistress, with whom she lived till she was twelve years old, was a kind, considerate friend, who taught her to read and spell. Thirdly, she was placed in favorable circumstances after she came to the North; having frequent intercourse with intelligent persons, who felt a friendly interest in her welfare, and were disposed to give her opportunities for self-improvement.

I am well aware that many will accuse me of <u>indecorum</u> for presenting these pages to the public; for the experiences of this intelligent and much-injured woman belong to a <u>class which some call delicate subjects, and others indelicate</u>. This peculiar phase of Slavery has generally been kept veiled; but the public ought to be made acquainted with its monstrous features, and I willingly take the responsibility of presenting them with the veil withdrawn. I do this for the sake of my sisters in bondage, who are suffering wrongs so foul, that our ears are too delicate to listen to them. I do it with the hope of arousing conscientious and reflecting women at the North to a sense of their duty in the exertion of moral influence on the question of Slavery, on all possible occasions. I do it with the hope that every man who reads this narrative will swear solemnly before God that, so far as he has power to prevent it, no fugitive from Slavery shall ever be sent back to suffer in that loathsome den of corruption and cruelty.

L. Maria Child.

The Trials of Girlhood.

During the first years of my service in Dr. Flint's family, I was accustomed to share some indulgences with the children of my mistress. Though this seemed to me no more than right, I was grateful for it, and tried to merit the kindness by the faithful discharge of my duties. But I now entered on my fifteenth year—a sad epoch in the life of a slave girl. My master began to whisper foul words in my ear. Young as I was, I could not remain ignorant of their import. I tried to treat them with indifference or contempt. The master's age, my extreme youth, and <u>the fear that his conduct would be reported</u> to my grandmother, made him bear this treatment for many months. He was a crafty man, and resorted to many means to accomplish his purposes. Sometimes he had stormy, terrific ways, that made his victims tremble; sometimes he assumed a gentleness that he thought must surely subdue. Of the two, I preferred his stormy moods, although they left me trembling. He tried his utmost to corrupt the pure principles my grandmother had instilled. He peopled my young mind with unclean images, such as only a vile monster could think of. I turned from him with disgust and hatred. But he was my master. I was compelled to live under the same roof with him—where I saw a man forty years my senior daily violating the most sacred commandments of nature. He told me I was his property; that I must be subject to his will in all things. My soul revolted against the mean tyranny. But where could I turn for protection? No matter whether the slave girl be as black as ebony or as fair as her mistress. In either case, there is no shadow of law to protect her from insult, from violence, or even from death; all these are inflicted by fiends who bear the shape of men. The mistress, who ought to protect the helpless victim, has no other feelings towards her but those of jealousy and rage. The degradation, the wrongs, the vices, that grow out of slavery, are more than I can describe. They are greater than you would willingly believe. Surely, if you credited one half the truths that are told you concerning the helpless millions suffering in this cruel bondage, you at the north would not help to tighten the yoke. You surely would refuse to do for the master, on your own soil, the mean and cruel work which trained bloodhounds and the lowest class of whites do for him at the south.

Every where the years bring to all enough of sin and sorrow; but in slavery the very dawn of life is darkened by these shadows. Even the little child, who is accustomed to wait on her mistress and her children, will learn, before she is twelve years old, why it is that her mistress hates such and such a one among the slaves. Perhaps the child's own mother is among those hated ones. She listens to violent outbreaks of jealous passion, and cannot help understanding what is the cause. She will become prematurely knowing in evil things. Soon she will learn to tremble when she hears her master's footfall. She will be compelled to realize that she is no longer a child. If God has bestowed beauty upon her, it will prove her greatest curse. That which commands admiration in the white woman only hastens the degradation of the female slave. I know that some are too much brutalized by slavery to feel the humiliation of their position; but many slaves feel it most acutely, and shrink from the memory of it. I cannot tell how much I suffered in the presence of these wrongs, nor how I am still pained by the retrospect. My master met me at every turn, reminding me that I belonged to him, and swearing by heaven and earth that he would compel me to submit to him. If I went out for a breath of fresh air, after a day of unwearied toil, his footsteps dogged me. If I knelt by my mother's grave, his dark shadow fell on me even there. The light heart which nature had given me became heavy with sad forebodings. The other slaves in my master's house noticed the change. Many of them pitied me; but none dared to ask the cause. They had no need to inquire. They knew too well the guilty practices under that roof; and they were aware that to speak of them was an offence that never went unpunished.

I longed for some one to confide in. I would have given the world to have laid my head on my grandmother's faithful bosom, and told her all my troubles. But Dr. Flint swore he would kill me, if I was not as silent as the grave. Then, although my grandmother was all in all to me, I feared her as well as loved her. I had been accustomed to look up to her with a respect bordering upon awe. I was very young, and felt shame-faced about telling her such impure things, especially as I knew her to be very strict on such subjects. Moreover, she was a woman of a high spirit. She was usually very quiet in her demeanor; but if her indignation was once roused, it was not very easily quelled. I had been told that she once chased a white gentleman with a loaded pistol, because he insulted one of her daughters. I dreaded the consequences of a violent outbreak; and both pride and fear kept me silent. But though I did not confide in my grandmother, and even evaded her vigilant watchfulness and inquiry, her presence in the neighborhood was some protection to me. Though she had been a slave, Dr. Flint was afraid of her. He dreaded her scorching rebukes. Moreover, she was known and patronized by many people; and he did not wish to have his villany made public. It was lucky for me that I did not live on a distant plantation, but in a town not so large that the inhabitants were ignorant of each other's affairs. Bad as are the laws and customs in a slaveholding community, the doctor, as a professional man, deemed it prudent to keep up some outward show of decency.

O, what days and nights of fear and sorrow that man caused me! Reader, it is not to awaken sympathy for myself that I am telling you truthfully what I suffered in slavery. I do it to kindle a flame of compassion in your hearts for my sisters who are still in bondage, suffering as I once suffered.

I once saw two beautiful children playing together. One was a fair white child; the other was her slave, and also her sister. When I saw them embracing each other, and heard their joyous laughter, I turned sadly away from the lively sight. I foresaw the inevitable blight that would fall on the little slave's heart. I knew how soon her laughter would be changed to sighs. The fair child grew up to be a still fairer woman. From childhood to womanhood her pathway was blooming with flowers, and overarched by a sunny sky. Scarcely one day of her life had been clouded when the sun rose on her happy bridal morning.

How had those years dealt with her slave sister, the little playmate of her childhood? She, also, was very beautiful; but the flowers and sun-shine of love were not for her. She drank the cup of sin, and shame, and misery, whereof her persecuted race are compelled to drink.

In view of these things, why are ye silent, ye free men and women of the north? Why do your tongues falter in maintenance of the right? Would that I had more ability! But my heart is so full, and my pen is so weak! There are noble men and women who plead for us, striving to help those who cannot help themselves. God bless them! God give them strength and courage to go on! God bless those, every where, who are laboring to advance the cause of humanity!

From THE MAIMIE PAPERS

by

MAIMIE PINZER

(1885–19??)

Born in Philadelphia of immigrant Polish and Russian parents, Maimie Pinzer left school at thirteen when the murder of her father plunged the family into poverty. Rejected by her mother and other relatives for her sexual activity, she became a prostitute. She was befriended by certain benefactors, including Fanny Howe, a prominent Bostonian. Her letters to Mrs. Howe show that she was capable of real friendship, which helped her in her struggles to leave "the life." Her whereabouts after 1922, when her letters ceased, remains a mystery.

• ———————————————————— •

Philadelphia, January 12, 1911

. . . And yet I could not buckle down to cutting out entirely all the things I had summed up while in the hospital as being empty and not worthwhile. At times, I would go all over the thoughts that passed through my mind while in the various hospitals and would decide that I would keep my word to myself and cut it out. Of course, the attending luxuries that go with loose living I did not want to give up. But, summed all up, it is anything but a pleasant road to travel; and I saw how the few luxuries did not make up for the indignities offered me and the cautious way I had to live. As, for instance, I love women—that is, I would like to have women friends—but I can't have; or rather, I couldn't have. I avoided them, even though very often I would meet one who would want to be friendly, and even now, the habit is so strong in me that I never encourage any advances from them—much as I should like to—for I couldn't find any enjoyment in being on friendly terms with a woman who lived a sporting sort of life, and the others, I dreaded would find out, perhaps inadvertently, something about me, and perhaps cut me, and I couldn't stand that; so I always repel any advances they make—so much so, that Mr. Jones thinks I am rude about it. . . .

When I was in the hospital in St. Louis in 1909, again I came to the conclusion that I would live right and perhaps be happy. I thought my mode of life explained why I was lying there all alone, without the visits

of a human being other than the general nurse and no word from anyone—besides the letters from my husband, which are always the very
kindest and affectionate. I would see all about me at the visiting hour
people hurrying and scurrying to the various beds to see the other patients, bringing them fruit and flowers and magazines. I don't think I
ever wanted anything in my life so much as I did some grapes while I
was there, but I had no friends to bring or send them to me. Then the
conviction was strong in me again that it was surely my fault that I was
so friendless and that I would surely try living straight and start to make
friends that were real. But, while I had that thought in my brain, I tucked
it conveniently out of my road—and hadn't been out of the hospital three
weeks before I went to San Antonio, Texas, with a circuit attorney of St.
Louis who too had been ill in the St. Agnes Hospital when I was, and
who had the same doctor. The doctor ordered the trip for his health and I
went along, writing my husband some absurd story about my uncle
Louis who lives thirty miles out of San Antonio sending me the ticket to
go there. (Fact of the matter was, when I did go to this small town to
visit my uncle whom I hadn't seen in ten years, he treated me as one
would an acquaintance and never even asked me to stop for a meal.) At
any rate, when I returned from San Antonio, went to Oklahoma City to
join Mr. Jones, I was again thoroughly and heartily weary of my precari-
ous way of living, for I had another belittling experience in San Antonio.
And then I just sat down and waited. For what, I didn't know, but I had
an idea that I wasn't going to meet anyone and would just cut it all out.
Then came Mr. Welsh's first letter; and no sooner was that correspondence started than I knew why, before that, I could only *think* to live
decent. For I found that which is the reason people keep diaries. It records
these thoughts, and once they are carefully taken apart and written, you
can follow the lines of your thoughts more clearly; and then it is a clear-
ing-house, and from one writing to the next, one's brain is cleared, ready
to follow out the line of thought or perhaps start a new line of thought.
In that way, Mr. Welsh helped me most, for I kept a sort of diary in my
letters to him of my thoughts as they came to me each day. And then,
when I felt I was responsible to a real live father for my actions, I was
very careful as to what I did. And I never did anything (even the most
ridiculous detail) that I didn't write to him of it; and I was happier than
ever before in my life. And because I believed in him, he readily convinced me that I had a Father in Heaven; and when I think back to the
first few weeks I was in the hospital last spring, I doubt whether it was
really I who had such childlike faith in prayers. I haven't even the slightest atom of that left, but I wish I had. It was very comforting. In a measure I'm like a child for I love to show off, provided I have the right sort
of an audience. I know when I procured the work at the *North American*,
it was because I wanted to show everyone how clever I was; and then
when Mr. Welsh left and I had no one to applaud, I quit being clever. . . .

I know you are worrying as to how I intend to manage this winter. And though I will tell you not to let it worry you, I know that isn't easy. You will probably think I've thought it all out as to how I will do—but really, I haven't, because I just can't. . . . Conditions are bad enough—couldn't be worse—but if any person knew that they were going to exist for a given period, they would act, knowing there was no recourse. But as it is, "hope springs eternal." And in my case, hardly a day—two at the most—but something seems to clear the way for a change in the near future, but unfortunately so far hasn't materialized. Here, as everywhere, I've no doubt, everyone hangs on to the hopes that at the end of each season, the war will be over, and with it the hard times. . . .

It is an old story, that the way is blocked for me to take up many of the situations that I am mentally fitted for—and which now also there are few of. Aside from these where mental ability is necessary, it is absolutely impossible for me to get those of the other sort. Salesperson, waitress, worker (physical) of any sort in a shop (due to insurance which prevents their employing anyone who has defective eyesight)—and sifted down, there is nothing else but housework. Which, since living here, I am fitted for—but can you think of any house that is fairly well kept that would have me? . . . Figured down, and logically, there doesn't seem much chance for me unless I happen on the proper place and I have no doubt there is such a place, provided I could wait long enough for it.

In the various agencies where I have applied, that are maintained by the city or otherwise to cope with this "unemployed problem," I was given a blank to fill out, and that I never heard from them is because they no doubt find others whose plight is worse, and leave me to find help elsewhere. You think (perhaps) how could anything I wrote make my plight seem less pitiful than others? Well I'll tell you. One question was: "Should you not find work, would you starve unless you resorted to unlawful acts?" (I suppose they meant stealing, or adultery, etc.) I answered in the negative, for could I say truthfully that I would starve when I know that you, Miss Huntington, Miss Payson, Mr. Welsh, Miss Outerbridge and one or two more, would not let me do that? Now bear in mind that I do not keep in mind that I can depend on any of these friends, and were these not abnormal times, I am sure I'd not have to put them to the test. But just the same, when a point-blank question of that sort is put before me, how else can I answer it and stick to my determination to be above deceit?

Other questions, such as, "Have you received an education?" (which no doubt is asked to determine one's ability) made me appear less needy than others; for though in the strict sense of the word I did not recieve [sic] an education, yet I am not to be classed as "uneducated":

"How many languages can you speak?"
"How many languages can you read?"

"How many languages can you write?"

And I answered "five" to the first (German, French, English, Yiddish and Russian); "four" to the second question, and "two" to the last. All this, I am sure, made me seem less hopeless than some of the others who, at the most (French Canadians), are only bi-lingual.

I bring all this out to show you, then, why I can expect no help from such sources. Though I did write in the proper classification that I was unable to cope with conditions mainly because of my impaired sight, and even more defective appearance, I received not a word from them—though Stella (who also registered) did. Though in her case she was referred to the Catholic Church—who recommended that she leave all worldly cares and enter the Sacred Heart Convent as a penitent. Sweet outlook! That means for life. So, you see—here I am, right where I started and no nearer to the solution than when I started. . . .

When every other consideration fails, there comes a thought which I can't eliminate any more than I can that I have friends who will not let me starve—and that is Mr. Benjamin. We have never discussed this phase of the situation—but I know he realizes it as I do, that if I have no means, and work of some sort isn't available, I will have to return to live with him.

Just now he hasn't a dollar in the world. I mean just that. On Tuesday, he bought me a strip of war tax stamps; and when he got his change, he said, "This is my all," (and it was 20 cents) "until I put something over"— meaning selling some stock. The only reason that the plan of living with him comes to my mind is because, for the same rent he pays, I could live; and though food for two costs more than food for one—eaten together, and with care, I could live on what his food costs him in the restaurants (for he eats only in absolutely clean places, and they are always expensive). I haven't discussed this probability with him; and I believe— if it were necessary—I'd have to suggest it, because he never has in any way referred to this possibility ever occurring again. . . .

When I think about the possibility of returning to that life again, I feel more puzzled at what the girls would think of me, and the fact that my brother James's prophecy would come true (for he says I am a prostitute at heart—he didn't tell me that, but I saw it in writing to my oldest brother, who scarcely knows me, and whom I wouldn't know if I met him) than I do about the actual wrong I should be committing. For I have the knowledge that I don't want to be bad. But I don't see what else I shall do, if I don't soon find some way of earning my keep. When writing to Mr. Welsh several days ago, I didn't mention this possibility. I hope you won't consider this deceit. I couldn't do it—it would pain him, and I hadn't the courage to inflict it on him. I know too that you won't welcome the thought; so I say, don't let it fret you, for perhaps it may not come to that.

I cast about in my mind for excuses for myself, and I can think of many. . . .

POEM ABOUT MY RIGHTS

by

JUNE JORDAN
(b. 1936)

Born in Harlem, June Jordan grew up in the slums of the Bedford-Stuyvesant section of Brooklyn. Educated at Barnard, the University of Michigan, and the University of Chicago, she is now a professor at the University of California at Berkeley. She was the founder and director of The Voice of the Children and co-founder of Afro-Americans against Famine. She has held several fellowships and has been writer-in-residence at many colleges. She has written biography, political essays, two plays, four young adult novels, and six volumes of poetry. Jordan sees herself as a public poet in the tradition of Walt Whitman, speaking for the inarticulate and silent. Recent works include On Call: Political Essays *(1985)* and Naming Our Destiny: New and Selected Poems *(1989).*

Even tonight and I need to take a walk and clear
my head about this poem about why I can't
go out without changing my clothes my shoes
my body posture my gender identity my age
my status as a woman alone in the evening/
alone on the streets/alone not being the point/
the point being that I can't do what I want
to do with my own body because I am the wrong
sex the wrong age the wrong skin and
suppose it was not here in the city but down on the beach/
or far into the woods and I wanted to go
there by myself thinking about God/or thinking
about children or thinking about the world/all of it
disclosed by the stars and the silence:
I could not go and I could not think and I could not
stay there
alone
as I need to be

alone because I can't do what I want to do with my own
body and
who in the hell set things up
like this
and in France they say if the guy penetrates
but does not ejaculate then he did not rape me
and if after stabbing him if after screams if
after begging the bastard and if even after smashing
a hammer to his head if even after that if he
and his buddies fuck me after that
then I consented and there was
no rape because finally you understand finally
they fucked me over because I was wrong I was
wrong again to be me being me where I was/wrong
to be who I am
which is exactly like South Africa
penetrating into Namibia penetrating into
Angola and does that mean I mean how do you know if
Pretoria ejaculates what will the evidence look like the
proof of the monster jackboot ejaculation on Blackland
and if
after Namibia and if after Angola and if after Zimbabwe
and if after all of my kinsmen and women resist even to
self-immolation of the villages and if after that
we lose nevertheless what will the big boys say will they
claim my consent:
Do You Follow Me: We are the wrong people of
the wrong skin on the wrong continent and what
in the hell is everybody being reasonable about
and according to the *Times* this week
back in 1966 the C.I.A. decided that they had this problem
and the problem was a man named Nkrumah so they
killed him and before that it was Patrice Lumumba
and before that it was my father on the campus
of my Ivy League school and my father afraid
to walk into the cafeteria because he said he
was wrong the wrong age the wrong skin the wrong
gender identity and he was paying my tuition and
before that
it was my father saying I was wrong saying that
I should have been a boy because he wanted one/a
boy and that I should have been lighter skinned and
that I should have had straighter hair and that
I should not be so boy crazy but instead I should
just be one/a boy and before that

it was my mother pleading plastic surgery for
my nose and braces for my teeth and telling me
to let the books loose to let them loose in other
words
I am very familiar with the problems of the C.I.A.
and the problems of South Africa and the problems
of Exxon Corporation and the problems of white
America in general and the problems of the teachers
and the preachers and the F.B.I. and the social
workers and my particular Mom and Dad/I am very
familiar with the problems because the problems
turn out to be
me
I am the history of rape
I am the history of the rejection of who I am
I am the history of the terrorized incarceration of
my self
I am the history of battery assault and limitless
armies against whatever I want to do with my mind
and my body and my soul and
whether it's about walking out at night
or whether it's about the love that I feel or
whether it's about the sanctity of my vagina or
the sanctity of my national boundaries
or the sanctity of my leaders or the sanctity
of each and every desire
that I know from my personal and idiosyncratic
and indisputably single and singular heart
I have been raped
be-
cause I have been wrong the wrong sex the wrong age
the wrong skin the wrong nose the wrong hair the
wrong need the wrong dream the wrong geographic
the wrong sartorial
I have been the meaning of rape
I have been the problem everyone seeks to
eliminate by forced
penetration with or without the evidence of slime and/
but let this be unmistakable this poem
is not consent I do not consent
to my mother to my father to the teachers to
the F.B.I. to South Africa to Bedford-Stuy
to Park Avenue to American Airlines to the hardon
idlers on the corners to the sneaky creeps in
cars

JUNE JORDAN
337

I am not wrong: Wrong is not my name
My name is my own my own my own
and I can't tell you who the hell set things up like this
but I can tell you that from now on my resistance
my simple and daily and nightly self-determination
may very well cost you your life

IMAGE FIVE

· ———————————— ·

Women
without Men

Throughout history women who have lived alone have been looked on
with suspicion, either as unnatural or as having failed: the witch has
been feared and persecuted; the "old maid" treated with contempt or, at
best, viewed with pity. Women who shared their lives with other women,
even sisters, elicited the negative attitudes directed toward any woman
without a man of her own. Even today, when more women than ever
voluntarily live without men, their status is still viewed pejoratively.
Those who assert their happiness in choosing to have a sexual relationship with a female partner share with male homosexuals in the oppro-
brium of the general public. The power of the wife-mother ideal and their
nonavailability as sex objects makes women without men the target of
the ridicule that hides a fear that women's freedom will cost men what
they believe are their rightful perquisites as fathers, husbands, and lovers.
The fear is augmented, of course, by knowledge that women can now be
free from the inevitable childbearing that had always been the result of
heterosexual unions; if more and more women are not forced into dependency, the wife-mother ideal is threatened. Dr. Johnson's eighteenth-
century argument for chastity still seems relevant: "Upon that all the
property in the world depends." He was referring to the need to be sure
of paternity for purposes of property inheritance; women's sexual freedom threatens not only property but all male rights to be and feel superior. It is no wonder that easily accessible contraceptives and abortion

are the targets of such deep rage, persisting in the face of a much more rational fear, that of world overpopulation.

The old maid stereotype may seem to be out of date; actually, it underlies attitudes toward widows, toward women who live together in groups or as couples, and often toward old women, whether they are alone or not; any woman not in a reproductive relationship with a man is suspect in many societies. In Russia and other countries where the shortage of workers has forced the majority of women into dual roles as workers and wives, the "old maid" is still an anathema because she does not contribute to the population. In China, even though each couple is allowed only one child because of population pressures, women who live apart from a family situation have no place in society; women as young as forty-five are expected to retire from other work to be primarily child caretakers.

An attitude of scorn and an assumption of biological peculiarity seem to underlie the portrait of "Miss Gee" by W. H. Auden—himself a homosexual. Physically repugnant, poor, and old, she is shown as contemptible because she fears sexuality; her cancer is ascribed to her lack of "creativity," her barrenness. Though in the poem these attitudes are ascribed to other figures—the cold medical men who treat her like a specimen and the "Oxford Groupers" who do not feel Christian charity for her—it is hard not to feel venom from the author himself. But he may be mocking the ballad form, which often elicits a vague sentimentality instead of true pity. It may be that Auden is rejecting the falsity of a society that has allowed Miss Gee's existence without the dignity of full personhood that would elicit sympathy.

In "The Bedquilt," Dorothy Canfield Fisher clearly elicits sympathy for Aunt Mehetabel; her doing so contributed to her dismissal by literary critics as a writer of "domestic" fiction, a genre first scorned three-quarters of a century earlier by Nathaniel Hawthorne as the product of "scribbling women," whom he could not imitate or outsell. Though very successful in her day, Fisher does not often appear in curricula today. She is very modern in showing creativity as an avenue to self-esteem; her story is almost a model for Alice Walker's claims in "In Search of Our Mothers' Gardens" (1983) that women denied access to literacy and high art have throughout history found ways of expressing their creative talents in art, whether gardening or quilting. The respect Aunt Mehetabel wins through her art is a sign of hope that women will be admired for traits other than beauty or reproductive power.

"The Women Men Don't See" exemplifies the reactions of incredulity and anger that have caused a backlash to the women's movement. In the story a mother and daughter, disgusted by their invisibility as workers and their secondary roles, choose to escape to another planet. Faced with eyewitness knowledge of the women's competence, James Tiptree's macho narrator finds incredible his growing realization that they have rejected not only their roles but the entire society. Caught in his own ideology, he is totally unable to understand their reasons; he can deal with his fantastic experience only by getting drunk.

Agnes Smedley reports on a group of women who have also happily escaped traditional roles; living independently together while working in a silk factory, these young women fulfill their filial duty by supporting their parents even though they reject the traditional duty of marrying. Though their economic status gives them a higher social role than that of wives, they are accused of being lesbians because they enjoy the company of their fellow workers; even the young Western-trained "expert" accompanying Smedley speaks of them with "hostility and contempt." It is clear that he resents their prosperity and their freedom to speak out when he does not dare. Smedley concludes with thoughts of "the common humanity, the goodness and unity of the common people of all lands"; she seems not to perceive the irony that the young expert's attitude is far more common than the happiness of the silk workers. Camaraderie has accompanied the continuing exploitation of Third World workers in the manufacturing of clothing and computers, but it cannot compensate for the injustices they suffer. It is sad to realize that in many parts of the world the new exploitation, like that of the silk workers in 1930, is perceived by many women and even child laborers as preferable to any alternative available to them.

In the past two women living together might be tolerated; in nineteenth-century New England, as Henry James showed in *The Bostonians* (1886), a "Boston marriage," though spoken of patronizingly, could be acknowledged publicly. But no mention was made of sexuality. For a long time, the many women who were couples were tacitly assumed to be asexual and were described merely as women living together; even when referred to as "women loving women," their sexual relationship was not mentioned. In an important article, one historian claims that ardent friendships between women in the nineteenth century were means of exchanging tender caresses as a substitute for the formality and distance, if not frigidity, experienced in heterosexual relationships (Smith-Rosenberg, 1975). Only very recently have lesbians spoken out as strongly as does Pat Parker's speaker, a black who wishes her love for a white woman could insulate her from the racism, sexism, and homophobia she has experienced. Valerie Miner's lesbian lovers are ordinary women, going on a weekend vacation to the country home they own collectively with other women. But, lacking male protection, they respond with fear when an armed intruder appears on their land. Like all women, Kate and Josie fear male hostility, especially when it appears without warning and seems almost invincible. The sheriff and the legal system seem to be on the side of the intruder. Though not physically harmed, the lovers are psychologically damaged and can return only with difficulty to their idyllic joy in one another.

The lesbian lovers in Shirley Ann Grau's story are of disparate ages; the older one has had a child. In spite of their happiness together, the younger woman cannot overcome her longing to have a child of her own; she is thirty-six and feels the biological clock running out. Feeling "hollow and empty and useless . . . so light that the wind will blow . . . her away," Vicky exemplifies the traditional stereotype of a woman who needs to fill her interior empty space in order to be fully human. This attitude has been expressed by many psychologists, most cogently and influentially by Erik Erikson (1964), who sees childless women as developmentally weak. Angela wearily realizes that she cannot contend with Vicky's desire; both are sad that they cannot as lovers have a child together. A lesbian couple's sorrow over their inability to be biological parents together may be real, but it is based on the unfounded assumption that only the physical experience of childbirth can satisfy the longing for maternity, and it prioritizes maternity over sexuality.

The other selections in this section focus on women who are involuntarily alone. The two widows portrayed by Kate Chopin and William Carlos Williams have diametrically opposite attitudes toward their position. Obviously, a woman's attitude toward widowhood depends on the quality of the marriage. The unconventional attitude of Chopin's widow makes us realize that the stereotype of helpless grief is too narrow to take into account the circumstances of all marriages. Our language has no word to designate the position of May Sarton's speaker in "Mourning to Do," who is the survivor of a long-term lesbian relationship; this means that she is free from any tradition of mourning. Sarton focuses on the comfort of remembering the dead woman, who can continue to be loved and live in her lover's memory.

Bobbie Ann Mason's two widows console each other for the reality of their lives without men. Neighbors, they are sympathetic to each other's feelings; the childless Rita Jean cherishes her cat and vicariously enjoys the excitement of Cleo's children's lives. But Cleo disapproves of her daughter's decision to leave her husband and resents her parking her children at Cleo's house. Cleo is not ready to function as a grandmother; she needs freedom to earn her living as a seamstress and to enjoy Rita Jean's understanding company. At a flea market Cleo finds a knick-knack that reminds her of her happy marriage, and she finds fantasizing about it a way of being happy without living in the past. Mason has given us a minimalist picture of how to make the best of a limited situation.

Whether voluntarily or not, most women will at some time live without men; changes in negative views of this inevitable status may accompany new attitudes toward other roles.

MISS GEE

by

W. H. AUDEN
(1907–1973)

Born in England, W. H. Auden became a U.S. citizen in 1939 and divided his time between the two countries and a summer home in Austria. A major American poet, Auden turned from his early interest in Marxism to a deep commitment to Christianity; his long poem For the Time Being *(1941) expresses his belief in the need for faith in our time. His poems, many of which are light in tone, reflect a wide interest in politics, literature, and music. His last poems,* Thank You, Fog, *were published posthumously in 1975.*

Let me tell you a little story
    About Miss Edith Gee;
She lived in Clevedon Terrace
    At Number 83.

She'd a slight squint in her left eye,
    Her lips they were thin and small,
She had narrow sloping shoulders
    And she had no bust at all.

She'd a velvet hat with trimmings,
    And a dark-grey serge costume;
She lived in Clevedon Terrace
    In a small bed-sitting room.

She'd a purple mac for wet days,
    A green umbrella too to take,
She'd a bicycle with shopping basket
    And a harsh back-pedal brake.

The Church of Saint Aloysius
    Was not so very far;
She did a lot of knitting,
    Knitting for that Church Bazaar.

Miss Gee looked up at the starlight
    And said: 'Does anyone care
That I live in Clevedon Terrace
    On one hundred pounds a year?'

She dreamed a dream one evening
    That she was the Queen of France
And the Vicar of Saint Aloysius
    Asked Her Majesty to dance.

But a storm blew down the palace,
    She was biking through a field of corn,
And a bull with the face of the Vicar
    Was charging with lowered horn.

She could feel his hot breath behind her,
    He was going to overtake;
And the bicycle went slower and slower
    Because of that back-pedal brake.

Summer made the trees a picture,
    Winter made them a wreck;
She bicycled to the evening service
    With her clothes buttoned up to her neck.

She passed by the loving couples,
    She turned her head away;
She passed by the loving couples
    And they didn't ask her to stay.

Miss Gee sat down in the side-aisle,
    She heard the organ play;
And the choir it sang so sweetly
    At the ending of the day,

Miss Gee knelt down in the side-aisle,
    She knelt down on her knees;

'Lead me not into temptation
     But make me a good girl, please.'

The days and nights went by her
     Like waves round a Cornish wreck;
She bicycled down to the doctor
     With her clothes buttoned up to her neck.

She bicycled down to the doctor,
     And rang the surgery bell;
'O, doctor, I've a pain inside me,
     And I don't feel very well.'

Doctor Thomas looked her over,
     And then he looked some more;
Walked over to his wash-basin,
     Said, 'Why didn't you come before?'

Doctor Thomas sat over his dinner,
     Though his wife was waiting to ring;
Rolling his bread into pellets,
     Said, 'Cancer's a funny thing.

'Nobody knows what the cause is,
     Though some pretend they do;
It's like some hidden assassin
     Waiting to strike at you.

'Childless women get it,
     And men when they retire;
It's as if there had to be some outlet
     For their foiled creative fire.'

His wife she rang for the servant,
     Said, 'Don't be so morbid, dear,'
He said; 'I saw Miss Gee this evening
     And she's a goner, I fear.'

They took Miss Gee to the hospital,
     She lay there a total wreck,
Lay in the ward for women
     With the bedclothes right up to her neck.

W. H. AUDEN

They laid her on the table,
  The students began to laugh;
And Mr. Rose the surgeon
  He cut Miss Gee in half.

Mr. Rose he turned to his students,
  Said; 'Gentlemen, if you please,
We seldom see a sarcoma
  As far advanced as this.'

They took her off the table,
  They wheeled away Miss Gee
Down to another department
  Where they study Anatomy.

They hung her from the ceiling,
  Yes, they hung up Miss Gee;
And a couple of Oxford Groupers
  Carefully dissected her knee.

THE BEDQUILT

by

DOROTHY CANFIELD FISHER
(1879–1958)

Dorothy Canfield Fisher does not fit the stereotype of the neglected woman author. Her novels, such as Understood Betsy *(1917),* The Home-Maker *(1924), and* Seasoned Timber *(1939), were very popular when they were published; several were dramatized or made into films. Her work shows her to be very much a feminist in her concern for women's education and equality. Highly educated herself (Ph.D., Columbia University), she was also an antiwar and environmental activist, especially in Vermont, the locus of* Hillsboro People *(1915), a short story collection from which "The Bedquilt" is taken.*

• ———————————————— •

Of all the Elwell family Aunt Mehetabel was certainly the most unimportant member. It was in the New England days, when an unmarried woman was an old maid at twenty, at forty was everyone's servant, and at sixty had gone through so much discipline that she could need no more in the next world. Aunt Mehetabel was sixty-eight.

She had never for a moment known the pleasure of being important to anyone. Not that she was useless in her brother's family; she was expected, as a matter of course, to take upon herself the most tedious and uninteresting part of the household labors. On Mondays she accepted as her share the washing of the men's shirts, heavy with sweat and stiff with dirt from the fields and from their own hard-working bodies. Tuesdays she never dreamed of being allowed to iron anything pretty or even interesting, like the baby's white dresses or the fancy aprons of her younger lady nieces. She stood all day pressing out a tiresome monotonous succession of dish-cloths and towels and sheets.

In preserving-time she was allowed to have none of the pleasant responsibility of deciding when the fruit had cooked long enough, nor did she share in the little excitement of pouring the sweet-smelling stuff into the stone jars. She sat in a corner with the children and stoned cherries incessantly, or hulled strawberries until her fingers were dyed red to the bone.

The Elwells were not consciously unkind to their aunt, they were even in a vague way fond of her; but she was so utterly insignificant a figure in their lives that they bestowed no thought whatever on her. Aunt Mehetabel did not resent this treatment; she took it quite as unconsciously as they gave it. It was to be expected when one was an old-maid dependent in a busy family. She gathered what crumbs of comfort she could from their occasional careless kindnesses and tried to hide the hurt which even yet pierced her at her brother's rough joking. In the winter when they all sat before the big hearth, roasted apples, drank mulled cider, and teased the girls about their beaux and the boys about their sweethearts, she shrank into a dusky corner with her knitting, happy if the evening passed without her brother saying, with a crude sarcasm, "Ask your Aunt Mehetabel about the beaux that used to come a-sparkin' her!" or, "Mehetabel, how was't when you was in love with Abel Cummings." As a matter of fact, she had been the same at twenty as at sixty, a quiet, mouse-like little creature, too timid and shy for anyone to notice, or to raise her eyes for a moment and wish for a life of her own.

Her sister-in-law, a big hearty housewife, who ruled indoors with as autocratic a sway as did her husband on the farm, was rather kind in an absent, offhand way to the shrunken little old woman, and it was through her that Mehetabel was able to enjoy the one pleasure of her life. Even as a girl she had been clever with her needle in the way of patching bedquilts. More than that she could never learn to do. The garments which she made for herself were the most lamentable affairs, and she was humbly grateful for any help in the bewildering business of putting them together. But in patchwork she enjoyed a tepid importance. She could really do that as well as anyone else. During years of devotion to this one art she had accumulated a considerable store of quilting patterns. Sometimes the neighbors would send over and ask "Miss Mehetabel" for such and such a design. It was with an agreeable flutter at being able to help someone that she went to the dresser, in her bare little room under the eaves, and extracted from her crowded portfolio the pattern desired.

She never knew how her great idea came to her. Sometimes she thought she must have dreamed it, sometimes she even wondered reverently, in the phraseology of the weekly prayer-meeting, if it had not been "sent" to her. She never admitted to herself that she could have thought of it without other help; it was too great, too ambitious, too lofty a project for her humble mind to have conceived. Even when she finished drawing the design with her own fingers, she gazed at it incredulously, not daring to believe that it could indeed be her handiwork. At first it seemed to her only like a lovely but quite unreal dream. She did not think of putting it into execution—so elaborate, so complicated, so beautifully difficult a pattern could be only for the angels in heaven to quilt. But so curiously does familiarity accustom us even to very wonderful things, that as she lived with this astonishing creation of her mind, the longing grew stronger and stronger to give it material life with her nimble old fingers.

She gasped at her daring when this idea first swept over her and put it away as one does a sinfully selfish notion, but she kept coming back to it again and again. Finally she said compromisingly to herself that she would make one "square," just one part of her design, to see how it would look. Accustomed to the most complete dependence on her brother and his wife, she dared not do even this without asking Sophia's permission. With a heart full of hope and fear thumping furiously against her old ribs, she approached the mistress of the house on churning-day, knowing with the innocent guile of a child that the country woman was apt to be in a good temper while working over the fragrant butter in the cool cellar.

Sophia listened absently to her sister-in-law's halting, hesitating petition. "Why, yes, Mehetabel," she said, leaning far down into the huge churn for the last golden morsels—"why, yes, start another quilt if you want to. I've got a lot of pieces from the spring sewing that will work in real good." Mehetabel tried honestly to make her see that this would be no common quilt, but her limited vocabulary and her emotion stood between her and expression. At last Sophia said, with a kindly impatience: "Oh, there! Don't bother me. I never could keep track of your quiltin' patterns, anyhow. I don't care what pattern you go by."

With this overwhelmingly, although unconsciously, generous permission Mehetabel rushed back up the steep attic stairs to her room, and in a joyful agitation began preparations for the work of her life. It was even better than she hoped. By some heaven-sent inspiration she had invented a pattern beyond which no patchwork quilt could go.

She had but little time from her incessant round of household drudgery for this new and absorbing occupation, and she did not dare sit up late at night lest she burn too much candle. It was weeks before the little square began to take on a finished look, to show the pattern. Then Mehetabel was in a fever of impatience to bring it to completion. She was too conscientious to shirk even the smallest part of her share of the work of the house, but she rushed through it with a speed which left her panting as she climbed to the little room. This seemed like a radiant spot to her as she bent over the innumerable scraps of cloth which already in her imagination ranged themselves in the infinitely diverse pattern of her masterpiece. Finally she could wait no longer, and one evening ventured to bring her work down beside the fire where the family sat, hoping that some good fortune would give her a place near the tallow candles on the mantelpiece. She was on the last corner of the square, and her needle flew in and out with inconceivable rapidity. No one noticed her, a fact which filled her with relief, and by bedtime she had but a few more stitches to add.

As she stood up with the others, the square fluttered out of her trembling old hands and fell on the table. Sophia glanced at it carelessly. "Is that the new quilt you're beginning on?" she asked with a yawn. "It looks like a real pretty pattern. Let's see it." Up to that moment Mehetabel had labored in the purest spirit of disinterested devotion to an ideal, but as Sophia held her work toward the candle to examine it, and exclaimed in amazement and admiration, she felt an astonished joy to know that her creation would stand the test of publicity.

"Land sakes!" ejaculated her sister-in-law, looking at the many-colored square. "Why, Mehetabel Elwell, where'd you git that pattern?"

"I made it up," said Mehetabel quietly, but with unutterable pride.

"No!" exclaimed Sophia incredulously. "*Did* you! Why, I never see such a pattern in my life. Girls, come here and see what your Aunt Mehetabel is doing."

The three tall daughters turned back reluctantly from the stairs. "I don't seem to take much interest in patchwork," said one listlessly.

"No, nor I neither!" answered Sophia; "but a stone image would take an interest in this pattern. Honest Mehetabel, did you think of it yourself? And how under the sun and stars did you ever git your courage up to start in a-making it? Land! Look at all those tiny squinchy little seams! Why the wrong side ain't a thing *but* seams!"

The girls echoed their mother's exclamations, and Mr. Elwell himself came over to see what they were discussing. "Well, I declare!" he said, looking at his sister with eyes more approving than she could ever remember. "That beats old Mis' Wightman's quilt that got the blue ribbon so many times at the county fair."

Mehetabel's heart swelled within her, and tears of joy moistened her old eyes as she lay that night in her narrow, hard bed, too proud and excited to sleep. The next day her sister-in-law amazed her by taking the huge pan of potatoes out of her lap and setting one of the younger children to peeling them. "Don't you want to go on with that quiltin' pattern?" she said; "I'd kind o' like to see how you're goin' to make the grape-vine design come out on the corner."

By the end of the summer the family interest had risen so high that Mehetabel was given a little stand in the sitting-room where she could keep her pieces, and work in odd minutes. She almost wept over such kindness, and resolved firmly not to take advantage of it by neglecting her work, which she performed with a fierce thoroughness. But the whole atmosphere of her world was changed. Things had a meaning now. Through the longest task of washing milk-pans there rose the rainbow of promise of her variegated work. She took her place by the little table and put the thimble on her knotted, hard finger with the solemnity of a priestess performing a sacred rite.

She was even able to bear with some degree of dignity the extreme honor of having the minister and the minister's wife comment admiringly on her great project. The family felt quite proud of Aunt Mehetabel as Minister Bowman had said it was work as fine as any he had ever seen, "and he didn't know but finer!" The remark was repeated verbatim to the neighbors in the following weeks when they dropped in and examined in a perverse silence some astonishingly difficult *tour de force* which Mehetabel had just finished.

The family especially plumed themselves on the slow progress of the quilt. "Mehetabel has been to work on that corner for six weeks, come Tuesday, and she ain't half done yet," they explained to visitors. They fell out of the way of always expecting her to be the one to run on errands, even for the children. "Don't bother your Aunt Mehetabel," Sophia would call. "Can't you see she's got to a ticklish place on the quilt?"

The old woman sat up straighter and looked the world in the face. She was a part of it at last. She joined in the conversation and her remarks were listened to. The children were even told to mind her when she asked them to do some service for her, although this she did but seldom, the habit of self-effacement being too strong.

One day some strangers from the next town drove up and asked if they could inspect the wonderful quilt which they had heard of, even down in their end of the valley. After that such visitations were not uncommon, making the Elwells' house a notable object. Mehetabel's quilt came to be one of the town sights, and no one was allowed to leave the town without having paid tribute to its worth. The Elwells saw to it that their aunt was better dressed than she had ever been before, and one of the girls made her a pretty little cap to wear on her thin white hair.

A year went by and a quarter of the quilt was finished; a second year passed and half was done. The third year Mehetabel had pneumonia and lay ill for weeks and weeks, overcome with terror lest she die before her work was completed. A fourth year and one could really see the grandeur of the whole design; and in September of the fifth year, the entire family watching her with eager and admiring eyes, Mehetabel quilted the last stitches in her creation. The girls held it up by the four corners, and they all looked at it in a solemn silence. Then Mr. Elwell smote one horny hand within the other and exclaimed: "By ginger! That's goin' to the county fair!" Mehetabel blushed a deep red at this. It was a thought which had occurred to her in a bold moment, but she had not dared to entertain it. The family acclaimed the idea, and one of the boys was forthwith dispatched to the house of the neighbor who was chairman of the committee for their village. He returned with radiant face. "Of course he'll take it. Like's not it may git a prize, so he says; but he's got to have it right off, because all the things are goin' to-morrow morning."

Even in her swelling pride Mehetabel felt a pang of separation as the bulky package was carried out of the house. As the days went on she felt absolutely lost without her work. For years it had been her one preoccupation, and she could not bear even to look at the little stand, now quite bare of the litter of scraps which had lain on it so long. One of the neighbors, who took the long journey to the fair, reported that the quilt was hung in a place of honor in a glass case in "Agricultural Hall." But that meant little to Mehetabel's utter ignorance of all that lay outside of her brother's home. The family noticed the old woman's depression, and one day Sophia said kindly, "You feel sort o' lost without the quilt, don't you, Mehetabel?"

"They took it away so quick!" she said wistfully; "I hadn't hardly had one real good look at it myself."

Mr. Elwell made no comment, but a day or two later he asked his sister how early she could get up in the morning.

"I dun'no'. Why?" she asked.

"Well, Thomas Ralston has got to drive clear to West Oldton to see a lawyer there, and that is four miles beyond the fair. He says if you can git up so's to leave here at four in the morning he'll drive you over to the fair, leave you there for the day, and bring you back again at night."

Mehetabel looked at him with incredulity. It was as though someone had offered her a ride in a golden chariot up to the gates of heaven. "Why, you can't *mean* it!" she cried, paling with the intensity of her emotion. Her brother laughed a little uneasily. Even to his careless indifference this joy was a revelation of the narrowness of her life in his home. "Oh, 'tain't so much to go to the fair. Yes, I mean it. Go git your things ready, for he wants to start to-morrow morning."

All that night a trembling, excited old woman lay and stared at the rafters. She, who had never been more than six miles from home in her life, was going to drive thirty miles away—it was like going to another world. She who had never seen anything more exciting than a church supper was to see the county fair. To Mehetabel it was like making the tour of the world. She had never dreamed of doing it. She could not at all imagine what it would be like.

Nor did the exhortations of the family, as they bade good-by to her, throw any light on her confusion. They had all been at least once to the scene of gayety she was to visit, and as she tried to eat her breakfast they called out conflicting advice to her till her head whirled. Sophia told her to be sure and see the display of preserves. Her brother said not to miss inspecting the stock, her nieces said the fancywork was the only thing worth looking at, and her nephews said she must bring them home an account of the races. The buggy drove up to the door, she was helped in, and her wraps tucked about her. They all stood together and waved good-by to her as she drove out of the yard. She waved back, but she scarcely saw them. On her return home that evening she was very pale, and so tired and stiff that her brother had to lift her out bodily, but her lips were set in a blissful smile. They crowded around her with thronging questions, until Sophia pushed them all aside, telling them Aunt Mehetabel was too tired to speak until she had had her supper. This was eaten in an enforced silence on the part of the children, and then the old woman was helped into an easy-chair before the fire. They gathered about her, eager for news of the great world, and Sophia said, "Now, come, Mehetabel, tell us all about it!"

Mehetabel drew a long breath. "It was just perfect!" she said; "finer even than I thought. They've got it hanging up in the very middle of a sort o' closet made of glass, and one of the lower corners is ripped and turned back so's to show the seams on the wrong side."

"What?" asked Sophia, a little blankly.

"Why, the quilt!" said Mehetabel in surprise. "There are a whole lot of other ones in that room, but not one that can hold a candle to it, if I do say it who shouldn't. I heard lots of people say the same thing. You ought to have heard what the women said about that corner, Sophia. They said— well, I'd be ashamed to *tell* you what they said. I declare if I wouldn't!"

Mr. Elwell asked, "What did you think of that big ox we've heard so much about?"

"I didn't look at the stock," returned his sister indifferently. "That set of pieces you gave me, Maria, from your red waist, come out just lovely!" she assured one of her nieces. "I heard one woman say you could 'most smell the red silk roses."

"Did any of the horses in our town race?" asked young Thomas.

"I didn't see the races."

"How about the preserves?" asked Sophia.

"I didn't see the preserves," said Mehetabel calmly. "You see, I went right to the room where the quilt was, and then I didn't want to leave it. It had been so long since I'd seen it. I had to look at it first real good my-self, and then I looked at the others to see if there was any that could come up to it. And then the people begun comin' in and I got so inter-ested in hearin' what they had to say I couldn't think of goin' anywheres else. I ate my lunch right there too, and I'm as glad as can be I did, too; for what do you think?"—she gazed about her with kindling eyes— "while I stood there with a sandwich in one hand didn't the head of the hull concern come in and open the glass door and pin 'First Prize' right in the middle of the quilt!"

There was a stir of congratulation and proud exclamation. Then Sophia returned again to the attack. "Didn't you go to see anything else?" she queried.

"Why, no," said Mehetabel. "Only the quilt. Why should I?"

She fell into a reverie where she saw again the glorious creation of her hand and brain hanging before all the world with the mark of highest approval on it. She longed to make her listeners see the splendid vision with her. She struggled for words; she reached blindly after unknown superlatives. "I tell you it looked like—— " she said, and paused, hesitat-ing. Vague recollections of hymn-book phraseology came into her mind, the only form of literary expression she knew; but they were dismissed as being sacrilegious, and also not sufficiently forcible. Finally, "I tell you it looked real *well*!" she assured them, and sat staring into the fire, on her tired old face the supreme content of an artist who has realized his ideal.

THE WOMEN
MEN DON'T SEE

by

JAMES TIPTREE, JR.
(b. 1918?)

Embarrassed by the praise for "The Women Men Don't See" as an example of how well a man could write about women, Alice Sheldon disclosed in 1974 that she is James Tiptree, Jr. A semi-retired psychologist, Sheldon has received four prizes since 1968 for science fiction writing. Widely traveled, she lives—or at least receives her mail—at McLean, Virginia. Sheldon's collection, Star Songs of an Old Primate *(1978), has an introduction by Ursula Le Guin; recent works are* Crown of Stars *(1988) and* Houston, Houston, Do You Read *(1989).*

• ———————————————— •

I see her first while the Mexicana 727 is barreling down to Cozumel Island. I come out of the can and lurch into her seat, saying "Sorry," at a double female blur. The near blur nods quietly. The younger one in the window seat goes on looking out. I continue down the aisle, registering nothing. Zero. I never would have looked at them or thought of them again.

Cozumel airport is the usual mix of panicky Yanks dressed for the sand pile and calm Mexicans dressed for lunch at the Presidente. I am a used-up Yank dressed for serious fishing; I extract my rods and duffel from the riot and hike across the field to find my charter pilot. One Captain Estéban has contracted to deliver me to the bonefish flats of Belize three hundred kilometers down the coast.

Captain Estéban turns out to be four-feet nine of mahogany Mayan *puro*. He is also in a somber Maya snit. He tells me my Cessna is grounded somewhere and his Bonanza is booked to take a party to Chetumal.

Well, Chetumal is south; can he take me along and go on to Belize after he drops them off? Gloomily he concedes the possibility—*if* the other party permits, and *if* there are not too many *equipajes*.

The Chetumal party approaches. It's the woman and her young companion—daughter?—neatly picking their way across the gravel and yucca apron. Their Ventura two-suiters, like themselves, are small, plain and neutral-colored. No problem. When the captain asks if I may ride along, the mother says mildly "Of course," without looking at me.

I think that's when my inner tilt-detector sends up its first faint click. How come this woman has already looked me over carefully enough to accept me on her plane? I disregard it. Paranoia hasn't been useful in my business for years, but the habit is hard to break.

As we clamber into the Bonanza, I see the girl has what could be an attractive body if there was any spark at all. There isn't. Captain Estéban folds a serape to sit on so he can see over the cowling and runs a meticulous check-down. And then we're up and trundling over the turquoise Jello of the Caribbean into a stiff south wind.

The coast on our right is the territory of Quintana Roo. If you haven't seen Yucatán, imagine the world's biggest absolutely flat green-gray rug. An empty-looking land. We pass the white ruin of Tulum and the gash of the road to Chichén Itzá, a half-dozen coconut plantations, and then nothing but reef and low scrub jungle all the way to the horizon, just about the way the conquistadors saw it four centuries back.

Long strings of cumulus are racing at us, shadowing the coast. I have gathered that part of our pilot's gloom concerns the weather. A cold front is dying on the henequen fields of Mérida to the west, and the south wind has piled up a string of coastal storms: what they call *llovisnos*. Estéban detours methodically around a couple of small thunderheads. The Bonanza jinks, and I look back with a vague notion of reassuring the women. They are calmly intent on what can be seen of Yucatán. Well, they were offered the copilot's view, but they turned it down. Too shy?

Another *llovisno* puffs up ahead. Estéban takes the Bonanza upstairs, rising in his seat to sight his course. I relax for the first time in too long, savoring the latitudes between me and my desk, the week of fishing ahead. Our captain's classic Maya profile attracts my gaze: forehead sloping back from his predatory nose, lips and jaw stepping back below it. If his slant eyes had been any more crossed, he couldn't have made his license. That's a handsome combination, believe it or not. On the little Maya chicks in their minishifts with iridescent gloop on those cockeyes, it's also highly erotic. Nothing like the oriental doll thing; these people have stone bones. Captain Estéban's old grandmother could probably tow the Bonanza . . .

I'm snapped awake by the cabin hitting my ear. Estéban is barking into his headset over a drumming racket of hail; the windows are dark gray.

One important noise is missing—the motor. I realize Estéban is fighting a dead plane. Thirty-six hundred; we've lost two thousand feet!

He slaps tank switches as the storm throws us around; I catch something about *gasolina* in a snarl that shows his big teeth. The Bonanza reels down. As he reaches for an overhead toggle, I see the fuel gauges are high. Maybe a clogged gravity feed line; I've heard of dirty gas down here. He drops the set; it's a million to one nobody can read us through the storm at this range anyway. Twenty-five hundred—going down.

His electric feed pump seems to have cut in: the motor explodes— quits—explodes—and quits again for good. We are suddenly out of the bottom of the clouds. Below us is a long white line almost hidden by rain: the reef. But there isn't any beach behind it, only a big meandering bay with a few mangrove flats—and it's coming up at us fast.

This is going to be bad, I tell myself with great unoriginality. The women behind me haven't made a sound. I look back and see they've braced down with their coats by their heads. With a stalling speed around eighty, all this isn't much use, but I wedge myself in.

Estéban yells some more into his set, flying a falling plane. He is do- ing one jesus job, too—as the water rushes up at us he dives into a hair- raising turn and hangs us into the wind—with a long pale ride of sandbar in front of our nose.

Where in hell he found it I never know. The Bonanza mushes down, and we belly-hit with a tremendous tearing crash—bounce—hit again— and everything slews wildly as we flat-spin into the mangroves at the end of the bar. Crash! Clang! The plane is wrapping itself into a mound of strangler fig with one wing up. The crashing quits with us all in one piece. And no fire. Fantastic.

Captain Estéban pries open his door, which is now in the roof. Behind me a woman is repeating quietly, "Mother. Mother." I climb up the floor and find the girl trying to free herself from her mother's embrace. The woman's eyes are closed. Then she opens them and suddenly lets go, sane as soap. Estéban starts hauling them out. I grab the Bonanza's aid kit and scramble out after them into brilliant sun and wind. The storm that hit us is already vanishing up the coast.

"Great landing, Captain."

"Oh, yes! It was beautiful." The women are shaky, but no hysteria. Estéban is surveying the scenery with the expression his ancestors used on the Spaniards.

If you've been in one of these things, you know the slow-motion inan- ity that goes on. Euphoria, first. We straggle down the fig tree and out onto the sandbar in the roaring hot wind, noting without alarm that there's nothing but miles of crystalline water on all sides. It's only a foot or so deep, and the bottom is the olive color of silt. The distant shore around us is all flat mangrove swamp, totally uninhabitable.

"Bahía Espiritu Santo." Estéban confirms my guess that we're down in that huge water wilderness. I always wanted to fish it.

"What's all that smoke?" The girl is pointing at the plumes blowing around the horizon.

"Alligator hunters," says Estéban. Maya poachers have left burn-offs in the swamps. It occurs to me that any signal fires we make aren't going to be too conspicuous. And I now note that our plane is well-buried in the mound of fig. Hard to see it from the air.

Just as the question of how the hell we get out of here surfaces in my mind, the older woman asks composedly, "If they didn't hear you, Captain, when will they start looking for us? Tomorrow?"

"Correct," Estéban agrees dourly. I recall that air-sea rescue is fairly informal here. Like, keep an eye open for Mario, his mother says he hasn't been home all week.

It dawns on me we may be here quite some while.

Furthermore, the diesel-truck noise on our left is the Caribbean piling back into the mouth of the bay. The wind is pushing it at us, and the bare bottoms on the mangroves show that our bar is covered at high tide. I recall seeing a full moon this morning in—believe it, St. Louis—which means maximal tides. Well, we can climb up in the plane. But what about drinking water?

There's a small splat! behind me. The older woman has sampled the bay. She shakes her head, smiling ruefully. It's the first real expression on either of them; I take it as the signal for introductions. When I say I'm Don Fenton from St. Louis, she tells me their name is Parsons, from Bethesda, Maryland. She says it so nicely I don't at first notice we aren't being given first names. We all compliment Captain Estéban again.

His left eye is swelled shut, an inconvenience beneath his attention as a Maya, but Mrs. Parsons spots the way he's bracing his elbow in his ribs.

"You're hurt, Captain."

"*Roto*—I think is broken." He's embarrassed at being in pain. We get him to peel off his Jaime shirt, revealing a nasty bruise in his superb dark-bay torso.

"Is there tape in that kit, Mr. Fenton? I've had a little first-aid training."

She begins to deal competently and very impersonally with the tape. Miss Parsons and I wander to the end of the bar and have a conversation which I am later to recall acutely.

"Roseate spoonbills," I tell her as three pink birds flap away.

"They're beautiful," she says in her tiny voice. They both have tiny voices. "He's a Mayan Indian, isn't he? The pilot, I mean."

"Right. The real thing, straight out of the Bonampak murals. Have you seen Chichén and Uxmal?"

"Yes. We were in Mérida. We're going to Tikal in Guatemala . . . I mean, we were."

"You'll get there." It occurs to me the girl needs cheering up. "Have they told you that Maya mothers used to tie a board on the infant's fore-head to get that slant? They also hung a ball of tallow over its nose to make the eyes cross. It was considered aristocratic."

She smiles and takes another peek at Estéban. "People seem different in Yucatán," she says thoughtfully. "Not like the Indians around Mexico City. More, I don't know, independent."

"Comes from never having been conquered. Mayas got massacred and chased a lot, but nobody ever really flattened them. I bet you didn't know that the last Mexican-Maya war ended with a negotiated truce in nineteen thirty-five?"

"No!" Then she says seriously, "I like that."

"So do I."

"The water is really rising very fast," says Mrs. Parsons gently from behind us.

It is, and so is another *llovisno*. We climb back into the Bonanza. I try to rig my parka for a rain catcher, which blows loose as the storm hits fast and furious. We sort a couple of malt bars and my bottle of Jack Daniels out of the jumble in the cabin and make ourselves reasonably comfortable. The Parsons take a sip of whiskey each, Estéban and I considerably more. The Bonanza begins to bump soggily. Estéban makes an ancient one-eyed Mayan face at the water seeping into his cabin and goes to sleep. We all nap.

When the water goes down, the euphoria has gone with it, and we're very, very thirsty. It's also damn near sunset. I get to work with a bait-casting rod and some treble hooks and manage to foul-hook four small mullets. Estéban and the women tie the Bonanza's midget life raft out in the mangroves to catch rain. The wind is parching hot. No planes go by.

Finally another shower comes over and yields us six ounces of water apiece. When the sunset envelops the world in golden smoke, we squat on the sandbar to eat wet raw mullet and Instant Breakfast crumbs. The women are now in shorts, neat but definitely not sexy.

"I never realized how refreshing raw fish is," Mrs. Parsons says pleasantly. Her daughter chuckles, also pleasantly. She's on Mamma's far side away from Estéban and me. I have Mrs. Parsons figured now; Mother Hen protecting only chick from male predators. That's all right with me. I came here to fish.

But something is irritating me. The damn women haven't complained once, you understand. Not a peep, not a quaver, no personal manifestations whatever. They're like something out of a manual.

"You really seem at home in the wilderness, Mrs. Parsons. You do much camping?"

"Oh goodness no." Diffident laugh. "Not since my girl scout days. Oh, look—are those man-of-war birds?"

Answer a question with a question. I wait while the frigate birds sail nobly into the sunset.

"Bethesda . . . Would I be wrong in guessing you work for Uncle Sam?"

"Why yes. You must be very familiar with Washington, Mr. Fenton. Does your work bring you there often?"

Anywhere but on our sandbar the little ploy would have worked. My hunter's gene twitches.

"Which agency are you with?"

She gives up gracefully. "Oh, just GSA records. I'm a librarian."

Of course. I know her now, all the Mrs. Parsonses in records divisions, accounting sections, research branches, personnel and administration offices. Tell Mrs. Parsons we need a recap on the external service contracts for fiscal '73. So Yucatán is on the tours now? Pity . . . I offer her the tired little joke. "You know where the bodies are buried."

She smiles deprecatingly and stands up. "It does get dark quickly, doesn't it?"

Time to get back into the plane.

A flock of ibis are circling us, evidently accustomed to roosting in our fig tree. Estéban produces a machete and a Mayan string hammock. He proceeds to sling it between tree and plane, refusing help. His machete stroke is noticeably tentative.

The Parsons are taking a pee behind the tail vane. I hear one of them slip and squeal faintly. When they come back over the hull, Mrs. Parsons asks, "Might we sleep in the hammock, Captain?"

Estéban splits an unbelieving grin. I protest about rain and mosquitoes.

"Oh, we have insect repellent and we do enjoy fresh air."

The air is rushing by about force five and colder by the minute.

"We have our raincoats," the girl adds cheerfully.

Well, okay, ladies. We dangerous males retire inside the damp cabin. Through the wind I hear the women laugh softly now and then, apparently cosy in their chilly ibis roost. A private insanity, I decide. I know myself for the least threatening of men; my non-charisma has been in fact an asset jobwise, over the years. Are they having fantasies about Estéban? Or maybe they really are fresh-air nuts . . . Sleep comes for me in invisible diesels roaring by on the reef outside.

We emerge dry-mouthed into a vast windy salmon sunrise. A diamond chip of sun breaks out of the sea and promptly submerges in cloud. I go to work with the rod and some mullet bait while two showers detour around us. Breakfast is a strip of wet barracuda apiece.

The Parsons continue stoic and helpful. Under Estéban's direction they set up a section of cowling for a gasoline flare in case we hear a plane, but nothing goes over except one unseen jet droning toward Panama. The wind howls, hot and dry and full of coral dust. So are we.

"They look first in the sea." Estéban remarks. His aristocratic frontal slope is beaded with sweat; Mrs. Parsons watches him concernedly. I watch the cloud blanket tearing by above, getting higher and dryer and thicker. While that lasts nobody is going to find us, and the water business is now unfunny.

Finally I borrow Estéban's machete and hack a long light pole. "There's a stream coming in back there, I saw it from the plane. Can't be more than two, three miles."

"I'm afraid the raft's torn." Mrs. Parsons shows me the cracks in the orange plastic; irritatingly, it's a Delaware label.

"All right," I hear myself announce. "The tide's going down. If we cut the good end of that air tube, I can haul water back in it. I've waded flats before."

Even to me it sounds crazy.

"Stay by plane," Estéban says. He's right, of course. He's also clearly running a fever. I look at the overcast and taste grit and old barracuda. The hell with the manual.

When I start cutting up the raft, Estéban tells me to take the serape. "You stay one night." He's right about that, too; I'll have to wait out the tide.

"I'll come with you," says Mrs. Parsons calmly.

I simply stare at her. What new madness has got into Mother Hen? Does she imagine Estéban is too battered to be functional? While I'm being astounded, my eyes take in the fact that Mrs. Parsons is now quite rosy around the knees, with her hair loose and a sunburn starting on her nose. A trim, in fact a very neat shading-forty.

"Look, that stuff is horrible going. Mud up to your ears and water over your head."

"I'm really quite fit and I swim a great deal. I'll try to keep up. Two would be much safer, Mr. Fenton, and we can bring more water."

She's serious. Well, I'm about as fit as a marshmallow at this time of winter, and I can't pretend I'm depressed by the idea of company. So be it.

"Let me show Miss Parsons how to work this rod."

Miss Parsons is even rosier and more windblown, and she's not clumsy with my tackle. A good girl, Miss Parsons, in her nothing way. We cut another staff and get some gear together. At the last minute Estéban shows how sick he feels: he offers me the machete. I thank him, but, no; I'm used to my Wirkkala knife. We tie some air into the plastic tube for a float and set out along the sandiest looking line.

Estéban raises one dark palm. *"Buen viaje."* Miss Parsons has hugged her mother and gone to cast from the mangrove. She waves. We wave.

An hour later we're barely out of waving distance. The going is surely god-awful. The sand keeps dissolving into silt you can't walk on or swim through, and the bottom is spiked with dead mangrove spears. We flounder from one pothole to the next, scaring up rays and turtles and hoping to god we don't kick a moray eel. Where we're not soaked in slime, we're desiccated, and we smell like the Old Cretaceous.

Mrs. Parsons keeps up doggedly. I only have to pull her out once. When I do so, I notice the sandbar is now out of sight.

Finally we reach the gap in the mangrove line I thought was the creek. It turns out to open into another arm of the bay, with more mangroves ahead. And the tide is coming in.

"I've had the world's lousiest idea."

Mrs. Parsons only says mildly, "It's so different from the view from the plane."

I revise my opinion of the girl scouts, and we plow on past the mangroves toward the smoky haze that has to be shore. The sun is setting in our faces, making it hard to see. Ibises and herons fly up around us, and once a big permit spooks ahead, his fin cutting a rooster tail. We fall into more potholes. The flashlights get soaked. I am having fantasies of the mangrove as universal obstacle; it's hard to recall I ever walked down a street, for instance, without stumbling over or under or through mangrove roots. And the sun is dropping down, down.

Suddenly we hit a ledge and fall over it into a cold flow.

"The stream! It's fresh water!"

We guzzle and garble and douse our heads; it's the best drink I remember. "Oh my, oh my—!" Mrs. Parsons is laughing right out loud.

"That dark place over to the right looks like real land."

We flounder across the flow and follow a hard shelf, which turns into solid bank and rises over our heads. Shortly there's a break beside a clump of spiny bromels, and we scramble up and flop down at the top, dripping and stinking. Out of sheer reflex my arm goes around my companion's shoulder—but Mrs. Parsons isn't there; she's up on her knees peering at the burnt-over plain around us.

"It's so good to see land one can walk on!" The tone is too innocent. *Noli me tangere.*

"Don't try it." I'm exasperated; the muddy little woman, what does she think? "That ground out there is a crush of ashes over muck, and it's full of stubs. You can go in over your knees."

"It seems firm here."

"We're in an alligator nursery. That was the slide we came up. Don't worry, by now the old lady's doubtless on her way to be made into handbags."

"What a shame."

"I better set a line down in the stream while I can still see."

I slide back down and rig a string of hooks that may get us breakfast. When I get back Mrs. Parsons is wringing muck out of the serape.

"I'm glad you warned me, Mr. Fenton. It *is* treacherous."

"Yeah." I'm over my irritation; god knows I don't want to *tangere* Mrs. Parsons, even if I weren't beat down to mush. "In its quiet way, Yucatán is a tough place to get around in. You can see why the Mayas built roads. Speaking of which—look!"

The last of the sunset is silhouetting a small square shape a couple of kilometers inland; a Maya *ruina* with a fig tree growing out of it.

"Lot of those around. People think they were guard towers."

"What a deserted-feeling land."

"Let's hope it's deserted by mosquitoes."

We slump down in the 'gator nursery and share the last malt bar, watching the stars slide in and out of the blowing clouds. The bugs aren't too bad; maybe the burn did them in. And it isn't hot any more, either—in fact, it's not even warm, wet as we are. Mrs. Parsons continues tranquilly interested in Yucatán and unmistakably uninterested in togetherness.

Just as I'm beginning to get aggressive notions about how we're going to spend the night if she expects me to give her the serape, she stands up, scuffs at a couple of hummocks and says, "I expect this is as good a place as any, isn't it, Mr. Fenton?"

With which she spreads out the raft bag for a pillow and lies down on her side in the dirt with exactly half the serape over her and the other corner folded neatly open. Her small back is toward me.

The demonstration is so convincing that I'm halfway under my share of serape before the preposterousness of it stops me.

"By the way. My name is Don."

"Oh, of course." Her voice is graciousness itself, "I'm Ruth."

I get in not quite touching her, and we lie there like two fish on a plate, exposed to the stars and smelling the smoke in the wind and feeling things underneath us. It is absolutely the most intimately awkward moment I've had in years.

The woman doesn't mean one thing to me, but the obtrusive recessiveness of her, the defiance of her little rump eight inches from my fly—for two pesos I'd have those shorts down and introduce myself. If I were twenty years younger. If I wasn't so bushed . . . But the twenty years and the exhaustion are there, and it comes to me wryly that Mrs. Ruth Parsons has judged things to a nicety. If I *were* twenty years younger, she wouldn't be here. Like the butterfish that float around a sated barracuda, only to vanish away the instant his intent changes, Mrs. Parsons knows her little shorts are safe. Those firmly filled little shorts, so close . . .

A warm nerve stirs in my groin—and just as it does I become aware of a silent emptiness beside me. Mrs. Parsons is imperceptibly inching away. Did my breathing change? Whatever, I'm perfectly sure that if my hand reached, she'd be elsewhere—probably announcing her intention to take a dip. The twenty years bring a chuckle to my throat, and I relax.

"Good night, Ruth."

"Good night, Don."

And believe it or not, we sleep, while the armadas of the wind roar overhead.

Light wakes me—a cold white glare.

My first thought is 'gator hunters. Best to manifest ourselves as *turistas* as fast as possible. I scramble up, noting that Ruth has dived under the bromel clump.

"*Quién estás? A secorro!* Help, *señores!*"

No answer except the light goes out, leaving me blind.

I yell some more in a couple of languages. It stays dark. There's a vague scrabbling, whistling sound somewhere in the burn-off. Liking everything less by the minute, I try a speech about our plane having crashed and we need help.

A very narrow pencil of light flicks over us and snaps off.

"Eh-ep," says a blurry voice and something metallic twitters. They for sure aren't locals. I'm getting unpleasant ideas.

"Yes, help!"

Something goes *crackle-crackle whish-whish,* and all sounds fade away.

"What the holy hell!" I stumble toward where they were.

"Look." Ruth whispers behind me. "Over by the ruin."

I look and catch a multiple flicker which winks out fast.

"A camp?"

And I take two more blind strides. My leg goes down through the crust, and a spike spears me just where you stick the knife in to unjoint a drumstick. By the pain that goes through my bladder I recognize that my trick kneecap has caught it.

For instant basket-case you can't beat kneecaps. First you discover your knee doesn't bend any more, so you try putting some weight on it, and a bayonet goes up your spine and unhinges your jaw. Little grains of gristle have got into the sensitive bearing surface. The knee tries to buckle and can't, and mercifully you fall down.

Ruth helps me back to the serape.

"What a fool, what a god-forgotten imbecile—"

"Not at all, Don. It was perfectly natural." We strike matches; her fingers push mine aside, exploring. "I think it's in place, but it's swelling fast. I'll lay a wet handkerchief on it. We'll have to wait for morning to check the cut. Were they poachers, do you think?"

"Probably," I lie. What I think they were is smugglers.

She comes back with a soaked bandanna and drapes it on. "We must have frightened them. That light . . . it seemed so bright."

"Some hunting party. People do crazy things around here."

"Perhaps they'll come back in the morning."

"Could be."

Ruth pulls up the wet serape, and we say goodnight again. Neither of us are mentioning how we're going to get back to the plane without help.

I lie staring south where Alpha Centauri is blinking in and out of the overcast and cursing myself for the sweet mess I've made. My first idea is giving way to an even less pleasing one.

Smuggling, around here, is a couple of guys in an outboard meeting a shrimp boat by the reef. They don't light up the sky or have some kind of swamp buggy that goes whoosh. Plus a big camp . . . paramilitary-type equipment?

I've seen a report of Guevarista infiltrators operating on the British Honduran border, which is about a hundred kilometers—sixty miles— south of here. Right under those clouds. If that's what looked us over, I'll be more than happy if they don't come back . . .

I wake up in pelting rain, alone. My first move confirms that my leg is as expected—a giant misplaced erection bulging out of my shorts. I raise up painfully to see Ruth standing by the bromels, looking over the bay. Solid wet nimbus is pouring out of the south.

"No planes today."

"Oh, good morning, Don. Should we look at that cut now?"

"It's minimal." In fact the skin is hardly broken, and no deep puncture. Totally out of proportion to the havoc inside.

"Well, they have water to drink," Ruth says tranquilly. "Maybe those hunters will come back. I'll go see if we have a fish—that is, can I help you in any way, Don?"

Very tactful. I emit an ungracious negative, and she goes off about her private concerns.

They certainly are private, too; when I recover from my own sanitary efforts, she's still away. Finally I hear splashing.

"It's a big fish!" More splashing. Then she climbs up the bank with a three-pound mangrove snapper—and something else.

It isn't until after the messy work of filleting the fish that I begin to notice.

She's making a smudge of chaff and twigs to singe the fillets, small hands very quick, tension in that female upper lip. The rain has eased off for the moment; we're sluicing wet but warm enough. Ruth brings me my fish on a mangrove skewer and sits back on her heels with an odd breathy sigh.

"Aren't you joining me?"

"Oh, of course." She gets a strip and picks at it, saying quickly, "We either have too much salt or too little, don't we? I should fetch some brine." Her eyes are roving from nothing to noplace.

"Good thought." I hear another sigh and decide the girl scouts need an assist. "Your daughter mentioned you've come from Mérida. Have you seen much of Mexico?"

"Not really. Last year we went to Mazatlán and Cuernavaca . . . " She puts the fish down, frowning.

"And you're going to see Tikal. Going to Bonampak too?"

"No." Suddenly she jumps up brushing rain off her face. "I'll bring you some water, Don."

She ducks down the slide, and after a fair while comes back with a full bromel stalk.

"Thanks." She's standing above me, staring restlessly round the horizon.

"Ruth, I hate to say it, but those guys are not coming back and it's probably just as well. Whatever they were up to, we looked like trouble. The most they'll do is tell someone we're here. That'll take a day or two to get around, we'll be back at the plane by then."

"I'm sure you're right, Don." She wanders over to the smudge fire.

"And quit fretting about your daughter. She's a big girl."

"Oh, I'm sure Althea's all right . . . They have plenty of water now." Her fingers drum on her thigh. It's raining again.

"Come on, Ruth. Sit down. Tell me about Althea. Is she still in college?"

She gives that sighing little laugh and sits. "Althea got her degree last year. She's in computer programming."

"Good for her. And what about you, what do you do in GSA records?"

"I'm in Foreign Procurement Archives." She smiles mechanically, but her breathing is shallow. "It's very interesting."

"I know a Jack Wittig in Contracts, maybe you know him?"

It sounds pretty absurd, there in the 'gator slide.

"Oh, I've met Mr. Wittig. I'm sure he wouldn't remember me."

"Why not?"

"I'm not very memorable."

Her voice is factual. She's perfectly right, of course. Who was that woman, Mrs. Jannings, Janny, who coped with my per diem for years? Competent, agreeable, impersonal. She had a sick father or something. But dammit, Ruth is a lot younger and better-looking. Comparatively speaking.

"Maybe Mrs. Parsons doesn't want to be memorable."

She makes a vague sound, and I suddenly realize Ruth isn't listening to me at all. Her hands are clenched around her knees, she's staring inland at the ruin.

"Ruth. I tell you our friends with the light are in the next country by now. Forget it, we don't need them."

Her eyes come back to me as if she'd forgotten I was there, and she nods slowly. It seems to be too much effort to speak. Suddenly she cocks her head and jumps up again.

"I'll go look at the line, Don. I thought I heard something—" She's gone like a rabbit.

While she's away I try getting up onto my good leg and the staff. The pain is sickening; knees seem to have some kind of hot line to the stomach. I take a couple of hops to test whether the Demerol I have in my belt would get me walking. As I do so, Ruth comes up the bank with a fish flapping in her hands.

"Oh, no, Don! *No!*" She actually clasps the snapper to her breast.

"The water will take some of my weight. I'd like to give it a try."

"You mustn't!" Ruth says quite violently and instantly modulates down. "Look at the bay, Don. One can't see a thing."

I teeter there, tasting bile and looking at the mingled curtains of sun and rain driving across the water. She's right, thank god. Even with two good legs we could get into trouble out there.

"I guess one more night won't kill us."

I let her collapse me back onto the gritty plastic, and she positively bustles around, finding me a chunk to lean on, stretching the serape on both staffs to keep rain off me, bringing another drink, grubbing for dry tinder.

"I'll make us a real bonfire as soon as it lets up, Don. They'll see our smoke, they'll know we're all right. We just have to wait." Cheery smile. "Is there any way we can make you more comfortable?"

Holy Saint Sterculius: playing house in a mud puddle. For a fatuous moment I wonder if Mrs. Parsons has designs on me. And then she lets out another sigh and sinks back onto her heels with that listening look. Unconsciously her rump wiggles a little. My ear picks up the operative word: *wait*.

Ruth Parsons is waiting. In fact, she acts as if she's waiting so hard it's killing her. For what? For someone to get us out of here, what else? . . . But why was she so horrified when I got up to try to leave? Why all this tension?

My paranoia stirs. I grab it by the collar and start idly checking back. Up to when whoever it was showed up last night, Mrs. Parsons was, I guess, normal. Calm and sensible, anyway. Now she's humming like a high wire. And she seems to want to stay here and wait. Just as an intellectual pastime, why?

Could she have intended to come here? No way. Where she planned to be was Chetumal, which is on the border. Come to think, Chetumal is an odd way round to Tikal. Let's say the scenario was that she's meeting somebody in Chetumal. Somebody who's part of an organization. So now her contact in Chetumal knows she's overdue. And when those types appeared last night, something suggests to her that they're part of the same organization. And she hopes they'll put one and one together and come back for her?

"May I have the knife, Don? I'll clean the fish."

Rather slowly I pass the knife, kicking my subconscious. Such a decent ordinary little woman, a good girl scout. My trouble is that I've bumped into too many professional agilities under the careful stereotypes. *I'm not very memorable . . .*

What's in Foreign Procurement Archives? Wittig handles classified contracts. Lots of money stuff; foreign currency negotiations, commodity price schedules, some industrial technology. Or—just as a hypothesis—it could be as simple as a wad of bills back in that modest beige Ventura, to be exchanged for a packet from say, Costa Rica. If she were a courier, they'd want to get at the plane. And then what about me and maybe Estéban? Even hypothetically, not good.

I watch her hacking at the fish, forehead knotted with effort, teeth in her lip. Mrs. Parsons of Bethesda, this thrumming, private woman. How crazy can I get? *They'll see our smoke . . .*

"Here's your knife, Don. I washed it. Does the leg hurt very badly?"

I blink away the fantasies and see a scared little woman in a mangrove swamp.

"Sit down, rest. You've been going all out."

She sits obediently, like a kid in a dentist chair.

"You're stewing about Althea. And she's probably worried about you. We'll get back tomorrow under our own steam, Ruth."

"Honestly I'm not worried at all, Don." The smile fades; she nibbles her lip, frowning out at the bay.

"You know, Ruth, you surprised me when you offered to come along. Not that I don't appreciate it. But I rather thought you'd be concerned about leaving Althea alone with our good pilot. Or was it only me?"

This gets her attention at last.

"I believe Captain Estéban is a very fine type of man."

The words surprise me a little. Isn't the correct line more like "I trust Althea," or even, indignantly, "Althea is a good girl"?

"He's a man. Althea seemed to think he was interesting."

She goes on staring at the bay. And then I notice her tongue flick out and lick that prehensile upper lip. There's a flush that isn't sunburn around her ears and throat too, and one hand is gently rubbing her thigh. What's she seeing, out there in the flats?

Oho.

Captain Estéban's mahogany arms clasping Miss Althea Parsons' pearly body. Captain Estéban's archaic nostrils snuffling in Miss Parsons' tender neck. Captain Estéban's copper buttocks pumping into Althea's creamy upturned bottom . . . The hammock, very bouncy. Mayas know all about it.

Well, well. So Mother Hen has her little quirks.

I feel fairly silly and more than a little irritated. *Now* I find out . . . But even vicarious lust has much to recommend it, here in the mud and rain. I settle back, recalling that Miss Althea the computer programmer had waved good-bye very composedly. Was she sending her mother to flounder across the bay with me so she can get programmed in Maya? The memory of Honduran mahogany logs drifting in and out of the opalescent sand comes to me. Just as I am about to suggest that Mrs. Parsons might care to share my rain shelter, she remarks serenely, "The Mayas seem to be a very fine type of people. I believe you said so to Althea."

The implications fall on me with the rain. *Type.* As in breeding, blood-line, sire. Am I supposed to have certified Estéban not only as a stud but as a genetic donor?

"Ruth, are you telling me you're prepared to accept a half-Indian grandchild?"

"Why, Don, that's up to Althea, you know."

Looking at the mother, I guess it is. Oh, for mahogany gonads.

Ruth has gone back to listening to the wind, but I'm not about to let her off that easy. Not after all that *noli me tangere* jazz.

"What will Althea's father think?"

Her face snaps around at me, genuinely startled.

"Althea's father?" Complicated semismile. "He won't mind."

"He'll accept it too, eh?" I see her shake her head as if a fly were bothering her, and add with a cripple's malice: "Your husband must be a very fine type of a man."

Ruth looks at me, pushing her wet hair back abruptly. I have the impression that mousy Mrs. Parsons is roaring out of control, but her voice is quiet.

"There isn't any Mr. Parsons, Don. There never was. Althea's father was a Danish medical student . . . I believe he has gained considerable prominence."

"Oh." Something warns me not to say I'm sorry. "You mean he doesn't know about Althea?"

"No." She smiles, her eyes bright and cuckoo.

"Seems like rather a rough deal for her."

"I grew up quite happily under the same circumstances."

Bang, I'm dead. Well, well, well. A mad image blooms in my mind: generations of solitary Parsons women selecting sires, making impregnation trips. Well, I hear the world is moving their way.

"I better look at the fish line."

She leaves. The glow fades. *No.* Just no, no contact. Good-bye, Captain Estéban. My leg is very uncomfortable. The hell with Mrs. Parsons' long-distance orgasm.

We don't talk much after that, which seems to suit Ruth. The odd day drags by. Squall after squall blows over us. Ruth singes up some more fillets, but the rain drowns her smudge; it seems to pour hardest just as the sun's about to show.

Finally she comes to sit under my sagging serape, but there's no warmth there. I doze, aware of her getting up now and then to look around. My subconscious notes that she's still twitchy. I tell my subconscious to knock it off.

Presently I wake up to find her penciling on the water-soaked pages of a little notepad.

"What's that, a shopping list for alligators?"

Automatic polite laugh. "Oh, just an address. In case we—I'm being silly, Don."

"Hey," I sit up, wincing, "Ruth, quit fretting. I mean it. We'll all be out of this soon. You'll have a great story to tell."

She doesn't look up. "Yes . . . I guess we will."

"Come on, we're doing fine. There isn't any real danger here, you know. Unless you're allergic to fish?"

Another good-little-girl laugh, but there's a shiver in it.

"Sometimes I think I'd like to go . . . really far away."

To keep her talking I say the first thing in my head.

"Tell me, Ruth. I'm curious why you would settle for that kind of lonely life, there in Washington? I mean, a woman like you—"

"Should get married?" She gives a shaky sigh, pushing the notebook back in her wet pocket.

"Why not? It's the normal source of companionship. Don't tell me you're trying to be some kind of professional man-hater."

"Lesbian, you mean?" Her laugh sounds better. "With my security rating? No, I'm not."

"Well, then. Whatever trauma you went through, these things don't last forever. You can't hate all men."

The smile is back. "Oh, there wasn't any trauma, Don, and I *don't* hate men. That would be as silly as—as hating the weather." She glances wryly at the blowing rain.

"I think you have a grudge. You're even spooky of me."

Smooth as a mouse bite she says, "I'd love to hear about your family, Don?"

Touché. I give her the edited version of how I don't have one any more, and she says she's sorry, how sad. And we chat about what a good life a single person really has, and how she and her friends enjoy plays and concerts and travel, and one of them is head cashier for Ringling Brothers, how about that?

But it's coming out jerkier and jerkier like a bad tape, with her eyes going round the horizon in the pauses and her face listening for something that isn't my voice. What's wrong with her? Well, what's wrong with any furtively unconventional middle-aged woman with an empty bed. And a security clearance. An old habit of mind remarks unkindly that Mrs. Parsons represents what is known as the classic penetration target.

"—so much more opportunity now." Her voice trails off.

"Hurrah for women's lib, eh?"

"The lib?" Impatiently she leans forward and tugs the serape straight. "Oh, that's doomed."

The apocalyptic word jars my attention.

"What do you mean, doomed?"

She glances at me as if I weren't hanging straight either and says vaguely, "Oh . . ."

"Come on, why doomed? Didn't they get that equal rights bill?"

Long hesitation. When she speaks again her voice is different.

"Women have no rights, Don, except what men allow us. Men are more aggressive and powerful, and they run the world. When the next real crisis upsets them, our so-called rights will vanish like—like that smoke. We'll be back where we always were: property. And whatever has gone wrong will be blamed on our freedom, like the fall of Rome was. You'll see."

Now all this is delivered in a gray tone of total conviction. The last time I heard that tone, the speaker was explaining why he had to keep his file drawers full of dead pigeons.

JAMES TIPTREE, JR.

"Oh, come on. You and your friends are the backbone of the system; if you quit, the country would come to a screeching halt before lunch."

No answering smile.

"That's fantasy." Her voice is still quiet. "Women don't work that way. We're a—a toothless world." She looks around as if she wanted to stop talking. "What women do is survive. We live by ones and twos in the chinks of your world-machine."

"Sounds like a guerrilla operation." I'm not really joking, here in the 'gator den. In fact, I'm wondering if I spent too much thought on mahogany logs.

"Guerrillas have something to hope for." Suddenly she switches on a jolly smile. "Think of us as opossums, Don. Did you know there are opossums living all over? Even in New York City."

I smile back with my neck prickling. I thought I was the paranoid one.

"Men and women aren't different species, Ruth. Women do everything men do."

"Do they?" Our eyes meet, but she seems to be seeing ghosts between us in the rain. She mutters something that could be "My Lai" and looks away. "All the endless wars . . . " Her voice is a whisper. "All the huge authoritarian organizations for doing unreal things. Men live to struggle against each other; we're just part of the battlefields. It'll never change unless you change the whole world. I dream sometimes of—of going away—" She checks and abruptly changes voice. "Forgive me, Don, it's so stupid saying all this."

"Men hate wars too, Ruth," I say as gently as I can.

"I know." She shrugs and climbs to her feet. "But that's your problem, isn't it?"

End of communication. Mrs. Ruth Parsons isn't even living in the same world with me.

I watch her move around restlessly, head turning toward the ruins. Alienation like that can add up to dead pigeons, which would be GSA's problem. It could also lead to believing some joker who's promising to change the whole world. Which could just probably be my problem if one of them was over in that camp last night, where she keeps looking. *Guerrillas have something to hope for . . . ?*

Nonsense. I try another position and see that the sky seems to be clearing as the sun sets. The wind is quieting down at last too. Insane to think this little woman is acting out some fantasy in this swamp. But that equipment last night was no fantasy; if those lads have some connection with her, I'll be in the way. You couldn't find a handier spot to dispose of the body . . . Maybe some Guevarista is a fine type of man?

Absurd. Sure . . . The only thing more absurd would be to come through the wars and get myself terminated by a mad librarian's boyfriend on a fishing trip.

A fish flops in the stream below us. Ruth spins around so fast she hits the serape. "I better start the fire," she says, her eyes still on the plain and her head cocked, listening.

All right, let's test.

"Expecting company?"

It rocks her. She freezes, and her eyes come swiveling around at me like a film take captioned Fright. I can see her decide to smile.

"Oh, one never can tell!" She laughs weirdly, the eyes not changed. "I'll get the—the kindling." She fairly scuttles into the brush.

Nobody, paranoid or not, could call *that* a normal reaction.

Ruth Parsons is either psycho or she's expecting something to happen—and it has nothing to do with me; I scared her pissless.

Well, she could be nuts. And I could be wrong, but there are some mistakes you only make once.

Reluctantly I unzip my body belt, telling myself that if I think what I think, my only course is to take something for my leg and get as far as possible from Mrs. Ruth Parsons before whoever she's waiting for arrives.

In my belt also is a .32 caliber asset Ruth doesn't know about—and it's going to stay there. My longevity program leaves the shoot-outs to TV and stresses being somewhere else when the roof falls in. I can spend a perfectly safe and also perfectly horrible night out in one of those mangrove flats . . . Am I insane?

At this moment Ruth stands up and stares blatantly inland with her hand shading her eyes. Then she tucks something into her pocket, buttons up and tightens her belt.

That does it.

I dry-swallow two 100 mg tabs, which should get me ambulatory and still leave me wits to hide. Give it a few minutes. I make sure my compass and some hooks are in my own pocket and sit waiting while Ruth fusses with her smudge fire, sneaking looks away when she thinks I'm not watching.

The flat world around us is turning into an unearthly amber and violet light show as the first numbness sweeps into my leg. Ruth has crawled under the bromels for more dry stuff; I can see her foot. Okay. I reach for my staff.

Suddenly the foot jerks, and Ruth yells—or rather, her throat makes that *Uh-uh-hhh* that means pure horror. The foot disappears in a rattle of bromel stalks.

I lunge upright on the crutch and look over the bank at a frozen scene.

Ruth is crouching sideways on the ledge, clutching her stomach. They are about a yard below, floating on the river in a skiff. While I was making up my stupid mind, her friends have glided right under my ass. There are three of them.

They are tall and white. I try to see them as men in some kind of white jumpsuits. The one nearest the bank is stretching out a long white arm toward Ruth. She jerks and scuttles further away.

The arm stretches after her. It stretches and stretches. It stretches two yards and stays hanging in the air. Small black things are wiggling from its tip.

I look where their faces should be and see black hollow dishes with vertical stripes. The stripes move slowly . . .

There is no more possibility of their being human—or anything else I've ever seen. What has Ruth conjured up?

The scene is totally silent. I blink, blink—this cannot be real. The two in the far end of the skiff are writhing those arms around an apparatus on a tripod. A weapon? Suddenly I hear the same blurry voice I heard in the night.

"Guh-give," it groans. "G-give . . . "

Dear god, it's real, whatever it is. I'm terrified. My mind is trying not to form a word.

And Ruth—Jesus, of course—Ruth is terrified too; she's edging along the bank away from them, gaping at the monsters in the skiff, who are obviously nobody's friends. She's hugging something to her body. Why doesn't she get over the bank and circle back behind me?

"G-g-give." That wheeze is coming from the tripod. "Pee-eeze give." The skiff is moving upstream below Ruth, following her. The arm undulates out at her again, its black digits looping. Ruth scrambles to the top of the bank.

"Ruth!" My voice cracks. "Ruth, get over here behind me!"

She doesn't look at me, only keeps sidling farther away. My terror detonates into anger.

"Come back here!" With my free hand I'm working the .32 out of my belt. The sun has gone down.

She doesn't turn but straightens up warily, still hugging the thing. I see her mouth working. Is she actually trying to *talk* to them?

"Please . . . " She swallows. "Please speak to me. I need your help."

"RUTH!!"

At this moment the nearest white monster whips into a great S-curve and sails right onto the bank at her, eight feet of snowy rippling horror.

And I shoot Ruth.

I don't know that for a moment—I've yanked the gun up so fast that my staff slips and dumps me as I fire. I stagger up, hearing Ruth scream "No! No! No!"

The creature is back down by his boat, and Ruth is still farther away, clutching herself. Blood is running down her elbow.

"Stop it, Don! They aren't attacking you!"

"For god's sake! Don't be a fool, I can't help you if you won't get away from them!"

No reply. Nobody moves. No sound except the drone of a jet passing far above. In the darkening stream below me the three white figures shift uneasily; I get the impression of radar dishes focusing. The word spells itself in my head: *Aliens.*

Extraterrestrials.

What do I do, call the President? Capture them single-handed with my peashooter? . . . I'm alone in the arse end of nowhere with one leg and my brain cuddled in meperidine hydrochloride.

"Prrr-eese," their machine blurs again. "Wa-wat help . . . "

"Our plane fell down," Ruth says in a very distinct, eerie voice. She points up at the jet, out towards the bay. "My—my child is there. Please take us *there* in your boat."

Dear god. While she's gesturing, I get a look at the thing she's hugging in her wounded arm. It's metallic, like a big glimmering distributor head. What—?

Wait a minute. This morning: when she was gone so long, she could have found that thing. Something they left behind. Or dropped. And she hid it, not telling me. That's why she kept going under that bromel clump—she was peeking at it. Waiting. And the owners came back and caught her. They want it. She's trying to bargain, by god.

"—Water," Ruth is pointing again. "Take us. Me. And him."

The black faces turn toward me, blind and horrible. Later on I may be grateful for that "us." Not now.

"Throw your gun away, Don. They'll take us back." Her voice is weak.

"Like hell I will. You—who are you? What are you doing here?"

"Oh god, does it matter? He's frightened," she cries to them. "Can you understand?"

She's as alien as they, there in the twilight. The beings in the skiff are twittering among themselves. Their box starts to moan.

"Ss-stu-dens," I make out. "S-stu-ding . . . not—huh-arm-ing . . . w-we . . . buh . . . " It fades into garble and then says "G-give . . . we . . . g-go . . . "

Peace-loving cultural-exchange students—on the interstellar level now. Oh, no.

"Bring that thing here, Ruth—right now!"

But she's starting down the bank toward them saying, "Take me."

"Wait! You need a tourniquet on that arm."

"I know. Please put the gun down, Don."

She's actually at the skiff, right by them. They aren't moving.

"Jesus Christ." Slowly, reluctantly, I drop the .32. When I start down the slide, I find I'm floating; adrenaline and Demerol are a bad mix.

The skiff comes gliding toward me, Ruth in the bow clutching the thing and her arm. The aliens stay in the stern behind their tripod, away from me. I note the skiff is camouflaged tan and green. The world around us is deep shadowy blue.

"Don, bring the water bag!"

As I'm dragging down the plastic bag, it occurs to me that Ruth really is cracking up, the water isn't needed now. But my own brain seems to have gone into overload. All I can focus on is a long white rubbery arm with black worms clutching the far end of the orange tube, helping me fill it. This isn't happening.

"Can you get in, Don?" As I hoist my numb legs up, two long white pipes reach for me. *No you don't.* I kick and tumble in beside Ruth. She moves away.

A creaky hum starts up, it's coming from a wedge in the center of the skiff. And we're in motion, sliding toward dark mangrove files.

I stare mindlessly at the wedge. Alien technological secrets? I can't see any, the power source is under that triangular cover, about two feet long. The gadgets on the tripod are equally cryptic, except that one has a big lens. Their light?

As we hit the open bay, the hum rises and we start planing faster and faster still. Thirty knots? Hard to judge in the dark. Their hull seems to be a modified trihedral much like ours, with a remarkable absence of slap. Say twenty-two feet. Schemes of capturing it swirl in my mind. I'll need Estéban.

Suddenly a huge flood of white light fans out over us from the tripod, blotting out the aliens in the stern. I see Ruth pulling at a belt around her arm still hugging the gizmo.

"I'll tie that for you."

"It's all right."

The alien device is twinkling or phosphorescing slightly. I lean over to look, whispering, "Give that to me, I'll pass it to Estéban."

"No!" She scoots away, almost over the side. "It's theirs, they need it!"

"What? Are you crazy?" I'm so taken aback by this idiocy I literally stammer. "We have to, we—"

"They haven't hurt us. I'm sure they could." Her eyes are watching me with feral intensity; in the light her face has a lunatic look. Numb as I am, I realize that the wretched woman is poised to throw herself over the side if I move. With the alien thing.

"I think they're gentle," she mutters.

"For Christ's sake, Ruth, they're *aliens!*"

"I'm used to it," she says absently. "There's the island! Stop! Stop here!"

The skiff slows, turning. A mound of foliage is tiny in the light. Metal glints—the plane.

"Althea! Althea! Are you all right?"

Yells, movement on the plane. The water is high, we're floating over the bar. The aliens are keeping us in the lead with the light hiding them. I see one pale figure splashing toward us and a dark one behind, coming more slowly. Estéban must be puzzled by that light.

"Mr. Fenton is hurt, Althea. These people brought us back with the water. Are you all right?"

"A-okay." Althea flounders up, peering excitedly. "You all right? Whew, that light!" Automatically I start handing her the idiotic water bag.

"Leave that for the captain," Ruth says sharply. "Althea, can you climb in the boat? Quickly, it's important."

"Coming."

"No, no!" I protest, but the skiff tilts as Althea swarms in. The aliens twitter, and their voice box starts groaning. "Gu-give . . . now . . . give . . . "

"*Que llega?*" Estéban's face appears beside me, squinting fiercely into the light.

"Grab it, get it from her—that thing she has—" but Ruth's voice rides over mine. "Captain, lift Mr. Fenton out of the boat. He's hurt his leg. Hurry, please."

"Goddamn it, wait!" I shout, but an arm has grabbed my middle. When a Maya boosts you, you go. I hear Althea saying, "Mother, your arm!" and fall onto Estéban. We stagger around in water up to my waist; I can't feel my feet at all.

When I get steady, the boat is yards away. The two women are head-to-head, murmuring.

"Get them!" I tug loose from Estéban and flounder forward. Ruth stands up in the boat facing the invisible aliens.

"Take us with you. Please. We want to go with you, away from here."

"Ruth! Estéban, get that boat!" I lunge and lose my feet again. The aliens are chirruping madly behind their light.

"Please take us. We don't mind what your planet is like; we'll learn—we'll do anything! We won't cause any trouble. Please. Oh *please*." The skiff is drifting farther away.

"Ruth! Althea! Are you crazy? Wait—" But I can only shuffle night-marelike in the ooze, hearing that damn voice box wheeze, "N-not come . . . more . . . not come . . . " Althea's face turns to it, open-mouthed grin.

"Yes, we understand," Ruth cries. "We don't want to come back. Please take us with you!"

I shout and Estéban splashes past me shouting too, something about radio.

"Yes-s-s" groans the voice.

Ruth sits down suddenly, clutching Althea. At that moment Estéban grabs the edge of the skiff beside her.

"Hold them, Estéban! Don't let her go."

He gives me one slit-eyed glance over his shoulder, and I recognize his total uninvolvement. He's had a good look at that camouflage paint and the absence of fishing gear. I make a desperate rush and slip again. When I come up Ruth is saying, "We're going with these people, Captain. Please take your money out of my purse, it's in the plane. And give this to Mr. Fenton."

She passes him something small; the notebook. He takes it slowly.

"Estéban! No!"

He has released the skiff.

"Thank you so much," Ruth says as they float apart. Her voice is shaky; she raises it. "There won't be any trouble, Don. Please send this cable. It's to a friend of mine, she'll take care of everything." Then she adds the craziest touch of the entire night. "She's a grand person; she's director of nursing training at N.I.H."

As the skiff drifts, I hear Althea add something that sounds like "Right on."

Sweet Jesus . . . Next minute the humming has started; the light is receding fast. The last I see of Mrs. Ruth Parsons and Miss Althea Parsons is two small shadows against that light, like two opossums. The light snaps off, the hum deepens—and they're going, going, gone away.

In the dark water beside me Estéban is instructing everybody in general to *chingarse* themselves.

"Friends, or something," I tell him lamely. "She seemed to want to go with them."

He is pointedly silent, hauling me back to the plane. He knows what could be around here better than I do, and Mayas have their own longevity program. His condition seems improved. As we get in I notice the hammock has been repositioned.

In the night—of which I remember little—the wind changes. And at seven thirty next morning a Cessna buzzes the sandbar under cloudless skies.

By noon we're back in Cozumel, Captain Estéban accepts his fees and departs laconically for his insurance wars. I leave the Parsons' bags with the Caribe agent, who couldn't care less. The cable goes to a Mrs. Priscilla Hayes Smith, also of Bethesda. I take myself to a medico and by three PM I'm sitting on the Cabañas terrace with a fat leg and a double margharita, trying to believe the whole thing.

The cable said, *Althea and I taking extraordinary opportunity for travel. Gone several years. Please take charge our affairs. Love, Ruth.*

She'd written it that afternoon, you understand.

I order another double, wishing to hell I'd gotten a good look at that gizmo. Did it have a label. Made by Betelgeusians? No matter how weird it was, *how* could a person be crazy enough to imagine—?

Not only that but to hope, to plan? *If I could only go away* . . . That's what she was doing, all day. Waiting, hoping, figuring how to get Althea. To go sight unseen to an alien world . . .

With the third margharita I try a joke about alienated women, but my heart's not in it. And I'm certain there won't be any bother, any trouble at all. Two human women, one of them possibly pregnant, have departed for, I guess, the stars; and the fabric of society will never show a ripple. I brood: do all Mrs. Parsons' friends hold themselves in readiness for any eventuality, including leaving Earth? And will Mrs. Parsons somehow one day contrive to send for Mrs. Priscilla Hayes Smith, that grand person?

I can only send for another cold one, musing on Althea. What suns will Captain Estéban's sloe-eyed offspring, if any, look upon? "Get in, Althea, we're taking off for Orion." "A-okay, Mother." Is that some system of upbringing? *We survive by ones and twos in the chinks of your world-machine . . . I'm used to aliens . . .* She'd meant every word. Insane. How could a woman choose to live among unknown monsters, to say good-bye to her home, her world?

As the margharitas take hold, the whole mad scenario melts down to the image of those two small shapes sitting side by side in the receding alien glare.

Two of our opossums are missing.

SILK WORKERS

by

AGNES SMEDLEY
(1892–1950)

Agnes Smedley was born in Missouri and grew up in poverty in Colorado coal-mining camps. Her autobiographical novel Daughter of Earth *(1929) reveals her trying life with a drunken father and an overworked mother who died when Smedley was sixteen. Determined not to suffer her mother's fate, she spent a brief time at college and for the rest of her life was self-educated. She became a journalist and a political activist, involving herself for ten years in New York and Berlin in the effort to free India from British rule. In 1928 she went to participate in the Chinese revolution and traveled with the Red Army until ill health caused her to return to the United States in 1941. In the 1950s she was investigated by the McCarthy committee because of her radical views, even though she had never joined the Communist Party. She died in London and was buried with great honor in China. A posthumous collection of her essays was published in 1976 as* Portraits of Chinese Women in Revolution. *"Silk Workers" is from* Battle Hymn of China *(1943).*

Just as I arrived in Canton in the hot summer months of 1930, another General was killed by his bodyguard for the sake of the fifty Chinese dollars offered by a rival General. Such events had begun to strike me as sardonic. The Kwangtung Provincial Government was semi-independent, but in the hands of generals who took by violence what they considered their share in the loot of the south. They whirled around the city in bullet-proof cars with armed bodyguards standing on the running boards. Such was the spirit of the generals and of the officials whom they brought to power with them.

I interviewed them all and put no stock in what they said. They treated me magnificently, for foreign journalists seldom or never went south in the hot summer months. So I had a Government launch to myself, with an official guide to show me factories, paved roads, new waterworks and the Sun Yat-sen Memorial Hall. For truth I depended on Chinese university professors, an occasional newspaper reporter or editor, teachers and writers, the German Consul in Canton—and on my own eyes and ears.

The real reason I went south in the hottest part of the year was to study the lot of the millions of "silk peasants" in a silk industry which was rapidly losing its American markets to Japanese magnates. But I did not wish to see the silk regions as a guest of the powerful Canton Silk Guild, for the Guild, after all, was like a big laughing Buddha, naked to the waist, his fat belly hanging over his pajama belt. At last I found a group of Lingnan Christian University professors who were engaged in research in the industry. One young expert was leaving for the Shuntek silk region for a six weeks' inspection tour. I went with him to the Canton Silk Guild, where he argued with a suspicious Guild official until given permission to travel on Guild river steamers and enter the region in which millions of peasants toiled. There the millionaires of the South Seas had erected many large filatures; the spinners were all young women.

Next day the young expert and I boarded a river steamer. Some twenty or thirty Guild merchants were the only other passengers. The steamers had armor plating and machine-guns to protect the merchants from "bandits." The "bandits," I learned, were peasants who took to the highway for a part of each year in order to earn a living.

I once calculated that, if these "bandits" had attacked and captured our steamer, they would have secured enough food to feed a whole village for months. At meal times the merchants hunched over the tables, eating gargantuan meals and dropping the chicken bones on the floor. They talked of silk, money, markets, and of how much their firms were losing. The silk industry was indeed fighting for its life, but if there were losses, it clearly did not come out of the hides of these men. I pined a little for Jesse James.

My young escort was awed by these men, but when he spoke of the silk peasants or the girl filature workers, hostility and contempt crept into his voice. His particular hatred seemed to be the thousands of women spinners, and only with difficulty could I learn why. He told me that the women were notorious throughout China as Lesbians. They refused to marry, and if their families forced them, they merely bribed their husbands with a part of their wages and induced them to take concubines. The most such a married girl would do was bear one son; then she would return to the factory, refusing to live with her husband any longer. The Government had just issued a decree forbidding women to escape from marriage by bribery, but the women ignored it.

"They're too rich—that's the root of the trouble!" my young escort explained. "They earn as much as eleven dollars a month, and become proud and contemptuous." He added that on this money they also supported parents, brothers and sisters, and grandparents. "They squander their money!" he cried. "I have never gone to a picture theater without seeing groups of them sitting together, holding hands."

Until 1927, when they were forbidden, there had been Communist cells and trade unions in the filatures, he charged, and now these despicable girls evaded the law by forming secret "Sister Societies." They had even dared strike for shorter hours and higher wages. Now and then two or three girls would commit suicide together because their families were forcing them to marry.

For weeks my escort and I went by foot or small boat from village to village, from market town to market town. The fierce sun beat down upon us until our clothing clung to our bodies like a surgeon's glove and the perspiration wilted our hat bands and our shoes. At night we took rooms in village inns or pitched our camp beds under mosquito nets in family temples. All the roads and paths were lined with half-naked peasants bending low under huge baskets of cocoons swung from the ends of bamboo poles. Market towns reeked with the cocoons and hanks of raw silk piled up to the rafters in the warehouses. Every village was a mass of trays on which the silkworms fed, tended night and day by gaunt careworn peasants who went about naked to the waist.

At first curiously, then with interest, my escort began to translate for me as I questioned the peasants on their life and work. Their homes were bare huts with earthen floors, and the bed was a board covered by an old mat and surrounded by a cotton cloth, once white, which served as a mosquito net. There was usually a small clay stove with a cooking utensil or two, a narrow bench, and sometimes an ancient, scarred table. For millions this was home. A few owned several mulberry trees—for wealth was reckoned in trees. But almost all had sold their cocoon crops in advance in order to get money or food. If the crop failed, they were the losers. Wherever we traveled the story was the same: the silk peasants were held in pawn by the merchants and were never free from debt.

Only as we neared big market towns, in which silk filatures belched forth the stench of cocoons, did we come upon better homes and fewer careworn faces. The daughters of such families were spinners. It was then that I began to see what industrialism, bad as it had seemed elsewhere, meant to the working girls. These were the only places in the whole country where the birth of a baby girl was an occasion for joy, for here girls were the main support of their families. Consciousness of their worth was reflected in their dignified independent bearing. I began to understand the charges that they were Lesbians. They could not but compare the dignity of their positions with the low position of married women. Their independence seemed a personal affront to officialdom.

The hatred of my escort for these girls became more marked when we visited the filatures. Long lines of them, clad in glossy black jackets and trousers, sat before boiling vats of cocoons, their parboiled fingers twinkling among the spinning filaments. Sometimes a remark passed along their lines set a whole mill laughing. The face of my escort would grow livid.

"They call me a running dog of the capitalists, and you a foreign devil of an imperialist! They are laughing at your clothing and your hair and eyes!" he explained.

One evening the two of us sat at the entrance of an old family temple in the empty stone halls of which we had pitched our netted camp cots. On the other side of the canal rose the high walls of a filature, which soon began pouring forth black-clad girl workers, each with her tin dinner pail. All wore wooden sandals which were fastened by a single leather strap across the toes and which clattered as they walked. Their glossy black hair was combed back and hung in a heavy braid to the waist. At the nape of the neck the braid was caught in red yarn, making a band two or three inches wide—a lovely splash of color.

As they streamed in long lines over the bridge arching the canal and past the temple entrance, I felt I had never seen more handsome women.

I urged my young escort to interpret for me, but he refused, saying he did not understand their dialect. He was so irritated that he rose and walked toward the town. When he was gone, I went down the steps. A group of girls gathered around me and stared. I offered them some of my malt candy. There was a flash of white teeth and exclamations in a sharp staccato dialect. They took the candy, began chewing, then examined my clothing and stared at my hair and eyes. I did the same with them and soon we were laughing at each other.

Two of them linked their arms in mine and began pulling me down the flagstone street. Others followed, chattering happily. We entered the home of one girl and were welcomed by her father and mother and two big-eyed little brothers. Behind them the small room was already filled with other girls and curious neighbors. A candle burned in the center of a square table surrounded by crowded benches. I was seated in the place of honor and served the conventional cup of tea.

Then a strange conversation began. Even had I known the most perfect Mandarin, I could not have understood these girls, for their speech was different from that spoken in any other part of the country. I had studied Chinese spasmodically—in Manchuria, in Peking, in Shanghai— but each time, before I had more than begun, I had had to move on to new fields, and all that I had previously learned became almost useless. Shanghai had its own dialect, and what I had learned there aroused laughter in Peking and was utterly useless in the south. Only missionaries and consular officials could afford to spend a year in the Peking Language School. Journalists had to be here, there, and everywhere.

I therefore talked with the filature girls in signs and gestures. Did I have any children, they asked, pointing to the children. No? Not married either? They seemed interested and surprised. In explanation I unclamped my fountain pen, took a notebook from my pocket, tried to make a show of thinking, looked them over critically, and began to write. There was great excitement.

A man standing near the door asked me something in Mandarin and I was able to understand him. I was an American, a reporter, he told the crowded room. Yes, I was an intellectual—but was once a worker. When he interpreted this, they seemed to find it very hard to believe.

Girls crowded the benches and others stood banked behind them. Using my few words of Mandarin and many gestures, I learned that some of them earned eight or nine dollars a month, a few eleven. They worked ten hours a day—not eight, as my escort had said. Once they had worked fourteen.

My language broke down, so I supplemented it with crude pictures in my notebook. How did they win the ten-hour day? I drew a sketch of a filature with a big fat man standing on top laughing, then a second picture of the same with the fat man weeping because a row of girls stood holding hands all around the mill. They chattered over these drawings, then a girl shouted two words and all of them began to demonstrate a strike. They crossed their arms, as though refusing to work, while some rested their elbows on the table and lowered their heads, as though refusing to move. They laughed, began to link hands, and drew me into this circle. We all stood holding hands in an unbroken line, laughing. Yes, that was how they got the ten-hour day!

As we stood there, one girl suddenly began to sing in a high sweet voice. Just as suddenly she halted. The whole room chanted an answer. Again and again she sang a question and they replied, while I stood, excited, made desperate by the fact that I could not understand.

The strange song ended and they began to demand something of me. They wanted a song! The *Marseillaise* came to mind, and I sang it. They shouted for more and I tried the *Internationale*, watching carefully for any reaction. They did not recognize it at all. So, I thought, it isn't true that these girls had Communist cells!

A slight commotion spread through the room, and I saw that a man stood in the doorway holding a flute in his hand. He put it to his lips and it began to murmur softly. Then the sound soared and the high sweet voice of the girl singer followed. She paused. The flute soared higher and a man's voice joined it. He was telling some tale, and when he paused, the girl's voice answered. It was surely some ballad, some ancient song of the people, for it had in it the universal quality of folk-music.

In this way I spent an evening with people whose tongue I could not speak, and when I returned to my temple, many went with me, one lighting our way with a swinging lantern. I passed through the silent stone courtyards to my room and my bed. And throughout the night the village watchman beat his brass gong, crying the hours. His gong sounded first from a distance, passed the temple wall, and receded again, saying to the world that all was well.

I lay thinking of ancient things . . . of the common humanity, the goodness and unity of the common people of all lands.

MY LOVER IS A WOMAN

by

PAT PARKER
(1944–1989)

Born in poverty in Houston, Pat Parker became a militant spokes-person against stereotypes of blacks and lesbians and the kind of violence she recorded in Womanslaughter *(1978), the story of her sister's murder by her husband. Her second book of poems,* Pit Stop *(1973), dealt with alcoholism among women. In the 1970s she became part of a community of other activist poets in San Francisco, and for many years she read her poetry and lectured widely. Her poems were collected in* Movement in Black *(1978).* Jonestown and Other Madness *appeared in 1985 and* All Good Women *in 1988. Parker died of cancer in June, 1989.*

•————————————•

I

My lover is a woman
   & when i hold her -
      feel her warmth -
      i feel good - feel safe

then/ i never think of
   my families' voices -
   never hear my sisters say -
   bulldaggers, queers, funny -
   come see us, but don't
   bring your friends -
   it's okay with us,
   but don't tell mama
      it'd break her heart
   never feel my father
   turn in his grave
   never hear my mother cry
   Lord, what kind of child is this?

2

My lover's hair is blonde
   & when it rubs across my face
      it feels soft -
   feels like a thousand fingers
   touch my skin & hold me
   and i feel good.

then/ i never think of the little boy
   who spat & called me nigger
   never think of the policemen
   who kicked my body and said crawl
   never think of Black bodies
   hanging in trees or filled
   with bullet holes
   never hear my sisters say
   white folks hair stinks
   don't trust any of them
   never feel my father
   turn in his grave
   never hear my mother talk
   of her back ache after scrubbing floors
   never hear her cry -
Lord, what kind of child is this?

3

My lover's eyes are blue
& when she looks at me
i float in a warm lake
   feel my muscles go weak with want
      feel good - feel safe

Then/ i never think of the blue
   eyes that have glared at me -
   moved three stools away from me
      in a bar
   never hear my sisters rage
   of syphilitic Black men as
      guinea pigs -
   rage of sterilized children -
   watch them just stop in an

intersection to scare *the old*
   white bitch.
never feel my father turn
   in his grave
never remember my mother
teaching me the yes sirs & mams
   to keep me alive -
never hear my mother cry,
Lord, what kind of child is this?

4

And when we go to a gay bar
   & my people shun me because i crossed
      the line
   & her people look to see what's
wrong with her - what defect
drove her to me -

And when we walk the streets
   of this city - forget and touch
   or hold hands and the people
   stare, glare, frown, & taunt
   at those queers -

I remember -
   Every word taught me
   Every word said to me
   Every deed done to me
   & then i hate -
   i look at my lover
   & for an instant - doubt -

Then/ i hold her hand tighter
And i can hear my mother cry.
Lord, what kind of child is this.

TRESPASSING

by

VALERIE MINER
(b. 1947)

Born in New York City, Valerie Miner has traveled widely and taught at the University of California at Berkeley for a decade. In 1990 she began teaching in the master of fine arts program at Arizona State University at Tempe. She has written fiction about working-class women, sexual harassment in the classroom, growing up in the women's movement, and women sharing their lives. Her five novels are Movement *(1982),* Blood Sisters *(1982),* Murder in the English Department *(1983),* Winter's Edge *(1985), and* All Good Women *(1987). She is the co-author of* Competition: A Feminist Taboo? *published in 1987 by The Feminist Press.*

Exhausted from four hours of traffic, Kate and Josie almost missed seeing the two doe and their fawn drinking at the pond. The women waited in the car, cautious lest the noise of opening doors disturb the animals. The deer lingered another five minutes and then stepped off gracefully into the wings of sequoias. Last sun settled on the golden hills. Night noises pulsed: frogs, crickets, mallards. Wind whispered across dry grass. Jays barked from the top of the hill. As the sky grew roses, Kate and Josie watched Jupiter blaze over the Eastern mountains.

They unloaded the Chevy quickly and sloppily, eager for the comfort of the compact wooden cabin they had built with their friends over five summers. Josie opened the gas line outside the house. Kate lit a fire, reflecting on the joys of collective ownership when the rest of the collective was absent. She could hardly believe it—two whole days away from Meredith High School; forty-eight hours of privacy and peace.

Suddenly starving, they decided to eat right away. Afterwards they would sit in front of the fire and read to each other. Kate chopped salad while Josie made pasta and whistled. The sky got redder and then, abruptly, the cabin was dark. With heavy reluctance, Kate walked around and lit the lanterns.

'Oh,' Kate said.

Josie turned and caught a flick of brown before her, like an insect crashing on a windshield.

'Damn bats.' Kate shook her head and picked up the broom.

'Bats!' Josie screamed. 'I thought Iris got rid of those gruesome things last month.'

'Must still be some holes in the sun porch.'

A dark object dropped beside Josie, like a small turd falling, from the eaves. It disappeared. She fretted the wooden spoon through the pasta, watching another tiny brown mass cut its fall in mid-air and swoop across the room. It was too much. 'Bats!'

Josie ran outside. She felt safer in the dark.

Kate stayed in the house, sweeping bats out of the windows and back door.

Staring up at the stars, so benign in their distance, Josie considered vast differences between Kate and herself. Rational, taciturn Kate was probably calculating the increasing velocity of wing movement as the bats ignited to wakefulness. Josie, herself, still cringed at Grandma's tales about bats nesting in little girls' hair. And raised as she was in a wilful family where intentionality was more important than action, where danger didn't exist if one closed one's imagination to it, Josie was given to the substitution of 'good thoughts.' Let's see, she forced herself to concentrate on a pleasant memory: how she and Kate met. It was a miracle if you thought about it; *who* would have expected romance at the school xerox machine? But there was Kate copying quark diagrams for her physics students while Josie waited to xerox a new translation of *La Cigale et La Fourmi*. If Kate hadn't run out of toner, they might never have become acquainted.

'All clear,' Kate called. There was no disdain in her voice for she had always envied Josie's ability to show fear. She should tell Josie this.

Josie craned her neck and stared at the sky. 'Glorious night,' she called back. 'Wanna see?'

Ducking out the front door, Kate ran through the pungent pennyroyal to her friend. Josie took her hand. Together they stood quietly until they could hear the frogs and the crickets once more.

They slept late and spent the next morning eating eggs and fried potatoes and rye toast. Josie noticed some wasps dancing around the table, so they cleaned up and went outside to lie on the warm deck.

Later they spent an hour fitting moulding around the edges of the sun porch's glass door, sealing the house seams against nocturnal trespassers.

At noon the women drove five miles to town for forgotten country necessities—ice, water and flashlight batteries. Josie secretly checked the grocery shelves for bat killer, but she didn't find any and she knew Kate wouldn't approve.

As they drove back to the land, Josie tried to renew her enthusiasm for the weekend. She stopped in front of the cabin. Kate, now completely restored by country air, bounded into the house with the grocery bag.

Josie moved the Chevy into the shade of an oak tree which was being gradually occupied by Spanish moss. As she locked up the car, she saw a fat man with a rifle waddling out of the forest. He wore a yellow cap, a striped T-shirt and bluejeans.

A giant bumblebee, she thought. Then she warned herself to get serious. The land was clearly posted, 'No Trespassing. No Hunting'. A shiver ran along her collarbone. They were half-a-mile from the highway here. It could be weeks before anyone investigated.

Josie decided to be friendly and waved.

'Hello there.' He was winded, hustling to meet her.

Josie closed her eyes and hoped Kate would stay in the house until it was all over.

'I got lost,' he said, nodding his whole body. 'How do you get back to the highway?'

'That direction.' Josie tried to calm herself. 'Up the road there.'

He looked her over. 'You got any water? A glass of water? I've been walking for hours.'

Biblical tales filled her head. 'The Woman at the Well', 'The Wedding at Cana', 'The Good Samaritan'. 'Sure,' she said as noncommittally as possible. 'I'll be right back.'

'Who's that?' Kate greeted her.

Josie tried to be calm. 'Water man. I mean, a lost man who needs water.' She watched Kate's jaw stiffen. 'Now let me handle it. He just wants a glass of water and then he'll be on his way.' Josie poured water from a plastic jug into an old jam jar they used for drinking.

'Water, my foot, what is he doing on the land? It's posted "No Trespassing", for God's sake.'

'Listen, Kate, he was hunting and . . .'

Kate took the glass and poured half the water back into the jug. 'Don't *spoil* him. He may return.'

She stalked out to the man, who was leaning on their car, his gun on the ground. Josie stood at the door, watching.

'Thanks, ma'am.' He reached for the water.

'No shooting on this land,' Kate said as she released the glass.

'Sorry, ma'am. I was hunting up there on the North Ridge and I hit a buck. But he got away. I followed, to make sure I got him good. Then I got lost and I guess I wound up here.'

'Guess so,' Kate said. She held her hand against her leg to stop it from shaking.

'I'll be off your land soon's I finish the water,' he promised.

'That's right.' She kept her voice even.

'But I'll need to be coming back to get the buck. See, I finally did get him. But since I was lost, I couldn't drag him all over tarnation.'

'We don't want a dead buck on the land,' Kate conceded. 'When're you coming?'

'Tomorrow morning?' he asked. 'About eight o'clock?'

'Fine, and no guns,' she said.

'No, ma'am, no guns.'

'Right then.' She held her hand out for the jam jar. 'Road's that way.'

'Yes, ma'am.'

Kate watched him climb the hill and walked back to the house, shaking her head. Josie reached to hug her, but Kate pulled away. 'God damned hunter.' She was on the verge of tears.

'How about some coffee or lunch?'

'Naw, are you nuts, after all we ate this morning? No, I think I'll just go for a walk. See if I can find the buck. If there *is* a buck.'

Josie nodded. 'Want company?' She wasn't keen on viewing a dead animal, but she didn't care to admit being afraid to stay in the house alone, not after her melodramatic performance with the bats last night.

'Sure.' Kate was grateful. 'Let's go.'

Josie locked the ice chest and dropped the jam jar in the brown paper garbage bag on the way out.

It was hotter now, about 85 degrees. The pennyroyal smelled mintier than last night. The day was dry and still–bleached grass, golden hills scumbled against teal sky. A turkey vulture glided above the oak grove. As they walked around the pond, they could hear frogs scholop into the water. Kate stopped to inspect the eucalyptus trees they had planted in the spring. Four out of five still alive, not bad. Further along, a salamander skittered across their path. Josie felt cool even before she entered the woods. In a way, she hoped they wouldn't find the buck. But if there was no buck, who knew what the bumblebee man really wanted?

The woods were thick with madrone and manzanita and poison oak. It was always a balance on the land, Kate thought, pleasure and danger.

Josie wished she had worn sneakers instead of sandals. But Kate didn't seem to be bothered about her feet as she marched ahead. Right, Josie reminded herself, this wasn't a ramble. They continued in silence for half-an-hour.

''Round here, I guess,' called Kate, who was now several yards ahead. 'See the way branches have broken. Yes, here. Oh, my god, it's still alive. God damned hunter.'

They stared at the huge animal, its left front leg broken in a fall, panting and sweating, blind fear in its wide eyes.

'I told Myla we should keep a gun at the house.' Kate cried. 'What are we going to do?'

Josie didn't think about it. She probably wouldn't have been able to lift the boulder if she had thought about it. But she heard herself shouting to Kate, 'Stand back,' and watched herself drop the big rock on the buck's head. They heard a gurgling and saw a muscle ripple along the animal's belly. Then nothing. There was nothing alive under the boulder.

Josie stared at the four bullet wounds scattered up the right side of the buck. The animal's blood was a dark, cinnamon colour. She noticed sweat along the hip joints.

VALERIE MINER

389

Kate walked over to her quietly and took her hand. 'Good, brave,' she stuttered. 'That was good, Josie.'

'Yeah, it seemed the right thing.'

Kate hugged Josie and gently drew her away from the dead buck and the broken bush.

They walked straight out to the trail. Neither one seemed to want to stay in the woods for their customary ramble. Kate watched her friend closely, waiting for the explosion. This silence was so uncharacteristic of Josie. Soon, soon, she would erupt with anger and aggravation and guilt and a long examination of what she had done in the woods. For her own part, Kate could only think of one word. Brave.

'Let's go swimming,' Josie said, trying to focus on the trail. 'It'll cool us off.'

The two women stripped on the makeshift dock and lay in the sun beside one another. Kate was slim, her legs long and shapely. She didn't think much about this body which had always served her well. She never felt too thin or too plump. Josie, in contrast, fretted about her zoftig breasts and hips. Her skin was pinker than Kate's, a faint pink. Kate curled up beside Josie, her legs across Josie's legs, her head on Josie's shoulder.

Josie closed her eyes and told herself it was over. They were all right. She had never killed anything before and she felt terribly sad. Of course, the animal had been dying. It was a humane act. Still, her chest ached with a funny hollowness.

'What's that?' Kate sat up.

They listened, Josie flat and Kate leaning forward from her waist.

The noise came again.

A loud whirr.

Like an engine.

Whirr.

'Quail.' Kate relaxed back on her elbow. 'Come on, let's wash off the feeling of that creepy guy.'

She lowered herself into the water from the wooden ladder, surprised as Josie jumped in.

'Freezing!' Josie laughed, swimming around her friend and noticing how Kate's blonde curls sprang back the minute she lifted her head from the water. 'Freezing!'

'You'll warm up,' Kate said, herself breathless from the cold.

'You're always telling me to stop daydreaming, to stay in the present. The present is freezing.' Josie giggled and splashed her friend.

Kate laughed. She ducked under the water, swimming deep enough to catch Josie's feet, which were treading earnestly.

'Hey, watch it.' But Josie called too late. Now she was below the surface, tangled in Kate's legs and the long roots of silky grass. It was green down here and very cold.

They dried out on the sunny dock and dressed before starting towards the house. Often they walked naked across the land, especially after swimming when they didn't want to wear sweaty clothes. Today that didn't feel safe.

Back at the cabin, the afternoon grew long and restless. Both women felt fidgety. Kate put aside her equations and washed all the windows in the house. Josie couldn't concentrate on her translation, so she worked up lesson plans for the following week.

About five o'clock, she glanced at Kate, stretching recklessly to the skylight from the top of a ladder.

'Careful up there.'

'Sure, hon!'

'What did we bring for dinner?' Josie's mind was blank.

'That beef chilli you made last week. And rye bread.'

'Why don't we go out?' Josie paced in front of the wood stove. God, she wished Kate would be careful on that ladder.

'Out? But the whole point of being here, oops,' she tipped precariously and then straightened. 'Hey, just let me get one more lick in here and we can talk. There.' She started down the steps. 'But the whole point of being in the country is to retreat together in solitary bliss. And what's wrong with your chilli? I thought this batch was perfect?'

Josie shrugged and looked out the big bay window across the grass. She told herself to watch the horses ambling along the ridge or the hawk hovering over the pond. Instead she was caught by a line of lint Kate had left in the middle of the frame. 'I don't know. Not in the mood. Guess I'd like vegetarian tonight.' Her eyes stung.

Kate stood behind her; still, Josie could sense her nodding.

'Why not,' Kate said. 'Be nice to take a ride this time of evening.'

Edna's Café was practically empty. But then—Kate checked her watch—it *was* only five-thirty. Edna waved menus from behind the counter. Josie and Kate said yes.

'Coffee, girls?' Edna carried the menus under her arm, pot of coffee in one hand and mugs in the other.

'Thanks,' Josie said.

'Not just yet,' Kate smiled. Edna reminded her of Aunt Bella who worked in a coffee shop back East.

While Kate studied the menu, Josie excused herself to the rest-room.

Kate breathed easier when Josie returned to the table looking relaxed. She felt a great surge of affection as her companion intently appraised the menu.

'I think I'll have the chef's salad with Jack cheese,' Josie decided.

'Sound's good.' Kate nodded. She was relieved to see Josie looking happy. 'Two chef salads, with Jack cheese,' she called over to Edna.

They talked about plans for the following summer when they could spend four consecutive weeks on the land.

'You two girls sisters?' Edna served the enormous salads.

VALERIE MINER

391

'No,' laughed Kate. 'Why?'

'Don't know. You kinda look alike. 'Course when I stare straight at you like this, there's not much resemblance. I don't know. And you always order the same thing.'

'In that case, I'll have tea,' Kate laughed again. 'With lemon.'

They ate silently, self-conscious of being the only ones in the restaurant. Kate could hardly get down the lettuce. She'd feel better after she made the phone call. She wouldn't tell Josie, who would get nervous. But it was responsible to report the intruder to the sheriff. 'Excuse me. Now I've got to use the bathroom,' she said to Josie. 'Don't let Edna take my salad.'

'I'll guard it with my life,' Josie grinned.

The sheriff's number was posted beneath the fire station number. She dialled and heard a funny, moist sound, as if the man were eating or maybe clicking in his dentures. She concentrated on the sturdy black plastic of the phone.

'Hello,' he said finally.

She began to report the incident.

'Listen, you're the second lady to call me about this in twenty minutes. Like I told the other one, there's nothing I can do unless the man is actually trespassing on your land. Since you've invited him back tomorrow, he ain't exactly trespassing.'

'We didn't exactly invite him.'

'OK, if it makes you feel easier, I said I'll swing by about eight a.m. That's when the other lady said he'd be coming.'

'Thank you, sir.'

'Sir,' she shook her head as she walked back to the table. She hadn't said 'sir' in fifteen years.

Josie had finished her salad and was doodling on a paper napkin. Definitely signs of a good mood. Kate sat down and stared at her until she looked up. 'So I hear you have a date with the law tomorrow morning.'

Josie smiled. 'Hope you don't think I'm stepping out on you.'

By the time Kate finished her salad, the café was getting crowded.

'Refills?' Edna approached with a pot of coffee and a pot of hot water. 'No thanks, just the cheque,' Josie said.

'Guess you girls didn't mind my asking if you was sisters?'

'No, no, not at all.' They spoke in unison.

It was a warm, richly scented evening and they drove home with the top down. Jupiter came out early again. Josie thought how much she preferred Jupiter to the cold North Star.

They were both worn out as they collapsed on the couch together. Their feet on the fruit crate coffee table, they watched pink gain the horizon. It was almost pitch dark when Josie reached up to light the lanterns.

She hesitated a moment, remembering last night, and then proceeded.

Light, *voilá*, the room was filled with sharp corners and shiny surfaces. Kate picked up her book, but Josie drew it away, cuddling closer.

'Here?' Kate was surprised by her own resistance. After all, they were alone, five miles from town.

'Where then?' Josie tried to sound like Lauren Bacall.

Kate sighed with a breath that moved her whole body, a body, she noticed, which was becoming increasingly sensitive to the body next to her. 'Mmmmm,' she kissed Josie on her neck, sweet with late summer sweat.

When Josie opened her eyes, she thought she saw something. No, they had sealed off the sun porch this morning. She kissed Kate on the lips and was startled by a whisssh over her friend's head. 'Bats,' she said evenly, pulling Kate lower on the couch.

'Don't worry,' Kate said. 'I'll get rid of him.'

Worry, Josie cringed. She wasn't worried; she was hysterical. Calm down, she told herself. Think about the invasion of Poland. This was her mother's approach to anxiety—distract yourself by thinking about people with *real* problems. Worry is a perversion of imagination.

Kate opened the windows and set forth again with the broom, but the bat wouldn't leave. Eventually it spiralled upstairs into the large sleeping loft. Kate shook her head and closed up the house against further intrusion. She shrugged and returned to the couch, where Josie was sitting up, considerably more collected than the previous night.

'It'll be OK,' Kate said. 'It'll just go to sleep. You know, they're not really Transylvanian leeches. They're harmless little herbivores. And rather inept.'

Herbivores. Josie thought about eating salad for absolution after she murdered the buck.

Kate reached over and brushed her lover's breast, but Josie pulled away. 'Not now, sweetie. I can't just now.'

Kate nodded. She picked up her book. Josie fiddled with a crossword puzzle. At about ten o'clock, Kate yawned, 'Bed?'

'OK,' Josie was determined to be brave. 'I'll go up first.'

'Sure,' Kate regarded her closely. 'You light the candle up there. I'll get the lantern down here.'

They settled comfortably in the double nylon sleeping bag. Kate blew out the light. She reached over to rub Josie's back in the hope something more might develop. Suddenly she heard a whissh, whissh, whissh.

'Looks like our friend is back.' Kate tried to keep her voice light.

'Just a harmless little herbivore.' Josie rolled to her side of the bed, putting a pillow over her head.

That night Josie dreamt that she had become Mayor of Lincoln, Nebraska.

Kate slept fitfully, hardly dreaming, and waking with the first sun.

She lay and watched Josie breathing evenly, blowing the edges of her black hair, her body ripe and luscious in the soft light. If she woke up early enough, they could make love before Mr Creepo arrived. And the sheriff. Had they made a mistake in phoning the sheriff?

The loft grew lighter. Kate lay on her back with her head on her palms, wondering where the bat had nested, about the reliability of her research assistant, whether she would go home for Christmas this year. Then she heard the noise.

Her entire body stiffened. No mistaking the sound of a car crawling down the gravel road toward their cabin. She checked her watch. Seven a.m. Shit. The sheriff wouldn't arrive until their bodies were cold. Maybe Josie would be safer if she just stayed in the house; maybe she wouldn't wake her. Yes, Kate pulled out of the sleeping bag. She was grabbed by the night-gown.

'Not so quick, brown fox,' Josie said sleepily. 'How about a cuddle?'

She was adorable in the morning, thought Kate, completely *dérangé*, as Josie herself would admit, before the second cup of coffee.

The noise outside grew closer and Kate tightened.

'Don't you even want to hear how I got elected Mayor of Lincoln . . . ?'

'Not now.' Kate couldn't stem the panic in her own voice.

Josie sat up. 'What is it?' Then she heard the truck's motor dying.

'I'll just go check in with him,' Kate said nonchalantly. 'You wait here and I'll come back to snuggle.' She pulled on her clothes.

'No you don't, Joan of Arc.' Josie stood up and tucked her night-shirt into a pair of jeans.

The two walked downstairs together.

The fat man was approaching the house, empty-handed. His friend, also bulky and middle-aged, stayed behind, leaning against the red pick-up truck.

Kate called out to him when he was three yards from the house. 'Back again.'

'Sorry to bother you, ma'am. As you can see we didn't bring no guns. We'll just get that deer and then git offa yer property as soon's we can.'

His friend shuffled and looked at his feet.

'OK,' Kate said gruffly. 'We don't want dead animals on the land. By the way, we finished him off for you yesterday.'

The man opened his mouth in surprise. His friend moved forward, tugging him back. They closed up the truck and headed into the woods.

Josie watched until they were out of sight. Kate went inside to make coffee.

Half-an-hour later, as they sat down to breakfast, another vehicle crunched down the hill. Josie looked out at the black and white sedan. 'Our hero, the sheriff.'

They walked over to greet the sheriff, a solid man, who looked them over carefully.

'You the girls who called me yesterday?'

'Yes, we did.' Josie smiled.

'Yes.' Kate nodded, the 'sir' gone as quickly as it had come. She didn't like his expression.

'Only ladies listed on the deed to this land, I see. Looked it up last night. All schoolteachers. Some kind of commune? Something religious?'

'Just friends.' Kate stepped back.

'Edna says she thought you were sisters.' He squinted against the bright sun. 'One sort or another.'

'Just friends.' Kate's voice was more distant.

'Soooo.' The sheriff held his ground. 'You want to run through the nature of that problem again?'

As Kate talked with the sheriff, Josie inspected the hunters' pick-up truck. The bumper sticker read, 'I live in a cave and one good fuck is all I crave.' Inside, dice hung from the rearview mirror. On the seat were a parka and two empty cans of Dr. Pepper. The dashboard was plastered with several iridescent signs. The sun glared so that she could read only one. 'Gas, Ass or Grass—No one rides for free.'

The sheriff noticed her and observed, 'Leon's truck. Just as I figured. Leon Bates, a local man. He's, well, he's strayed off the hunting trail before.'

'Isn't there something you can do about him?' Josie felt the heat rising to her face. 'He might have killed one of us. On our property. With a gun.'

'Today,' the sheriff's voice was cool, 'today your friend tells me that he has no gun. That in fact, you said he could come back here to get his buck. That right?'

Josie closed her eyes, feeling naive for imagining this man might protect them. Now bureaucracy seemed the only recourse. 'Right. Can't we make some kind of complaint about what he did yesterday?'

'Sure can,' the sheriff nodded. 'If that's what you want.'

'What do you mean?' Kate's back tightened.

'You're weekend folks, right?' He lit a cigarette.

'We work in the city, if that's what you mean,' Kate spoke carefully, 'and don't live here year round.'

'None of my business what you all have going on here. None of Leon's business either. But if you file a complaint and we take it to court, well, he's bound to do some investigating and . . .'

'There's nothing illegal about our land group,' Josie snapped.

'Miss, Miss, I never said anything about legal, illegal, but you know there are natural pests the law can't control. And it's better maybe not to get them roused.'

Kate and Josie exchanged glances. 'Well, perhaps we'll check with Loretta; her sister's a lawyer. We'll get back to you.'

'Yes, ma'am.' He grew more serious. 'That about all for today, ma'am? I mean you said they didn't bring no guns with them. You feel safe enough on your own?'

'Yes,' Josie said. 'We're safe enough on our own.'

'Then if you'll excuse me, it's almost eight o'clock and services start early around here.' He stamped out his cigarette and softened. 'Church is always open to outsiders and weekend people, by the way. Just three miles down, on the road by the gas station.'

'I know where it is,' Josie said. 'Goodbye, sheriff.'

They watched him roll up the hill, then returned to the house for breakfast. They were both too furious to talk. Kate hardly touched her food, watching out the window for the trespassers.

About ten o'clock, she saw two pregnant-looking men pulling a buck through the dust by its antlers. Her first thought was how powerful those antlers must be. She tightened and Josie looked up from her book. 'At last.'

It took the men ten minutes to reach the truck. They were huffing and sweating and Josie had to resist the urge to bring them a pitcher of water. She followed Kate out on the front porch.

Leon Bates glowered at them, as if weighing the value of wasting breath for talk. He and his friend heaved the buck into the truck. On the second try, they made it.

Leon's friend wiped his hands on his jeans, waiting with an expression of excruciating embarrassment.

Leon straightened up, drew a breath and shouted, 'That'll do it.'

'Good,' called Kate.

'Gotta ask one question.' Leon leaned forward on his right leg. 'What'd you have to go and bust his head for? Ruined a perfect trophy. Just look at the antlers. Would have been perfect.'

'Come on, Leon,' his friend called.

Kate stood firmly, hands on her hips. Josie tried to hold back the tears, but she couldn't and pivoted toward the cabin.

'The road's that way,' Kate pointed. 'Only goes in one direction.'

Kate stamped into the house. 'Damn them. Damn them!' she screamed.

'Hey, now.' Josie reached up to her shoulders and pulled Kate toward her. 'Hey now, relax, love.'

'Don't tell me to relax. This man comes on our land, shoots living things, threatens us. And you tell me to relax.' She banged her hand on the table.

Josie inhaled heavily and pulled Kate a little closer. 'They've gone now.' She looked over Kate's shoulder and out the back window, which gleamed in the mid-morning sun. 'See, they're over the hill.'

'Out of sight, that's what you think, you fool.' Kate tried to draw apart.

Josie held tight, hoping to melt the contortions from her friend's face.

Kate pushed her away. Josie lost balance, hitting her head against a pane of glass in the sun porch door.

The glass cracked, sending a high-pitched rip through the room.

Josie ducked forward, her eyes tightly shut, just in time to avoid most of the showering glass fragments.

Drenched in sweat, Kate shook her and shouted, 'Josie, Josie, are you all right? Oh, my God, Josie, are you all right?'

'We'll never keep out the bats this way,' Josie laughed nervously, on the verge.

'Josie, I didn't mean it.' Tears welled in Kate's eyes. 'I love you, Josie, are you all right?'

Josie nodded. They held each other, shivering.

Josie stepped forward, 'OK, yes, but I feel a little like Tinkerbell. Scattering all this glitter.'

'Tinkerbell!' Kate laughed and cried and choked. The room seemed to be closing in on them. Hot, tight, airless. She could feel herself listing.

'But you, hey.' Josie frowned. 'Let's go upstairs and have *you* lie down.'

They sat on the bed, holding hands and staring out at the land. The day was hot, even dryer than yesterday and the golden grass shimmered against the shadowy backdrop of the woods.

'We really should go down and clean up the glass, put a board over the shattered pane.' Kate whispered.

'Yeah, if we don't head home soon, traffic's gonna be impossible.'

Kate rested her head on Josie's breast. She smelled the musk from the black feathers beneath her arms. Her hand went to the soft nest at the bottom of Josie's generous belly. Josie slipped off her clothes. Kate followed. They sank down on the bed, swimming together again, sucked into the cool sleeping bag.

'Home,' Josie murmured.

'Hmmmm?' Kate inhaled the scents of Josie's sweat and sex. Forcing herself to be alert, she pulled back. Was her friend delirious? Maybe she had a concussion.

'Home.' Josie kissed her with a passion so conscious as to take away both Kate's concern and her breath.

'Yes.' Kate moved her fingers lower, separating the labia, swirling the honey thicker. 'Yes.'

Josie crawled on top of Kate, licking her shoulders, her breasts; burying her nose in her navel; kissing her thighs. Then she was distracted by a slow fizzzz, as if their air-mattress were deflating.

Josie looked up. Two wasps hovered over them, bobbing and weaving and then lifting themselves abruptly out of vision. Maybe if she just continued Kate wouldn't notice. But it was too late.

'They always come out in the middle of the day,' Kate said drearily. 'For food. For their nests.'

Josie shook her head, staring at the unsteady, fragile creatures.

'What the hell,' Kate shrugged, inching away from Josie.

'What the hell,' Josie whispered seductively. They returned to the pleasures between them. When they finished making love, Josie curled around Kate. She explained how she had been elected Mayor of Lincoln, Nebraska.

The wasps wove over and around the two women. Even as they fell asleep.

HOME

by

SHIRLEY ANN GRAU
(b. 1929)

Shirley Ann Grau still lives in her native Louisiana but summers on Martha's Vineyard. The Keepers of the House, *the third of her five novels, won the Pulitzer Prize in 1965; it shows how a young woman transcends the stereotype of the Southern woman when she learns of her grandfather's love for a strong black woman. Frequent themes of Grau's work are the power of nature and of money and the violence associated with them. She has received awards for her short stories, of which* Nine Women *(1985) is the third collection.*

At five-fifteen when Angela Taylor got back to her office, there were six telephone messages waiting for her.

Dinny, who worked afternoons at the reception desk, said, "Mrs. Marshall called twice. She was getting impatient."

"*The* Mrs. Marshall? *My* Mrs. Marshall? God."

Dinny giggled. Mrs. Marshall was old, rich, difficult, and fond of buying and selling houses. Of the fifteen agents at Peerless Realty, only Angela Taylor dealt with her successfully.

"Well," Angela twirled the note in small circles, "she pays my commission, so I don't care. How long has she been in her present house, Dinny?"

"A couple of years," Dinny said.

"A year to remodel, a year to live in it. And now she's getting restless. Maybe I can talk her into selling this house and moving into a hotel while we look for another. That would make it easier on me." She flicked through the other messages, began whistling quietly through her front teeth. It was a childhood habit she had never corrected, and it meant that she was extremely pleased.

Dinny said, "Good news?"

"If this is what I think it is, I have just sold that monster of a Boudreaux place. I'll get on this right now."

In her glass-walled office cubicle, she kicked off her shoes, wiggled her toes against the soft carpeting. Her back was aching—wrong shoes again. She'd just have to start wearing sensible laced oxfords. They looked dreadful, but she was on her feet too much and the days were just too long. . . . She dropped into her chair and fought off the desire to put her feet on the desk—hardly proper office behavior. She rubbed her face briskly; her makeup had worn off, leaving the skin slightly rough to the touch. It was time to go back to Monsieur Raoul for another series of treatments.

She tossed a half pack of cigarettes into the wastebasket; she would take a fresh one tomorrow morning. She always did. She'd discovered that no matter how annoying or stupid a client was, how devious, uncertain, and utterly exhausting, she needed only to light a cigarette, slowly, slowly, and after the first puff consider the burning tip as if it were the most interesting thing in the world—her annoyance would vanish, her calm return. (Even clients seemed impressed by her solemn ponderous movements.) In all this time—and she'd been a successful agent for twenty years—she'd never grown to like tobacco. She needed it, and it became part of her working day, like the pale pastel suits she wore all year round, very smooth, very well-tailored, with never a pleat or a ruffle on them.

She arranged her telephone messages carefully in order of importance. Took a deep breath and began. It was then five-thirty.

"Miss Prescott, please." A pause. "Look, Vicky, just wait for me. I think I'm finally getting rid of the Boudreaux house and I've got to close before they change their mind. I'm running late, I just got back here, and I've got a list of other calls—a good half hour before I can leave. Okay?"

She scarcely waited for Vicky's answer, she was so eager to get on with the business of the Boudreaux property. The old uptown Victorian house had been on the market for two years, it was way overpriced—and now she had a buyer.

It wasn't until she'd finished—all calls answered, details for the Boudreaux transaction settled, Mrs. Marshall put off until the end of the week—that she remembered the edge in Vicky's voice.

Angela paused, hand holding the phone halfway to the cradle. Dear lord, not one of Vicky's moods. Not when things were going so well and she was feeling so very pleased with herself. . . . She remembered that cool edgy voice. . . . Another mood, probably made worse by that hasty phone call.

She shrugged away her annoyance. Vicky was like that—constantly demanding assurance as if she were a child and not a nearly middle-aged woman.

And that, Angela thought, never would change.

She put her shoes back on, grimacing. She was the last in the office; she switched off the lights and set the burglar alarm as she left.

In the parking lot the summer air was still and hot, the fading light an uncertain pale yellow. She hurried to her car, turned on air conditioner and radio, and took her place in the slow-moving lines of traffic.

SHIRLEY ANN GRAU

Vicky was waiting just outside the shop. Over her head, across the entire second-floor facade, a five-foot signature announced *Victoria*.

Angela looked with approval at the large flowing white script. My idea, she thought, and a damn good one. Flash without trash, she chuckled to herself.

There were still people in the shop: late afternoon was always busy. The last customers often didn't finish until nearly seven, crossing paths with the incoming night security guard.

She'd been right about the location: Angela gave herself another little pat on the back. She didn't usually handle commercial property, but that didn't mean she didn't know a good thing when she saw it. And this location was perfect for an expensive shopping area. She knew it and she worked hard to see that it developed correctly. She even put a lot of her own money into the area—at the start when things needed a push. Eventually she sold out very profitably, so that now the only thing she owned, with Vicky, was the handsome two-story building that housed the dress shop.

Angela brought the car to a stop. Vicky, small, trim, dark, wearing a lavender dress, slipped quickly inside. Bal à Versailles filled the car.

Ever so much the trim businesswoman, Angela thought with a glint of amusement, except for that perfume. Too heavy a scent, too many flowers had died to produce it.

"I thought you'd never come," Vicky snapped. "Another half hour and I'd have called a cab."

"And be deprived of my charming company?" Yes, Vicky was in one of her moods; the only thing was to pretend not to see it, to be flip and casual. "A good day?"

"Average." Vicky wiped an invisible speck of dust from the dashboard. "The shipment from Arnold didn't arrive, of course."

"They're always late," Angela said. "Don't I remember some terrible confusion with last fall's line?"

"You do." Vicky slumped back in her seat and stared straight ahead. "I don't know why I keep dealing with them. They are so impossible."

"Because, luv, you like their clothes, and your customers like their clothes and they pay ridiculous prices for them and you turn a tidy little profit. Which is why you put up with all the nonsense from Arnold."

"Huum," Vicky said. And fell silent.

The flowers of Bal à Versailles were as suffocating as smoke.

Except for a single lamp in the entrance foyer, their apartment was dark. "Well now," Angela said as she flipped the wall switches that filled the rooms with soft irregular patterns of light, "home at last, far from the madding crowd, the bustle of commerce. Now we discover what Madame Papa has left for us to have with our cocktails."

"Angela, why do you call her that? If she hears, she's going to quit and she is such a good housekeeper."

Angela raised her eyebrows. So the silence is over, she thought. How nice of you to make your first words criticism. . . . I was really getting used to the quiet. I really enjoyed whistling and humming to the radio all that long drive home.

But she said nothing aloud. In their fifteen years together she had learned that nothing she could do would alter Vicky's moods. Sometimes she wondered if Vicky herself controlled them. Sometimes she knew she did not, that they were seizures or spasms quite independent of the body they inhabited.

Ignoring the neatly stacked mail, Angela crossed the living room. "I'm having a drink. You want one?" The curtains were closed, and she wondered if she should open them—there was still a bit of soft twilight in the park outside their windows. No, she thought, drink first. "A drink, Vicky?"

"You're not going to open the curtains?"

She reads my thoughts. Angela gave a mental shrug. . . . "Later. I need my drink to celebrate. This was a very good day."

In the small bar the glasses and bottles and ice were waiting. God bless Madame Papa, Angela thought fervently. She filled the largest glass with ice and poured the gin, not bothering to measure. The feel of the bottle in her hand cheered her immensely, as did the small dish of lemon peel. Madame Papa, whose name was Papadopoulous, was a most efficient housekeeper. And, Angela thought, taking the first long taste of her martini, she makes the most marvelous baklava; why didn't I ever have baklava when I was a child . . .

She stopped abruptly and laughed out loud. The thought was so silly, so utterly silly. The kitchen in her mother's house had been staffed by large black women who presided over greasy black stoves that were never cleaned and large black pots whose outsides were crinkled with grease and age until they resembled an alligator's skin. The pots rattled, half-burned wood spoons thumped against their sides, and the kitchen filled with steam and loud voices and laughter. The food was greasy and heavy and delicious. But, she thought, it wasn't baklava.

She waved her glass and laughed again.

"What did you say?" Vicky called.

"Nothing."

"You were laughing."

So shoot me, Angela thought. But she only said calmly, "I was thinking of the kitchen when I was a child." She added more gin and ice to her glass and turned back to the living room, where Vicky was thumbing through the mail.

"Here," Vicky said. "A fund-raiser for Hart."

"For who?"

"Gary Hart. You know, the next President of the United States."

"Ah," Angela said. "Didn't we just go to something for him? Cocktails in the park with little zoo animals wandering around underfoot."

"That was cocktails and only twenty-five dollars." Vicky was studying the heavy card carefully. "This one is two hundred and fifty."

"Good lord," Angela said, "he must really be serious."

"Look at the list of sponsors." Vicky's practiced eye scanned the long list. "At least ten are customers. We'll have to go."

"I suppose," Angela said to the ice cubes, "you are going to sell them dresses for that event and you are going to make a lot more than the five hundred dollars it's going to cost us."

Vicky said, "I'll put it in the book. The twenty-second."

"I suppose," Angela went on ruminatively to her martini, "your Hart-inclined customers see you there and think you are one of them. And your Reagan customers aren't there to see that you are not one of *them*."

"What?" Vicky frowned slightly. "We are going to a Reagan lunch, I forget the exact date, but it's in the book."

"Behold the devious mind of a retailer." The alcohol was filtering into her blood now. A pleasant warmth began in the pit of her stomach and spread upward, washing over her ears like some soft tropical sea. She sat down and kicked off her shoes.

Vicky went on thumbing through the mail, opening and sorting quickly. For a fraction of a second she hesitated over one letter, then with an impatient gesture tossed all remaining ones aside.

Oh, oh . . . Angela watched the quick flip of the small hand, the flash of rings . . . what's this? That letter annoyed her very much. What do we have here?

"Angela, I asked you about the curtains."

"Open them if you like," Angela said, wiggling her toes.

"I was asking if *you* wanted them. I don't. I don't like this time of day at all. The way the light hits the windows and they shine back like blank eyes, like eyes with cataracts. You know that."

"No, I didn't know that. I don't think you ever said that before."

"I hate this time of day."

"A martini?" Angela suggested again.

"I'll get it," Vicky said. "You put in too much vermouth."

"Ah well." Angela lifted her glass and toasted the ceiling. Things were going to be very difficult, but at least Vicky was talking. Once last year she had not said a word for three days. The absolute silence had eaten into Angela's nerves, though she'd managed to maintain her calm indifferent exterior. She'd even considered some kind of record keeping, some sort of cryptic numbers on a calendar. But Vicky might have found it, might have guessed. And that would have hurt her—she thought of herself as even-tempered and easygoing.

Angela whistled at the ceiling, a bit of the Colonel Bogie march. I wonder if I could stand another one of those, she thought, another record-breaking tantrum.

Vicky tossed herself into the opposite chair. She'd made her drink carelessly. Her lavender dress showed a broad pattern of splash marks.

Angela waited for the liquor to soften her mood. Patient, unmoving, almost not breathing . . .

Vicky drank very fast, and at the end gave a little sigh, a tiny sound like an echo.

Angela said, "I had one fantastic sale today. The old Boudreaux place."

Vicky stared directly at her, round blue eyes registering no comprehension, no acknowledgment.

"Just about everybody in the office had tried with it and no luck. Then I remembered that couple from Clarksdale—we met them somewhere about a year ago—they talked about wanting to move to town, and they said they wanted a big old house to do over. A period piece, I remember them saying. So I called them and because they have far more money than sense, they bought that ghastly monster."

Vicky's eyes didn't change.

This is going to be quite an evening, Angela thought. And then, aloud, "We have tickets for that experimental theater tonight. Do you want to go?"

Vicky's eyes snapped suddenly into focus. "No."

"It probably isn't very good." Angela kept her voice even and toneless. "Let's have dinner downstairs at Paul's and then come home."

"I have been to Paul's so often I know that menu by heart. I know how every single thing is going to taste before I taste it."

"When you live in a building, you tend to eat downstairs fairly often because it is so convenient."

"I hate it."

"Well now"—the smallest trace of anger appeared in Angela's voice—"I certainly don't feel like fixing supper here. I think I'll go to dinner and then have a look at that foolish play or multimedia presentation or whatever they call it."

Vicky's eyes glittered and changed, sparkles like tinsel appeared in the blue irises.

Her eyes were so damned expressive, Angela thought. They showed hurt too clearly, you could see the blood of invisible wounds. Faced by their pain, Angela retreated to the pantry for another drink. Deliberately, measuring carefully, she fixed the martini, tossed both lemon and olive on top the ice. Still elaborately casual, she sauntered back, stopping to pick up the mail Vicky had tossed aside. On top, with its clear printing, its elaborately scrolled capitals, was a letter from Angela's daughter, Louise. Why had that upset Vicky?

The paper crackled loudly in the silence as she smoothed the folded sheets. "Your glass is empty, Vicky. Why don't you have another drink while I read this."

Angela was not sure how she felt about her daughter, that beautiful young woman who seemed capable of endless understanding without a hint of malice or anger. She'd adjusted to her parents' divorce, had lived happily with her father, had grown to love her stepmother. With Vicky, she'd been quietly friendly, relaxed, and quite free of embarrassment. Cool, disciplined, well organized, a model student in college, now working on an MFA, she was married to an associate professor of economics who looked like a young John Wayne.

Perfection, Angela thought. How could I have produced anything so damn perfect. . . . And where was Vicky?

She was standing at the refrigerator, one finger rubbing a small circle on the door. Carefully Angela put her arms around her. In the softness of that body and the muskiness of that hair, Angela felt again the familiar rush of pain and love and tenderness. And something else, something darker and stronger. Something she could not name, something she refused to think about, a force that gave a restless desperation to her life.

Wearily, for the uncounted thousandth time, Angela pushed back the thing that crouched waiting in the shadows. She heard the crackling of its voice and the swishing of its tail. Not yet, she told it, not yet. Not this time.

And softly into Vicky's ear, pink curves under wisps of black hair, "We're both tired, honey. Come on, let's finish our drinks now. I saw some kind of dip in the refrigerator. And after a while we'll go and have dinner at Paul's, but we won't try the theater. Not tonight, when we're both so tired."

Vicky nodded silently, eyes closed, anger lines fading from her small face—the wistful, heart-shaped face that had haunted Angela ever since they first met, years ago, when Vicky was a college student, Angela a young matron with a husband and child.

Now again, as always, seeing Vicky's face close up, seeing the perfect porcelain skin, the lash-fringed eyes, naturally shadowed as some Irish eyes are, the thin-lipped and very small mouth—the face of a mannequin—Angela was reminded again of the toys of her childhood, the dolls whose china heads she had smashed open against rocks just to see the glass eyes spring out and roll away.

Dinner was pleasant. They knew a dozen people in the restaurant, they waved to them. The Bartons, their neighbors down the hall, joined them in the bar for an after-dinner brandy. It was the sort of evening Angela liked best—lively, amusing, time filled with people who were not close to you. Nice people, people you liked, people who were gone before they became tiresome.

Vicky's moodiness vanished. She talked gaily with the Bartons, laughing at their long stories of misfortune and confusion during a trip to Hong Kong.

By eleven they were home. "Huuuu." Angela closed the door and leaned against it. "I am tired!" She stretched, rubbed her eyes. "Bed is going to feel so good."

They had separate bedrooms now that the first frenzy of love had passed and they no longer required a presence within arm's reach all night. Angela shook her head, still puzzled by the lust of those early years, the rhythmic beating of blood that silenced everything else. They had been, she thought, more than a little crazy.

Eventually balance and control had come back. Or was it weariness? Angela yawned. Age and habit finally muffled everything, that was sure.

She ran her bath, poured in oil, and eased herself into the slippery tub, sighing with comfort. These pleasures were becoming more and more important to her—the perfumed hot tub, the wide bed all to herself, the smooth cool sheets with their embroidered edges.

She soaked, half asleep, remembering the first time she met Vicky, fifteen years ago. It seemed even longer than that, all the figures were fuzzy and out of focus, softened by time and distance.

It was a Thursday. Angela and Neal always went out to dinner on Thursday. Their ten-year-old daughter stayed with the housekeeper, Felicia, a thin pious spinster who left the house only for early Sunday mass, who never touched the television, and who turned on the radio only for the evening rosary in Spanish. All her salary went into a savings account. One day she would return to Guatemala and start a shop, a fabric shop that also sold candies and baked goods, she told Angela. But years passed and Felicia did not go home. She seemed to have forgotten her plans. After the divorce she stayed with Neal and the child. When they moved, she went with them. She was still there; Louise's letters mentioned her occasionally: "Felicia, dour as ever."

On that Thursday night fifteen years ago, the night her life changed, Angela and her husband had dinner early and went to the University Theater for a production of *The Glass Menagerie*, directed by Neal's sister. Angela was bored: the actors were painfully amateur, the staging was awkward. Still, remembering Neal's sister, she applauded dutifully and smiled and tried very hard to be encouraging. Afterwards they went to the cast party in the student center, where they hugged and kissed everybody and laughed loudly and made silly toasts in beer. And Angela met Vicky.

She remembered the exact moment she first saw her—a jolt, a shock. Too violent to be pleasant. (Vicky remembered it differently: "I didn't notice you until you spoke to me, Angela. And then I thought you had a lovely voice.")

Angela remembered it all—the way the room smelled: beer, dust, sweat, the sourish odor of makeup, the sweet smell of cold cream. Somebody broke a confetti egg against the roof and bits of colored paper whirled in the air like bright midges. Neal and his sister were at the bar filling their mugs, laughing and talking as they worked their way through the crowd. A group of student stagehands in T-shirts and blue jeans gathered in one corner, fifteen or twenty of them, stretched on the dusty floor, perched on the windowsills. Vicky was there. She was standing in the bewildered way that was so characteristic of her, hands limply at her sides, a small frail figure in large overalls, dark hair cut short in fashionable imitation of Mia Farrow. She seemed utterly alone in the midst of the crowd.

Angela walked briskly across the room and touched Vicky's sleeve. "I feel that I know you," she said. "Isn't your name Vicky?"

"No," Vicky said.

"It should be. Vicky Prescott."

"It's not."

"It is now," Angela said. "I just gave you a new name."

Three months later they moved into a small apartment near the campus. Angela took four suitcases of clothes—nothing else—with her.

When she told Neal, he said nothing, absolutely nothing. His face froze, then gradually drained of color until the bones showed as dark shadows. His lips turned white and then a clear pale blue. Without a word he went upstairs into the bedroom and locked the door.

Felicia said he stayed in the room all that day, and there hadn't been a sound. The morning of the second day he appeared at breakfast, he read the paper and talked with his daughter; he asked Felicia formally to stay on as housekeeper, and he drove the child to school. She was delighted; usually she took the bus.

A year later, to the day, Neal sued for divorce. Angela did not contest child custody, finding that weekend afternoons with her daughter were quite enough. She and Neal met occasionally at lunch to agree on the details of the dissolution of their marriage. "You know I have quite enough income of my own," she told him. "I do not think I should ask you for anything."

He nodded gravely. (He seemed to have become very ponderous and solemn, she thought.) "When will you come to the house to select the things you want to keep?"

She shook her head.

"Things of sentimental value? Things from your family?"

"There is nothing," she said. "Nothing at all."

Three years later Neal moved to the West Coast, to begin his own consulting firm. Angela supervised the packing and the moving. And declined again the offer of furniture. Neal kissed her good-bye on one cheek, her daughter on the other. (Vicky had not come, she had always refused to meet Neal.) Then they were gone, astonished at how very simple and easy it all had been.

Six months later there was a formal announcement of Neal's marriage. After that, from a distance, Angela saw her daughter through the rituals of growing up—birthday presents, summer visits, graduation presents, wedding presents. All conducted quietly and factually and coolly, like the business transactions they really were.

Drowsy and comforted by the warm perfumed waters, Angela left the tub, toweled carelessly, reached for a nightgown without looking at it.

She patted the heavy embroidery on the edge of the sheet once or twice and fell into a deep black sleep.

When Vicky slipped into her bed next to her, she scarcely stirred. "Tomorrow." She pulled away. "Vicky, it's late and I'm tired."

"I don't want to make love," Vicky whispered so close to her ear that her breath tickled unpleasantly.

"You can't be this spoiled," Angela muttered. "Go away."

"I have to talk to you." There was that rasping note of decision in the soft voice.

Oh, oh, oh, Angela thought in her comfortable sleepy haze, I hope this isn't going to be one of Vicky's long rambling middle-of-the-night talks. "I'm dead tired, Vicky. You can't be this selfish."

"I have to talk to you now." The small voice was cool and steady.

Well, Angela thought, maybe it won't be such a long talk. . . . She rolled over, reaching for the lamp switch. Vicky's hand closed over hers, stopping it.

"No. I want to talk in the dark," Vicky said. "I always talk better in the dark."

"You always talk longer in the dark." Angela squinted at the green dial on the clock: three-fifteen. "I've got a nine-fifteen appointment, and just look at the time."

"Now," Vicky repeated.

Angela sighed deeply, pulled the pillows up behind her, and settled back against them. For a moment she dozed—then shook herself awake. Vicky remained curled in the middle of the bed.

"My dear," Angela said, stifling a yawn, "this had better be important or I am going to be perfectly furious with you."

"I want a child," Vicky said. "I want to get pregnant."

In the silence a far-off clock ticked steadily. A police siren waved a thin finger of sound down a distant street.

"That is important," Angela said dryly.

Vicky was silent, unmoving.

"Is there anything more you want?"

A small despairing hiss, like air from a balloon. "I knew you'd misunderstand."

"You must give me a moment," Angela said, "to catch up with you." (Is this how Neal felt when I told him—when the unthinkable happens?)

"I knew you'd be angry . . . and I knew you'd misunderstand. I've been dreading this so much that I've been putting it off and putting it off. For months. I just couldn't tell you."

"You have lost your mind."

The bed moved slightly. Vicky was shaking her head. "I don't want to want a child, you see. I know it would be trouble, and I thought you might even leave."

Did you? Angela thought. I don't believe that.

"It got so bad, I even began going to a psychiatrist."

"I didn't know."

"I thought at first it would go away, so I waited. But it didn't. I thought about a tranquilizer or an energizer or lithium if I was really crazy."

"A strange pharmacopoeia," Angela said into the dark. "Was the shrink any help?"

"No drugs," Vicky said sadly, raising her head slightly so that she showed briefly as a silhouette against the pale yellow wallpaper. "He said it would be months or years before anything could change. If then."

"No help from him."

"No," Vicky said.

The clock was still ticking, but the siren had vanished. The room was filled with a faint humming, the building's air-conditioning system. Like the far-off hum of bees, Angela thought. There'd been hives on her family's summer place in Maine.

Vicky was talking again, rapidly, slurring her words. Angela noticed the heavy smell of brandy. She'd been drinking, and she probably hadn't been to bed at all.

"I didn't want you to be angry. I tried every way I knew. But nothing helped. It's even getting worse."

"The urge to procreate."

Vicky sobbed softly.

Dear God, Angela thought, if I still believed in you, I would think that you are punishing me for my sins. But I left Sunday school too long ago for that. . . .

"You've got to understand," Vicky said. "You've always helped before. Even when my parents died. You were so kind then."

They'd been killed in a highway accident and Vicky, wild with grief, neither ate nor slept. Finally Angela took her, dizzy with Librium, for a six months' trip through Europe. They worked their way page by page through the points of interest listed in their Baedekers. They climbed mountains, hiked through forests, they exhausted themselves in the thin Jura air and staggered through the smells of Naples.

"Listen to me now." Vicky spoke clearly and slowly, as if she were instructing a child. "I am thirty-six. How much longer can I have children. One child. I feel, I don't know, I feel hollow and empty and useless. Sometimes I feel so light I think the wind will blow me away."

"It won't," Angela said.

"You have a child." The harsh accusation startled Angela. "You have a child. Every time a letter comes from her, every time she telephones and talks to us, I want to die. Because I have nothing."

Nothing, Angela thought dully, sadly. You have me. And your career. You are the owner of a very successful shop. You have friends. You have a lovely apartment. And just today I saw a carriage house uptown, not too large, early nineteenth century, with lovely cypress woodwork, and a garden that is completely enclosed by a high brick wall, a perfect house for us. And you have love.

"Nothing," Vicky repeated as if she had heard.

"I'm going to get a drink."

"Take mine." Vicky put her glass carefully into Angela's hand. "I want you to understand, but I'm not saying it very well."

"I understand," Angela said.

"No," Vicky said. "I love my life. I love you and I love my work. There isn't anybody else, you know that. I make more money every year. So it isn't any of the things it's supposed to be—not sex, not money, not boredom."

"That what the psychiatrist said?" Angela drained the glass, almost choking on the straight brandy. She hated drinking like this, in a race for comfort.

"Not exactly, but I guess so, really."

"Look, Vicky." Angela tried to put the glass on the night table, missed in the dark, and heard the glass roll across the rug. "It's late, we have to work tomorrow. Why don't we both come home early and have a sensible discussion."

"No," Vicky said. "I know what I'm going to do."

"Get pregnant?"

"Yes." The darkness and the small voice and the absolute determination.

I am angry, Angela thought, I am white hot and frozen with anger. "You seem to have thought it out. Have you decided how? I mean, you are an attractive woman, you can certainly find a man. You could even shop around until you found a man whose face you'd like to have repeated in a child."

A small sigh. And silence. Vicky was not going to be lured into an argument.

"I suppose," Angela went on, "you could always have it done artificially. Like a cow."

This time Vicky was silent so long that Angela thought that she had fallen into a drunken sleep. Her own eyelids strained in the confining dark, dry and aching.

Eventually Vicky said, "At least then my bones and blood will be quiet."

"Just what I always wanted: quiet blood." Angela bounced out of bed, went to the pantry. She poured a large brandy, noticing that the bottle was almost empty. I ought to get out, she thought, I ought to take the car and go for a long drive and just keep driving around until things make more sense to me.

But she didn't. She went back into the bedroom. "Time's winged chariot."

"It's like being thirsty," Vicky said. "You have to have water."

"Brandy. Do you know how much brandy you've drunk? The bottle is almost empty."

"To give me courage," Vicky said simply.

And there it was, the tone, the motion, the gesture that ended all discussion, all argument. Why am I like this, Angela thought, why can she always do this to me. . . . Why does she turn me around? Why can't I leave, even for a drive. Is there so much of my life invested here?

"You are proposing that you and I raise this child together?"

"Yes," Vicky said. "At first I thought you might want to leave, but now I don't think so. I think it will be all right and you will love the child because it's half me."

"Jesus Christ." Angela made another trip to the pantry to empty the bottle of brandy into her glass and top it with soda and the bits of ice that remained in the bucket. The clock there said four-thirty.

Vicky uncurled and lay stretched crosswise on the foot of the bed. Angela sat down Indian-fashion to keep from touching her. "All right, Vicky, we'll raise the child together. If that's what you want."

Vicky's voice was thick with sleep and alcohol. "I knew you would."

"How the hell could you know that?"

Vicky stretched and prepared to fall asleep where she was. "I knew."

Do you know how much of my life I have invested in you? Do you? You, a small arrangement of bones and skin and flesh and blood that I would kill if it would free me. But it wouldn't.

Vicky lay so still Angela thought she had fallen asleep. She got up slowly, carefully, not to disturb her, and began tiptoeing toward the door.

Vicky said clearly, without the slur of alcohol, "You're going to love the child. And I'm going to come to hate it."

"Go to sleep, Vicky." And stop talking, let me alone for a while anyway. Before something I can't imagine or control happens . . .

"You're going to love the part that's me, and I'm going to hate the part that isn't you."

"Vicky, you are terribly drunk. You're not making sense."

"I want your child," Vicky said. "A child that's you and me. Now tell me why that's so stupid."

And with a slight movement and a small sigh, she turned face down and fell asleep. The mattress moved softly with her sudden increase in weight.

Angela went into the living room. She felt strange and detached and very calm. She opened the curtains and stared at the city that stretched beyond the pale reflection of herself. She raised an arm, saluting herself in the imperfect mirror. She was breathing regularly and slowly, all anger and fear were gone. But the moving arm didn't belong to her, nor did that figure reflected distantly back to her.

Traffic flickered slowly through the leaf-obscured streets, lights were beginning to show in some of the distant hill houses, it would not be long until daylight.

She sat at her desk and began a note to Mrs. Papadopoulous, saying that Vicky was not to be disturbed, no matter how long she slept. She herself would call the shop to tell them that Miss Prescott would be late, if indeed she came in at all today, please do not call, any decisions can wait until tomorrow.

She watched the sky. Despite the brandy, she was not drunk, she wasn't even tired. Her mind moved lightly, decisively, thoughts clicking like high heels on marble.

When the first gray morning streaks showed, she would make coffee and scramble a couple of eggs. She would shower and dress, and go to her office earlier than usual. She would finish the paperwork there and then she would make an offer for that uptown carriage house, whose small walled garden would be a lovely safe place for a child to play.

THE STORY OF AN HOUR

by

KATE CHOPIN
(1850–1904)

In the past few years Kate Chopin has been rediscovered. Her novel The Awakening *(1899) has had several editions, and Per Seyersted edited her collected works and a selection,* The Storm and Other Stories *(1974), for* The Feminist Press. *Chopin shows the difficulties a woman trying to be herself faces in a traditional society such as that of New Orleans. She wrote most of her works as a widow with six children.*

Knowing that Mrs. Mallard was afflicted with a heart trouble, great care was taken to break to her as gently as possible the news of her husband's death.

It was her sister Josephine who told her, in broken sentences; veiled hints that revealed in half concealing. Her husband's friend Richards was there, too, near her. It was he who had been in the newspaper office when intelligence of the railroad disaster was received, with Brently Mallard's name leading the list of "killed." He had only taken the time to assure himself of its truth by a second telegram, and had hastened to forestall any less careful, less tender friend in bearing the sad message.

She did not hear the story as many women have heard the same, with a paralyzed inability to accept its significance. She wept at once, with sudden, wild abandonment, in her sister's arms. When the storm of grief had spent itself she went away to her room alone. She would have no one follow her.

There stood, facing the open window, a comfortable, roomy armchair. Into this she sank, pressed down by a physical exhaustion that haunted her body and seemed to reach into her soul.

She could see in the open square before her house the tops of trees that were all aquiver with the new spring life. The delicious breath of rain was in the air. In the street below a peddler was crying his wares.

The notes of a distant song which some one was singing reached her faintly, and countless sparrows were twittering in the eaves.

There were patches of blue sky showing here and there through the clouds that had met and piled one above the other in the west facing her window.

She sat with her head thrown back upon the cushion of the chair, quite motionless, except when a sob came up into her throat and shook her, as a child who has cried itself to sleep continues to sob in its dreams.

She was young, with a fair, calm face, whose lines bespoke repression and even a certain strength. But now there was a dull stare in her eyes, whose gaze was fixed away off yonder on one of those patches of blue sky. It was not a glance of reflection, but rather indicated a suspension of intelligent thought.

There was something coming to her and she was waiting for it, fearfully. What was it? She did not know; it was too subtle and elusive to name. But she felt it, creeping out of the sky, reaching toward her through the sounds, the scents, the color that filled the air.

Now her bosom rose and fell tumultuously. She was beginning to recognize this thing that was approaching to possess her, and she was striving to beat it back with her will—as powerless as her two white slender hands would have been.

When she abandoned herself a little whispered word escaped her slightly parted lips. She said it over and over under her breath: "free, free, free!" The vacant stare and the look of terror that had followed it went from her eyes. They stayed keen and bright. Her pulses beat fast, and the coursing blood warmed and relaxed every inch of her body.

She did not stop to ask if it were or were not a monstrous joy that held her. A clear and exalted perception enabled her to dismiss the suggestion as trivial.

She knew that she would weep again when she saw the kind, tender hands folded in death; the face that had never looked save with love upon her, fixed and gray and dead. But she saw beyond that bitter moment a long procession of years to come that would belong to her absolutely. And she opened and spread her arms out to them in welcome.

There would be no one to live for her during those coming years; she would live for herself. There would be no powerful will bending hers in that blind persistence with which men and women believe they have a right to impose a private will upon a fellow-creature. A kind intention or a cruel intention made the act seem no less a crime as she looked upon it in that brief moment of illumination.

And yet she had loved him—sometimes. Often she had not. What did it matter! What could love, the unsolved mystery, count for in face of this possession of self-assertion which she suddenly recognized as the strongest impulse of her being!

"Free! Body and soul free!" she kept whispering.

Josephine was kneeling before the closed door with her lips to the keyhole, imploring for admission. "Louise, open the door! I beg; open the door—you will make yourself ill. What are you doing, Louise? For heaven's sake open the door."

"Go away. I am not making myself ill." No; she was drinking in a very elixir of life through that open window.

Her fancy was running riot along those days ahead of her. Spring days, and summer days, and all sorts of days that would be her own. She breathed a quick prayer that life might be long. It was only yesterday she had thought with a shudder that life might be long.

She rose at length and opened the door to her sister's importunities. There was a feverish triumph in her eyes, and she carried herself unwittingly like a goddess of Victory. She clasped her sister's waist, and together they descended the stairs. Richards stood waiting for them at the bottom.

Some one was opening the front door with a latchkey. It was Brently Mallard who entered, a little travel-stained, composedly carrying his grip-sack and umbrella. He had been far from the scene of the accident, and did not even know there had been one. He stood amazed at Josephine's piercing cry; at Richards' quick motion to screen him from the view of his wife.

But Richards was too late.

When the doctors came they said she had died of heart disease—of joy that kills.

THE WIDOW'S LAMENT
IN SPRINGTIME

by

WILLIAM CARLOS WILLIAMS
(1883–1963)

Even though he was a hard-working New Jersey physician, William Carlos Williams managed to write more than twenty-five volumes of poetry and fiction. His epic poem Paterson *(1946–1958) reflects his knowledge of and compassion for people, his sense of history, and his use of the language and rhythms of speech.*

Sorrow is my own yard
where the new grass
flames as it has flamed
often before but not
with the cold fire
that closes round me this year.
Thirtyfive years
I lived with my husband.
The plumtree is white today
with masses of flowers.
Masses of flowers
load the cherry branches
and color some bushes
yellow and some red
but the grief in my heart
is stronger than they
for though they were my joy
formerly, today I notice them
and turned away forgetting.
Today my son told me

that in the meadows,
at the edge of the heavy woods
in the distance, he saw
trees of white flowers.
I feel that I would like
to go there
and fall into those flowers
and sink into the marsh near them.

MOURNING TO DO

by

MAY SARTON
(b. 1912)

Born in Belgium, May Sarton came to Cambridge, Massachusetts, in 1916 and was educated there before going to New York City to study acting. She left the theater in 1937 to become a writer; she has been prolific as a poet, novelist, and autobiographer. She has lectured widely and has received many fellowships, awards, and honorary doctorates. Her novel The Education of Harriet Hatfield *(1989) is about a sixty-year-old lesbian who learns about homophobia when running a bookstore. Her autobiographical works focus on her solitary life in York, Maine; she vividly reports thoughts on aging and illness.*

The new year and a fresh fall of snow,
The new year and mourning to do
Alone here in the lovely silent house,
Alone as the inner eye opens at last—
Not as the shutter of a camera with a click,
But like a gentle waking in a dark room
Before dawn when familiar objects take on
Substance out of their shadowy corners
And come to life. So with my lost love,
For years lost in the darkness of her mind,
Tied to a wheelchair, not knowing where she was
Or who she had been when we lived together
In amity, peaceful as turtledoves.

Judy is dead.   Judy is gone forever.

I cannot fathom that darkness, nor know
Whether the true spirit is alive again.
But what I do know is the peace of it,
And in the darkened room before dawn, I lie

Awake and let the good tears flow at last,
And as light touches the chest of drawers
And the windows grow transparent, rest,
Happy to be mourning what was singular
And comforting as the paintings on the wall,
All that can now come to life in my mind,
Good memories fresh and sweet as the dawn—
Judy drinking her tea with a cat on her lap,
And our many little walks before suppertime.
So it is now the gentle waking to what was,
And what is and will be as long as I am alive.
"Happy grieving," someone said who knew—
Happy the dawn of memory and the sunrise.

OLD THINGS

by

BOBBIE ANN MASON
(b. 1940)

*Bobbie Ann Mason's writing focuses on people on the farms and in
the small towns of her native Kentucky. She completed her doctorate at the University of Connecticut in 1972 and has taught English
and journalism at Mansfield State College in Pennsylvania, where
she now lives. Her stories began winning awards in 1981, and she
has held fellowships from the National Endowment for the Arts
and the Guggenheim Foundation. In 1982* Shiloh and Other Stories
*won the Ernest Hemingway award for the most distinguished first
work of fiction. Mason has published a scholarly book,* The Girl
Sleuth: A Feminist Guide to Detective Fiction *(1982); a novel
about Vietnam,* In Country *(1985); a novella,* Spence + Lila *(1988);
and a second collection of short stories,* Love Life *(1988).*

Cleo Watkins makes invisible, overlapping rings on the table with her
cup as she talks.

"The kids just got off to school and I'm still in one piece," she says.
"Last night we was up till all hours watching that special and my eyes is
pasted together this morning. After the weekend we've been through,
now everybody's going off and I'll be so lonesome all day!"

Cleo puts her elbow on the kitchen table and switches the receiver to
the other ear. Her friend Rita Jean Wiggins says she had trouble getting
her car started yesterday in time for church; it flooded and she had to let
it sit for a while. Rita Jean is worried sick about her cat Dexter and is
going to take him to the vet again. As Cleo listens, she notices that Tom
Brokaw is introducing a guest who is going to talk about men as single
parents. Cleo doesn't know whether to listen to Tom or Rita Jean. For a
minute she loses the train of Rita Jean's story.

"Just a minute, I better turn this television down." Cleo crosses the
kitchen and lowers the volume. "This house is such a mess," says Cleo,
sitting down again. "And you don't know how embarrassing it all is—
Linda's car here all the time, the kids going in and out. She's making an
old woman out of me."

"Did she bring much from home?" Rita Jean asks.

"Mostly things the kids needed, and a lot of her clothes," Cleo says, watching the faces move on the television screen. "I told her wasn't no use carrying all that over here, they'd be going back before long, but she wouldn't listen. You can't walk here."

Rita Jean's voice is sympathetic. "I'm sure she'll get straightened out with Bob in no time."

"I don't know. Looks like she's moved in. She went to trade day out here at the stockyard, and she come back with the awfulest conglomeration you ever saw."

"What all did she get?"

"A rocking chair she's going to refinish, and a milk glass lamp, and some kind of whatnot, and a big grabbag—a box of junk you buy for a dollar and then there might be one thing in it you want. I never saw such par'phenalin."

"Was there anything in it she could use?" asks Rita Jean. Rita Jean, who has no children, is always intensely concerned about Cleo's family.

"She found a wood spoon she said was antique."

"People are antique-crazy."

"You're telling me." Cleo has spent years trying to get rid of things she has collected. After her husband died, she moved to town, to a little brick house with a dishwasher and wall-to-wall carpet. Cleo's two sons haven't mentioned it, but Linda says it's awful that Cleo has gotten rid of every reminder of Jake. There is nothing but the picture album left. All his suits were given away, and the rest of his things boxed up and sold. She gave away all his handkerchiefs, neatly washed and ironed. They were monogrammed with the initials RJW, for Robert Jacob Watkins. And now somebody with totally different initials is carrying them around and blowing his nose on them. Linda reminds her of this every so often but Cleo isn't sorry. She doesn't want to live in the past.

After talking to Rita Jean, Cleo cleans the house with unusual attention. The kids have scattered their things everywhere. Cleo hangs up Tammy's clothes and puts Davey's toys in the trunk Linda has brought. The trunk is yellow enamel with thin black swirls that make it look old. Linda has antiqued it.

Cleo pins patterns down on the length of material laid on the table. She is cutting out a set of cheerleader outfits that have to be done by next week. The cheeerleader outfits are red and gray, made like bib overalls, with shorts. Everything is double seams, and the bibs have pockets with flaps.

"Get down from there, Prissy-Tail!" The cat has attacked the flimsy pattern and torn it. "You know you're not supposed to be on Mama's sewing." Cleo waves the scissors at Prissy-Tail, who scampers onto Cleo's shoulder. Cleo sets her down on a pillow, saying, "I can't cut out with you dancing on my shoulder." Prissy-Tail struts around on the divan, purring.

"I could tell you things that would sizzle your tailfeathers," Cleo says.

Cleo backs in the front door, pulling the storm door shut with her foot. On TV there is a wild west shoot-out, and the radio is blaring out an accompanying song with a heavy, driving beat. Tammy is talking on the telephone.

"What do you mean, what do I mean? Oh, you know what I mean. Anyway, we're at my grandmother's and my mother's going out tonight—Davey, quit it!—that was my little brother. He's a meanie. I just stuck my tongue out at him. Anyway, do you think he'll ask you or what? Unh-huh. That's what I thought."

Cleo stands in the hallway, adjusting to the sounds. Tammy's patter on the phone is meaningless to her. Linda had never done that. Linda had been such a quiet child. She hears Tammy speaking in a knowing tone.

"You know what April told Kevin? I nearly died! Kevin was going to ask her for her homework? And he said to her could she meet him at the Dairy Queen and she said she might and she might not, and he said to her could she carry him because his car was broke down? And she said he had legs, he could walk! I think he's mad at her."

"Watch out, Tammy, I'm coming through," says Cleo. Davey has returned to the television, and Tammy is sprawled out in the kitchen doorway. Tammy is wearing ripped bluejeans and a velour pullover with stripes down the sleeves. Tammy bends her knees so half the doorway is clear, and Cleo squeezes by, balancing the groceries on her hip.

Tammy hangs up and pokes into the grocery sack. "Chicken! Not again!"

"Chicken was ninety-nine cents a pound," says Cleo. "You better be glad you're where there's food on the table, kid."

"Ick! All that yellow fat."

"The yellower a chicken is, the better it is. That's how you tell when they're good. If they're blue they're not any 'count. Or if they've got spots."

"Oooh!" Tammy makes a twisted face. "Why can't you just buy it already fried?"

"Hah! We're lucky we don't have to pull the feathers off. I used to kill chickens, you know. Whack their heads off, dip 'em in boiling water, pick off the feathers. I'd like to see you pick a chicken!"

Cleo reaches around Tammy and hugs her. Tammy squeals. "Hey, why don't we just eat the cat?"

"Now you're going to hurt somebody's feelings," says Cleo, as Tammy squirms away from her.

Tammy prances out of the room and the noises return. The television; the radio; the buzz of the electric clock; the whir of the furnace making its claim for attention. The kids never hear the noises. Kids never seem to care about anything anymore, Cleo thinks. Tammy had a complete toy kitchen, with a stove and refrigerator, when she was five, and she didn't care anything about it. It cost a fortune. Linda's children always make Cleo feel old.

BOBBIE ANN MASON

421

"I'm old enough to be a grandmother," Rita Jean said early in their acquaintance. Rita Jean had lost her husband, too.

"I think of you as a spring chicken," Cleo told her.

"You're not that much older than me. Louise Brown is two years younger than me, and she's a grandmother. Imagine, thirty-five and a grandmother."

"That makes me feel old."

"I feel old," said Rita Jean. "To think that the war could be that long ago."

Rita Jean's husband was twenty-one when he left for Vietnam. It was early in the war and nobody thought it would turn out so bad. She has a portrait on her dresser of a young man she hardly knew, a child almost. Now Rita Jean is old enough to be the mother of a boy like that.

Cleo told Rita Jean she could still get married and have a baby. She could start all over again.

"If anybody would have me," said Rita Jean.

"You don't try."

"Sometimes I think I'm just waiting to get into Senior Citizens."

"Listen to yourself," said Cleo. "That's the most ridiculous thing I ever heard. Why, *I'm* not but fifty-two."

"They say that's the prime of life," said Rita Jean.

"Where are you going, Mama? Tell me where you're going." Davey is pulling at Linda's belt.

"Oh, Davey, look. You're going to mess up Mama's outfit. I told you seven times, Shirley and me's going to Paducah to hear some music. It's not anything you're interested in, so don't be saying you want to go too."

Linda has washed her hair and put on a new pants suit, a tangerine color. Cleo knows Linda cannot afford it, but Linda always has to have the best.

Tammy, sitting with her legs propped up on the back of the divan, says, with mock surprise, "You mean you're going to miss *Charlie's Angels*? You ain't *never* missed *Charlie's Angels*!"

"Them younguns want you to stay home," Cleo says as Linda combs her hair. It is wet and falls in skinny black ringlets.

"I can't see what difference it makes." Linda lights a cigarette.

"These children need a daddy around."

"You're full of prunes if you think I'm going back to Bob!" Linda says, turning on the blow dryer. She raises her voice. "I don't feel like hanging around the same house with somebody that can go for three hours without saying a word. He might as well not be there."

"Hush. The children might hear you."

Linda works on her hair, holding out damp strands and brushing them under with the dryer to style them. Cleo admires the way her daughter keeps up her appearance. She can't imagine Bob would ever look at another woman when he has Linda. Cleo cannot believe Bob has mistreated

Linda. It is just as though she has been told some wild tale about outer space, like something on a TV show.

Cleo says, "I bet he's just held in and held in till he's tight as a tick. People do that. I know you—impatient. Listen. A man takes care of a woman. But it works the other way round too. If he thinks you're not giving him enough loving, he'll draw up—just like a morning glory at evening. You think he's not paying any attention to you, but maybe you've been too busy for him."

Cleo knows Linda thinks she is silly. Daughters never believe their mothers. "You have to remember to give each other some loving," she says, her confidence fading. "Don't take each other for granted."

"Bob's no morning glory." Linda puts on lip gloss and works her lips together.

"You'll be wondering how to buy them kids fine things. You'll be off on your own, girl."

Linda says nothing. She examines her face in the mirror and picks at a speck on her cheek.

Davey gets his lessons on the floor in front of the television. He is learning a new kind of arithmetic Cleo has never heard of. Later, Cleo watches *Charlie's Angels* with Tammy, and after Tammy goes to bed, she watches the *10 O'Clock Report*. She tells herself that she has to wait up to unlock the doors for Linda. She has put a chain on the door, because young people are going wild, breaking in on defenseless older women. Cleo is afraid Linda's friend Shirley is a bad influence. Shirley had to get married and didn't finish school. Now she is divorced. She even let her husband have her kids, while she went gallivanting around. Cleo cannot imagine a mother giving her kids away. Shirley's husband moved to Alabama with the kids, and Shirley sees them only occasionally. On TV, Johnny Carson keeps breaking into the funny dance he does when a joke flops. Cleo usually gets a kick out of that, but it doesn't seem funny this time, with him repeating it so much. Johnny has been divorced twice, but now he is happily married. He is the stay-at-home type, she has read.

Cleo is well into the *Tomorrow* show, which is a disturbing discussion of teenage alcoholism, when Linda returns. Linda's cheeks are glowing and she looks happy.

"I thought Duke Ellington was dead," says Cleo, when Linda tells her about the concert.

"He is. But his brother leads the band. He directs the band like this." Linda makes her hands dive in fishlike movements. "He danced around, with his back to the audience, swaying along in a trance. He had on this dark pink suit the exact same color of Miss Imogene's panties that time in fifth grade—when she fell off the desk?"

Cleo groans. Everything seems to distress her, she notices. She is afraid Linda has been drinking.

BOBBIE ANN MASON

423

"And the band had this great singer!" Linda goes on. "She wore a tight skullcap with sequins on it? And a brown tuxedo, and she sounded for all the world like Ella Fitzgerald. Boy, was she sexy. She had a real deep voice, but she could go real high at times."

Linda unscrews the top of a quart of Coke and pours herself a glass. She drinks the Coke thirstily. "I wouldn't be explaining all this to you if you had gone. I tried to get you to go with me."

"And leave the kids here?" Cleo turns off the TV.

"Shirley had on the darlingest outfit. It had these pleats—what do you want, Davey?"

Davey is trailing a quilt into the living room. "I couldn't sleep," he whines. "The big girls was going to get me."

"He means Charlie's Angels," says Cleo. "We were watching them and they kept him awake."

"He's had a bad dream. Here, hon." Linda hugs Davey and takes him back to bed.

"I worked myself to death yesterday getting this house in shape and it looks like a cyclone hit it," Cleo says to Rita Jean on the telephone the next morning. "First, tell me how's Dexter."

Cleo listens to Rita Jean's account of Dexter's trip to the vet. "He said there's nothing to do now but wait. He's not suffering any, and the vet said it would be all right if I keep him at home. He's asleep most of the time. He's the pitifulest thing."

Rita Jean's cat is thirteen. After the news came from Vietnam, Rita Jean got a cat and then another cat when the first one got run over. The present cat she has kept in the house all its life.

"The one thing about cats," says Cleo, trying to sound comforting, "is that there's more where that one come from. You'll grieve, but you'll get over it and get you another cat."

"I guess so."

Cleo tells about Linda's night out. "She was dolled up so pretty, she looked like she was going out on a date. It made me feel so funny. She had on a new pants suit. The kids didn't want her to go, either. They know something's wrong. They never miss a thing."

"Kids don't miss much," Rita Jean agrees.

"And how in the world does she think they can afford to keep on like they've been doing? But I think they'll get back together."

"Surely they will."

"Knock on wood." Cleo has to stretch to reach the door facing. She is getting a headache. Absently, she watches the *Today* credits roll by as Rita Jean tells about her brother's trip out West. He tried to get her to go along, but she couldn't think of closing her house up and she wouldn't leave Dexter. "They went to the Grand Canyon and Yosemite and a bunch of other places," Rita Jean says. "You should see the load of pictures they took. They must of takened a bushel."

"It must be something to be able to take off like that," Cleo says. "I never had the chance when we lived on the farm, but now there are too many maniacs on the road." Cleo sips her coffee, knowing it will aggravate her headache. "The way things are going around here, I think maybe I ought to go out West. I think I'll just get me a wig and go running around!" Cleo laughs at herself, but a pain jabs at her temple. Rita Jean laughs, and Cleo goes on, "I thinks Linda's going to have it out with Bob finally. They're going to meet over at the lake one day next week. It wasn't none of my business, but I tried to tell her she ought to simmer down and think it over."

"I think they'll patch it up, Cleo. I really do."

"That Bob Isbell was always the best thing!" Cleo leans back in her chair, almost dreamily. "I tell you, girl, I couldn't have survived if it hadn't been for him when Jake passed away. He was here every hour; he seen to it that we all got to where we was going; he took care of the house here and then went back and took care of their house. He was even washing dishes. Davey was little-bitty then. Of course, none of us could think straight and we didn't see right then all he was doing, but don't you know we appreciated it. I never will forget how good he was."

"He always was good to the kids."

"They had to pinch them pennies, but those kids never did without. He makes good at the lumberyard, and with what Linda brings in from the K Mart, they're pretty well off. That house is just as fine as can be—and Linda walks off and leaves it! You just can't tell me he done her that way, the way she said. And she don't seem to care!"

"She's keeping it in."

"I keep halfway expecting Bob to pull in the driveway, but he hasn't called or said boo to the kids or anything. I don't want to run them out, but I'll be glad when they get this thing worked out! They're tearing up jack! There's always something a-going. A washing machine or the dishwasher. The television, of course. I never saw so many dishes as these younguns can mess up. I never aimed to be feeding Coxey's Army! And they just strow like you've never seen. Right through the middle of the living room. Here comes one dropping this and that, and then right behind here comes the other one. Prissy-Tail's got her tail tied up in knots with all the combustion here!"

Cleo stands up. She has to get an aspirin. "Well, I'll let you get back to your doodling!"

When Cleo starts toward the refrigerator to get ice water, Prissy-Tail bounds straight out of the living room and beats her to the refrigerator.

"You're going to throw me down," she cries.

She gives Prissy-Tail some milk and takes two aspirins. Phil Donahue is talking to former dope addicts. Cleo turns off the TV and finishes her coffee. She looks around at all the extra objects that have accumulated. A tennis racket. Orange-and-blue-striped shoes. Bluejeans in heaps like rag dolls. Tammy's snapshots scattered around on the divan and end tables.

BOBBIE ANN MASON

425

A collapsible plaid suitcase. Tote bags with dirty clothes streaming out the tops. Davey's Star Wars toys and his red computer toy that resembles a Princess phone. Tammy's Minute Maker camera. Cleo has forgotten how to move effortlessly through the clutter children make. She pours more coffee and looks at the mail. She looks at a mail-order catalog which specializes in household gadgets. She is impressed with the number of things you can buy to help you organize things, items such as plastic pockets for grocery coupons and accessory chests for closets. She spends a long time then studying the luxurious compartments of a Winnebago in a magazine ad. She imagines traveling out West in it, doing her cooking in the tiny kitchen, but she can't think why she would be going out West by herself.

The cheerleaders' outfits are taking a week. Everything has to be done over. Cleo puts zippers in upside down, allows too much on seams, has to cut plackets out twice. The cheerleaders come over for a fitting and everything is the wrong size. Cleo tells the cheerleaders, "I'm just like a wiggleworm in hot ashes." In comparison to the overalls, the blouses are easy, but she has trouble with the interfacing.

"You don't charge enough," Linda tells her. "You should charge twenty-five dollars apiece for those things."

"People here won't pay that much," Cleo says.

Linda is in and out. The kids visit Bob at home during the weekend. It is more peaceful, but it makes Cleo worry. She is almost glad when they return Sunday evening, carrying tote bags of clothes and playthings. Bob has taken them out for pizza every meal, and they turn up their noses at what she has on the table—fried channel cat and hush puppies. Linda doesn't eat either. She is going out with Shirley. Cleo gives Prissy-Tail more fish than she can eat.

"Smile, Grandma."

"Well, hurry up," Cleo says, her body poised as if about to take off and fly. "I can't hold like this all day."

"Just a minute." Tammy moves the camera around. It looks like the mask on a space suit. "Say cheese!"

Cleo holds her smile, which is growing halfhearted and strained. The camera clicks, and the flashbulb flares. Together, they watch the picture take shape. Like the dawn, it grows in intensity until finally Cleo's features appear. The Cleo in the picture stands there vacantly, like a scared cat.

"I look terrible," says Cleo.

"You look old, Grandma."

On the cheerleader outfits, Cleo is down to finger work. As she whips the facings, she imagines Bob alone in the big ranch house. What would a man do in a house like that by himself? Linda had left him late one night and brought Tammy and Davey over, right in the middle of *The Tonight Show* (John Davidson was the guest host). The children were half asleep. Cleo imagines them groggy and senseless, one day hooked on dope.

The cheerleader outfits are finished. There are some flaws, Cleo knows, where she has had to take out and put in again so many times, but she tells herself that only somebody who sews will notice them. She pulls out bright blue basting thread.

She does some wash, finishes this week's *Family Circle* and cuts out a hamburger casserole recipe she thinks the kids might like. She throws away the *Family Circle* and the old *TV Guide*. She carries out trash. Then she straightens up her sewing corner and sorts her threads. She collects Tammy's scattered pictures and puts them in a pile. As she tries to find a box they will fit in, she accidentally steps on the cat's tail. "Oh, I'm sorry!" she cries, shocked. Prissy-Tail hides under the couch. Cleo can't find a box the right size.

When the cheerleaders try on their new outfits, Cleo spots bits of blue basting thread she has missed. Embarrassed, she pulls out the threads. She knows the cheerleaders will go to the ball game and someone will see blue basting thread sticking out.

Later, thinking she will go to the show if there is a decent one on, Cleo drives to the shopping center. There isn't. An invasion from outer space and Jane Fonda. Cleo parks and goes to the K Mart. She waves at Linda, who is busy with a long line of people at her register. Cleo walks around the store and finds a picture album with plastic pockets for Tammy. She will pay for it with some of the money she collected from the cheerleaders. Davey will want something too, but she doesn't know what to buy that he will like. After rejecting all the toys she sees, she buys a striped turtleneck sweater on sale. The album and sweater are roughly the same price. She doesn't see Linda when she goes through the checkout line.

Cleo sits in the parking lot of the shopping center for a long time and then she goes home and makes the hamburger recipe.

"You all go on about your cats like they was babies," says Linda. Linda is sanding a rocking chair, which is upside down on newspapers in the hall.

"They're a heap sight less trouble," says Cleo, who is dusting. Rita Jean has called to say Dexter is home from the hospital, but there isn't much hope.

"Stop fanning doors, Tammy," Linda says. "Grandma's got a present for you."

Cleo brings out the picture album and the sweater.

"Now I want you to keep all them pictures in this," she tells Tammy. "Here, squirt," she says to Davey. "Here's something else for me to pick up."

The children take the presents wordlessly, examining them. Tammy turns the pages and pokes her fingers into the picture pockets. Davey rips the plastic wrapper off the sweater and holds it up. "It fits!" he says.

Davey turns on the television and Tammy sits on the divan, turning the empty pages of the picture album.

"You didn't have to do that," says Linda to Cleo.

"I'm just keeping up with the times," Cleo says. "Spend, spend, spend."

"Nothing wrong with keeping up with the times," says Linda.

"I see you are. With all that old-timey stuff you're collecting. Explain that."

"Everybody's going back to old-timey stuff. Furniture like yours is out of style."

"Then maybe one day it'll be antique. If I live that long." Cleo pokes the dusting broom at the ceiling.

"We're getting on your nerves," says Linda. "We're going to be getting out before long."

"I hope you mean going back home where you belong. Not that I mean to kick you out. You know what I mean."

"We're going back home, all right," Linda says. "This is the big night—I'm going to meet Bob at Kenlake. I'm going to have it out with him. I can't wait." She wipes the rocker with a rag and turns it right side up. "There, I think that's enough. What a job. If I could just find a twin to it. Tammy, turn that radio down; you're bothering Grandma."

Cleo has to sit down. She is out of breath. The broom falls to the floor as she sinks onto the divan. "I'm not sixteen anymore," she says. "I give out too quick."

"Mama, there's not a thing wrong with you. You just don't do anything with yourself."

"What do you mean?"

"Look at you; you're still a young woman. You could go to school, make a nurse or something. That Mrs. Smith over yonder is sixty-eight and flies an airplane. By herself too."

"I can see me doing that." Cleo clutches a needlepoint pillow. Tammy and Davey are arguing, sounding like wild Indians, but the racket is losing its definition around her. She finds it hard to pick out individual sounds. It is just a racket, something like a prolonged, steady snore—with lots of tuneful snorts and snuffles and puffs. Jake used to snore like that, but she could always tug the covers or kick at him gently and he would stop.

"Rita Jean said I was in the prime of life," says Cleo.

"Rita Jean should talk. Look at her. She petted that cat to death, if you ask me. And I never heard anything so ridiculous as her not wanting to go out West when she had the chance! I'd be gone in a minute!"

"People can't just have everything they want, all the time," Cleo says.

"I'm not mad at you, Mama. But people don't have to do what they don't want to as much now as they used to."

"I should know that," Cleo says. "It's all over television. You make me feel awful."

"I don't mean to. It's for your own good."

Prissy-Tail jumps up on the divan and Cleo grabs her. She squirms up onto Cleo's shoulder.

"You sure are lucky, Prissy-Tail, that you don't have to worry," Cleo says.

Linda pulls the rocker through the doorway into the living room. It scrapes the paint on the door facing.

Cleo is behind on supper. She is making a blackberry cobbler and she is confused about the timing. The children's favorite show comes on before supper is ready. They take their plates into the living room. *Mork and Mindy* is the one thing Tammy and Davey agree on. Cleo fills her plate and watches it with them. It isn't one of her regular stories, and it seems strange to her. Mork is from outer space and drinks through his finger. Otherwise, he is like a human being. Cleo finds his nonstop wisecracks hard to follow. Also, he wears galluses and sleeps hanging upside down. Jake used to wear galluses, Cleo thinks suddenly. Mork lives with Mindy, but Davey and Tammy seem to think nothing of it. Cleo is pleased that they eat the hamburger casserole without complaining. During the commercial she gets them large helpings of hot blackberry cobbler.

In the light she sees that Tammy is wearing blue eye shadow. "It makes you look holler-eyed," Cleo tells her, but Tammy shrugs.

When Tammy and Davey are asleep, Cleo gets out her family picture album. It has few pictures, compared to the way people take pictures nowadays, she thinks. The little black corners are coming loose, and some of the pictures are lying at crazy angles. She tries to put them back in place, knowing they won't stay. She looks through the pictures of her parents' wedding trip to Biloxi. Her parents look so young. Her mother looks like Linda in the picture. She is wearing a long baggy dress in style at the time. Cleo's father is a slim, dark-haired man in the picture. He is smiling. He always smiled. Cleo's parents are both dead. She turns the pages to her own honeymoon pictures. One, in which she and Jake look like children, was taken by a stranger in front of the Jefferson Davis monument. She looks carefully at Jake's face, realizing that the memory of the snapshots is more real than the memory of his actual face. As she turns the pages she sees herself and Jake get slightly older. A picture of Linda shows a stubborn child with bangs.

Cleo looks at a picture of Jake on the tractor. He is grinning into the sun. That was Jake when he was happy. He was a quiet man. Cleo studies a picture taken the year he died, and she wonders suddenly if Jake had ever cheated on her. He could have that time he went to the state fair, she thinks. When he returned he acted strangely, bringing back a red ribbon he had won, and talking in a peculiar way about the future of the family farm. Jake would never forgive her for selling the farm. It was surely her way of cheating on him, she thinks uncomfortably, but she never would have thought of divorcing him, just as she has not been able later to think of remarrying.

On the last pages of the album she sees a surprise, a picture she does not recognize at first. It is dim figures on a television screen. Then she remembers. Tammy took pictures of *Charlie's Angels* the night Linda missed it.

"Here, Mama, that's you." Tammy had pointed to the dark-haired actress, whose face was no bigger than a pencil eraser and hard to make out.

"Just give me her money and I'll do without her looks," Linda had replied.

Tammy has put this picture in Cleo's family album. Cleo cannot think why Tammy would do this. Then she sees on the next page that Tammy has also put in the picture she took of Cleo. The picture is the last one in the scrapbook. Again, Cleo sees herself, looking scared and old.

"The roof fell in," Cleo tells Rita Jean the next day. "Linda says she's not going back to Bob. She says she wants a separation and he's agreed to move out. Them children will be packed from pillar to post. I didn't sleep a wink all night last night."

Cleo is at Rita Jean's. Cleo has driven over, skipping the *Today* show and her morning phone conversation. Now she feels more comfortable at Rita Jean's than at home. The house is brightly decorated with handmade objects. Rita belongs to a mail-order craft club which sends a kit every month. She has made a new embroidered wall hanging of an Arizona sunset. Cleo admires it and says, as she gazes at a whipstitch, "What I don't understand is how my daughter can carry on like she does. She chirps like a bird!"

"I just don't know," says Rita Jean. "Don't look at this mess," she says as she leads Cleo to the back room, where Dexter is sleeping in a box. "The vet said there's not a thing wrong with him. He's just wearing out. He said keep him warm, have food for him whenever he wants it, and pet him and talk to him. It might be that I kept him in too long and he's just pined away. Do you think that was right, to keep him in like that all this time?"

"If you had let him out he would have just got run over," says Cleo. She strokes Dexter and he stirs slightly. His fur is dull and thin.

"I'll just have to accept it," says Rita Jean.

"Maybe it will be good for you," says Cleo, more harshly than she intends. "I've about decided there's no use trying to hang on to anything. You just lose it all in the end. You might as well just not care."

"Don't talk that way, Cleo."

"I must be getting old." Cleo laughs. "I'm saying what I think more.

Or younger, one. Old people and children—they always say what they think."

Over coffee, Cleo talks Rita Jean into going to trade day at the stock-yard.

"Linda said we've got to get out, keep up with the times," Cleo says. "Just what I need—more junk. But it's the style."

"Maybe it will take our minds off of everything," says Rita Jean, getting her scarf.

Most of the traders at the stockyard are farmers who trade in second-hand goods on the side. Cleo is shocked to realize this, though she knows nobody can make a living on a farm these days. She recognizes some of the farmers, behind their folding tables of dusty old objects. Even at the time of Jake's death, feeding the cows was costing almost as much as the milk brought. She cannot imagine Jake in a camper, peddling some old junk from the barn. That would kill him if the heart attack hadn't.

Cleo and Rita Jean drift from table to table, touching Depression glass, crystal goblets, cracked china, cast-off egg beaters and mixers, rusted farm implements, and greasy wooden boxes stuffed with buttons and papers.

"I never saw so much old stuff," says Cleo.

"Look at this," says Rita Jean, pointing to a box of plastic jump ropes. "These aren't old."

They look at hand-tooled leather belts and billfolds, made by prison-ers. And paintings of bright scenes on black velvet—bullfights and sky-lines and sunsets. A man in a cowboy hat displays the paintings from a fancy camper called a Sports Coach.

"He must have come from far away," says Rita Jean.

"I used to have a set of these." Cleo holds a tiny crystal salt shaker, without the pepper. There is a syrup holder to match.

"You could spend all day here," says Rita Jean, looking around like a lost child.

Cleo doesn't hear her. All of a sudden her blood is rushing to her head and her stomach is churning. She is looking at a miniature Early American whatnot, right in front of her. It is imitation mahogany. She holds it, touch-ing it, turning it, amazed.

"If it had been a snake it would have bit me!" cries Cleo, astonished. But Rita Jean is intent on examining a set of enamel canisters with cat decals on them and doesn't notice.

The whatnot cannot be the same one. Cleo cannot remember what happened to the little whatnot that sat on the dresser, the box in which Jake kept his stamps, his receipts, and his bankbook.

This whatnot has a door held in place by a wooden button, and on the top, like books on a shelf, is a series of tiny boxes, with sliding covers like match boxes. The little boxes have names: Book Plates, Mending Tape, Gummed Patches, Rubber Bands, Gummed Labels, Mailing Labels.

There are pictures on the spines of the boxes, together forming a scene—an old-fashioned train running through a meadow past a river, with black smoke trailing across three of the boxes and meeting a distant mountain. A steamboat is in the background. The curved track extends from the first box to the last. The scene is faded green and yellow, and there are lacy ferns and a tree in the foreground. The boxes are a simple picture puzzle to put in order. Cleo's children played with the puzzle when they were small, but her grandchildren were never interested in it. It cannot be the very same whatnot, she thinks.

"I'm going to buy this!" Cleo says.

"That's high," says Rita Jean, fingering the price sticker. The whatnot is three dollars.

Cleo looks at the train. Two of the pictures are out of order, and she rearranges them so that the caboose is at the end. For a moment she can see the train gliding silently through the pleasant scene, as quietly as someone dreaming, and she can imagine her family aboard the train as it crosses a fertile valley—like the place down by the creek that Jake loved—on its way out West. On the train, her well-behaved sons and their children are looking out the windows, and Linda and Bob are driving the train, guiding the cowcatcher down the track, while Tammy and Davey patiently count telephone poles and watch the passing scenery. Cleo is following unafraid in the caboose, as the train passes through the golden meadow and they all wave at the future and smile perfect smiles.

PART
II

WOMAN BECOMING

But every contradiction
Has the condition of resolving
Itself through the process
Through the process
Through the process of
Becoming, becoming, becoming,
Becoming, BECOMING.
                                    Megan Terry
                        Approaching Simone

In her 1970 play about the French philosopher Simone Weil, Megan Terry suggests that we cannot actually *reach* Simone, we can only *approach* an understanding of her. Terry's emphasis on "the process of/Becoming" as the means of resolving contradictions is still appropriate as we try to see the changes that have occurred and will occur in woman's position in the world and in her representation of herself. All of the selections in this section show women characters and speakers coming to an awareness of themselves and other women and somehow creating a sense of self, an identity different from any prescribed by traditional images. Selections in Part I portrayed emergence from roles; here the emphasis is on the means of emerging, on the process itself. Not content to *be*, the women in these selections are agents, actors, doers. They refuse "to move to the rhythms of others," they speak out, stand up, dive alone, choose, learn to read, learn to write, defy the law, work, dance, sing, walk, help others, dream, hope. Some works emphasize the pain of process, the slowness of change; others focus on the outcome, the rewards. All indicate that "becoming" is oriented toward improvement.

One has to read doubly to discover hope in some of these works. Emily Dickinson's speaker sees no relief from captivity even in heaven. She recognizes the subtle appeal of captivity. The illusion of safety, the comfort of the familiar, and the illusory nature of freedom make the captive concur in her own imprisonment. Dickinson gives us a metaphor for understanding why women not only have accepted their secondary status but have even sought it as a haven. Long before Freud, Dickinson perceived the submergence of our deepest consciousness in adult life: her speaker has forgotten the joy of freedom experienced in childhood. But even though this speaker includes herself among the "we" in prison, she is also an observer. She analyzes and describes for the reader—who may through her insight escape from "the narrow Round" of limitation imposed by stereotypes. The hope for change lies in the writer/reader relationship; Dickinson has stated the case, but the poem works for us only if we grasp the tone of longing for freedom that underlies the knowledge of its absence.

Tillie Olsen is a passionate reader of Dickinson. Her "Tell Me a Riddle" could almost be an exemplum of Dickinson's assertion that "A Prison gets to be a friend." Marriage and motherhood constitute the prison for Eva and cause her to feel disconnected from her young self, who fought for freedom in czarist Russia. Though her husband had been her fellow revolutionary, "her springtide love," in her old age she feels estranged from him, separated by the years of motherhood for her, job and union work for him. She wants to find coherence as she looks back over her life and yearns for a "reconciled peace," a time when she will never again need to "move to the rhythms of others." In the year of her final illness, as they travel to visit their children, her husband realizes that she has continued to dream of their youthful ideals and marvels at the strength of her faith that "These things shall be." By returning imaginatively to her youth Eva has found the "coherence, transport, meaning" that make her life a completed circle. Olsen's story is an elegy for the waste of human talent when traditional roles for both men and women deprive them of personal fruition and of the opportunity to work toward a "loftier race." Not content with the "nobility" of her children—with reproduction—Eva laments the lack of production—of work for others—she might also have achieved. Both Dickinson and Olsen go beyond description of gender problems to make universal statements. Their work illustrates how greatly literature has been warped by the omission of women's perspective.

Marge Piercy evokes images of a woman student's socialization into passivity and enjoins her to speak both in the singular and in the plural as she learns to overcome others' negative views. Hisaye Yamamoto's story is a grim reminder that even learning to speak—to write poems— may not be a strong enough weapon against tradition and male anger at a wife's change of roles. The poet warns her daughter not to marry; in telling her story, she injects some realism into her daughter's first sexual fantasies in the hope that she will escape the prison that sexual experience has made for her mother.

Charlotte Perkins Gilman's play is more optimistic: warned by her mother never to marry and by her career-woman aunt never to have a career, the heroine Aline finds a third way out. She will "have it all"—

but only because there is an economic arrangement available that supports her wish to continue her career as a teacher and to marry the man she loves. By boarding out—living communally—she can manage both. If children arrive, Aline will need group kitchen and child care arrangements, proposed by Gilman as an economist. Such arrangements might have given some freedom to Olsen's Eva earlier in her life so that she might have worked to fulfill her dreams for all humankind.

Like Gilman, Marietta Holley uses a light touch to show the injustice of traditional limitations for women. In "A Allegory on Wimmen's Rights," Holley pokes fun at the stereotype of the husband as provider and at the arguments against women's voting. She illustrates what can happen when women not only "learn to unspeak" but speak out.

Lucille Clifton and Susan Griffin emphasize the power of role models. In the "brown bag of a woman" she sees, Clifton's speaker recognizes a strong young woman, a survivor, and is inspired to stand up. Griffin tells the story of the former slave Harriet Tubman, who dressed as a man and led hundreds of other slaves to freedom; she draws a parallel to the necessity for standing up against men who make laws that do not provide for human needs.

In her autobiographical novel *Work: A Story of Experience*, Louisa May Alcott takes her hero Christie through almost every kind of work open to a woman. The selection presented here shows Christie's start. Like the mythical heroes of epics and sagas and Horatio Alger success stories, Christie leaves home at age twenty-one to face the world alone with very few resources. Though she is an orphan, she has as a guide the memory of her own mother's refusal to be confined to traditional expectations. Her mother died young after marrying "beneath" her, but Christie sees her story as having a happy ending because she is left to fulfill her mother's dream. Unlike Dickinson's speaker, Christie can remember a happier time. She will seek her own path, refusing marriage for now and hoping to earn her own living and be a benefactor to other girls. That this was a romantic fantasy for a woman of her time is summed up by her uncle's attitude that experience in the world will give her the "breakin' in" she needs to become docile and accept her place in life. Christie manages to earn a meager living in such stereotypical women's jobs as laundress, seamstress, maid, teacher, factory worker; she even tries acting. But like all good nineteenth-century American heroines (Baym, 1978), after a brief period of independence, Christie marries. Soon widowed, however, and left with a daughter, she, like Alcott herself and many other women of her time, continues to work for the rest of her life, more a hero than a heroine. Alcott has subverted the dominant marry-and-live-happily-ever-after plot.

The next three selections stress the importance of education as a resource for entering the world. Anna Julia Cooper, born into slavery but freed by the Civil War, uses an autobiographical anecdote to illustrate her plea for the education of black girls, telling how as a bright child she managed to worm her way into a class in Greek for male students preparing to become ministers. Though the teacher did admit her, he was as pessimistic as Christie's uncle in his expectations, agreeing with her bitter perception that "the only mission opening before a girl in his school was to marry one of those candidates." We know that Cooper, like Christie, had "spunk," and she went on to become a distinguished teacher and lecturer. Like Cooper, Rebecca Jackson, a black woman born in Philadelphia in the late eighteenth century, wanted education; she wished to read the Bible and to be able to write her own thoughts. Although her brother attributed her success to having memorized a passage she had heard, she considered her accomplishment miraculous, a gift from God, and determined to use it.

Jackson was thirty-five when she learned to read, forty-eight when she became a poet. At the time described in "A Person as Well as a Female," Jade Snow Wong was a high school senior, a Chinese-American in San Francisco, who wanted to go to college. She had worked as a maid in four different Caucasian households in which her education about Americans had been greatly augmented; in one family, for example, who "gave dinners in honor of up-and-coming young California political figures, there were always many men but few women." Her own father's refusal to help her to go to college was based on Chinese tradition; he believed in education, but only for sons. Jade Snow had to fight against double prejudice, and she went on to accomplish her goal on her own.

Though loving in many ways, neither Christie's Aunt Betsey nor Jade Snow's mother can stand up against their husbands. The mother in Margaret Atwood's poem "Spelling" is fiercely determined to give her daughter the power of words, the power to speak out that has been denied many women who have suffered torture. If her daughter can learn to spell her own name—to know who she is from the beginning—then she may also know "how to make spells"—how to change the world. "This is a metaphor," Atwood's speaker says of her image of the female body as a mouth that "speaks the truth." The use of a metaphor points to the power of the imagination to expand the world, a power writers have. In her recent novel *The Handmaid's Tale*, for example, Atwood portrays women being used as breeders in a totalitarian society. In a television interview about the filming of the novel, she said that everything in the book is based on reality, on something that has happened in the past. Putting all the parts together results in a new vision, the re-vision Adrienne Rich (1983) has asked for. Atwood's horrific picture of what present trends in society can lead to is a cautionary tale.

Susan Glaspell's "Trifles" takes us one step further on the quest for ways of achieving equity for women. Two women join together to find a way to help an acquaintance accused of having murdered her husband. When the two women discover the other's pet bird with its neck twisted, they deduce the sequence of events from the clues, showing their ability to think logically. But they decide to hide their knowledge from the male authorities, who dismiss their concerns as "trifles." Like Harriet Tubman, these women defy the law because it is an unjust one. They see more justice in defending the victim of cruelty than in punishing her, basing their concept of what is right on human relationships instead of an abstract principle such as "an eye for an eye." Showing more capability in logical deduction than the men, they act on their own moral values. Glaspell wrote this story in dramatic form, traditionally the most openended genre, one that allows viewers to form their own opinions; but her focus on the women's mutuality—their sisterhood—and her dismissal of the men's reasoning weight our sympathies toward the accused wife.

Like young Christie, Adrienne Rich's diver sets off into the unknown alone. She has the knowledge, skill, and tools needed to succeed. Her lonely voyage to watery depths symbolizes a search for origins, which she will find only beyond history and myth: women's names do not appear in the "book of myths" about quests for identity. The diver must learn to be at home in the water, which—unlike earth—frees her from the force of gravity. This is a new environment, where power is not an issue; she breathes differently. Discovering the wreck itself—the reality—she has changed: she is now androgynous, both mermaid and merman. The diver has gone beyond gender to full humanity. Perhaps her name and the pictures she takes will revise the book of myths; perhaps the earthly environment will become free of domination. The poem implies that the quest has been worthwhile; there is hope. Nadya Aisenberg's poem, dedicated to a Russian poet whose first name means *hope* (as does Nadya), asks whether the courage to plunge "through breakers" is all that is required to overcome hesitation, fear, and doubt and brave the barracuda that "swim alongside." The poet implies that Hope—her name capitalized as if she were a goddess—can give the courage to act, although she does not have the supernatural power to compel action or to promise success. We must risk everything—poems, children, the future, in order to "change our name."

The speaker in Martha Collins's "Homecoming" stakes her relationship with her lover, who is returning from war, on his observing her new boundaries and respecting her newfound sense of self. Collins reverses the myth of Odysseus, who returned home to find his patient wife Penelope waiting unchanged. Nellie Wong's woman at the window also has a new self-image as a poet as well as secretary. By searching her memories, she can imagine herself occupying "other skins," knowing from the inside women of different ages, experiences, and situations. Through this power she transcends time and space. Sonia Sanchez's black woman thinks back through her mother and grandmothers, creates herself, and becomes the women she remembers. "Womb ripe," fully adult, the speaker of Sanchez's poem is a new person. The title of Alice Walker's poem "Beyond What" is in the form of a question but has no question mark. Her speaker is very sure that there are destinies "beyond/what we have come to know," beyond stereotypical expectations that lovers will become one person, two halves of one whole, as in the Platonic myth. These lovers will not gaze raptly into each others' eyes: they will "see the world" and be equally free to make decisions. The poem goes beyond conventional heterosexual allusion: in the myth the two halves could be of the same gender. And "Shared. But inviolate." implies that separate *and* equal, not separate but equal, is true equality. Gender equality is an aspect of justice for all men and women.

Olive Schreiner includes all "brave women and brave men hand in hand" in her vision of the future; like Olsen's Eva, the dreamer is sure that "these things shall be," on earth, not in heaven. Schreiner's *Dreams* was an inspiration to militant women of her time in both England and South Africa. Reminding ourselves of their sacrifices and suffering, we can hope to reach goals beyond what they imagined. We need a sense that we will not be abandoned, that we have a chance to succeed. Alaíde Foppa both addresses and describes a woman who can be trusted. She does not fulfill any traditional image; she "begins to know who she is / and starts to live." Like all of us, this woman is in the process of becoming.

A PRISON GETS TO BE A FRIEND

by

EMILY DICKINSON
(1830–1886)

Famous for being a recluse, Emily Dickinson spent her entire life in Amherst, Massachusetts, except for a year at Mount Holyoke Female Seminary. At her death, over 900 poems were found in manuscript, only 7 of which had been published. An additional 900 poems have since been discovered, many not published until 1945. Now recognized as a major poet, Dickinson wrote of love, death, God, and nature. Unconventional both in form and content, her work seems very modern. Her letters were published in three volumes in 1958.

A Prison gets to be a friend–
Between its Ponderous face
And Ours–a Kinsmanship express–
And in its narrow Eyes–

We come to look with gratitude
For the appointed Beam
It deal us–stated as our food–
And hungered for–the same–

We learn to know the Planks–
That answer to Our feet–
So miserable a sound–at first–
Nor ever now–so sweet–

As plashing in the Pools–
When Memory was a Boy–
But a Demurer Circuit–
A Geometric Joy–

The Posture of the Key
That interrupt the Day
To Our Endeavor–Not so real
The Cheek of Liberty–

As this Phantasm Steel–
Whose features–Day and Night–
Are present to us–as Our Own–
And as escapeless–quite–

The narrow Round–the Stint–
The slow exchange of Hope–
For something passiver–Content
Too steep for looking up–

The Liberty we knew
Avoided–like a Dream–
Too wide for any Night but Heaven–
If That–indeed–redeem–

TELL ME A RIDDLE

"These Things Shall Be"

by

TILLIE OLSEN
(b. 1913)

Born in Nebraska, Tillie Olsen has lived most of her adult life in San Francisco. A Depression-era high-school dropout, self-taught in public libraries, she wrote and published when young, but the necessity of raising and supporting four children silenced her for twenty years. Tell Me a Riddle, *a collection of short stories first published in 1962, is now regarded as a classic. Her novel* Yonnondio: From the Thirties, *"lost" for forty years, was published in 1974, and* Silences, *a collection of essays on human creativity, appeared in 1978. She edited* Mother to Daughter, Daughter to Mother *(1984), a collection of poems published by the Feminist Press. In recent years Tillie Olsen has received many awards and honors and has taught and lectured widely.*

• ——————————————————— •

1

For forty-seven years they had been married. How deep back the stubborn, gnarled roots of the quarrel reached, no one could say—but only now, when tending to the needs of others no longer shackled them together, the roots swelled up visible, split the earth between them, and the tearing shook even to the children, long since grown.

Why now, why now? wailed Hannah.

As if when we grew up weren't enough, said Paul.

Poor Ma. Poor Dad. It hurts so for both of them, said Vivi. They never had very much; at least in old age they should be happy.

Knock their heads together, insisted Sammy; tell 'em: you're too old for this kind of thing; no reason not to get along now.

Lennie wrote to Clara: They've lived over so much together; what could possibly tear them apart?

Something tangible enough.

Arthritic hands, and such work as he got, occasional. Poverty all his life, and there was little breath left for running. He could not, could not turn away from this desire: to have the troubling of responsibility, the fretting with money, over and done with; to be free, to be *carefree* where success was not measured by accumulation, and there was use for the vitality still in him.

There was a way. They could sell the house, and with the money join his lodge's Haven, cooperative for the aged. Happy communal life, and was he not already an official; had he not helped organize it, raise funds, served as a trustee?

But she—would not consider it.

"What do we need all this for?" he would ask loudly, for her hearing aid was turned down and the vacuum was shrilling. "Five rooms" (pushing the sofa so she could get into the corner) "furniture" (smoothing down the rug) "floors and surfaces to make work. Tell me, why do we need it?" And he was glad he could ask in a scream.

"Because I'm use't."

"Because you're use't. This is a reason, Mrs. Word Miser? Used to can get unused!"

"Enough unused I have to get used to already. . . . Not enough words?" turning off the vacuum a moment to hear herself answer. "Because soon enough we'll need only a little closet, no windows, no furniture, nothing to make work, but for worms. Because now I want room. . . . Screech and blow like you're doing, you'll need that closet even sooner. . . . Ha, again!" for the vacuum bag wailed, puffed half up, hung stubbornly limp. "This time fix it so it stays; quick before the phone rings and you get too important busy."

But while he struggled with the motor, it seethed in him. Why fix it? Why have to bother? And if it can't be fixed, have to wring the mind with how to pay the repair? At the Haven they come in with their own machines to clean your room or your cottage; you fish, or play cards, or make jokes in the sun, not with knotty fingers fight to mend vacuums.

Over the dishes, coaxingly: "For once in your life, to be free, to have everything done for you, like a queen."

"I never liked queens."

"No dishes, no garbage, no towel to sop, no worry what to buy, what to eat."

"And what else would I do with my empty hands? Better to eat at my own table when I want, and to cook and eat how I want."

"In the cottages they buy what you ask, and cook it how you like. *You* are the one who always used to say: better mankind born without mouths and stomachs than always to worry for money to buy, to shop, to fix, to cook, to wash, to clean."

"How cleverly you hid that you heard. I said it then because eighteen hours a day I ran. And you never scraped a carrot or knew a dish towel sops. Now—for you and me—who cares? A herring out of a jar is enough. But when *I* want, and nobody to bother." And she turned off her ear button, so she would not have to hear.

But as *he* had no peace, juggling and rejuggling the money to figure: how will I pay for this now?; prying out the storm windows (there they take care of this); jolting in the streetcar on errands (there I would not have to ride to take care of this or that); fending the patronizing relatives just back from Florida (at the Haven it matters what one is, not what one can afford), he gave *her* no peace.

"Look! In their bulletin. A reading circle. Twice a week it meets."

"Haumm," her answer of not listening.

"A reading circle. Chekhov they read that you like, and Peretz. Cultured people at the Haven that you would enjoy."

"Enjoy!" She tasted the word. "Now, when it pleases you, you find a reading circle for me. And forty years ago when the children were morsels and there was a Circle, did you stay home with them once so I could go? Even once? You trained me well. I do not need others to enjoy. Others!" Her voice trembled. "Because *you* want to be there with others. Already it makes me sick to think of you always around others. Clown, grimacer, floormat, yesman, entertainer, whatever they want of you."

And now it was he who turned on the television loud so he need not hear.

Old scar tissue ruptured and the wounds festered anew. Chekhov indeed. She thought without softness of that young wife, who in the deep night hours while she nursed the current baby, and perhaps held another in her lap, would try to stay awake for the only time there was to read. She would feel again the weather of the outside on his cheek when, coming late from a meeting, he would find her so, and stimulated and ardent, sniffing her skin, coax: "I'll put the baby to bed, and you—put the book away, don't read, don't read."

That had been the most beguiling of all the "don't read, put your book away" her life had been. Chekhov indeed!

"Money?" She shrugged him off. "Could we get poorer than once we were? And in America, who starves?"

But as still he pressed:

"Let me alone about money. Was there ever enough? Seven little ones— for every penny I had to ask—and sometimes, remember, there was nothing. But always *I* had to manage. Now *you* manage. Rub your nose in it good."

But from those years she had had to manage, old humiliations and terrors rose up, lived again, and forced her to relive them. The children's needings; that grocer's face or this merchant's wife she had had to beg credit from when credit was a disgrace; the scenery of the long blocks walked around when she could not pay; school coming, and the desperate going over the old to see what could yet be remade; the soups of meat bones begged "for-the-dog" one winter. . . .

Enough. Now they had no children. Let *him* wrack his head for how they would live. She would not exchange her solitude for anything. *Never again to be forced to move to the rhythms of others.*

For in this solitude she had won to a reconciled peace.

Tranquillity from having the empty house no longer an enemy, for it stayed clean—not as in the days when it was her family, the life in it, that had seemed the enemy: tracking, smudging, littering, dirtying, engaging her in endless defeating battle—and on whom her endless defeat had been spewed.

The few old books, memorized from rereading; the pictures to ponder (the magnifying glass superimposed on her heavy eyeglasses). Or if she wishes, when he is gone, the phonograph, that if she turns up very loud and strains, she can hear: the ordered sounds and the struggling.

Out in the garden, growing things to nurture. Birds to be kept out of the pear tree, and when the pears are heavy and ripe, the old fury of work, for all must be canned, nothing wasted.

And her one social duty (for she will not go to luncheons or meetings) the boxes of old clothes left with her, as with a life-practised eye for finding what is still wearable within the worn (again the magnifying glass superimposed on the heavy glasses) she scans and sorts—this for rag or rummage, that for mending and cleaning, and this for sending away.

Being able at last to live within, and not move to the rhythms of others, as life had forced her to: denying; removing; isolating; taking the children one by one; then deafening, half-blinding—and at last, presenting her solitude.

And in it she had won to a reconciled peace.

Now he was violating it with his constant campaigning: *Sell the house and move to the Haven.* (You sit, you sit—there too you could sit like a stone.) He was making of her a battleground where old grievances tore. (Turn on your ear button—I am talking.) And stubbornly she resisted—so that from wheedling, reasoning, manipulation, it was bitterness he now started with.

And it came to where every happening lashed up a quarrel.

"I will sell the house anyway," he flung at her one night. "I am putting it up for sale. There will be a way to make you sign."

The television blared, as always it did on the evenings he stayed home, and as always it reached her only as noise. She did not know if the tumult was in her or outside. Snap! she turned the sound off. "Shadows," she whispered to him, pointing to the screen, "look, it is only shadows." And in a scream: "Did you say that you will sell the house? Look at me, not at that. I am no shadow. You cannot sell without me."

"Leave on the television. I am watching."

"Like Paulie, like Jenny, a four-year-old. Staring at shadows. *You cannot sell the house.*"

"I will. We are going to the Haven. There you would not hear the television when you do not want it. I could sit in the social room and watch. You could lock yourself up to smell your unpleasantness in a room by yourself—for who would want to come near you?"

"No, no selling." A whisper now.

"The television is shadows. Mrs. Enlightened! Mrs. Cultured! A world comes into your house—and it is shadows. People you would never meet in a thousand lifetimes. Wonders. When you were four years old, yes, like Paulie, like Jenny, did you know of Indian dances, alligators, how they use bamboo in Malaya? No, you scratched in your dirt with the chickens and thought Olshana was the world. Yes, Mrs. Unpleasant, I will sell the house, for there better can we be rid of each other than here."

She did not know if the tumult was outside, or in her. Always a ravening inside, a pull to the bed, to lie down, to succumb.

"Have you thought maybe Ma should let a doctor have a look at her?" asked their son Paul after Sunday dinner, regarding his mother crumpled on the couch, instead of, as was her custom, busying herself in Nancy's kitchen.

"Why not the President too?"

"Seriously, Dad. This is the third Sunday she's lain down like that after dinner. Is she that way at home?"

"A regular love affair with the bed. Every time I start to talk to her."

Good protective reaction, observed Nancy to herself. The workings of hos-til-ity.

"Nancy could take her. I just don't like how she looks. Let's have Nancy arrange an appointment."

"You think she'll go?" regarding his wife gloomily. "All right, we have to have doctor bills, we have to have doctor bills." Loudly: "Something hurts you?"

She startled, looked to his lips. He repeated: "Mrs. Take It Easy, something hurts?"

"Nothing. . . . Only you."

"A woman of honey. That's why you're lying down?"

"Soon I'll get up to do the dishes, Nancy."

"Leave them, Mother, I like it better this way."

"Mrs. Take It Easy, Paul says you should start ballet. You should go to see a doctor and ask: how soon can you start ballet?"

"A doctor?" she begged. "Ballet?"

"We were talking, Ma," explained Paul, "you don't seem any too well. It would be a good idea for you to see a doctor for a checkup."

"I get up now to do the kitchen. Doctors are bills and foolishness, my son. I need no doctors."

"At the Haven," he could not resist pointing out, "a doctor is *not* bills. He lives beside you. You start to sneeze, he is there before you open up a Kleenex. You can be sick there for free, all you want."

"Diarrhea of the mouth, is there a doctor to make you dumb?"

"Ma. Promise me you'll go. Nancy will arrange it."

"It's all of a piece when you think of it," said Nancy, "the way she attacks my kitchen, scrubbing under every cup hook, doing the inside of the oven so I can't enjoy Sunday dinner, knowing that half-blind or not, she's going to find every speck of dirt. . . ."

"Don't, Nancy, I've told you—it's the only way she knows to be useful. What did the *doctor* say?"

"A real fatherly lecture. Sixty-nine is young these days. Go out, enjoy life, find interests. Get a new hearing aid, this one is antiquated. Old age is sickness only if one makes it so. Geriatrics, Inc."

"So there was nothing physical."

"Of course there was. How can you live to yourself like she does without there being? Evidence of a kidney disorder, and her blood count is low. He gave her a diet, and she's to come back for follow-up and lab work. . . . But he was clear enough: Number One prescription—start living like a human being. . . . When I think of your dad, who could really play the invalid with that arthritis of his, as active as a teenager, and twice as much fun. . . ."

"You didn't tell me the doctor says your sickness is in you, how you live." He pushed his advantage. "Life and enjoyments you need better than medicine. And this diet, how can you keep it? To weigh each morsel and scrape away each bit of fat, to make this soup, that pudding. There, at the Haven, they have a dietician, they would do it for you."

She is silent.

"You would feel better there, I know it," he says gently. "There there is life and enjoyments all around."

"What is the matter, Mr. Importantbusy, you have no card game or meeting you can go to?"—turning her face to the pillow.

For a while he cut his meetings and going out, fussed over her diet, tried to wheedle her into leaving the house, brought in visitors:

"I should come to a fashion tea. I should sit and look at pretty babies in clothes I cannot buy. This is pleasure?"

"Always you are better than everyone else. The doctor said you should go out. Mrs. Brem comes to you with goodness and you turn her away."

"Because *you* asked her to, she asked me."

"They won't come back. People you need, the doctor said. Your own cousins I asked; they were willing to come and make peace as if nothing had happened. . . ."

"No more crushers of people, pushers, hypocrites, around me. No more in *my* house. You go to them if you like."

"Kind he is to visit. And you, like ice."

"A babbler. All my life around babblers. Enough!"

"She's even worse, Dad? Then let her stew a while," advised Nancy.

"You can't let it destroy you; it's a psychological thing, maybe too far gone for any of us to help."

So he let her stew. More and more she lay silent in bed, and sometimes did not even get up to make the meals. No longer was the tongue-lashing inevitable if he left the coffee cup where it did not belong, or forgot to take out the garbage or mislaid the broom. The birds grew bold that summer and for once pocked the pears, undisturbed.

A bellyfull of bitterness and every day the same quarrel in a new way and a different old grievance the quarrel forced her to enter and relive. And the new torment: I am not really sick, the doctor said it, then why do I feel so sick?

One night she asked him: "You have a meeting tonight? Do not go. Stay . . . with me."

He had planned to watch "This Is Your Life," but half sick himself from the heavy heat, and sickening therefore the more after the brooks and woods of the Haven, with satisfaction he grated:

"Hah, Mrs. Live Alone And Like It wants company all of a sudden. It doesn't seem so good the time of solitary when she was a girl exile in Siberia. 'Do not go. Stay with me.' A new song for Mrs. Free As A Bird. Yes, I am going out, and while I am gone chew this aloneness good, and think how you keep us both from where if you want people, you do not need to be alone."

"Go, go. All your life you have gone without me."

After him she sobbed curses he had not heard in years, old-country curses from their childhood: Grow, oh shall you grow like an onion, with your head in the ground. Like the hide of a drum shall you be, beaten in life, beaten in death. Oh shall you be like a chandelier, to hang, and to burn. . . .

She was not in their bed when he came back. She lay on the cot on the sun porch. All week she did not speak or come near him; nor did he try to make peace or care for her.

He slept badly, so used to her next to him. After all the years, old harmonies and dependencies deep in their bodies; she curled to him, or he coiled to her, each warmed, warming, turning as the other turned, the nights a long embrace.

It was not the empty bed or the storm that woke him, but a faint singing. *She* was singing. Shaking off the drops of rain, the lightning riving her lifted face, he saw her so; the cot covers on the floor.

"This is a private concert?" he asked. "Come in, you are wet."

"I can breathe now," she answered; "my lungs are rich." Though indeed the sound was hardly a breath.

"Come in, come in." Loosing the bamboo shades. "Look how wet you are." Half helping, half carrying her, still faint-breathing her song.

A Russian love song of fifty years ago.

He had found a buyer, but before he told her, he called together those children who were close enough to come. Paul, of course, Sammy from New Jersey, Hannah from Connecticut, Vivi from Ohio.

With a kindling of energy for her beloved visitors, she arrayed the house, cooked and baked. She was not prepared for the solemn after-dinner conclave, they too probing in and tearing. Her frightened eyes watched from mouth to mouth as each spoke.

His stories were eloquent and funny of her refusal to go back to the doctor; of the scorned invitations; of her stubborn silence or the bile "like a Niagara"; of her contrariness: "If I clean it's no good how I cleaned; if I don't clean, I'm still a master who thinks he has a slave."

(Vinegar he poured on me all his life; I am well marinated; how can I be honey now?)

Deftly he marched in the rightness for moving to the Haven; their money from social security free for visiting the children, not sucked into daily needs and into the house; the activities in the Haven for him; but mostly the Haven for *her*: her health, her need of care, distraction, amusement, friends who shared her interests.

"This does offer an outlet for Dad," said Paul; "he's always been an active person. And economic peace of mind isn't to be sneezed at, either. I could use a little of that myself."

But when they asked: "And you, Ma, how do you feel about it?" could only whisper:

"For him it is good. It is not for me. I can no longer live between people."

"You lived all your life *for* people," Vivi cried.

"Not with." Suffering doubly for the unhappiness on her children's faces.

"You have to find some compromise," Sammy insisted. "Maybe sell the house and buy a trailer. After forty-seven years there's surely some way you can find to live in peace."

"There is no help, my children. Different things we need."

"Then live alone!" He could control himself no longer. "I have a buyer for the house. Half the money for you, half for me. Either alone or with me to the Haven. You think I can live any longer as we are doing now?"

"Ma doesn't have to make a decision this minute, however you feel, Dad," Paul said quickly, "and you wouldn't want her to. Let's let it lay a few months, and then talk some more."

"I think I can work it out to take Mother home with me for a while," Hannah said. "You both look terrible, but especially you, Mother. I'm going to ask Phil to have a look at you."

"Sure," cracked Sammy. "What's the use of a doctor husband if you can't get free service out of him once in a while for the family? And absence might make the heart . . . you know."

"There was something after all," Paul told Nancy in a colorless voice. "That was Hannah's Phil calling. Her gall bladder. . . . Surgery."

"Her *gall* bladder. If that isn't classic. 'Bitter as gall'—talk of psycho-som——"

He stepped closer, put his hand over her mouth, and said in the same colorless, plodding voice. "We have to get Dad. They operated at once. The cancer was everywhere, surrounding the liver, everywhere. They did what they could . . . at best she has a year. Dad . . . we have to tell him."

2

Honest in his weakness when they told him, and that she was not to know. "I'm not an actor. She'll know right away by how I am. Oh that poor woman. I am old too, it will break me into pieces. Oh that poor woman. She will spit on me: 'So my sickness was how I live.' Oh Paulie, how she will be, that poor woman. Only she should not suffer. . . . I can't stand sickness, Paulie, I can't go with you."

But went. And play-acted.

"A grand opening and you did not even wait for me. . . . A good thing Hannah took you with her."

"Fashion teas I needed. They cut out what tore in me; just in my throat something hurts yet. . . . Look! so many flowers, like a funeral. Vivi called, did Hannah tell you? And Lennie from San Francisco, and Clara; and Sammy is coming." Her gnome's face pressed happily into the flowers.

It is impossible to predict in these cases, but once over the immediate effects of the operation, she should have several months of comparative well-being.

The money, where will come the money?

Travel with her, Dad. Don't take her home to the old associations. The other children will want to see her.

The money, where will I wring the money?

Whatever happens, she is not to know. No, you can't ask her to sign papers to sell the house; nothing to upset her. Borrow instead, then after. . . .

I had wanted to leave you each a few dollars to make life easier, as other fathers do. There will be nothing left now. (Failure! you and your "business is exploitation." Why didn't you make it when it could be made?——Is that what you're thinking, Sammy?)

Sure she's unreasonable, Dad——but you have to stay with her; if there's to be any happiness in what's left of her life, it depends on you.

Prop me up, children, think of me, too. Shuffled, chained with her, bitter woman. No Haven, and the little money going. . . . How happy she looks, poor creature.

The look of excitement. The straining to hear everything (the new hearing aid turned full). Why are you so happy, dying woman?

How the petals are, fold on fold, and the gladioli color. The autumn air.

Stranger grandsons, tall above the little gnome grandmother, the little spry grandfather. Paul in a frenzy of picture-taking before going.

She, wandering the great house. Feeling the books; laughing at the maple shoemaker's bench of a hundred years ago used as a table. The ear turned to music.

"Let us go home. See how good I walk now." "One step from the hospital," he answers, "and she wants to fly. Wait till Doctor Phil says."

"Look—the birds too are flying home. Very good Phil is and will not show it, but he is sick of sickness by the time he comes home."

"Mrs. Telepathy, to read minds," he answers; "read mine what it says: when the trunks of medicines become a suitcase, then we will go."

The grandboys, they do not know what to say to us. . . . Hannah, she runs around here, there, when is there time for herself?

Let us go home. Let us go home.

Musing; gentleness—*but for the incidents of the rabbi in the hospital, and of the candles of benediction.*

Of the rabbi in the hospital:

Now tell me what happened, Mother.

From the sleep I awoke, Hannah's Phil, and he stands there like a devil in a dream and calls me by name. I cannot hear. I think he prays. Go away, please, I tell him, I am not a believer. Still he stands, while my heart knocks with fright.

You scared *him*, Mother. He thought you were delirious.

Who sent him? Why did he come to me?

It is a custom. The men of God come to visit those of their religion they might help. The hospital makes up the list for them—race, religion—and you are on the Jewish list.

Not for rabbis. At once go and make them change. Tell them to write: Race, human; Religion, none.

And of the candles of benediction:

Look how you have upset yourself, Mrs. Excited Over Nothing. Pleasant memories you should leave.

Go in, go back to Hannah and the lights. Two weeks I saw candles and said nothing. But she asked me.

So what was so terrible? She forgets you never did, she asks you to light the Friday candles and say the benediction like Phil's mother when she visits. If the candles give her pleasure, why shouldn't she have the pleasure?

Not for pleasure she does it. For emptiness. Because his family does. Because all around her do.

That is not a good reason too? But you did not hear her. For heritage, she told you. For the boys, from the past they should have tradition.

Superstition! From our ancestors, savages, afraid of the dark, of themselves: mumbo words and magic lights to scare away ghosts.

She told you: how it started does not take away the goodness. For centuries, peace in the house it means.

Swindler! does she look back on the dark centuries? Candles bought instead of bread and stuck into a potato for a candlestick? Religion that stifled and said: in Paradise, woman, you will be the footstool of your husband, and in life—poor chosen Jew—ground under, despised, trembling in cellars. And cremated. And cremated.

This is religion's fault? You think you are still an orator of the 1905 revolution? Where are the pills for quieting? Which are they?

Heritage. How have we come from our savage past, how no longer to be savages—this to teach. To look back and learn what humanizes—this to teach. To smash all ghettos that divide us—not to go back, not to go back—this to teach. Learned books in the house, will humankind live or die, and she gives to her boys—superstition.

Hannah that is so good to you. Take your pill, Mrs. Excited For Nothing, swallow.

Heritage! But when did I have time to teach? Of Hannah I asked only hands to help.

Swallow.

Otherwise—musing; gentleness.

Not to travel. To go home.

The children want to see you. We have to show them you are as thorny a flower as ever.

Not to travel.

Vivi wants you should see her new baby. She sent the tickets—airplane tickets—a Mrs. Roosevelt she wants to make of you. To Vivi's we have to go.

A new baby. How many warm, seductive babies. She holds him stiffly, *away* from her, so that he wails. And a long shudder begins, and the sweat beads on her forehead.

"Hush, shush," croons the grandfather, lifting him back. "You should forgive your grandmamma, little prince, she has never held a baby before, only seen them in glass cases. Hush, shush."

"You're tired, Ma," says Vivi. "The travel and the noisy dinner. I'll take you to lie down."

(A long travel from, to, what the feel of a baby evokes.)

In the airplane, cunningly designed to encase from motion (no wind, no feel of flight), she had sat severely and still, her face turned to the sky through which they cleaved and left no scar.

So this was how it looked, the determining, the crucial sky, and this was how man moved through it, remote above the dwindled earth, the concealed human life. Vulnerable life, that could scar.

TILLIE OLSEN

453

There was a steerage ship of memory that shook across a great, circular sea: clustered, ill human beings; and through the thick-stained air, tiny fretting waters in a window round like the airplane's—sun round, moon round. (The round thatched roofs of Olshana.) Eye round—like the smaller window that framed distance the solitary year of exile when only her eyes could travel, and no voice spoke. And the polar winds hurled themselves across snows trackless and endless and white—like the clouds which had closed together below and hidden the earth.

Now they put a baby in her lap. Do not ask me, she would have liked to beg. Enough the worn face of Vivi, the remembered grandchildren. I cannot, cannot. . . .

Cannot what? Unnatural grandmother, not able to make herself embrace a baby.

She lay there in the bed of the two little girls, her new hearing aid turned full, listening to the sound of the children going to sleep, the baby's fretful crying and hushing, the clatter of dishes being washed and put away. They thought she slept. Still she rode on.

It was not that she had not loved her babies, her children. The love—the passion of tending—had risen with the need like a torrent; and like a torrent drowned and immolated all else. But when the need was done—oh the power that was lost in the painful damming back and drying up of what still surged, but had nowhere to go. Only the thin pulsing left that could not quiet, suffering over lives one felt, but could no longer hold nor help.

On that torrent she had borne them to their own lives, and the riverbed was desert long years now. Not there would she dwell, a memoried wraith. Surely that was not all, surely there was more. Still the springs, the springs were in her seeking. Somewhere an older power that beat for life. Somewhere coherence, transport, meaning. If they would but leave her in the air now stilled of clamor, in the reconciled solitude, to journey on.

And they put a baby in her lap. Immediacy to embrace, and the breath of *that* past: warm flesh like this that had claims and nuzzled away all else and with lovely mouths devoured; hot-living like an animal—intensely and now; the turning maze; the long drunkenness; the drowning into needing and being needed. Severely she looked back—and the shudder seized her again, and the sweat. Not that way. Not there, not now could she, not yet. . . .

And all that visit, she could not touch the baby.

"Daddy, is it the . . . sickness she's like that?" asked Vivi. "I was so glad to be having the baby—for her. I told Tim, it'll give her more happiness than anything, being around a baby again. And she hasn't played with him once."

He was not listening, "Aahh little seed of life, little charmer," he crooned, "Hollywood should see you. A heart of ice you would melt.

Kick, kick. The future you'll have for a ball. In 2050 still kick. Kick for your grandaddy then."

Attentive with the older children; sat through their performances (command performance; we command you to be the audience); helped Ann sort autumn leaves to find the best for a school program; listened gravely to Richard tell about his rock collection, while her lips mutely formed the words to remember: *igneous, sedimentary, metamorphic*; looked for missing socks, books, and bus tickets; watched the children whoop after their grandfather who knew how to tickle, chuck, lift, toss, do tricks, tell secrets, make jokes, match riddle for riddle. (Tell me a riddle, Grammy. I know no riddles, child.) Scrubbed sills and woodwork and furniture in every room; folded the laundry; straightened drawers; emptied the heaped baskets waiting for ironing (while he or Vivi or Tim nagged: You're supposed to rest here, you've been sick) but to none tended or gave food—and could not touch the baby.

After a week she said: "Let us go home. Today call about the tickets."

"You have important business, Mrs. Inahurry? The President waits to consult with you?" He shouted, for the fear of the future raced in him. "The clothes are still warm from the suitcase, your children cannot show enough how glad they are to see you, and you want home. There is plenty of time for home. We cannot be with the children at home."

"Blind to around you as always: the little ones sleep four in a room because we take their bed. We are two more people in a house with a new baby, and no help."

"Vivi is happy so. The children should have their grandparents a while, she told to me. I should have my mommy and daddy. . . ."

"Babbler and blind. Do you look at her so tired? How she starts to talk and she cries? I am not strong enough yet to help. Let us go home."

(To reconciled solitude.)

For it seemed to her the crowded noisy house was listening to her, listening for her. She could feel it like a great ear pressed under her heart. And everything knocked: quick constant raps: let me in, let me in.

How was it that soft reaching tendrils also became blows that knocked?

C'mon, Grandma, I want to show you. . . .

Tell me a riddle, Grandma. (*I know no riddles.*)

Look, Grammy, he's so dumb he can't even find his hands. (Dody and the baby on a blanket over the fermenting autumn mould.)

I made them—for you. (Ann) (Flat paper dolls with aprons that lifted on scalloped skirts that lifted on flowered pants; hair of yarn and great ringed questioning eyes.)

Watch me, Grandma. (Richard snaking up the tree, hanging exultant, free, with one hand at the top. Below Dody hunching over in pretend-cooking.) (*Climb too, Dody, climb and look.*)

TILLIE OLSEN
455

Be my nap bed, Grammy. (The "No!" too late.) Morty's abandoned heaviness, while his fingers ladder up and down her hearing-aid cord to his drowsy chant: eentsiebeentsiespider. (*Children trust.*)

It's to start off your own rock collection, Grandma. That's a trilobite fossil, 200 million years old (millions of years on a boy's mouth) and that one's obsidian, black glass.

Knocked and knocked.

Mother, I *told* you the teacher said we had to bring it back all filled out this morning. Didn't you even ask Daddy? Then tell *me* which plan and I'll check it: evacuate or stay in the city or wait for you to come and take me away. (Seeing the look of straining to hear.) It's for Disaster, Grandma. (*Children trust.*)

Vivi in the maze of the long, the lovely drunkenness. The old old noises: baby sounds; screaming of a mother flayed to exasperation; children quarreling; children playing; singing; laughter.

And Vivi's tears and memories, spilling so fast, half the words not understood.

She had started remembering out loud deliberately, so her mother would know the past was cherished, still lived in her.

Nursing the baby: My friends marvel, and I tell them, oh it's easy to be such a cow. I remember how beautiful my mother seemed nursing my brother, and the milk just flows. . . . Was that Davy? It must have been Davy. . . .

Lowering a hem: How did you ever . . . when I think how you made everything we wore . . . Tim, just think, seven kids and Mommy sewed everything . . . do I remember you sang while you sewed? That white dress with the red apples on the skirt you fixed over for me, was it Hannah's or Clara's before it was mine?

Washing sweaters: Ma, I'll never forget, one of those days so nice you washed clothes outside; one of the first spring days it must have been. The bubbles just danced while you scrubbed, and we chased after, and you stopped to show us how to blow our own bubbles with green onion stalks . . . you always. . . .

"Strong onion, to still make you cry after so many years," her father said, to turn the tears into laughter.

While Richard bent over his homework: Where is it now, do we still have it, the Book of the Martyrs? It always seemed so, well—exalted, when you'd put it on the round table and we'd all look at it together; there was even a halo from the lamp. The lamp with the beaded fringe you could move up and down; they're in style again, pulley lamps like that, but without the fringe. You know the book I'm talking about, Daddy, the Book of the Martyrs, the first picture was a bust of Spartacus . . . Socrates? I wish there was something like that for the children, Mommy, to give them what you. . . . (And the tears splashed again.)

(What I intended and did not? Stop it, daughter, stop it, leave that time. And he, the hypocrite, sitting there with tears in his eyes—it was nothing to you then, nothing.)

. . . The time you came to school and I almost died of shame because of your accent and because I knew you knew I was ashamed; how could I? . . . Sammy's harmonica and you danced to it once, yes you did, you and Davy squealing in your arms. . . . That time you bundled us up and walked us down to the railway station to stay the night 'cause it was heated and we didn't have any coal, that winter of the strike, you didn't think I remembered that, did you, Mommy? . . . How you'd call us out to see the sunsets. . . .

Day after day, the spilling memories. Worse now, questions, too. Even the grandchildren: Grandma, in the olden days, when you were little. . . .

It was the afternoons that saved.

While they thought she napped, she would leave the mosaic on the wall (of children's drawings, maps, calendars, pictures, Ann's cardboard dolls with their great ringed questioning eyes) and hunch in the girls' closet on the low shelf where the shoes stood, and the girls' dresses covered.

For that while she would painfully sheathe against the listening house, the tendrils and noises that knocked, and Vivi's spilling memories. Sometimes it helped to braid and unbraid the sashes that dangled, or to trace the pattern on the hoop slips.

Today she had jacks and children under jet trails to forget. Last night, Ann and Dody silhouetted in the window against a sunset of flaming man-made clouds of jet trail, their jacks ball accenting the peaceful noise of dinner being made. Had she told them, yes she had told them of how they played jacks in her village though there was no ball, no jacks. Six stones, round and flat, toss them out, the seventh on the back of the hand, toss, catch and swoop up as many as possible, toss again. . . .

Of stones (repeating Richard) there are three kinds: earth's fire jetting; rock of layered centuries; crucibled new out of the old *(igneous, sedimentary, metamorphic)*. But there was that other—frozen to black glass, never to transform or hold the fossil memory . . . (let not my seed fall on stone). There was an ancient man who fought to heights a great rock that crashed back down eternally—eternal labor, freedom, labor . . . (stone will perish, but the word remain). And you, David, who with a stone slew, screaming: Lord, take my heart of stone and give me flesh.

Who was screaming? Why was she back in the common room of the prison, the sun motes dancing in the shafts of light, and the informer being brought in, a prisoner now, like themselves. And Lisa leaping, yes, Lisa, the gentle and tender, biting at the betrayer's jugular. Screaming and screaming.

No, it is the children screaming. Another of Paul and Sammy's terrible fights?

TILLIE OLSEN

457

In Vivi's house. Severely: you are in Vivi's house.

Blows, screams, a call: "Grandma!" For her? Oh please not for her. Hide, hunch behind the dresses deeper. But a trembling little body hurls itself beside her—surprised, smothered laughter, arms surround her neck, tears rub dry on her cheek, and words too soft to understand whisper into her ear (Is this where you hide too, Grammy? It's my secret place, we have a secret now).

And the sweat beads, and the long shudder seizes.

It seemed the great ear pressed inside now, and the knocking. "We have to go home," she told him, "I grow ill here."

"It's your own fault, Mrs. Bodybusy, you do not rest, you do too much." He raged, but the fear was in his eyes. "It was a serious operation, they told you to take care. . . . All right, we will go to where you can rest."

But where? Not home to death, not yet. He had thought to Lennie's, to Clara's; beautiful visits with each of the children. She would have to rest first, be stronger. If they could but go to Florida—it glittered before him, the never-realized promise of Florida. California: of course. (The money, the money, dwindling!) Los Angeles first for sun and rest, then to Lennie's in San Francisco.

He told her the next day. "You saw what Nancy wrote: snow and wind back home, a terrible winter. And look at you—all bones and a swollen belly. I called Phil: he said: 'A prescription, Los Angeles sun and rest.'"

She watched the words on his lips. "You have sold the house," she cried, "that is why we do not go home. That is why you talk no more of the Haven, why there is money for travel. After the children you will drag me to the Haven."

"The Haven! Who thinks of the Haven any more? Tell her, Vivi, tell Mrs. Suspicious: a prescription, sun and rest, to make you healthy. . . . And how could I sell the house without *you?*"

At the place of farewells and greetings, of winds of coming and winds of going, they say their good-byes.

They look back at her with the eyes of others before them: Richard with her own blue blaze; Ann with the nordic eyes of Tim; Morty's dreaming brown of a great-grandmother he will never know; Dody with the laughing eyes of him who had been her springtide love (who stands beside her now); Vivi's, all tears.

The baby's eyes are closed in sleep.

Good-bye, my children.

3

It is to the back of the great city he brought her, to the dwelling places of the cast-off old. Bounded by two lines of amusement piers to the north and to the south, and between a long straight paving rimmed with black benches facing the sand—sands so wide the ocean is only a far fluting.

In the brief vacation season, some of the boarded stores fronting the sands open, and families, young people and children, may be seen. A little tasselled tram shuttles between the piers, and the lights of roller coasters prink and tweak over those who come to have sensation made in them.

The rest of the year it is abandoned to the old, all else boarded up and still; seemingly empty, except the occasional days and hours when the sun, like a tide, sucks them out of the low rooming houses, casts them onto the benches and sandy rim of the walk—and sweeps them into decaying enclosures once again.

A few newer apartments glint among the low bleached squares. It is in one of these Lennie's Jeannie has arranged their rooms. "Only a few miles north and south people pay hundreds of dollars a month for just this gorgeous air, Grandaddy, just this ocean closeness."

She had been ill on the plane, lay ill for days in the unfamiliar room. Several times the doctor came by—left medicine she would not take. Several times Jeannie drove in the twenty miles from work, still in her Visiting Nurse uniform, the lightness and brightness of her like a healing.

"Who can believe it is winter?" he asked one morning. "Beautiful it is outside like an ad. Come, Mrs. Invalid, come to taste it. You are well enough to sit in here, you are well enough to sit outside. The doctor said it too."

But the benches were encrusted with people, and the sands at the sidewalk's edge. Besides, she had seen the far ruffle of the sea: "there take me," and though she leaned against him, it was she who led.

Plodding and plodding, sitting often to rest, he grumbling. Patting the sand so warm. Once she scooped up a handful, cradling it close to her better eye; peered, and flung it back. And as they came almost to the brink and she could see the glistening wet, she sat down, pulled off her shoes and stockings, left him and began to run. "You'll catch cold," he screamed, but the sand in his shoes weighed him down—he who had always been the agile one—and already the white spray creamed her feet.

He pulled her back, took a handkerchief to wipe off the wet and the sand. "Oh no," she said, "the sun will dry," seized the square and smoothed it flat, dropped on it a mound of sand, knotted the kerchief corners and tied it to a bag—"to look at with the strong glass" (for the first time in years explaining an action of hers)—and lay down with the little bag against her cheek, looking toward the shore that nurtured life as it first crawled toward consciousness the millions of years ago.

He took her one Sunday in the evil-smelling bus, past flat miles of blister houses, to the home of relatives. Oh what is this? she cried as the light began to smoke and the houses to dim and recede. Smog, he said, everyone knows but you. . . . Outside he kept his arms about her, but she walked with hands pushing the heavy air as if to open it, whispered: who

TILLIE OLSEN

has done this? sat down suddenly to vomit at the curb and for a long while refused to rise.

One's age as seen on the altered face of those known in youth. Is this they he has come to visit? This Max and Rose, smooth and pleasant, introducing them to polite children, disinterested grandchildren, "the whole family, once a month on Sundays. And why not? We have the room, the help, the food."

Talk of cars, of houses, of success: this son that, that daughter this. And *your* children? Hastily skimped over, the intermarriages, the obscure work—"my doctor son-in-law, Phil"—all he has to offer. She silent in a corner. (Car-sick like a baby, he explains.) Years since he has taken her to visit anyone but the children, and old apprehensions prickle: "no incidents," he silently begs, "no incidents." He itched to tell them. "A very sick woman," significantly, indicating her with his eyes, "a very sick woman." Their restricted faces did not react. "Have you thought maybe she'd do better at Palm Springs?" Rose asked. "Or at least a nicer section of the beach, nicer people, a pool." Not to have to say "money" he said instead: "would she have sand to look at through a magnifying glass?" and went on, detail after detail, the old habit betraying of parading the queerness of her for laughter.

After dinner—the others into the living room in men- or women-clusters, or into the den to watch TV—the four of them alone. She sat close to him, and did not speak. Jokes, stories, people they had known, beginning of reminiscence, Russia fifty-sixty years ago. Strange words across the Duncan Phyfe table: *hunger; secret meetings; human rights; spies; betrayals; prison; escape*—interrupted by one of the grandchildren: "Commercial's on; any Coke left? Gee, you're missing a real hair-raiser." And then a granddaughter (Max proudly: "look at her, an American queen") drove them home on her way back to U.C.L.A. No incident— except there had been no incidents.

The first few mornings she had taken with her the magnifying glass, but he would sit only on the benches, so she rested at the foot, where slatted bench shadows fell, and unless she turned her hearing aid down, other voices invaded.

Now on the days when the sun shone and she felt well enough, he took her on the tram to where the benches ranged in oblongs, some with tables for checkers or cards. Again the blanket on the sand in the striped shadows, but she no longer brought the magnifying glass. He played cards, and she lay in the sun and looked towards the waters; or they walked— two blocks down to the scaling hotel, two blocks back—past chili-hamburger stands, open-doored bars, Next-to-New and perpetual rummage sale stores.

Once, out of the aimless walkers, slow and shuffling like themselves, someone ran unevenly towards them, embraced, kissed, wept: "dear friends, old friends." A friend of *hers*, not his: Mrs. Mays who had lived next door to them in Denver when the children were small.

Thirty years are compressed into a dozen sentences; and the present, not even in three. All is told: the children scattered; the husband dead; she lives in a room two blocks up from the sing hall—and points to the domed auditorium jutting before the pier. The leg? phlebitis; the heavy breathing? that, one does not ask. She, too, comes to the benches each day to sit. And tomorrow, tomorrow, are they going to the community sing? Of course he would have heard of it, everybody goes—the big doings they wait for all week. They have never been? She will come to them for dinner tomorrow and they will all go together.

So it is that she sits in the wind of the singing, among the thousand various faces of age.

She had turned off her hearing aid at once they came into the auditorium.—as she would have wished to turn off sight.

One by one they streamed by and imprinted on her—and though the savage zest of their singing came voicelessly soft and distant, the faces still roared—the faces densened the air—chorded into

children-chants, mother-croons, singing of the chained
love serenades, Beethoven storms, mad Lucia's scream
drunken joy-songs, keens for the dead, work-singing

while from floor to balcony to dome a bare-footed sore-covered little girl threaded the sound-thronged tumult, danced her ecstasy of grimace to flutes that scratched at a cross-roads village wedding

Yes, faces became sound, and the sound became faces; and faces and sound became weight—pushed, pressed

"Air"—her hands claw his.

"Whenever I enjoy myself. . . ." Then he saw the gray sweat on her face. "Here. Up. Help me, Mrs. Mays," and they support her out to where she can gulp the air in sob after sob.

"A doctor, we should get for her a doctor."

"Tch, it's nothing," says Ellen Mays, "I get it all the time. You've missed the tram; come to my place. Fix your hearing aid, honey . . . close . . . tea. My view. See, she *wants* to come. Steady now, that's how." Adding mysteriously: "Remember your advice, easy to keep your head above water, empty things float. Float."

The singing a fading march for them, tall woman with a swollen leg, weaving little man, and the swollen thinness they help between.

The stench in the hall: mildew? decay? "We sit and rest then climb. My gorgeous view. We help each other and here   we   are."

TILLIE OLSEN

461

The stench along into the slab of room. A washstand for a sink, a box
with oilcloth tacked around for a cupboard, a three-burner gas plate.
Artificial flowers, colorless with dust. Everywhere pictures foaming:
wedding, baby, party, vacation, graduation, family pictures. From the narrow couch under a slit of window, sure enough the view: lurching roof-
tops and a scallop of ocean heaving, preening, twitching under the moon.

"While the water heats. Excuse me . . . down the hall." Ellen Mays
has gone.

"You'll live?" he asks mechanically, sat down to feel his fright; tried
to pull her alongside.

She pushed him away. "For air," she said; stood clinging to the dresser.
Then, in a terrible voice:

After a lifetime of room. Of many rooms.

Shhh.

You remember how she lived. Eight children. And now one room   like
a coffin.

She pays rent!

Shrinking the life of her   into one room   like a coffin   Rooms and
rooms like this   I lie on the quilt and hear them talk

Please, Mrs. Orator-without-Breath.

Once you went for coffee   I walked   I saw   A Balzac   a Chekhov to
write it   Rummage   Alone   On scraps

Better old here than in the old country!

On scraps   Yet they sang like   like   Wondrous!   *Humankind   one
has to believe*   So strong   for what?   To rot   not grow?

Your poor lungs beg you. They sob between each word.

Singing.   Unused   the life in them.   She   in this poor room   with
her   pictures   Max   You   The children   Everywhere unused the
life   And who has meaning?   Century after century   still all in us   not
to grow?

Coffins, rummage, plants: sick woman. Oh lay down. We will get for
you the doctor.

"And when will it end. Oh, *the end*." *That* nightmare thought, and
this time she writhed, crumpled against him, seized his hand (for a
moment again the weight, the soft distant roaring of humanity) and
on the strangled-for breath, begged: "Man . . . we'll destroy ourselves?"

And looking for answer—in the helpless pity and fear for her (for *her*)
that distorted his face—she understood the last months, and knew that
she was dying.

4

"Let us go home," she said after several days.

"You are in training for a cross-country race? That is why you do not
even walk across the room? Here, like a prescription Phil said, till you
are stronger from the operation. You want to break doctor's orders?"

She saw the fiction was necessary to him, was silent; then: "At home I will get better. If the doctor here says?"

"And winter? And the visits to Lennie and to Clara? All right," for he saw the tears in her eyes, "I will write Phil, and talk to the doctor."

Days passed. He reported nothing. Jeannie came and took her out for air, past the boarded concessions, the hooded and tented amusement rides, to the end of the pier. They watched the spent waves feeding the new, the gulls in the clouded sky; even up where they sat, the wind-blown sand stung.

She did not ask to go down the crooked steps to the sea.

Back in her bed, while he was gone to the store, she said: "Jeannie, this doctor, he is not one I can ask questions. Ask him for me, can I go home?"

Jeannie looked at her, said quickly: "Of course, poor Granny. You want your own things around you, don't you? I'll call him tonight. . . . Look, I've something to show you," and from her purse unwrapped a large cookie, intricately shaped like a little girl. "Look at the curls—can you hear me well, Granny?—and the darling eyelashes. I just came from a house where they were baking them."

"The dimples, there in the knees," she marveled, holding it to the better light, turning, studying, "like art. Each singly they cut, or a mold?"

"Singly," said Jeannie, "and if it is a child only the mother can make them. Oh Granny, it's the likeness of a real little girl who died yesterday—Rosita. She was three years old. *Pan del Muerto*, the Bread of the Dead. It was the custom in the part of Mexico they came from."

Still she turned and inspected. "Look, the hollow in the throat, the little cross necklace. . . . I think for the mother it is a good thing to be busy with such bread. You know the family?"

Jeannie nodded. "On my rounds. I nursed. . . . Oh Granny, it is like a party; they play songs she liked to dance to. The coffin is lined with pink velvet and she wears a white dress. There are candles. . . ."

"In the house?" Surprised, "They keep her in the house?"

"Yes," said Jeannie, "and it is against the health law. The father said it will be sad to bury her in this country; in Oaxaca they have a feast night with candles each year; everyone picnics on the graves of those they loved until dawn."

"Yes, Jeannie, the living must comfort themselves." And closed her eyes.

"You want to sleep, Granny?"

"Yes, tired from the pleasure of you. I may keep the Rosita? There stand it, on the dresser, where I can see; something of my own around me."

In the kitchenette, helping her grandfather unpack the groceries, Jeannie said in her light voice:

"I'm resigning my job, Grandaddy."

"Ah, the lucky young man. Which one is he?"

"Too late. You're spoken for." She made a pyramid of cans, unstacked, and built again.

"Something is wrong with the job?"

"With me. I can't be"—she searched for the word—"What they call professional enough. I let myself feel things. And tomorrow I have to report a family. . . ." The cans clicked again. "It's not that, either. I just don't know what I want to do, maybe go back to school, maybe go to art school. I thought if you went to San Francisco I'd come along and talk it over with Momma and Daddy. But I don't see how you can go. She wants to go home. She asked me to ask the doctor."

The doctor told her himself. "Next week you may travel, when you are a little stronger." But next week there was the fever of an infection, and by the time that was over, she could not leave the bed—a rented hospital bed that stood beside the double bed he slept in alone now.

Outwardly the days repeated themselves. Every other afternoon and evening he went out to his newfound cronies, to talk and play cards. Twice a week, Mrs. Mays came. And the rest of the time, Jeannie was there.

By the sickbed stood Jeannie's FM radio. Often into the room the shapes of music came. She would lie curled on her side, her knees drawn up, intense in listening (Jeannie sketched her so, coiled, convoluted like an ear), then thresh her hand out and abruptly snap the radio mute—still to lie in her attitude of listening, concealing tears.

Once Jeannie brought in a young Marine to visit, a friend from high-school days she had found wandering near the empty pier. Because Jeannie asked him to, gravely, without self-consciousness, he sat himself cross-legged on the floor and performed for them a dance of his native Samoa.

Long after they left, a tiny thrumming sound could be heard where, in her bed, she strove to repeat the beckon, flight, surrender of his hands, the fluttering footbeats, and his low plaintive calls.

Hannah and Phil sent flowers. To deepen her pleasure, he placed one in her hair. "Like a girl," he said, and brought the hand mirror so she could see. She looked at the pulsing red flower, the yellow skull face; a desolate, excited laugh shuddered from her, and she pushed the mirror away—but let the flower burn.

The week Lennie and Helen came, the fever returned. With it the excited laugh, and incessant words. She, who in her life had spoken but seldom and then only when necessary (never having learned the easy, social uses of words), now in dying, spoke incessantly.

In a half-whisper: "Like Lisa she is, your Jeannie. Have I told you of Lisa who taught me to read? Of the highborn she was, but noble in herself. I was sixteen; they beat me; my father beat me so I would not go to her. It was forbidden, she was a Tolstoyan. At night, past dogs that howled, terrible dogs, my son, in the snows of winter to the road, I to ride in her carriage like a lady, to books. To her, life was holy, knowledge was holy, and she taught me to read. They hung her. Everything that happens one must try to understand. She killed one who betrayed many. Because of betrayal, betrayed all she lived and believed. In one minute she killed, before my eyes (there is so much blood in a human being, my son), in prison with me. All that happens, one must try to understand.

"The name?" Her lips would work. "The name that was their pole star; the doors of the death houses fixed to open on it; I read of it my year of penal servitude. Thuban!" very excited, "Thuban, in ancient Egypt the pole star. Can you see, look out to see it, Jeannie, if it swings around *our* pole star that seems to *us* not to move.

"Yes, Jeannie, at your age my mother and grandmother had already buried children . . . yes, Jeannie, it is more than oceans between Olshana and you . . . yes, Jeannie, they danced, and for all the bodies they had they might as well be chickens, and indeed, they scratched and flapped their arms and hopped.

"And Andrei Yefimitch, who for twenty years had never known of it and never wanted to know, said as if he wanted to cry: but why my dear friend this malicious laughter?" Telling to herself half-memorized phrases from her few books. "Pain I answer with tears and cries, baseness with indignation, meanness with repulsion . . . for life may be hated or wearied of, but never despised."

Delirious: "Tell me, my neighbor, Mrs. Mays, the pictures never lived, but what of the flowers? Tell them who ask: no rabbis, no ministers, no priests, no speeches, no ceremonies: ah, false—let the living comfort themselves. Tell Sammy's boy, he who flies, tell him to go to Stuttgart and see where Davy has no grave. And what? . . . And what? where millions have no graves—save air."

In delirium or not, wanting the radio on; not seeming to listen, the words still jetting, wanting the music on. Once, silencing it abruptly as of old, she began to cry, unconcealed tears this time. "You have pain, Granny?" Jeannie asked.

"The music," she said, "still it is there and we do not hear; knocks, and our poor human ears too weak. What else, what else we do not hear?"

Once she knocked his hand aside as he gave her a pill, swept the bottles from her bedside table: "no pills, let me feel what I feel," and laughed as on his hands and knees he groped to pick them up.

Nighttimes her hand reached across the bed to hold his.

A constant retching began. Her breath was too faint for sustained speech now, but still the lips moved:

> When no longer necessary   to injure others
> Pick   pick pick   Blind   chicken
> As a human being   responsibility

"David!" imperious, "Basin!" and she would vomit, rinse her mouth, the wasted throat working to swallow, and begin the chant again.

She will be better off in the hospital now, the doctor said.

He sent the telegrams to the children, was packing her suitcase, when her hoarse voice startled. She had roused, was pulling herself to sitting.

"Where now?" she asked. "Where now do you drag me?"

"You do not even have to have a baby to go this time," he soothed, looking for the brush to pack. "Remember, after Davy you told me—worthy to have a baby for the pleasure of the ten day rest in the hospital?"

"Where now? Not home yet?" Her voice mourned. "Where *is* my home?"

He rose to ease her back. "The doctor, the hospital," he started to explain, but deftly, like a snake, she had slithered out of bed and stood swaying, propped behind the night table.

"Coward," she hissed, "runner."

"You stand," he said senselessly.

"To take me there and run. Afraid of a little vomit."

He reached her as she fell. She struggled against him, half slipped from his arms, pulled herself up again.

"Weakling," she taunted, "to leave me there and run. Betrayer. All your life you have run."

He sobbed, telling Jeannie. "A Marilyn Monroe to run for her virtue. Fifty-nine pounds she weighs, the doctor said, and she beats at me like a Dempsey. Betrayer, she cries, and I running like a dog when she calls; day and night, running to her, her vomit, the bedpan. . . ."

"She needs you, Grandaddy," said Jeannie. "Isn't that what they call love? I'll see if she sleeps, and if she does, poor worn-out darling, we'll have a party, you and I: I brought us rum babas."

They did not move her. By her bed now stood the tall hooked pillar that held the solutions—blood and dextrose—to feed her veins. Jeannie moved down the hall to take over the sickroom, her face so radiant, her grandfather asked her once: "you are in love?" (Shameful the joy, the pure overwhelming joy from being with her grandmother; the peace, the serenity that breathed.) "My darling escape," she answered incoherently, "my darling Granny"—as if that explained.

Now one by one the children came, those that were able. Hannah, Paul, Sammy. Too late to ask: and what did you learn with your living, Mother, and what do we need to know?

Clara, the eldest, clenched:

Pay me back, Mother, pay me back for all you took from me. Those others you crowded into your heart. The hands I needed to be for you, the heaviness, the responsibility.

Is this she? Noises the dying make, the crablike hands crawling over the covers. The ethereal singing.

She hears that music, that singing from childhood; forgotten sound—

*not heard since, since. . . . And the hardness breaks like a cry: Where
did we lose each other, first mother, singing mother?*

*Annulled: the quarrels, the gibing, the harshness between; the fall
into silence and the withdrawal.*

I do not know you, Mother. Mother, I never knew you.

Lennie, suffering not alone for her who was dying, but for that in her
which never lived (for that which in him might never live). From him
too, unspoken words: *good-bye Mother who taught me to mother myself.*

Not Vivi, who must stay with her children; not Davy, but he is already here, having to die again with *her* this time, for the living take
their dead with them when they die.

Light she grew, like a bird, and, like a bird, sound bubbled in her throat
while the body fluttered in agony. Night and day, asleep or awake (though
indeed there was no difference now) the songs and the phrases leaping.

And he, who had once dreaded a long dying (from fear of himself, from
horror of the dwindling money) now desired her quick death profoundly,
for *her* sake. He no longer went out, except when Jeannie forced him; no
longer laughed, except when, in the bright kitchenette, Jeannie coaxed
his laughter (and she, who seemed to hear nothing else, would laugh too,
conspiratorial wisps of laughter).

Light, like a bird, the fluttering body, the little claw hands, the beaked
shadow on her face; and the throat, bubbling, straining.

He tried not to listen, as he tried not to look on the face in which only
the forehead remained familiar, but trapped with her the long nights in
that little room, the sounds worked themselves into his consciousness,
with their punctuation of death swallows, whimpers, gurglings.

Even in reality (swallow) *life's lack of it*

Slaveships   deathtrains   clubs   eeenough

The bell   summon   what enobles

    78,000 in one minute (whisper of a scream) *78,000*

human beings   we'll destroy ourselves?

"Aah, Mrs. Miserable," he said, as if she could hear, "all your life working, and now in bed you lie, servants to tend, you do not even need to
call to be tended, and still you work. Such hard work it is to die? Such
hard work?"

The body threshed, her hand clung in his. A melody, ghost-thin, hovered on her lips, and like a guilty ghost, the vision of her bent in listening to it, silencing the record instantly he was near. Now, heedless of his
presence, she floated the melody on and on.

"Hid it from me," he complained, "how many times you listened to
remember it so?" And tried to think when she had first played it, or first
begun to silence her few records when he came near—but could reconstruct nothing. There was only this room with its tall hooked pillar and
its swarm of sounds.

TILLIE OLSEN

No man one   except through others
Strong   with the not yet   in the now
Dogma dead   war dead   one country

"It helps, Mrs. Philosopher, words from books? It helps?" And it seemed to him that for seventy years she had hidden a tape recorder, infinitely microscopic, within her, that it had coiled infinite mile on mile, trapping every song, every melody, every word read, heard, and spoken—and that maliciously she was playing back only what said nothing of him, of the children, of their intimate life together.

"Left us indeed, Mrs. Babbler," he reproached, "you who called others babbler and cunningly saved your words. A lifetime you tended and loved, and now not a word of us, for us. Left us indeed? Left me."

And he took out his solitaire deck, shuffled the cards loudly, slapped them down.

Lift high   banner of reason (tatter of an orator's voice)
justice   freedom   light
Humankind   life   worthy   capacities
Seeks (blur of shudder) *belong   human being*

"Words, words," he accused, "and what human beings did *you* seek around you, Mrs. Live Alone, and what humankind think worthy?"

Though even as he spoke, he remembered she had not always been isolated, had not always wanted to be alone (as he knew there had been a voice before this gossamer one; before the hoarse voice that broke from silence to lash, make incidents, shame him—a girl's voice of eloquence that spoke their holiest dreams). But again he could reconstruct, image, nothing of what had been before, or when, or how, it had changed.

Ace, queen, jack. The pillar shadow fell, so, in two tracks; in the mirror depths glistened a moonlike blob, the empty solution bottle. And it worked in him: *of reason and justice and freedom . . . Dogma dead:* he remembered the full quotation, laughed bitterly. "Hah, good you do not know what you say; good Victor Hugo died and did not see it, his twentieth century."

Deuce, ten, five. Dauntlessly she began a song of their youth of belief:

> *These things shall be, a loftier race*
> *than e'er the world hath known shall rise*
> *with flame of freedom in their souls*
> *and light of knowledge in their eyes*

King, four, jack "In the twentieth century, hah!"

> *They shall be gentle, brave and strong*
> *to spill no drop of blood, but dare*
> *all . . .*
>
> *on earth and fire and sea and air*

"To spill no drop of blood, hah! So, cadaver, and you too, cadaver Hugo, 'in the twentieth century ignorance will be dead, dogma will be dead, war will be dead, and for all mankind one country—of fulfilment?' Hah!"

> *And every life* (long strangling cough) *shall*
> *be a song*

The cards fell from his fingers. Without warning, the bereavement and betrayal he had sheltered—compounded through the years—hidden even from himself—revealed itself,

uncoiled,
released,
sprung

and with it the monstrous shapes of what had actually happened in the century.

A ravening hunger or thirst seized him. He groped into the kitchenette, switched on all three lights, piled a tray—"you have finished your night snack, Mrs. Cadaver, now I will have mine." And he was shocked at the tears that splashed on the tray.

"Salt tears. For free. I forgot to shake on salt?"

Whispered: "Lost, how much I lost."

Escaped to the grandchildren whose childhoods were childish, who had never hungered, who lived unravaged by disease in warm houses of many rooms, had all the school for which they cared, could walk on any street, stood a head taller than their grandparents, towered above—beautiful skins, straight backs, clear straightforward eyes. "Yes, you in Olshana," he said to the town of sixty years ago, "they would be nobility to you."

And was this not the dream then, come true in ways undreamed? he asked.

And are there no other children in the world? he answered, as if in her harsh voice.

And the flame of freedom, the light of knowledge?

And the drop, to spill no drop of blood?

And he thought that at six Jeannie would get up and it would be his turn to go to her room and sleep, that he could press the buzzer and she would come now; that in the afternoon Ellen Mays was coming, and this time they would play cards and he could marvel at how rouge can stand half an inch on the cheek; that in the evening the doctor would come, and he could beg him to be merciful, to stop the feeding solutions, to let her die.

To let her die, and with her their youth of belief out of which her bright, betrayed words foamed; stained words, that on her working lips came stainless.

Hours yet before Jeannie's turn. He could press the buzzer and wake her to come now; he could take a pill, and with it sleep; he could pour more brandy into his milk glass, though what he had poured was not yet touched.

Instead he went back, checked her pulse, gently tended with his knotty fingers as Jeannie had taught.

She was whimpering; her hand crawled across the covers for his. Compassionately he enfolded it, and with his free hand gathered up the cards again. Still was there thirst or hunger ravening in him.

That world of their youth—dark, ignorant, terrible with hate and disease—how was it that living in it, in the midst of corruption, filth, treachery, degradation, they had not mistrusted man nor themselves; had believed so beautifully, so . . . falsely?

"Aaah, children," he said out loud, "how we believed, how we belonged." And he yearned to package for each of the children, the grandchildren, for everyone, *that joyous certainty, that sense of mattering, of moving and being moved, of being one and indivisible with the great of the past, with all that freed, ennobled.* Package it, stand on corners, in front of stadiums and on crowded beaches, knock on doors, give it as a fabled gift.

"And why not in cereal boxes, in soap packages?" he mocked himself. "Aah. You have taken my senses, cadaver."

Words foamed, died unsounded. Her body writhed; she made kissing motions with her mouth. (Her lips moving as she read, poring over the Book of the Martyrs, the magnifying glass superimposed over the heavy eyeglasses.) *Still she believed?* "Eva!" he whispered. "Still you believed? You lived by it? These Things Shall Be?"

"One pound soup meat," she answered distinctly, "one soup bone."

"My ears heard you. Ellen Mays was witness: 'Humankind . . . one has to believe.'" Imploringly: "Eva!"

"Bread, day-old." She was mumbling. "Please, in a wooden box . . . for kindling. The thread, hah, the thread breaks. Cheap thread"—and a gurgling, enormously loud, began in her throat.

"I ask for stone; she gives me bread—day-old." He pulled his hand away, shouted: "Who wanted questions? Everything you have to wake?" Then dully, "Ah, let me help you turn, poor creature."

Words jumbled, cleared. In a voice of crowded terror:

"Paul, Sammy, don't fight.

"Hannah, have I ten hands?

"How can I give it, Clara, how can I give it if I don't have?"

"You lie," he said sturdily, "there was joy too." Bitterly: "Ah how cheap you speak of us at the last."

As if to rebuke him, as if her voice had no relationship with her flailing body, she sang clearly, beautifully, a school song the children had taught her when they were little; begged:

"Not look   my hair   where they cut. . . ."

(The crown of braids shorn.) And instantly he left the mute old woman poring over the Book of the Martyrs; went past the mother treading at the sewing machine, singing with the children; past the girl in her wrinkled prison dress, hiding her hair with scarred hands, lifting to him her awkward, shamed, imploring eyes of love; and took her in his arms, dear, personal, fleshed, in all the heavy passion he had loved to rouse from her.

"Eva!"

Her little claw hand beat the covers. How much, how much can a man stand? He took up the cards, put them down, circled the beds, walked to the dresser, opened, shut drawers, brushed his hair, moved his hand bit by bit over the mirror to see what of the reflection he could blot out with each move, and felt that at any moment he would die of what was unendurable. Went to press the buzzer to wake Jeannie, looked down, saw on Jeannie's sketch pad the hospital bed, with *her*; the double bed alongside, with him; the tall pillar feeding into her veins, and their hands, his and hers, clasped, feeding each other. And as if he had been instructed he went to his bed, lay down, holding the sketch (as if it could shield against the monstrous shapes of loss, of betrayal, of death) and with his free hand took hers back into his.

So Jeannie found them in the morning.

That last day the agony was perpetual. Time after time it lifted her almost off the bed, so they had to fight to hold her down. He could not endure and left the room; wept as if there never would be tears enough.

Jeannie came to comfort him. In her light voice she said: Grandaddy, Grandaddy don't cry. She is not there, she promised me. On the last day, she said she would go back to when she first heard music, a little girl on the road of the village where she was born. She promised me. It is a wedding and they dance, while the flutes so joyous and vibrant tremble in the air. Leave her there. Grandaddy, it is all right. She promised me. Come back, come back and help her poor body to die.

For two of that generation
Seevya and Genya
Infinite, dauntless, incorruptible

Death deepens the wonder

TILLIE OLSEN

471

UNLEARNING TO NOT SPEAK

by

MARGE PIERCY
(b. 1936)

Marge Piercy was born in Detroit and was the first in her family to attend college. She now lives at Wellfleet on Cape Cod. She has published eight novels, including Woman on the Edge of Time *(1976), a science fiction work in which she experimented with a "woman's language." She has also written a play, essays, and nine volumes of poetry. Recent works include a volume of poems,* Available Light *(1988), an edition of American women's poetry,* Early Ripening *(1988), and a novel,* Summer People *(1989). Piercy has lectured widely at colleges and feminist meetings.*

Blizzards of paper
in slow motion
sift through her.
In nightmares she suddenly recalls
a class she signed up for
but forgot to attend.
Now it is too late.
Now it is time for finals:
losers will be shot.
Phrases of men who lectured her
drift and rustle in piles:
Why don't you speak up?
Why are you shouting?
You have the wrong answer,
wrong line, wrong face.
They tell her she is womb-man,
babymachine, mirror image, toy,
earth mother and penis-poor,
a dish of synthetic strawberry icecream
rapidly melting.

She grunts to a halt.
She must learn again to speak
starting with *I*
starting with *We*
starting as the infant does
with her own true hunger
and pleasure
and rage.

SEVENTEEN SYLLABLES

by

HISAYE YAMAMOTO
(b. 1921)

*Born in Redondo Beach, California, of Japanese immigrant parents,
Hisaye Yamamoto was interned in a concentration camp from 1942
to 1945. She majored in languages at Compton Junior College, after
attending Japanese school for twelve years. She worked as a journalist in both Los Angeles and New York. The success of her earliest
short stories won her a Whitney Foundation fellowship in 1950.
Her work has been widely published in periodicals and anthologies,
and in 1986 she won the American Book Award for Lifetime Achievement from the Before Columbus Foundation. Her collection* Seventeen Syllables, *representing the work of forty years, appeared in
1988. (In this story Mrs. Hayashi's pen name means roughly
"flowering plum tree.")*

• ——————————————————— •

The first Rosie knew that her mother had taken to writing poems was
one evening when she finished one and read it aloud for her daughter's
approval. It was about cats, and Rosie pretended to understand it thoroughly and appreciate it no end, partly because she hesitated to disillusion her mother about the quantity and quality of Japanese she had
learned in all the years now that she had been going to Japanese school
every Saturday (and Wednesday, too, in the summer). Even so, her mother
must have been skeptical about the depth of Rosie's understanding,
because she explained afterwards about the kind of poem she was trying
to write.

See, Rosie, she said, it was a *haiku*, a poem in which she must pack
all her meaning into seventeen syllables only, which were divided into
three lines of five, seven, and five syllables. In the one she had just read,
she had tried to capture the charm of a kitten, as well as comment on
the superstition that owning a cat of three colors meant good luck.

"Yes, yes, I understand. How utterly lovely," Rosie said, and her
mother, either satisfied or seeing through the deception and resigned,
went back to composing.

The truth was that Rosie was lazy; English lay ready on the tongue
but Japanese had to be searched for and examined, and even then put
forth tentatively (probably to meet with laughter). It was so much easier

to say yes, yes, even when one meant no, no. Besides, this was what was in her mind to say: I was looking through one of your magazines from Japan last night, Mother, and towards the back I found some *haiku* in English that delighted me. There was one that made me giggle off and on until I fell asleep—

> *It is morning, and lo!*
> *I lie awake, comme il faut,*
> *sighing for some dough.*

Now, how to reach her mother, how to communicate the melancholy song? Rosie knew formal Japanese by fits and starts, her mother had even less English, no French. It was much more possible to say yes, yes.

It developed that her mother was writing the *haiku* for a daily newspaper, the *Mainichi Shimbun*, that was published in San Francisco. Los Angeles, to be sure, was closer to the farming community in which the Hayashi family lived and several Japanese vernaculars were printed there, but Rosie's parents said they preferred the tone of the northern paper. Once a week, the *Mainichi* would have a section devoted to *haiku*, and her mother became an extravagant contributor, taking for herself the blossoming pen name, Ume Hanazono.

So Rosie and her father lived for awhile with two women, her mother and Ume Hanazono. Her mother (Tome Hayashi by name) kept house, cooked, washed, and, along with her husband and the Carrascos, the Mexican family hired for the harvest, did her ample share of picking tomatoes out in the sweltering fields and boxing them in tidy strata in the cool packing shed. Ume Hanazono, who came to life after the dinner dishes were done, was an earnest, muttering stranger who often neglected speaking when spoken to and stayed busy at the parlor table as late as midnight scribbling with pencil on scratch paper or carefully copying characters on good paper with her fat, pale green Parker.

The new interest had some repercussions on the household routine. Before, Rosie had been accustomed to her parents and herself taking their hot baths early and going to bed almost immediately afterwards, unless her parents challenged each other to a game of flower cards or unless company dropped in. Now if her father wanted to play cards, he had to resort to solitaire (at which he always cheated fearlessly), and if a group of friends came over, it was bound to contain someone who was also writing *haiku*, and the small assemblage would be split in two, her father entertaining the non-literary members and her mother comparing ecstatic notes with the visiting poet.

If they went out, it was more of the same thing. But Ume Hanazono's life span, even for a poet's, was very brief—perhaps three months at most.

One night they went over to see the Hayano family in the neighboring town to the west, an adventure both painful and attractive to Rosie. It was attractive because there were four Hayano girls, all lovely and each one named after a season of the year (Haru, Natsu, Aki, Fuyu), painful because something had been wrong with Mrs. Hayano ever since the birth of her first child. Rosie would sometimes watch Mrs. Hayano, reputed to have been the belle of her native village, making her way about a room, stooped, slowly shuffling, violently trembling (*always* trembling), and she would be reminded that this woman, in this same condition, had carried and given issue to three babies. She would look wonderingly at Mr. Hayano, handsome, tall, and strong, and she would look at her four pretty friends. But it was not a matter she could come to any decision about.

On this visit, however, Mrs. Hayano sat all evening in the rocker, as motionless and unobtrusive as it was possible for her to be, and Rosie found the greater part of the evening practically anaesthetic. Too, Rosie spent most of it in the girls' room, because Haru, the garrulous one, said almost as soon as the bows and other greetings were over, "Oh, you must see my new coat!"

It was a pale plaid of grey, sand, and blue, with an enormous collar, and Rosie, seeing nothing special in it, said, "Gee, how nice."

"Nice?" said Haru, indignantly. "Is that all you can say about it? It's gorgeous! And so cheap, too. Only seventeen-ninety-eight, because it was a sale. The saleslady said it was twenty-five dollars regular."

"Gee," said Rosie. Natsu, who never said much and when she said anything said it shyly, fingered the coat covetously and Haru pulled it away.

"Mine," she said, putting it on. She minced in the aisle between the two large beds and smiled happily. "Let's see how your mother likes it."

She broke into the front room and the adult conversation and went to stand in front of Rosie's mother, while the rest watched from the door. Rosie's mother was properly envious. "May I inherit it when you're through with it?"

Haru, pleased, giggled and said yes, she could, but Natsu reminded gravely from the door, "You promised me, Haru."

Everyone laughed but Natsu, who shamefacedly retreated into the bedroom. Haru came in laughing, taking off the coat. "We were only kidding, Natsu," she said. "Here, you try it on now."

After Natsu buttoned herself into the coat, inspected herself solemnly in the bureau mirror, and reluctantly shed it, Rosie, Aki, and Fuyu got their turns, and Fuyu, who was eight, drowned in it while her sisters and Rosie doubled up in amusement. They all went into the front room later, because Haru's mother quaveringly called to her to fix the tea and rice cakes and open a can of sliced peaches for everybody. Rosie noticed that her mother and Mr. Hayano were talking together at the little table— they were discussing a *haiku* that Mr. Hayano was planning to send to the *Mainichi*, while her father was sitting at one end of the sofa looking through a copy of *Life*, the new picture magazine. Occasionally, her father would comment on a photograph, holding it toward Mrs. Hayano and speaking to her as he always did—loudly, as though he thought someone such as she must surely be at least a trifle deaf also.

The five girls had their refreshments at the kitchen table, and it was while Rosie was showing the sisters her trick of swallowing peach slices without chewing (she chased each slippery crescent down with a swig of tea) that her father brought his empty teacup and untouched saucer to the sink and said, "Come on, Rosie, we're going home now."

"Already?" asked Rosie.

"Work tomorrow," he said.

He sounded irritated, and Rosie, puzzled, gulped one last yellow slice and stood up to go, while the sisters began protesting, as was their wont. "We have to get up at five-thirty," he told them, going into the front room quickly, so that they did not have their usual chance to hang onto his hands and plead for an extension of time.

Rosie, following, saw that her mother and Mr. Hayano were sipping tea and still talking together, while Mrs. Hayano concentrated, quivering, on raising the handleless Japanese cup to her lips with both her hands and lowering it back to her lap. Her father, saying nothing, went out the door, onto the bright porch, and down the steps. Her mother looked up and asked, "Where is he going?"

"Where is he going?" Rosie said. "He said we were going home now."

"Going home?" Her mother looked with embarrassment at Mr. Hayano and his absorbed wife and then forced a smile. "He must be tired," she said.

Haru was not giving up yet. "May Rosie stay overnight?" she asked, and Natsu, Aki, and Fuyu came to reinforce their sister's plea by helping her make a circle around Rosie's mother. Rosie, for once having no desire to stay, was relieved when her mother, apologizing to the perturbed Mr. and Mrs. Hayano for her father's abruptness at the same time, managed to shake her head no at the quartet, kindly but adamant, so that they broke their circle and let her go.

Rosie's father looked ahead into the windshield as the two joined him. "I'm sorry," her mother said. "You must be tired." Her father, stepping on the starter, said nothing. "You know how I get when it's *haiku*," she continued, "I forget what time it is." He only grunted.

As they rode homeward silently, Rosie, sitting between, felt a rush of hate for both—for her mother for begging, for her father for denying her mother. I wish this old Ford would crash, right now, she thought, then immediately, no, no, I wish my father would laugh, but it was too late: already the vision had passed through her mind of the green pick-up crumpled in the dark against one of the mighty eucalyptus trees they were just riding past, of the three contorted, bleeding bodies, one of them hers.

Rosie ran between two patches of tomatoes, her heart working more rambunctiously than she had ever known it to. How lucky it was that

Aunt Taka and Uncle Gimpachi had come tonight, though, how very lucky. Otherwise she might not have really kept her half-promise to meet Jesus Carrasco. Jesus was going to be a senior in September at the same school she went to, and his parents were the ones helping with the tomatoes this year. She and Jesus, who hardly remembered seeing each other at Cleveland High where there were so many other people and two whole grades between them, had become great friends this summer—he always had a joke for her when he periodically drove the loaded pick-up up from the fields to the shed where she was usually sorting while her mother and father did the packing, and they laughed a great deal together over infinitesimal repartee during the afternoon break for chilled watermelon or ice cream in the shade of the shed.

What she enjoyed most was racing him to see which could finish picking a double row first. He, who could work faster, would tease her by slowing down until she thought she would surely pass him this time, then speeding up furiously to leave her several sprawling vines behind. Once he had made her screech hideously by crossing over, while her back was turned, to place atop the tomatoes in her green-stained bucket a truly monstrous, pale green worm (it had looked more like an infant snake). And it was when they had finished a contest this morning, after she had pantingly pointed a green finger at the immature tomatoes evident in the lugs at the end of his row and he had returned the accusation (with justice), that he had startlingly brought up the matter of their possibly meeting outside the range of both their parents' dubious eyes.
"What for?" she had asked.
"I've got a secret I want to tell you," he said.
"Tell me now," she demanded.
"It won't be ready till tonight," he said.
She laughed. "Tell me tomorrow then."
"It'll be gone tomorrow," he threatened.
"Well, for seven hakes, what is it?" she had asked, more than twice, and when he had suggested that the packing shed would be an appropriate place to find out, she had cautiously answered maybe. She had not been certain she was going to keep the appointment until the arrival of mother's sister and her husband. Their coming seemed a sort of signal of permission, of grace, and she had definitely made up her mind to lie and leave as she was bowing them welcome.
So as soon as everyone appeared settled back for the evening, she announced loudly that she was going to the privy outside, "I'm going to the *benjo!*" and slipped out the door. And now that she was actually on her way, her heart pumped in such an undisciplined way that she could hear it with her ears. It's because I'm running, she told herself, slowing to a walk. The shed was up ahead, one more patch away, in the middle of the fields. Its bulk, looming in the dimness, took on a sinisterness that was

funny when Rosie reminded herself that it was only a wooden frame with a canvas roof and three canvas walls that made a slapping noise on breezy days.

Jesus was sitting on the narrow plank that was the sorting platform and she went around to the other side and jumped backwards to seat herself on the rim of a packing stand. "Well, tell me," she said without greeting, thinking her voice sounded reassuringly familiar.

"I saw you coming out the door," Jesus said. "I heard you running part of the way, too."

"Uh-huh," Rosie said. "Now tell me the secret."

"I was afraid you wouldn't come," he said.

Rosie delved around on the chicken-wire bottom of the stall for number two tomatoes, ripe, which she was sitting beside, and came up with a left-over that felt edible. She bit into it and began sucking out the pulp and seeds. "I'm here," she pointed out.

"Rosie, are you sorry you came?"

"Sorry? What for?" she said. "You said you were going to tell me something."

"I will, I will," Jesus said, but his voice contained disappointment, and Rosie fleetingly felt the older of the two, realizing a brand-new power which vanished without category under her recognition.

"I have to go back in a minute," she said. "My aunt and uncle are here from Wintersburg. I told them I was going to the privy."

Jesus laughed. "You funny thing," he said. "You slay me!"

"Just because you have a bathroom *inside*," Rosie said. "Come on, tell me."

Chuckling, Jesus came around to lean on the stand facing her. They still could not see each other very clearly, but Rosie noticed that Jesus became very sober again as he took the hollow tomato from her hand and dropped it back into the stall. When he took hold of her empty hand, she could find no words to protest; her vocabulary had become distressingly constricted and she thought desperately that all that remained intact now was yes and no and oh, and even these few sounds would not easily out. Thus, kissed by Jesus, Rosie fell for the first time entirely victim to a helplessness delectable beyond speech. But the terrible, beautiful sensation lasted no more than a second, and the reality of Jesus' lips and tongue and teeth and hands made her pull away with such strength that she nearly tumbled.

Rosie stopped running as she approached the lights from the windows of home. How long since she had left? She could not guess, but gasping yet, she went to the privy in back and locked herself in. Her own breathing deafened her in the dark, close space, and she sat and waited until she could hear at last the nightly calling of the frogs and crickets. Even then, all she could think to say was oh, my, and the pressure of Jesus' face against her face would not leave.

No one had missed her in the parlor, however, and Rosie walked in and through quickly, announcing that she was next going to take a bath. "Your father's in the bathhouse," her mother said, and Rosie, in her room, recalled that she had not seen him when she entered. There had been only Aunt Taka and Uncle Gimpachi with her mother at the table, drinking tea. She got her robe and straw sandals and crossed the parlor again to go outside. Her mother was telling them about the *haiku* competition in the *Mainichi* and the poem she had entered.

Rosie met her father coming out of the bathhouse. "Are you through, Father?" she asked. "I was going to ask you to scrub my back."

"Scrub your own back," he said shortly, going toward the main house.

"What have I done now?" she yelled after him. She suddenly felt like doing a lot of yelling. But he did not answer, and she went into the bathhouse. Turning on the dangling light, she removed her denims and T-shirt and threw them in the big carton for dirty clothes standing next to the washing machine. Her other things she took with her into the bath compartment to wash after her bath. After she had scooped a basin of hot water from the square wooden tub, she sat on the grey cement of the floor and soaped herself at exaggerated leisure, singing "Red Sails in the Sunset" at the top of her voice and using da-da-da where she suspected her words. Then, standing up, still singing, for she was possessed by the notion that any attempt now to analyze would result in spoilage and she believed that the larger her volume the less she would be able to hear herself think, she obtained more hot water and poured it on until she was free of lather. Only then did she allow herself to step into the steaming vat, one leg first, then the remainder of her body inch by inch until the water no longer stung and she could move around at will.

She took a long time soaking, afterwards remembering to go around outside to stoke the embers of the tin-lined fireplace beneath the tub and to throw on a few more sticks so that the water might keep its heat for her mother, and when she finally returned to the parlor, she found her mother still talking *haiku* with her aunt and uncle, the three of them on another round of tea. Her father was nowhere in sight.

At Japanese school the next day (Wednesday, it was), Rosie was grave and giddy by turns. Preoccupied at her desk in the row for students on Book Eight, she made up for it at recess by performing wild mimicry for the benefit of her friend Chizuko. She held her nose and whined a witticism or two in what she considered was the manner of Fred Allen; she assumed intoxication and a British accent to go over the climax of the Rudy Vallee recording of the pub conversation about William Ewart Gladstone; she was the child Shirley Temple piping, "On the Good Ship Lollipop"; she was the gentleman soprano of the Four Inkspots trilling, "If I Didn't Care." And she felt reasonably satisfied when Chizuko wept and gasped, "Oh, Rosie, you ought to be in the movies!"

Her father came after her at noon, bringing her sandwiches of minced ham and two nectarines to eat while she rode, so that she could pitch right into the sorting when they got home. The lugs were piling up, he said, and the ripe tomatoes in them would probably have to be taken to the cannery tomorrow if they were not ready for the produce haulers tonight. "This heat's not doing them any good. And we've got no time for a break today."

It *was* hot, probably the hottest day of the year, and Rosie's blouse stuck damply to her back even under the protection of the canvas. But she worked as efficiently as a flawless machine and kept the stalls heaped, with one part of her mind listening in to the parental murmuring about the heat and the tomatoes and with another part planning the exact words she would say to Jesus when he drove up with the first load of the afternoon. But when at last she saw that the pick-up was coming, her hands went berserk and the tomatoes started falling in the wrong stalls, and her father said, "Hey, hey! Rosie, watch what you're doing!"

"Well, I have to go to the *benjo*," she said, hiding panic.

"Go in the weeds over there," he said, only half-joking.

"Oh, Father!" she protested.

"Oh, go on home," her mother said. "We'll make out for awhile."

In the privy Rosie peered through a knothole toward the fields, watching as much as she could of Jesus. Happily she thought she saw him look in the direction of the house from time to time before he finished unloading and went back toward the patch where his mother and father worked. As she was heading for the shed, a very presentable black car purred up the dirt driveway to the house and its driver motioned to her. Was this the Hayashi home, he wanted to know. She nodded. Was she a Hayashi? Yes, she said, thinking that he was a good-looking man. He got out of the car with a huge, flat package and she saw that he warmly wore a business suit. "I have something here for your mother then," he said, in a more elegant Japanese than she was used to.

She told him where her mother was and he came along with her, patting his face with an immaculate white handkerchief and saying something about the coolness of San Francisco. To her surprised mother and father, he bowed and introduced himself as, among other things, the *haiku* editor of the *Mainichi Shimbun*, saying that since he had been coming as far as Los Angeles anyway, he had decided to bring her the first prize she had won in the recent contest.

"First prize?" her mother echoed, believing and not believing, pleased and overwhelmed. Handed the package with a bow, she bobbed her head up and down numerous times to express her utter gratitude.

"It is nothing much," he added, "but I hope it will serve as a token of our great appreciation for your contributions and our great admiration of your considerable talent."

"I am not worthy," she said, falling easily into his style. "It is I who should make some sign of my humble thanks for being permitted to contribute."

"No, no, to the contrary," he said, bowing again.

But Rosie's mother insisted, and then saying that she knew she was being unorthodox, she asked if she might open the package because her curiosity was so great. Certainly she might. In fact, he would like her reaction to it, for personally, it was one of his favorite *Hiroshiges*.

Rosie thought it was a pleasant picture, which looked to have been sketched with delicate quickness. There were pink clouds, containing some graceful calligraphy, and a sea that was a pale blue except at the edges, containing four sampans with indications of people in them. Pines edged the water and on the far-off beach there was a cluster of thatched huts towered over by pine-dotted mountains of grey and blue. The frame was scalloped and gilt.

After Rosie's mother pronounced it without peer and somewhat prodded her father into nodding agreement, she said Mr. Kuroda must at least have a cup of tea after coming all this way, and although Mr. Kuroda did not want to impose, he soon agreed that a cup of tea would be refreshing and went along with her to the house, carrying the picture for her.

"Ha, your mother's crazy!" Rosie's father said, and Rosie laughed uneasily as she resumed judgment on the tomatoes. She had emptied six lugs when he broke into an imaginary conversation with Jesus to tell her to go and remind her mother of the tomatoes, and she went slowly.

Mr. Kuroda was in his shirtsleeves expounding some *haiku* theory as he munched a rice cake, and her mother was rapt. Abashed in the great man's presence, Rosie stood next to her mother's chair until her mother looked up inquiringly, and then she started to whisper the message, but her mother pushed her gently away and reproached, "You are not being very polite to our guest."

"Father says the tomatoes . . . " Rosie said aloud, smiling foolishly.

"Tell him I shall only be a minute," her mother said, speaking the language of Mr. Kuroda.

When Rosie carried the reply to her father, he did not seem to hear and she said again, "Mother says she'll be back in a minute."

"All right, all right," he nodded, and they worked again in silence. But suddenly, her father uttered an incredible noise, exactly like the cork of a bottle popping, and the next Rosie knew, he was stalking angrily toward the house, almost running in fact, and she chased after him crying, "Father! Father! What are you going to do?"

He stopped long enough to order her back to the shed. "Never mind!" he shouted. "Get on with the sorting!"

And from the place in the fields where she stood, frightened and vacillating, Rosie saw her father enter the house. Soon Mr. Kuroda came out alone, putting on his coat. Mr. Kuroda got into his car and backed out down the driveway onto the highway. Next her father emerged, also alone, something in his arms (it was the picture, she realized), and, going over to the bathhouse woodpile, he threw the picture on the ground and picked up the axe. Smashing the picture, glass and all (she heard the explosion faintly), he reached over for the kerosene that was used to encourage the bath fire and poured it over the wreckage. I am dreaming, Rosie said to herself, I am dreaming, but her father, having made sure that his act of cremation was irrevocable, was even then returning to the fields.

Rosie ran past him and toward the house. What had become of her mother? She burst into the parlor and found her mother at the back window watching the dying fire. They watched together until there remained only a feeble smoke under the blazing sun. Her mother was very calm.

"Do you know why I married your father?" she said without turning.

"No," said Rosie. It was the most frightening question she had ever been called upon to answer. Don't tell me now, she wanted to say, tell me tomorrow, tell me next week, don't tell me today. But she knew she would be told now, that the telling would combine with the other violence of the hot afternoon to level her life, her world to the very ground.

It was like a story out of the magazines illustrated in sepia, which she had consumed so greedily for a period until the information had somehow reached her that those wretchedly unhappy autobiographies, offered to her as the testimonials of living men and women, were largely inventions: Her mother, at nineteen, had come to America and married her father as an alternative to suicide.

At eighteen she had been in love with the first son of one of the well-to-do families in her village. The two had met whenever and wherever they could, secretly, because it would not have done for his family to see him favor her—her father had no money; he was a drunkard and a gambler besides. She had learned she was with child; an excellent match had already been arranged for her lover. Despised by her family, she had given premature birth to a stillborn son, who would be seventeen now. Her family did not turn her out, but she could no longer project herself in any direction without refreshing in them the memory of her indiscretion. She wrote to Aunt Taka, her favorite sister in America, threatening to kill herself if Aunt Taka would not send for her. Aunt Taka hastily arranged a marriage with a young man of whom she knew, but lately arrived from Japan, a young man of simple mind, it was said, but of kindly heart. The young man was never told why his unseen betrothed was so eager to hasten the day of meeting.

The story was told perfectly, with neither groping for words nor untoward passion. It was as though her mother had memorized it by heart, reciting it to herself so many times over that its nagging vileness had long since gone.

"I had a brother then?" Rosie asked, for this was what seemed to matter now; she would think about the other later, she assured herself, pushing back the illumination which threatened all that darkness that had hitherto been merely mysterious or even glamorous. "A half-brother?"

"Yes."

"I would have liked a brother," she said.

HISAYE YAMAMOTO

Suddenly, her mother knelt on the floor and took her by the wrists. "Rosie," she said urgently, "Promise me you will never marry!" Shocked more by the request than the revelation, Rosie stared at her mother's face. Jesus, Jesus, she called silently, not certain whether she was invoking the help of the son of the Carrascos or of God, until there returned sweetly the memory of Jesus' hand, how it had touched her and where. Still her mother waited for an answer, holding her wrists so tightly that her hands were going numb. She tried to pull free. Promise, her mother whispered fiercely, promise. Yes, yes, I promise, Rosie said. But for an instant she turned away, and her mother, hearing the familiar glib agreement, released her. Oh, you, you, you, her eyes and twisted mouth said, you fool. Rosie, covering her face, began at last to cry, and the embrace and consoling hand came much later than she expected.

THREE WOMEN

A One-Act Play

by

CHARLOTTE PERKINS GILMAN
(1860–1935)

Born in Hartford, Connecticut, Charlotte Perkins Gilman was the niece of Harriet Beecher Stowe and shared her aunt's zeal for reforming society nearer to women's values of loving relationships. A prolific lifelong writer, Gilman produced two major works that have been rediscovered by feminist scholars: Women and Economics *(1898), the original title of which was* Economic Relation of the Sexes as a Factor in Social Development, *and* "The Yellow Wallpaper," *a short story about a wife's descent into madness when her husband confines her to her room. First published in a journal in 1892, the story has been separately republished by The Feminist Press.*

• ───────────────────────────── •

Characters

ALINE MORROW   A kindergartner of about twenty-five, at first plainly dressed; a good-looking, pleasant, friendly girl; kind, strong, reliable. Later, blossoms out into an ultra-feminine and attractive gown, coiffure, manner, etc.

MRS. MORROW   Her mother. A quiet, rather sad-faced, very domestic, elderly-looking woman of about fifty, somewhat old-fashioned, dressed in black.

MISS UPTON   Her aunt. Some ten years younger than Mrs. Morrow, vivacious, handsome, richly dressed, successful and popular.

MRS. ELLIS   Mother of some of Aline's pupils. Excitable, staccato little woman, devoted to Aline and her work.

DR. RUSSELL   A physician. Wishes to marry Aline.

A MAID

Scene

Parlor in Mrs. Morrow's home. Evening. Center table with shaded light. Mrs. Morrow discovered rocking in a low chair and darning stockings, humming a little hymn tune, as "Abide With Me."

(Bell heard. Enter maid.)

MAID   Mrs. Ellis.

MRS. MORROW   Show her right in.

(Enter Mrs. Ellis.)

MRS. MORROW   Glad to see you, Mrs. Ellis. Won't you sit down—and lay off your things?

MRS. ELLIS   Oh, no, thank you! I can't stop but a *moment*—just a *moment! Excuse* my intruding, but I just couldn't wait to show her the babies' pictures! Where is she?

MRS. MORROW   She's at Mrs. Anderson's. More of her babies there, you know. But she'll be here directly, I'm sure. Won't you show them to me?

MRS. ELLIS   Why, yes, of course! Do *you* care for children as she does? Now, Mrs. Morrow, I wonder if you *appreciate* that daughter of yours! The children simply *worship* her!

MRS. MORROW   And she seems to worship them, Mrs. Ellis.

MRS. ELLIS   Oh, she does! She *does!* If ever there was a world-mother it's that girl! She has genius—absolute *genius!*

(Enter Miss Upton. She is in evening dress and carries an evening wrap over her arm.)

MISS UPTON   What genius have you discovered now, Mrs. Ellis?

MRS. ELLIS   Oh, good *evening*, Miss Upton! I'm so *glad* to see you. It's that *wonderful* niece of yours, Miss Upton. She has such a genius for her work, her *beautiful* work—the kindergarten, you know.

MISS UPTON   Yes, Aline's an artist in her line—a real one.

MRS. ELLIS   Of course, it's not like yours—not like *Art!* We hear *wonderful* things about you, Miss Upton.

MISS UPTON   Thank you, Mrs. Ellis. I wish I *were* doing wonderful things.

MRS. ELLIS   Oh, you *are!* You *are!* Why, that article about you in the Centurion quite staggered me, Miss Upton. To think that I really knew a woman who could paint such marvelous pictures!

MISS UPTON   I see you've brought us some marvelous pictures, Mrs. Ellis. *(Takes photos.)* These are excellent—excellent.

MRS. MORROW   Clara is very fond of children's pictures, Mrs. Ellis.

MRS. ELLIS   Yes, I know. What was it the great critic said? That you not only painted mothers and children—you painted motherhood!

(Enter Aline.)

ALINE   Well, mother. Good evening, all. *(All rise to welcome her. She greets Mrs. Ellis cordially, puts an arm about both mother and aunt, kisses each affectionately. Sees photos.)* Ah, my babies! *(Takes pictures and looks at them with evident delight.)*

MRS. ELLIS   *(Admiringly.)* I do believe you love our babies as well as we mothers do!

MISS UPTON   Better than some mothers I've seen, Mrs. Ellis. I believe that mothers are born and not made.

MRS. MORROW   You're right, Clara.

MRS. ELLIS   I'm so glad you like them, Miss Morrow! These are for you. I couldn't wait to show them. *Good* evening, all! I have to go back and put the children to bed. *Good* night, Miss Upton. *Good* night, Mrs. Morrow. *Good* night, *dear* Miss Morrow! *(Exit Mrs. Ellis.)*

MRS. MORROW   How fond those children's mothers are of you, Aline!

ALINE   They are very kind indeed—most of them. Aren't you rather unusually gorgeous, Aunt Clara? Going out, of course!

MISS UPTON   Yes—later. It's the Jainville's reception.

ALINE   And which of your forty adorers is coming for you, Auntie?

MISS UPTON   A woman of forty needs forty adorers, Aline. But, speaking of gorgeousness—aren't you going to change *your* dress?

ALINE   What for? I don't have forty adorers.

MISS UPTON   No, but you have *one*, and that's much more important. *(Bell heard. Maid appears.)*

MAID   Dr. Russell.

MISS UPTON   Come, now, run along and put on a pretty frock, child—do!

ALINE   Why should I? *(Looks in mirror.)* This is a perfectly good dress.

MISS UPTON   *(Kissing her.)* You are a perfectly good—goose, Aline Morrow. *(Enter Dr. Russell. Coat on, gloves in hand. Greets them all most politely.)*

DR. RUSSELL   Good evening, Mrs. Morrow—Miss Upton. Good evening, Miss Morrow.

MRS. MORROW   Sit down, Dr. Russell, sit down. Take your coat off, won't you?

DR. RUSSELL   Thank you, Mrs. Morrow. I've only a moment. *(Looks at watch.)* On my way to a patient.

(Miss Upton rises, gathers cloak about her.)

DR. RUSSELL   Allow me. *(Offers to [help.])*

MISS UPTON   No, thank you. I need a practiced hand for a few moments. Sister, you'll have to come and help me.

MRS. MORROW   Yes, certainly, Clara. *(Exit both.)*

DR. RUSSELL   Your aunt is a very popular lady.

ALINE   Isn't she! She's like a young girl! Everybody likes her. It's a beautiful life. Don't you admire her work, Dr. Russell?

DR. RUSSELL   I do, indeed. And yet—even with all her friends, and her successes—it is a pity that so lovely a woman is not married. Don't you think so, Miss Morrow?

ALINE   Oh—I don't know! I've seen many married women that couldn't compare with Aunt Clara for happiness. Look at the last addition to my family. *(Shows him the photographs.)*

DR. RUSSELL   Very pretty, very pretty.

ALINE   Did I ever show you my jewels—a la Cornelia? *(Brings out a great array of photos of children and sets them up.)*

DR. RUSSELL   You are very fond of children, aren't you?

ALINE   Fond of children! Of course. What are women for?

DR. RUSSELL   I thought you held they were for many other purposes.

ALINE   Oh, yes—as *persons*—for any kind of work they like. You always forget that women are persons. But as *women*—they are for children.

DR. RUSSELL   I can't see the difference—I see only the woman. *(Looks at her admiringly. She is looking at the photos. He rises. Comes to her, takes the pictures from her hands, seizes her hands.)*

DR. RUSSELL   I cannot wait another day, Aline! When will you marry me?

ALINE   Marry you! Why, I did not know—*(Laughs softly.)* I can't lie to save me. I did know you wanted me to—at least, I hoped so.

DR. RUSSELL   Hoped? Oh, Aline! My Aline! *(She holds him at arm's length.)*

ALINE   Wait! Wait! I haven't said I would yet.

DR. RUSSELL   You said you loved me. At least, you said you hoped I— Aline! You do love me?

ALINE   *(Soberly.)* I do love you, Gordon. I've loved you—ever so long. *(He tries to embrace her.)* No! No! We've got to talk a little first.

DR. RUSSELL   What is there to talk about? If you love me that's all there is to it. *(He takes one hand and kisses it over and over. She withdraws it with a little breathless sob.)*

ALINE   Don't do that—yet! I can't think—and I've got to think now! *(She stands away from him, puts a chair before her and confronts him.)*

DR. RUSSELL   What do you mean, Aline? *(Half seriously.)* Is there A Past between us?

ALINE   No—but there is a Future!

DR. RUSSELL   *(Puzzled.)* The future will be ours together, surely.

ALINE   *(Slowly.)* Some of it will—and some of it won't. We may have a beautiful future together—*(She drops her voice lovingly at the word, then lifts her head and goes on clearly.)* but we also want a beautiful future separately.

DR. RUSSELL   Separately? What do you mean?

ALINE   Didn't you have a big, bright future before you knew me—hopes of advancement in your profession—ambition to do great work—to serve humanity?

DR. RUSSELL   Of course I had—and have yet. But that is not *separate*, dear. My whole life will be yours. All that I have—all that I do—all my hope and ambition and success—it is all for you. You shall share it.

ALINE   That is true, I hope. I should, gladly, share in your professional ambition and success—but would you also share in mine?

DR. RUSSELL   *(Looks puzzled.)* In yours?

ALINE   *(Watches him eagerly, gives a little disappointed cry.)* Oh, haven't you even *thought* that my work was dear to me—as dear as yours to you? *(Comes a little toward him.)*

DR. RUSSELL   *(Regarding her confusedly.)* Do you mean that you would wish to go on teaching school—after we were married?

ALINE   Yes.

DR. RUSSELL   For a while, you mean.

ALINE   All my life.

DR. RUSSELL   You never mentioned this before.

ALINE   How could I?

DR. RUSSELL   *(Turns, walks up and down. He crosses to her suddenly.)* You love me? Say it again!

ALINE   *(Solemnly.)* I love you.

DR. RUSSELL   Do you not love me well enough to give up teaching school?

ALINE   Do you love me well enough to give up practicing medicine?

DR. RUSSELL *(Hotly.)* Aline! It is not the same thing.

ALINE Why not?

DR. RUSSELL A man does not have to give up his work to marry.

ALINE Neither does a woman, nowadays.

DR. RUSSELL Nowadays! Women haven't left off being women nowadays, have they?

ALINE No—but they have begun to be something more.

DR. RUSSELL *(Coming closer, holding her hand. Draws her to a sofa.)* Come, dear. Let us sit and talk it over. I love you too well to deny you anything in reason, but surely—the duties of the wife and mother come first in a woman's life. You believe that, don't you?

ALINE No honestly—I don't agree with you. I think the first duty of anybody—man or woman—is to do their best work for the world. Oh, my dear, don't make it so—hard! See—I am willing to be your wife. I should hope to be *(her voice drops reverently)* a mother. But I am by nature, by habit, by seven years' training, a *teacher*—and I cannot give it up.

DR. RUSSELL *(Takes both her hands and leans nearer.)* Not for love's sake? *(She hesitates. He slips his arm around her, draws her to him.)* Look at me, Aline! Ah, my dearest! Only marry me and I will engage to make you forget your school-teaching. *(She starts up; he follows her.)* Trust me, Aline. You love me; that is enough. I have not had one kiss yet—not one. And I've been wanting it so—ever since I first saw you— for two years. *(He tries to turn her face to his, but she breaks from him breathlessly.)*

ALINE No! No! Gordon—not yet! You—move me so—I find it hard to be wise. *(He comes nearer.)* Don't touch me—go and sit over there. *(He sits.)* Don't look at me—please. Look at the table. *(He looks at it, smiling. They sit opposite.)* We must be perfectly agreed about this before it is too late.

DR. RUSSELL It is too late already, Aline. If a woman gives her heart to a man—

ALINE She may still refuse to marry him if she so choose—even if it breaks her heart.

DR. RUSSELL And his?

ALINE Yes—even that. Two broken hearts are better than one broken marriage.

DR. RUSSELL *(Drumming on the table—trying to be patient.)* I wish you would consider this thing practically, dear.

ALINE *(Eagerly.)* That is just what I am trying to do. Now, see. You know how we live here—you know how good the food is—and how cheap—and how little service is required, or management. If we had a house this way—with meals and service from outside—I could be as free as I am now.

DR. RUSSELL *(Rising.)* You forget Aline. A girl does. There is more than housekeeping to consider. The best use of all your kindergartening will be to help you when your own little ones demand your care. Can you not foresee?

ALINE *(Rising, facing him squarely, standing tall and pale.)* Can I not foresee? You, a man, ask me, a woman, if I cannot foresee motherhood! I have foreseen it since I was a child. Since I was a girl of fifteen I have planned and worked and tried to live my best, in the hope that some day—I tell you I am not a girl. I am a woman.

DR. RUSSELL You glorious woman! I knew your heart would guide you. I knew the Teacher would give way to the Mother. *(Approaches her, tries to embrace her, she holding him off.)*

ALINE *(Pleadingly.)* Don't misunderstand me, Gordon. I should still be a teacher—and a better mother because of it.

DR. RUSSELL *(Angry, disappointed, hurt, stands by, folds his arms.)* You propose, then, that my home shall be the adjunct of a boarding-house—and that I rent an office as I do now, and live as the husband of a school-teacher?

ALINE I propose nothing, Dr. Russell. I understood you to propose marriage. Do you withdraw the proposal?

(They stand facing one another. Both take a step forward. He holds out his arms to her.)

DR. RUSSELL I love you better than anything else in life! Aline!

ALINE Except your prejudices!

DR. RUSSELL *(Clock strikes. Starts and looks at his watch.)* Please do not decide now! Please wait a little. I must keep my appointment. I will be back as soon as I can. Let me beg you to consider—ask your own heart. Consult your mother.

ALINE I will—and my aunt.

DR. RUSSELL And don't forget that we love each other! *(Exit Dr. Russell.)*

(Aline, left alone, gradually loses her determined air, runs to window and looks after him. The curtains partly conceal her. Re-enter Mrs. Morrow. Takes her chair again, looks for thimble, wets her finger and slips it on. Seats herself and begins to rock and hum and darn again. Aline turns and comes to her. Kisses her daintily, affectionately.)

CHARLOTTE PERKINS GILMAN

ALINE   There's a dear little curl in the back of your neck, Motherkin. It's so pretty. *(Mrs. Morrow kisses her warmly.)* Now you go right on being a picture of contented domesticity—I want to ask you something. *(Brings low stool or cushion and sits at her mother's feet. Lays her arm on her mother's knees, chin on hands and looks at her. Mother strokes her hair lovingly.)* Can you darn stockings and give advice at the same time, Motherkin?

MRS. MORROW   *(Darning.)* What do you want advice about? I thought you never took any.

ALINE   I may not take this. Asking advice and taking it are two quite different things. *(Plays with darning cotton.)* It's about marrying—or not marrying. Or, rather, it's about giving up my profession—or not giving it up.

MRS. MORROW   Dr. Russell? *(Aline nods.)* And he wants you to give up your work—insists upon it?

ALINE   Yes. It amounts to that. I thought he knew how I felt about it. It is rather difficult, you see—to tell a man your views on post-matrimonial industry before he proposes!

MRS. MORROW   *(With sudden change of feeling.)* Of course it's difficult! Whatever the girl does is difficult! She's supposed to be blankly innocent and unsuspecting, and to say "This is so sudden!" else she's unwomanly. On the other hand, "a true woman" always knows if a man loves her! If she does not foresee it all and stave him off in what they call "a thousand delicate ways"—then she's accused of leading him on. So there you are! *(Nods defiantly.)*

ALINE   *(Gently.)* Well—I've often said what I thought about a woman's working after she was married, but he seemed as surprised as if he'd never met the idea.

MRS. MORROW   Did you put it to him at once?

ALINE   Yes. That is *(a little embarrassed)* we discussed it. He's coming back for an answer.

MRS. MORROW   Seems to me, in your case, there's no difficulty at all. Here's this blessed "Dunham" answers all the housekeeping problem. Delicious and cheap. Meals sent in hot. Service by the hour. He knows about that.

ALINE   Yes, of course. And he's often eaten with us, and knows how nice it is; but he says he wants a home of his own.

MRS. MORROW   That is—a cook of his own. And he doesn't even know what he would escape. *(Lays down her work.)* Look here, child. You could manage perfectly. He could rent our lower floor. Clara would be glad to get her a studio down town; she only stays here to help me out—bless her! The rooms would be better for him than where he is now, and on the same block. He wouldn't lose anything.

ALINE I wish he thought so.

MRS. MORROW Why, what does the man want? I'd rent you the house and we'd all go into The Dunham. He *couldn't* live as cheaply any other way.

ALINE He doesn't like the idea.

MRS. MORROW Then when the children come you could substitute for a while—and go right on teaching. I could supervise, you know, till they are big enough for the kindergarten—and there you are.

ALINE I'd have to be out mornings—

MRS. MORROW Well? He'd have to be *in* mornings, wouldn't he? Office hours! And in case children were in mortal peril I guess a grandmother and a doctor-father—with a trained nurse—could keep 'em alive until you were telephoned for. Why it's ideal!

ALINE But, Mother—he won't see it. He—he's a man. It's feeling. You can't reason against feeling. *(She meditates, smiling softly. Her mother watches her anxiously.)*

MRS. MORROW I know—I know, dear. It is delicious—at first. It is hard— very hard—to decide. *(Pause.)* You ask my advice, Aline. I know you won't take it. *(She rises, stands upright with clenched hands.)* DON'T GIVE UP YOUR PROFESSION FOR THE BEST MAN ON EARTH!

ALINE Why, Mother! Why, *Mother!* (Mrs. Morrow drops limply into a chair again and buries her face in the pile of stockings and sobs despairingly. Aline kneels by her, puts her arms around her, caresses, tries to soothe her.) Mother! Mother, dear! Don't cry so! Oh, Mother, I'd no idea that you felt this way! You have me—isn't that something?

MRS. MORROW Something? *(Turns and embraces her with intense fervor.)* Something! You are everything. You are *all*—all there is.

ALINE *(Holding her close.)* Dearest Mother! I wouldn't leave you in any case. Whoever takes me has got to take you, too.

MRS. MORROW *(Draws away sharply, almost angrily.)* It's not that! I never even thought of *that*. Did I object to your going to college, or to Germany to study? I'm not a common pig-mother! It's your *work* I'm thinking of. My own life has gone—gone forever—except as it is in you. I can't lose yours, too.

ALINE *(Puzzled, grieved, asks softly.)* Weren't you happy with Father?

MRS. MORROW *(Trying to speak composedly.)* Yes. Yes, I was. I loved him dearly. I loved him enough to give up my work to please him. But, my child, do not believe Eros himself if he tells you that "love is enough." It isn't. We have other interests—other powers and desires. I had a Voice— once.

ALINE   Why, Mother! I never heard you sing.

MRS. MORROW   No. You never heard me sing.

ALINE   And you gave it up—for him?

MRS. MORROW   Yes—for love. And I had love—until he died. He didn't intend to die—but the Voice went first. You see, dear, he didn't care for music at all—especially vocal music. He didn't like the people who did care for it. He hated to have me go out without him. There was no money for lessons, no time for practice. It is all gone.

ALINE   You had the home—the children.

MRS. MORROW   Yes, thank God! I loved my home, and I loved my children dearly. But even while I had them—even while my heart and my hands were full—there was always this great empty place. You have grown up. It's ten years since I lost your father. I am fifty now. I may live ten—twenty—thirty years more, and, except for you, my life is empty. (She rises, puts all her work neatly into basket. Aline watches her, silent.) If you do care for my advice, if the loss of my life can be of any use to save yours, you will stick to your work as your aunt did. She was wiser than I. She refuses to give up. Now she is a happy woman—successful, popular, known, honored, well paid. She has lived. Yours is real mother-work, too. You can love and help more children than you ever could have of your own. Oh, you'll be hungry, of course! You'll be hungry for love— for your own babies. But I tell you, if you have them, and don't have your work, you'll starve!

(Re-enter Miss Upton. Mrs. Morrow controls herself and gathers up her darning.)

ALINE   (With an effort.) Carriage not come yet, Aunt Clara?

MISS UPTON   (Looks at clock.) No, it's really not time yet. (To Mrs. Morrow.) Why will you waste time darning stockings, Molly? I can't afford it. I can earn a dozen pair—silk ones—in the time it would take me to darn six.

MRS. MORROW   My time isn't as valuable as yours, Clara. I've left my cotton upstairs-—(Rises.)

ALINE   Let me get it, Mother. (Her mother kisses her and whispers to her, Aline nods understandingly. Mrs. Morrow goes out. Aline goes and stands by the fire. Miss Upton looks at papers on table, walks about a bit, hangs her cloak over the back of a tall carved chair by table, sits on arm, swings one dainty foot, picks up silver cigarette case.)

MISS UPTON   You don't mind if I have a cigarette, Aline? (Takes one.)

ALINE *(Turning and coming to her.)* I think you're entitled to whatever you want, Aunt Clara. You certainly are a successful woman.

MISS UPTON I'm doing very well.

ALINE Your free, happy life! And your beautiful work—your own real work! I congratulate you with all my heart. *(Her aunt puts an arm around her, kisses her, goes on smoking, and looking about, swinging her foot a little, airy, successful, complacent.)*

ALINE But, Auntie, can you talk to me a little? Can you give me some sagacious advice on a very solemn question?

MISS UPTON Of course I will. Giving advice is a pleasure to all of us— more especially to women—most especially to unmarried women. Is it whom you shall marry? Marry Dr. Russell, by all means. I'd like to marry him myself.

ALINE Neither you nor Mother seems to have been in any doubt as to Dr. Russell's intentions.

MISS UPTON Why, no. Were you? He's all right, Aline. You've spoken to your mother, then. Has he asked you?

ALINE Yes. He's coming back for his answer.

MISS UPTON You say "yes." If that's the question, I wonder you want advice.

ALINE No; that's not the question. The question is, shall I drop my work, give up my profession, to be his wife?

MISS UPTON *(Stops smiling and sits up straight.)* Does he make it a condition?

ALINE I'm afraid he does.

MISS UPTON *(Fiercely, intensely, starting to her feet.)* Then do it! Do it in a minute! Drop it once and for all. Forswear it; forget it—and thank God for a good man's love.

ALINE Why, Aunt Clara! I—thought—you—I thought you were—

MISS UPTON You thought I was happy in my work, no doubt. Everyone does. I mean they shall. I had my chance of happiness once—and lost it. But I made my choice and I stand by it. I'm a good loser. We Uptons are. I never let even your mother know. She had her happiness. She thought I had mine. *(Aline listens. Miss Upton walks about much excited. Turns to Aline.)* But you are young, Aline. You have your best years all before you. You have the crown and glory and blessing of your life in your hands. Take it, Aline! Take it. *(Aline stares, amazed.)* I've never spoken of this to a living soul, but I love you, Aline. You are a splendid girl, and I don't want you to spoil your life as I have spoiled mine.

CHARLOTTE PERKINS GILMAN

ALINE   Don't, Aunt Clara—don't speak of it if it hurts you. I understand—

MISS UPTON   *(Interrupting.) Understand?* You don't understand. No woman could understand unless she had lived twenty years without love—and knew she had thrown it away.

ALINE   *(Earnestly.)* Isn't the work a comfort, Aunt Clara? Your success, your wide, free life?

MISS UPTON   *(Fiercely.)* Of course it is—and my clothes are a comfort—and my dinner! But they do not, unfortunately, meet the same want. You need not say a word, Aline. I know. I stood in your shoes, I had the same ideas, and I chose the work. Well—I can make money. I can do as I please, but—*(She stretches out empty arms and snatches them back, empty, to her heart.)* I've never held my baby in my arms. *(She stands silent. Aline goes to her, tries to comfort her. She waves her away.)* It's not only babies, though that's ache enough—just the physical ache for them, for their little blundering, crumpling fingers on your face; their foolish, delicious curly feet; the down on their heads; the sweetness of the backs of their necks; the hugableness of them! It's not only the babies, Aline. It's the husband! Women are not supposed to care—They do—!

ALINE   You have so many friends, Aunt Clara.

MISS UPTON   Oh, you make me angry! You girl! You child! How can I make you see? Ten thousand friends are not the same as the man you love! Haven't you a heart, child, in your body?

ALINE   Yes—I have. But I have a head, too, and I thought—

MISS UPTON   Stop thinking. Feel. Just make sure that you love—plain *love* him—and then marry him.

ALINE   But I'm not sure. I do love him, but after loving him, after marrying him, there remain the years of a lifetime.

MISS UPTON   They do, indeed. I was twenty when I refused my lover—for my work. Twenty years have gone by. I suppose there may be thirty more—I'm a strong woman. Fifty years—without any one of my own! *(She throws up her arms in a wild gesture, sinks on a seat by the table, buries her face, and bursts into heavy sobs—strained agonizing sobs. Aline stands, trying to soothe her.)*

MISS UPTON   Go away. It's only a little hysteria. I'll be quieter when I'm alone. I'm used to being alone. Go away. *But take my advice.*

(Aline goes out.)
(Mrs. Morrow re-enters.)

MRS. MORROW   Tired of waiting, Clara?

MISS UPTON   *(Raises her head.)* Yes, I am. *(Rises, walks about, looks at clock. Mrs. Morrow is gathering up her work.)* Well, Molly, I guess you and I are going to lose a daughter soon.

MRS. MORROW   I hope not! Oh, I hope not!

MISS UPTON   Hope not? I'd like to know why! She'll never get a finer man than Gordon Russell—nor one more devoted to her. You don't want her to live single, do you?

MRS. MORROW   No, but she'd much better do that than give up her profession.

MISS UPTON   Why, Molly Morrow! *You* talk that way! *You* have been happy with your husband and children. You certainly do not want her to miss all that?

MRS. MORROW   That sounds well from you, *Clara.* After all your success! Actions speak louder than words. *(Miss Upton looks at her, hesitates.)* Just remember that Aline was fairly *born* a kindergartner as you were a painter. Think of all her years of study and training—and how she loves it—and how useful she is to all those little children, and their mothers!

MISS UPTON   And what are all those little children and their mothers— and all those years of study and training—and all her love of it, to the love of one little child of her own, in her own arms?

MRS. MORROW   Why, Clara! *Clara!* Do you mean—?

MISS UPTON   Do I mean—what? And what do you mean?

MRS. MORROW   Why, I always thought—that you—oh, Clara! You don't mean to tell me that you've been—sorry—all these years?

MISS UPTON   I did not mean to tell you, but it seems I have. You were happy. Why should I distress you with my unhappiness?

MRS. MORROW   Happy? *I—*

MISS UPTON   *(Whirling upon her.)* You were NOT? Molly!

MRS. MORROW   I have been wretched all my life, Clara, because I gave up my work for love.

MISS UPTON   And I because I didn't.

MRS. MORROW   Two lives ruined! But Aline shan't waste hers. I have told her.

MISS UPTON   So have I.

MRS. MORROW   You haven't advised her to give up?

MISS UPTON   I certainly have. *(They stand opposed. Bell heard. They do not notice it. Dr. Russell appears at the door.)*

CHARLOTTE PERKINS GILMAN

DR. RUSSELL   I beg pardon. *(Both turn upon him.)*

MRS. MORROW   Come in, Dr. Russell.

MISS UPTON   Yes. Come in. *(He enters.)*

DR. RUSSELL   Is Miss Morrow—?

MRS. MORROW   Yes, she's here. She'll be in presently. She—Dr. Russell—

DR. RUSSELL   Yes, Mrs. Morrow.

MRS. MORROW   Why can't you be willing for Aline to keep on with her work? She'll never be happy without it.

MISS UPTON   She'll never be happy with it—and without love.

MRS. MORROW   Clara, stop! She is *my* child, Dr. Russell. I am her mother. But not even motherhood makes up for losing one's own work. I know what it costs to give up all one's personal life for love!

MISS UPTON   And I know what it costs *not to.* Dr. Russell, don't let her refuse you. If she loves you—and I'm pretty sure she does—you marry her.

DR. RUSSELL   I wish for her happiness—

MRS. MORROW   Then let her keep her work.

MISS UPTON   Then marry her.

DR. RUSSELL   After all, she must decide. Believe me, Mrs. Morrow, all my life shall be given to make her happy—if she will take it. But a woman must choose between her career and marriage. She must choose.

MISS UPTON   Well, Molly, he's right. You chose—I chose—now she must choose. Come. We must leave it to her. *(They go out much depressed.)*

(Dr. Russell proceeds to walk up and down the room, sits, tries to read, plays with flowers, gets very impatient. Rings. Maid appears.)

DR. RUSSELL   Does Miss Morrow know I'm here?

MAID   I'll see, sir. *(Exit maid. Reappears after a bit.)* Miss Morrow will be down presently, sir.

DR. RUSSELL   *(Continuing to show great strain and impatience.)* She never kept me waiting before—I wonder if it means—

(Finally she enters. He is standing with his back to the door; does not see her. She is exquisitely dressed in a white, misty, clinging, shimmering gown with an elusive sparkle in it. Her hair is beautifully done, much more softly and richly than her usual method. A red and white rose are tucked in her hair, and she carries one of each in her hand. She comes softly behind him, stands a moment, looks mischievously at him, reaches out a rose and touches his hand with it. He starts, turns, holds out his arms to her.)

DR. RUSSELL   My darling! *(She shakes her head, smiling, retreating, looking up at him archly.)*

ALINE   I don't know yet whether I'm your darling or not. That remains to be decided. This is a very serious matter, Dr. Russell.

DR. RUSSELL   I don't know you tonight, Aline. You are another woman, somehow.

ALINE   Well, do you like the other woman?

DR. RUSSELL   *(Starts toward her.)* Like her? Oh, my dear! I knew you were lovely, but I never knew you so enchanting.

ALINE   Thank you. I'm glad you're pleased with me. No—no—be patient a little yet. If we marry we have a lifetime before us to be happy in. If we don't—

DR. RUSSELL   If we don't! Aline! Have you not decided—yet?

ALINE   I? Oh, yes. *I* have decided, but you haven't.

DR. RUSSELL   I am too desperately in earnest to guess riddles, Aline. Please answer me. Will you be my wife?

ALINE   I cannot bear to give up my work, Gordon.

DR. RUSSELL   You mean—? Aline! You will not let that keep us apart?

ALINE   *(Fervently.)* Indeed I will not. It shall never come between us nor interfere with my love and duty to you.

DR. RUSSELL   *(Stands, his hands gripped together looking at her.)* Then you will—

ALINE   Listen, now. Let me say all I have to say, and then *you* may decide, if you please, whether to abide by *your* choice or not. You asked me to marry you—then made conditions. I am willing to marry you. *I* make no conditions. I do not say, "You must give up smoking," or "You must be a total abstainer," or "You must choose between me and something else you love." I love you, Gordon, unconditionally. *(He tries to embrace her, but she checks him.)* I love a man who is a doctor, a splendid doctor. I would marry the man and be proud of the doctor. You love a woman who is a teacher, a devoted one. You would marry the woman; she would be your wife. You wouldn't marry the teacher. She would go on teaching.

DR. RUSSELL   This is all sophistry, Aline. You expect the impossible. Oh, why not trust your heart—

ALINE   I expect nothing impossible, Gordon—only what I know to be practicable. You must leave the arrangements of the housework and the care of—the family—to me. That is plainly the woman's duty. I am no child, you know. *(Looks up at him, rose at lips, smiling.)*

CHARLOTTE PERKINS GILMAN
499

DR. RUSSELL   You look about sixteen to-night! You are deliciously beauti-ful! And puzzling beyond words! You say you love me. I feel that you love me. You do, don't you, dear? Yet you sit there talking like a judge. If I shut my eyes I seem to hear the New Woman laying down the law. If I open them—Lilith couldn't be lovelier. (*She looks at him with such mischievous sweetness, such tremor of soft withdrawal, that he comes to her. She lets him sit on the sofa beside her, and then faces him so calmly that he feels more remote than before.*)

DR. RUSSELL   You are being very cruel, Aline. Don't you know it? You are holding my heart in your hands. Tell me, dear; give me your answer. Will you be my wife?

ALINE   (*Very coldly and without interest.*) Yes.

DR. RUSSELL   You will give up your work?

ALINE   (*Gently, warmly, tenderly, with her heart in her eyes.*) No.

DR. RUSSELL   What *do* you mean, Aline? You torture me. Tell me your decision. You have had time to consider. You have advised with your family. (*Rises.*) You must have made up your mind.

ALINE   (*Rising, also.*) Yes, I have considered. I have advised with my family. I have seen the effects of this choice you require—the choice between living and loving. I have seen what it means to a woman to have love—and lose life. And what it means to have life—and lose love.

DR. RUSSELL   It is the woman's problem, and must be faced. You have your Life. I offer you—Love. Which will you choose?

ALINE   Both, if you please. (*He stands checked, astonished, angry, and hurt. She sinks down on the cushions, hides her face, sobs—or laughs. He sees a tear shine between her fingers, is beside her, his arms around her. She pushes him away. Then she turns her face and smiles up at him entrancingly, her head back on the velvet cushions, her two great roses lifted to her chin.*) If I were a man—and a lover—and the woman I loved was willing to marry me, I don't *think* I'd let a thing like this stand be-tween us. (*He drops beside her, draws her to him, his voice quite shaken.*)

DR. RUSSELL   I *thought* I knew best about this, Aline. But you may be right.

ALINE   My dear—you must take me as a teacher or not take me at all!

DR. RUSSELL   We will try it together, Aline. Only love me!

(*She comes to him.*)

(*Curtain*)

A ALLEGORY ON
WIMMEN'S RIGHTS

by

MARIETTA HOLLEY
(1836–1926)

*Marietta Holley lived her whole life—ninety years—on the farm
where she was born in Jefferson County, New York. She had to leave
school at fourteen but continued to educate herself by reading. She
turned to writing after teaching piano lessons for a living, and her
outspoken comic figure Samantha, better known as "Josiah Allen's
wife," was so successful that Holley's fame rivaled that of Mark
Twain. Josiah is the stereotypical henpecked husband; he and Betsy
Bobbett, an old maid, are the foils for Samantha's campaigns for
women's rights and other causes. Though Samantha's tongue is
sharp, she respects the individuality of her literary foils whose
prejudices she exposes. Her common sense and lack of venom
made Samantha into a heroine with whom a wide audience of
women could identify. A collection from Holley's sixteen very
popular novels was published in 1983 as* Samantha Rastles the
Woman Question *(edited by Jane Curry).*

About a couple of weeks after the quiltin', Thomas Jefferson said to Josiah,
one Saturday mornin',

"Father, can I have the old mare to go to Jonesville to-night?"

"What do you want to go to Jonesville for?" said his father, "you come
from there last night."

"There is goin' to be a lecture on wimmin's rights; can I have her,
father?"

"I s'pose so," says Josiah, kinder short, and after Thomas J. went out,
Josiah went on—

"Wimmin's rights, wimmin's rights, I wonder how many more fools
are goin' a caperin' round the country preachin' 'em up—I am sick of
wimmin's rights, I don't believe in 'em."

This riled up the old Smith blood, and says I to him with a glance that
went clear through to the back side of his head—

"I know you don't, Josiah Allen—I can tell a man that is for wimmin's
rights as fur as I can see 'em. There is a free, easy swing to their walk—
a noble look to thier faces—thier big hearts and soles love liberty and

justice, and bein' free themselves they want everybody else to be free. These men haint jealous of a woman's influence—haint afraid that she won't pay him proper respect if she haint obleeged to—and they needn't be afraid, for these are the very men that wimmin look up to, and worship,—and always will. A good, noble, true man is the best job old natur ever turned off her hands, or ever will—a man, that would wipe off a baby's tears as soft as a woman could, or 'die with his face to the foe.'

"They are most always big, noble-sized men, too," says I, with another look at Josiah that pierced him like a arrow. (Josiah don't weigh quite one hundred by the steelyards.)

"I don't know as I am to blame, Samantha, for not bein' a very hefty man."

"You can let your sole grow, Josiah Allen, by thinkin' big, noble-sized thoughts, and I believe if you did, you would weigh more by the steelyards."

"Wall, I don't care, Samantha, I stick to it, that I am sick of wimmin's rights; if wimmin would take care of the rights they have got now, they would do better than they do do."

Now I love to see folks use reason if they have got any—and I won't stand no importations cast on to my sect—and so I says to him in a tone of cold and almost freezin' dignity—

"What do you mean, Josiah?"

"I mean that women hain't no business a votin'; they had better let the laws alone, and tend to thier housework. The law loves wimmin and protects 'em."

"If the law loves wimmin so well, why don't he give her as much wages as men get for doin' the same work? Why don't he give her half as much, Josiah Allen?"

Josiah waved off my question, seemin'ly not noticin' of it—and continued with the doggy obstinacy of his sect—

"Wimmin haint no business with the laws of the country."

"If they haint no business with the law, the law haint no business with them," says I warmly. "Of the three classes that haint no business with the law—lunatics, idiots, and wimmin—the lunatics and idiots have the best time of it," says I, with a great rush of ideas into my brain that almost lifted up the border of my head-dress. "Let a idiot kill a man; 'What of it?' says the law; let a luny steal a sheep; again the law murmurs in a calm and gentle tone, 'What of it? they haint no business with the law and the law haint no business with them.' But let one of the third class, let a woman steal a sheep, does the law soothe her in these comfortin' tones? No, it thunders to her, in awful accents, 'You haint no business with the law, but the law has a good deal of business with you, vile female, start for State's prisen; you haint nothin' at all to do with the law, only to pay all the taxes it tells you to—embrace a license bill that is ruinin' your husband—give up your innocent little children to a wicked father if it tells you to—and a few other little things, such as bein' dragged off to prison by it—chained up for life, and hung, and et cetery.'"

Josiah sot motionless—and in a rapped eloquence I went on in the allegory way.

"'Methought I once heard the words,' sighs the female, 'True government consists in the consent of the governed;' did I dream them, or did the voice of a luny pour them into my ear?'

"'Haint I told you,' frouns the law on her, 'that that don't mean wimmin—have I got to explain to your weakened female comprehension again, the great fundymental truth, that wimmin haint included and mingled in the law books and statutes of the country only in a condemnin' and punishin' sense, as it were. Though I feel it to be bendin' down my powerful manly dignity to elucidate the subject further, I will consent to remind you of the consolin' fact, that though you wimmin are, from the tender softness of your natures, and the illogical weakness of your minds, unfit from ever havin' any voice in makin' the laws that govern you; you have the right, and nobody can ever deprive you of it, to be punished in a future world jest as hard as a man of the strongest intellect, and to be hung in this world jest as dead as a dead man; and what more can you ask for, you unreasonable female woman you?'

"Then groans the woman as the great fundymental truth rushes upon her—

"'I can be hung by the political rope, but I can't help twist it.'

"'Jest so,' says the law, 'that rope takes noble and manly fingers, and fingers of principle to twist it, and not the weak unprincipled grasp of lunatics, idiots, and wimmin.'

"'Alas!' sithes the woman to herself, 'would that I had the sweet rights of my wild and foolish companions, the idiots and lunys. But, says she, venturing with a beating heart, the timid and bashful inquiry, 'are the laws always just, that I should obey them thus implicitly? There is old Creshus, he stole two millions, and the law cleared him triumphantly. Several men have killed various other men, and the law insistin' they was out of their heads (had got out of 'em for the occasion, and got into 'em agin the minute they was cleared) let 'em off with sound necks. And I, a poor woman, have only stole a sheep, a small-sized sheep too, that my offspring might not perish with hunger—is it right to liberate in a triumphin' way the two million stealer and the man murderer, and inkarcerate the poor sheep stealer? and my children was *so* hungry, and it was such a small sheep,' says the woman in pleadin' accents.

"'Idiots! lunatics! and wimmin! are they goin' to speak?' thunders the law. 'Can I believe my noble right ear? can I bein' blindfolded trust my seventeen senses? I'll have you understand that it haint no woman's business whether the laws are just or unjust, all you have got to do is jest to obey 'em, so start off for prison, my young woman.'

"'But my house-work,' pleads the woman; 'woman's place is home: it is her duty to remain at all hazards within its holy and protectin' precincts; how can I leave its sacred retirement to moulder in State's prison?'

"'House-work!' and the law fairly yells the words, he is so filled with contempt at the idee. 'House-work! jest as if house-work is goin' to stand in the way of the noble administration of the law. I admit the recklessness and immorality of her leavin' that holy haven, long enough to vote— but I guess she can leave her house-work long enough to be condemned, and hung, and so forth.'

"'But I have got a infant,' says the woman, 'of tender days, how can I go?'

"'That is nothing to the case,' says the law in stern tones. 'The peculiar conditions of motherhood only unfits a female woman from ridin' to town with her husband, in a covered carriage, once a year, and layin' her vote on a pole. I'll have you understand it is no hindrance to her at all in a cold and naked cell, or in a public court room crowded with men.'

"'But the indelikacy, the outrage to my womanly nature?' says the woman.

"'Not another word out of your head, young woman,' says the law, 'or I'll fine you for contempt. I guess the law knows what is indelikacy, and what haint; where modesty comes in, and where it don't; now start for prison bareheaded, for I levy on your bunnet for contempt of me.'

"As the young woman totters along to prison, is it any wonder that she sithes to herself, but in a low tone, that the law might not hear her, and deprive her also of her shoes for her contemptas thoughts—

"'Would that I were a idiot; alas! is it not possible that I may become even now a luny?—then I should be respected.'"

As I finished my allegory and looked down from the side of the house, where my eyes had been fastened in the rapped eloquence of thought, I see Josiah with a contented countenance, readin' the almanac, and I said to him in a voice before which he quailed—

"Josiah Allen, you haint heard a word I've said, you know you haint."

"Yes I have," says he, shettin' up the almanac; "I heard you say wimmin ought to vote, and I say she hadn't. I shall always say that she is too fraguile, too delikate, it would be too hard for her to go to the pole."

"There is one pole you are willin' enough I should go to, Josiah Allen," and I stopped allegorin', and spoke with witherin' dignity and self respect—"and that is the hop pole." (Josiah has sot out a new hop yard, and he proudly brags to the neighbors that I am the fastest picker in the yard.) "You are willin' enough I should handle them poles!" He looked smit and conscience struck, but still true to the inherient principles of his sect, and thier doggy obstinacy, he murmured—

"If wimmin know when they are well off, they will let poles and 'lection boxes alone, it is too wearin for the fair sect."

"Josiah Allen," says I, "you think that for a woman to stand up straight on her feet, under a blazin' sun, and lift both her arms above her head, and pick seven bushels of hops, mingled with worms and spiders, into a gigantic box, day in, and day out, is awful healthy, so strengthenin' and stimulatin' to wimmin, but when it comes to droppin' a little slip of clean paper into a small seven by nine box, once a year in a shady room, you are afraid it is goin' to break down a woman's constitution to once."

He was speechless, and clung to Ayer'es almanac mechanically (as it were) and I continued—

"There is another pole you are willin' enough for me to handle, and that is our cistern pole. If you should spend some of the breath you waste— in pityin' the poor wimmin that have got to vote—in byin' a pump, you would raise 25 cents in my estimation, Josiah Allen. You have let me pull on that old cistern pole thirteen years, and get a ten quart pail of water on to the end of it, and I guess the political pole wouldn't draw much harder than that does."

"I guess I will get one, Samantha, when I sell the old critter. I have been a calculatin' to ever year, but things will kinder run along."

"I am aware of that," says I in a tone of dignity cold as a lump of cold ice. "I am aware of that. You may go into any neighborhood you please, and if there is a family in it, where the wife has to set up leeches, make soap, cut her own kindlin' wood, build fires in winter, set up stove-pipes, dround kittens, hang out clothes lines, cord beds, cut up pork, skin calves, and hatchel flax with a baby lashed to her side—I haint afraid to bet you a ten cent bill, that that womans husband thinks that wimmin are too feeble and delicate to go [to] the pole."

Josiah was speechless for pretty near half a minute, and when he did speak it was words calculated to draw my attention from contemplatin' that side of the subject. It was for reasons, I have too much respect for my husband to even hint at—odious to him, as odious could be—he wanted me to forget it, and in the gentle and sheepish manner men can so readily assume when they are talkin' to females he said, as he gently fingered Ayer's almanac, and looked pensively at the dyin' female re- vivin' at a view of the bottle—

"We men think too much of you wimmin to want you to lose your sweet, dignified, retirin' modesty that is your chieftest charm. How long would dignity and modesty stand firm before the wild Urena of public life? You are made to be happy wives, to be guarded by the stronger sect, from the cold blast and the torrid zone. To have a fence built around you by manly strength, to keep out the cares and troubles of life. Why, if I was one of the fair sect, I would have a husband to fence me in, if I had to hire one."

He meant this last, about hirin' a husband, as a joke, for he smiled feebly as he said it, and in other and happier times stern duty would have compelled me to laugh at it—but not now, oh no, my breast was heavin' with too many different sized emotions.

"You would hire one, would you? a woman don't lose her dignity and modesty a racin' round tryin' to get married, does she? Oh no," says I, as sarcastic as sarcastic could be, and then I added sternly, "If it ever does come in fashion to hire husbands by the year, I know of one that could be rented cheap, if his wife had the proceeds and avails in a pecuniary sense."

He looked almost mortified, but still he murmur'd as if mechanically. "It is wimmen's place to marry and not to vote."

"Josiah Allen," says I, "Anybody would think to hear you talk that a woman couldn't do but just one of the two things any way—marry or vote, and had got to take her choice of the two at the pint of the bayonet. And anybody would think to hear you go on, that if a woman could live in any other way, she wouldn't be married, and you couldn't get her to." Says I, looking at him shrewdly, "if marryin' is such a dreadful nice thing for wimmen I don't see what you are afraid of. You men act kinder guilty about it, and I don't wonder at it, for take a bad husband, and thier haint no kind of slavery to be compared to wife slavery. It is jest as natural for a mean, cowardly man to want to abuse and tyranize over them that they can, them that are dependent on 'em, as for a noble and generous man to want to protect them that are weak and in thier power. Figurin' accordin' to the closest rule of arithmetic, there are at least one-third mean, dis-sopated, drunken men in the world, and they most all have wives, and let them tread on these wives ever so hard, if they only tread accordin' to law, she can't escape. And suppose she tries to escape, blood-hounds haint half so bitter as public opinion on a woman that parts with her husband, chains and handcuffs haint to be compared to her pride, and her love for her children, and so she keeps still, and suffers agony enough to make four first class martyrs. Field slaves have a few hours for rest at night, and a hope, to kinder boy them up, of gettin' a better master. But the wife slave has no hope of a change of masters, and let him be ever so degraded and brutal is at his mercy day and night. Men seem to be awful afraid that wimmen wont be so fierce for marryin' anybody, for a home and a support, if they can support themselves independent, and be jest as respectable in the eyes of the world. But," says I,

"In them days when men and wimmen are both independent—free and equal, they will marry in the only true way—from love and not from necessity. They will marry because God will join thier two hearts and hands so you cant get 'em apart no how. But to hear you talk Josiah Allen, anybody would think that there wouldn't another woman marry on earth, if they could get rid of it, and support themselves without it." And then I added, fixin' my keen grey eyes upon his'en. "You act guilty about it Josiah Allen." "But," says I, "just so long as the sun shines down upon the earth and the earth answers back to it, blowin' all out full of beau-ty—Jest so long as the moon looks down lovin'ly upon old ocien makin' her heart beat the faster, jest so long will the hearts and souls God made for each other, answer to each other's call. God's laws can't be repealed, Josiah Allen, they wasn't made in Washington, D.C."

I hardly ever see a man quail more than he did, and to tell the truth, I guess I never had been quite so eloquent in all the 14 years we had lived together—I felt so eloquent that I couldn't stop myself and I went on.

"When did you ever see a couple that hated each other, or didn't care for each other, but what their children, was either jest as mean as pusley—or else wilted and unhappy lookin' like a potato sprout in a dark suller? What that potato sprout wants is sunshine, Josiah Allen. What them children wants is love. The fact is love is what makes a home—I don't care whether its walls are white, stone, marble or bass wood. If there haint a face to the winder a waitin' for you, when you have been off to the store, what good does all your things do you, though you have traded off ten pounds of butter? A lot of folks may get together in a big splendid house, and be called by the same name, and eat and sleep under the same roof till they die, and call it home, but if love don't board with 'em, give me an umbrella and a stump. But the children of these marriages that I speak of, when they see such perfect harmony of mind and heart in their father and mother, when they have been brought up in such a warm, bright, happy home—they can't no more help growin' up sweet, and noble, and happy, than your wheat can help growin' up straight and green when the warm rain and the sunshine falls on it. These children, Josiah Allen, are the future men and wimmens who are goin' to put their shoulder blades to the wheel and roll this world straight into millennium." Says Josiah,

"Wimmen are too good to vote with us men, wimmen haint much more nor less than angels any way."

When you have been soarin' in cloquence, it is always hard to be brought down sudden—it hurts you to light—and this speech sickened me, and says I, in a tone so cold that he shivered imperceptibly.

"Josiah Allen, there is one angel that would be glad to have a little wood got for her to get dinner with, there is one angel that cut every stick of wood she burnt yesterday, that same angel doin' a big washin' at the same time," and says I, repeatin' the words, as I glanced at the beef over the cold and chilly stove, "I should like a handful of wood Josiah Allen."

"I would get you some this minute Samantha," says he gettin' up and takin' down his plantin' bag, "but you know jest how hurried I be with my spring's work, can't you pick up a little for this forenoon? you haint got much to do have you?"

"Oh no!" says I in a lofty tone of irony, "Nothin' at all, only a big ironin', ten pies and six loves of bread to bake, a cheese curd to run up, 3 hens to scald, churnin' and moppin' and dinner to get. Jest a easy mornin's work for a angel."

"Wall then, I guess you'll get along, and to-morrow I'll try to get you some."

I said no more, but with lofty emotions surgin' in my breast, I took my axe and started for the wood-pile.

MARIETTA HOLLEY

MISS ROSIE

by

LUCILLE CLIFTON
(b. 1936)

*Born in New York State, Lucille Clifton attended Howard University
and Fredonia State Teachers College. She now teaches at the University of California at Santa Cruz. The mother of six children, she has
written several children's books. Both a collection of her previous
four volumes of poems,* Good Woman: Poems and a Memoir, 1969–80,
and a new volume, Next: New Poems, *appeared in 1987.*

——————————

When I watch you
wrapped up like garbage
sitting, surrounded by the smell
of too old potato peels
or
when I watch you
in your old man's shoes
with the little toe cut out
sitting, waiting for your mind
like next week's grocery
I say
when I watch you
you wet brown bag of a woman
who used to be the best looking gal in Georgia
used to be called the Georgia Rose
I stand up
through your destruction
I stand up

I LIKE TO THINK OF
HARRIET TUBMAN

by

SUSAN GRIFFIN
(b. 1943)

Susan Griffin has a bachelor of arts degree in English and experience in many different jobs usually filled by women: waitress, teacher, and artist's model. A divorcée and single parent, she lives in San Francisco with other women. She has published two collections of poems; a play, Voices *(1975); and two philosophical works,* Women and Nature *(1979) and* Pornography and Silence *(1981). More recent works include* Rape *(1986) and* Unremembered Country *(1987), a new collection of her poems.*

I like to think of Harriet Tubman.
Harriet Tubman who carried a revolver,
who had a scar on her head from a rock thrown
by a slave-master (because she
talked back), and who
had a ransom on her head
of thousands of dollars and who
was never caught, and who
had no use for the law
when the law was wrong,
who defied the law. I like
to think of her.
I like to think of her especially
when I think of the problem of
feeding children.

The legal answer
to the problem of feeding children
is ten free lunches every month,
being equal, in the child's real life,

to eating lunch every other day.
Monday but not Tuesday.
I like to think of the President
eating lunch Monday, but not
Tuesday.
And when I think of the President
and the law, and the problem of
feeding children, I like to
think of Harriet Tubman
and her revolver.

And then sometimes
I think of the President
and other men,
men who practice the law,
who revere the law,
who make the law,
who enforce the law
who live behind
and operate through
and feed themselves
at the expense of
starving children
because of the law,
men who sit in paneled offices
and think about vacations
and tell women
whose care it is
to feed children
not to be hysterical
not to be hysterical as in the word
hysterikos, the greek for
womb suffering,
not to suffer in their
wombs,
not to care,
not to bother the men
because they want to think
of other things
and do not want
to take the women seriously.
I want them
to take women seriously.

I want them to think about Harriet Tubman,
and remember,
remember she was beat by a white man
and she lived
and she lived to redress her grievances,
and she lived in swamps
and wore the clothes of a man
bringing hundreds of fugitives from
slavery, and was never caught,
and led an army,
and won a battle,
and defied the laws
because the laws were wrong. I want men
to take us seriously.
I am tired wanting them to think
about right and wrong.
I want them to fear.
I want them to feel fear now
as I have felt suffering in the womb, and
I want them
to know
that there is always a time
there is always a time to make right
what is wrong,
there is always a time
for retribution
and that time
is beginning.

From WORK: A STORY OF EXPERIENCE

by

LOUISA MAY ALCOTT
(1832–1888)

Louisa May Alcott spent most of her life in Concord, Massachusetts, and Boston, as part of the intellectual circle of the Transcendentalists. She supported her father, an improvident philosopher, by teaching and writing. Alcott gained fame during her lifetime for a wide variety of books, ranging from Hospital Sketches *(1863), based on her experience at the front during the Civil War, to books on suffrage, temperance, prison reform, and child labor. Her long-range reputation is based on her series of girls' books beginning with* Little Women *(1868), which was an instant best-seller. Only recently has it become known that she also published many thrillers under various pseudonyms. Although always motivated by economic considerations, Alcott maintained a high literary standard in all her publications. She is now viewed as a major American author.*

• ——————————————————— •

"Aunt Betsey, there's going to be a new Declaration of Independence."

"Bless and save us, what do you mean, child?" And the startled old lady precipitated a pie into the oven with destructive haste.

"I mean that, being of age, I'm going to take care of myself, and not be a burden any longer. Uncle wishes me out of the way; thinks I ought to go, and, sooner or later, will tell me so. I don't intend to wait for that, but, like the people in fairy tales, travel away into the world and seek my fortune. I know I can find it."

Christie emphasized her speech by energetic demonstrations in the bread-trough, kneading the dough as if it was her destiny, and she was shaping it to suit herself; while Aunt Betsey stood listening, with uplifted pie-fork, and as much astonishment as her placid face was capable of expressing. As the girl paused, with a decided thump, the old lady exclaimed:

"What crazy idee you got into your head now?"

"A very sane and sensible one that's got to be worked out, so please listen to it, ma'am. I've had it a good while, I've thought it over thoroughly, and I'm sure it's the right thing for me to do. I'm old enough to take care of myself; and if I'd been a boy, I should have been told to do it long ago. I hate to be dependent; and now there's no need of it, I can't bear it any longer. If you were poor, I wouldn't leave you; for I never forget how kind *you* have been to me. But Uncle doesn't love or understand me; I *am* a burden to him, and I must go where I can take care of myself. I can't be happy till I do, for there's nothing here for me. I'm sick of this dull town, where the one idea is eat, drink, and get rich; I don't find any friends to help me as I want to be helped, or any work that I can do well; so let me go, Aunty, and find my place, wherever it is."

"But I do need you, deary; and you mustn't think Uncle don't like you. He does, only he don't show it; and when your odd ways fret him, he ain't pleasant, I know. I don't see why you can't be contented; I've lived here all my days, and never found the place lonesome, or the folks unneighborly." And Aunt Betsey looked perplexed by the new idea.

"You and I are very different, ma'am. There was more yeast put into my composition, I guess; and, after standing quiet in a warm corner so long, I begin to ferment, and ought to be kneaded up in time, so that I may turn out a wholesome loaf. You can't do this; so let me go where it can be done, else I shall turn sour and good for nothing. Does that make the matter any clearer?" And Christie's serious face relaxed into a smile as her aunt's eye went down from her to the nicely moulded loaf offered as an illustration.

"I see what you mean, Kitty; but I never thought on't before. You be better riz than me; though, let me tell you, too much emptins makes bread poor stuff, like baker's trash; and too much workin' up makes it hard and dry. Now fly 'round, for the big oven is most het, and this cake takes a sight of time in the mixin'."

"You haven't said I might go, Aunty," began the girl, after a long pause devoted by the old lady to the preparation of some compound which seemed to require great nicety of measurement in its ingredients; for when she replied, Aunt Betsey curiously interlarded her speech with inaudible directions to herself from the receipt-book before her.

"I ain't no right to keep you, dear, ef you choose to take (a pinch of salt). I'm sorry you ain't happy, and think you might be ef you'd only (beat six eggs, yolks and whites together). But ef you can't, and feel that you need (two cups of sugar), only speak to Uncle, and ef he says (a squeeze of fresh lemon), go, my dear, and take my blessin' with you (not forgettin' to cover with a piece of paper)."

Christie's laugh echoed through the kitchen; and the old lady smiled benignly, quite unconscious of the cause of the girl's merriment.

"I shall ask Uncle to-night, and I know he won't object. Then I shall write to see if Mrs. Flint has a room for me, where I can stay till I get something to do. There is plenty of work in the world, and I'm not afraid of it; so you'll soon hear good news of me. Don't look sad, for you know I never could forget *you*, even if I should become the greatest lady in the land." And Christie left the prints of two floury but affectionate hands on the old lady's shoulders, as she kissed the wrinkled face that had never worn a frown to her.

Full of hopeful fancies, Christie salted the pans and buttered the dough in pleasant forgetfulness of all mundane affairs, and the ludicrous dismay of Aunt Betsey, who followed her about rectifying her mistakes, and watching over her as if this sudden absence of mind had roused suspicions of her sanity.

"Uncle, I want to go away, and get my own living, if you please," was Christie's abrupt beginning, as they sat round the evening fire.

"Hey! what's that?" said Uncle Enos, rousing from the doze he was enjoying, with a candle in perilous proximity to his newspaper and his nose.

Christie repeated her request, and was much relieved, when, after a meditative stare, the old man briefly answered:

"Wal, go ahead."

"I was afraid you might think it rash or silly, sir."

"I think it's the best thing you could do; and I like your good sense in pupposin' on't."

"Then I may really go?"

"Soon's ever you like. Don't pester me about it till you're ready; then I'll give you a little suthing to start off with." And Uncle Enos returned to "The Farmer's Friend," as if cattle were more interesting than kindred.

Christie was accustomed to his curt speech and careless manner; had expected nothing more cordial; and, turning to her aunt, said, rather bitterly:

"Didn't I tell you he'd be glad to have me go? No matter! When I've done something to be proud of, he will be as glad to see me back again." Then her voice changed, her eyes kindled, and the firm lips softened with a smile. "Yes, I'll try my experiment; then I'll get rich; found a home for girls like myself; or, better, still, be a Mrs. Fry, a Florence Nightingale, or"—

"How are you on't for stockin's, dear?"

Christie's castles in the air vanished at the prosaic question; but, after a blank look, she answered pleasantly:

"Thank you for bringing me down to my feet again, when I was soaring away too far and too fast. I'm poorly off, ma'am; but if you are knitting these for me, I shall certainly start on a firm foundation." And, leaning on Aunt Betsey's knee, she patiently discussed the wardrobe question from hose to head-gear.

"Don't you think you could be contented any way, Christie, ef I make the work lighter, and leave you more time for your books and things?" asked the old lady, loth to lose the one youthful element in her quiet life.

"No, ma'am, for I can't find what I want here," was the decided answer.

"What *do* you want, child?"

"Look in the fire, and I'll try to show you."

The old lady obediently turned her spectacles that way; and Christie said in a tone half serious, half playful:

"Do you see those two logs? Well that one smouldering dismally away in the corner is what my life is now; the other blazing and singing is what I want my life to be."

"Bless me, what an idee! They are both a-burnin' where they are put, and both will be ashes to-morrow; so what difference *does* it make?"

Christie smiled at the literal old lady; but, following the fancy that pleased her, she added earnestly:

"I know the end is the same; but it *does* make a difference *how* they turn to ashes, and *how* I spend my life. That log, with its one dull spot of fire, gives neither light nor warmth, but lies sizzling despondently among the cinders. But the other glows from end to end with cheerful little flames that go singing up the chimney with a pleasant sound. Its light fills the room and shines out into the dark; its warmth draws us nearer, making the hearth the cosiest place in the house, and we shall all miss the friendly blaze when it dies. Yes," she added, as if to herself, "I hope my life may be like that, so that, whether it be long or short, it will be useful and cheerful while it lasts, will be missed when it ends, and leave something behind besides ashes."

Though she only half understood them, the girl's words touched the kind old lady, and made her look anxiously at the eager young face gazing so wistfully into the fire.

"A good smart blowin' up with the belluses would make the green stick burn most as well as the dry one after a spell. I guess contentedness is the best bellus for young folks, ef they would only think so."

"I dare say you are right, Aunty; but I want to try for myself; and if I fail, I'll come back and follow your advice. Young folks always have discontented fits, you know. Didn't you when you were a girl?"

"Shouldn't wonder ef I did; but Enos came along, and I forgot 'em."

"My Enos has not come along yet, and never may; so I'm not going to sit and wait for any man to give me independence, if I can earn it for myself." And a quick glance at the gruff, gray old man in the corner plainly betrayed that, in Christie's opinion, Aunt Betsey made a bad bargain when she exchanged her girlish aspirations for a man whose soul was in his pocket.

"Jest like her mother, full of hifalutin notions, discontented, and sot in her own idees. Poor capital to start a fortin' on."

Christie's eye met that of her uncle peering over the top of his paper with an expression that always tried her patience. Now it was like a dash of cold water on her enthusiasm, and her face fell as she asked quickly:

"How do you mean, sir?"

"I mean that you are startin' all wrong; your redic'lus notions about independence and self-cultur won't come to nothin' in the long run, and you'll make as bad a failure of your life as your mother did of her'n."

"Please, don't say that to me; I can't bear it, for *I* shall never think her life a failure, because she tried to help herself, and married a good man in spite of poverty, when she loved him! You call that folly; but I'll do the same if I can; and I'd rather have what my father and mother left me, than all the money you are piling up, just for the pleasure of being richer than your neighbors."

"Never mind, dear, he don't mean no harm!" whispered Aunt Betsey, fearing a storm.

But though Christie's eyes had kindled and her color deepened, her voice was low and steady, and her indignation was of the inward sort.

"Uncle likes to try me by saying such things, and this is one reason why I want to go away before I get sharp and bitter and distrustful as he is. I don't suppose I can make you understand my feeling, but I'd like to try, and then I'll never speak of it again;" and, carefully controlling voice and face, Christie slowly added, with a look that would have been pathetically eloquent to one who could have understood the instincts of a strong nature for light and freedom: "You say I am discontented, proud and ambitious; that's true, and I'm glad of it. I am discontented, because I can't help feeling that there is a better sort of life than this dull one made up of everlasting work, with no object but money. I can't starve my soul for the sake of my body, and I mean to get out of the treadmill if I can. I'm proud, as you call it, because I hate dependence where there isn't any love to make it bearable. You don't say so in words, but I know you begrudge me a home, though you will call me ungrateful when I'm gone. I'm willing to work, but I want work that I can put my heart into, and feel that it does me good, no matter how hard it is. I only ask for a chance to be a useful, happy woman, and I don't think that is a bad ambition. Even if I only do what my dear mother did, earn my living honestly and happily, and leave a beautiful example behind me, to help one other woman as hers helps me, I shall be satisfied."

Christie's voice faltered over the last words, for the thoughts and feelings which had been working within her during the last few days had stirred her deeply, and the resolution to cut loose from the old life had not been lightly made. Mr. Devon had listened behind his paper to this unusual outpouring with a sense of discomfort which was new to him. But though the words reproached and annoyed, they did not soften him, and when Christie paused with tearful eyes, her uncle rose, saying, slowly, as he lighted his candle:

"Ef I'd refused to let you go before, I'd agree to it now; for you need breakin' in, my girl, and you are goin' where you'll get it, so the sooner you're off the better for all on us. Come, Betsey, we may as wal leave, for we can't understand the wants of her higher nater, as Christie calls it, and we've had lecterin' enough for one night." And with a grim laugh the old man quitted the field, worsted but in good order.

"There, there, dear, hev a good cry, and forgit all about it!" purred Aunt Betsey, as the heavy footsteps creaked away, for the good soul had a most old-fashioned and dutiful awe of her lord and master.

"I shan't cry but act; for it is high time I *was* off. I've stayed for your sake; now I'm more trouble than comfort, and away I go. Good-night, my dear old Aunty, and don't look troubled, for I'll be a lamb while I stay."

Having kissed the old lady, Christie swept her work away, and sat down to write the letter which was the first step toward freedom. When it was done, she drew nearer to her friendly *confidante* the fire, and till late into the night sat thinking tenderly of the past, bravely of the present, hopefully of the future. Twenty-one to-morrow, and her inheritance a head, a heart, a pair of hands; also the dower of most New England girls, intelligence, courage, and common sense, many practical gifts, and, hidden under the reserve that soon melts in a genial atmosphere, much romance and enthusiasm, and the spirit which can rise to heroism when the great moment comes.

Christie was one of that large class of women who, moderately endowed with talents, earnest and true-hearted, are driven by necessity, temperament, or principle out into the world to find support, happiness, and homes for themselves. Many turn back discouraged; more accept shadow for substance, and discover their mistake too late; the weakest lose their purpose and themselves; but the strongest struggle on, and, after danger and defeat, earn at last the best success this world can give us, the possession of a brave and cheerful spirit, rich in self-knowledge, self-control, self-help. This was the real desire of Christie's heart; this was to be her lesson and reward, and to this happy end she was slowly yet surely brought by the long discipline of life and labor.

Sitting alone there in the night, she tried to strengthen herself with all the good and helpful memories she could recall, before she went away to find her place in the great unknown world. She thought of her mother, so like herself, who had borne the commonplace life of home till she could bear it no longer. Then had gone away to teach, as most country girls are forced to do. Had met, loved, and married a poor gentleman, and, after a few years of genuine happiness, untroubled even by much care and poverty, had followed him out of the world, leaving her little child to the protection of her brother.

Christie looked back over the long, lonely years she had spent in the old farm-house, plodding to school and church, and doing her tasks with kind Aunt Betsey while a child; and slowly growing into girlhood, with a world of romance locked up in a heart hungry for love and a larger, nobler life.

She had tried to appease this hunger in many ways, but found little help. Her father's old books were all she could command, and these she wore out with much reading. Inheriting his refined tastes, she found nothing to attract her in the society of the commonplace and often coarse people about her. She tried to like the buxom girls whose one ambition was to "get married," and whose only subjects of conversation were "smart bonnets" and "nice dresses." She tried to believe that the admiration and regard of the bluff young farmers was worth striving for;

but when one well-to-do neighbor laid his acres at her feet, she found it impossible to accept for her life's companion a man whose soul was wrapped up in prize cattle and big turnips.

Uncle Enos never could forgive her for this piece of folly, and Christie plainly saw that one of three things would surely happen, if she lived on there with no vent for her full heart and busy mind. She would either marry Joe Butterfield in sheer desperation, and become a farmer's household drudge; settle down into a sour spinster, content to make butter, gossip, and lay up money all her days; or do what poor Mary Stone had done, try to crush and curb her needs and aspirations till the struggle grew too hard, and then in a fit of despair end her life, and leave a tragic story to haunt their quiet river.

To escape these fates but one way appeared; to break loose from this narrow life, go out into the world and see what she could do for herself. This idea was full of enchantment to the eager girl, and, after much earnest thought, she had resolved to try it.

"If I fail, I can come back," she said to herself, even while she scorned the idea of failure, for with all her shy pride she was both brave and ardent, and her dreams were of the rosiest sort.

"I won't marry Joe; I won't wear myself out in a district-school for the mean sum they give a woman; I won't delve away here where I'm not wanted; and I won't end my life like a coward, because it is dull and hard. I'll try my fate as mother did, and perhaps I may succeed as well." And Christie's thoughts went wandering away into the dim, sweet past when she, a happy child, lived with loving parents in a different world from that.

Lost in these tender memories, she sat till the old moon-faced clock behind the door struck twelve, then the visions vanished, leaving their benison behind them.

As she glanced backward at the smouldering fire, a slender spire of flame shot up from the log that had blazed so cheerily, and shone upon her as she went. A good omen, gratefully accepted then, and remembered often in the years to come.

From A VOICE FROM THE SOUTH

by

ANNA JULIA COOPER
(1859–1964)

Anna Julia Cooper was born in Raleigh, North Carolina to a slave mother and a white father. The most important event in her long and full life was being selected at age six to be a student at a church school founded during Reconstruction. At eighteen she married one of her teachers and was widowed at twenty. She continued her education at Oberlin College and received a doctoral degree from the Sorbonne in Paris in 1925 at the age of sixty-six. Her thesis on French attitudes toward slavery during the Revolution was translated into English in 1988. Cooper never stopped learning and teaching. For thirty years she taught in the only high school in Washington, D.C., open to blacks; during a term as principal, she won accreditation for the school. Later she founded a school for employed adults, which she continued to run until 1941, when she was eighty-two. A Voice from the South by a Black Woman of the South *(1892) is a collection of her essays; she lectured widely on women's roles and was well-known as an advocate of higher education for blacks.*

My readers will pardon my illustrating my point and also giving a reason for the fear that is in me, by a little bit of personal experience. When a child I was put into a school near home that professed to be normal and collegiate, i.e. to prepare teachers for colored youth, furnish candidates for the ministry, and offer collegiate training for those who should be ready for it. Well, I found after a while that I had a good deal of time on my hands. I had devoured what was put before me, and, like Oliver Twist, was looking around to ask for more. I constantly felt (as I suppose many an ambitious girl has felt) a thumping from within unanswered by any beckoning from without. Class after class was organized for these ministerial candidates (many of them men who had been preaching before I was born). Into every one of these classes I was expected to go, with the sole intent, I thought at the time, of enabling the dear old principal, as he looked from the vacant countenances of his sleepy old class over to where I sat, to get off his solitary pun—his never-failing pleasantry, especially in hot weather—which was, as he called out "Any one!" to the effect that "*any* one" then meant "*Annie* one."

Finally a Greek class was to be formed. My inspiring preceptor informed me that Greek had never been taught in the school, but that he was going to form a class *for the candidates for the ministry*, and if I liked I might join it. I replied—humbly I hope, as became a female of the human species—that I would like very much to study Greek, and that I was thankful for the opportunity, and so it went on. A boy, however meager his equipment and shallow his pretentions, had only to declare a floating intention to study theology and he could get all the support, encouragement and stimulus he needed, be absolved from work and invested beforehand with all the dignity of his far away office. While a self-supporting girl had to struggle on by teaching in the summer and working after school hours to keep up with her board bills, and actually to fight her way against positive discouragements to the higher education; till one such girl one day flared out and told the principal "the only mission opening before a girl in his school was to marry one of those candidates." He said he didn't know but it was. And when at last that same girl announced her desire and intention to go to college it was received with about the same incredulity and dismay as if a brass button on one of those candidate's coats had propounded a new method for squaring the circle or trisecting the arc.

Now this is not fancy. It is a simple unvarnished photograph, and what I believe was not in those days exceptional in colored schools, and I ask the men and women who are teachers and co-workers for the highest interests of the race, that they give the girls a chance! We might as well expect to grow trees from leaves as hope to build up a civilization or a manhood without taking into consideration our women and the home life made by them, which must be the root and ground of the whole matter. Let us insist then on special encouragement for the education of our women and special care in their training. Let our girls feel that we expect something more of them than that they merely look pretty and appear well in society. Teach them that there is a race with special needs which they and only they can help; that the world needs and is already asking for their trained, efficient forces. Finally, if there is an ambitious girl with pluck and brain to take the higher education, encourage her to make the most of it. Let there be the same flourish of trumpets and clapping of hands as when a boy announces his determination to enter the lists; and then, as you know that she is physically the weaker of the two, don't stand from under and leave her to buffet the waves alone. Let her know that your heart is following her, that your hand, though she sees it not, is ready to support her. To be plain, I mean let money be raised and scholarships be founded in our colleges and universities for self-supporting, worthy young women, to offset and balance the aid that can always be found for boys who will take theology.

The earnest well trained Christian young woman, as a teacher, as a home-maker, as wife, mother, or silent influence even, is as potent a missionary agency among our people as is the theologian; and I claim that at the present stage of our development in the South she is even more important and necessary.

Let us then, here and now, recognize this force and resolve to make the most of it—not the boys less, but the girls more.

From GIFTS OF POWER

by

REBECCA JACKSON
(1795–1871)

A religious visionary in the Shaker tradition, Rebecca Jackson was born in Philadelphia; though her diary was not known until this century, she made her mark in her lifetime as an independent itinerant preacher. Her spiritual awakening at thirty-five, which led her to learn to read so that she could understand the Bible on her own, was met with disapproval by many. However, she won many followers and left behind a black Shaker community she had founded.

• —————————————————— •

. . . I can truly say that my prayers have been answered again and again, for which I give the glory to that God to whom it belongs. I am only a pen in His hand. Oh, that I may prove faithful to the end.

[1831?]

The Gift of Reading

A remarkable providence of God's love for me. After I received the blessing of God, I had a great desire to read the Bible. I am the only child of my mother that had not learning. And now, having the charge of my brother and his six children to see to, and my husband, and taking in sewing for a living, I saw no way that I could now get learning without my brother would give me one hour's lesson at night after supper or before he went to bed. His time was taken up as well as mine. So I spoke to him about it. He said he would give me one or two lessons, I being so desirous to learn. (He was a tolerable scholar, so that he was able to teach his own children at home, without sending them to school. For a time, he fulfilled the offices of seven men in the Methodist church. And when he ceased from this, he worked hard and earned his bread by the sweat of his brow.) And my brother so tired when he would come home that he had not power so to do, and it would grieve me. Then I would pray to God to give me power over my feelings that I might not think hard of my brother. Then I would be comforted.

So I went to get my brother to write my letters and to read them. So he was awriting a letter in answer to one he had just read. I told him what to put in. Then I asked him to read. He did. I said, "Thee has put in more than I told thee." This he done several times. I then said, "I don't want thee to *word* my letter. I only want thee to *write* it." Then he said, "Sister, thee is the hardest one I ever wrote for!" These words, together with the manner that he had wrote my letter, pierced my soul like a sword. (As there was nothing I could do for him or his children that I thought was too hard to me to do for their comfort, I felt hurt, when he refused me these little things.) And at this time, I could not keep from crying. And these words were spoken in my heart, "Be faithful, and the time shall come when you can write." These words were spoken in my heart as though a tender father spoke them. My tears were gone in a moment.

One day I was sitting finishing a dress in haste and in prayer. This word was spoken in my mind, "Who learned the first man on earth?" "Why, God." "He is unchangeable, and if He learned the first man to read, He can learn you." I laid down my dress, picked up my Bible, ran upstairs, opened it, and kneeled down with it pressed to my breast, prayed earnestly to Almighty God if it was consisting to His holy will, to learn me to read His holy word. And when I looked on the word, I began to read. And when I found I was reading, I was frightened—then I could not read one word. I closed my eyes again in prayer and then opened my eyes, began to read. So I done, until I read the chapter. I came down. "Samuel, I can read the Bible." "Woman, you are agoing crazy!" "Praise the God of heaven and of earth, I can read His holy word!" Down I sat and read through. And it was in James. So Samuel praised the Lord with me. When my brother came to dinner I told him, "I can read the Bible! I have read a whole chapter!" "One thee has heard the children read, till thee has got it by heart." What a wound that was to me, to think he would make so light of a gift of God! But I did not speak. Samuel reproved him and told him all about it. He sat down very sorrowful. I then told him, "I had a promise, the day thee wrote my letter to sister Diges, that if I was faithful I would see the day when I can write." (I repeated this conditional promise to him at the time and said then "I will write thee a letter." He said, he had no doubt of it. This soon after took place.) So I tried, took my Bible daily and praying and read until I could read anywhere. The first chapter that I read I never could know it after that day. I only knowed it was in James, but what chapter I never can tell.

Oh how thankful I feel for this unspeakable gift of Almighty God to me! Oh may I make a good use of it all the days of my life!

REBECCA JACKSON

523

Then I woke and found the burden of my people heavy upon me. I had borne a burden of my people for twelve years, but now it was double, and I cried unto the Lord and prayed this prayer, "Oh, Lord God of Hosts, if Thou art going to make me useful to my people, either temporal or spiritual,—for temporally they are held by their white brethren in bondage, not as bound man and bound woman, but as bought beasts, and spiritually they are held by their ministers, by the world, the flesh, and the devil. And if these are not a people in bondage, where are there any on the earth?—Oh, my Father and my God, make me faithful in this Thy work and give me wisdom that I may comply with Thy whole will."

This was March the 12th, 1843, in [a house in] Albany, New York State.

March 13th, I laid down and slept. When I woke the wind was blowing as if it would seize the house into the air. And I was afraid of the suffering of my body under the moving of the house. And in this feeling, I prayed to the Lord to give me strength. And in a few minutes, I was brought into the shower of flowers. And as I looked through, I seen the blessed saints come through the flowers. And I was in the house that I was, in the dream the night before. So it pleased the Lord to show me in a dream and prepare me for this heavenly interview.

These saints came until they filled the house, and the wind was ablowing as if it would destroy everything on the earth. They told me that they came to comfort me, and to give me understanding. The wind, they told me, this was the way God made known his power to his little ones in these last days. For this wind could not hurt his saints, for the Holy Ghost carried them over all danger. And if the house was lifted into the air, I would be carried over all and be made happy (in the wind as they were in it coming to me. While they were talking I was made happy). And the wind was to me like a shower of glory. And they carried me away with them. And when I found myself again, I woke out of a sweet sleep. It was morning, and the wind was not unusual for a high wind. And oh, the blessed instruction that them blessed saints gave me! May I never forget it, but live to the glory of God in all things!

March 24, 1843, at supper, it pleased the Lord to give me the following lines.

> The Lord is good to them that serve Him.
> Oh how good, oh how good.
> He will save us from all danger,
> Oh how good, oh how good.
>
> The Lord will save the soul that serves Him,
> Oh how good, oh how good.

He will give them peace forever,
Oh how good, oh how good.

He will clear the way before them,
Oh how good, oh how good.
He will give them strength and wisdom,
For to conquer, for to conquer.

Let us hasten then to serve Him,
Oh how sweet, oh how sweet.
He has filled me like a bottle,
With new wine, with new wine.

For to empty unto others,
Oh how precious, oh how precious.
Oh that I may be so faithful,
As to finish, as to finish.

And then soar away into Heaven,
Into glory, into glory,
There to see my Blessed Savior,
Whom I love here, oh how I love here.

This is the first spiritual song given to me, that I have been permitted to write, and when I received it, I was forty-eight years, one month, and nine days old. Though I had often received heavenly songs and sung them in the spirit, they were taken away, and then given me again as was needful. . . .

A PERSON AS WELL AS
A FEMALE

by

JADE SNOW WONG
(b. 1922)

*Jade Snow Wong is a journalist, a prize-winning ceramicist, and a
writer of nonfiction about Chinese-Americans in her native San
Francisco. She is a graduate of Mills College. The owner of a travel
agency, she has traveled widely, to China and elsewhere. She speaks
English and Cantonese and is learning Mandarin. Her books include*
The Immigrant Experience *(1971) and* No Chinese Stranger *(1975).*
Fifth Chinese Daughter *(1950), her autobiography, of which this
selection is a chapter, has been widely used in schools since it was
written forty years ago.*

• ──────────────────── •

After graduation from the Chinese school, Jade Snow seriously sought a
solution to her money problem. For two reasons, she decided that she
would try working outside their factory-home. She thought that she could
make a little more money, and even if she didn't, she would at least escape from some of the continuous family friction. She sought help from
the state employment service, which found openings for her in house-
work. Within the following six months, Jade Snow worked in seven different homes and was exposed to a series of candid views of the private
lives of these American families. Jade Snow made her own decisions. At
no time did she consult her family about the various jobs; she simply told
them when her mind was made up.

Daddy and Mama did give her one bit of serious advice when she
started her first job. Mama said, "I have done my best to teach you to be
honest and diligent. Now you are about to emerge on your own. You
must follow your best judgment and conscience and, above all, do not be
greedy in your work. If you were to see your employer's diamonds and
gold pieces lying around, do not covet them."

Daddy was reminded to reminisce a bit: "When my father began his
business training as an apprentice, one of the duties assigned to him was
to sweep the floor daily. At times, he found a coin on the floor. Without

a word, he picked up the coin each time and put it away. After many months, his employer complained. 'I do not know who can be trusted around here. I have been missing some coins.' Whereupon your grandfather calmly went to his quarters and produced all of the salvaged coins, each wrapped carefully in a memorandum dated with the time your grandfather found it. He effectively proved himself to be trustworthy."

Her parents probably did not remember the incident of the peddler specifically but Jade Snow had never forgotten. Aloud, she simply answered, "Yes."

First she worked for the Schmidts, who ran a small soft-drink fountain and poolroom near their home in a residential district of San Francisco. The mother was a big-hearted, merry-eyed, stout woman who worked hard and continuously. She usually cooked one hot dish a day, to be served at the fountain as the luncheon special. Jade Snow helped her with the cooking and the light housework, and quickly became great friends with her employer, who treated her with utmost kindness. There were two things Jade Snow always thought of when she looked back on this job: the perpetually darkened "front room" with its heavy velvet drapes, drawn to keep the sun from fading the plush furniture, and her own weeping eyes as she peeled and ground vast mounds of onions for the endless hamburgers ordered at the fountain.

After a brief period with the Schmidts, Jade Snow moved on to their good friends, the Jeffersons, because young Mrs. Jefferson was ill after an operation. Mrs. Schmidt said that she could manage somehow, but her friend really needed help; she had several small children, and her husband, who operated a service station, was busy all day.

Jade Snow's most persistent memory of her first day in this new position was a big galvanized pail of string beans set on the back of the kitchen stove. The husband, struggling to work, shop, and care for the children as well as to nurse his wife, had cooked quantities of this vegetable to feed all of them for several days. Perhaps ten pounds of beans were boiling through their second hour. Jade Snow, trained in the Chinese tradition of quick cooking of finely cut vegetables, who had never cooked string beans more than seven or eight minutes, suppressed her surprise and politely asked the reason.

Mr. Jefferson replied, "Where I come from in the South, we don't think a bean is tender until it has been cooked at least two hours!"

However, the Jeffersons good-naturedly let Jade Snow take over their very informal household. For a month, while the mother was getting well, Jade Snow was busy from morning until night with all the familiar home chores; but now she was paid fifty cents an hour, and there was no criticism.

At the end of the summer Jade Snow was a senior in high school, and could take on only part-time work. She decided to try working at several odd jobs so that she would not be tied down completely. By word-of-mouth referrals, she made four contacts which kept her busy. She really liked these odd jobs better, since all that was involved was serving party dinners and washing dishes, which was not so tiring as the entire management of a household.

Mentally she tabulated these four families by type rather than by name—" the horsy family," "the apartment-house family," "the political couple," and the "bridge-playing group."

The "horsy family" was composed of an elderly, mild father who said scarcely a word, an ambitious, tense mother, and two equally ambitious and mutually antagonistic daughters in their thirties, whose chief purpose in life was to be "smart." They were unrelenting in their efforts to get their names on the social page of the local newspapers, and their method was horses. They had their pictures taken in horsy poses, and they gave parties, but only for guests who "mattered." They owned a large house patterned after English cottage architecture, which the mother tried to keep in perfect order as a setting for her daughters' activities. The father, who worked all day, said nothing when he came home, but the daughters argued continuously about the best means to achieve their common goal.

The "political" middle-aged couple gave dinners in honor of up-and-coming young California political figures; there were always many men but few women at these parties. Here, Jade Snow was initiated into a new wrinkle in the American pattern—the off-color story.

Needless to say, the Wong household, if not always gentle, had high standards. Between Confucian decorum and Christian ideals, even unessential or boisterous laughing was dissonant. There an off-color story had never reared its ugly head. However, at this home, toward ten o'clock when everyone had had many cocktails, and the waiting dinner was turning to ruin in the oven, a group of men, including the political star of honor, howling with laughter, would burst into the kitchen to get away from the women in the living room. Here they would start on their gleeful "Have you heard the latest one?" slap each other, and roar with gales of laughter over each tale.

The small, lone female, Jade Snow, must have been to them merely another kitchen fixture for they never recognized her. Stoically she continued her work, trying not to blush at their remarks and double talk and to drive them out of her memory.

What would Daddy and Mama think about this? They never knew that in these months their fifth daughter saw and heard things that broadened and humanized the American world beyond the realm of typewriters and stenographers, which had provided her first and only childhood associations with Caucasians. Needless to say, she never talked about these new experiences at home. Mama and Daddy were comfortable in their knowledge that Jade Snow had found honest work and was performing it satisfactorily. She was making about twenty dollars a month, and now paid for her own lunches, carfare, clothes, and all the other necessities of a fifteen-year-old schoolgirl. She had completed Chinese school, was about to complete the American high school, and was apparently establishing firm habits for earning a living and being a good homemaker, in accordance with the traditional Chinese pattern for women.

The "apartment-house" dwellers had one little girl about three, who was the light of their life. Everything Arleen did or said was the most astounding thing in the world, and had never been done or said so well before. If Arleen threw her dinner at the window of the kitchen door, she was not reproved or punished; she was excused for being "full of spirit." The only reason Jade Snow continued to oblige Arleen's fond parents was that once their angel child was asleep, she could use the evening to study, while being paid.

Finally, there were the Gilberts, or rather, Mrs. Gilbert, who loved bridge parties. The Gilberts' home was large, beautiful, adequately landscaped, and they were very proud of it. Mr. Gilbert liked golf. "Nothing like it in the world for relaxation and public relations," he always said. Every Saturday afternoon which did not see a downpour of rain found him at his favorite activity.

Mrs. Gilbert's passion for bridge demanded every Saturday, rain or shine. On the afternoons when she entertained "the girls" in her own home, Jade Snow helped her. On other Saturdays, she was at "the other girls'" homes.

When Mrs. Gilbert was hostess for a "simple" buffet luncheon, she set her table with her best lace cloth and polished silver. It was Jade Snow's first acquaintance with buffet meals. "The girls," from thirty-five to fifty in years, arrived, gushed, giggled, gossiped, ate, and played bridge all afternoon—and what was most amazing to Jade Snow—all the while with their hats on! It was always the same crowd of faces under different hats. Jade Snow wondered what it would be like to be one of them, to have so much time that you would try to spend it playing bridge, and so much money that you could pay someone to come in and wash the dishes while you played.

Jade Snow now concentrated intensely on her American schoolwork, since there were no more Chinese lessons to divide her energy. As her graduation was approaching, she began inquiries about qualifications for college entrance. She found that she had met the academic requirements for the state university; but the registration and other fees, together with commutation and books, would be beyond her part-time earning capacity, and more than she could possibly save, since she was using all her earnings for current expenses.

But if not college, what was her future?

"Education is your path to freedom," Daddy had said. "In China, you would have had little private tutoring and no free advanced schooling. Make the most of your American opportunity."

"Be a good girl—and study hard," Grandmother had said.

"Daddy thinks that Jade Snow is so intelligent," she had overheard her older sisters say skeptically, "but let's see if she can bring any honors home to our family."

"I resolve to be a credit to Mama and prove that the unkind predictions about her children were wrong," she had vowed once when Daddy was ill.

"Give me the strength and the ability to prove to my family that they have been unjust and make them prouder of me than anyone else," Jade Snow had pleaded later in unnumbered prayers.

Constantly, she remembered these challenges.

Moreover, she was most curious about college, and eager to learn more about the new worlds which her high school subjects were just opening up to her.

Yes, Jade Snow agreed with Daddy that education was the path to freedom. Forgotten was her early ambition to be a stenographer. She resolved to ask Daddy to help her with the college fees. After all, he had financed Older Brother's education.

Her next free night, when she was alone with Daddy in the dining room after dinner, Jade Snow broached the subject.

"Daddy, I have been studying the state university catalogue, and I should like to continue my education there, but it will cost more than I can manage, even though I still worked all I could. Would you help me to meet the college expenses?"

Daddy reluctantly pulled himself away from his evening paper and settled back in the large, square, straight, black armchair that was his alone. He took off his dark-rimmed reading glasses, and looked thoughtfully but distractedly at the figure standing respectfully before him. Then he chose his words seriously and deliberately.

"You are quite familiar by now with the fact that it is the sons who perpetuate our ancestral heritage by permanently bearing the Wong family name and transmitting it through their blood line, and therefore the sons must have priority over the daughters when parental provision for advantages must be limited by economic necessity. Generations of sons, bearing our Wong name, are those who make pilgrimages to ancestral burial grounds and preserve them forever. Our daughters leave home at marriage to give sons to their husbands' families to carry on the heritage for other names.

"Jade Snow, you have been given an above-average Chinese education for an American-born Chinese girl. You now have an average education for an American girl. I must still provide with all my powers for your Older Brother's advanced medical training."

"But Daddy, I want to be more than an average Chinese or American girl. If I stay here, I want to be more than average. If I go to China, I shall advance further with an American college degree," Jade Snow pleaded earnestly.

"I have no other means even though you desire to be above average," Daddy replied evenly, and Jade Snow could not detect either regret or sympathy in his statement of fact. She did not know whether his next words were uttered in challenge or in scorn as he added, "If you have the talent, you can provide for your own college education."

Daddy had spoken. He returned to his Chinese paper with finality and clamped on his glasses again. By habit, Jade Snow questioned aloud no more. She had been trained to make inquiry of Daddy with one question, and to accept his answer; she never asked twice. But her mind was full of questions as it echoed his words, "If you have the talent, you can provide for your own college education."

Tonight his statement did not leave Jade Snow with the customary reaction, "Daddy knows better. Daddy is fair. Even though I do not like what he says, he has eaten more salt than I have eaten rice, and in time I shall understand why this is my own problem and must be endured."

No, his answer tonight left Jade Snow with a new and sudden bitterness against the one person whom she had always trusted as fair to her.

"How can Daddy know what an American advanced education can mean to me? Why should Older Brother be alone in enjoying the major benefits of Daddy's toil? There are no ancestral pilgrimages to be made in the United States! I can't help being born a girl. Perhaps, even being a girl, I don't want to marry, *just* to raise sons! Perhaps I have a right to want more than sons! I am a person, besides being a female! Don't the Chinese admit that women also have feelings and minds?"

Jade Snow retreated to her little bedroom, but now she felt imprisoned. She was trapped in a mesh of tradition woven thousands of miles away by ancestors who had had no knowledge that someday one generation of their progeny might be raised in another culture. Acknowledging that she owed her very being and much of her thinking to those ancestors and their tradition, she could not believe that this background was meant to hinder her further development either in America or in China.

Beyond this point, she could not think clearly. Impulsively, she threw on her coat and left the house—the first time that she had done so without notifying Mama.

In a lonely walk, she wandered in the darkness over the San Francisco hills. She went first to the waterfront, saw a few tramps sleeping in empty railroad cars, hid from some drunken brawlers in front of the saloons, climbed up Telegraph Hill, came down and went up again over Russian Hill, to Van Ness Avenue, then back to Chinatown and home.

As she walked, she pushed away her bitterness in order to organize a practical course of action. To begin with, she was not going to give up her education. She felt that it was right to go on with it, and she must try to provide for it alone. She would try to get a scholarship to college.

But Daddy had also said, "If you have the talent. . . . " Jade Snow reasoned: talent is what you were born with—in combination with what you have learned. Did she have talent? Older Brother had said that she had no imagination nor personality, but did she have talent? She reasoned further: she had always tried to make the most of her ability.

Often her classmates seemed to get the right answer much more quickly than she did, but she always hung on, and eventually she caught up with them. If she continued to do her very best, and if what she had set her eyes on was the right thing for her to do, she had to believe that the talent part would somehow be taken care of.

She decided as simply as that. She would try her best to do the right things; somehow things would work out, and she would not worry. She was concerned only with doing what was immediately at hand, and putting her best into it. So she continued to keep people's houses clean, exhausted herself studying, ignored her family, got straight A's except in physical education, and left it to God to take care of His share in bringing her college education to reality.

SPELLING

by

MARGARET ATWOOD
(b. 1939)

*Born in Ottawa, Margaret Atwood studied at the University of
Toronto and Harvard. She lives in Toronto with her husband and
daughter when she is not teaching, lecturing, or reading from her
works. Prolific as both poet and fiction writer, Atwood has published
more than twenty works, including seven volumes of poetry, two
collections of short stories, and six novels. The Handmaid's Tale
(1986) won a Los Angeles Times award for best fiction and has been
made into a movie; its chilling image of a possible future has been
compared to George Orwell's 1984. Her novel Surfacing (1972),
about a woman's quest for identity, has become a classic of feminist literature.*

My daughter plays on the floor
with plastic letters,
red, blue & hard yellow,
learning how to spell,
spelling,
how to make spells

*

and I wonder how many women
denied themselves daughters,
closed themselves in rooms,
drew the curtains
so they could mainline words.

*

A child is not a poem,
a poem is not a child.
There is no either/or.
However.

*

I return to the story
of the woman caught in the war
& in labour, her thighs tied
together by the enemy
so she could not give birth.

Ancestress: the burning witch,
her mouth covered by leather
to strangle words.

A word after a word
after a word is power.

         *

At the point where language falls away
from the hot bones, at the point
where the rock breaks open and darkness
flows out of it like blood, at
the melting point of granite
when the bones know
they are hollow & the word
splits & doubles & speaks
the truth & the body
itself becomes a mouth.

This is a metaphor.

         *

How do you learn to spell?
Blood, sky & the sun,
your own name first,
your first naming, your first name,
your first word.

TRIFLES

by

SUSAN GLASPELL

(1882–1948)

Perhaps best known as a dramatist and a founder of the Province-town Players, Susan Glaspell won a Pulitzer Prize in 1930 for her play Alison's House, *based on the life of Emily Dickinson. She wrote several novels and short stories, of which "A Jury of Her Peers" is the most famous; it was reprinted in* The Best Short Stories of 1917. Trifles *is Glaspell's earlier dramatic version of that story.*

• ——————————————— •

Scene

The kitchen in the now abandoned farm-house of John Wright, a gloomy kitchen, and left without having been put in order—unwashed pans under the sink, a loaf of bread outside the bread-box, a dish-towel on the table— other signs of incompleted work. At the rear the outer door opens and the SHERIFF *comes in followed by the* COUNTY ATTORNEY *and* HALE. *The* SHERIFF *and* HALE *are men in middle life, the* COUNTY ATTORNEY *is a young man; all are much bundled up and go at once to the stove. They are followed by the two women—the Sheriff's wife first; she is a slight wiry woman, with a thin nervous face.* MRS. HALE *is larger and would ordinarily be called more comfortable looking, but she is disturbed now and looks fearfully about as she enters. The women have come in slowly, and stand close together near the door.*

COUNTY ATTORNEY   *(rubbing his hands)* This feels good. Come up to the fire, ladies.

MRS. PETERS   *(after taking a step forward)* I'm not—cold.

SHERIFF   *(unbuttoning his overcoat and stepping away from the stove as if to mark the beginning of official business)* Now, Mr. Hale, before we move things about, you explain to Mr. Henderson just what you saw when you came here yesterday morning.

COUNTY ATTORNEY By the way, has anything been moved? Are things just as you left them yesterday?

SHERIFF *(looking about)* It's just the same. When it dropped below zero last night I thought I'd better send Frank out this morning to make a fire for us—no use getting pneumonia with a big case on, but I told him not to touch anything except the stove—and you know Frank.

COUNTY ATTORNEY Somebody should have been left here yesterday.

SHERIFF Oh—yesterday. When I had to send Frank to Morris Center for that man who went crazy—I want you to know I had my hands full yesterday. I knew you could get back from Omaha by to-day and as long as I went over everything here myself—

COUNTY ATTORNEY Well, Mr. Hale, tell just what happened when you came here yesterday morning.

HALE Harry and I had started to town with a load of potatoes. We came along the road from my place and as I got here I said, "I'm going to see if I can't get John Wright to go in with me on a party telephone." I spoke to Wright about it once before and he put me off, saying folks talked too much anyway, and all he asked was peace and quiet—I guess you know about how much he talked himself; but I thought maybe if I went to the house and talked about it before his wife, though I said to Harry that I didn't know as what his wife wanted made much difference to John—

COUNTY ATTORNEY Let's talk about that later, Mr. Hale. I do want to talk about that, but tell now just what happened when you got to the house.

HALE I didn't hear or see anything; I knocked at the door, and still it was all quiet inside. I knew they must be up, it was past eight o'clock. So I knocked again, and I thought I heard somebody say "Come in." I wasn't sure, I'm not sure yet, but I opened the door—this door *(indicating the door by which the two women are still standing)* and there in that rocker—*(pointing to it)* sat Mrs. Wright.

(They all look at the rocker.)

COUNTY ATTORNEY What—was she doing?

HALE She was rockin' back and forth. She had her apron in her hand and was kind of—pleating it.

COUNTY ATTORNEY And how did she—look?

HALE Well, she looked queer.

COUNTY ATTORNEY How do you mean—queer?

HALE Well, as if she didn't know what she was going to do next. And kind of done up.

COUNTY ATTORNEY   How did she seem to feel about your coming?

HALE   Why, I don't think she minded—one way or other. She didn't pay much attention. I said, "How do, Mrs. Wright, it's cold, ain't it?" And she said "Is it?"—and went on kind of pleating at her apron. Well, I was surprised; she didn't ask me to come up to the stove, or to set down, but just sat there, not even looking at me, so I said, "I want to see John." And then she—laughed. I guess you would call it a laugh. I thought of Harry and the team outside, so I said a little sharp: "Can't I see John?" "No," she says, kind o' dull like. "Ain't he home?" says I. "Yes," says she, "he's home." "Then why can't I see him?" I asked her out of patience. "'Cause he's dead," says she. "*Dead?*" says I. She just nodded her head, not getting a bit excited, but rockin' back and forth. "Why—where is he?" says I, not knowing what to say. She just pointed upstairs—like that *(himself pointing to the room above).* I got up, with the idea of going up there. I walked from there to here—then I says, "Why, what did he die of?" "He died of a rope round his neck," says she, and just went on pleatin' at her apron. Well, I went out and called Harry. I thought I might—need help. We went upstairs and there he was lyin'—

COUNTY ATTORNEY   I think I'd rather have you go into that upstairs, where you can point it all out. Just go on now with the rest of the story.

HALE   Well, my first thought was to get that rope off. It looked . . . *(Stops, his face twitches.)* . . . but Harry, he went up to him, and he said, "No, he's dead all right, and we'd better not touch anything." So we went back down stairs. She was still sitting that same way. "Has anybody been notified?" I asked. "No," says she, unconcerned. "Who did this, Mrs. Wright?" said Harry. He said it business-like—and she stopped pleatin' of her apron. "I don't know," she says. "You don't *know?*" says Harry. "No," says she. "Weren't you sleepin' in the bed with him?" says Harry. "Yes," says she, "but I was on the inside." "Somebody slipped a rope round his neck and strangled him and you didn't wake up?" says Harry. "I didn't wake up," she said after him. We must 'a looked as if we didn't see how that could be, for after a minute she said, "I sleep sound." Harry was going to ask her more questions, but I said maybe we ought to let her tell her story first to the coroner, or the sheriff, so Harry went fast as he could to Rivers' place, where there's a telephone.

COUNTY ATTORNEY   And what did Mrs. Wright do when she knew that you had gone for the coroner?

HALE   She moved from that chair to this over here . . . *(Pointing to a small chair in the corner.)* . . . and just sat there with her hands held together and looking down. I got a feeling that I ought to make some conversation, so I said I had come in to see if John wanted to put in a telephone, and at that she started to laugh, and then she stopped and looked at me—scared. *(The* COUNTY ATTORNEY, *who has had his note-*

book out, makes a note.) I dunno, maybe it wasn't scared. I wouldn't like to say it was. Soon Harry got back, and then Dr. Lloyd came, and you, Mr. Peters, and so I guess that's all I know that you don't.

COUNTY ATTORNEY   *(looking around)* I guess we'll go upstairs first—and then out to the barn and around there. *(To the* SHERIFF.*)* You're convinced that there was nothing important here—nothing that would point to any motive?

SHERIFF   Nothing here but kitchen things.

(The COUNTY ATTORNEY, *after again looking around the kitchen, opens the door of a cupboard closet. He gets up on a chair and looks on a shelf. Pulls his hand away, sticky.)*

COUNTY ATTORNEY   Here's a nice mess.

(The women draw nearer.)

MRS. PETERS   *(to the other woman)* Oh, her fruit; it did freeze. *(To the Lawyer.)* She worried about that when it turned so cold. She said the fire'd go out and her jars would break.

SHERIFF   Well, can you beat the women! Held for murder and worryin' about her preserves.

COUNTY ATTORNEY   I guess before we're through she may have something more serious than preserves to worry about.

HALE   Well, women are used to worrying over trifles.

(The two women move a little closer together.)

COUNTY ATTORNEY   *(with the gallantry of a young politician)* And yet, for all their worries, what would we do without the ladies? *(The women do not unbend. He goes to the sink, takes a dipperful of water from the pail and, pouring it into a basin, washes his hands. Starts to wipe them on the roller-towel, turns it for a cleaner place.)* Dirty towels! *(Kicks his foot against the pans under the sink.)* Not much of a housekeeper, would you say, ladies?

MRS. HALE   *(stiffly)* There's a great deal of work to be done on a farm.

COUNTY ATTORNEY   To be sure. And yet . . . *(With a little bow to her.)* . . . I know there are some Dickson county farmhouses which do not have such roller towels.

(He gives it a pull to expose its full length again.)

MRS. HALE   Those towels get dirty awful quick. Men's hands aren't always as clean as they might be.

COUNTY ATTORNEY   Ah, loyal to your sex, I see. But you and Mrs. Wright were neighbors. I suppose you were friends, too.

MRS. HALE   *(shaking her head)* I've not seen much of her of late years. I've not been in this house—it's more than a year.

COUNTY ATTORNEY   And why was that? You didn't like her?

MRS. HALE   I like her all well enough. Farmers' wives have their hands full, Mr. Henderson. And then—

COUNTY ATTORNEY   Yes—?

MRS. HALE   *(looking about)* It never seemed a very cheerful place.

COUNTY ATTORNEY   No—it's not cheerful. I shouldn't say she had the homemaking instinct.

MRS. HALE   Well, I don't know as Wright had, either.

COUNTY ATTORNEY   You mean that they didn't get on very well?

MRS. HALE   No, I don't mean anything. But I don't think a place'd be any cheerful for John Wright's being in it.

COUNTY ATTORNEY   I'd like to talk more of that a little later. I want to get the lay of things upstairs now.
(He goes to the left, where three steps lead to a stair door.)

SHERIFF   I suppose anything Mrs. Peters does'll be all right. She was to take in some clothes for her, you know, and a few little things. We left in such a hurry yesterday.

COUNTY ATTORNEY   Yes, but I would like to see what you take, Mrs. Peters, and keep an eye out for anything that might be of use to us.

MRS. PETERS   Yes, Mr. Henderson.
(The women listen to the men's steps on the stairs, then look about the kitchen.)

MRS. HALE   I'd hate to have men coming into my kitchen, snooping around and criticizing.
(She arranges the pans under sink which the Lawyer had shoved out of place.)

MRS. PETERS   Of course it's no more than their duty.

MRS. HALE   Duty's all right, but I guess that deputy sheriff that came out to make the fire might have got a little of this on. *(Gives the roller towel a pull.)* Wish I'd thought of that sooner. Seems mean to talk about her for not having things slicked up when she had to come away in such a hurry.

MRS. PETERS   *(who has gone to a small table in the left rear corner of the room, and lifted one end of a towel that covers a pan)* She had bread set. *(Stands still.)*

MRS. HALE   *(eyes fixed on a loaf of bread beside the bread-box, which is on a low shelf at the other side of the room. Moves slowly toward it.)* She was going to put this in there. *(Picks up loaf, then abruptly drops it. In a manner of returning to familiar things.)* It's a shame about her fruit.

I wonder if it's all gone. *(Gets up on the chair and looks.)* I think there's some here that's all right, Mrs. Peters. Yes—here; *(Holding it toward the window.)* this is cherries, too. *(Looking again.)* I declare I believe that's the only one. *(Gets down, bottle in her hand. Goes to the sink and wipes it off on the outside.)* She'll feel awful bad after all her hard work in the hot weather. I remember the afternoon I put up my cherries last summer.

(She puts the bottle on the big kitchen table, center of the room, front table. With a sigh, is about to sit down in the rocking-chair. Before she is seated realizes what chair it is: with a slow look at it, steps back. The chair which she has touched rocks back and forth.)

MRS. PETERS   Well, I must get those things from the front room closet. *(She goes to the door at the right, but after looking into the other room, steps back.)* You coming with me, Mrs. Hale? You could help me carry them.

(They go in the other room: reappear, MRS. PETERS carrying a dress and skirt, MRS. HALE following with a pair of shoes.)

MRS. PETERS   My, it's cold in there.

(She puts the clothes on the big table, and hurries to the stove.)

MRS. HALE   *(examining the skirt)* Wright was close. I think maybe that's why she kept so much to herself. She didn't even belong to the Ladies' Aid. I suppose she felt she couldn't do her part, and then you don't enjoy things when you feel shabby. She used to wear pretty clothes and be lively, when she was Minnie Foster, one of the town girls singing in the choir. But that—oh, that was thirty years ago. This all you was to take in?

MRS. PETERS   She said she wanted an apron. Funny thing to want, for there isn't much to get you dirty in jail, goodness knows. But I suppose just to make her feel more natural. She said they was in the top drawer in this cupboard. Yes, here. And then her little shawl that always hung behind the door. *(Opens stair door and looks.)* Yes, here it is.

(Quickly shuts door leading upstairs.)

MRS. HALE   *(abruptly moving toward her)* Mrs. Peters?

MRS. PETERS   Yes, Mrs. Hale?

MRS. HALE   Do you think she did it?

MRS. PETERS   *(in a frightened voice)* Oh, I don't know.

MRS. HALE   Well, I don't think she did. Asking for an apron and her little shawl. Worrying about her fruit.

MRS. PETERS   *(starts to speak, glances up, where footsteps are heard in the room above. In a low voice)* Mr. Peters says it looks bad for her. Mr. Henderson is awful sarcastic in a speech and he'll make fun of her sayin' she didn't wake up.

MRS. HALE   Well, I guess John Wright didn't wake when they was slipping that rope under his neck.

MRS. PETERS   No, it's strange. It must have been done awful crafty and still. They say it was such a—funny way to kill a man, rigging it all up like that.

MRS. HALE   That's just what Mr. Hale said. There was a gun in the house. He says that's what he can't understand.

MRS. PETERS   Mr. Henderson said coming out that what was needed for the case was a motive; something to show anger, or—sudden feeling.

MRS. HALE   *(who is standing by the table)* Well, I don't see any signs of anger around here. *(She puts her hand on the dish towel which lies on the table, stands looking down at table, one half of which is clean, the other half messy.)* It's wiped here. *(Makes a move as if to finish work, then turns and looks at loaf of bread outside the bread-box. Drops towel. In that voice of coming back to familiar things.)* Wonder how they are finding things upstairs? I hope she had it a little more red-up up there. You know, it seems kind of *sneaking.* Locking her up in town and then coming out here and trying to get her own house to turn against her!

MRS. PETERS   But, Mrs. Hale, the law is the law.

MRS. HALE   I s'pose 'tis. *(Unbuttoning her coat.)* Better loosen up your things, Mrs. Peters. You won't feel them when you go out.

(MRS. PETERS takes off her fur tippet, goes to hang it on hook at back of room, stands looking at the under part of the small corner table.)

MRS. PETERS   She was piecing a quilt. *(She brings the large sewing basket and they look at the bright pieces.)*

MRS. HALE   It's log cabin pattern. Pretty, isn't it? I wonder if she was goin' to quilt it or just knot it?

(Footsteps have been heard coming down the stairs. The SHERIFF enters, followed by HALE and the COUNTY ATTORNEY.)

SHERIFF   They wonder if she was going to quilt it or just knot it.

(The men laugh, the women look abashed.)

COUNTY ATTORNEY   *(rubbing his hands over the stove)* Frank's fire didn't do much up there, did it? Well, let's go out to the barn and get that cleared up.

(The men go outside.)

MRS. HALE   *(resentfully)* I don't know as there's anything so strange, our takin' up our time with little things while we're waiting for them to get the evidence. *(She sits down at the big table smoothing out a block with decision.)* I don't see as it's anything to laugh about.

MRS. PETERS   *(apologetically)* Of course they've got awful important things on their minds.

(Pulls up a chair and joins MRS. HALE at the table.)

SUSAN GLASPELL

541

MRS. HALE *(examining another block)* Mrs. Peters, look at this one. Here, this is the one she was working on, and look at the sewing! All the rest of it has been so nice and even. And look at this! It's all over the place! Why, it looks as if she didn't know what she was about!

(After she has said this they look at each other, then start to glance back at the door. After an instant MRS. HALE *has pulled at a knot and ripped the sewing.)*

MRS. PETERS   Oh, what are you doing, Mrs. Hale?

MRS. HALE   *(mildly)* Just pulling out a stitch or two that's not sewed very good. *(Threading a needle.)* Bad sewing always made me fidgety.

MRS. PETERS   *(nervously)* I don't think we ought to touch things.

MRS. HALE   I'll just finish up this end. *(Suddenly stopping and leaning forward.)* Mrs. Peters?

MRS. PETERS   Yes, Mrs. Hale?

MRS. HALE   What do you suppose she was so nervous about?

MRS. PETERS   Oh—I don't know. I don't know as she was nervous. I sometimes sew awful queer when I'm just tired. *(*MRS. HALE *starts to say something, looks at* MRS. PETERS, *then goes on sewing.)* Well, I must get these things wrapped up. They may be through sooner than we think. *(Putting apron and other things together.)* I wonder where I can find a piece of paper, and string.

MRS. HALE   In that cupboard, maybe.

MRS. PETERS   *(looking in cupboard)* Why, here's a bird-cage. *(Holds it up.)* Did she have a bird, Mrs. Hale?

MRS. HALE   Why, I don't know whether she did or not—I've not been here for so long. There was a man around last year selling canaries cheap, but I don't know as she took one; maybe she did. She used to sing real pretty herself.

MRS. PETERS   *(glancing around)* Seems funny to think of a bird here. But she must have had one, or why should she have a cage? I wonder what happened to it?

MRS. HALE   I s'pose maybe the cat got it.

MRS. PETERS   No, she didn't have a cat. She's got that feeling some people have about cats—being afraid of them. My cat got in her room and she was real upset and asked me to take it out.

MRS. HALE   My sister Bessie was like that. Queer, ain't it?

MRS. PETERS   *(examining the cage)* Why, look at this door. It's broke. One hinge is pulled apart.

MRS. HALE (*looking too*) Looks as if some one must have been rough with it.

MRS. PETERS Why, yes.

(*She brings the cage forward and puts it on the table.*)

MRS. HALE I wish if they're going to find any evidence they'd be about it. I don't like this place.

MRS. PETERS. But I'm awful glad you came with me, Mrs. Hale. It would be lonesome for me sitting here alone.

MRS. HALE It would, wouldn't it? (*Dropping her sewing.*) But I tell you what I do wish, Mrs. Peters. I wish I had come over some times when *she* was here. I—(*Looking around the room.*)—wish I had.

MRS. PETERS But of course you were awful busy, Mrs. Hale—your house and your children.

MRS. HALE I could've come. I stayed away because it weren't cheerful— and that's why I ought to have come. I—I've never liked this place. Maybe because it's down in a hollow and you don't see the road. I dunno what it is, but it's a lonesome place and always was. I wish I had come over to see Minnie Foster sometimes. I can see now—

(*Shakes her head.*)

MRS. PETERS Well, you mustn't reproach yourself, Mrs. Hale. Somehow we just don't see how it is with other folks until—something comes up.

MRS. HALE Not having children makes less work—but it makes a quiet house, and Wright out to work all day, and no company when he did come in. Did you know John Wright, Mrs. Peters?

MRS. PETERS Not to know him; I've seen him in town. They say he was a good man.

MRS. HALE Yes—good; he didn't drink, and kept his word as well as most, I guess, and paid his debts. But he was a hard man, Mrs. Peters. Just to pass the time of day with him. (*Shivers.*) Like a raw wind that gets to the bone. (*Pauses, her eye falling on the cage.*) I should think she would 'a wanted a bird. But what do you suppose went with it?

MRS. PETERS I don't know, unless it got sick and died.

(*She reaches over and swings the broken door, swings it again, both women watch it.*)

MRS. HALE You weren't raised round here, were you? (MRS. PETERS *shakes her head.*) You didn't know—her?

MRS. PETERS Not till they brought her yesterday.

MRS. HALE She—come to think of it, she was kind of like a bird herself— real sweet and pretty, but kind of timid and—fluttery. How—she—did—

SUSAN GLASPELL

change. *(Silence; then as if struck by a happy thought and relieved to get back to every day things.)* Tell you what, Mrs. Peters, why don't you take the quilt in with you? It might take up her mind.

MRS. PETERS   Why, I think that's a real nice idea, Mrs. Hale. There couldn't possibly be any objection to it, could there? Now, just what would I take? I wonder if her patches are in here—and her things.

(They look in the sewing basket.)

MRS. HALE   Here's some red. I expect this has got sewing things in it. *(Brings out a fancy box.)* What a pretty box. Looks like something somebody would give you. Maybe her scissors are in here. *(Opens box. Suddenly puts her hand to her nose.)* Why— *(MRS. PETERS bends nearer, then turns her face away.)* There's something wrapped up in this piece of silk.

MRS. PETERS   Why, this isn't her scissors.

MRS. HALE   *(lifting the silk)* Oh, Mrs. Peters—it's—

(MRS. PETERS bends closer.)

MRS. PETERS   It's the bird.

MRS. HALE   *(jumping up)* But, Mrs. Peters—look at it. Its neck! Look at its neck! It's all—other side *to.*

MRS. PETERS   Somebody—wrung—its neck.

(Their eyes meet. A look of growing comprehension, of horror. Steps are heard outside. MRS. HALE slips box under quilt pieces, and sinks into her chair. Enter SHERIFF and COUNTY ATTORNEY. MRS. PETERS rises.)

COUNTY ATTORNEY   *(as one turning from serious things to little pleasantries)* Well, ladies, have you decided whether she was going to quilt it or knot it?

MRS. PETERS   We think she was going to—knot it.

COUNTY ATTORNEY   Well, that's interesting, I'm sure. *(Seeing the birdcage.)* Has the bird flown?

MRS. HALE   *(putting more quilt pieces over the box)* We think the—cat got it.

COUNTY ATTORNEY   *(preoccupied)* Is there a cat?

(MRS. HALE glances in a quick covert way at MRS. PETERS.)

MRS. PETERS   Well, not now. They're superstitious, you know. They leave.

COUNTY ATTORNEY   *(to SHERIFF PETERS, continuing an interrupted conversation)* No sign at all of any one having come from the outside. Their own rope. Now let's go up again and go over it piece by piece. *(They start upstairs.)* It would have to have been some one who knew just the—

(MRS. PETERS *sits down. The two women sit there not looking at one another, but as if peering into something and at the same time holding back. When they talk now it is in the manner of feeling their way over strange ground, as if afraid of what they are saying, but as if they cannot help saying it.*)

MRS. HALE   She liked the bird. She was going to bury it in that pretty box.

MRS. PETERS   (*in a whisper*) When I was a girl—my kitten—there was a boy took a hatchet, and before my eyes—and before I could get there— (*Covers her face an instant.*) If they hadn't held me back I would have— (*Catches herself, looks upstairs where steps are heard, falters weakly*)— hurt him.

MRS. HALE   (*with a slow look around her*) I wonder how it would seem never to have had any children around. (*Pause.*) No, Wright wouldn't like the bird—a thing that sang. She used to sing. He killed that, too.

MRS. PETERS   (*moving uneasily*) We don't know who killed the bird.

MRS. HALE   I knew John Wright.

MRS. PETERS   It was an awful thing was done in this house that night, Mrs. Hale. Killing a man while he slept, slipping a rope around his neck that choked the life out of him.

MRS. HALE   His neck. Choked the life out of him.

(*Her hand goes out and rests on the bird-cage.*)

MRS. PETERS   (*with rising voice*) We don't know who killed him. We don't *know.*

MRS. HALE   (*her own feeling not interrupted*) If there'd been years and years of nothing, then a bird to sing to you, it would be awful—still, after the bird was still.

MRS. PETERS   (*something within her speaking*) I know what stillness is. When we homesteaded in Dakota, and my first baby died—after he was two years old, and me with no other then—

MRS. HALE   (*moving*) How soon do you suppose they'll be through, looking for the evidence?

MRS. PETERS   I know what stillness is. (*Pulling herself back.*) The law has got to punish crime, Mrs. Hale.

MRS. HALE   (*not as if answering that*) I wish you'd seen Minnie Foster when she wore a white dress with blue ribbons and stood up there in the choir and sang. (*A look around the room.*) Oh, I *wish* I'd come over here once in a while. That was a crime! That was a crime! Who's going to punish that?

MRS. PETERS   (*looking upstairs*) We mustn't—take on.

SUSAN GLASPELL
545

MRS. HALE   I might have known she needed help! I know how things can be—for women. I tell you, it's queer, Mrs. Peters. We live close together and we live far apart. We all go through the same things—it's all just a different kind of the same thing. *(Brushes her eyes, noticing the bottle of fruit, reaches out for it.)* If I was you I wouldn't tell her her fruit was gone. Tell her it *ain't.* Tell her it's all right. Take this in to prove it to her. She—she may never know whether it was broke or not.

MRS. PETERS   *(takes the bottle, looks about for something to wrap it in; takes petticoat from the clothes brought from the other room, very nervously begins winding this around the bottle. In a false voice)* My, it's a good thing the men couldn't hear us. Wouldn't they just laugh. Getting all stirred up over a little thing like a—dead canary. As if that could have anything to do with—with—wouldn't they *laugh!*

(The men are heard coming down stairs.)

MRS. HALE   *(under her breath)* Maybe they would—maybe they wouldn't.

COUNTY ATTORNEY   No, Peters, it's all perfectly clear except a reason for doing it. But you know juries when it comes to women. If there was some definite thing. Something to show—something to make a story about—a thing that would connect up with this strange way of doing it.

(The women's eyes meet for an instant. Enter HALE from outer door.)

HALE   Well, I've got the team around. Pretty cold out there.

COUNTY ATTORNEY   I'm going to stay here a while by myself. *(To the SHERIFF.)* You can send Frank out for me, can't you? I want to go over everything. I'm not satisfied that we can't do better.

SHERIFF   Do you want to see what Mrs. Peters is going to take in?

(The Lawyer goes to the table, picks up the apron, laughs.)

COUNTY ATTORNEY   Oh, I guess they're not very dangerous things the ladies have picked out. *(Moves a few things about, disturbing the quilt pieces which cover the box. Steps back.)* No, Mrs. Peters doesn't need supervising. For that matter, a sheriff's wife is married to the law. Ever think of it that way, Mrs. Peters?

MRS. PETERS   Not—just that way.

SHERIFF   *(chuckling)* Married to the law. *(Moves toward the other room.)* I just want you to come in here a minute, George. We ought to take a look at these windows.

COUNTY ATTORNEY   *(scoffingly)* Oh, windows!

SHERIFF   We'll be right out, Mr. Hale.

(HALE goes outside. The SHERIFF follows the COUNTY ATTORNEY into the other room. Then MRS. HALE rises, hands tight together, looking intensely at MRS. PETERS, whose eyes make a slow turn, finally meeting MRS. HALE'S.

A moment MRS. HALE *holds her, then her own eyes point the way to where the box is concealed. Suddenly* MRS. PETERS *throws back quilt pieces and tries to put the box in the bag she is wearing. It is too big. She opens box, starts to take bird out, cannot touch it, goes to pieces, stands there helpless. Sound of a knob turning in the other room.* MRS. HALE *snatches the box and puts it in the pocket of her big coat. Enter* COUNTY ATTORNEY *and* SHERIFF.)

COUNTY ATTORNEY   *(facetiously)* Well, Henry, at least we found out that she was not going to quilt it. She was going to—what is it you call it, ladies?

MRS. HALE   *(her hand against her pocket)* We call it—knot it, Mr. Henderson.

(*Curtain*)

DIVING INTO THE WRECK

by

ADRIENNE RICH
(b. 1929)

*A graduate of Radcliffe College, Adrienne Rich has described her
life as one of privilege. Her early poems reflect the anguish of her
role conflict as wife, mother, and writer. More recently she has written of the lesbian experience. In addition to writing many volumes
of poetry, Rich has become a leader in feminist thought and literary
theory. A book on motherhood,* Of Woman Born, *appeared in 1976
and a collection of essays,* On Lies, Secrets, and Silences, *in 1979.
Collections of her poetry include* The Dream of a Common Language
(1978), The Fact of a Doorframe: Poems Selected and New, 1950–84
(1984), Your Native Land and Your Life *(1986), and* Time's Power:
Poems, 1985–88 *(1989).*

First having read the book of myths,
and loaded the camera,
and checked the edge of the knife-blade,
I put on
the body-armor of black rubber
the absurd flippers
the grave and awkward mask.
I am having to do this
not like Cousteau with his
assiduous team
aboard the sun-flooded schooner
but here alone.

There is a ladder.
The ladder is always there
hanging innocently
close to the side of the schooner.
We know what it is for,
we who have used it.

Otherwise
it's a piece of maritime floss
some sundry equipment.

I go down.
Rung after rung and still
the oxygen immerses me
the blue light
the clear atoms
of our human air.
I go down.
My flippers cripple me,
I crawl like an insect down the ladder
and there is no one
to tell me when the ocean
will begin.

First the air is blue and then
it is bluer and then green and then
black I am blacking out and yet
my mask is powerful
it pumps my blood with power
the sea is another story
the sea is not a question of power
I have to learn alone
to turn my body without force
in the deep element.

And now: it is easy to forget
what I came for
among so many who have always
lived here
swaying their crenellated fans
between the reefs
and besides
you breathe differently down here.

I came to explore the wreck.
The words are purposes.
The words are maps.
I came to see the damage that was done
and the treasures that prevail.

I stroke the beam of my lamp
slowly along the flank
of something more permanent
than fish or weed
the thing I came for:
the wreck and not the story of the wreck
the thing itself and not the myth
the drowned face always staring
toward the sun
the evidence of damage
worn by salt and sway into this threadbare beauty
the ribs of the disaster
curving their assertion
among the tentative haunters.

This is the place.
And I am here, the mermaid whose dark hair
streams black, the merman in his armored body
We circle silently
about the wreck
we dive into the hold.
I am she: I am he

whose drowned face sleeps with open eyes
whose breasts still bear the stress
whose silver, copper, vermeil cargo lies
obscurely inside barrels
half-wedged and left to rot
we are the half-destroyed instruments
that once held to a course
the water-eaten log
the fouled compass

We are, I am, you are
by cowardice or courage
the one who find our way
back to this scene
carrying a knife, a camera
a book of myths
in which
our names do not appear.

HOPE

by

NADYA AISENBERG
(b. 1928)

The holder of a doctorate in English from the University of Wisconsin, Nadya Aisenberg has taught widely in the Boston area. She was a co-founder of the Boston/Cambridge Alliance of Independent Scholars and co-author of Women of Academe: Outsiders in the Sacred Grove *(1988). She has edited a book of Charles Dickens's short stories and an anthology of poems about the environment,* We Animals: Poems of Our World *(1989). A founder of the Rowan Tree Press, which publishes poetry, Aisenberg is the author of three volumes of poetry.* Before We Were Strangers, *in which "Hope" appeared, was published in London and Boston in 1989. She is completing a second volume of literary criticism on contemporary women writers.*

• ——————————————————— •

for Nadezhda Mandelstam

One moment without hesitation—
can this be all it takes,

plunging through breakers
to come up sleek and dripping

like the travel poster of a girl
who never wakes up crying

but, glistening with oil,
can pose serenely at Persepolis

knowing it will rain
before she needs water?

For us there is
too much to guard against

we hesitate to lop even a branch
so the tree will be hardy,

seeing with our other eye
a future of always-falling blossoms,

the cardinal's red shriek
a crack in the observable universe

And although we hold hands
like children entering a wood

flowers still sharpen their edges
swordblades of grass catch fire from the sun

and although we set sail
in a pretty lateen rig

barracuda swim alongside
who can hone their teeth against water

If we change our name
will only the body die in battle

leaving all the poems and children
for Hope,

though she was never a goddess,
was never in the pantheon at all?

HOMECOMING

by

MARTHA COLLINS
(b. 1940)

Born in Nebraska, Martha Collins was raised in Iowa and educated at Stanford University and the University of Iowa. A professor of English at the University of Massachusetts at Boston, she has published her poems widely in periodicals. Her first collection, A Catastrophe of Rainbows, appeared in 1985. She has recently completed a novel, and the first part of her narrative poem Images of Women in American Literature appeared in Poet Lore, 1988–89. Formerly the winner of a fellowship from the National Endowment for the Humanities, she won a fellowship for 1990–1991 from the National Endowment for the Arts.

———————————————

So you're home from the wars,
or at least a summer
facsimile of them.
You're welcome, but
please don't rush.
There are some things
to be seen.

First you'll notice
these guests. You'll call
them suitors, and be
mistaken: they've
not cluttered
the hearth or changed
the order of things.

You'll find the bed
in the same quiet place,
neatly spread as before.
But you should know

I've grown accustomed
to sleeping in all
its spaces.

The sun-colored table
sits in the kitchen, prepared
for the usual
feasts, you'll think.
But I'm not quite ready
to serve your dinners,
to pour your wines.

I'd rather sit by the big
bay window, the one we saved
for special times.
There's an extra chair,
but please be still,
for it's here I've come
to reflect.

Perhaps you'll resent
the uncommon manner
in which I've come
to possess our rooms.
But you can't conceive
of the more extreme measures
I've thought of taking,

like pounding stakes
in the floor and stretching
ropes to inform you
this or that is mine,
stamping my name
on favorite walls,
carving initials

on window sills,
or merely breathing
autograph spaces
on panes of glass.
But of course
we're bound
to share, and it's more

than a neat
arrangement
of tables and chairs and beds.
And perhaps it's as
simple as getting familiar,
accepting
the common places again.

But please
understand,
and try to find
your own space
where you can see beyond
these ceilings and floors
and windows and walls.

It shouldn't be hard:
you have been miles
away, after all,
while I have been
making myself at home.

A WOMAN AT THE WINDOW

by

NELLIE WONG
(b. 1934)

Working in San Francisco as a secretary, Nellie Wong describes herself as a socialist, feminist, activist poet. She has contributed to many feminist, Third World, and Asian-American periodicals, and her work has appeared in several anthologies. She has published two volumes of poetry, Dreams in Harrison Railroad Park *(1977) and* Death of a Long Steam Lady *(1986).*

• ———————————————————— •

sees herself in a white silk linen blazer,
a black skirt with a slit, a cinnabar-red blouse,
and she sees herself through the plateglass
standing there with her hands thrust deep
into her pockets standing there watching the sun
sparkle in a thousand lights in pools of silver needles
as she wanders in search of memories
As usual the sun intrudes her darkness
her feelings of aloneness and privacy
and when the phone rings she dashes
to answer it, changes her mood from aloneness
to sounding office official sounding
like the secretary she is
though sometimes she forgets that she is a poet
and prefers to stand at the window, imagine
herself a mannequin in a shop window
posing with a vacuous stare with her hands extended
like hammers ready to crash through the plateglass
breaking loose from the wool and the silk
from the neon lights the store decorator

has knotted around her neck
If she crashes through the window she would
see blood dripping from her fingers
but she wouldn't lick them
she doesn't always like to taste red
but she knows the violence that is contained
inside her body as she feels trapped
like a silver fox desired for her skin
to be worn by a woman who passes her by
She knows instinctively that she is a woman
who wants to float in and out of other skins
a witch, a princess, a bag lady, a diem sum shop girl,
her mother dying of cancer, her grandmother who feeds
pigeons in the park, or a sewing factory woman
who plans to organize for higher wages,
for music and bright lights, for time to play
with her infant daughter
She doesn't understand her feelings of floating
water hyacinths or lilies
as a dragon imbued with powers
as wind that rages through her limbs
as a lion at the electric typewriter
as a voice of women and men of Asian America
She knows that she isn't alone or lonely
that the memories will find her standing
twenty-three floors above a city lake
that sunlight is her companion that the air
she breathes though filled with pollutants that she will
fight them with the swallowing of antihistamines
that she will fight them, a woman at the window
with her fingers that desire to become wings

PRESENT

by

SONIA SANCHEZ
(b. 1934)

Sonia Sanchez was born in Birmingham, Alabama and grew up in Harlem; she is now a professor at Temple University in Philadelphia. The title of one of her five plays reflects her respect for the African oral tradition: I'm Black When I'm Singing, I'm Blue When I Ain't *(1982). Her readings from her thirteen volumes of poems at hundreds of college campuses and in many foreign countries reflect her view of her writing and performances as black feminist activism. A recent book is* Under a Soprano Sky *(1987).*

This woman vomiting her
hunger over the world
this melancholy woman forgotten
before memory came
this yellow movement bursting forth like
coltrane's melodies all mouth
buttocks moving like palm trees,
this honeycoatedalabamianwoman
raining rhythm of blue/black/smiles
this yellow woman carrying beneath her breasts
pleasures without tongues
this woman whose body weaves
desert patterns,
this woman, wet with wandering,
reviving the beauty of forests and winds
is telling you secrets
gather up your odors and listen
as she sings the mold from memory.

       there is no place
for a soft/black/woman.

WOMAN BECOMING

there is no smile green enough or
summertime words warm enough to allow my growth.
and in my head
i see my history
standing like a shy child
and i chant lullabies
as i ride my past on horseback
tasting the thirst of yesterday tribes
hearing the ancient/black/woman
me, singing   hay-hay-hay-hay-ya-ya-ya.
                                         hay-hay-hay-hay-ya-ha-ya.

like a slow scent
beneath the sun
          and i dance my
creation and my grandmothers gathering
from my bones like great wooden birds
spread their wings
while their long/legged/laughter
stretches the night.
          and i taste the
seasons of my birth. mangoes. papayas.
drink my woman/coconut/milks
stalk the ancient grandfathers
sipping on proud afternoons
walk like a song round my waist
tremble like a new/born/child troubled
with new breaths
          and my singing
becomes the only sound of a
blue/black/magical/woman. walking.
womb ripe. walking. loud with mornings. walking.
making pilgrimage to herself. walking.

BEYOND WHAT

by

ALICE WALKER
(b. 1944)

*Born in Georgia, Alice Walker was educated at Spelman College
and Sarah Lawrence College. She spent many years in Mississippi
but currently lives in San Francisco. She has been a fellow of the
Radcliffe Institute and has taught and read her poetry in many
colleges. An influential essay, "In Search of Our Mothers' Gardens"
(1972), explores the problems of women as artists and is the title
essay of* In Search of Our Mothers' Gardens: Womanist Prose *(1983).
Her novel* The Color Purple *(1983) won a Pulitzer Prize. A more
recent novel,* The Temple of My Familiar *(1989), traces the history
and legendary past of Afro-Americans.* Revolutionary Petunias
*(1973), from which "Beyond What" is taken, was nominated for the
National Book Award and received the Lillian Smith Award from
the Southern Regional Council.*

• ———————————————— •

We reach for destinies beyond
what we have come to know
and in the romantic hush
of promises
perceive each
the other's life
as known mystery.
Shared. But inviolate.
No melting. No squeezing
into One.
We swing our eyes around
as well as side to side
to see the world.

To choose, renounce,
this, or that—
call it a council between equals
call it love.

THREE DREAMS
IN THE DESERT
UNDER A MIMOSA TREE

by

OLIVE SCHREINER
(1855–1920)

Born in Capetown, South Africa, Olive Schreiner became well-known in England as a novelist, an advocate of women's rights to work and to political and sexual freedom, and an anti-apartheid spokesperson. The Story of an African Farm *(1883) is the best known of her three novels; her allegories, collected in* Dreams *(1890), were eagerly used by British feminists as images of an ideal future.*

• ——————————————————— •

As I traveled across an African plain the sun shone down hotly. Then I drew my horse up under a mimosa-tree, and I took the saddle from him and left him to feed among the parched bushes. And all to right and to left stretched the brown earth. And I sat down under the tree, because the heat beat fiercely, and all along the horizon the air throbbed. And after a while a heavy drowsiness came over me, and I laid my head down against my saddle, and I fell asleep there. And, in my sleep, I had a curious dream.

I thought I stood on the border of a great desert, and the sand blew about everywhere. And I thought I saw two great figures like beasts of burden of the desert, and one lay upon the sand with its neck stretched out, and one stood by it. And I looked curiously at the one that lay upon the ground, for it had a great burden on its back, and the sand was thick about it, so that it seemed to have piled over it for centuries.

And I looked very curiously at it. And there stood one beside me watching. And I said to him, "What is this huge creature who lies here on the sand?"

And he said, "This is woman; she that bears men in her body."

And I said, "Why does she lie here motionless with the sand piled round her?"

And he answered, "Listen, I will tell you! Ages and ages long she has lain here, and the wind has blown over her. The oldest, oldest, oldest man living has never seen her move: the oldest, oldest book records that she lay here then, as she lies here now, with the sand about her. But listen! Older than the oldest book, older than the oldest recorded memory of man, on the Rocks of Language, on the hard-baked clay of Ancient Customs, now crumbling to decay, are found the marks of her footsteps! Side by side with his who stands beside her you may trace them; and you know that she who now lies there once wandered free over the rocks with him."

And I said, "Why does she lie there now?"

And he said, "I take it, ages ago the Age-of-dominion-of-muscular-force found her, and when she stooped low to give suck to her young, and her back was broad, he put his burden of subjection on to it, and tied it on with the broad band of Inevitable Necessity. Then she looked at the earth and the sky, and knew there was no hope for her; and she lay down on the sand with the burden she could not loosen. Ever since she has lain here. And the ages have come, and the ages have gone, but the band of Inevitable Necessity has not been cut."

And I looked and saw in her eyes the terrible patience of the centuries; the ground was wet with her tears, and her nostrils blew up the sand.

And I said, "Has she ever tried to move?"

And he said, "Sometimes a limb has quivered. But she is wise; she knows she cannot rise with the burden on her."

And I said, "Why does not he who stands by her leave her and go on?"

And he said, "He cannot. Look—"

And I saw a broad band passing along the ground from one to the other, and it bound them together.

He said, "While she lies there he must stand and look across the desert."

And I said, "Does he know why he cannot move?"

And he said, "No."

And I heard a sound of something cracking, and I looked, and I saw the band that bound the burden on to her back broken asunder; and the burden rolled on to the ground.

And I said, "What is this?"

And he said, "The Age-of-muscular-force is dead. The Age-of-nervous-force has killed him with the knife he holds in his hand; and silently and invisibly he has crept up to the woman, and with that knife of Mechanical Invention he has cut the band that bound the burden to her back. The Inevitable Necessity is broken. She might rise now."

And I saw that she still lay motionless on the sand, with her eyes open and her neck stretched out. And she seemed to look for something on the far-off border of the desert that never came. And I wondered if she were awake or asleep. And as I looked her body quivered, and a light came into her eyes, like when a sunbeam breaks into a dark room.

I said, "What is it?"

He whispered "Hush! the thought has come to her, 'Might I not rise?'"

And I looked. And she raised her head from the sand, and I saw the dent where her neck had lain so long. And she looked at the earth, and she looked at the sky, and she looked at him who stood by her: but he looked out across the desert.

And I saw her body quiver; and she pressed her front knees to the earth, and veins stood out; and I cried, "She is going to rise!"

But only her sides heaved, and she lay still where she was.

But her head she held up; she did not lay it down again. And he beside me said, "She is very weak. See, her legs have been crushed under her so long."

And I saw the creature struggle: and the drops stood out on her.

And I said, "Surely he who stands beside her will help her?"

And he beside me answered, "He cannot help her: *she must help herself*. Let her struggle till she is strong."

And I cried, "At least he will not hinder her! See, he moves farther from her, and tightens the cord between them, and he drags her down."

And he answered, "He does not understand. When she moves she draws the band that binds them, and hurts him, and he moves farther from her. The day will come when he will understand, and will know what she is doing. Let her once stagger on to her knees. In that day he will stand close to her, and look into her eyes with sympathy."

And she stretched her neck, and the drops fell from her. And the creature rose an inch from the earth and sank back.

And I cried, "Oh, she is too weak! she cannot walk! The long years have taken all her strength from her. Can she never move?"

And he answered me, "See the light in her eyes!"

And slowly the creature staggered on to its knees.

And I awoke: and all to the east and to the west stretched the barren earth, with the dry bushes on it. The ants ran up and down in the red sand, and the heat beat fiercely. I looked up through the thin branches of the tree at the blue sky overhead. I stretched myself, and I mused over the dream I had had. And I fell asleep again, with my head on my saddle. And in the fierce heat I had another dream.

I saw a desert and I saw a woman coming out of it. And she came to the bank of a dark river; and the bank was steep and high. And on it an old man met her, who had a long white beard; and a stick that curled was in his hand, and on it was written Reason. And he asked her what she wanted; and she said "I am woman; and I am seeking for the land of Freedom."

And he said, "It is before you."

And she said, "I see nothing before me but a dark flowing river, and a bank steep and high, and cuttings here and there with heavy sand in them."

And he said, "And beyond that?"

She said, "I see nothing, but sometimes, when I shade my eyes with my hand, I think I see on the further bank trees and hills, and the sun shining on them!"

OLIVE SCHREINER
563

He said, "That is the Land of Freedom."

She said, "How am I to get there?"

He said, "There is one way, and one only. Down the banks of Labour through the water of Suffering. There is no other."

She said, "Is there no bridge?"

He answered. "None."

She said, "Is the water deep?"

He said, "Deep."

She said, "Is the floor worn?"

He said, "It is. Your foot may slip at any time, and you may be lost."

She said, "Have any crossed already?"

He said, "Some have *tried!*"

She said, "Is there a track to show where the best fording is?"

He said, "It has to be made."

She shaded her eyes with her hand; and she said, "I will go."

And he said, "You must take off the clothes you wore in the desert: they are dragged down by them who go into the water so clothed."

And she threw from her gladly the mantle of Ancient-received-opinions she wore, for it was worn full of holes. And she took the girdle from her waist that she had treasured so long, and the moths flew out of it in a cloud. And he said, "Take the shoes of dependence off your feet."

And she stood there naked, but for one white garment that clung close to her.

And he said, "That you may keep. So they wear clothes in the Land of Freedom. In the water it buoys; it always swims."

And I saw on its breast was written Truth; and it was white; the sun had not often shone on it; the other clothes had covered it up. And he said, "Take this stick; hold it fast. In that day when it slips from your hand you are lost. Put it down before you; feel your way; where it cannot find a bottom do not set your foot."

And she said, "I am ready; let me go."

And he said, "No—but stay; what is that—in your breast?"

She was silent.

He said, "Open it, and let me see."

And she opened it. And against her breast was a tiny thing, who drank from it, and the yellow curls above his forehead pressed against it; and his knees were drawn up to her, and he held her breast fast with his hands.

And Reason said, "Who is he, and what is he doing here?"

And she said, "See his little wings—"

And Reason said, "Put him down."

And she said, "He is asleep, and he is drinking! I will carry him to the Land of Freedom. He has been a child so long, so long, I have carried him. In the Land of Freedom he will be a man. We will walk together there, and his great white wings will overshadow me. He has lisped one word only to me in the desert—'Passion!' I have dreamed he might learn to say 'Friendship' in that land."

And Reason said, "Put him down!"

And she said, "I will carry him so—with one arm, and with the other I will fight the water."

He said, "Lay him down on the ground. When you are in the water you will forget to fight, you will think only of him. Lay him down." He said, "He will not die. When he finds you have left him alone he will open his wings and fly. He will be in the Land of Freedom before you. Those who reach the Land of Freedom, the first hand they see stretching down the bank to help them shall be Love's. He will be a man then, not a child. In your breast he cannot thrive; put him down that he may grow."

And she took her bosom from his mouth, and he bit her, so that the blood ran down on to the ground. And she laid him down on the earth; and she covered her wound. And she bent and stroked his wings. And I saw the hair on her forehead turned white as snow, and she had changed from youth to age.

And she stood far off on the bank of the river. And she said, "For what do I go to this far land which no one has ever reached? *Oh, I am alone! I am utterly alone!*"

And Reason, that old man, said to her, "Silence! what do you hear?"

And she listened intently, and she said, "I hear a sound of feet, a thousand times ten thousand and thousands of thousands, and they beat this way!"

He said, "They are the feet of those that shall follow you. Lead on! make a track to the water's edge! Where you stand now, the ground will be beaten flat by ten thousand times ten thousand feet." And he said, "Have you seen the locusts how they cross a stream? First one comes down to the water-edge, and it is swept away, and then another comes and then another, and then another, and at last with their bodies piled up a bridge is built and the rest pass over."

She said, "And, of those that come first, some are swept away, and are heard of no more; their bodies do not even build the bridge?"

"And are swept away, and are heard of no more—and what of that?" he said.

"And what of that—" she said.

"They make a track to the water's edge."

"They make a track to the water's edge—." And she said, "Over that bridge which shall be built with our bodies, who will pass?"

He said, *"The entire human race."*

And the woman grasped her staff.

And I saw her turn down that dark path to the river.

And I awoke; and all about me was the yellow afternoon light: the sinking sun lit up the fingers of the milk bushes; and my horse stood by me quietly feeding. And I turned on my side, and I watched the ants run by thousands in the red sand. I thought I would go on my way now—the

OLIVE SCHREINER

afternoon was cooler. Then a drowsiness crept over me again, and I laid back my head and fell asleep.

And I dreamed a dream.

I dreamed I saw a land. And on the hills walked brave women and brave men, hand in hand. And they looked into each other's eyes, and they were not afraid.

And I saw the women also hold each other's hands.

And I said to him beside me, "What place is this?"

And he said, "This is heaven."

And I said, "Where is it?"

And he answered, "On earth."

And I said, "When shall these things be?"

And he answered, "IN THE FUTURE."

And I awoke, and all about me was the sunset light; and on the low hills the sun lay, and a delicious coolness had crept over everything; and the ants were going slowly home. And I walked towards my horse, who stood quietly feeding. Then the sun passed down behind the hills; but I knew that the next day he would arise again.

WOMAN

by

ALAÍDE FOPPA
(1915–1980?)

*Alaíde Foppa was born in Barcelona, Spain, raised in Italy, married
in Guatemala, and exiled to Mexico in 1954. She was a political
and feminist activist, working through organizations, in publications,
and on radio. She published four books of poetry. In 1980 she was
kidnapped by the Guatemalan army and has disappeared.*

Woman,
unfinished being
not the remote angelical rose sung by poets of old
nor the sinister witch burned at Inquisition's stake
nor the lauded and desired prostitute
nor the blessed mother.
Neither the withering, taunted old maid
nor she who is obliged to be beautiful
Nor she who is obliged to be bad
nor she who lives because they let her
Not she who must always say yes.
Woman, a being who begins to know who she is
and starts to live.

Translated by Margaret Randall

AFTERWORD:
IMAGES OF WRITING/
WRITING IMAGES

by

JEAN FERGUSON CARR

•───────────────•

Images of Women in Literature proposes that readers pay careful attention
to the constructed images that have represented women's diverse experiences and possibilities. The introduction to this anthology urges us to
test the boundaries of established categories, to reflect on the social construction of what may seem normal or natural. It argues for a double
reading of literary texts and of their relation to the social worlds from
which they emerge and in which they are read. It also calls for us to
reread our own acts of interpretation, to consider how we are positioned
to write about the texts that "image" us. As the introduction argues, "we
cannot see unless we look, self-conscious, aware that we are looking."
As we read self-reflexively, we also rethink what it means to write about
and through images. We can consider how we have been educated as
readers and as writers of literary texts and of images of women.

This anthology encourages us to ponder the power and continuity of
images, how they alter and resist alteration over time and in changing
circumstances. The diversity of selections allows us to explore how literary images are inflected by specific historical situations—by the shaping
power of class or race or ethnicity, by age and marital status, by sexual
orientation, and by work experiences. It also allows us to explore how
our own social perceptions are mediated by persistent literary and cultural conventions about women's roles, gender differences, and the relations between men and women. To write about images, then, is to

inspect the social world through the lens of a literary text *and* to reread that literary text in terms of its evocation of social worlds. Such writing also calls for careful reflection on what the writer brings to the text and what shapes readers' responses. It calls for us to question the terms or categories that organize our experience of the text.

To write differently through and about images of women in literature requires a rethinking not only of the subjects and their representation in literary texts, but of what it means to write about texts we read. Instead of accepting these images as privileged, we interrogate the acts of imaging that produced them, considering the strategies and gestures by which authors, readers, and their cultures construct multifaceted, complicated, and troubling images. This anthology can function, therefore, not just as a collection of authoritative readings, but as materials that provoke our entry into an ongoing argument about the representation of women and about the practice of interpretation. As readers and writers using this anthology, we need to account for how we determine the questions we ask of the texts, how we decide what is important to notice and what will remain part of the background. We need to account for where we choose to begin our critique and where we come to an end. What legitimizes certain interpretations over others? What relationship do our own experiences and knowledge have to our responses? One way to begin this accounting is to reflect on the images of writing that shape our own work and expectations.

Images of Writing

In her 1972 essay "When We Dead Awaken: Writing as Re-Vision," Adrienne Rich notes the difficulty of finding realistic images in literature of women as writers. According to Rich, what "the girl or woman who tries to write" finds in this search "negates everything she is about. . . . [P]recisely what she does not find is that absorbed, drudging, puzzled, sometimes inspired creature, herself, who sits at a desk trying to put words together." Rich is describing the lack of productive models for a creative writer, but her critique is equally applicable to those of us trying to recreate a literary text and our relationship to what it proposes. The writer Rich imagines is in the midst of a complex task characterized by the oppositions of drudgery and inspiration, of being puzzled and of being able to put things together. Accepting this complexity, this necessity for working things through, is the beginning of reformulating images of writing that will allow for the necessary complications of how we read and strive to articulate our responses.

Since this anthology is a textbook designed for use in college courses, designed to initiate the kind of writing possible in such circumstances, let us begin by examining how a sampling of American students have been instructed to write about literary texts. Such a historical excursion can help us to rethink our learned habits of response, to consider ways of reading and writing about literature other than those we have inherited. One of the dualities that this anthology invites us to rethink, for example, is a commonly accepted distinction between personal response (sometimes called opinion or prejudice) and what might be called "authorized" response (sometimes called criticism or judgment). What is at stake in this opposition is how individual responses and experiences get formed into socially sanctioned or agreed-upon positions. How a student learns to write about a literary text may involve a struggle between approved "images" of expert writing and the complex kind of image represented by Rich's drudging, inspired writer, an image that addresses the contradictions and tensions of writing as a cultural activity.

Let us focus, then, on how these writing textbooks from the past marked the distinction between students' "personal" responses to literature and the more approved views. This distinction takes on many forms: it was variously characterized as innocence versus experience, personal versus public, unschooled versus educated, and unruly versus disciplined. The multiple oppositions by which students were set off from "educated" culture indicate the tensions surrounding such "unlearned" responses. In some educational settings the individual side of the opposition was valued over the more social, public version, and in others that side was made to seem ridiculous, embarrassing, or, as an 1803 writing text argued, "vulgar." The preface to *The Young Gentleman and Lady's Monitor, and English Teacher's Assistant*, a writing textbook compiled and published by J. Hamilton Moore in Albany, New York, proposed to "eradicate vulgar prejudices and rusticity of manners" and to "facilitate" "reading, writing, and speaking the English language, with elegance and propriety." Students' past experiences and ways of noticing were expected to be "vulgar" and "rustic," that is, needing improvement and correction. Without proper schooling, students could only produce what the textbook dismissed as "prejudice." But the standard held up for students' writing, a socially correct value of "elegance and propriety," offered little direction for developing critical positions or extending the limits of prejudice. The textbook's instructions focused on issues of fault and failure, on what needed to be *eradicated* rather than on what could be improved. What could be learned was discussed almost entirely in terms of grammatical and rhetorical rules or stylistic conventions. The implication of such an image of writing is that students cannot investigate their own cultural assumptions; these are, presumably, too embarrassing to be acknowledged or discussed publicly, except as signs of error or failure. But neither can students question the construction of the standards of "propriety"; to do so would be, by definition, evidence of their "vulgar" impertinence or naive "rusticity of manners."

Bronson Alcott, the nineteenth-century essayist and educator, wrote in opposition to such a constrained image of what a writer could ask of a literary text and of the culture assigning it as material for study. In his journal of 1826, he wrote a critical fable about the results of bowing to the authority of books. In this fable, reading is so humble and obedient an activity that no writing is imaginable, since to write would require overthrowing the reigning tyranny:

> Ideas, when vended in a book, carry with them a kind of dignity and certainty which awe many into implicit belief. They often impose the most irrational and absurd conclusions on the fearful understanding. It dare not doubt. Fear keeps it ignorant. Authority lifts her head and commands instant belief. Reason, thus hushed into slumber, sleeps in secure repose. To dare to think, to think for oneself, is denominated pride and arrogance. And millions of human minds are in this state of slavery and tyranny.

In Alcott's fable, the personified figure of Authority and the unnamed individual collaborate, unknowingly, in the production of the irrational and the absurd. Neither of these "positions" can be read in and of itself as an essential value; Authority does not earn her position by being voted into power or acceded to after debate and consultation. She takes advantage of fear and uses the power of "denominating" to cancel out the possible differences of "millions" of minds. She can thus "vend" ideas that might otherwise go unpurchased and is effective because Reason is "hushed into slumber, sleeps in secure repose," because "understanding" is "fearful" and "dare[s] not doubt."

Alcott's image of the reader's position is socially constrained, apocalyptic; it is the condition of slavery and the sleep of reason. Emerging from this narrative is, however, a counterimage of an active reader, who could question how something becomes authoritative, who could ask who names and through what power. Such a reader could be, then, a writer, one who takes on the responsibility to produce—or to reproduce—a text. Alcott questions whether the positions of the millions of minds can be so readily dismissed as prejudice, or as what he calls "pride and arrogance." He reminds us of what Authority does to maintain her position of power: Alcott's Authority is not a distant neutrality, but is associated with active intervention in the politics of daily life (she vends, awes, imposes, commands, denominates). Her busy ordering of relations exposes the myth of the "naturalness" of the hierarchy's values and reminds us that one person's "prejudice" is another's reasoned opinion.

Even when prejudice is understood as a produced social position, however, a response different from the expected one can be explained away (denominated) as showing lack of education or as willful resistance to authority. A question on the 1916 College Entrance Examination reflects such an image, as it offered students a second chance to respond to texts in the appropriate manner: "You have been prejudiced against certain books by hearing them called 'classics,' by being urged to read them, or by being obliged to read them. What has been your attitude toward such books after reading them?" Most students would, one imagines, recognize that such a question called for a penitent renunciation of former opinions, clearly labeled prejudice and described as the reactions of those who have not yet read the texts properly. The question does not seem to allow for a response that is both learned *and* different; it does not admit a form of critique of "classics" that would be other than "prejudiced." Similarly, a 1927 correspondence course warned against "exaggerated" and "personal" responses to literature, advising instead a "neutral" accounting of the text's features. Students were instructed to "mention the author's philosophy" and to avoid "praise or censure." The slogan for the lesson on reading catchily summed up the opposing ways of discussing a literary text, rejecting opinion or social consideration in favor of an apolitical appraisal:

> Not, *"Do I Like?"* or, *"Do I flout?"*
> But—*"What's the book or play about?"*

Both of these early twentieth-century educational books put into opposition the acts of accounting for a text and reacting to a text; they offered little advice about how to make textual analysis responsive to social and personal issues, about how to examine one's reactions in a critical or questioning way. In both cases, writing about literature was seen as requiring certain proprieties of expression and a neutralizing of one's political or cultural reactions. Something labeled "personal" response is excluded from "proper" response.

Writing about and through images foregrounds the impossibility of separating the personal from the public, the political from the natural. Instead of excluding personal, social, and political response as inappropriate, as something that cannot be addressed in writing about literature, such writing reconstructs the authority of experience *and* of the text. Experience becomes something by which we measure whether a text has carried out its possibilities or has constrained or masked them by its social constructs and characters, by the situation it produces. The nineteenth-century American essayist Ralph Waldo Emerson wrote, "The use of literature is to afford us a platform whence we may command a view of our present life, a purchase by which we may move it" ("Circles," 1841). Conversely, our "present life," examined and questioned and tested, can be a "platform" from which to "view" and "move" the literary images that construct us, to critique and extend their insights.

These historical examples detail only one of the many ways of writing about literature, but the recognition that literary response is always culturally and historically shaped has many other implications. The delineation of some experience as personal rather than public, as natural rather than culturally constructed, similarly shapes critical debates about whether a focus on images of women may be seen as special pleading. The attention to images of women has often been challenged as political, that is, in opposition to something that gets named universal, and attention to a social-literary structure of images has often been labeled non-literary or merely sociological. We could extend this scrutiny of writing practices to question many other images of writing and the assumptions they perpetuate. We could have focused, for example, on the situating of the literary text in a formal realm, in which texts are compared and explicated according to their adherence to qualities of genre or technique. ("Explicate the following lyric." "Discuss the meter and diction of the following passages.") Or we could have focused on the construction of literature as a reflection or exemplification of a reality that exists somewhere else, or is figured only through an abstracted "ism." ("What attitude is reflected by American literature toward the following: nature, idealism, individualism, social problems, science, political democracy, humor, industrialism, religion, war?") Or we could have discussed the belief in the explanatory value of literary history, of literary periods and influences, of the "progress" of literature toward the improved text. ("Place X in the context of other literary works of the period." "Read carefully each of the five passages below. Give an approximate date for the composition of each passage, and name either the author or some poet who represents the school or period to which it belongs. [Do not give reasons; simply state your conclusions in one or two sentences for each passage.] Write a detailed analysis of any one of the passages. Show briefly how it differs from each of the other passages and, more fully, how it is characteristic of its period and author or school.")

The focus here reflects a concern suggested by many of the selections in this anthology as to how images of women get produced and become solidified, immune to the passing of time or changes in material conditions, sheltered—but also imprisoned—under such rubrics as the "personal," the "domestic," the "romantic." To disentangle the ways in which counterpositions get labeled prejudice and in which the personal is associated with women or with lack of authority is important in writing about images of women and in rereading the images that have been written. In any case, it is important to reflect on how we are using our own experiences to read a literary text, how that text represents such experiences, and how it allows us to consider what may be missing or skewed or not capable of being represented. As the French cultural critic Michel Foucault argued in his *Archaeology of Knowledge* (1969), it is important to examine the notions that have been previously accepted without question by one's intellectual community:

> What we must do is to tear away from their virtual self-evidence, and to free the problems that they pose; to recognize that they are not the

tranquil locus on the basis of which other questions . . . may be posed, but that they themselves pose a whole cluster of questions. . . . We
must recognize that they may not, in the last resort, be what they seem at first sight.

Such a self-questioning way of reading and writing will allow us to construct different notions of what is proper to ask, of what is productive
and helpful in articulating our personal responses as texts that others
must take seriously.

Writing Images

In "When We Dead Awaken: Writing as Re-Vision," Adrienne Rich suggests that such reading and writing depend on what she calls "re-vision—
the act of looking back, of seeing with fresh eyes, of entering an old text
from a new critical direction." *Images of Women in Literature* shares
this sense of reading and writing as social activities, not limited to the
production of a narrowly defined literary criticism or evaluation, but
implicated in our efforts to read ourselves culturally. Rich's catalogue of
the work of re-vision offers a plan of action for students reading and writing about images of women:

A radical critique of literature, feminist in impulse, would take the work first of all as a clue
to how we live, how we have been living, how
we have been led to imagine ourselves, how our
language has trapped as well as liberated us,
how the very act of naming has been till now a
male prerogative, and how we can begin to see
and name—and therefore live—afresh.

This insistence on the power and necessity of re-vision counters many
dominant views of reading and writing about literary texts. Rich suggests
treating a text as a *clue*, not to some arcane interpretive value, but to
something we normally think we know—"how we live, how we have
been living." Our attention needs to be drawn to the words that shape
behavior and relationships, to the categories that arrange value and importance, to the associations and oppositions that mark what is "woman"
and what is "man" in a particular culture and time. We must also attend
to the social acts of construction in the text. Who speaks the shaping
words? Who gets to answer? Who gets to frame or to challenge the terms?
Who is left silent?

Instead of reading just for information or for "the gist," we can look
back at our habits and through the authority of our experiences and

knowledge. Instead of learning what have been the "standard" views of a text or confirming the vision of a "master" reader, we can examine our points of entry to a text. According to Rich's essay, such personal self-scrutiny is a complex and demanding task, requiring the sternest discipline and habits of critical questioning. Rather than dismissing such self-reflection as beside the point or as unprofessional, Rich encourages us to read ourselves reading. She reminds us that what we read is not fact, but a produced image by which "we have been led to imagine ourselves." Language can both trap and liberate, and the power to give names and to change them has not been evenly allocated. The practice of reading as re-vision, and of writing stimulated by that re-vision, depends on our scrutiny of the language, images, and plots by which our habits and values have been shaped. "Until we can understand the assumptions in which we are drenched we cannot know ourselves"—Rich's metaphor of drenching emphasizes our immersion in culture, which is not something we can take on and off, like clothing, or something we can exit, like a play. Assumptions are, rather, what we breathe, or what prevents us from breathing something more sustaining.

I do not wish to offer rules for writing about and through images—to explain what is improper or impolitic, to demark a sphere for the vulgar or the rustic, or to name the appropriate or the correct. What I offer instead is a set of entry points, of ways into the issues raised by this anthology's selections and argument. These suggest the kinds of critical and cultural projects that make use of the specific texts and their collection as *Images of Women in Literature*.

Who gets to speak? Who is silent?   In "The Bridal Veil," Alice Cary's speaker addresses the man who thinks he has "won" her by making her his bride. She recognizes that what she has to say is "matter to vex" him, "matter to grieve" him. Yet her words are curiously framed by that amorphous social "they" who get to define what it means to be a woman married ("We're married, they say"), by her groom's prior definitions, and by her sense of his responses. The woman speaks the poem, but it is full of other powerful voices that contend with her for space, for terms, for value. Other monologues, such as Jane Augustine's "Secretive" or Gwendolyn Brooks's "The Mother," are also hemmed in by expected comments from the outside, from those with the power to judge or to censure. In Ntozake Shange's angry poem "With no immediate cause," the speaker's litany of horror is interrupted by the quoted official words "there is some concern . . . ," words set off by more than their quotation marks and indentation, words that haunt the poem—disembodied, uncaring, abstracted from the social realm they legislate. Perhaps the most important line of W. H. Auden's "Miss Gee" is its opening casual request, "Let me tell you a little story." Who, we might ask, is this "I"? Why should we grant the request? Who says it is a "little" story? Such questions remind us that the material of the story is not fact, not presented neutrally, without some investment on the part of the teller. They also remind us to examine carefully all representations, to take seriously even offhanded or understated claims to authority.

How is speech heard? Who listens?   Alice Cary's bride introduces her counterimage of marriage with the conversational "Well." Like the poems of her contemporary Emily Dickinson, Cary's poem dramatizes the hesitance and self-effacement of a woman's speech. The speaker interrupts herself, qualifies what she has said, and effaces her argument by stringing it together with unprepossessing dashes rather than with the more formal order of semicolons and subordinate clauses. She repeats herself, changing the meaning of "we're married" not so much by overt argument as by erosion, wearing away its conventional meanings until it can begin to stand for something she wants to amplify. Cary's poem thus reminds us that we need to attend to how speakers are positioned to be heard, to how their ways of articulating and expressing themselves are likely to be weighed by those with power to assign value. As the women in Susan Glaspell's play dramatize, what seem "trifles" to one set of critics may be of crucial import to another. But it takes a radical transformation of meaning and authority for Glaspell's women to act on their own sense of priorities and significance. And it would take an even more radical transformation for them to be able to articulate and justify their covert behavior in terms their culture would understand and respect.

As many of the selections in this volume suggest, it is not easy to alter the value of things, to shift the perspective. The speaker of Marge Piercy's poem "Unlearning to Not Speak" has nightmares about classes "she signed up for / but forgot to attend." She is besieged by "blizzards of paper," by "phrases of men who lectured her," by texts that preface whatever she might say, that mark it as "the wrong answer," simultaneously too quiet and too loud to be heard. She must "learn to speak again," with all the hesitance and vulnerability of an infant. In "Secretive," Jane Augustine examines how even such private spaces as personal journals are infused with the categories of the dominant culture. Although Augustine's narrator is writing without the expectation of publication and to a "secret friend," she worries: "Even my nonsecrets look bad when written out in words. . . . You see how my journal would sound— just a list of absurd concerns."

Starting from these texts' suggestions, a writer might focus on how women are positioned so that their writing or speech seems inarticulate, hesitant, or unprofessional. Or a writer could investigate the suggestive metaphors for change such texts offer. What, for example, does Piercy suggest is the value of "unlearning to not speak"? What would such unlearning require? What would it change? What does it take to notice "trifles" or to revalue a "list of absurd concerns"?

JEAN FERGUSON CARR

Whose words? Whose meanings?   In "Spelling," Margaret Atwood asserts: "A word after a word / after a word is power." How do writers get their words and their connections taken seriously rather than dismissed as nonsense or seen as trivial? And which words? With what meanings? In Lewis Carroll's *Alice through the Looking-Glass,* the heroine is outraged at the suggestion that words can mean whatever their speaker chooses to have them mean. She opposes both the arbitrary claim to power and the accompanying destruction of social discourse. Many of the selections in this anthology investigate the political and cultural claims to power that are implicit in the valuation of certain words. Harriet Jacobs's narrative warns of the dangers of "imaginary pictures" that perpetuate slavery, the "romantic notions of a sunny clime, and of the flowing vines that all the year round shade a happy home." She shows how the misuse of an empty phrase such as "happy home" or "sunny clime" covers over the actual horrors of the Southern domestic scene. Jacobs calls attention to the use of a particular language of romantic landscape and domesticity, as William Blake does in "Song," exposing a masculine dream of love, in which a woman is caught in man's "silken net," shut "in his golden cage," doing what "he loves."

Many of the selections treat common terms as unfamiliar, needing to be redefined or re-established. They mark off social language as quoted from someone else, indicating how the words have been invested with cultural authority by others, by past traditions or differing values. The outcome of this attention to language can be a recognition that a word— and the assumptions that attend its use—does not retain its ordering power. Erica Jong's speaker, for example, is struck by how puzzling the phrase "second sex" will seem to her newborn daughter, who will wonder "how anyone, / except a madman, / could call you 'second' / when you are so splendidly / first." Adrienne Rich claimed in "Writing as Re-Vision" that "poems are like dreams: in them you put what you don't know you know." One of the ways in which literature transmits what we don't know we know is by focusing our attention on the words that structure our lives—making them strange, repeating them, making us notice their form and rhetoric. Another way is to make words enter the arena of social debate, to move them from the protected sphere of what in "Discourse in the Novel" (1975) the Russian critic Mikhail Bakhtin called "the word of the fathers," where language seems to pre-exist, unquestionable, unchallenged, absolute.

Renegotiating the struggle between languages, the struggle to name and rename, is not a simple matter of will. Indeed, Alaíde Foppa's poem "Woman" reminds us how difficult it is to strip an image of its historical associations. Her poem suggests that to write about "woman" may first require defining what she is *not*: "not the remote angelical rose sung by poets of old / . . . Not she who must always say yes." As Rich argued in "Writing as Re-Vision," powerful writing requires a certain freedom to experiment, to try on other meanings, to try to invert or replace terms with others: "You have to be free to play around with the notion that . . . nothing can be too sacred for the imagination to turn into its opposite or to call experimentally by another name." It is important to recognize that women are not the only audience for such possibilities. As Rich and Dickinson and other authors represented in this anthology might argue, images of women become an organizing principle for a wide range of cultural activities; the oppositions that male and female come to represent and depend on serve as a grammar or syntax for how a widely construed "we" can live and imagine ourselves. Similarly, a writer using a book such as this one has the opportunity to investigate how an image is constructed over time, over a series of texts, and how it comes to stand for and also to illuminate reality. By attending to images produced over a range of times and cultural situations and by different authors for different audiences, we can begin to notice how images are constructed, what qualities get conjoined or opposed.

Images of Women in Literature offers a wide array of the pretexts, the uses of language, the images, and the narratives that construct what we believe are "our" assumptions. It offers the opportunity for a cultural retrospection, a looking back at what has shaped our current sense of reality and possibility. In her poem "Diving into the Wreck," Adrienne Rich explores the exhilaration and danger of searching without the aid of the usual guidebooks, procedures, and landmarks. In "Writing as Re-Vision," she explains such exploration as "a difficult and dangerous walking on the ice, as we try to find language and images for the consciousness we are just coming into, and with little in the past to support us." Indeed, the writing called for by such retrospection may well seem initially like walking on ice—sliding across dangerous surfaces without any certainty, seeing reflections everywhere but not being able to discern what is image and what is real, what appears frozen into solidity only to shift as the weather changes. But as Ralph Waldo Emerson suggested, in his 1844 essay "The Poet," recognizing that you are walking on glass may be a crucial aspect of your power as a writer. "The poet," Emerson proposed, "turns the world to glass, and shows us all things in their right series and procession." In *Nature* (1836) Emerson argued that the writer "unfixes the land and the sea, makes them revolve around the axis of [her] primary thought, and disposes them anew." It is by such acts of unsettlement that we are able to investigate how things come into being, how they establish and maintain their power and how they can be shifted or rethought. These acts of unsettling the past and the present may be necessary to allow an exploration of the new, of the possible, of what Rich calls "the challenge and promise of a whole new psychic geography to be explored," what Alice Walker termed "beyond what," and what is gathered here to represent "Woman Becoming."

To read and write about images, we need to take on what Emily Dickinson called "a discerning Eye" (#435, "Much Madness is divinest

Sense"), an ability to separate things that have been elided, to perceive differences in what have come to seem natural unities. We need to question the values assigned, to reconsider hierarchies and priorities. We need to investigate by what logic events are linked together into a narrative, into a sequence of causes and events, into what comes first and what comes last. "We noticed smallest things," Dickinson wrote in another poem (#422, "The last Night that She lived"): "Things overlooked before / By this great light upon our Minds / Italicized—as 'twere." Reading and writing through images can allow us to see things in relationship to what surrounds them, "italicized—as 'twere." It can allow us to question that relationship, to consider what happens when we bring "smallest things" or "trifles" into the foreground, separated from what in daily life obscures their origins and their various cultural uses.

References

Alcott, Bronson. *The Journals of Bronson Alcott*. Ed. Odell Shepard. Port Washington: Kennikat, 1938.

Bakhtin, Mikhail. "Discourse in the Novel." *The Dialogic Imagination: Four Essays*. 1975. Ed. Michael Holquist. Trans. Caryl Emerson and Michael Holquist. Austin: U of Texas P, 1981. 259–422.

Carroll, Lewis. *Alice through the Looking-Glass*. London: Macmillan, 1872.

College Entrance Examination Board Comprehensive Examination Questions. Boston: Ginn, 1916.

de Beauvoir, Simone. *The Second Sex*. 1949. Trans. and ed. H. M. Parshley. New York: Knopf, 1953.

Emerson, Ralph Waldo. *The Collected Works*. Eds. Alfred R. Ferguson, Jean Ferguson Carr, et al. Cambridge: Harvard UP, 1971– .

The Ethel Cotton Correspondence Course. 1927. London: Marcus-Campbell, 1948.

Foucault, Michel. *The Archaeology of Knowledge*. 1969. Trans. A. M. Sheridan Smith. New York: Harper, 1976.

Johnson, Thomas H., ed. *The Poems of Emily Dickinson*. Cambridge: Harvard UP, 1955.

Moore, J. Hamilton, ed. *The Young Gentleman and Lady's Monitor, and English Teacher's Assistant*. Albany: Webster, 1803.

Rich, Adrienne. "When We Dead Awaken: Writing as Re-Vision." *On Lies, Secrets, and Silence: Selected Prose 1966–1978*. New York: Norton, 1979. 33–49.

SUGGESTIONS FOR
FURTHER READING

. ——————————————— .

In 1989 a two-volume bibliography on women and literature listed about ten thousand articles and books published between 1974 and 1981; a third volume covering through 1985 is forthcoming (see Boos and Miller below). Clearly, any suggestions for further reading given here must be very selective. In order to help readers identify the most important types of aids for independent study and research, this section is divided into six lists, as follows:

Works cited in the introductions
Selections appearing in previous editions but omitted here
Reference works, with annotations detailing their scope and use
Periodicals currently publishing women's literature, criticism, and
    reviews
Specialized anthologies of literature by women
Selected recent literary criticism and theory

Works Cited in the Introductions

The works listed here provide insight into the theoretical background as well as a rationale for the selections of this edition. Some are already considered "classic"; most are recent works exemplifying research and criticism in several disciplines.

Barry, Kathleen, Charlotte Bunch, and Shirley Castley, eds. *Global Feminist Workshop to Organize against Traffic in Women*. Proc. of a conference. Rotterdam, 6 Apr. 1983. New York: Intl. Women's Tribune Ctr., 1984.

Baym, Nina. *Woman's Fiction: A Guide to Novels by and about Women in America, 1820–1870*. Ithaca: Cornell UP, 1978.

Bell, Lee Anne. "Something's Wrong Here and It's Not Me: Challenging the Dilemmas That Block Girls' Success." *Journal for the Education of the Gifted* 12 (Winter 1989), 118–30.

Berger, John. *Ways of Seeing*. Hammondsworth, Eng.: Penguin, 1972.

Betterton, Rosemary, ed. *Images of Femininity in the Visual Arts and Media*. London: Pandora, 1987.

Blicksilver, Edith, ed. *The Ethnic American Woman: Problems, Protests, Lifestyle*. Dubuque: Kendall Hunt, 1979.

Borysenko, Joan. *Minding the Body, Mending the Mind . . . .* New York: Warner, 1990.

Brown, Rosellen. *Autobiography of My Mother*. Garden City: Doubleday, 1976.

Bulkin, Elly, and Joan Larkin, eds. *Amazon Poetry: An Anthology of Lesbian Poetry*. Brooklyn: Out and Out, 1975.

Chodorow, Nancy. *The Reproduction of Mothering: Psychoanalysis and the Sociology of Gender*. Berkeley: U of California P, 1978.

———. *Feminism and Psychoanalytic Theory*. New Haven: Yale UP, 1989.

Christian, Barbara. *Black Women Novelists: The Development of a Tradition, 1892–1976*. Westport: Greenwood, 1980.

———, ed. *Black Feminist Criticism: Perspectives on Black Women Writers*. New York: Pergamon, 1985.

Cott, Nancy F. "Passionlessness: An Interpretation of Victorian Sexual Ideology, 1790–1850." *Signs* 4 (1978), 219–36. Reprinted in *A Heritage of Her Own: Toward a New Social History of American Women*. Eds. Nancy F. Cott and Elizabeth H. Pleck. New York: Simon, 1979.

Crowther, Bosley. Review of "Meet Me in St. Louis," musical. *New York Times*, 29 Nov. 1944, 20.

de Beauvoir, Simone. *The Second Sex*. Trans. and ed. H. M. Parshley. New York: Knopf, 1953.

Dinnerstein, Dorothy. *The Mermaid and the Minotaur: Sexual Arrangements and Human Malaise*. New York: Harper, 1977.

Erikson, Erik H. "Womanhood and the Inner Space." *The Woman in America*. Ed. Robert J. Lifton. Boston: Houghton, 1964.

Evans, Mari, ed. *Black Women Writers (1950–1980): A Critical Evaluation*. New York: Anchor, 1984.

Fisher, Dexter, ed. *The Third Woman: Minority Women Writers of the United States*. Boston: Houghton, 1980.

Flynn, Elizabeth, and Patricinio P. Schweickart, eds. *Gender and Reading: Texts, Contexts*. Baltimore: Johns Hopkins UP, 1986.

Gilbert, Sandra, and Susan Gubar. *The Madwoman in the Attic: The Woman Writer and the Nineteenth-Century Literary Imagination.* New Haven: Yale UP, 1979.

Gilligan, Carol. *In a Different Voice: Psychological Theory and Women's Development.* Cambridge: Harvard UP, 1982.

Gittelsohn, John. "No Time for Korean Girls: In 'Year of Horse,' Superstition, Sexism, Abortions." *Boston Globe* 23 Jan. 1990: 2.

Gordon, Margaret T., and Stephanie Riger. *The Female Fear.* New York: Macmillan, 1989.

Government of India. "National Perspective Plan for Women, 1988–2000." Report of the Core Group, Dept. of Women and Child Development. New Delhi: 1988.

Gray, Francine du Plessix. *Soviet Women: Walking the Tightrope.* New York: Doubleday, 1990.

Hertz, Rosanna. *More Equal Than Others: Women and Men in Dual-Career Marriages.* Berkeley: U of California P, 1986.

Hyde, Janet S., and Marcia C. Linn. *The Psychology of Gender: Advances through Meta-Analysis.* Baltimore: Johns Hopkins UP, 1986.

Johnson, Miriam M. *Strong Mothers, Weak Wives: The Search for Gender Equality.* Berkeley: U of California P, 1988.

Johnson, Richard. "What Is Cultural Studies Anyway?" *Social Text* 16 (Winter 1986–87), 38–80.

Keller, Suzanne. "Women in the 21st Century: Summing Up and Moving Forward." Paper given at Radcliffe College Conference, 2–3 Dec. 1988.

Lakoff, George. *Women, Fire, and Dangerous Things: What Categories about the Mind Reveal.* Chicago: U of Chicago P, 1987.

Latza, Berit. *Sextourismas in Südöstasien.* Frankfort: Fischer Verlag, 1987.

Lawson, Carol. "Toys: Girls Still Apply Makeup, Boys Fight Wars." *New York Times* 15 June 1989: 1, 10.

Lindholm, Charles. "Demystifying Romance." *Harvard Gazette* 9 Feb. 1990.

Luria, Zella. "Sex and Gender: A Young Child's View." Lecture. The Bunting Institute, Radcliffe College, 10 Jan. 1990.

MacCannell, Dean, and Juliet Flower MacCannell. "The Beauty System." *The Ideology of Conduct: Essays in Literature and the History of Sexuality.* Eds. Nancy Armstrong and Leonard Tennenhouse. New York: Methuen, 1987. 206–235.

Mitchell, W. J. T. *Iconology, Image, Text, Ideology.* Chicago: U of Chicago P, 1986.

Olsen, Tillie. "One Out of Twelve." *Silences: Why Writers Don't Write.* New York: Delacorte, 1978. 22–46. (Originally presented at the 1971 convention of the Modern Language Association.)

Pacheco, Patrick. Review of new "Meet Me in St. Louis," musical. *New York Times* 29 Oct. 1989: 11, 3:1.

Perry, Ruth, and Martine W. Brownley, eds. *Mothering the Mind: Twelve Studies of Writers and Their Silent Partners.* New York: Holmes and Meier, 1984.

Pheterson, Gail, ed. *A Vindication of the Rights of Whores.* Seattle: Seal, 1989. (Articles from World Whores' Conferences, Amsterdam, 1985; Brussels, 1986.)

Phongpaikit, Pasuk. *From Peasant Girls to Bangkok Masseuses.* Women, Work, and Development 2. Geneva: Intl. Development Office, 1982.

Philips, Susan, Susan Steele, and Christine Tanz. *Language, Gender, and Sex in Comparative Perspective.* London: Cambridge UP, 1987.

Radway, Janet. *Reading the Romance: Women, Patriarchy, and Popular Literature.* Chapel Hill: U of North Carolina P, 1984.

Reynolds, Helen. *The Economics of Prostitution.* Springfield: Thomas, 1986.

Rich, Adrienne. "When We Dead Awaken: Writing as Re-Vision." *On Lies, Secrets, and Silence: Selected Prose, 1966–78.* New York: Norton, 1979. 33–49. (Originally presented at the 1971 convention of the Modern Language Association.)

Rich, Frank. Review of new "Meet Me in Saint Louis," musical. *New York Times* 3 Nov. 1989: 111, 3:1.

Ruddick, Sara. *Maternal Thinking: Toward a Politics of Peace.* Boston: Beacon, 1989.

Russell, Diana E. *The Secret Trauma: Incest in the Lives of Girls and Women.* New York: Basic, 1986.

Scott, Joan W. *Gender and the Politics of History.* New York: Columbia UP, 1988.

Showalter, Elaine. *A Literature of Their Own: British Women Novelists from Brontë to Lessing.* Princeton: Princeton UP, 1977.

———. "Feminist Criticism in the Wilderness." *Critical Inquiry* 8 (Winter 1981). Reprinted in *The New Feminist Criticism: Essays on Women, Literature, & Theory.* Ed. Elaine Showalter. New York: Pantheon, 1985.

———, ed. *Speaking of Gender.* New York: Routledge, 1989.

Smith-Rosenberg, Carol. "The Female World of Love and Ritual: Relations between Women in Nineteenth-Century America." *Signs* 1 (1975), 1–29.

Spivack, Gayatri Chakravorty. *In Other Worlds: Essays in Cultural Politics.* New York: Methuen, 1987.

Stevens, Evelyn P. "Marianismo: The Other Face of Machismo in Latin America." *Female and Male in Latin America: Essays.* Ed. Ann Pescatello. Pittsburgh: U of Pittsburgh P, 1973. 89–100.

Walker, Alice. *In Search of Our Mothers' Gardens: Womanist Prose.* New York: Harcourt, 1983.

Washington, Mary Helen, ed. *Black-Eyed Susans: Classic Stories by and about Black Women.* New York: Doubleday, 1975.

_____. *Midnight Birds: Stories of Contemporary Black Women.* New York: Doubleday, 1980.

Yale French Studies 62. *Feminist Readings: French Texts, American Contexts.* Eds. Dartmouth Feminist Collective. 1981.

Yellin, Jean. "Written by Herself: Harriet Jacobs' Slave Narrative." *American Literature* 53 (November, 1981), 479–86.

Zimmermann, Bonnie. "What Has Never Been: An Overview of Lesbian Feminist Criticism." *Feminist Studies* 7 (1981). Reprinted in *The New Feminist Criticism: Essays on Women, Literature, & Theory.* Ed. Elaine Showalter. New York: Pantheon, 1985. 200–224.

Works Included in Previous Editions

This list of works that appeared in previous editions of this book is presented for the convenience of readers wishing to expand the range of materials for each image and the possibilities for comparison. Most of the works listed here are now widely available. The works are listed by image and author's name, with the date(s) of the edition(s) in which each appeared.

The Wife

Anderson, Sherwood. "Death in the Woods." 1973, 1977, 1981, 1986.

Chekhov, Anton. "The Darling." 1973, 1977.

Cohen, Florence. "Mrs. Poe." 1981.

Hemingway, Ernest. "The Short Happy Life of Francis Macomber." 1973, 1977, 1981, 1986.

Morris, Wright. "The Ram in the Thicket." 1973, 1977.

O'Neill, Eugene. *Before Breakfast.* 1977, 1981, 1986.

Parker, Dorothy. "Big Blonde." 1973.

Plath, Sylvia. "The Jailor." 1977, 1981.

Slesinger, Tess. "On Being Told That Her Second Husband Has Taken His First Lover." 1977, 1981.

Stanford, Ann. "Cassandra's Wedding Song." 1977.

Swenson, May. "Women." 1977, 1981, 1986.

Walker, Alice. "Her Sweet Jerome." 1973, 1977.

Wharton, Edith. "The Other Two." 1973, 1977.

The Mother

Betts, Doris. "Still Life with Fruit." 1977, 1981.

Boyle, Kay. "His Idea of a Mother." 1973, 1977.

Brodkey, Harold. "Verona: A Young Woman Speaks." 1981.

Calisher, Hortense. "The Middle Drawer." 1986.

Davis, Catherine. "SHE." 1977, 1981, 1986.

Gaines, Ernest J. "The Sky Is Gray." 1973, 1977, 1981, 1986.

Gardner, Isabella. "At a Summer Hotel." 1977, 1981, 1986.

Goldberg, Myra. "Gifts." 1981.

LeSueur, Meridel. "Biography of My Daughter." 1986.

Munro, Alice. "Royal Battles." 1981.

Rich, Adrienne. "Night Pieces: The Crib." 1973, 1977.

Williams, Shirley Anne. "Tell Martha Not to Moan." 1986.

Woman on a Pedestal

Fitzgerald, F. Scott. "The Last of the Belles." 1973, 1977.

Frost, Robert. "The Pauper Witch of Grafton." 1973, 1977.

Gorky, Maxim. "26 Men and a Girl." 1981.

Hawthorne, Nathaniel. "Rappacini's Daughter." 1973, 1977.

Howells, William Dean. "Editha." 1973, 1981.

Toomer, Jean. "Fern." 1973, 1977, 1981, 1986.

The Sex Object

Atwood, Margaret. "Circe: Mud Poems." 1981.

Davis, Helene. "Affair." 1973, 1977, 1981, 1986.

Gilbert, Sandra. "Daguerrotype: 'Fallen' Woman." 1986.

Jaffe, Rona. "Rima the Bird Girl." 1977, 1981, 1986.

Mailer, Norman. "The Time of Her Time." 1973, 1977, 1981, 1986.

Moravia, Alberto. "The Chase." 1973, 1977, 1981.

Oates, Joyce Carol. "The Girl." 1981, 1986.

Piercy, Marge. "Barbie Doll." 1977.

Wakowski, Diane. "Belly Dancer." 1977.

Welty, Eudora. "At the Landing." 1973, 1977.

Women without Men

Freeman, Mary E. Wilkins. "A New England Nun." 1977, 1981, 1986.

Jewett, Sarah Orne. "Aunt Cynthy Dallett." 1986.

Lessing, Doris. "Our Friend Judith." 1977.

Levertov, Denise. "Living Alone." 1986.

Mansfield, Katherine. "Miss Brill." 1973, 1977.

O'Brien, Edna. "The Call." 1981, 1986.

Rule, Jane. "Middle Children." 1981, 1986.

Sarton, May. "Joy in Provence." 1981, 1986.

Schultz, Elizabeth. "Bone." 1981.

Tramblay, Estela Portilla. "The Burning." 1986.

Woman Becoming

Adams, Alice. "Roses, Rhododendron." 1981.

Beattie, Ann. "Tuesday Night." 1981. (Moved to *The Wife*, 1986.)

Broumas, Olga. "Artemis." 1981. (Moved to *Women without Men*, 1986.)

Childress, Alice. "Wine in the Wilderness." 1977.

Levertov, Denise. "Stepping Westward." 1977, 1981.

Luce, Clare Booth. "A Doll's House, 1970." 1973.

Nin, Anaïs. "Alraune." 1973.

Olds, Sharon. "Best Friends." 1986.

Stanford, Ann. "The Descent." 1981.

Terry, Megan. *Approaching Simone*. 1981.

Vroman, Mary Ellen. *See How They Run*. 1973.

*Self-Images**

Field, Joanna. From *A Life of One's Own*. 1986.

Hughes, Mary Gray. "A Thousand Springs." 1986.

Kollwitz, Käthe. From *Diaries and Letters*. 1986.

Nin, Anaïs. From *Diary*. 1986.

Noël, Marie. From *Notes for Myself*. 1986.

Perkins, Arozina. From *Diary*. 1986.

Reference Works

The Library of Congress publishes periodically a *Subject Index to Books in Print*. Under the major heading "Women" appear such subheadings as "Women–Literary Collections," "Women Authors," "Women in Literature," "Women's Writings," "Women's Rights," and "Women's Studies" (see Dickstein, Mills, and Waite, below, for a full list). A search under several headings should help update the sources below, which cannot be absolutely current.

Another invaluable source is *Contemporary Authors*, published by the Gale Research Company in Detroit. In 1990 there were 128 volumes, covering about 94,000 authors (of nontechnical works) writing in or

*This category, new in 1986, was merged with the other images in 1991.

translated into English. The aim is inclusion of all such authors still alive in 1960 or later; some famous authors who died as early as 1900 are also listed. Each article gives biographical, bibliographical, and critical information; many are based on interviews. There are frequent cumulative indexes, as well as cross references to other Gale publications, such as the ten-volume *Autobiography Series*, which lists autobiographies by famous writers, and *Contemporary Literary Criticism*.

Another important source of information is a listing of series being published by various presses. For example, Indiana University Press has two series of scholarly books about women writers: Key Women Writers and Women of Letters; Rutgers University Press issues volumes by nineteenth-century American women writers; Nebraska University Press publishes European women writers in translation; the Feminist Press is bringing out works by forgotten American writers of the 1930s; and Virago publishes British women writers. In an important new series, the Oxford University Press is republishing works by nineteenth-century black writers, including a new edition of Anna Julia Cooper's *A Voice from the South* (1990), edited by Mary Helen Washington.

The editors of ongoing series often change; the works are listed here under the editors' names appropriate at the time this book went to press.

Ariel, Joan. *Building Women's Studies Collections: A Resource Guide.* Choice Bibliographical Series #8. Middletown: Choice, 1987.
This guide lists and furnishes addresses for feminist periodicals, publishers, catalogs, audiovisual materials, and bookdealers.

Ballou, Patricia K. *Women: A Bibliography of Bibliographies.* 2nd ed. Boston: Hall, 1986.
This work lists and annotates several hundred specific bibliographies, including ones on literature and literary criticism. It covers 1979–1985; further volumes are promised.

Boos, Florence, and Lynn Miller. *Bibliography of Women and Literature: Articles and Books by and about Women from 600 to 1975.* Vol. 1, 1974–1978; vol. 2, 1979–1981. New York: Holmes and Meier, 1989. (Vol. 3 forthcoming.)

Briscoe, Mary Louise, with Barbara Tobias and Lynn Z. Bloom. *American Autobiography, 1945–80: A Bibliography.* Madison: U of Wisconsin P, 1982.
Women's autobiographies are starred in this listing of more than five thousand. Annotations describe the main aspects of each work.

Capek, Mary Ellen. *A Woman's Thesaurus: An Index of Language Used to Describe and Locate Information by and about Women.* New York: Harper, 1987.
This work lists and defines headings and subheadings useful for pursuing information in indexes other than the Library of Congress *Subject Headings*. It is especially helpful for working with periodicals and

books not based on the Library of Congress system. For example, under "Sexism" is the subheading "Institutional Sexism," which lists "Discrimination," "Gatekeeping," and "Glass Ceiling"; the last two appear in newspaper and periodical articles but not in the Library of Congress lists.

Cardinale, Susan. *Anthologies by and about Women: An Analytical Index*. Westport: Greenwood, 1982.
This 822-page index reproduces the tables of contents of 375 anthologies in various fields, with cross-indexes to individual authors, to the titles of separate works anthologized, and to forty subject headings. These subjects include biography, autobiography, literary criticism, drama, poetry, fiction, science fiction, black women, older women, and lesbians. A keyword index includes *image, self-image, lesbian, myth,* and *stereotype.*

Chapman, Dorothy Hilton. *Index to Poetry by Black American Women*. Westport: Greenwood, 1986.
This work covers from 1746 to the present. It indexes 120 individuals and 83 anthologies by author, subject, and more than a thousand themes, such as death, love, religion, Africa, slavery, dreams, and children.

Cline, Cheryl. *Women's Diaries, Journals, and Letters: An Annotated Bibliography*. New York: Garland, 1989.
This bibliography lists published private writings in English and several foreign languages, including books, articles, and extracts in larger works. It includes an index of anthologies and a bibliography of critical works.

Dickstein, Ruth, Victoria A. Mills, and Ellen J. Waite. *Women in LC's Terms: A Thesaurus of Library of Congress Subject Headings Related to Women*. Phoenix: Oryx, 1988.
Compiled at the request of the women's studies program at the University of Arizona, this work lists thirty-five hundred terms and cross references; it is organized with the same chapter headings as Capek's thesaurus (see above), so the two supplement each other. Chapter 7 covers literature and language. There is an extensive alphabetical list of subject headings as well as a separate list of call numbers used by the Library of Congress: PN, PR, and PS are the most important for literature.

Glikin, Ronda. *Black American Women in Literature: A Bibliography, 1976–87*. Jefferson: McFarland, 1989.
This bibliography covers three hundred writers in all genres, listing works by each and critical articles and reviews on each.

Guy, Patricia. *A Woman's Poetry Index*. Phoenix: Oryx, 1985.
This work indexes the contents of fifty-one anthologies by author and title.

Maggiore, Delores J. *Lesbianism: An Annotated Bibliography and Guide to the Literature, 1976–86*. Metuchen: Scarecrow, 1987.

This comprehensive bibliography of books, articles, and theses on lesbianism includes mainly social science materials but some literary sources. An analytical article discusses definitions of lesbianism.

Mainiero, Lina. *American Women Writers, from Colonial Times to the Present*. 4 vols. New York: Ungar, 1979.
This work covers writers in all genres. Articles are substantial, with biographical, critical, and bibliographical information. A volume updating living writers and listing new ones is in preparation.

Parker, Linda. *Feminist Periodicals: A Current Listing of Contents*. Madison: U of Wisconsin P, 1981–present.
Prepared by the women's studies librarian at the University of Wisconsin, this bibliography appears twice yearly and prints the tables of contents from current issues of seventy major feminist journals.

Reardon, Joan, and Kristine A. Thorsen. *Poetry by American Women, 1900–1975: A Bibliography*. Metuchen, NJ: Scarecrow, 1979.
This bibliography of works by and about poets is comprehensive for the period covered.

Searing, Susan. *New Books on Women and Feminism*. Madison: U of Wisconsin P, 1979–present.
Books and periodicals selected by the women's studies librarian at the University of Wisconsin are listed and annotated; the coverage is selective but extensive—2,391 items in the Spring 1988 listing, for example. Items are organized by subjects, which include biography, autobiography, diaries, letters, essays, literature, drama, fiction, poetry, mixed genres, history, and criticism; there is a separate list of children's literature.

Todd, Janet. *British Women Writers: A Critical Reference Guide*. New York: Continuum, 1989.
This guide covers writers from the fourteenth century to the present in all genres; the articles, though brief, are authoritative sources of biography, criticism, and bibliography.

Periodicals

Belles Lettres, A Review of Books by Women. 1985–   . This quarterly review of books by and about women, published by trade, university, and independent presses, frequently has interviews, review articles, and a feature on a rediscovery. Examples of special topics include "Jewish Women Writers," Sept./Oct. 1987; "Short Stories," Spring 1989; and "Women's Autobiography," Winter 1990.

Conditions: A Feminist Magazine of Writing by Women with an Emphasis on Writing by Lesbians. 1977–   . Published annually, this journal has recently expanded its scope to include international writing; in addition to reviews, it includes poetry, fiction, and essays. No. 15

(1988) focused on AIDS; no. 16 (1989) was a selection of the best of the past twelve years.

Differences, A Journal of Feminist Cultural Studies. 1989– . Published by the Pembroke Women's Center at Brown University, this journal has had few literary articles, but its focus on culture provides important background for literature and theory.

Feminist Studies. 1972– . Published with support from the women's studies program of the University of Maryland, this journal focuses on social and political issues but frequently has essays and reviews dealing with literature and interdisciplinary topics. Occasionally, original poetry and fiction are published.

Frontiers: A Journal of Women's Studies. 1966– . Published by a collective at the University of Colorado at Boulder, this journal has many short interdisciplinary articles. It often includes book reviews of literary works and literary criticism and sometimes review articles. Vol. 14 (Spring 1988) focused on the literary theory of deconstruction.

NWSA Journal. 1989– . Published quarterly by the women's studies program at Ohio State University for the National Women's Studies Association, this journal includes articles and extensive book reviews in all fields.

Sage: A Scholarly Journal on Black Women. 1984– . Published quarterly by the women's studies program at Spelman College, this journal often has literary criticism and short book reviews and occasionally biographical and autobiographical articles.

Signs: Journal of Women in Culture and Society. 1975– . This is an interdisciplinary journal with an emphasis on theory; it has articles, review articles of work in specific fields, and book reviews. Special issues have focused on lesbianism, race, and "The Ideology of Mothering" (vol. 15, Spring 1990). (Originally at the University of Chicago, the editorial headquarters moved from Duke to the University of Minnesota for 1990–1995.)

Tulsa Studies in Women's Literature. 1982– . This journal originally focused entirely on women's writing from previous centuries, but its scope is now all-inclusive. Its many book reviews are largely on literary criticism and theory.

Women's Review of Books. 1984– . Published monthly except in August by the Wellesley College Center for Research on Women, this journal has in-depth interdisciplinary reviews, many on literary matters.

Women's Studies: An Interdisciplinary Journal. 1972– . Frequent articles on literary topics appear in this quarterly, edited in the United States and published in England; there are no book reviews.

Women's Studies International Forum. 1985–   . Published monthly in
England by Pergamon Press, this journal aims for "rapid publication"
of research findings in all fields and also publishes many book reviews.
Its focus is on the actual lives of women worldwide. Vol. 12, no. 1
(1989), for example, was on nonviolent direct action by women; vol.
11, no. 4 (1988) was on feminism in Ireland and included some original
fiction and poetry.

Women's Studies Quarterly. 1972–   . This publication of the Feminist
Press often focuses on teaching. Vol. XVII (1989) was on women's non-
traditional literature—diaries, autobiographies, and letters.

Anthologies of Women's Writings

These collections are only a few of the hundreds currently available; all
of those listed here are in print, most in paperback. Many contain theoretical introductions, and some present a mixture of forms.

Asian Women United of California, eds. *Making Waves: An Anthology
of Writings by Asian-American Women*. Boston: Beacon, 1989.

Allen, Paula Gunn, ed. *Spider Woman's Granddaughters: Traditional
Tales and Contemporary Writing by Native American Women*.
Boston: Beacon, 1989.

Canan, Janine, ed. *She Rises like the Sun: Invocations of the Goddess by
Contemporary American Poets*. Freedom: Crossing, 1989.

DeSalvo, Louise, Kathleen D'Arcy, and Katherine Hogan, eds. *Territories
of the Voice: Contemporary Stories by Irish Women Writers*. Boston:
Beacon, 1990.

Flores, Angel, et al., eds. and trans. *The Defiant Muse: Feminist Poems
from the Middle Ages to the Present*. 4 vols. (Hispanic, French, Italian,
German). New York: Feminist, 1986–1989.

Garfield, Evelyn Picon, ed. *Women's Fiction from Latin America:
Selections from Twelve Contemporary Authors*. Detroit: Wayne State
UP, 1988.

Gibson, Mary Ellis, ed. *New Stories by Southern Women*. Columbia: U
of South Carolina P, 1987.

Goscilo, Helena, ed. *Contemporary Stories by Russian Women*.
Bloomington: Indiana UP, 1989.

———, ed. and trans. *Russian and Polish Women's Fiction*. Knoxville: U
of Tennessee P, 1985.

Honig, Emily, and Gail Hershatter, eds. *Personal Voices: Chinese
Women in the 1980's*. Palo Alto: Stanford UP, 1988.

Lim, Shirley Geok-Lin, and Mayumi Tsutakawa, eds. *Forbidden Stitch: An Asian American Women's Anthology*. Corvallis: Calyx, 1989.

Miles, Julia, ed. *Women's Work: Five New Plays from the Women's Project*. New York: Applause Theatre, 1989.

Nestle, Joan, and Naomi Holock, eds. *Women on Women: An Anthology of American Lesbian Short Fiction*. New York: NAL, 1990.

Perkins, Kathy A., ed. *Black Female Playwrights: An Anthology of Plays before 1950*. Bloomington: Indiana UP, 1989.

Piercy, Marge, ed. *Early Ripening: American Women's Poetry Now*. New York: Pantheon, 1987.

Piekarski, Vicki, ed. *Westward the Women: An Anthology of Western Stories by Women*. 2nd ed. Albuquerque: U of New Mexico P, 1988.

Saxton, Marsha, and Florence Howe, eds. *With Wings: An Anthology of Literature by and about Women with Disabilities*. New York: Feminist, 1987.

Scheffler, Judith A., ed. *Wall Tappings: An Anthology of Writings by Women Prisoners*. Boston: Northeastern UP, 1986.

Sok-kyǒng, Kang, Kim Chi-wǒn, and O. Chǒng-Rui. *Words of Farewell: Stories by Korean Women Writers*. Trans. Bruce and Ju-Chan Fulton. Seattle: Seal, 1989.

Stanton, Domna, ed. *The Female Autograph: Theory and Practice of Autobiography from the Tenth to the Twentieth Century*. Chicago: U of Chicago P, 1987.

Ueda, Makoto, ed. *The Mother of Dreams and Other Short Stories: Portrayals of Women in Modern Japanese Fiction*. Palo Alto: Stanford UP, 1986.

Velez, Diana, ed. and trans. *Reclaiming Medusa: Short Stories by Puerto Rican Women*. San Francisco: Spinsters/Aunt Lute, 1988.

Walker, Nancy, and Zita Dresner, eds. *Redressing the Balance: American Women's Literary Humor from Colonial Times to the 1980's*. Jackson: UP of Mississippi, 1988.

Washington, Mary Helen, ed. *Invented Lives: Narratives of Black Women, 1860–1960*. New York: Doubleday, 1987.

Selected Recent Literary Criticism and Theory

The crucial word here is *selected*. Almost all the works listed here have been published since 1985. This list cannot be used as a kind of history of critical works as could related lists in previous editions; it is not even a complete list of recent works but rather a sample of the many diverse kinds of topics and approaches used in the last five years. It should be used in conjunction with the list of works cited that was presented first in this section, in which many "classic" works appear.

Acosta-Belén, Edna, ed. *The Puerto-Rican Woman: Perspectives on Culture, History, and Society.* 2nd ed. New York: Praeger, 1986.

Albinski, Nan Bowman. *Women's Utopias in British and American Fiction.* London: Routledge, 1988.

Baddes, Barbara, and Suzanne Gossett. *Declarations of Independence: Women and Political Power in Nineteenth-Century American Fiction.* New Brunswick: Rutgers UP, 1990.

Banta, Martha. *Imaging American Women: Idea and Ideals in Cultural History.* New York: Columbia UP, 1987.

Barr, Marleen S. *Alien to Femininity: Speculative Fiction and Feminist Theory.* Westport: Greenwood, 1987.

Bartkowski, Frances. *Feminist Utopias.* Lincoln: U of Nebraska P, 1989.

Benstock, Sheri. *Feminist Issues in Literary Scholarship.* Bloomington: Indiana UP, 1987.

————, ed. *The Private Self: Theory and Practices of Women's Auto-biographical Writings.* Chapel Hill: U of North Carolina P, 1988.

Brater, Enoch, ed. *Feminine Focus: The New Women Playwrights.* New York: Oxford UP, 1989.

Braxton, Joanne M. *Black Women Writing Biography: A Tradition within a Tradition.* Philadelphia: Temple UP, 1989.

————, and Andree McLaughlin, eds. *Wild Women in the Whirlwind: Afra-American Culture and the Contemporary Literary Renaissance.* New Brunswick: Rutgers UP, 1989.

Brodzki, Bella, and Celeste Schenck. *Life/Lines: Theorizing Women's Autobiography.* Ithaca: Cornell UP, 1988.

Carby, Hazel V. *Reconstructing Womanhood: The Emergence of the Afro-American Woman Novelist.* New York: Oxford UP, 1987.

Felski, Rita. *Beyond Feminist Aesthetics: Feminist Literature and Social Change.* Cambridge: Harvard UP, 1989.

Ferguson, Margaret W., Maureen Quilligan, and Nancy J. Vickers, eds. *Rewriting the Renaissance: The Discourses of Sexual Difference in Early Modern Europe.* Chicago: U of Chicago P, 1986.

Ferris, Lesley. *Acting Women: Images of Women in Theater.* New York: New York UP, 1989.

Gilbert, Sandra, and Susan Gubar. *No Man's Land: The Place of the Woman Writer in the Twentieth Century.* 3 vols. New Haven: Yale UP.

Vol. 1: *The War of Words*, 1988; vol. 2: *Sexchanges*, 1989; vol. 3, forthcoming.

Gilligan, Carol, Janie V. Ward, and Jill M. Taylor. *Mapping the Moral Domain: A Contribution of Women's Thinking to Psychological Theory and Education*. Cambridge: Harvard UP, 1988.

Graham-Brown, Sarah. *Images of Women: The Portrayal of Women in Photography of the Middle East, 1860–1950*. New York: Columbia UP, 1988.

Grahn, Judy. *The Highest Apple: Sappho and the Lesbian Poetic Tradition*. San Francisco: Spinsters Ink, 1985.

Hart, Lynda, ed. *Making a Spectacle: Feminist Essays on Contemporary Women's Theatre*. Ann Arbor: U of Michigan P, 1989.

Heilbrun, Carolyn G. *Writing a Woman's Life*. New York: Norton, 1988.

Hirsch, Marianne. *The Mother/Daughter Plot: Narrative, Psychoanalysis, Feminism*. Bloomington: Indiana UP, 1989.

Howe, Florence, ed. *Tradition and the Talents of Women*. Champaign: U of Illinois P, 1990.

LaBelle, Jenijoy. *Herself Beheld: The Literature of the Looking Glass*. Ithaca: Cornell UP, 1988.

Ling, Amy. *Between Worlds: Women Writers of Chinese Ancestry*. New York: Pergamon, 1990.

Lipking, Lawrence. *Abandoned Women and Poetic Tradition*. Chicago: U of Chicago P, 1988.

Miller, Nancy, ed. *The Poetics of Gender*. New York: Columbia UP, 1987.

Mills, Sara, et al. *Feminist Readings/Feminists Reading*. Charlottesville: UP of Virginia, 1989.

Minh-ha, Trinh T. *Woman, Native, Other: Writing Postcoloniality and Feminism*. Bloomington: Indiana UP, 1989.

Palmer, Paulina. *Contemporary Women's Fiction: Narrative Practice and Feminist Theory*. Jackson: UP of Mississippi, 1989.

Pearlman, Mickey, ed. *American Women Writing Fiction: Memory, Identity, Space*. Lexington: U of Kentucky P, 1988.

———. *Mother Puzzles: Daughters and Mothers in Contemporary American Literature*. Westport: Greenwood, 1990.

Personal Narratives Group. *Interpreting Women's Lives: Feminist Theory and Women's Lives*. Bloomington: Indiana UP, 1989.

Poovey, Mary. *Uneven Developments: The Ideological Work of Gender in Mid-Victorian England*. Chicago: U of Chicago P, 1988.

Rubinstein, Roberta. *Boundaries of the Self: Gender, Culture, Fiction.* Champaign: U of Illinois P, 1990.

Smith, Sidonie. *A Poetics of Women's Autobiography: Marginality and the Fictions of Self-Representation.* Bloomington: Indiana UP, 1987.

Van Buren, Jane Silverman. *The Modernist Madonna: Semiotics of the Maternal Metaphor.* Bloomington: Indiana UP, 1989.

Wall, Cheryl A., ed. *Changing Our Own Words: Essays on Criticism, Theory, and Writing by Black Women.* New Brunswick: Rutgers UP, 1989.

Willis, Susan. *Specifying: Black Women Writing the American Experience.* Madison: U of Wisconsin P, 1987.

Zandy, Janet, ed. *Calling Home: Working Class Women's Writing.* New Brunswick: Rutgers UP, 1990.

ACKNOWLEDGMENTS

———————————————

NADYA AISENBERG "Hope" from *Before We Were Strangers, Poems by Nadya Aisenberg*. Poems copyright © by Nadya Aisenberg. Reprinted by permission of Forest Books.

ALTA "Pretty" from *No Visible Means of Support* by Alta. Copyright © 1980 by Alta Gerrey. Reprinted by permission of the Shameless Hussey Press.

MAYA ANGELOU Excerpt from pp. 65–74 in *I Know Why the Caged Bird Sings* by Maya Angelou. Copyright © 1969 by Maya Angelou. Reprinted by permission of Random House, Inc.

GLORIA ANZALDÚA "Cihuatlyotl, Woman Alone" from *Borderlands–La Frontera: The New Mestiza* by Gloria Anzaldúa. Copyright © 1987 by Gloria Anzaldúa. Reprinted by permission of Aunt Lute Books.

MAX APPLE "Bridging" from *Free Agents* by Max Apple. Copyright © 1984 by Max Apple. Reprinted by permission of Harper & Row, Publishers, Inc.

MARGARET ATWOOD "Spelling." Copyright by Margaret Atwood, in *True Stories*. Reprinted by permission of the author.

W. H. AUDEN "Miss Gee," copyright 1940 and renewed 1968 by W. H. Auden. Reprinted from *W. H. Auden: Collected Poems*, edited by Edward Mendelson, reprinted by permission of Random House, Inc.; and reprinted by permission of Faber and Faber Ltd. from *Collected Poems* by W. H. Auden.

JANE AUGUSTINE "Secretive," first published in *Aphra, The Feminist Literary Magazine*, vol. 4, #4, Fall, 1973. Reprinted by permission of the author.

SALLY BENSON "Little Woman." Reprinted by permission; © 1938, 1966 The New Yorker Magazine, Inc.

RAY BRADBURY "I Sing the Body Electric!" Originally published in *McCall's*, August 1969. Reprinted by permission of Don Congdon Associates, Inc. Copyright © 1969 by Ray Bradbury.

GWENDOLYN BROOKS "The Mother" from *Blacks* by Gwendolyn Brooks. Copyright © 1987, The David Company, Chicago. Reprinted by permission of the author.

LARRY BROWN Copyright © 1987 by Larry Brown, "Facing the Music" by Larry Brown. First published in *Mississippi Review*, Spring 1987. Excerpted from *Facing the Music* by permission of Algonquin Books of Chapel Hill, a division of Workman Publishing Company, Inc. Copyright © 1988 by Larry Brown.

JAN CLAUSEN "Daddy" from *Mother Sister Daughter Lover* by Jan Clausen, reprinted by permission of The Crossing Press.

CAROL GREGORY "Migration." Reprinted by permission of the author.

LUCILLE CLIFTON "Miss Rosie" from *Good Times* by Lucille Clifton. Copyright © 1969 by Lucille Clifton. Reprinted by permission of Random House, Inc.

COLETTE "The Patriarch" from *The Collected Stories* by Colette. Translation copyright © 1957, 1966, 1983 by Farrar, Straus and Giroux, Inc. Reprinted by permission of Farrar, Straus and Giroux, Inc.

MARTHA COLLINS "Homecoming," reprinted by permission of the author. Copyright © 1972 by Martha Collins. This poem originally appeared in *Southern Review*.

ADELAIDE CRAPSEY "Susanna and the Elders" reprinted from *Complete Poems and Collected Letters of Adelaide Crapsey*, ed. Susan Sutton Smith, by permission of the State University of New York Press. © 1977 State University of New York; all rights reserved.

TOI DERRICOTTE "Transition" from *Natural Birth: Poems* by Toi Derricotte; published by The Crossing Press, 1983. Reprinted by permission of the author.

EMILY DICKINSON Poem #652 from *The Complete Poems of Emily Dickinson*, ed. by Thomas H. Johnson. Copyright 1929 by Martha Dickinson Bianchi; © renewed 1957 by Mary L. Hampson. By permission of Little, Brown and Company. Four lines from #652 reprinted by permission of the publishers and the Trustees of Amherst College from *The Poems of Emily Dickinson*, Thomas H. Johnson, ed., Cambridge, Mass.: The Belknap Press of Harvard University Press, Copyright 1951, © 1955, 1979, 1983 by the President and Fellows of Harvard College.

RUTH FAINLIGHT "Flower Feet." Reprinted by permission; © 1989 by Ruth Fainlight. Originally in *The New Yorker*.

JULIE FAY "Metonymy" by Julie Fay. Originally published in *Calyx, A Journal of Art and Literature by Women*, Vol. 12, No. 3, Summer 1990. Reprinted by permission of the author.

DOROTHY CANFIELD FISHER "The Bedquilt" from *Hillsboro People* by Dorothy Canfield Fisher (New York: Henry Holt and Company, 1915).

ALAÍDE FOPPA "Woman" by Alaíde Foppa from *Women Brave in the Face of Danger* by Margaret Randall, Crossing Press, 1985. Reprinted by permission of Margaret Randall.

SUSAN GLASPELL "Trifles" from *Plays* by Susan Glaspell. Copyright 1920 by Dodd, Mead & Co., copyright renewed 1948 by Susan Glaspell. Reprinted by permission of Daphne Cook, 21 Stuyvesant Oval, Manhattan, NY 10009.

SHIRLEY ANN GRAU "Home" from *Nine Women* by Shirley Ann Grau. Copyright © 1985 by Shirley Ann Grau. Reprinted by permission of Alfred A. Knopf, Inc.

SUSAN GRIFFIN "I Like to Think of Harriet Tubman" from *Like the Iris of An Eye* by Susan Griffin. Copyright © 1976 by Susan Griffin. Reprinted by permission of Harper & Row, Publishers, Inc.

HEINRICH HEINE "The Loreley" from *Heinrich Heine: Paradox and Poet: The Poems* by Louis Untermeyer, copyright 1937 by Harcourt Brace Jovanovich, Inc.; renewed 1965 by Louis Untermeyer. Reprinted by permission of the publisher.

MARIETTA HOLLEY "A Allegory on Wimmen's Rights" by Marietta Holley from *My Opinions and Betsey Bobbett's* (Hartford: American Publishing Company, 1873).

ZORA NEALE HURSTON Excerpt from pp. 143–51 in *Tell My Horse* by Zora Neale Hurston. Copyright 1938 by Zora Neale Hurston, renewed © 1966 by Joel Hurston and John C. Hurston. Reprinted by permission of Harper & Row, Publishers, Inc.

REBECCA JACKSON Excerpt from pp. 559–62 reprinted from *Gifts of Power: The Writings of Rebecca Jackson, Black Visionary, Shaker Eldress*, Jean Humez, ed. (Amherst: University of Massachusetts Press, 1981). Copyright © by The University of Massachusetts Press.

HARRIET JACOBS Excerpt from *Incidents in the Life of a Slave Girl, Written by Herself*, by Linda Brent, edited by L. Maria Child, Boston: Published for the author, 1861.

ERICA JONG Excerpts from "On the First Night" from *Ordinary Miracles* by Erica Jong. Copyright © 1983 by Erica Mann Jong. Reprinted by permission of Viking Penguin, a division of Penguin Books USA Inc.

JUNE JORDAN "Poem about My Rights" from *Passion: New Poems, 1977–80* by June Jordan. Copyright © 1990 by June Jordan. Reprinted by permission of the author.

SUZANNE KELLER Excerpts from Radcliffe paper by Suzanne Keller, used by permission.

ACKNOWLEDGMENTS

JAMAICA KINCAID "Girl" from *At the Bottom of the River* by Jamaica Kincaid. Copyright © 1983 by Jamaica Kincaid. Reprinted by permission of Farrar, Straus and Giroux, Inc.

MAXINE KUMIN "The Envelope" from *Our Ground Time Here Will Be Brief* by Maxine Kumin. Copyright © 1978 by Maxine Kumin. Reprinted by permission of Viking Penguin, a division of Penguin Books USA Inc.

LI-YOUNG LEE "I Ask My Mother to Sing," copyright © 1986 by Li-Young Lee. Reprinted from *Rose* by Li-Young Lee with the permission of BOA Editions, Ltd., 92 Park Ave., Brockport, NY 14420.

GEORGE LEFFERTS "The Glamour Trap" by George Lefferts from *George Lefferts' Special for Women: Eight Plays*, Avon Books, 1961. Reprinted by permission of the author.

ELLEN LESSER "Pressure for Pressure" from *The Shoplifter's Apprentice* by Ellen Lesser. Copyright © 1989 by Ellen Lesser. Reprinted by permission of Simon & Schuster, Inc.

DORIS LESSING "One off the Short List" from *A Man and Two Women* by Doris Lessing. Copyright © 1958, 1962, 1963 by Doris Lessing. Reprinted by permission of Simon & Schuster, Inc. and Jonathan Clowes Ltd, London, on behalf of Doris Lessing.

AUDRE LORDE "Dear Toni Instead of a Letter . . ." is reprinted from *Chosen Poems, Old and New* by Audre Lorde, by permission of W. W. Norton & Company, Inc. Copyright © 1982, 1976, 1974, 1973, 1970, 1968 by Audre Lorde.

PAULE MARSHALL "Brooklyn" By Paule Marshall. Copyright © 1983 by The Feminist Press at CUNY. From the book *Reena and Other Stories* by Paule Marshall.

BOBBIE ANN MASON "Old Things" from *Shiloh and Other Stories* by Bobbie Ann Mason. Copyright © 1982 by Bobbie Ann Mason. Reprinted by permission of Harper & Row, Publishers, Inc.

SUE MILLER "Expensive Gifts" from *Inventing the Abbotts and Other Stories* by Sue Miller. Copyright © 1987 by Sue Miller. Reprinted by permission of Harper & Row, Publishers, Inc.

VALERIE MINER "Trespassing" from *Trespassing and Other Stories, 1989* by Valerie Miner, reprinted by permission of Valerie Miner and The Crossing Press.

NICHOLASA MOHR "Aunt Rosana's Rocker." First published in *Rituals of Survival: A Woman's Portfolio* by Nicholasa Mohr (Houston: Arte Publico Press/University of Houston, 1985). Reprinted by permission of the publisher.

BHARATI MUKHERJEE "A Wife's Story" from *The Middleman and Other Stories* by Bharati Mukherjee. Reprinted by permission of Grove Weidenfeld. Copyright © 1988 by Bharati Mukherjee.

GLORIA C. ODEN "Speculation" by Gloria C. Oden. Copyright © 1969 by Media Plus, Inc. Reprinted by permission of the author and Ann Grifalconi/Greyfalcon House.

TILLIE OLSEN "Tell Me a Riddle" from *Tell Me a Riddle* by Tillie Olsen, copyright © 1956, 1957, 1960, 1961 by Tillie Olsen. Used by permission of Delacorte Press/Seymour Lawrence, a division of Bantam, Doubleday, Dell Publishing Group, Inc.

PAT PARKER "My Lover Is a Woman" by Pat Parker from *Movement in Black, Poetry by Pat Parker, 1961–1978*. Reprinted by permission of Firebrand Books.

LINDA PASTAN "Marks" is reprinted from *The Five Stages of Grief, Poems by Linda Pastan*, by permission of W. W. Norton & Company, Inc. Copyright © 1978 by Linda Pastan.

JAYNE ANNE PHILLIPS Excerpts from "Souvenir" from *Black Tickets* by Jayne Anne Phillips, copyright © 1979 by Jayne Anne Phillips. Used by permission of Delacorte Press/Seymour Lawrence, a division of Bantam, Doubleday, Dell Publishing Group, Inc.

MARGE PIERCY "Unlearning to Not Speak" from *Circles on the Water* by Marge Piercy. Copyright © 1982 by Marge Piercy. Reprinted by permission of Alfred A. Knopf, Inc.

MAIMIE PINZER Reproduced by permission of the Schlesinger Library, Radcliffe College, from the "Maimie" manuscript collection.

ADRIENNE RICH "Diving into the Wreck" is reprinted from *Diving into the Wreck, Poems 1971–1972* by Adrienne Rich, by permission of W. W. Norton & Company, Inc. Copyright © 1973 by W. W. Norton & Company, Inc.

MARY JO SALTER "Dead Letters" from *Unfinished Paintings* by Mary Jo Salter. Copyright © 1989 by Mary Jo Salter. Reprinted by permission of Alfred A. Knopf, Inc.

SONIA SANCHEZ "Present" from *I've Been a Woman: New and Selected Poems* by Sonia Sanchez. Reprinted by permission of The Black Scholar.

MAY SARTON "Mourning to Do" is reprinted from *Letters from Maine, New Poems* by May Sarton, by permission of W. W. Norton & Company, Inc. Copyright © 1984 by May Sarton.

OLIVE SCHREINER "Three Dreams in the Desert, Under a Mimosa-Tree" from *Dreams*, published in 1890.

VICKIE L. SEARS "Grace" is reprinted from *Simple Songs, Stories* by Vickie Sears, published by Firebrand Books (Ithaca, New York), 1990, and is used with permission.

NTOZAKE SHANGE "With no immediate cause" from *Nappy Edges* by Ntozake Shange. Copyright © 1972, 1974, 1975, 1976, 1977, 1978 by Ntozake Shange. Reprinted by permission of St. Martin's Press, Inc., New York.

IRWIN SHAW "The Girls in Their Summer Dresses" from *Five Decades*, copyright © 1978 by Irwin Shaw. Used by permission of Dell Books, a division of Bantam, Doubleday, Dell Publishing Group, Inc.

AGNES SMEDLEY Excerpt from pp. 86–92 (titled: "Silk Workers") in *Battle Hymn of China* by Agnes Smedley. Copyright 1943 and renewed 1971 by Agnes Smedley. Reprinted by permission of Alfred A. Knopf, Inc.

JEAN STAFFORD "The End of a Career" from *The Collected Stories* by Jean Stafford. Copyright © 1956, 1969 by Jean Stafford. Reprinted by permission of Farrar, Straus and Giroux, Inc.

RUTH STONE "Between the Lines" from *Second-Hand Coat* by Ruth Stone. Copyright © 1987 by Ruth Stone. Published by permission of David R. Godine, Publisher, Inc.

MEGAN TERRY Lines from *Approaching Simone*, reprinted by permission of Elizabeth Marton.

JEAN THOMPSON "Driving to Oregon" from *The Gasoline Wars*, copyright © 1979 by Jean Thompson. "Driving to Oregon" originally appeared in *Carolina Quarterly XXIX* (Spring/Summer 1977). Reprinted by permission of the University of Illinois Press.

JAMES TIPTREE, JR. "The Women Men Don't See," copyright © 1974 by James Tiptree, Jr. Reprinted by permission of the author and the author's agent, Virginia Kidd.

ALICE WALKER "Beyond What" from *Revolutionary Petunias and Other Poems*, copyright © 1973 by Alice Walker, reprinted by permission of Harcourt Brace Jovanovich, Inc.

RUTH WHITMAN "Cutting the Jewish Bride's Hair" from *The Marriage Wig and Other Poems*, Copyright © 1968 by Ruth Whitman, reprinted by permission of Harcourt Brace Jovanovich, Inc.

KATE WILHELM "Baby, You Were Great!" from *Orbit 2*, reprinted by permission of the author. Copyright © 1969 by Damon Knight.

WILLIAM CARLOS WILLIAMS "The Widow's Lament in Springtime." *William Carlos Williams: Collected Poems, 1909–1939, Vol. I.* Copyright 1939 by New Directions Publishing Corporation. US & Canadian rights. Reprinted by permission of New Directions Publishing Corporation.

JADE SNOW WONG "A Person as Well as a Female" from *Fifth Chinese Daughter* by Jade Snow Wong. Copyright © 1945, 1948, 1950 by Jade Snow Wong; copyright renewal 1978 by Jade Snow Wong. Reprinted by permission of the University of Washington Press.

NELLIE WONG "A Woman at the Window" from *The Death of a Long Steam Lady* by Nellie Wong. Copyright © 1984 by Nellie Wong. Reprinted by permission of West End Press, Box 27334, Albuquerque, NM 87122.

HISAYE YAMAMOTO "Seventeen Syllables" from *Seventeen Syllables* by Hisaye Yamamoto, with permission of Kitchen Table: Women of Color Press and the author.

AUTHOR / TITLE INDEX

• ───────────────────────────── •